Interest in the life and work of the Nobel prize-winning writer Rabindranath Tagore is now enjoying a revival after many years of neglect outside India. Tagore wrote thousands of letters in both Bengali and English. Most of the significant Bengali letters have been published in the half-century since his death, but not translated, while few of the noteworthy English letters are in print. Those English letters that are in print have appeared mainly in journals, magazines and newspapers that are unavailable to most scholars. They are also, generally speaking, inadequately presented. The Bengali letters are, of course, accessible only to scholars who read Bengali, and mostly lack adequate introductions and notes too.

This book, which consists of about 350 letters spanning Tagore's entire life, is the first to reveal the range of his letters to English readers. Individually introduced and comprehensively annotated, the letters have been selected to show as many facets of Tagore's experience, interests and ideas as possible, and to impart a new understanding of the complexity of his personality.

UNIVERSITY OF CAMBRIDGE ORIENTAL PUBLICATIONS 53
SELECTED LETTERS OF RABINDRANATH TAGORE

A series list is shown at the back of the book

Rabindranath Tagore, in Shantiniketan, 1938/9

Selected letters of
Rabindranath Tagore

Edited by
KRISHNA DUTTA and ANDREW ROBINSON

with a foreword by Amartya Sen

PUBLISHED BY THE PRESS SYNDICATE OF THE UNIVERSITY OF CAMBRIDGE
The Pitt Building, Trumpington Street, Cambridge CB2 1RP, United Kingdom

CAMBRIDGE UNIVERSITY PRESS
The Edinburgh Building, Cambridge, CB2 2RU, United Kingdom
40 West 20th Street, New York, NY 10011-4211, USA
10 Stamford Road, Oakleigh, Melbourne 3166, Australia

© Letters Visva-Bharati University 1997
© Translations of letters, introductions, notes and other editorial matter Krishna Dutta and Andrew Robinson 1997
© Foreword Amartya Sen 1997
This book is in copyright. Subject to statutory exception and to the provisions of relevant collective licensing agreements, no reproduction of any part may take place without the written permission of Cambridge University Press.

First published 1997

Printed in the United Kingdom at the University Press, Cambridge

Typeset in Monotype Times New Roman

A catalogue record for this book is available from the British Library

Library of Congress Cataloguing in Publication data
Tagore, Rabindranath, 1861–1941.
[Correspondence. Selections]
Selected letters of Rabindranath Tagore / edited by Krishna Dutta and Andrew Robinson.
    p.   cm. – (University of Cambridge oriental publications; 53)
Includes bibliographical references and index.
ISBN 0 521 59018 3
1. Tagore, Rabindranath, 1861–1941 – Correspondence. 2. Authors, Bengali – 19th century – Correspondence. 3. Authors., Bengali – 20th century – Corrrespondence. I. Dutta, Krishna. II. Robinson, Andrew. III. Title. IV. Series: University of Cambridge oriental publications; no. 53.
PK1725.A45 1997
891'.4414–dc20 [B]   96–38903   CIP

ISBN 0521 59018 3 hardback

For Anita
who also has Rabindranath 'in custody'

It is a long while since I have written to you but you have not been out of my thoughts. Your *Autobiography* especially has been a great pleasure. I wish you could give us the latter half – your thoughts on your own life work, and on the different movements of modern Bengal. The more is now written for Bengal, the more it would interest Europe.

W. B. Yeats to Rabindranath Tagore,
London, 24 April 1918

A number of my Bengali letters written in my young days had been collected some years ago. I gave my permission to publish them when I was convinced that they could be of great help to explain my writings which appeared unintelligible to some part of my readers. My nephew . . . has translated these letters into English. They cover those very years which were most productive for me and therefore they act like a footpath in my life history, unconsciously laid by the treading of my thoughts. I feel sure these letters, when published, will present to you pictures and ideas concerning me and my surroundings more vividly and truly than anything I have yet written.

Rabindranath Tagore to W. B. Yeats,
Shantiniketan, 17 June 1918

CONTENTS

Tagore's correspondents		*page* xi
List of plates		xv
Foreword		xvii
Acknowledgements		xxvi
Editorial note		xxviii
List of abbreviations		xxx
Introduction		1
Letters		
1–4	Youthful bravado (1879–1889)	6
5–23	Zamindar (1890–1897)	15
24–30	Family life (1898–1904)	45
31–45	Shantiniketan and Swadeshi (1905–1911)	61
46–69	Voyage to the West (1912–1913)	89
70–87	The Nobel prize (1913–1914)	126
88–110	The crest of a wave (1914–1916)	149
111–136	The ebbing of faith (1917–1918)	180
137–149	Anti-imperialist (1919–1920)	215
150–179	The founding of a university (1920–1921)	233
180–194	Anti-noncooperator (1921–1923)	285
195–215	Travels east and west (1924–1926)	307
216–231	Nationalism and internationalism (1927–1930)	344
232–248	Farewell to the West (1930)	372
249–271	Against the Raj (1931–1933)	396
272–301	International nationalist (1934–1936)	432
302–331	The Great Sentinel (1937–1939)	470
332–346	The crisis in civilisation (1939–1941)	509

Appendix 1: Tagore and Einstein 527
Appendix 2: The Bihar earthquake 536
Appendix 3: Gandhi the man 538

Bibliography 541
Index 549

TAGORE'S CORRESPONDENTS

(in alphabetical order with letter numbers)

Rafiuddin Ahmed	299
James Drummond Anderson	120
John Anderson	309
Charles Freer Andrews	70, 92, 134, 135, 138–41, 149, 151, 153, 156, 157, 160, 161, 163–5, 168, 172, 188, 189, 211, 257, 321, 323
Annie Besant	133
S. R. Bomanji	238
Aurobindo Mohan Bose	36
Jagadish Chandra Bose	27
Rash Behari Bose	313, 325
Subhash Chandra Bose	314
Robert Bridges	87, 101, 104
Amiya Chakravarty	274, 287, 303
Madhurilata Chakravarty (Tagore)	60, 61
Ramananda Chatterji [Chattopadhyay]	39, 44, 64, 269
Sarat Chatterji [Chattopadhyay]	217
Suniti Chatterji [Chattopadhyay]	224, 229, 230
Pramathanath Chaudhuri	89
Lord Chelmsford	126, 142
Kamla Chowdhury	346
James H. Cousins	106, 136
Ramakrishna Dalmia	329
Frieda Hauswirth Das	265
Mahadev Desai	176, 302
John Graham Drummond	147
Sudhindranath Dutta	233
Frederik van Eeden	67
Dorothy Elmhirst (Straight)	200, 235, 243
Leonard Knight Elmhirst	181, 187, 194, 197, 204, 210, 214, 259, 312, 317, 327, 334, 340, 343
Mrs George Engel	276

N. E. B. Ezra	275
Schlomith Flaum	298
Carlo Formichi	212
Mahatma Gandhi	94, 137, 260, 262, 264, 266–8, 270, 272, 289, 304, 305, 311, 330, 333, 336, 344
Mira Gangulee (Tagore)	32, 41, 48, 66, 150, 154, 240, 258
Nagendranath Gangulee	33, 35, 63, 99, 152, 191
Nitindranath Gangulee	253
Arthur Geddes	208
Patrick Geddes	184
Moti Lal Ghosh	112
André Gide	237
Gopal Krishna Gokhale	75
Robert Gourlay	116
Gretchen Green	295
Malcolm Hailey	279
Daniel Hamilton	239
Sven Hedin	318
Amal Home	227
Lord Irwin	231
Andrée Karpelès	284
Hermann Keyserling	170
Ajit Singh Khatau	337
Sten Konow	185
Nandita Kripalani	292
Vincenc Lesny	324
Muriel Lester	273, 278
Sylvain Lévi	221
Ramsay MacDonald	261
Macmillan & Co. (London)	93, 100, 300
Macmillan & Co. (New York)	123, 143
Nirmal Kumari Mahalanobis	228, 242
Prashanta Chandra Mahalanobis	175, 222
G. R. S. Mead	113
Hertha Mendel	250
Helen Meyer-Franck	285
Harriet Monroe	78
Maria Montessori	207
Harriet Moody	69, 79, 127
Ashutosh Mookerjee [Mukhopadhyay]	192
Thomas Sturge Moore	81, 86, 171, 178, 196, 286
Benito Mussolini	247
Sarojini Naidu	111, 271
Jawaharlal Nehru	283, 290, 296, 297, 301, 326, 332
Henry Nevinson	335

Yone Noguchi	322
Akiki Nyabongo	306
Victoria Ocampo	198, 199, 205, 236, 277, 328, 342
Okuma Shigenobu	124
Immanuel Olsvanger	310
Kostís Palamás	234
William Winstanley Pearson	98, 103, 114, 119, 155, 158, 159, 186
Myron Phelps	37
Ezra Pound	55, 58
Sarvepalli Radhakrishnan	125
Robert Fleming Rattray	339
Hemanta Bala Ray	254
Ernest Rhys	88, 293, 320
Romain Rolland	146, 195, 203, 209
Lord Ronaldshay	117, 118
Franklin Delano Roosevelt	341
Ronald Ross	216
Rachel Rothenstein	130
William Rothenstein	47, 51, 53, 54, 56, 59, 62, 68, 71, 73, 76, 77, 82, 95, 97, 115, 129, 144, 166, 167, 169, 218, 232, 249, 263, 307, 331
Bidhan Chandra Roy	251
Dilip Kumar Roy	223
Bertrand Russell	50
Michael Sadler	132
Margaret Sanger	202
Sharashi Lal Sarkar	256
C. P. Scott	213
Brajendranath Seal	179
Ellery Sedgwick	244
Atul Prashad Sen	190
Dinesh Chandra Sen	31
Gertrude Emerson Sen	308, 316
Kshiti Mohan Sen	34, 46
Priyanath Sen	3, 4, 26
Mayce Seymour	128
George Bernard Shaw	219
Upton Sinclair	193
Abanindranath Tagore	109
Gaganendranath Tagore	25, 108
Indira Tagore	5, 7–23, 65
Jnanadanandini Tagore	43
Jyotirindranath Tagore	1, 52
Kadambari Tagore	2
Mrinalini Tagore	6, 24, 28, 29

xiv Tagore's Correspondents

Nandini Tagore	241
Pratima Tagore	38, 42, 248
Rathindranath Tagore	30, 45, 96, 110, 121, 145, 201, 245, 246
Satyendranath Tagore	180
Edward John Thompson	72, 74, 80, 83–5, 90, 107, 148, 162, 173, 174, 177, 182, 183, 206, 225, 252, 280–2, 291, 315, 319, 338
Giuseppe Tucci	215
Boyd Tucker	226
Thanwardas Lilaram Vaswani	40
Vidyavati Devi (of Kasmunda)	294
Foss Westcott	345
Woodrow Wilson	122
William Butler Yeats	49, 57, 91, 102, 105, 131, 255, 288
N. Zwager	220

PLATES

All illustrations are identified from left to right. The name of the photographer, where known, is given first in roman, followed by our source in italics (*RB* stands for Rabindra Bhavan, Shantiniketan).

Frontispiece Rabindranath Tagore, in Shantiniketan, 1938/9 (Sambhu Shaha/*RB*)	*page* iv
1 Rabindranath, in England, *c.* 1879 (*RB*)	6
2 Rabindranath as zamindar, on his estates in East Bengal (*RB*)	17
3 Rabindranath at the wedding of his son, at Jorasanko, Calcutta, 1910: daughter Mira, son Rathindranath, daughter-in-law Pratima, daughter Bela (Upendrakishore Ray/*RB*)	47
4 Rabindranath as patriot, Swadeshi Movement, 1905/6 (Sukumar Ray, *RB*)	63
5 Somendra Chandra Dev Burman, D. N. Maitra, Rabindranath, John and William Rothenstein, Rathindranath Tagore, in Hampstead, London,1912 (John Trevor/*RB*)	91
6 Rabindranath, in Calcutta, 1914 (Johnston and Hoffmann/*RB*)	126
7 Tagore, in Japan, 1916, at the villa of Okakura Kakuzo (*Andrew Robinson*)	151
8 Gaganendranath Tagore as 'Father', Ashamukul as Amal, Rabindranath as Fakir, in *Dak Ghar* (*The Post Office*), Jorasanko, Calcutta, 1917	180
9 Tagore, with Buddha (place and date unknown) (*Martin Kämpchen*)	217
10 Kurt Wolff and Tagore, in Germany, 1921 (*RB*)	235
11 Leonard Elmhirst and Rabindranath, in Shantiniketan, 1920s/30s (*RB*)	287
12 Madeleine Rolland, Prashanta Chandra Mahalanobis, Tagore, Rani Mahalanobis, Romain Rolland (*seated*), Pratima Tagore, in Villeneuve, Switzerland, 1926 (Rod Schlemmer/*Bibliothèque Nationale*)	309
13 Tagore at the opening of an exhibition of his paintings, Galerie Pigalle, Paris, 1930: Countess Anna de Noailles, French minister of fine art, Victoria Ocampo (*RB*)	344
14 Albert Einstein and Tagore, New York, 1930 (Martin Vos/*RB*)	372
15 Rabindranath as public leader (protesting against the shooting of prisoners at Hijli detention camp), on the Maidan, Calcutta, 1931 (Kanchan Mukherjee/*RB*)	396

16 Jawaharlal Nehru and Rabindranath, in Shantiniketan, 1939 (*RB*) 432
17 Letter from Tagore to W. B. Yeats, 1935 (*Michael Yeats*) 456
18 Rabindranath and Mahatma Gandhi, in Shantiniketan, 1940 (*RB*) 470
19 The funeral of Rabindranath Tagore, in Calcutta, 7 August 1941 (*RB*) 510

FOREWORD

Amartya Sen

If something is 'secret', I was told at Oxford, then it can be shared with only one person at a time. A letter, similarly, is an essay written for one person at a time. Most letters are meant to go no further; indeed had they all circulated, the world would have perished under the weight of stupendous boredom. However, many letters, not unlike Oxford secrets, are destined to become – sometimes even planned to become – common knowledge.

Rabindranath Tagore belonged to a tradition – and to an age – in which the art of letter writing for eventual public communication was in full bloom. While many of the letters in this book, selected by Krishna Dutta and Andrew Robinson, were intended only for the addressee, quite a few of them were clearly meant to be shared. The letters bring out the effectiveness of this special genre. Despite the eventual possibility of sharing, the form of a letter can give its content an immediacy and directness that would seem inappropriate in essays meant directly for 'all'. The reader of the eventually published letter has to take note of the contingency of the context, but the author does not have to build the context into the content of the letter itself (as would be demanded of an essay for publication in a general journal). We find here Rabindranath explaining and defending his beliefs and speculations with great care, in letters addressed mostly to people he cared about, whose general concerns provided the particular occasion for addressing one issue rather than another. We get a close and undetached account of the beliefs, commitments and hopes of one of the most creative writers of this century.

Like all such selections, this one too reflects a compromise between distinct interests and pursuits which would demand quite different selections. While some readers with particular interests might wish that more letters were included in some fields rather than others, we have here a wide-ranging selection that should serve as a good introduction to Tagore's general ideas for the uninitiated and yet offer something substantial even to the well initiated. There is no 'optimum subset' of letters uniquely deserving of priority in publication, and a compromise has to be made paying attention to range as well as depth and reach. The compromise reflected here serves this purpose well.

An assigned identity?

Rabindranath saw himself primarily as a poet. To a great extent, that is also how others saw him; for example, the citation for his Nobel prize focused on his poetry. And yet he was a great short-story writer and novelist, a powerful author of essays and lectures, a composer whose songs reverberate around a lot of India and much of Bangladesh, and also an outstanding painter, whose pictures are now beginning to receive the acclaim that they have all along deserved. This breadth in the choice of medium is matched by his extensive interests in ideas and arguments. His essays have ranged over literature, politics, culture, social organisation, religious beliefs, philosophical claims, international relations, and a lot else.

Given this range, perhaps the most astonishing aspect of the standard image of Tagore in the West is the recurrent attempt to see him in extremely narrow terms, as 'the great mystic from the East', with a putative message for the West, which some would welcome, others dislike, and still others find profoundly boring. To some extent, this Tagore was the West's own creation, following a tradition of message-seeking from the East, particularly from India, which – as Hegel put it – had 'existed for millennia in the imagination of the Europeans'. What had happened in the two previous centuries in the hands of Schlegel, Schelling, Herder, Schopenhauer and many others, with attributed wisdom from India first praised and then denounced, happened again – this time to Rabindranath. Ezra Pound, W. B. Yeats and others, who had led the chorus of adoration of the almost unfathomable spirituality of Rabindranath Tagore's poetry, moved soon to firm neglect or even shrill denunciation.

Tagore himself played a somewhat bemused part in this 'boom and bust', accepting the massive praise with much surprise as well as pleasure, and then receiving the denunciations with even greater surprise and barely concealed pain. He had a deep respect for western intellectual circles, and for their commitment to fairness, even though from time to time he registered his protest at the crudeness of the excited treatment he was receiving (as he wrote to C. F. Andrews in 1920: 'These people . . . are like drunkards who are afraid of their lucid intervals').[1] And he did think that in the Indian cultural traditions there was wisdom of real importance, including universalism, toleration and the need for directness in seeking God (an idea that is plentifully present in *Gitanjali*, the poems that first caught the western imagination).

Rabindranath also thought, especially in the context of the brutalities of the First World War, that the co-existence of many cultures and many contradictory beliefs in India's past did have something to offer both to contemporary India and to the world about living with each other despite differences. But he had many other things to say, and while he said very practical things, in plain English, about nationalism, war and peace, cross-cultural education, the role of toleration, the need for openness and so on, the listening in the West was firmly tuned to more other-worldly themes. Sometimes when people came to hear him on one of these grander, transcendental themes, and got instead lectures on right political behaviour, there was, as E. P. Thompson reports, some resentment, particularly of his criticism of contemporary politics, 'at $700 a scold'.[2]

Letters and themes

Some of the letters tell us about the themes that Rabindranath wanted to talk about in his international tours, and sometimes express his frustration at not being heard.

Others deal with different issues more linked to preoccupations at home, in India. His attitude to the nationalist movements included sympathy and commitment as well as deep criticism of narrowness and chauvinism. His insistence on the need to be both strongly local and strongly global – at the same time – is a persistent theme that influenced his practical work in politics, education, social reform and literature, and this theme as well as its implications get a good airing in the letters published here. His forceful criticism as well as deep admiration of the British also receive much attention in the letters. Above all, the image of the single-minded Tagore created by his early admirers in the West gets handsomely buried under the massive expressions of his interests, commitments, speculations and proposals on an astonishing variety of subjects.

A collection of letters cannot, however, give a representative view of an author's work, especially in the case of a person whose poetry is as important as Tagore's is. The letters are inevitably more geared to prose than to poetry, and to non-fiction over fiction. While readers will find a few things of interest in what Tagore himself thought of his poetry, novels and short stories, and how he explained his inspirations and objectives, it is on deliberative subjects that the letters provide the greatest insight. In a brief foreword such as this, it would be futile to try to cover, even catalogue, all the themes that Tagore takes up in these letters. Instead, I shall choose a small number of subjects in which, I believe, Rabindranath's ideas remain particularly relevant today.

On nationalism

Tagore was strongly involved in protesting against the Raj on a number of occasions, and his insistence on the need for Indian independence was firmly rooted. His letter of 1919 to the viceroy, requesting that he should be relieved of his knighthood, in protest against the Amritsar massacre, includes an analysis of the brutal nature of the alien rule of India.[3] Political leaders such as Mahatma Gandhi and Jawaharlal Nehru expressed great appreciation for what Tagore did to strengthen the struggle for independence.[4]

And yet Rabindranath persistently rebelled against the sectarian forms that Indian nationalist movements took, and this made him withdraw, again and again, from an active role in the contemporary political movements. For example, while he took a leading part in the agitations against the British decision to partition Bengal in 1905 – a movement that was very important in the emergence of the nationalist struggle later on – he felt compelled to withdraw from it as he saw the forces of resistance turn chauvinist and even lead to violent action against particular groups within the country. His attitude to Mahatma Gandhi's 'noncooperation' movement remained partly – but firmly – critical, and he resented the 'patriotism' of the movement, while wanting to support its stress on self-reliance.

Tagore's censure of patriotism has been a persistent theme in his writings. As early as 1908, he put his position succinctly in a letter defending himself against criticism from the wife (Abala Bose) of a great Indian scientist (Jagadish Chandra Bose): 'Patriotism cannot be our final spiritual shelter; my refuge is humanity. I will not buy glass for the price of diamonds, and I will never allow patriotism to triumph over humanity as long as I live.'⁵ In his immensely successful novel *Ghare Baire* (*The Home and the World*), Nikhil expresses what Rabindranath clearly stood for: 'I am willing to serve my country; but my worship I reserve for Right which is far greater than my country. To worship my country as a god is to bring a curse upon it.'⁶

Rabindranath's dual attitude to nationalism is well illustrated by his reaction to nationalism in Japan. He saw the need to build the self-confidence of a defeated and humiliated people (as in the case of India), and of people left behind by developments elsewhere (as in the case of Japan before its new emergence). He noted at the very beginning of his lecture on 'Nationalism in Japan', given in Japan in 1916, that 'the worst form of bondage is the bondage of dejection, which keeps men hopelessly chained in loss of faith in themselves'. He expressed great admiration for the fact that Japan 'in giant strides left centuries of inaction behind, overtaking the present time in its foremost achievement'. This was inspirational for other nations outside the West, and it 'has broken the spell under which we lay in torpor for ages, taking it to be the normal condition of certain races living in certain geographical limits'.⁷

But then Tagore went on to criticise the emergence of strong nationalism in Japan and its new role as a possible imperialist. As E. P. Thompson notes, 'Tagore's outspoken criticisms did not please Japanese audiences and the welcome given to him on first arrival soon cooled.'⁸ Twenty-one years later, in 1937, when Tagore received a letter from an anti-British Indian revolutionary in Japan requesting support for efforts for Indian independence in warlike Japan, Tagore returned to the same theme, with fresh evidence of what he had feared earlier. He replied to Rash Behari Bose:

> Your cable has caused me many restless hours, for it hurts me very much to have to ignore your appeal. I wish you had asked for my cooperation in a cause against which my spirit did not protest. I know, in making this appeal, you counted on my great regard for the Japanese for, I, along with the rest of Asia, did once admire and look up to Japan and did once fondly hope that in Japan Asia had at last discovered its challenge to the West, that Japan's new strength would be consecrated in safeguarding the culture of the East against alien interests. But Japan has not taken long to betray that rising hope and repudiate all that seemed significant in her wonderful, and, to us symbolic, awakening, and has now become itself a worse menace to the defenceless peoples of the East.⁹

India and Indianness

Tagore's 'dual' attitude to nationalism – supporting its emphasis on self-respect but rejecting its patriotism – was not an easy one to get across, even in India. His criticism of Japan and of Britain were received with easy understanding in India, but when similar criticisms were made of India and Indians, there were many attempts to see Rabindranath as a lukewarm Indian. But Tagore remained deeply committed to his Indianness, while rejecting both patriotism and the advocacy of cultural isolation.

Isaiah Berlin summarises Tagore's complex position on Indian nationalism in these words:

> Tagore stood fast on the narrow causeway, and did not betray his vision of the difficult truth. He condemned romantic overattachment to the past, what he called the tying of

India to the past 'like a sacrificial goat tethered to a post', and he accused men who displayed it – they seemed to him reactionary – of not knowing what true political freedom was, pointing out that it is from English thinkers and English books that the very notion of political liberty was derived. But against cosmopolitanism he maintained that the English stood on their own feet, and so must Indians. In 1917 he once more denounced the danger of 'leaving everything to the unalterable will of the Master', be he Brahmin or Englishman.[10]

This duality is well reflected also in Tagore's attitude to cultural diversity. He wanted Indians to learn what was going on elsewhere, how others lived, what they valued, and so on, while remaining interested and involved in their own culture and heritage. Indeed, in his educational writings this synthesis is strongly stressed. It can also be found in his advice to Indian students abroad. For example, he wrote the following to his son-in-law Nagendranath in 1907 when he had gone to America to study agriculture:

> To get on familiar terms with the local people is a part of your education. To know only agriculture is not enough; you must know America too. Of course if, in the process of knowing America, one begins to lose one's identity and falls into the trap of becoming an Americanised person contemptuous of everything Indian, it is preferable to stay in a locked room.[11]

Despite his great pride in Indian traditions and culture, Rabindranath was often deeply critical of many things happening in India. Towards the end of his life he was particularly saddened by the fact that India's traditional problems (including poverty and hunger) were being supplemented by politically organised communal violence. His letter to Leonard Elmhirst written in December 1939 expresses his concerns:

> But what about India? It does not need a defeatist to feel deeply anxious about the future of millions who with all their innate culture and their peaceful traditions are being simultaneously subjected to hunger, disease, exploitations foreign and indigenous, and the seething discontents of communalism. Our people do not possess the vitality that you have in Europe, and the crisis, even before this war started in the West, has become acute in India. Needless to say, interested groups led by ambition and outside instigation, are today using the communal motive for destructive political ends.[12]

Traditionalism, Gandhi and Tagore

Tagore's dualist position applied to the issue of tradition and modernity as well. Isaiah Berlin, once again, captures Tagore's position well when he describes Rabindranath as 'choosing the difficult middle path, drifting neither to the Scylla of radical modernism, nor the Charybdis of proud and gloomy traditionalism'.[13] This description can be supplemented by noting that Tagore's position involves something more than just avoiding each extreme, and includes combining a non-extreme and non-exclusive version of both traditionalism and modernism within oneself. Tagore expresses the tyranny of being bound to the past in his amusing yet profoundly serious short story, 'Kartar Bhoot' (The Ghost of the Leader), where the wishes of a respected but dead leader make present lives impossibly restrained.

The issue of traditionalism was a subject of some tension with Mahatma Gandhi. Tagore had the greatest admiration for Gandhi as a person and as a political leader, but also harboured some scepticism of his traditionalism (in addition to disagreeing on nationalism). Many illustrations of his admiration as well as reservation can be found in the letters included in this selection.

Tagore's 1938 essay on 'Gandhi the man', included here in appendix 3, shows the combination well. The admiration for Mahatma Gandhi is at the profoundest level. What he describes as 'the significant fact about Gandhiji' finds the following expression in Tagore's words: 'Great as he is as a politician, as an organiser, as a leader of men, as a moral reformer, he is greater than all these as a man, because none of these aspects and activities limits his humanity. They are rather inspired and sustained by it.'[14] And yet there is an equally profound division between the two. Here is Tagore's view of what he could not agree with:

> We who often glorify our tendency to ignore reason, installing in its place blind faith, valuing it as spiritual, are ever paying for its cost with the obscuration of our mind and destiny. I blamed Mahatmaji for exploiting this irrational force of credulity in our people, which might have had a quick result in a superstructure, while sapping the foundation. Thus began my estimate of Mahatmaji, as the guide of our nation, and it is fortunate for me that it did not end there.[15]

But while it 'did not end there', that difference of vision was a powerful divider of the respective attitudes of Gandhi and Tagore on a variety of issues.

Rabindranath remained unconvinced of the merit of Gandhiji's attempt at making spinning at home (with the *charka* – the primitive spinning wheel) an important part of India's self-realization. 'The *charka* does not require anyone to think; one simply turns the wheel of the antiquated invention endlessly, using the minimum of judgment and stamina.' He could not see how the search for 'ways to liberate the country' can be helped by 'the ideology of the *charka*'.[16]

Tagore was more gentle regarding his difference with Gandhiji on the latter's attitude to sexual life.

> [Gandhiji] condemns sexual life as inconsistent with the moral progress of man, and has a horror of sex as great as that of the author of *The Kreutzer Sonata*, but, unlike Tolstoy, he betrays no abhorrence of the sex that tempts his kind. In fact, his tenderness for women is one of the noblest and most consistent traits of his character, and he counts among the women of his country some of his best and truest comrades in the great movement he is leading.[17]

An occasion on which Mahatma Gandhi and Rabindranath Tagore rather severely clashed with each other, which is the subject of appendix 2 of this book, involved their totally different attitudes to science. A devastating earthquake in Bihar, which killed many people, occurred in January 1934. Gandhi, who was then deeply involved in the fight against untouchability, decided to turn this tragic event into a positive move. He described the earthquake as 'divine chastisement sent by God for our sins' – in particular the sins of untouchability. Tagore, who was equally committed to the removal of untouchability, protested vehemently against this interpretation of an event that had caused suffering and death to so many innocent people, and he also hated the implicit epistemology of seeing earthquakes as an ethical phenomenon.

In the exchange that followed on this subject with Gandhiji, Tagore expressed his dismay at this association of 'ethical principles with cosmic phenomena'. He also wondered how, if Gandhi were right, so many atrocities could have occurred in the past without precipitating any natural catastrophe:

> Though we cannot point out any period of human history that is free from iniquities of the darkest kind, we still find citadels of malevolence yet remain unshaken, that the factories that cruelly thrive upon abject poverty and the ignorance of the famished cultivators, or prison-houses in all parts of the world where a penal system is pursued, which most often is a special form of licensed criminality, still stand firm. It only shows that the law of gravitation does not in the least respond to the stupendous load of callousness that accumulates till the moral foundations of our society begin to show dangerous cracks and civilisations are undermined.[18]

Interpretational epistemology

While Tagore was totally opposed not only to ignoring modern science in trying to understand physical phenomena, and particularly critical of giving ethical failures a role in explaining natural catastrophes, his views on epistemology were interestingly heterodox. The report of his conversation with Einstein, included here in appendix 1, brings out how insistent Tagore was in interpreting truth through observations and reflective concepts. In this framework, assertions about truth in the absence of anyone to observe or perceive or conceptualize it appeared to Tagore to be deeply problematic. When Einstein asks, 'If there were no human beings any more, the Apollo Belvedere no longer would be beautiful?', Tagore asserts, 'No.' Going further – and into much more interesting territory – Einstein says, 'I agree with regard to this conception of beauty, but not with regard to truth.' Tagore's response is: 'Why not? Truth is realised through men?'[19]

This is, alas, not the occasion to discuss this engaging issue further. We could ask for clarification as to the sense in which 'realisation' is being used. Some would compare Tagore's position with certain recent philosophical works on the nature of reality, particularly Hilary Putnam's argument that 'truth depends on conceptual schemes and it is nonetheless "real truth"'.[20] Tagore's speculations on these issues, which were invariably interesting, were never systematically followed.

Educational commitments

The dispute with Mahatma Gandhi on the Bihar earthquake touched on a subject that was closest to Tagore's passions and commitments: the importance of being educated in science as well as literature and the humanities. Much of Rabindranath's life was spent in developing the school he had founded at Santiniketan. The '$700 a scold' to which E. P. Thompson had referred (in describing Tagore's lectures in America) were accepted by Tagore on behalf of the school, which was perpetually short of money.

Tagore attempted to reflect his dual emphases, mentioned earlier, in the educational arrangements at Santiniketan. There were strong elements of nationalism in the focus on Indian traditions, including classics, and in the use of Bengali rather than English as the medium of instruction, and at the same time, there were many courses on western culture and traditions, and facilities also for studying China, Japan and the Middle East. Tagore was happy that many foreigners came to Santiniketan and that the fusion of studies did seem to work. In October 1920, he wrote to C. F. Andrews: 'Now I know more clearly than ever before that Shantiniketan belongs to all the world and we shall have to be worthy of this great fact.'[21]

I am personally rather partial to seeing Tagore as an educationist, having been educated myself at Santiniketan. There was something totally remarkable about the ease with which discussions in the school could move from Indian traditional literature to contemporary as well as classical western thought and to China, Japan and elsewhere. The celebration of *variety* is also in sharp contrast with the cultural conservatism and separatism that has tended to grip India from time to time. Tagore's own vision of the contemporary world, with its give and take, has close parallels with the inclusive vision presented by the great film director Satyajit Ray, an outstanding alumnus of Santiniketan.[22]

Freedom of mind

I end with a final remark on the importance of freedom in the broadest sense in Rabindranath Tagore's thinking. His attitude to politics and culture, nationalism and internationalism, tradition and modernity, and cross-cultural education, can all be seen in the light of his strong attachment to the importance of living and reasoning in freedom. His support for nationalist movements came from that commitment – against the unfreedom of an alien rule – and so did his reservations about patriotism, which can narrow the freedom with which one can accept ideas from the whole world and have commitments towards people who are distant as well as those who are near.

In a little-remembered interview, given by Tagore to *Izvestia* in 1930, he criticised the unfreedom that he saw in Russia, despite his admiration for many other things happening there, including educational expansion and economic development (the English translation of his *Letters from Russia* was banned by the British Raj largely because he had compared favourably Russian policy – especially educational policy – towards Soviet Asia with British policy in India):

> I must ask you: Are you doing your ideal a service by arousing in the minds of those under your training anger, class-hatred, and revengefulness against those whom you consider to be your enemies? . . . Freedom of mind is needed for the reception of truth; terror hopelessly kills it . . . For the sake of humanity I hope you may never create a vicious force of violence, which will go on weaving an interminable chain of violence and cruelty . . . You have tried to destroy many of the other evils of [the czarist] period. Why not try to destroy this one also.[23]

This critique remains valuable – sadly – even today, for the world in which we live. It is in the defence of freedom and fearless reasoning that we can find the lasting voice of Rabindranath Tagore.

Notes

1 See p. 246.
2 E. P. Thompson, 'Introduction', in Rabindranath Tagore, *Nationalism* (London, 1991), p. 11.
3 See pp. 223–4. See also RT's letters to C. F. Andrews around this time, pp. 219–22.
4 See for example Nehru's description of RT in *The Discovery of India* (Delhi, 1946; centenary edn, 1989), pp. 340–1.
5 See p. 72.
6 *The Home and the World* (London, 1919), p. 22/*RR*, VIII, p. 157. Martha Nussbaum initiates her wide-ranging critique of patriotism (in a debate that is joined by Kwame Anthone Appiah, Sissela Bok, Judith Butler, Gertrude Himmelfarb, Hilary Putnam, Elaine Scarry, Charles Taylor, Michael Walzer and others) by quoting this passage from *The Home and the World*. She goes on to say: 'I believe, as do Tagore and his character Nikhil, that this emphasis on patriotic pride is both morally dangerous and, ultimately, subversive of some of the worthy goals patriotism sets out to serve – for example, the goal of national unity in devotion to worthy moral ideas of justice and equality' (Martha C. Nussbaum et al., *For Love of Country*, Boston, 1996, pp. 3–4).
7 Tagore, *Nationalism*, pp. 17–18.
8 *Ibid.*, p. 10.
9 See pp. 485–6.
10 Isaiah Berlin, 'Rabindranath Tagore and the consciousness of nationality', in his *The Sense of Reality: Studies in Ideas and their History* (Henry Hardy ed.; London, 1996), p. 265.
11 See p. 67.
12 See p. 515. Since the term 'communalism' used in India may not be readily understood, I should explain that the reference is to sectarian conduct and violence between members of different religious communities, such as Hindus, Muslims and Sikhs.
13 Berlin, *Sense of Reality*, pp. 260–1.
14 See p. 539.
15 See pp. 538–9.
16 See p. 365.
17 See p. 539.
18 See p. 537.
19 See p. 531.
20 Hilary Putnam, *The Many Faces of Realism* (La Salle, Ill., 1987). See also Thomas Nagel, *The View from Nowhere* (New York, 1989).
21 See p. 240.
22 See Satyajit Ray, *Our Films Their Films* (New Delhi, 1976). I have tried to discuss these issues in my Satyajit Ray Memorial Lecture, 'Our Culture, Their Culture', *New Republic*, 1 April 1996.
23 The interview (in English) was published in the *Manchester Guardian* and is reproduced in Krishna Dutta and Andrew Robinson, *Rabindranath Tagore: The Myriad-Minded Man* (London, 1995), p. 297. It was not published in *Izvestia* until 1988.

ACKNOWLEDGEMENTS

This book has grown out of at least three other books. In 1990, we retranslated *Glimpses of Bengal*, Rabindranath Tagore's vibrant letters to his niece, and in 1991 we edited and published the correspondence of Tagore and Leonard K. Elmhirst, the founder of Dartington. At the same time, we were researching Tagore's life for our biography, *The Myriad-Minded Man*. Burying ourselves in the wonderful collections of the Tagore archives at Rabindra Bhavan, in the beautiful setting of Shantiniketan, we discovered that Tagore's letters, particularly his English letters, were a relatively untapped resource. We also turned up a number of significant letters in other, non-Indian archives that were not at all familiar. Some of these letters found their way into quotations in the biography, but a great many important ones did not. Having finished writing the biography, it was clear to us that a selection of these letters – both those written in English and those written in Bengali – ought to be made available to a wider circle than simply scholars devoted to Tagore.

After surviving various pitfalls in both Britain and India, the project received a welcome from Gordon Johnson, general editor of *The New Cambridge History of India* and chairman of the Cambridge University Press Syndicate. His comment that the publication of Tagore's letters would help to 'unwrap' a figure whose true importance has been unjustly obscured by poor translations and his earlier cult reputation echoed our own feeling. As E. P. Thompson, another advocate of the project, observed in 1993 just before his death: 'The West is still, after half a century, groping in the half-light to discern the features of Tagore's genius.' We hope that this book will serve to increase the light level.

In Bengal, we are grateful to the authorities of Visva-Bharati, Tagore's university, for giving permission to reproduce the letters, in particular to the director of the publishing department, Ashoke Mukhopadhyay. The generous assistance of Amartya Sen, whose family has close links with Tagore and Shantiniketan, was invaluable in this regard.

Many people have been of help in answering the detailed queries that inevitably arise in editing a book of letters, either because they knew the answer or because they could put us in touch with someone who did. Nirad C. Chaudhuri heads our list of debts: not only could we draw upon his unique knowledge of Bengali and western literature of Tagore's time, we also benefited from his formidable memory for Bengali life in the first half of this century. Despite his great age, he never failed to respond to questions with prompt and entertaining letters.

Prashanta Kumar Paul has been a prodigious source of information, both in person and through his ongoing biography of Rabindranath. Probably no one has read his *Rabijibani* more thoroughly than we have, bar its author!

Thanks for copies of letters and/or useful information are due to the late Alex Aronson (letter to Schlomith Flaum), Richard Bowen (Shinzo Takagaki), Lionel Carter (J. G. Drummond), Uma Das Gupta (E. J. Thompson), l'Ecole d'Humanité, Switzerland (Aurobindo Mohan Bose), John Erickson (F. N. Petrov), Dipali Ghosh (viceroys and secretaries of state for India), Nemai Ghosh (Harindranath Chatterji), Leonard A. Gordon (Margaret Sanger), Jews' College, London (Immanuel Olsvanger), Martin Kämpchen (Helen Meyer-Franck), John Kelly (W. B. Yeats), the London Library (as always), Indrani Majumdar (Jawaharlal Nehru, Gertrude Emerson Sen and Frieda Hauswirth Das), Musée départemental Albert-Kahn, France (Albert Kahn), Erin O'Donnell (Harriet Monroe and Harriet Moody), Asko Parpola (Carlo Formichi), Richard Popplewell (Myron Phelps), R. P. Pudumjee (S. R. Bomanji), William T. Starr (Madeleine Rolland), Sandip Tagore (Kampo Arai), Anne Taylor (G. R. S. Mead), Michael Yeats (W. B. Yeats), Michael Young (Dorothy Elmhirst); also to Lucy Bartlett and Maggie Giraud of the Elmhirst archives, High Cross House, Dartington.

Thanks are also due to Debnath Bandopadhyay, Michael D. Coe, Peter Cox, Sankho Ghosh, Sandy Hall, Ashish Hazra, Walter Holzhausen, Dipankar Home, Eivind Kahrs, Samiran Nandy, Marie-Laure Prévost, Dilip K. Roy, Supriya Roy, Tushar Sinha, K. G. Subramanyan, E. P. Thompson and Ronald Warwick, for other kinds of help.

We are also grateful to Marigold Acland and Mary Starkey at Cambridge University Press.

After Satyajit Ray finished his deep and stirring documentary film, *Rabindranath Tagore*, made for the 1961 Tagore birth centenary, he wrote a letter to a film-maker friend in Sri Lanka: '*Tagore* was a back-breaking chore with research, scenario, shooting, editing each an exhausting and time-consuming process, and the whole taking up twice as long as a normal feature.' Having finished editing this selection of Tagore's letters, we can sympathise. We also feel a bit like Deven, devotee of the great, dying Urdu poet Nur in that poignant and comic novel, *In Custody*, by Anita Desai – to whom this book is dedicated. Deven 'had imagined he was taking Nur's poetry into safe custody, and not realised that if he was to be the custodian of Nur's genius, then Nur would become his custodian and place him in custody too. This alliance could be considered an unendurable burden – or else a shining honour. Both demanded an equal strength.' Working on Rabindranath Tagore over the past ten and more years has been both an honour and a burden for us. This, we expect, is our last book on him.

EDITORIAL NOTE

Any editor of Tagore's writing in English is faced with the problem of whether to leave his text entirely as Tagore wrote it or instead to correct his slips of grammar and syntax, so as to bring out his meaning better, in the manner of his early editors, beginning with W. B. Yeats. With some reservations, we have adopted the latter approach – but we have altered Tagore's original *only* where the English is unclear or ambiguous, not where his grammatical slip, such as a dropped definite article or a slightly wrong preposition, makes no difference to the sense. Changes are indicated by square brackets, except for cuts and changes in punctuation, which are not indicated.

None of the letters has been abridged, except for letter 1 (see p. 8 for our reasons). However, Tagore himself edited his letters to his niece Indira, and we have been obliged to follow the fullest available Bengali text. Other letters contain occasional omissions or obscurities, which we have indicated with three dots.

Spellings of non-Indian words have been standardised throughout the book, and so have the spellings of non-Indian names. The spelling of Indian words and names in the English letters presents more of a problem. While the personal names have been standardised, i.e. the name of any one individual, e.g. Subhash Chandra Bose, is spelt the same way wherever it appears, the place names have been left as Tagore spelt them, with their modern standard form added afterwards in square brackets, where this differs significantly from the old spelling, e.g. Chandernagore [Chandannagar]. Place names in the Bengali letters have been converted into their modern standard form, e.g. Barddhaman, not Burdwan. Since there is no agreed standard form for Shantiniketan/Santiniketan, we have used Shantiniketan in our own text, but left the spelling used by Tagore in his letter (he used both spellings of the place serendipitously).

The transliteration of Bengali words and names in English is a tricky and unsatisfactory business. We have spelt them all without scholarly but cumbersome diacritical marks, and have tried instead to use a spelling that reproduces the sound not the orthography of Bengali. In the case of 's', since almost every 's' in Bengali is pronounced 'sh', rather than employing the conventional but confusing 's' and 'sh' to represent the three Bengali letters for 's', we have transliterated all three letters as 'sh' – except where there is an established spelling, as in the word sari, the name of the Tagore house Jorasanko, or the name of Tagore's brother, Satyendranath.

Editorial note

Salutations

The translation of salutations at the beginning and end of letters is difficult, because they generally have a customary meaning different from their literal meaning, which also alters over time. We have therefore not translated Tagore's salutations, with the occasional exception. He used a wide variety, many of them Sanskritic, making their translation even more problematic than usual. However, their literal meanings and/or close English equivalents are given below in alphabetical order:

Anugata	Obediently
Apnader	Yours
Apnar	Yours
Apnar sneher	Yours affectionately
Ashirbbadak	With my blessing
Bahumanbhajaneshu	To one most revered
Bhabadiya	Yours ever
Bhai	Brother
Bhai Chhota Bou	My dear little wife
Bhai Dada	My dear elder brother
Bhai Meja Bouthan	My dear elder sister-in-law
Bhai Meja Dada	My dear elder brother
Binayshambhashanpurbbak nibedan	With cordial and humble submission
Briddha	Old girl
Ekanta shubhanudhyayi	Sincere well-wisher
Kabi bandhu	My poet friend
Kalyaniyashu	To her who deserves my good wishes
Kalyaniyeshu	To him who deserves my good wishes
Pratinamashkar nibedan	With cordial and humble submission
Pritishambhashanametat	With cordial greetings
Priya bandhu	Dear friend
Shraddhashpadeshu	My revered friend
Shubhakangkshi	One who wishes you well
Shubhanudhyayi	Well-wisher
Shuhridwar	My excellent friend
Shuhrittameshu	My great-hearted friend
Snehanurakta	Yours affectionately
Snehashakta	Yours affectionately
Sneher	Affectionately
Tomader	Yours
Tomar	Your
Tomar sneher	Your affectionate

ABBREVIATIONS

Rabindranath Tagore is abbreviated to RT throughout the notes on the letters, while the following abbreviations are used for books and journals:

CMG	*Calcutta Municipal Gazette* (Tagore Memorial Special Supplement), 13 Sept. 1941
CP	*Chithipatra* (letters)
CPB	*Chhinnapatrabali* (letters)
CWMG	*Collected Works of Mahatma Gandhi*
GB	*Gitabitan* (collected songs of RT)
MR	*Modern Review* (Calcutta monthly)
My Rem	*My Reminiscences* (memoirs of RT)
RR	*Rabindra Rachanabali* (collected works of RT)
RR (AS)	*Rabindra Rachanabali (Achalita Shangraha)* (addenda to collected works)
TUM	*Towards Universal Man* (essays)
VBN	*Visva-Bharati News*
VBP	*Visva-Bharati Patrika*
VBQ	*Visva-Bharati Quarterly*

The abbreviations for the manuscript sources, given in square brackets, e.g. [London], are listed in the bibliography on p. 541.

Introduction

In 1939, when Rabindranath Tagore was nearly eighty and a national institution, the coming Calcutta poet and critic Buddhadeva Bose went to see him in his setting at Shantiniketan and afterwards wrote this lively description for an Indian magazine:[1]

> Shaded by a leafy mango tree, he was sitting at a little table covered with books and papers. Every dawn sees him there, and there, under the mango tree, he sits, works and sees people till the sun gets too hot. On the table were some volumes of Bengali poetry by younger poets (he was then working on an anthology of Bengali poetry which has since been published), and in his hands was a recent book of e. e. cummings. Vivacious, playful, irresistibly charming, this young man of eighty ragged us over cummings and modern poetry; and we felt it to be great fun rather than the oracular utterances of a prophet. And this, I think, is where most westerners are mistaken. An English journalist, who had been to Santiniketan has recently said in the *London Mercury* that Tagore never smiles and that his conversation is poor.[2] We cannot say how really it strikes a foreigner; but one need only look at that noble face, a face somewhere between Tennyson's and Tolstoy's creased with good-humoured smiles, and listen once to that rich, if feminine voice to know how mistaken those impressions are. Or is it that the incisive fineness of his conversation cannot be put across in any foreign language, depending as it does, for its effects, on the very idioms of the Bengali language . . . Tagore is always a word wizard, with his pen as well as with his tongue: brilliant talk flows from him as easily as water from a fountain; lightning-like, his wit flashes and sears the object of sarcasm. He is a star actor in his own way, for his voice and features can express every conceivable shade and tone of feeling. But he has very few gestures; rigorous discipline from childhood has made him a master of poise; he can sit for hours on end in exactly the same position, the red-shot, classical Oriental eyes alone serving to reflect the changing tones of thought and feeling. Minimum physical movement combined with a musical flow of intense words – this is Tagore as a speaker and talker.

The letters of Tagore, taken together, bring us nearer to this complex, compelling, mercurial personality – which attracted people as varied as Ezra Pound, Albert Einstein and Mahatma Gandhi – than any other part of his vast oeuvre of poetry, songs, drama, short stories, novels, memoirs, essays and paintings. His letters, in both Bengali and English, are some of his most alert writings: they also express his ideas in a more concise and vivid manner than many of his published writings, and show him struggling (and generally failing) to put these ideas into practice; and his unique sense of humour, which so easily evaporates in translations of his work, shines out of the more intimate correspondence.

The letters run into many thousands (though not as many as Gandhi wrote), and that excludes the descriptive letters Tagore wrote on foreign visits that were deliberately written to be published as books of travel.[3] They span sixty years, from 1878 to the final months of Tagore's life in 1941. Almost all the significant ones written in Bengali have been published (though not translated) in the decades since his death, unlike those written in English, many of which remain virtually or wholly unknown, even to Tagore scholars; not even the prolific correspondence with Charles Freer Andrews, Tagore's closest English collaborator, is fully published (the fraction that is available was mangled by Andrews as editor of *Letters to a Friend*, so as to make it practically useless for scholarly purposes).[4] About half of the English letters in this book have not previously appeared in print.

In selecting a few hundred from all of Tagore's letters for publication, we have been guided principally by a desire to show as many facets of his experience, interests and ideas as possible. Thus there are letters on most aspects of the arts, eastern and western, letters about many of the places that Tagore visited between 1912 and the 1930s, and letters on the history of India and on Indian social, religious, educational, economic and political questions, including even a letter (to the mayor of Calcutta) recommending that the Calcutta Corporation support a Japanese judo expert whom Tagore had brought from Japan to Shantiniketan at his own expense – thereby becoming the pioneer of judo in India.[5] There are also many letters to the members of the Tagore family, dealing with matters that are personal yet which also shed much light on the other spheres of Rabindranath's activities, such as his attempts to direct his son and son-in-law to begin 'rural reconstruction' work on the Tagore estates in East Bengal (predating Gandhi's village development programme by over two decades), and his efforts to persuade his painter nephews Gaganendranath and Abanindranath (founder of the Bengal School) to travel outside India to Japan and broaden their artistic horizons.

His correspondents were predictably wide ranging, covering family members, estate workers and staff at Shantiniketan, Bengali litterateurs and writers such as Pramatha Chaudhuri, Sarat Chandra Chatterji [Chattopadhyay] and Dilip Kumar Roy, poets such as W. B. Yeats, Ezra Pound and Robert Bridges, the artist William Rothenstein, the Tagore biographer and historian of India Edward J. Thompson, editors such as C. P. Scott, Harriet Monroe and Ramananda Chatterji [Chattopadhyay], thinkers such as Romain Rolland, Bertrand Russell and Brajendranath Seal, the scientist Jagadish Chandra Bose, educationists such as Michael Sadler and Patrick Geddes, scholars of Indian religion and philology such as Kshiti Mohan Sen, Sylvain Lévi and Suniti Kumar Chatterji [Chattopadhyay], religious leaders such as Foss Westcott (metropolitan of India), the agricultural economist Leonard Elmhirst (who co-founded the Dartington Trust), politicians and statesman such as Mahatma Gandhi, Jawaharlal Nehru, Subhash Chandra Bose, Benito Mussolini and Woodrow Wilson, as well as British viceroys, governors and other Indian government officials. In addition, many interesting letters were written to comparative unknowns, for example Hemanta Bala Ray, a Bengali woman from an orthodox Hindu *zamindari* family, to whom Rabindranath wrote 264 letters, including some penetrating comments on Hindu–Muslim relations.

The Bengali letters, which we have translated ourselves, make up about a quarter of the book. Rabindranath's letters to his niece Indira, mostly written from the Tagore estates where he was the manager in the 1890s, are among his most celebrated letters, and we have chosen many of them; it is these letters that (as he told Yeats in 1918) 'will present to you pictures and ideas concerning me and my surroundings more vividly and truly than anything I have yet written'.[6] Instead of translating the letters in the form in which they were abridged by Tagore in 1912 for publication as *Chhinnapatra* (and later, in English translation, as *Glimpses of Bengal*), we have retained the original letters in the fullest available form.

In translating, we have aimed to make all the Bengali letters sound as fluent in English as they do in Bengali, without any of the stiltedness that, as Tagore himself well knew, tends to affect his own writing in English. We agree with Satyajit Ray, who remarked: 'I don't think Rabindranath ever wrote idiomatic English. To me it seemed that he was always translating from Bengali.'[7]

When, for instance, Tagore tells Edward J. Thompson in 1935, with characteristic irony, that he is suffering from his past English literary reputation, built upon what he now admits were poor translations of his poetry, 'which, as the saying is in our own language, proves itself as a living bear which originally offered its boon as a blanket', we can guess what he meant by using this Bengali proverb. That is, once upon a time (in Nobel prize days, twenty years previously), Rabindranath thought English was something he could slip around him like a blanket, but now, with the decline in his literary standing in English, he has realised that the language is more like a hair-shirt or straitjacket that he cannot take off.[8] But had Rabindranath been writing to Thompson in Bengali, rather than English, we, as translators, would probably have replaced the innocent-looking blanket that turned out to be a bear with something like a purring cat that while being stroked suddenly shows its claws. And we believe that Tagore would have required the change. He ruthlessly altered his original images when translating, where necessary, and he was more than capable of subtle wordplay in English, of which this book contains many examples. He once wrote to his niece (a letter not included here) that he had just received a telegram stating 'Missing gown lying post office' – which made him wonder idly to her (of course in Bengali), was the gown lying in the post office or was it really missing, with the post office lying about its disappearance?[9]

To turn to the content of the letters, it is, as might be expected, extraordinarily diverse, ranging from the miseries of the peasants on the Tagore estates in what is now Bangladesh, and Tagore's efforts to relieve their poverty, to the stresses and strains of fundraising for Shantiniketan in New York, where a furious Tagore felt compelled to read his poetry to millionaire lovers of mysticism. Indeed, the friction between cultures, between East and West – a dichotomy so much sharper in Tagore's day than in ours – is perhaps the only theme that is common to almost all the letters.

Consequently, rather than attempting to introduce our selection *en masse* with one long piece at the beginning of the book, or, alternatively, with shorter pieces spread through the book each introducing a group of letters, we have chosen to provide a separate introduction to almost every letter, along with comprehensive notes. Without such individual introductions, many of the letters would be virtually meaningless, even to Tagore scholars. Inevitably, some of the introductions are of necessity longer than the letters they introduce.

Nevertheless, we have grouped the letters into eighteen chronological sections, corresponding to phases in Tagore's life, such as 'Zamindar (1890–1897)' and 'International nationalist (1934–1936)', each of which has a very brief introduction giving merely a sketch of Tagore's activities, travels and concerns during the period in question. We recognise that there is an element of artifice in these divisions – after all, Tagore had many preoccupations other than politics in the period 1934–6 – but we believe the divisions both correspond with reality to a considerable extent and also serve to impose some order on what would otherwise be too disparate and overwhelming a mass of material for the reader to absorb. They have also helped us to some extent in winnowing all the letters written in each period of Tagore's multifarious life so as to make our selection.

It is no accident that the divisions resemble, though not exactly, the chapters of our biography of Tagore, *The Myriad-Minded Man*, published in 1995. We regard this book of letters as a companion to that book. This introduction, and indeed the book as a whole, aims to avoid repeating the material in the biography. Instead, readers will find regular citations of the biography, where appropriate (as well as of numerous other articles and books on Tagore, duly referenced in our notes and bibliography). Many of the English letters part-quoted in the biography – often for the first time in print – are here given in full; and so this book may be seen as offering the full evidence for the sometimes controversial statements we have made in the biography. For example, there are a number of letters here that show the way in which the demands of Shantiniketan took precedence over the needs of Tagore's family, with unhappy consequences for all concerned; others show clearly the ambivalence of Rabindranath towards Shantiniketan and its inmates once he had established the institution; and yet others demonstrate his contradictory attitude towards his western literary fame, symbolised by his repeated (and doubtful) claim that he did not relish foreign appreciation of his English translations from 1912. Whatever may be the reader's judgement of these letters, it is important that their evidence be made available for all to read.

At the conclusion of the introduction to our biography, we quoted a comment by Tagore in a short and appreciative review he wrote of a book by an Indian scholar writing on architecture. He remarked:

> Ordinarily research scholars seem to ignore the fact that the past is of interest to us only in so far as it was *living* and that unless they discover it for us in such a way as to make us feel its life, we may admire them for their patience and industry but will not be the wiser for their labours. I have often felt sad that so much human talent and industry should disappear in the publication of matter where bones keep on rattling without forming for us an outline of the figure which once moved.[10]

There could scarcely be a more demanding human being for a biographer to attempt to bring to life than Rabindranath Tagore. We hope that this selection of his own, largely spontaneous, words will add up to more than mere rattling old bones; that it will be a fruitful contribution to a continuing scholarly effort in many countries to rebuild the reputation of a great writer who was one of the most fascinating figures ever to emerge from India.

Notes

1 'Rabindranath Tagore at home', *Hindusthan Standard*, 6 Aug. 1939 (first published in *India Monthly Magazine*).
2 Ranald Newson, 'Some recollections of Tagore', *London Mercury*, Dec. 1938, p. 186.
3 No one, so far as we are aware, has yet counted all the known letters of Tagore, and more turn up from time to time. They are scattered all over the world, but the majority are kept in either original or copy form at Rabindra Bhavan, Shantiniketan.
4 The only book of Tagore's English letters that has been adequately edited is his correspondence with William Rothenstein, elegantly published in 1972 as *Imperfect Encounter* (see Mary M. Lago (ed.), *Imperfect Encounter: Letters of William Rothenstein and Rabindranath Tagore, 1911–1941* (Cambridge, Mass., 1972)).
5 See letter 251.
6 See letter 131.
7 Ray to Andrew Robinson, 23 Dec. 1987.
8 See letter 282.
9 Tagore to Indira Devi Chaudhurani, 30 Baishakh 1300 [12 May 1893], *Glimpses of Bengal* (Krishna Dutta and Andrew Robinson trans.; London, 1991), p. 85/*Chhinnapatrabali* (1367 [1960]), p. 150.
10 'Dr P. K. Acharya on Indian architecture', *VBQ*, *1*, No. 1, May–July 1935, p. 115.

1 Rabindranath in England, *c.* 1879

Youthful bravado (1879–1889)

Introduction

Tagore's earliest existing letters were prompted by his first stay in Britain. He arrived there from India in October 1878 and remained until February 1880. Though he spent some months living with his elder brother Satyendranath, a civil servant, and his family, in Brighton and Torquay, much of his time was spent away from his family. The idea was that he should train as a barrister, but nothing came of it.

On return to Bengal, he began publishing in earnest his writing, including the letters written from Britain, which he would later call mere 'youthful bravado'. His first major volume of poetry appeared in mid-1882 and was welcomed by Bankim Chandra Chatterji [Chattopadhyay], the leading Bengali writer of the time. It was followed, in the period up to 1890, by more poetry, plays, songs, 'operas', a novel, stories and essays.

In the meantime, Rabindranath became a family man. He married Mrinalini in December 1883, and they produced a daughter, Madhurilata (Bela), in 1886, and a son, Rathindranath, in 1888. In the late 1880s, the family lived in different places in India for varying periods, but Tagore's base remained the family house at Jorasanko in north Calcutta, where he soon became the centre of artistic (especially musical) attention, helped by his talented elder brother, Jyotirindranath.

In April 1884, Kadambari, Jyotirindranath's wife, committed suicide. She had been Rabindranath's closest companion since he was a boy – many of the letters sent from Britain were meant for her – and her death was his first great loss. The experience helped to mature him as an artist.

1

To Jyotirindranath Tagore[1]

Rabindranath was only seventeen when he first went to England in 1878. Throughout his stay he wrote long and witty letters home describing English life and the life of Bengalis in England, comparing and contrasting the two; letters soon published, after editing by his elder brother Dwijendranath, in the Tagore family magazine *Bharati* and then, in 1881, in book form as *Yurop Prabashir Patra* (Letters from an Exile in Europe) – the first book to be written in colloquial, as opposed to literary, Bengali. It was 'an unlucky moment', the adult Rabindranath recalled in 1911, when writing his memoir of his early life:

Now it is beyond my power to call them back. They were nothing but the outcome of youthful bravado. At that age the mind refuses to admit that its greatest cause for pride is in its power to understand, to accept, to respect; and that modesty is the best means of enlarging its domain. To admire and praise becomes a sign of weakness or surrender, and the desire to cry down and hurt and demolish with argument gives rise to a kind of intellectual fireworks. These attempts of mine to establish my superiority by revilement might have amused me today, had not their want of straightforwardness and common courtesy been too painful.[2]

Though the published letters were included in his collected works published in 1904, when Rabindranath republished the letters in 1936 as *Pashchatya Bhraman* (Western Journey), he further edited them very substantially. His abridged text was followed by Visva-Bharati until 1961, when the complete text of *Yurop Prabashir Patra* was republished.

Tagore was certainly correct in thinking the letters pointed: even today parts should make both English and Bengali readers wince. But they are also truthful, amusing and a unique record of the Anglo-Bengali cultural collision at the zenith of the British empire. They paint a most distinct picture of a sensitive young Bengali able to love English culture, especially English literature, quite independently of his feelings for Englishmen and women. As Rabi wryly remarks of an ordinary middle-aged English doctor whom he shocked by not knowing the purpose of a woman's muff: 'Dr M– must have thought, "It's quite absurd that someone who doesn't know what a muff is has read Shakespeare!"'[3]

But if he could be devastating about little Englanders and the artificial charms of Victorian Englishwomen, Rabi was even more critical of the Bengalis who sucked up to them. His letter selected here concerns this species, dubbed by Dwijendranath *ingabangas*, an almost untranslatable nickname meaning anglicised or England-worshipping Bengalis – anglomaniacs.[4]

Rabindranath's observations of the *ingabanga* appeared first in his letters from England – supplemented, as he admitted, by his fertile imagination. Later they entered his short stories too, as satirical characterisations (and later still his nephew, the artist Gaganendranath, produced a series of brilliant caricatures). Although pukka *ingabangas* were the product of their Victorian age – Rabindranath reckoned them 'almost extinct' in his preface to the revised 1936 edition of the letters from Europe – their descendants are recognisable in both India and Britain today.[5]

Following the example of Tagore himself in 1936, we have edited his letter – but not, as in his case, because we want to omit sharp criticisms, simply because the published letter in Bengali is very long and often needlessly repetitive.[6] (Excisions are indicated by three dots.) Furthermore, the original letter is lost; thus the available text is already an edited version. This is, however, the only letter in our selection of 346 letters that we have abridged.

[London?, UK]
[1879][7]

[?]

By and by the ship arrives and docks at Southampton. The Bengali passengers have reached the shores of England. They set off for London. As they disembark from the train an English porter approaches them. Politely he enquires if he can be of service. As he takes down their luggage and ushers them into a carriage, the Bengali thinks to himself, How extraordinary! How polite the English are! That Englishmen could be so polite, he had no idea. He presses a whole shilling into the porter's hand. Never mind the cost, the newly arrived Bengali youth tells himself; the salaam of a white man was worth every penny of that shilling . . .

Before the Bengalis arrive in England, their friends who are already here have arranged rooms for them. As the Bengali enters his room, he sees a carpet on the floor, pictures hanging on the walls, a large mirror in its proper place, a sofa, stools and chairs, one or two glass flower vases, and to one side a baby piano. Good heavens! The Bengalis summon their friends: 'We aren't here as rich men, you know! My dear fellows, we haven't much cash on us, we can't afford to stay in rooms like these.' Their friends are highly amused, having completely forgotten their own precisely similar behaviour when *they* first arrived. Treating the new arrivals as throughgoing rice-eating rustics they tell them in voices full of experience, 'All rooms are like this over here.' This reminds the newcoming Bengalis of the rooms in our own country: damp, with a wooden cot covered by a wicker mat, here and there people puffing on hookahs, others lounging around a board game, their bodies bare to the waist, their shoes cast casually aside, while a cow lies tethered in the courtyard that has walls plastered in cow-dung cakes, and wet washing hangs drying over a verandah. For the first few days the Bengalis find themselves terribly embarrassed to sit on a chair or stool, lie on a bed, eat off a table or walk about a carpet. They sit very awkwardly on the sofas, fearful lest they make them dirty or damage them in any way. They imagine that the sofas have been put there for decoration, the owners surely cannot have intended them to be spoilt by use. But if that is their first impression of their rooms, there follows another impression, almost as immediate and even more significant.

In some smaller types of accommodation in England the figure called the 'landlord' still exists; but most Bengali lodgers must deal with a 'landlady'. Settling the rent, sorting out various problems, arranging food, is all down to the landlady. When my Bengali friends first stepped into their rooms, she quickly appeared, an Englishwoman waiting to greet them with the politest of 'good morning's. Hurriedly they returned the greeting in the most proper manner, and then stood struck dumb. And when they saw their various *ingabanga* friends strike up an easy conversation with the lady in question, their awkwardness turned to absolute awe. To think of it: they were talking to a real live memsahib, complete in shoes, hat and dress! Here was a sight to stir real respect in a Bengali heart. Would they ever acquire this courage shown by their *ingabanga* friends? Surely it was beyond the bounds of possibility.

Afterwards, having installed the newcomers, the *ingabanga* friends went off to their respective residences and spent the next few days making fun of Bengali ignorance – while the aforementioned landlady came each day to enquire, most politely, what my newly arrived friends liked to have, and what they did not like to have. My friends soon came to regard these occasions with real pleasure. One of them even told me that when he first ticked off this Englishwoman – ever so slightly – he felt thrilled with himself for the rest of the day. Notwithstanding, the sun did not rise in the West, mountains did not move and fire did not freeze that day . . .

To know the *ingabanga* – the England-worshipping Bengali – truly, one must observe him in three situations. One must see how he behaves with Englishmen; how he behaves with ordinary Bengalis; and how he behaves with fellow *ingabangas*. To see an *ingabanga* face to face with an Englishman is really a sight to gladden your eyes. The weight of courtesy in his words is like a burden making his shoulders droop; in debate he is the meekest and mildest of men; and if he is compelled to disagree, he will do so with an expression of extreme regret and with a thousand apologies. An *ingabanga* sitting with an Englishman, whether he be talking or listening, will appear in his every gesture and facial movement to be the acme of humility. But catch him with his own countrymen in his own sphere, and he will display genuine temper. One who has lived three years in England will regard himself as infinitely superior to one who has spent a mere one year here. Should the former type of resident happen to argue with the latter type, one may observe the 'three-year' man exert his prowess. Each word he utters, and each inflection he gives it, sounds like a dictum personally dictated to him by the lips of goddess Saraswati.[8] Anyone who dares to contradict him he will bluntly label 'mistaken', or even 'ignorant' – to his face . . .

Had you seen for yourself the thorough research these people put into which way up a knife or fork should be held when dining, your respect would surely be still further increased. What the currently fashionable cut of a jacket is, whether today's gentleman wears his trousers tight or loose, whether one should dance the waltz, the polka or the mazurka, and whether meat should follow fish or vice versa – these people know all these things with unerring accuracy. Their preoccupation with trivia – what is and is not 'done' – is far greater than that of the natives of this country. If you happen to use the wrong knife to eat fish, an Englishman would not think much of it; he would put it down to your being a foreigner. But if an *ingabanga* Bengali saw you, he would probably have to take smelling salts. Were you to drink champagne out of a sherry glass, he would stare at you aghast, as if your ignorant blunder had totally upset the world's tranquillity. And were you, God forbid, to wear a morning coat in the evening, had he a magistrate's power he would condemn you to solitary confinement . . .

There is one other special feature of the *ingabanga* I must tell you about. The majority of those who come here do not confess if they are married – because married men naturally command less attention from unmarried ladies. By pretending to be bachelors they can mix much more freely in society and have much more fun, otherwise their unmarried companions would never permit such goings on. There is a lot to be gained by declaring oneself unattached.

No doubt there are many *ingabanga* Bengalis who do not fit my description. I have written only of the general characteristics of the species as I have spotted them.

[?]
[Rabi?]

Source: RR, I, pp. 553–60. The original MS is lost.

1 Jyotirindranath Tagore (1849–1925): musician, composer, artist, poet, dramatist, translator into Bengali from Sanskrit, English and French; fifth son of Debendranath Tagore. See Krishna Dutta and Andrew Robinson, *Rabindranath Tagore: The Myriad-Minded Man* (London, 1995), pp. 38–9.
  No addressee of this letter is given – none is given throughout *Yurop Prabashir Patra* – but Jyotirindranath was the likely recipient, or his wife Kadambari Devi (see letter 2). The dedication of the

book is ambiguous; it reads (in translation): 'Brother Jyoti Dada. To the hands of the one whom I remembered most while in England, I dedicate this book. Affectionately Rabi.' Prashanta Kumar Paul (*Rabijibani*, II (1391 [1984]), p. 61) concludes that some of the letters were probably written to Kadambari.
2 *My Rem*, p. 115/*RR*, XVII, p. 358.
3 Krishna Dutta and Andrew Robinson (eds.), *Purabi: A Miscellany in Memory of Rabindranath Tagore, 1941–1991* (London, 1991), p. 46/*RR*, I, pp. 561–8.
4 Indira Devi Chaudhurani attributes the coining of *ingabanga* to Dwijendranath in her article, 'In memoriam Dwijendranath Tagore', *VBQ*, 10, No. 3, Nov. 1944–Jan. 1945, p. 130.
5 The preface appears as an appendix to the 1961 edition of *Yurop Prabashir Patra* (1368 [1961]), in the form of a letter to Charu Chandra Dutta.
6 A selection of letters from *Yurop Prabashir Patra*, translated by William Radice, appears as 'Letters from Europe' in Dutta and Robinson eds., *Purabi*, pp. 39–53.
7 The published letter is undated, but appears to have been written in the first half of 1879, between RT's arrival in London in January and his departure from London in the summer for Torquay.
8 Saraswati: goddess of learning and eloquence.

2

To Kadambari Tagore (Ganguli [Gangopadhyay])[1]

Considering Rabindranath's great reputation as a poet of nature in Bengali, and his admiration for an English nature poet such as Wordsworth, it is always surprising how little attention he paid in his writings to the beauties of the English rural scene. There are such passages in his works, but they are rare. This letter, again from *Yurop Prabashi Patra*, which was most likely written to his sister-in-law Kadambari Devi (also a worshipper of nature), is probably the most significant; Rabindranath's pleasure in escaping to Devon from grimy, claustrophobic London is almost palpable.

Almost half a century later, Tagore's early love of Devon helped to persuade his friend Leonard Elmhirst to found his school in Devon, in the village of Dartington. Elmhirst had already been pondering Dorset or Devon as the place for his institution; then he discussed the school with Tagore, who independently told him:

> As we have no right to deprive growing children of direct access to nature and to all the beauty that nature lavishes upon us, the most beautiful place you can find in England will not be too beautiful for your school. Why not look for a site in Devon? I still remember my visit with delight. I was only a boy. It was so beautiful.'[2]

[Torquay, Devon, UK]
[June–August 1879][3]

[?]

Summertime. The sun is shining wonderfully. It is two o'clock in the afternoon. A sweet breeze is blowing, similar to the one that blows at noontime in winter in our country. Everything basks in the sunshine. How pleasant it feels and how languid it makes my mind, I just can't tell you.

We are now staying in a town called Torquay in Devonshire.[4] It is beside the sea. Hills all around. Such a crystal-clear day – no clouds, no fog and no gloom; there are trees everywhere, birds chirping everywhere, flowers blooming everywhere. When I was in Tunbridge Wells, I used to think that if Madan [god of love] were to appear here he would have to grope his way through many thorny thickets and copses to find even a few wild flowers to decorate his bow.[5] But here in Torquay, even if he invented a weapon like a Gatling gun which could fling a thousand flower arrows per minute and he kept this rate up twenty-four hours in a day, there would still be no likelihood of his bankrupting his flower stock, so much is here. Wherever you tread there are flowers. Every day we go for walks in the hills. Cows and sheep are grazing; in places the road slopes so much that climbing up or down is hard going. In other places the path is very narrow, the trees close in on both sides and cast dark shadows, there are rough steps for the benefit of climbers, and creepers and shrubs grow in the middle of the path. All around the sun shines mildly. The air is quite warm and reminds you of India. This warmth, though little, seems to make the creatures more lethargic than those in London. Horses move rather slowly, people too do not rush around – everyone loiters.

The seaside here I like very much. When the tide comes in, the huge boulders on the shore are submerged, only their tops show. They look like small islands. There are many cliffs, large and small, rising above the water. The washing of the waves has formed caves beneath these cliffs; when the tide ebbs we sometimes go inside them and sit there. In the interiors pools of clear water collect, there are patches of lichen, the sea smell is invigorating and boulders lie scattered in all directions. Some days we all try to shift these boulders by pushing and shoving, and we pick up various shells such as snail shells and cockles. Certain of the cliffs practically lean over the ocean; from time to time we clamber up them with a lot of effort and sit at the top watching the rise and fall of the waves below. A roaring sound reaches us, small boats float past with raised sails, the sun shines down, and with a parasol shading us we lie back, heads against the rocks, and chat. Where else shall I find such a fine place for idling? Once in a while I go up into the hills, look out for a secret spot enclosed by boulders and covered by vegetation, drop down into it with my book, and sit and read.

[?]
[Rabi?]

Source: RR, I, pp. 578–9. The original MS is lost.

1 Kadambari Tagore (Ganguli [Gangopadhyay]) (1859–84): wife of Jyotirindranath Tagore, whom she married in 1868; her maiden name was Matangini Ganguli. Kadambari was Rabi's closest companion and literary confidante during his childhood and adolescence, to whom he dedicated several books and on whom he based his novella *Nashtanirh* (*The Broken Nest*), filmed by Satyajit Ray as *Charulata*. She remained childless and committed suicide in April 1884.
    No addressee of this letter is given (see letter 1, n. 1). The content suggests that the letter was written to Kadambari, rather than to Jyotirindranath.
2 Quoted in Nicholas Cottis and John Lane, *A Dartington Anthology 1925–75* (Dartington, 1975), p. 50. The conversation took place in Argentina in 1924/5, and was recalled by Elmhirst in *Dartington Hall News*, 9 June 1967.
3 The published letter is undated but it must postdate 12 June 1879, when RT was still in London attending a debate at the House of Commons.
4 RT's brother Satyendranath, his sister-in-law Jnanadanandini Devi and their two children had rented a house in Torquay.
5 RT probably stayed in Tunbridge Wells with cousins from the Pathuriaghat branch of the Tagores, who were the two daughters of Gnanendra Mohan Tagore, a Christian convert who settled in Britain after being disinherited by his father in Calcutta; but RT never says so explicitly (Paul, *Rabijibani*, II, p. 27).

3

To Priyanath Sen[1]

The marriage of Rabindranath, aged twenty-two, was arranged by his father on 9 December 1883 at his family home in Jorasanko, Calcutta, with the minimum of ceremony. Only a few members of the family and a few friends were present. The bride was a girl of about ten years, the daughter of an official on the Tagore estates in East Bengal, with little education and of no particular beauty, whom Rabindranath had never met. The ambivalent feelings of the bridegroom are suggested by the invitation letters he sent to his friends, such as this one.

[Calcutta, India][2]
[December 1883]

Priya Babu–

Next Sunday, on the 24th of Agrahayan, at the auspicious hour, my closest relative Shriman Rabindranath Thakur is engaged to be married.[3] You are requested to oblige me and my family by being present at the occasion on the aforesaid day at the house of Debendranath Thakur, Number 6 Jorasanko, to observe the wedding ceremony.

Anugata
Shri Rabindranath Thakur

Source: MS original at Rabindra Bhavan, Shantiniketan; letter published in *CP*, VIII, p. 11.

1 Priyanath Sen (1854–1916): close friend and literary companion of RT until the turn of the century. See Kshitish Roy, 'Rabindranath Tagore and Priyanath Sen', *VBN*, Dec. 1966, pp. 77–80.
2 There is no address on the letter, but it must have been written from Jorasanko. Instead, there is a crest containing a line from a poem by Michael Madhushudan Dutta, which translates as: 'How has it profited me to beguile myself with hope?' Beside this crest, in RT's handwriting, is the comment: 'not my motto'. Dutta's line forms the opening of his well-known poem 'Atma Bilap' (Lament for Myself), written in 1861, in which the poet laments, among other disappointments, the failure of his first marriage to an Englishwoman. Perhaps RT was making an oblique comment on his father's wish to keep him away from the English girls who had attracted him in London in 1878–80?
3 Agrahayan: Bengali month corresponding to mid-Nov.–mid-Dec.

4

To Priyanath Sen

Music was of the first importance to Tagore throughout his life. He was, however, far more responsive to Indian than to western music, though he liked western stringed instruments such as the violin and the cello. Strangely, for someone so intensely musical, he never learnt to play any instrument, Indian or western. But he became a celebrated singer early in his life. In January 1886, at Jorasanko, he sang hymns of his own composition for three thousand Brahmos at their annual festival, Maghotshab (11 Magh). Later he repeated the performance for his father, who was then bedridden. The Maharshi was so impressed that he gave his son a large cheque with the comment, recorded by Rabindranath in his memoirs: 'If the king of the country had known the language and could appreciate its literature, he would doubtless have rewarded the poet. Since that is not so, I suppose I must do it.'[1]

[Calcutta, India]
[20 January 1886]

Bhai

Today at 3.30 p.m. there is a violin concert by Reményi.[2] People who have heard him say that to hear him play the violin is a once-in-a-lifetime experience – they have yet to hear lovelier music. I shall go to hear it today with some of our boys – you really must join us, it is wrong to deprive oneself of such music. So be a good boy, skip your office and turn up at the Corinthian Theatre at the appointed time – that will be jolly nice. We have reserved four-rupee seats – you can choose which ones – but you must be there. If I had a moment's respite to draw breath, I should undoubtedly have come to you myself and compelled you to consent – but you must not take advantage of my lack of time to give me the slip.

After this comes 11 Magh – you are invited to both lunch and supper, and if you can make it in the morning I shall have the pleasure of your company all day. In the meantime there is another event – the joint prayer of the three Brahmo Samajes – that is on 9 Magh, i.e. tomorrow morning, when the leading figures from all three Samajes will gather here.[3] Your presence is required – seriously, I will be delighted if you come.

One more news item – *Meja Dada* has come.[4]

I am very busy.

Shri Rabindranath Thakur

Source: MS original at Rabindra Bhavan, Shantiniketan; letter published in *CP*, VIII, pp. 30–1.

1 *My Rem*, p. 73/*RR*, XVII, pp. 317–18.
2 Eduard Reményi (1828–98): Hungarian violinist, admired by Brahms and Liszt, who was solo violinist to Queen Victoria in 1854–9; in 1886 he undertook a world tour.
3 In fact, the occasion was mainly attended by members of the Adi Brahmo Samaj, started by Debendranath Tagore; the newspaper of the Sadharan Brahmo Samaj ignored it. (See Paul, *Rabijibani*, III (1393 [1986]), pp. 24–5.)
4 *Meja Dada*: Satyendranath Tagore; elder brother of RT, second son of Debendranath Tagore. See letter 180.

Zamindar (1890–1897)

Introduction

In 1889, at his father's behest, Rabindranath took over the management of the Tagore *zamindari* (estates) in East Bengal and Orissa from his elder brothers and other family members. He began living on the estates, in his houseboat *Padma* and in the estate buildings at Shelidah and Shahzadpur, two insignificant villages, for a substantial period of the year, but with frequent trips to Calcutta to see his family and friends and report on estate business to his father (and a brief abortive visit to Europe in the second half of 1890).

He did not at first welcome this opportunity, which seemed to offer nothing to a litterateur except the company of poor and illiterate peasants and the discomforts of village life. But in due course he realised that the change would enrich his entire life and work. In the 1890s, while living on the estates, he wrote some of his greatest lyrical poetry, many fine songs and perhaps the most distinctive of his short stories. He also developed a sympathy with the common man and woman, made the Tagore estates a byword for fairness, and took the first steps towards the 'rural reconstruction' programme that eventually took concrete shape around Shantiniketan in the 1920s. In the words of Satyajit Ray, in his documentary film, *Rabindranath Tagore*:

> With a worldly wisdom unusual in a poet but characteristic of the Tagores, Rabindranath . . . set about in a practical way to improve the lot of the poor peasants of his estates, and his varied work in this field is on record. But his own gain from this intimate contact with the fundamental aspects of life and nature, and the influence of this contact on his life and work – are beyond measure. Living mostly in his boat and watching life through the window, a whole new world of sights and sounds and feelings opened up before him.

5

To Indira Devi Chaudhurani (Tagore)[1]

As a zamindar in the *mofussil*, i.e. up-country, Tagore had periodically to entertain visiting British officials, such as magistrates and engineers. He regarded these visits with trepidation and described them to his niece with a lively mixture of self-mockery and indignation. In the earliest surviving letter to his wife, written in January 1890, he wrote: 'My sahib will come and perhaps bring his men too. They may come and dine here, or he may say, "Babu, I have no time!" Let me be so fortunate! I pray that his time will be too short.'[2] This amusing letter (to the niece) describes what transpired.

Shahzadpur, [Rajshahi, Bangladesh]
[25 January 1890]

[Bibi/Bob?]

And so at midday this zamindar babu placed his puggree on his head, picked up one of his visiting cards, climbed into his palanquin, and sallied forth. The magistrate was sitting in the verandah of his tent dispensing justice, flanked by constables. A crowd of supplicants waited nearby beneath the shade of a tree. My palanquin was set down under the sahib's nose and he received me cordially on his wooden cot. He was a young fellow with only the beginnings of a moustache. His hair was very fair with darker patches here and there, giving him an odd appearance – one could almost have mistaken him for a white-haired old man but for his extremely youthful face. Hospitality was required of me; I said, 'Do come and eat with me tomorrow night.' He said, 'I am due elsewhere to arrange for a pig sticking.' I (inwardly exultant) said, 'What a shame.' The sahib replied, 'I shall be back again on Monday.' I (now feeling despondent) said, 'Then please come and eat on Monday.' He instantly agreed. Never mind, I sighed to myself – Monday is a fair way off.

As I was returning to the house, terrific clouds rolled up and a tremendous storm began with torrents of rain. I had no desire to pick up a book, and writing was impossible, my mind was too disturbed for it – or to put my mood in more poetic language, I felt someone was missing, if only the person were here instead of being far away. So I took to wandering back and forth from room to room in a distracted frame of mind. It became quite dark. Thunder rumbled constantly, there was flash after flash of lightning, and every now and then gusts of wind got hold of the trunk of the big lychee tree outside the verandah and gave its shaggy top a thorough shaking. The dry pit in front of the house soon filled with water . . .[3] As I paced I was suddenly struck by the thought that I should offer shelter to the magistrate. I sent off a note, saying something like 'Sahib, to go out pig sticking in this weather will not work. Even though you are a strapping sahiblet, living in a watery tent can be trying for a land-based species – should you prefer dry land, my refuge awaits you.'

But having despatched the note, when I went to investigate the only spare room I found it a real sight. Two bamboo poles were hanging from the beams, over which were draped dirty old quilts and bolsters. Littering the floor were servants' belongings, tobacco pipes and two wooden chests containing a soiled quilt, a coverless oil-smeared pillow, a grimy mat, a bit of hessian variously stained and a layer of dirt . . . besides sundry packing cases full of broken odds and ends such as a rusty kettle lid, an iron stove without a bottom, a discoloured old zinc teapot, some bottles and old glasses, bits of glass shade from an oil lamp, a sooty lampstand, a couple of filters, a meat safe, a soup plate caked in treacle and dust, some broken and unbroken plates and a pile of soggy and dirty dusters. In a corner was a tub for washing clothes, Gophur Mia's cook's uniform, soiled, and his old velvet skull cap. The furniture and fittings consisted of one rickety, worm-eaten dressing table bearing water stains, oil stains, milk stains, black,

2 Rabindranath on his estates in East Bengal

brown and white stains and all kinds of mixed stains, with damaged legs and detached mirror resting against a wall and drawers which were receptacles for dust, toothpicks, napkins, old locks, the bases of broken glasses, wires from soda bottles and bed casters, rods and stuffing; one washhand stand, with broken legs; and four walls, with smelly stains and nails poking out of them.

For a moment I was overwhelmed with dismay, then it was a case of – send for everyone, the manager, the storekeeper, the cashier and all the servants, get hold of extra men, bring a broom, fetch water, put up ladders, unfasten ropes, pull down poles, take away bolsters, quilts and bedding, pick up broken glass bit by little bit, wrench nails from the wall one by one. Why are you people standing there staring? – grab hold of those and try not to break them. Bang, bang, crash! – there go three glass lamp holders – pick them up piece by piece. I myself whisk a wicker basket and mat encrusted with the filth of ages off the floor and out of the window, thereby dislodging a family of cockroaches that scatter in all directions, to whose business I have been unwitting host as they dined off my bread, my treacle and the polish on my shoes.

The magistrate's reply arrives: 'I'm on my way out of real trouble.' Hurry up everyone! You must hurry! Soon there's a shout: 'The sahib has arrived.' In a flurry I brush the dust off my hair, my beard, and the rest of my person, and try to look, as I receive my guest in the drawing room, like a gentleman who has been reposing there comfortably all afternoon. I shake the sahib's hand, converse and laugh without apparent concern; but inside I cannot stop thinking about his sleeping accommodation. When at last I showed him his room, I found it passable; he should have had a night's rest – if the homeless cockroaches did not tickle the soles of his feet. The sahib said, 'Tomorrow morning I shall go for a spot of shikar.' I refrained from making any comment. In the evening a routed footman from the sahib's camp turned up with the news that the storm had torn his sleeping tent to pieces; his office tent too was soaked and in a pretty bad state. And so the sahib had to put off hunting other animals and put with this zamindar babu.

[Uncle Rabi?]

Source: MS copy at Rabindra Bhavan, Shantiniketan; letter published in *CPB*, pp. 23–6.

1 Indira Devi Chaudhurani (1873–1960): musician, translator and close companion of RT from 1878 onwards; daughter of Satyendranath Tagore, husband of Pramatha Chaudhuri. Best known for her compilation of the notations of RT's songs, she was trained in both Indian and western music. Besides translating from Bengali into English and from French into Bengali, she published several books of her own in Bengali. See obituary in *VBN*, Sept. 1960, pp. 47–8.
2 *CP*, I, p. 2.
3 Partly illegible sentence omitted here: '... feel like writing something similar, but perhaps there is nothing more to write.'

6

To Mrinalini Tagore (Ray Chaudhuri)[1]

Rabindranath's simple affection for his young wife Mrinalini, and her lack of sophistication, are clear from this letter, written on board ship to Europe. Later letters reveal a more complex relationship.

[SS] *Siam* [en route to Europe]
Friday [29 August 1890]

Bhai Chhota Bou

Today we will reach a place called Aden and touch land again after a long time. But we cannot disembark, in case we pick up some contagious disease. On arrival in Aden we have to change ship, which will be a big bother. I cannot tell you how seasick I have been this time – for three days, whatever I swallowed just came up again, my head felt dizzy and the rest of me was in turmoil – I even wondered whether I would pull through. On Sunday night I distinctly felt my self leave my body and go to Jorasanko. You were lying on one side of the big bed, Beli and Khoka beside you. I caressed you a little and said, 'Little wife, remember this Sunday night when I left my body and came to see you – when I return from Europe I shall ask you if you saw me.' Then I kissed Beli and Khoka and came back.[2] When I was ill did you ever think of me? I became restless thinking of seeing you again. Nowadays I feel constantly that there is no place like home – this time when I get back I shall not stir out anymore. Today I had my first bath for a week. But baths here are not a pleasure: the salt in the seawater makes the whole body sticky and my hair becomes matted and horribly glued together – it is an odd sensation. I think I shall avoid bathing until I leave the ship. It will be another week before we reach Europe – when we get there, I shall be glad to set foot on land. I have had enough of the ocean day and night. But at present the sea is pretty calm, the ship hardly rolls, and I am no longer sick. All day I lie on deck in a long chair and either chat with Loken, ponder, or read a book.[3] At night too, we make our beds on deck and avoid entering our cabins if possible. Going inside the cabin makes you feel queasy. Last night, though, it suddenly rained – we had to drag our bedding to a place where the rain could not get at us. Since then it has not stopped raining, after being fine and sunny yesterday. On board there are some little girls, whose mother has died and whose father is taking them to England. When I look at them I feel pity. Their father goes everywhere with them, but he does not know how to dress them properly or how to look after them. When they go out in the rain and he warns them not to, they tell him 'we like going out in the rain' – which makes him laugh a bit; seeing them happily playing in the rain he cannot bring himself to stop them. To look at them reminds me of my own babies. Last night I dreamt of Beli – she had come on board the steamer, and she looked lovelier than I can say. You must tell me what sort of thing I should bring them when I return home. If you answer this letter immediately, I might receive your reply while I am in England. Remember that Tuesday is the day for mailing to England. Give the children lots of kisses from me – and have some yourself too.

Shri Rabindranath Thakur

Source: MS original at Rabindra Bhavan, Shantiniketan; letter published in *CP*, I, pp. 3–5.

1 Mrinalini Tagore (1873?–1902): wife of RT; they married in 1883 (see letter 3) and she bore him five children. See Visva-Bharati, *Mrinalini Devi*.
2 Beli, or Bela: familiar name of Madhurilata, daughter of RT, then aged nearly four. Khoka: familiar name of Rathindranath, son of RT, then aged almost two.
3 Loken: Lokendranath Palit (1865–1915): friend and literary companion of RT from 1879; he joined the Indian Civil Service in 1886 and served in Bengal and Bihar.

7

To Indira Devi Chaudhurani (Tagore)

Rabindranath was known to his tenants as an unusually conscientious, generous and innovative zamindar. His son wrote of this in his memoirs:

> Every morning [Father] would go through the accounts, hear reports from the staff, and dispose of important correspondence. But the most interesting function for him was to meet the tenants, hear their complaints and settle disputes. He did not treat them in the traditional manner. He talked with them freely and they too felt so much at ease with him that they would tell him about their land, their families, and their personal affairs. Father had made known that any tenant who wanted to see him could go straight to him; no officer was to interfere with this inherent right of the tenant. Thus was established a bond of love and respect between the landlord and the tenants, a tradition that lasted in our estates till the end.[1]

This letter shows how this 'bond' worked in practice, and also, incidentally, how Rabindranath collected material for his short stories.

Kaligram, [Rajshahi, Bangladesh]
[19? January 1891]

[Bibi/Bob?]

As I began to write to you, one of our clerks here came and chattered away about his sad state of poverty, the need for an increase in his wages and the necessity of a man getting married – he went on talking and I went on writing, until finally I paused and briefly tried to get him to understand the idea that when a sensible person grants someone's petition it is because the petition is reasonable, not because it has been repeated five times instead of once only. I had imagined that such a wise and wonderful remark would render the fellow speechless, but I saw that in fact it had the opposite effect. Instead of falling silent he asked me a question – if a child does not open its mind to its own parents, who will he talk to? This left me stumped for a satisfactory reply. So once again he started chattering and I for my part continued to write. To be nominated a parent out of the blue and for nothing is quite a trial.

Yesterday, while I was listening to the petitions of my tenants, five or six boys appeared and formed a disciplined line in front of me. Before I could open my mouth their spokesman launched into a high-flown speech: 'Sire! The grace of the Almighty and the good fortune of your benighted children have once more brought about your lordship's auspicious arrival in this locality.' He went on like this for nearly half an hour, pausing from time to time to stare at the sky when he forgot his lines, correct himself, and then continue. His subject was the shortage of school benches and stools. 'For want of these wooden supports,' as he put it, 'we know not where to seat ourselves, where to seat our revered teachers, or what to offer our most respected inspector when he pays a visit.' Such a torrent of eloquence from such a small boy made it hard for me to hide a smile. Particularly in a place like this, where the unlettered ryots normally voice their humble needs and sorrows in the plain and direct vernacular. The talk is usually of floods, famines, cows, calves and ploughs – in other words the unavoidable

Zamindar

facts of life – and even those words get twisted out of shape. So a speech about stools and benches in such refined language sounded really out of place! The clerks and ryots, however, were duly impressed by the boy's mastery of words – they seemed to be lamenting to themselves, 'Our parents failed to educate us properly, or we too could appear before the zamindar and make appeals in equally grand language.' One of them nudged another and said enviously, 'He must have been coached.'

In due course I interrupted and said, 'Well, boys, I shall arrange for the required benches and stools.' Undaunted, the boy took up where he had left off and, despite my having spoken, finished to the last word, bowed low in order to touch my feet with a *pranam*, and then took himself and the others home. He had lavished such pains over his learning by heart. Had I refused to supply the seats he probably would not have minded, but had I deprived him of his speech – that would have struck him as intolerable. Therefore, though it kept more important matters waiting, I gravely heard him out. If someone with the right sense of humour had been about, probably I would have jumped up and run next door to share the joke. But a *zamindari* is simply not the place for a humourmonger – here we display only solemnity and high learning.[2]

[Uncle Rabi?]

Source: MS copy at Rabindra Bhavan, Shantiniketan; letter published in *CPB*, pp. 32–3.

1 Rathindranath Tagore, *On the Edges of Time*, 2nd edn (Calcutta, 1981), p. 28. See also Annada Sankar Ray, 'Tagore as a zamindar', *Statesman* (Tagore Centenary Supplement), 8 May 1961, in which Ray gives examples of how RT's tenants loved him, drawn from the author's personal experience as a district official in East Bengal in the 1930s.
2 RT inspected the school on 20 Jan. 1890 and noted in its inspection book: 'I did not try to frighten the boys out of their wits by cursory examination, which I find they have often enough. I have every reason to believe that the headmaster is doing his duty conscientiously and I dare say the school is as good as any other of its kind' (Paul, *Rabijibani*, III, p. 130).

8

To Indira Devi Chaudhurani (Tagore)

As a prolific letter writer, Tagore was naturally concerned with the workings of the postal service. Needless to say, in the 1890s it was far more efficient than its equivalent a century later: letters posted on the Tagore estates would often reach Calcutta the following day; Shelidah was then less than half a day's journey from Calcutta by train and boat.

The postmaster of Shahzadpur, who is mentioned in this letter, reappears in letters 16 and 21. He is one of the few individuals in Tagore's letters whom he specifically links with a character in his short stories.

Shahzadpur, [Rajshahi, Bangladesh]
[9? February 1891]

[Bibi/Bob?]

Some evenings the postmaster comes upstairs to have a chat with me. His office is on the ground floor of our building – very convenient, for we get our letters as soon as they arrive. I enjoy our talks. He tells of the most improbable things in the gravest possible fashion. Yesterday he informed me of the reverence towards the Ganges shown by the people of the locality. If someone dies, he said, and the relatives do not have the means to take his ashes to the Ganges, they powder a piece of bone from the funeral pyre and keep it until they come across a person who at some time or other has drunk the water of the sacred river. To him they administer some of this powder, hidden in a courteous offering of betel, and so are content to think that their deceased relative has finally made his pilgrimage to the blessed waters – or at least a portion of him has. I smiled as I remarked, 'This must be a yarn.' He pondered for quite a while and then admitted, 'Sir, it probably is.'

[Uncle Rabi?]

Source: MS copy at Rabindra Bhavan, Shantiniketan; letter published in *CPB*, p. 41.

9

To Indira Devi Chaudhurani (Tagore)

Though he was born and brought up in Calcutta, and earned his initial celebrity there, Rabindranath never liked the city. As he grew older, and Calcutta itself became larger and more commercial, his antipathy turned to detestation and he spent less and less time there. In the early 1920s, he wrote:

> Calcutta is an upstart town with no depth of sentiment in her face and in her manners. It may truly be said about her genesis: In the beginning was the spirit of the Shop, which uttered through its megaphone, 'Let there be the Office!' and there was Calcutta. She brought with her no dower of distinction, no majesty of noble or romantic origin; she never gathered around her any great historical associations, any annals of brave sufferings, or memory of mighty deeds.[1]

This letter shows Tagore's dislike of Calcutta in an amusing and novel form, a dream, but incorporating a favourite preoccupation of his: education. He had a low opinion of all the educational institutions of Calcutta – and indeed Bengal as a whole – having himself attended several of them, including St Xavier's College.[2]

Shahzadpur, [Rajshahi, Bangladesh]
[June 1891]

[Bibi/Bob?]

Last night I had an extraordinary dream. The whole of Calcutta was enveloped by some formidable but peculiar power, the houses rendered only dimly visible by a dense dark mist, through which strange doings could be glimpsed. I was on my way down Park Street in a hackney carriage, and as I passed St Xavier's College I found it to be growing rapidly with its top fast vanishing into darkness and fog. I came to know that a band of men had come to town who could, if properly paid, perform many such magical tricks. When I reached our house at Jorasanko, I found the magicians had got there too. They were ugly-looking fellows, Mongolian in features, with wispy moustaches and a few long hairs sticking out of their chins. They had the power to make people, as well as houses, grow. All the ladies in our house were keen to become taller, and the magicians sprinkled some powder on their heads and they promptly shot up. I could only mutter: 'This is most extraordinary – just like a dream!' Then someone proposed that our house should be made to expand. Our visitors agreed, and as preparation they quickly demolished some portions. Dismantling done, they demanded money, or else they would not go on. Kunja Sarkar [the cashier] was aghast; how could payment be made before the job was completed? The magicians became wild. They twisted the building into a stupendous tangle, so that half of some occupants was set into the brickwork and the other half was left sticking out. It was a diabolical business. I said to my eldest brother: 'Just look at the mess we're in. We'd better start praying to God for help!' I went into the corridor and concentrated on praying. When I had finished I thought I would go and reprimand these creatures in the name of the God – but though my heart was bursting, no words came out of my throat. Then I woke up – I am not sure when. A curious dream, wasn't it? Calcutta entirely under the control of Satan: everything in it inflating tremendously in size and prosperity with his help, while enveloped in an infernal fog. One aspect was rather funny: with the whole city to choose from, why single out the Jesuit college for special satanic attention? . . .

The schoolmasters of the English school in Shahzadpur paid me a courtesy call yesterday. They showed no sign of leaving, even though I could not find a word to say. Every five minutes or so I managed a question, to which they offered the briefest of replies; and then I sat like a dunce, twirling my pen and scratching my head. At last I ventured a query about the crops, but being schoolmasters they knew nothing of this subject whatsoever. About their pupils I had already asked everything I could think of, so I had to start over again: 'How many boys had they in the school?' One said eighty, another a hundred and seventy-five. I hoped that this might provoke an argument, but no, they settled their difference. Why, an hour and a half later, they should have decided to take their leave, is hard to know. They might just as well have gone an hour earlier or, for that matter, twelve hours later. They seemed not to follow any rule but to rely on blind fate.

[Uncle Rabi?]

Source: MS copy at Rabindra Bhavan, Shantiniketan; letter published in *CPB*, pp. 51–3.

1 *Creative Unity* (London, 1922), p. 116.
2 RT attended St Xavier's for two-and-a-half months in 1875, an experience he describes in *My Rem*, pp. 84–6/*RR*, XVII, pp. 328–9.

10

To Indira Devi Chaudhurani (Tagore)

As a short-story writer (and indeed as a painter), Tagore has a particular gift for portraying women. One of his most touching stories, 'Shamapti' ('The Conclusion'), was based on the village girl he describes in this letter. As he reminisced to an Indian interviewer in 1936:

She was quite wild and extraordinary. There was nobody to restrain her freedom. She used to watch me every day from a distance and sometimes she brought a child with her and with finger pointed towards me she used to show me to the child. Day after day she came. Then one day she didn't come. That day I overheard the talk of the village women who had come to fetch water from the river. They were discussing with anxiety about the fate of that girl, who was now to go to her mother-in-law's house. 'She is quite wild. She doesn't know how to behave. What will happen to her!' they said. The next day I saw a small boat on the river. The poor girl was forced to go aboard. The whole scene was full of sadness and pathos. One of her girl companions was shedding tears stealthily, while others were persuading and encouraging her not to be afraid. The boat disappeared. It gave me the setting for a story named 'The End'.[1]

Shahzadpur, [Rajshahi, Bangladesh]
4 July 1891

[Bibi/Bob?]

There is a boat moored at our ghat, and on the bank in front of it is a crowd of village women . . . It looks as if someone is going to embark and the others have come to see her off. Infants, veiled faces and grey hairs are all present together in large number. One girl attracts my attention more than the rest. She must be twelve or so, but the fullness of her figure could let her pass for fourteen or fifteen. Her face is fine – very dark, yet very pretty – and her hair is cropped like a boy's; it goes well with her simple, frank and alert expression. She holds a child in her arms and stands staring at me with unabashed curiosity and certainly no lack of candour or intelligence in her eyes . . . In fact her entire face and body are pleasing to look at, as if they contained not a hint of silliness, crookedness or imperfection. Her half-boyish, half-girlish look is singularly appealing: a novel blend that combines an air of unconscious independence with feminine sweetness. That such women existed in the villages of Bengal I had never imagined. Apparently none of her family is much troubled by bashfulness. One of them has let her hair down and stands in the sun combing out the knots with her fingers while conversing with another on board at the top of her voice. I learn that she has only this daughter, no son, and that the girl is a dimwit who doesn't know how to behave or talk, or even the difference between family and strangers . . . I learn, too, that because her husband Gopal's son-in-law has turned out badly, now this daughter doesn't want to go to him.

At last, when it is time to start, I see my short-cropped, plump-bodied, gold-bangled damsel with the guileless radiant face being led towards the boat with much commotion; but she refuses to get on board. With a great deal of effort, they eventually cajole her into the boat. I grasp that she is being returned from her parents' to her husband's home. As the boat casts off, each woman and girl stands on the ghat following it with her gaze, one or two slowly wiping their eyes with the loose end of their saris. A small girl with her hair tightly knotted clings to the neck of an older woman and quietly weeps on her shoulder. Perhaps she has just lost a darling *didimani* who joined her in playing with dolls and also cuffed her when she was naughty.[2] The morning sun and the riverbank seem deeply melancholic. The whole morning feels bereft of hope like the sound of a mournful ragini, and the world, for all its beauty, seems full of pain to me . . . The life history of this unknown girl has become intimately familiar.

Zamindar 25

The floating away of a boat on a stream adds pathos to the moment of farewell – it is so like death. Those who watch wipe their eyes and return to their lives, while the one who floats away becomes invisible. True, the grief wears off, perhaps sooner than we expect, the feeling is transitory, while the forgetting is permanent. But if we pause for an instant, we can see that it is the pain that is real, and not the oblivion. Separation and death remind man clearly from time to time that grief is terribly true. They make us aware that we can remain untroubled only by remaining ignorant; that anxiety and grief are the world's true realities. No one lives on, nothing survives – so stark is this truth that we humans suppress our realisation of it, along with our grief – and if and when we do call it to mind, it deeply perplexes us that not only do we ourselves not live on, neither do we live on in the minds of others. We are totally obliterated from both the outer and the inner world. There cannot be any music suitable for man's condition, whether now or eternally, except the mournful raginis of our country.

[Uncle Rabi?]

Source: MS copy at Rabindra Bhavan, Shantiniketan; letter published in *CPB*, pp. 53–5.

1 'Discourse on short stories', *Forward*, Calcutta, 23 Feb. 1936 (interview in Shantiniketan with a group of visiting writers). According to Naresh Chandra Chakravarty of Shahzadpur, the girl was the daughter of a well-known local businessman, Gopal Shaha (Paul, *Rabijibani*, III, p. 279). 'Shamapti' ('The Conclusion') was published some two years after this letter in *Sadhana*, Ashwin–Kartik 1300 [Oct.–Dec. 1893]; a recent translation appears in *Selected Short Stories* (Krishna Dutta and Mary Lago trans.; London, 1991), pp. 80–102. Satyajit Ray filmed the story in 1961, with Aparna Das Gupta (later Aparna Sen), as the tomboy Mrinmayi, acting in her first film role.
2 *didimani*: literally, 'jewel of an elder sister'.

11

To Indira Devi Chaudhurani (Tagore)

Rabindranath lived frugally at Shelidah, especially when he was living there alone, which was most of the time between 1890 and 1898, when his family joined him. Visitors, particularly sahibs rather than Bengalis, posed a problem in terms of providing hospitality; provisions for looking after them, including supplies of champagne, had to be brought from Calcutta. Indeed most of Tagore's own food, simple though it was, came from Calcutta, because the quality and variety of local food was poor. This letter describes what happened when stocks ran low.

Shelidah, [Khulna, Bangladesh]
4 January [1892]

[Bibi/Bob?]

A few days ago the engineer sahib arrived from Pabna with his wife and children. You know, Bob, that looking after guests does not come easily to me – I become soft in the head – moreover I had no idea he would turn up with a couple of children. I had planned to be alone this time, so I was especially low on edibles. Somehow, by ignoring my creature comforts, I had been getting by on scraps. Now the memsahib likes tea, and I had none to give her; she has an aversion for dal formed in childhood, and I offered her dal for lack of any other food; she has not touched fish for years and years and I, little suspecting, gave her fish curry. Luckily she likes 'country sweets' and consumed an old and dried-up piece of *shandesh* with great determination by using a fork to break it.[1] Last year's biscuit box, whatever might be the state of its contents, is going to come in handy.

I have committed another major blunder. I told the sahib that though his wife drinks tea, most regrettably I lack tea and have only cocoa. He replied, the lady loves cocoa even more than tea. Well, I've raided my cupboard – no cocoa! It's all been sent back to Calcutta. So now I have to tell him there's no tea and no cocoa either – Padma water only, and a teapot. I wonder how he will react.

The two children are really unruly and mischievous, I must say. The memsahib, with her cropped hair, is not as bad looking as I had thought – she is moderately pretty. Periodic rows break out between husband and wife which I can hear from my boat. The combination of children squabbling, servants loudly chattering, and this couple bickering is bothersome. I can't see much writing getting done today. The memsahib has just shouted at her offspring: 'What a little pig you are!' What have I done to deserve this! What's more, this evening she wants to come ashore for a stroll and has asked me to keep her company – as though I haven't enough afflictions already. If you could see me now you would be itching to laugh – I myself, as I write these words, am having a sad laugh. I had never imagined I would go walking around my *zamindari* with a mem on my arm. My ryots will doubtless be astonished. If I can only bid them all farewell tomorrow morning, I will survive; but if they say they will be staying another day, I will be dead, Bob.

[Uncle Rabi?]

Source: MS copy at Rabindra Bhavan, Shantiniketan; letter published in *CPB*, pp. 68–9.

1 *shandesh*: traditional Bengali sweetmeat made of posset; when freshly made it is soft.

12

To Indira Devi Chaudhurani (Tagore)

Tagore's tendency to anthropomorphise nature is fundamental to his life and works, though it varies greatly in intensity. And the same may of course be said of Indian classical literature. Whatever its origin in Tagore's case, the years he spent on the rivers of Bengal undoubtedly accentuated the tendency. Sometimes (as in letters 22 and 23), he seems to regard nature as detached and indifferent; at other times, as in letter 18 and in this letter, she becomes his close confidante.[1]

Shelidah, [Khulna, Bangladesh]
9 January [1892]

[Bibi/Bob?]

For some days the weather here has been wavering between winter and spring. In the morning, land and water may be shivering at the touch of the north wind, while in the evening we quiver under the caresses of a southern breeze wafting through the bright moonlight. The fact that spring is well on its way is not in doubt. After a long interval the *papiya* once more calls from the groves on the opposite bank. The hearts of men too are stirred; when evening falls, the villages near the groves emit sounds of singing, which suggests that people are no longer in a hurry to close their doors and windows and cover up snugly for the night.

Tonight is a full moon. Its great disc observes me closely through the open window on my left, as if trying to make out whether I am criticising it in my letter; it suspects, perhaps, that we earthlings are more intrigued by its dark side than by its light. From the silent sand spit in the river a *titi* bird makes the cry that matches its name. The water is quite still, rendered even stiller by an unmoving band of shadow cast upon it by the thick fringe of trees on the bank. Though the moon is full, a slight haze gives it the look of a sleepy eye held open. From tonight onwards, darkness will gradually descend. Tomorrow when I come to cross the river on return from my office, the favourite consort of my exile will be slightly estranged from me, as if beginning to have doubts about having revealed the secret recesses of her heart so fully the previous night, and hence covering herself up once more little by little. So intimate does nature become in strange and solitary places that for days I have actually been worrying myself with the thought that from now on I shall see less and less of the moon. I shall feel my exile much more keenly when her familiar tranquil radiance is gone, leaving me to float back in darkness . . . But for the moment the moon is full – the first full moon of spring – and I simply record the fact. One day something may remind me of this night, with its cry of a *titi* bird, its glimmer of light from a boat on the far shore, its dazzling thread of river brushed by the umbra of the trees along its edge, and its hazy sky overhead, pale and aloof.

[Uncle Rabi?]

Source: MS copy at Rabindra Bhavan, Shantiniketan; letter published in *CPB*, pp. 70–1.

1 The oscillation between these two extremes of attitude to nature in RT is perhaps best seen in his 1930 conversation with Einstein on the 'nature of reality' and in his exchange with Gandhi concerning the great Bihar earthquake of 1934. See the appendixes.

13

To Indira Devi Chaudhurani (Tagore)

Rabindranath's family did not join him on the Tagore estates until 1898, though he often saw them in Calcutta and Shantiniketan. He was an affectionate father to all his children, but he was fondest of his eldest born, Bela – his 'favourite child', according to his son Rathindranath ('Khoka'). She inspired a well-known poem, 'Jete Nahi Dibo' (I'm Not Letting You Go), and a well-known short story, 'Kabulioala' ('The Kabuliwallah'), both of which he wrote during the latter half of 1892.[1] This letter describes Bela's sensitivity, which contrasts with the more conventional behaviour of her mother, Rabindranath's wife, known here as *Chhota Bou*.

Bolpur, [West Bengal, India]
6 Jaishtha 1299 [18 May 1892]

[Bibi/Bob?]

The other evening Khoka and Bela had an argument which is worth recounting to you. Khoka said: 'Bela, I'm feeling hungry for water.' Bela said: 'Oh Toothless, you don't say hungry for water. It's thirsty for water.' But Khoka was firm: 'No, hungry for water.' Bela: 'Oh Khoka! I'm three years older than you and are two years younger than me, you know! I know so much more than you do!' Khoka was suspicious: 'You are so old?' Bela: 'Alright, ask Father.' Khoka suddenly became excited: 'But I drink milk and you don't!' Bela was full of scorn: 'So what! Mother doesn't drink milk, and you can't say Mother isn't older than you!' Khoka went completely quiet, put his head on a pillow and was lost in thought. Then Bela began to chatter, 'O Father, there's someone I have ever such a close friendship with! She's really crazy and ever so lovely! Oh I can eat her up!' And then she ran over to Renu and gave her such an enormous shower of kisses that Renu began to cry.[2]

Yesterday Bela came to me feeling very sad. What happened was that Swayam Prabha and others were cooking fish curry in the small bungalow. A mad chap had taken refuge in there with some mangoes – *Chhota Bou*, Swayam Prabha and the rest were scared of him and so they shooed him out.[3] I was having a rest in my first-floor room, when Bela came back from the small bungalow and said to me in a distressed voice, 'Father, that man is very poor, poor man is hungry, so he went to the bungalow with some mangoes, and they pushed him out with sticks.' She kept on saying, 'Poor man is poor, he has nothing, he has almost nothing on, perhaps in winter he will have nothing to wear, so he'll be cold. He didn't do anything wrong. I asked him his name and he told me. He said he lives in heaven. They drove him away, poor man, and he said nothing. He just went away.' How sweetly she said all this to me! Beli is really full of kindness. She spoke with such genuine sympathy – cruelty of this kind seemed so needless to her. As I listened to her I was very touched. Beli will grow up to be an affectionate, honest and good-natured woman. Khoka too is very affectionate. He really adores Renu. He cuddles her so gently and puts up with all her antics more patiently than many a mother would.

[Uncle Rabi?]

Source: MS copy at Rabindra Bhavan, Shantiniketan; letter published in *CPB*, pp. 79–80.

1 'Jete Nahi Dibo' was written in Calcutta on 29 Oct. 1892 and is clearly about Bela. 'Kabulioala' was published in *Sadhana*, Agrahayan 1299 (Nov.–Dec. 1892) and is much more loosely based on Bela: RT once told C. F. Andrews that the five-year-old girl Mini was Bela, but in 1936, long after Bela's death, when asked about the origin of the story, he mentioned a real Kabuliwallah but did not mention Bela – perhaps the subject was too painful for him (Andrews to RT, 20 Oct. 1917 [RB]; 'Discourse on short stories', *Forward*, Calcutta, 23 Feb. 1936).
2 Madhurilata (Bela), born 25 Oct. 1888, was then four and a half; Rathindranath (Khoka), born 27 Nov. 1888, was three and a half; and Renuka (Renu), born 23 Jan. 1891, was not yet one and a half.
3 *Chhota Bou*: Mrinalini Devi, wife of RT; Swayam Prabha: wife of Shatya Prashad Ganguli [Gangopadhyay], a nephew of RT.

14

To Indira Devi Chaudhurani (Tagore)

Rabindranath often visited the ashram at Shantiniketan and stayed for some time in the years before he finally moved there for good in 1901. He was deeply attracted to both the arid plain around the ashram and the riverine landscape of the Tagore estates. 'But there is no doubt', according to his son Rathindranath,

> that [Father's] first and deepest love was for the country of mellow green fields with their clusters of bamboo shoots swaying gently in the south breeze and hiding villages in their midst, of majestic rivers with their stretches of gleaming white sand – the haunts of myriads of wild ducks . . . Such associations had entered deeper into his life than the parched and barren wastes that surrounded him at Santiniketan, the choice of his later years.[1]

This letter describes a storm at Shantiniketan, which makes an interesting comparison with the storm at Shahzadpur described in letter 5. The Shantiniketan storm strikes Rabindranath, significantly, as more fanatical than the storm at Shahzadpur.[2]

Bolpur, [West Bengal, India]
12 Jaishtha [1299] [24 May 1892]

[Bibi/Bob?]

As I wrote to you earlier, in the late afternoon I like to pace my roof terrace with only myself for company. Yesterday about this time it occurred to me that I ought to show the beauties of the area to two guests staying here, and so I strolled out with them, taking Aghore as guide.[3] At the horizon, where a blue fringe of trees met the sky, a line of dark-blue cloud had risen, magnificent to see. It prompted me to be poetical and say that it was like kohl on the lashes of a beautiful blue eye. One of my companions failed to catch the remark, another did not follow it, while the third dismissed it with the comment: 'Yes, very pretty.' I was not encouraged to attempt a second flight of fancy. We walked about a mile until we came to a dam with palmyra trees beside it, from which flows a natural spring. While we stood looking at this, we realised that the line of cloud we had seen in the north had swollen and darkened and was making for us with regular flashes of lightning.

Unanimously we decided that the beauties of nature were better viewed from the safety of the house, but no sooner had we turned homewards than the storm, with giant strides over the open ground, was on us with an angry roar. I had no idea, while I was admiring Nature's gorgeous kohl-rimmed eyes, that she would shortly fly at us like an irate housewife, threatening us with a tremendous slap! Dust made the sky so dark that we could not see beyond a few paces. The fury of the storm continued to increase, and grit driven by the wind stung our bodies like shot, while gusts took us by the scruff of the neck and thrust us along and drops of rain slapped and whipped our faces. Run! Run! But the ground was not level; it was deeply scarred with watercourses, and not easy to cross at any time, much less in a storm. I managed to get entangled in a thorny shrub, and as I was trying to escape, the wind grabbed me and practically threw me to the ground.

We had almost reached the house when a host of servants came hurrying towards us with a hullabaloo and fell upon us like a second storm. Some held our arms, some beat their breasts, some eagerly showed the way, others hung on our backs as if fearing that the storm might carry off their master altogether. We had a job to evade the attention of this retinue and get into the house, panting, hair dishevelled, skin dust-caked and clothing drenched.

Still, I had learnt one thing; never again to write in a poem or story a description of a hero, the image of his lady love imprinted in his mind, passing unruffled through wind and tempest. The idea is quite false. No one could keep any face in mind, however lovely, in such a gale; he would be too busy keeping grit out of his eyes. I was wearing my eye glasses. The wind was blowing so hard, I could hardly keep hold of them. So, clutching my glasses in one hand and the pleats of my dhoti in the other I stumbled along, catching against thorny bushes and falling into holes. Just imagine if my lady love had made her home on the banks of our own River Kopai – could I have been holding her image in my mind rather than my glasses and dhoti! The Vaishnava poets have sung ravishingly of Radha going calmly to her tryst with Krishna through a stormy night. I wonder if they ever paused to consider the state in which she must have reached him? The tangle of hair is easy to imagine; and so is the condition of her ornaments and toilet. Encrusted in dust and spattered all over with mud, she must have gained her bower looking quite a sight! But when we read Vaishnava poems, none of this comes to mind. Instead we conjure a picture of a lovely woman, passing beneath sheltering *kadamba* blossoms in the blackness of a stormy night in the month of Shraban towards the bank of the Yamuna, forgetful of wind or rain, drawn by her surpassing love, as if in a dream.[4] Lest she be heard, she has tied up her anklets, and lest she be seen she is clad in dark-blue raiment – but she holds no umbrella lest she get wet, she carries no lantern lest she fall. Too bad for such necessities – so essential in living, so redundant in poetry! Poetry strives vainly to free us from the bondage of a thousand practical demands. Umbrellas, shoes and shirts will forever be needed: it is poetry that people say will become obsolete with the march of civilisation, while patent after patent will be taken out on new designs of shoe and umbrella.

[Uncle Rabi?]

Source: MS copy at Rabindra Bhavan, Shantiniketan; letter published in *CPB*, pp. 84–6.

1 Rathindranath Tagore, *Edges of Time*, p. 34.
2 Satyajit Ray wrote of Shantiniketan that it was 'a world apart':

> It was a world of vast open spaces, vaulted over with a dustless sky, that on a clear night showed the constellations as no city sky could ever do. The same sky, on a clear day, could summon up in moments an awesome invasion of billowing darkness that seemed to engulf the entire universe. (Quoted in Andrew Robinson, *Satyajit Ray: The Inner Eye* (London, 1989), p. 55)

3 Aghorenath Chatterji [Chattopadhyay] (1861–1932): first resident of the Shantiniketan ashram, who described this early period in his memoirs (see bibliography).
4 Shraban: Bengali month corresponding to mid-July–mid-Aug.; monsoon.

15

To Indira Devi Chaudhurani (Tagore)

In 1930, Tagore told a Jewish interviewer in New York: 'For centuries the Arabs have neglected their land, because spiritually they were above political nationalism. Western civilisation calls this state primitive and uncivilised.'[1] He was being consistent with his famous line, 'Much rather would I be an Arab Bedouin!', in his 1888 poem 'Duranta Asha' (Wild Hopes). There he began to articulate the fierce individualism that throughout his life would be at war with his urge to reform his countrymen and indeed the world. This letter develops the poem's thought, and concludes with a sentence that is peculiarly ironic in today's Bengal, where the songs of Tagore, *Rabindrasangit*, have become a unique source of 'comfort and solace'.

> Shelidah, [Khulna, Bangladesh]
> 31 Jaishtha [1299] [12 June 1892]

[Bibi/Bob?]

I hate all the demands of good manners. Nowadays I keep repeating that line: 'Much rather would I be an Arab Bedouin!'[2] Oh for a healthy, strong, unfettered barbarity! I want to quit this creeping senility of mind and body, constantly preoccupied with ancient quibbles over custom and convention, and feel the joy of a vigorous incautious life; to hold confident, carefree, generous ideas and aspirations – for better or for worse; to break free of this perpetual friction between custom and reason, reason and desire, desire and action. If I could only escape utterly the bonds of this restricted life, I would storm the four quarters with wave upon wave of excitement, grab a sturdy wild horse and tear away on it to the very heights of ecstasy.

But I am a Bengali, not a Bedouin! I sit in my corner, moping and worrying and arguing. My mind is like a fish being fried – first this way up, now the other – blistered by the boiling oil on one side, and then on the other. Enough of this. Since it is impracticable to be uncivilised, I had better try to be thoroughly civil – why foment a quarrel between the two? . . .

I am by nature unsocial – human intimacy is almost unbearable to me. Unless I have a lot of space around me in all directions I cannot unpack my mind, mentally stretch my arms and legs. Let the human race flourish with my blessings, but let its members not lean on me . . . Let the general public leave me completely aside and most probably it will still find the good counsel it seeks. People will not lack for comfort and solace.

[Uncle Rabi?]

Source: MS copy at Rabindra Bhavan, Shantiniketan; letter published in *CPB*, pp. 89–90.

1 Quoted in Joseph Brainin, *Jewish Standard*, Toronto, 28 Nov. 1930 (interview with RT).
2 *RR*, II, p. 197.

16

To Indira Devi Chaudhurani

In letter 8, Tagore mentions the postmaster at Shahzadpur who became a basis for his story 'The Postmaster', noting the man's penchant for story-telling and myth-making. In this amusing letter, the postmaster reappears but now seems more sceptical about superstition. The story he tells Rabindranath, though ludicrous, is not as improbable as one might think a century later – especially when one recalls the willingness of some Indians worldwide to believe that images of Ganesh in various countries drank milk during a short period in 1995. It was even suggested at that time by one commentator that Tagore, were he alive, would have been sympathetic to these claims. This letter disproves such an assertion.

Shahzadpur, [Rajshahi, Bangladesh]
28? June [1892]

[Bibi/Bob?]

Yesterday I wrote to you that the following night at 7 p.m. I had an engagement with Kalidasa the poet. At the appointed hour I lit a lamp, drew up my chair to the table, and sat ready, book in hand – when instead of Kalidasa, the postmaster walked in. A live postmaster cannot but claim precedence over a dead poet. I could not very well say to him: kindly make way for Kalidasa, who is due any minute now – and if I had, he would not have understood me. So I pulled out a stool and quietly said goodbye to old Kalidasa. There is a kind of bond between this postmaster and me. When the post office was on the ground floor of the estate building, I used to meet him every day and in this very room upstairs I wrote my story 'The Postmaster'. When it came out in *Hitabadi* our postmaster touched on it after a series of bashful smiles.[1] I must say I like the man. He has a fund of anecdotes which I dip into and silently enjoy. He also has a nice sense of humour. That is how he catches and holds one's interest. After sitting all day on my own, as I do here, contact with a live human being produces ripples in my calm existence . . .

He was narrating to me the saga of our munsiff. Hearing the whole business told in his special style made me weak with laughter. What has happened is that the munsiff has all of a sudden perceived Lord Shiva in the bole of a tree. On the first day he saw Shiva, on the next day Kali, and on the day after that Radha-Krishna – as if the entire celestial abode of the gods had come down to roost in our Shahzadpur banyan tree. The munsiff grabs everyone and says: 'Look, look, can't you see it! There's his eye, there's her tongue!' Those who are dependent on him, such as his clerks, see these things too, but those who do not rely on him for anything do not see them. Our postmaster belongs to the latter group. On days when offerings of sweet *kshir* and jackfruit are made to the goddess, the postmaster manages to see something in the tree – but as soon as he has lapped up his *kshir*[2] he asks the munsiff, 'Which part did you say was the eye, sir?' The munsiff replies, 'Don't you see it? It's there, look up there!' Then the postmaster says gravely, 'Oh I see, I thought that was the head.' On one occasion the munsiff said to him, 'Well sir, did you see what happened? During today's worship, just when the bells and gongs were being struck, something flew into the tree and settled there and a few drops of water fell down.' And the postmaster, wearing his most serious face, replied, 'Of course – yes, certainly the tree moved.' The foot of the tree has now been paved – the munsiff is doing *puja* there twice daily, bells and conch shells are resounding, and a sanyasi is sitting smoking hashish and saying through closed eyes, 'I see Mother Kali here.' One or two local people are also experiencing trances, and speaking divine words while entranced. All sorts of quackery is starting to spring up. The postmaster said to me, 'When the magistrate visits your *zamindari* you call upon him. Now the gods have taken up residence in this banyan tree, you really must pay them a visit.' I am thinking I shall go to watch the fun. What's more, if this rumour persists a while longer, Shahzadpur will become a place of pilgrimage. We shall all gain from that.[3]

It was quite late when the postmaster left and I got started on [Kalidasa's] *Raghuvamsa*. I read the bit about the *swayamvara* of Indumati.[4] Seated on rows of thrones in the marriage hall, splendidly attired, striking-looking princes are kept waiting. Suddenly blasts of conch shell and bugle sound, and Indumati, in bridal finery supported by Shunanda, enters and stands between the rows of suitors. What a superb picture! Then she is introduced by Shunanda to the princes one by one, and to each of them Indumati makes a courteous *namashkar*, and passes on. How beautifully she does it! Though she rejects each one she is so respectful that her gesture seems like reverence. This is far superior to the haughty vanity of an English miss. These are all princes and all older than she – for Indumati is a mere girl – and yet she passes them by. Had she not wiped away the stain of that fact with the humility of her *pranam*, the scene would have lost its grace. But before Prince Aja could be garlanded, the night had become far advanced and I had to go to bed – and so Indumati's marriage could not be arranged yesterday, unlike our Priya's.[5]

[Uncle Rabi?]

Source: MS copy at Rabindra Bhavan, Shantiniketan; letter published in *CPB*, pp. 99–101.

1 *Hitabadi* began publishing on 30 May 1891, with RT as its literary editor. He contributed six stories to the magazine, including 'The Postmaster' (exact date of publication unknown).
2 *kshir*: milk condensed and sweetened by boiling.
3 Though RT evidently did not believe in gods roosting in banyan trees, the imagery must have appealed to him: in his (much later) paintings, the branches of trees are sometimes seen to conceal grotesque faces.
4 The *swayamvara* of Indumati is the subject of canto 6 of *Raghuvamsa*, which culminates in Indumati garlanding Prince Aja as her husband-to-be (Kalidasa, *The Dynasty of Raghu* (Robert Antoine trans.; Calcutta, 1972), pp. 67–78). On RT's view of *Raghuvamsa*, see 'The springhead of Indian civilisation', *MR*, Dec. 1912, pp. 566–7/*RR*, XIV, pp. 457–80.
5 Priya: Priyam Bada Devi (1871–1935): niece of Pramatha Chaudhuri; she married on 27 June 1892.

17

To Indira Devi Chaudhurani (Tagore)

In early 1893, Rabindranath visited Orissa on a tour of the family estates. At Cuttack, staying with a Bengali friend who was the district judge, he came in contact with various British officials and their wives. These encounters provoked him to write several letters to his niece, strongly criticising the British in India, as well as four essays.[1]

The irony present in letter 5 concerning the magistrate at Shahzadpur here turns into downright, even blimpish condemnation – of the arrogance of the official class and of the sycophancy of those babus waiting upon British favour. Many of his later stories about the Calcutta elite obviously benefited from such first-hand observation.[2]

This letter is especially interesting because it deals with the clash of cultures as well as the more superficial and familiar political friction between British and Indian. Rabindranath describes how each side sang to each other and then applauded, and then he asks, 'Can such people ever enjoy what I truly love?' He had been asked, or rather compelled, to sing for a British audience many times since his first visit to England in 1878 – with extremely mixed feelings. In his autobiography, he wrote of how at parties on his first visit, 'everyone clearly anticipated some extraordinary specimen of native music and added their entreaties . . . Afterwards, amidst much suppressed tittering, would come a chorus of "Thank you very much!" "How interesting!"' – and he would perspire all over.[3] Tagore came to the conclusion, which only deepened with age, that Indian music and European music affected the listener in completely different ways.[4]

Cuttack, [Orissa, India]
[6 March 1893]

[Bibi/Bob?]

You have asked me if I am happy with the applause I received at the magistrate's house in Puri. Your question has been prompted by my not writing to you openly about the whole affair. So let me give you a detailed account. When Bihari Babu and others first requested me to call on the magistrate of Puri, I hesitated, but given their assurances and their evident keenness, I reluctantly consented.[5] Having written my name on a couple of visiting cards I went along with Bihari Babu and his wife. They did not take their own cards, instead they sent in a note along with my two cards. After about five minutes word came – let us come back the following morning and the sahib will see us. Bihari Babu and Mrs Gupta were flabbergasted. Retreating from this ticklish situation we stepped out of the magistrate's house. Bihari Babu and wife were now livid. That evening a letter came from Mrs Walsh (the magistrate's name is Walsh) expressing deep regret. The message sent in by the judge sahib and his memsahib had not been delivered to her by the bearer. I had already expected this. But the basic fact remained that while the magistrate had not intended to show disrespect to the judge, had it been another 'native' gentleman calling, he would have been asked to come back the next day in order to meet the sahib. Perhaps the very idea of my sending a card had struck Mrs Magistrate as audacity. Of course the magistrate might say that he was short of time, but who is he – this son of a nabob – that I should have to come and pay him my respects at an hour appointed by him! Obviously I accept that our countrymen are to blame here, for the way they hang about the doors of the sahibs, salaam them and solicit their daily bread from them – and the idea that I, a person with a Bengali name, would have the nerve to make a social 'call' on the Magistrate and Mrs Magistrate had never crossed their minds. At the same time I think that to take great offence at the sahib's behaviour is to overreact. Yet I cannot help feeling that the effort to show respect to these people requires a degree of formality that is really bothersome.

However respectable and well born I may be, to them this is of no value. Until such time as I may erase the particular features of my race and put on a counterfeit badge of honour bestowed by the sahibs, they will not regard me as a person. Just look at what happens with our barristers: however much they cultivate English society and the English temperament, they still cannot get on intimate terms with the sahibs living here. Even in the bar library they naturally gravitate into a dark-complexioned circle estranged from the rest like the dark spots on the face of the full moon. So what is the use of trying, why do we force ourselves? Have we become so thoroughly unbearable to our own people! However dark-faced they may be, they cannot be any darker than us. As long as the English show me respect by denying my race, I will treat that respect as an intolerable insult. So you ask, was I happy when the Puri magistrate agreed to meet me the following day and invited me to dine? Don't even give it a thought. But had I rejected the invitation, I would clearly have been making an exhibition of my hurt feelings and also diminishing the importance of the hurt – in addition to mortifying Bihari Babu.

I therefore accepted it, went into dinner arm in arm with the magistrate's sister-in-law and sat at the table with a smile on my face; I agreed with my companion that the beach at Puri was indeed a beautiful one, and I expressed delight in the fact that the sea breeze keeps Puri from ever becoming too hot. After that I listened to some English singing and sang to the sahibs in reply. I applauded and so did they. But does such appreciation show that the heart has been touched? Or is it just the curiosity that has been satisfied? Does it not resemble the conducting of an experiment to see which titbit from our plates will feel tasty to a palate very different from ours? Can such people ever enjoy what I truly love? And if they do not like something, is that thing therefore worthless? Were this really so, what pleasure could their applause afford me? If we begin to rate the applause of Englishmen too highly we shall come to reject much that is good in us, and adopt much that is bad from them. We shall grow ashamed to go about without socks, for instance, and cease to feel shame at the sight of their ball dresses. We shall have no hesitation in throwing overboard our manners, and cheerfully emulating their customary lack of them. Our achkans will be cast aside as unsatisfactory apparel, but we shall replace them on our heads with hats that are hideous. Handshakes and applause from fair-skinned hands are terribly important to us, and they are indeed visible marks of respect – but they undermine our authentic self-respect. Consciously or unconsciously we come to mould our lives according to whether we are clapped or not, and thus we trivialise ourselves.

I therefore solemnly admonish myself as follows,

> O Earthen Pot! Keep away from that Metal Pot! Whether it smashes you in anger or merely gives you a patronising tap, you are done for, holed in either case. So pay heed to sage Aesop's counsel – and keep your distance.
> Let the Metal Pot serve the wealthy homes; your work is in the homes of the poor. Allow yourself to be broken and you will have no place in either home but will return to the clay from which you came, or at best you will secure yourself a corner of some rich person's drawing room bric-a-brac cabinet, as a curiosity. More glorious by far is to find your true worth beneath the arm of a lowly but virtuous village woman.[6]

[Uncle Rabi?]

Source: MS copy in Rabindra Bhavan, Shantiniketan; letter published in *CPB*, pp. 135–8.

1 The letters appear in *CPB*; the essays are collected in *RR*, X. Very little of this scathing criticism has been translated (during RT's lifetime, to avoid giving offence); but there is a letter in *Glimpses of Bengal*, p. 79. See also Nirad C. Chaudhuri, *Thy Hand, Great Anarch! India 1921–1952* (London, 1987), pp. 604–6.
2 For instance, 'Rajtika' ('The Raj Seal') in Krishna Dutta and Andrew Robinson, *Noon in Calcutta: Short Stories from Bengal* (London, 1992), pp. 1–12/*RR*, XXI, pp. 237–49.
3 *My Rem*, p. 123/*RR*, XVII, pp. 365–6.
4 See, for instance, *Glimpses of Bengal*, pp. 105–6/*CPB*, pp. 215–16. Arthur Fox Strangways, music critic and author of *The Music of Hindostan* (Oxford, 1914), wrote to RT on 23 March 1914:

> I am deeply conscious how impossible it is for an outsider to see things from the inside . . . I met others in India [besides you] with greater technical knowledge and more ready skill as performers, but none with such a sense of the dignity of music or so well prepared to believe that the likenesses between Indian and European music, though not more numerous, were more important than the differences. There is plenty to like and wonder at in both. ([RB]

5 Bihari Lal Gupta (1849–1916): he joined the Indian Civil Service in 1871, became a district and sessions judge in 1888 and eventually a judge in the Calcutta High Court and a member of the legislative council.
6 RT has paraphrased Iswar Chandra Vidyasagar, *Kathamala*, in *Rachanashambhar* (Pramathanath Bisi, ed.; 1364 [1957]), pp. 463–4. In 1856, Vidyasagar published a version of Aesop's fables based on the version by Revd Thomas James with illustrations by John Tenniel published in London in 1848 (see No. 125, 'The Two Pots'). Vidyasagar's version became popular in Bengal.

18

To Indira Devi Chaudhurani (Tagore)

Letter 15 introduced the conflict in Rabindranath between his need as an artist to be solitary and his urge as a reformer to be part of society. In this letter, on a related theme – the life of the mind versus the life of action – Rabindranath passingly compares his predicament with that of Rammohun Roy. Given that his admiration of Rammohun was already of heroic proportions, this remark would appear to indicate that he had a keen sense of his own future significance, coupled with a feeling that his true *métier*, unlike Rammohun's, might lie in thought more than in action, in art rather than in social reform. With age this Tagorean dilemma would become more acute.

Shelidah, [Khulna, Bangladesh]
16 May [1893]

[Bibi/Bob?]

In the evenings, at about half past six, feeling fresh and clean after my bath, I go for an hour's walk along the riverbank. Then I get into the new jolly-boat, anchor in midstream, make up a bed for myself and lie silently in the dark, feeling the breeze on my skin and staring at the heavens. Shailendra sits beside me and talks away.[1] Above us the night becomes more and more thickly studded with stars. Daily I find myself wondering: shall I see this spangled sky again in some future birth? If I do see it, shall I be able to make a bed on a jolly-boat and lie in the peace of an evening on the silent River Gorai in a beautiful corner of Bengal with such an enchanted tranquil mind? Perhaps I shall never recapture such an evening. My new setting will be different; and what kind of mind shall I be given? A similar evening will no doubt come many times more for me, but will she again fall as quietly as tonight, covering my body in her dark tresses and smothering me with love? And would I still be the man I am now! Oddly enough my greatest fear is of rebirth in Europe. For there one cannot lie out like this and expose oneself body and soul to the universe; loitering of this sort is considered a sin. There I would probably have to hustle my body and soul in some factory or bank, or in parliament. There the roads are stone metalled for the carriages of business, and so must minds be. Soft grass and redundant creepers forbidden! Everything to be right-angled, shipshape, regulated and durable. I am not sure why my indolent, self-absorbed, fancy-filled frame of mind seems to me the more desirable, and certainly not a subject for shame. When I recline in the jolly-boat I feel not a whit inferior to those men of affairs, however busy they are. And I perceive that had I girded my loins for action, I would have looked all too feeble beside those oaken-hearted young achievers. But does that make this jolly-boat-prone, infatuated youth any less important as an individual than Rammohun Roy?

[Uncle Rabi?]

Source: MS copy at Rabindra Bhavan, Shantiniketan; letter published in *CPB*, pp. 151–2.

1 Shailendra Majumdar: officer of Tagore estates, younger brother of RT's friend Shrish Chandra Majumdar.

19

To Indira Devi Chaudhurani (Tagore)

As already mentioned (in letter 11), Rabindranath's diet while living on the estates was generally simple. It included meat but at several times in his life he tried to give up eating meat.[1] In 1916, for instance, while undergoing a gruelling lecture tour in the United States, he came to the conclusion that his weakness was due to his vegetarianism; he began eating meat again, and immediately felt stronger.[2] This letter explains his fundamental feeling on the subject.

Patisar, [Rajshahi, Bangladesh]
22 March [1894]

[Bibi/Bob?]

Balu sent an essay on 'Love of animals' and I spent my entire morning on it.[3] Yesterday I was sitting at the window of the boat when something caught my attention. Some bird was struggling across the river to the opposite bank, pursued by a great commotion. Eventually I saw it was a hen; it must have escaped imminent death in the galley, jumped overboard and tried to swim across. It had almost made the bank when a grim reaper grabbed it by the neck and brought it back to the boat. I called Phatik and told him I would take no meat that night.[4] Then Balu's essay happened to arrive, and I was struck by the coincidence. I really must break the meat-eating habit [, Bob]. Only because we do not think about its injustice and cruelty can we continue to swallow flesh. There are many misfortunes in the world of which man is the author that are not clear-cut cases of right or wrong, deriving as they do from custom, culture and tradition – but cruelty is not one of them. It is a fundamental sin, admitting of no argument or nice distinctions, and if our feelings were not numb, our eyes and hearts not deliberately closed, we would hear the call for a ban on cruelty plainly. Instead, we gaily, even joyfully, commit cruelty, in fact those who do not are dubbed cranks.

How peculiar and artificial is our apprehension of sin and virtue. I feel that the highest commandment of all is that of sympathy for all sentient beings. Love is the foundation of all religion. Let me not bring sorrow into this world, let me spread happiness. Let me sympathise with the happiness, sorrow and pain of all creatures so that I hurt none – that is true religion, and we should try to live up to this holy ideal. The other day I read in one of the English-language papers that 50,000 lbs of carcasses had been sent to some army station in Africa, but as the meat had gone bad on the way, the consignment was returned and finally was auctioned off for a few pounds at Portsmouth. What a shocking waste [, Bob]! What callous disregard for life! And when we invite guests to dine how many lives are sacrificed in our dishes, and yet how few of these dishes are fully consumed. So long as we are unconscious of partaking in cruelty we do not sin. But if, when our pity is aroused, we throttle it simply to remain part of the carnivorous pack, we insult all that is highest in us. I have decided to try a vegetarian diet once again . . .

I have acquired a close friend in this solitude: a copy of Amiel's *Journal*, borrowed from Loken.[5] Whenever I have a moment I flick through it and it seems to be in conversation with me. I have rarely felt so intimate with a book. Though many books are better written, and it certainly has its shortcomings, it is after my heart. Often with a book, after glancing at a few pages one feels uncomfortable. It is like when one is ill and unable to find the right position in bed; one turns from side to side, props pillow on pillow or ejects a pillow. If in that state of mind I open Amiel's *Journal*, I immediately relax. My friend Amiel has an entry about cruelty to animals, and so I have included it as a note to Balu's essay. In general, I do not much like this piece by Balu – it seems artificial and overdone. It does not appear to be coming from the heart – it is too elaborate, there are too many made-up words – and so instead of having the ring of truth, it sounds like empty exaggeration . . . In many pieces of writing made-up words are not a weakness; but a subject such as this requires sincere and straightforward handling, or the reader will become irritated and hostile. I have suggested to Balu that he translate some portions of the deer hunting scenes in *Kadambari*.[6] Birds resemble us to some extent and in one respect there is little difference between them and us – in the way we both show spontaneous tenderness for our offspring. Banbhatta was able to feel this similarity in compassion through his imaginative faculty and give expression to it, as in the phrase '[one] touch of nature makes the whole world kin'.[7]

[Uncle Rabi?]

Source: MS copy at Rabindra Bhavan, Shantiniketan; letter published in *CPB*, pp. 176–8.

1 Paul, *Rabijibani*, III, p. 289.
2 As reported from the USA by W. W. Pearson in a letter to Rathindranath Tagore, 9 Nov. 1916 [RB].
3 Balu: Balendranath Tagore (1870–99): art and literary critic; nephew of RT, son of his elder brother Birendranath. See Partha Mitter, *Art and Nationalism in Colonial India: Occidental Orientations* (Cambridge, 1994), especially pp. 230–3. Balendranath's essay, 'Pashu priti' (Love of animals), extensively revised by RT, was published in *Sadhana*, Chaitra 1300 [March–April 1894].
4 Phatik: RT's cook. On many an evening RT would sit in his boat, watching the river, when 'the venerable

Phatik would appear and break the silence with his stentorian voice announcing dinner – a ceaseless monotony of chicken cutlets and bread-pudding' (Rathindranath Tagore, *Edges of Time*, p. 36).
5 On Loken Palit, see letter 6, n. 3. Henri Frederic Amiel (1821–81): Swiss philosopher and writer, who kept a journal between 1847 and his death. Published in 1883 in French, it was translated into English by Mrs Humphry Ward and published in 1889; RT had her version. The journal remained popular in Bengal in the generation after RT's, according to Nirad C. Chaudhuri (Chaudhuri to authors, 4 Dec. 1995).
6 *Kadambari*: a romance written in Sanskrit by the classical author Banbhatta. In 1900, RT published an essay inspired by a new painting of a scene from *Kadambari*; the story's descriptions of a forest ashram probably influenced his conception of Shantiniketan. 'For all the floweriness of his style [Banabhatta]'s outlook has more in common with that of the 20th century than that of any other early Indian writer' (A. L. Basham, *The Wonder That Was India* (London, 1954), p. 447).
7 Shakespeare, *Troilus and Cressida*, III. 3. 175.

20

To Indira Devi Chaudhurani (Tagore)

This wonderful letter is one of Tagore's clearest statements of his view of the nature of reality. When he met Albert Einstein many years later, he expressed similar ideas (see appendix 1). The stark contrast between his congested, social, time-bound milieu in north Calcutta and his spacious, solitary, timeless existence on the Tagore estates – physically only half a day's journey apart but in all other respects a world away – sharpened Rabindranath's sense of the dichotomy between the objective and the subjective. In Shelidah, he says here, 'it seems to me that the subdivisions of time and space are figments of my mind'.

Shelidah, [Khulna, Bangladesh]
24 June [1894]

[Bibi/Bob?]

I have been here just four days but already I have lost track of time. If I were to return to Calcutta immediately I feel I should find much of it transformed . . . It is as if I am now standing in a place outside the current of time, unconscious of the gradually altering set of the world. The fact is that here, away from Calcutta, time is quadrupled because I live in my inner world where time may be stretched or compressed and clocks do not work in the usual way. Duration is measured by intensity of feeling; the emotions of the moment seem endless. Where the outside world with its flow of incident is not constantly employed in checking on my daily activities, moments become hours and hours moments, as in a dream. And then it seems to me that the subdivisions of time and space are figments of my mind. Each atom is immeasurable and each moment infinite.

When I was very small I remember reading a Persian story about this idea of time, which I liked enormously. I think I understood, even then, something of the underlying notion. To show that time cannot be quantified a fakir put some magic water in a bathtub and invited the king to take a dip. No sooner had the king done so than he found himself in a strange country by the sea, where he experienced diverse sensations and encounters – in fact a whole lifetime of happiness and pain. He married and had many children and they died, as did his wife; he lost all his wealth; and then, while he writhed in grief, he suddenly found himself back in his palace room surrounded by his courtiers. He began to vent his anger on the head of the fakir, but his courtiers all said, 'Maharaj, you have but dipped your head in the water and withdrawn it!'

Our lives, with all their moods, are held too within a moment. They may seem immensely long and intensely felt at the time, but as soon as we finish our dip in the world, the entire experience seems no more than a few moments in a dream. Time itself cannot be short or long – only humans call it that. These thoughts have not been prompted by an attempt to ascertain the likely arrival time of your letter – I often find myself pondering the fact that our keenest happiness and sorrow are not permanent, and each time I conclude sadly that I can give no answer to the riddle. A possible answer is that though the experience of happiness and sorrow is not permanent, its consequence is permanent. But why are we lured with all sorts of false promises to embrace these consequences? Why do we say that 'love's treasure is everlasting'? Who has given mankind the false assurance that love triumphs over death – which has led to the composition of consoling legends about Savitri and Satyavan – and so many others.[1]

It was a fine day yesterday. The waterline on my side of the river, the sand spit beyond and the playfully repeating patterns of sun and cloud over the forest on the distant bank of the river struck me as gorgeously beautiful whenever I gazed through my open window. Like a dream! Why do we speak of beauty as being dreamlike? I don't know, unless it is because the sheerness of beauty requires the absence of all touch of reality – in other words that field of grain which provides food, this waterway which carries jute boats, that sandbank which generates revenue for zamindars, and all the hundred thousand other associations of this scene must be barred from consciousness before we can perceive the picture of sheer incalculable, superfluous, unadulterated joy, and call it 'dreamlike'. At other times we focus chiefly on the truth of the world, its reality, and we see beauty of other kinds. But when we concentrate on beauty itself, and neglect to assess whether it is true or not, then we call the scene dreamlike ... Human beings often try to differentiate truth from beauty – science tends to omit beauty from truth and poetry does not value truth as beautiful. The kind of beauty that can be experienced in science is the beauty that is inseparable from truth, while the truth that is experienced in poetry is the truth that is inseparable from beauty.[2] For lack of space you are spared a good deal more lecturing on this occasion.

[Uncle Rabi?]

Source: MS copy at Rabindra Bhavan, Shantiniketan; letter published in *CPB*, pp. 184–6.

1 Savitri and Satyavan: a legend in the *Mahabharata* similar to that of Orpheus and Euridyce. Savitri married Satyavan knowing that he had only a year to live. When he died, she followed Yama, the lord of death, and eventually brought Satyavan back to live by appeasing Yama.
2 See RT's exchange with Einstein in appendix 1.

21

To Indira Devi Chaudhurani (Tagore)

Rabindranath's sojourn on the family estates fed his writing in many ways, perhaps most of all through his proximity to nature, both on water and on land. Previous letters have tended to deal with the awesome and infinite aspects of nature, such as a storm or the night sky; this letter, by contrast, stresses the intoxicating immediacy of nature, especially at noontime.

Shahzadpur, [Rajshahi, Bangladesh]
5 September [1894]

[Bibi/Bob?]

    I love it when I move into the Shahzadpur house after living on the boat for a long period. The large doors and windows let in light and air on all sides without hindrance. And when I look out my eye falls on green branches and I hear constant birdsong – the moment I step into the south verandah every pore of my brain is saturated with the fragrance of *kamini* flowers. All of a sudden I realise how hungry for space I have become and so I take my fill of it. I am sole monarch of these four large rooms and so I throw open every door and window. I feel the mood and the will to write here as nowhere else. The living essence of the outside world floats in freely in verdurous waves of light and air and sound and scent that mingle with my bewitched mind and mould it into story after story after story. The intoxication is especially strong in the afternoons. Heat, hush, solitude, birdsong – especially the cawing of crows – and languid, limitless leisure remove me from reality. I believe, though I have no proof, that the *Arabian Nights* came into being upon such sun-baked afternoons in Damascus, Samarkand and Bokhara. I can see the bunches of grapes and the wild gardens of roses, hear the melody of *bulbuls*, taste the wines of Shiraz. In the desert there is only a file of camels, an itinerant horseman or a crystal spring beneath a date palm to be seen. But in the city, below bright canopies overhanging narrow alleys in the bazaar, there sit turbanned loosely attired merchants selling melons and pomegranates, while not far away in a great palace perfumed with incense, on bolsters and kincob-covered divans within balconies, reclines Zobedia or Amina or Sufia, dressed in a gaily decorated jacket, flowing pyjamas and gold-embroidered slippers, her hubble-bubble pipe coiled at her feet and her person guarded by gorgeously liveried Abyssinians. Such a prodigiously grand and mysterious setting in such a faraway country was bound to lead to a thousand tales – credible and incredible – of the deepest hopes and fears of mankind.

    Noontime in Shahzadpur is high noon for story writing. It was at this time, at this very table, I recall, that my story 'The Postmaster' took over my thoughts.[1] The light, the breeze and the movement of leaves on all sides combined and entered my writing. There are few kinds of happiness in the world more filling than the happiness of creating something in which the mind is totally immersed in its surroundings. This morning I set about writing a piece on folk literature, and I became so caught up in it that I enjoyed myself greatly.[2] These folk rhymes belong to an independent realm in which there are no rules and regulations, like cloud cuckoo land. Unfortunately, the mundane world always catches up and dominates this other world. And so all of a sudden, while I was writing away, officialdom irrupted in the form of my clerks, and blew away my fantasy kingdom. Sorting out the business matter took until lunchtime. It is an imbecile thing to eat to bellyful of food at midday, which stupefies one's imagination and other higher faculties. By overfilling themselves with food at midday,

Bengalis fail to drink in the moody intensity of noontime – instead they close their doors, puff away at tobacco, chomp on betel and prepare themselves for a thoroughly torpid siesta. That is how they become glistening and corpulent. But how can anywhere compare with the way in which the exhausted solitude of noontime soundlessly pervades the monotonous fields of the limitless plain of Bengal? Noontime has fascinated me since my early boyhood. In those days the second floor of our house was empty and I used to lie down alone in one of the rooms on a curved couch and feel the hot blast from outside through the open door – I spent whole days there lost in my imagination amid who knows what inarticulate fancies.[3]

[Uncle Rabi?]

Source: MS copy at Rabindra Bhavan, Shantiniketan; letter published in *CPB*, pp. 224–6.

1 See letter 16. RT's play *Visarjan* (*Sacrifice*) was written on his first visit to Shahzadpur in 1889.
2 'Meyeli chhara' (Women's rhymes), *Sadhana*, Ashwin–Kartik 1301 [Sept.–Nov. 1894]; a revised and renamed version appears in *RR*, VI, p. 577.
3 See various references in *My Rem*, e.g. p. 26/*RR*, XVII, p. 272.

22

To Indira Devi Chaudhurani (Tagore)

There are frequent references to the night sky in Rabindranath's letters to his niece. Its vastness and the brilliance of the stars in the clean air of rural Bengal was certainly a spur to feelings of mysticism; but Tagore had also a lifelong interest in astronomy, dating from the time when he was a boy in the Himalayas, and his father would point out the constellations and treat Rabi to an astronomical discourse. Tagore liked to read most of the popular astronomy books of the time (see letter 41), and himself wrote about the subject a number of times. Poetic feeling and scientific curiosity coalesce in letters such as this one.

Shelidah, [Khulna, Bangladesh]
7 December [1894]

[Bibi/Bob?]

Evenings on the sandbanks these days are so magnificent they are beyond my powers of description. When I go out on the sands alone, before long Shailendra usually comes after me and talks about business matters.[1] He came yesterday. After talking about the rent roll and so on for a while, he paused for a moment – and in a flash I sensed the vastness of the universe in the silent night sky before me. Then I felt astounded to think that one ordinary human voice in my ears could drown such a sky-filling hush – where in all the silence of Creation is there a place for talk of rent rolls and other office matters of our Berahimpur *zamindari*? I made no response to Shailendra's comments, and he thought I had not understood him. He repeated his question and once again I said nothing, to avoid conversation. He became very puzzled and fell silent. The moment he stopped the peace of the stars descended and transformed me; and I too found my place at the far edge of that boundless gathering of soundless celestial luminaries. All the stars have their places in infinite space, as I, for my part, have my place on this empty sandbank beside the River Padma; both they and I have our seats at the great reception known as existence.

We stayed out on the sandbanks in the moonlight until very late, then returned to the boat, lit a lamp, closed the doors, stretched ourselves out in chairs and resurrected our discussion about Berahimpur. Then we ate four *luchis* with fresh palm molasses and drank a glass of milk.[2] After that we had a bit of literary talk and eventually lay down to sleep.

[Uncle Rabi?]

Source: MS copy at Rabindra Bhavan, Shantiniketan; letter published in *CPB*, p. 270.

1 On Shailendra Majumdar, see letter 18, n. 1.
2 *luchi*: a kind of bread prepared from refined flour and water; the dough, rolled flat and circular, is fried in ghee, which makes it blow up like a balloon.

23

To Indira Devi Chaudhurani (Tagore)

Although Rabindranath was fairly well read in western poetry, he was not much attracted to the novel. One looks in vain in his writings for his response to the works of the great nineteenth-century novelists. There are stray references, but there is no sustained analysis. Tolstoy, for instance, got short shrift in a letter to his niece from the estates of August 1894: 'Tried to read *Anna Karenina*. Could not go on, found it so unpleasant. I cannot understand what pleasure can be had out of such a *sickly* [the word is in English] book . . . I cannot stand for long these complicated, bizarre, and perverse goings-on.'[1]

His life on the estates, so vastly different from his life in Calcutta, accentuated such feelings of revulsion. Its elemental quality, lived in direct communion with nature and the human heart, had little to do with modern western literary sensibility, though Rabindranath's power to distil it into the songs and poetry of *Gitanjali* could capture (albeit briefly) the attention of modern western readers seeking an alternative to this sensibility. This letter is a foretaste of *Gitanjali*.

Shelidah, [Khulna, Bangladesh]
12 December [1895]

[Bibi/Bob?]

The other evening an insignificant incident startled me. As I mentioned before, of late I have taken to lighting a lamp in the boat and sitting and reading till I feel sleepy. One should not seek to be alone always and everywhere, particularly in the evening, lest one falls prey to that old saw about wanting some aunt to die so that one can wallow in sorrow; and since, in the absence of a suitable aunt, one may be tempted to fall back on oneself, I prefer to take up a book. That evening I was reading a book of critical essays in English full of contorted disputation about poetry, art, beauty and so forth. As I plodded through these artificial discussions, my weary mind seemed to have strayed into a mirage, a land where things were constructed out of words. A deadening spirit seemed to dance before me like a mocking demon. The night was far advanced, so I shut the book with a snap and flung it on the table, intending to head for bed after blowing out the lamp. But the moment I extinguished the flame, moonlight burst through the open window and flooded the boat. It was like a shock to an infatuated man. The glare from a satanic little lamp had been mocking an infinite radiance. What on earth had I been hoping to find in the empty wordiness of that book? The heavens had been waiting for me soundlessly outside all the time. Had I chanced to miss them and gone off to bed in darkness, they would not have made the slightest protest. Had I never given them a glance during my mortal existence and remained unenlightened even on my deathbed, that lamp would have triumphed. But the moon would always have been there, silent and sweetly smiling, neither concealing nor advertising her presence.[2]

Since then I have begun doing without the lamp in the evenings.

[Uncle Rabi?]

Source: MS copy at Rabindra Bhavan, Shantiniketan; letter published in *CPB*, pp. 346–7.

1 Quoted in Chaudhuri, *Thy Hand*, p. 603; the original letter appears in *CPB*, p. 217. RT's reaction to *Anna Karenina* was similar to the reaction of most western readers to his only long novel, *Gora*. Nevertheless, RT encouraged his children to read novels by writers such as Dickens and George Eliot.
2 Contrast RT's view of the moon in letter 12.

Family life (1898–1904)

Introduction

Until mid-1898, Tagore's wife and young family remained in the family house in Calcutta, while he lived alone on the estates, though they of course paid visits to the estates. Then they too moved there, and the children began to be educated by their father. After 1901, they lived at Shantiniketan.

Rabindranath was ambivalent about family life. He was devoted to his wife and children, but he increasingly saw them less as individuals than as part of the greater cause to which he felt his life was dedicated. In 1896 he wrote a poem that expressed this tension. This is his own translation, revised by W. B. Yeats:

> At midnight the would-be ascetic announced:
> 'This is the time to give up my home and seek for God. Ah, who has held me so long in delusion here?'
> God whispered, 'I,' but the ears of the man were stopped.
> With a baby asleep at her breast lay his wife, peacefully sleeping on one side of the bed.
> The man said, 'Who are ye that have fooled me so long?'
> The voice said again, 'They are God,' but he heard it not.
> The baby cried out in its dream, nestling close to its mother.
> God commanded, 'Stop, fool, leave not thy home,' but still he heard not.
> God sighed and complained, 'Why does my servant wander to seek me, forsaking me?'[1]

Rabindranath's family life was, for the most part, tragic. His wife died in 1902, followed by his daughter Renuka in 1903; later he lost his youngest son, Shamindranath, his eldest daughter, Bela, and his only grandson. None of his children, except Bela, made a happy marriage.

1 *The Gardener* (London, 1913) (75), p. 130/*Chaitali*, RR, V, p. 11.

24

To Mrinalini Tagore (Ray Chaudhuri)

By 1898, Rabindranath was the father of five children. They had been living with their mother, Mrinalini, at Jorasanko, the family house in Calcutta, while their father lived on the estates in East Bengal, though he paid constant visits to Calcutta (at least once a month to read the estate accounts to his father, the Maharshi). But Rabindranath was now dissatisfied with this arrangement: the children needed educating; he disapproved of orthodox education; and he was unhappy (as was his wife) with the petty atmosphere of Jorasanko. In August of that year, he moved the whole family to Shelidah and began to educate them himself.

This letter to his wife prepares the ground for the move, and contains the seed of his later move (in 1901) to found the school at Shantiniketan. It is something of a sermon, though it is not sanctimonious: one senses, rather, Rabindranath's growing awareness of his wife's conventionality. He clearly feared that if she were to remain at Jorasanko, she and their children would become narrow minded and conventional like the majority of the family still living in the house.

There can be no doubt that Mrinalini was an average personality. There is no evidence of her having any pronounced talent beyond the household arts, though she seems to have had an affectionate disposition. While Rabindranath was certainly affectionate towards her, his feelings do not seem to have had the depth of genuine companionship. Almost all his letters to her suggest that it was nothing like a relationship of equals, despite his wishes; the letters she wrote to him he did not keep; and in the nearly forty years that he lived after her death, he referred to her very rarely, even in letters to his children.[1] In a long and informal discussion of marriage with a Bengali friend in 1928, there is not even a glancing reference to Mrinalini.[2] And in all Tagore's works, there is only a single group of poems that is clearly connected with Mrinalini – in contrast with many poems, songs, paintings and other works connected with other women.[3] Perhaps it could not have been otherwise; the wives of geniuses have seldom been more than shadowy figures.

[Shelidah, Khulna, Bangladesh]
[June 1898]

Bhai chhuti[4]

Returning from Dhaka today I found your letter. I shall complete my work at Kaligram speedily and come to Calcutta to settle matters appropriately. But dear, you must not let yourself be upset for nothing. Try to accept everything that happens in a calm, quiet and contented manner. This is the only rule I always observe and try to apply in my life. I do not succeed all the time – but if you too were to cherish peace of mind, perhaps I could draw strength from our mutual efforts and attain the peace that comes of being contented. Of course you are much younger than I am, your overall experience of life much more limited, but in some ways your nature is more disciplined and patient than mine. And so you have less need to protect your mind carefully from every kind of provocation. But in everyone's life, from time to time, there come real crises; then, the virtue of patience and the habit of being contented are effective. At such times the everyday slights, obstacles and hurts by which our minds are constantly agitated and offended, are set at naught. Let us give love and act for the good, discharging our duties to others with sweet cheerfulness – and whatever will happen will take care of itself. For the span of life is not very long and our joys and sorrows are perpetually shifting. I know it is difficult to treat lightly things that damage one's inter-

Family life 47

3 Rabindranath at the wedding of his son, at Jorasanko, Calcutta: with daughter Mira, son Rathindranath, daughter-in-law Pratima, daughter Bela

ests, to suffer or to be cheated, but if we do not take them in this calm spirit, the burden of life grows intolerable and our high ideals cannot remain unshaken. If we cannot respond in this way, if day after day we spend our time in dissatisfaction and distraction, in constant friction generated by unavoidable petty antagonisms – then we shall have lived in vain. Great peacefulness, lofty detachment, selfless affection and dispassionate service – these are the measures of success in life. If you can find peace within yourself and spread solace to all around you, your life will be more worthy than that of an empress. My dear, if you allow your mind to carp at all and sundry, it will turn against itself: the majority of our sorrows are self-inflicted. Do not be annoyed with me for giving you this high-sounding lecture. You cannot know with what intense longing I speak. My mind is illumined these days by the vision of an ideal before my eyes, that the strong bonds of my affection, respect and easy comradeship for you should grow ever closer, that this perfect peace and happiness should grow to matter more than anything else in our lives and that all our daily frustrations and despair should grow insignificant in comparison. There is a heady intoxication in the amour of a man and a woman when young, as you will have realised from your own life. Only at a maturer age, after experiencing the vicissitudes of the wider world does a true, lasting, deep, restrained and wordless kind of love manifest itself between a man and a woman. As one's inner world expands, the external world gradually retreats – which is why, despite the expansion, one feels in a sense more solitary and a corresponding desire to embrace the other person in greater intimacy. Nothing is more beautiful than the human soul. Wherever one gets close to it, wherever one confronts it face to face, there is to be found the fundamental origin of true love. Then, no more illusions remain, there is no need for one to deify the other, and there are no storms of passion at partings and reunions – in their stead shines forth a pure light of natural joy and unhesitating trust, whether we two are physically near or far apart, in safety or in danger, in riches or in poverty. I am aware that you have suffered because of me, but I also know for certain that as a result of bearing this sorrow you will in due course attain great joy. The happiness to be found in the acceptance of suffering and the forgiveness of love is a happiness not to be found in the fulfilment of desire and in self-gratification. These days the only yearning I have is that our lives become straight and simple. We should conduct our affairs with calmness and grace, without a trace of showiness but full of benevolence; our wants should be few; our ideals high; our efforts selfless; and the needs of our country should take precedence over our own needs. And if our children should gradually stray from these ideals, may the two of us remain, to the very end, advocates to each other of the principle of humanity, and sure refuges for each other's world-weary heart; thus we shall bring our lives to a beautiful conclusion. And this is why I am eager to take you away from Calcutta, that stone temple of self-interest, away to the secluded villages. In Calcutta one can never forget profit and loss, friend and foe, one is always being distracted by petty matters, until finally the noble purpose of life is sliced up into a thousand useless pieces. Here, by contrast, a little goes a long way and the false may not be mistaken for the true. Here it is not so difficult to keep in mind the injunction:

> Whether joy or sorrow, pain or pleasure –
> whatsoever may befall thee,
> Accept it serenely and with an unvanquished heart.[5]

Tomar
Rabi

[PS] Pramatha, Suren and Pramatha's Gujerati friend are here at Shelidah.[6]

Source: MS original at Rabindra Bhavan, Shantiniketan; letter published in *CP*, I, pp. 28–31.

1 See Visva-Bharati, *Mrinalini Devi*.
2 In conversation with Dilip Kumar Roy, 'The function of woman's shakti in society', *VBQ*, 6, No. 1, April 1928, pp. 68–78.
3 The group of poems is *Smaran* (Remembrance), *RR*, VIII, which bears the austere dedication '7 Agrahayan 1309', i.e. 23 Nov. 1902, the date of Mrinalini's death.
4 This greeting is untranslatable. It means, literally, 'Brother holiday'; *chhuti* recalls *chhota* in *Chhota Bou* (Little Wife), RT's earlier greeting to his wife.

5 *Mahabharata*, 12:25:26 and 12:174:39.
6 On Pramatha Chaudhuri, see letter 89. Suren: Surendranath Tagore (1872–1940): translator of several Tagore works into English; nephew of RT, son of elder brother Satyendranath.

25

To Gaganendranath Tagore[1]

Though he had moved to Shelidah, Rabindranath could not of course escape Calcutta politics altogether. This letter, written to his artist nephew Gaganendranath, who lived at Jorasanko, gives a flavour of Indian politics in the run-up to the Swadeshi Movement of 1905 and shows the stresses that politics imposed on the Tagore family as a whole.

In 1898, the Government introduced a bill into the Bengal Legislative Council to reform the Calcutta Corporation by reducing the power of its elected Bengali councillors and giving more power to British representatives. On the arrival of the new viceroy, Lord Curzon, in January 1899, this legislation effort was further strengthened in the interests of efficient local government, as Curzon declared. When the bill became law later in the year, twenty-eight Bengali councillors resigned.

Nationalists, including Rabindranath, naturally opposed the change. But the Bengalis in the British Indian Association, a group representing the interests of the zamindars, supported the Government. (Founded in 1851, this group had once had Debendranath, father of Rabindranath, as its honorary secretary, but had long since ceased to speak for national interests.) The leading figures included Maharaja Jotendra Mohan Tagore, the head of the Pathuriaghat branch of the Tagores, who was honorary secretary for a period from 1879. Yet again, therefore, the two main branches of the Tagores were now at loggerheads. Gagenendranath, though belonging to the Jorasanko Tagores, was more orthodox than Rabindranath (he was not a Brahmo, for instance) and seems to have wished to remain a member of the British Indian Association.

[Shelidah, Khulna, Bangladesh]
[September/October 1898]

Gagan

Ashu has written me a letter bemoaning the fact that you people are not willing to cancel your membership of the British Indian Association.[2] Given the way this body is opposing the country over the Municipal Bill, we should resign en masse. Only in the municipality do we have self-rule – this is one place in which we can learn and take pride; how the British Indian Association can be willing to inflict such a blow on the self-respect of our people is beyond me. On this issue the country really must reprimand the association. We naturally feel some hesitation because of family ties but is the British Indian Association to be held together only by such ties?

Just because Jotendra Mohan has not joined the Brahmo Samaj, must I quarrel with him?[3] There is no necessary conflict between the preserving of family relationships and the maintaining of one's own views and sense of duty.

These days there seems to be no end to conflict. The Music Association is also having a stormy time.[4] And you are not short of excitements.[5] Constant meetings, debates, argy-bargies and hot words. The plague seems to have gone, but these matters are no less virulent.[6]

In the meantime, you should go to Ashu and mollify him.

In the coming issue of *Bharati*, in an article called 'Ultraconservatism', I have rebuked the British Indian group with some harsh words.[7] The good news for them is that they cannot read Bengali – nor, it would appear, much English.[8]

The sky has been overcast and squally since the night before last. I hope that when it clears we might have a few days' respite.

Uncle Rabi

Source: MS original at Rabindra Bhavan, Shantiniketan; letter published in *VBP*, Magh–Chaitra 1353 [Jan.–April 1947], pp. 133–4.

1 Gaganendranath Tagore (1867–1938): painter and caricaturist; nephew of RT.
2 (Sir) Ashutosh Chaudhuri (1860–1924): judge of the Calcutta High Court from 1904. He married a niece of RT. Chaudhuri strongly attacked the British Indian Association's stand on the Municipal Bill in a speech at the Calcutta Town Hall on 31 Aug. 1898.
3 Maharaja Jotendra Mohan Tagore (1831–1908): zamindar, member of the Bengal Legislative Council. In 1866, the governor of Bengal, honouring him, noted: 'You come from a family great in the annals of Calcutta, I may say great in the annals of the British dominions in India, conspicuous for loyalty to the British Government and for acts of public beneficence' (James W. Furrell, *The Tagore Family: A Memoir* (Calcutta, 1882), p. 163).
4 The Music Association (Sangit Sabha), founded in Jan. 1898 by Jyotirindranath Tagore, RT's elder brother, with the enthusiastic support of RT, soon ran into opposition and spawned a rival group in Jan. 1899.
5 RT was probably referring to orthodox Bengali opposition to the downgrading of European art in favour of Indian art at the Calcutta Art School, with which Gaganendranath was associated. See Mitter, *Art and Nationalism*, pp. 279–82.
6 Plague had affected other parts of India very badly in 1897. In 1898 it reached Calcutta, but was stamped out by severe Government measures, though only after a riot on 4 May. RT cooperated with Sister Nivedita (Margaret Noble) in combating the disease, by, for instance, collecting up dead rats. See Punya Lata Chakravarty, *Chhelebelar Dinguli* (Calcutta, 1365 [1958]), pp. 61, 93. RT left his family at Shantiniketan during the worst period of the plague. (See Paul, *Rabijibani*, IV (1395 [1988]), p. 174.)
7 *Bharati*, Kartik 1305 [Oct.–Nov. 1898]; *RR*, X, pp. 587–92. RT wrote the article in response to an unsigned article in the *Pioneer*.
8 Many Bengali *bhadralok* were unused to reading Bengali at this time (English was the language even of the Congress). But how well did they read English, jibed Rabindranath – if they could allow the Municipal Bill to deprive them of their power over municipal affairs?

26

To Priyanath Sen

Generally speaking, throughout his life, Rabindranath lacked intellectual companionship with Bengalis. Priyanath Sen, a slightly older man, was one of the exceptions, though the relationship seems to have faltered in later years. Referring to the 1880s and his own early attempts at poetry, Tagore described the modest Sen in his autobiography as 'an expert navigator of all seven seas of literature, whose highways and byways he is constantly traversing in almost all languages, Indian and foreign. To converse with him is to gain glimpses of the most out-of-the-way scenery in the world of ideas.' This wide reading helped to make Sen a good critic, said Tagore. 'His authoritative criticism assisted me more than I can tell. I used to read him everything I wrote, and, but for his timely showers of discriminating appreciation my early ploughings and sowings might not have yielded what they did.'[1]

Though the main bond between Rabindranath and Priyanath was literary, as demonstrated by this letter, Sen also helped Tagore in borrowing money to pay off debts. In 1900–1 he assisted in the arranging of the marriage of Madhurilata (Bela), eldest daughter of Rabindranath.[2]

[Shelidah, Khulna, Bangladesh]
20 August [1900]/4 Bhadra [1307]

Bhai

If you are placing an order with Chunder & Brothers please include the following books:
Choice Works of Mark Twain
Mark Twain's Library of Humour
published by Chatto and Windus.[3]

Each evening I sit surrounded by my family circle and read to them by lamplight. I have discovered that Mark Twain's humour is the family favourite – Bela and Bela's mother find it particularly funny. I have copies of *Tramps Abroad* and *Innocents Abroad* but I have nearly exhausted the humorous sections. If you happen to know of any short books, humorous or tragic, suitable for reading aloud to children, please export them to me. I remember noticing in Thacker's some time ago some short English farces in two or three acts – can you send me a basketful?[4] I can select from them for reading aloud. They are also quite cheap to buy. My reading stocks are running low and will not last more than a couple of days or so: unless you send me some rations pretty soon, my condition will resemble that of the Pekin legation; I shall be unable to ward off an attack by my offspring. Given that you go to office every day, and your route takes you past Thacker's – and that you will leave for office shortly after receiving this letter – I am not afraid of inconveniencing you much or overstraining your memory.

When Vidyarnava was here, I suppose I did boast a little of my friendship with you, but any hyperbole was not such as to cause you to reproach me or cause me to feel repentant. Therefore I shall turn a deaf ear to your remonstrations.[5]

Pramatha Babu wants to know the details of Chandranath Babu's appreciation, but I do not want to copy it all again.[6] Will you do me a favour? Will you show Pramatha Babu the passages I quoted in my previous letter to you? If you can send him a copy of those that would be even better – you seem to have made your boys thoroughly trained as copyists. At any rate treat this letter as a request which I trust you will not dishonour.

No one else puts as much faith in the dating of my letters as you do. You should depend upon an almanac instead.[7]

The sky has become overcast. There are signs that rain is imminent. Moreover, Suren is due here any minute.[8] I must send this letter off.

Shri Rabindranath Thakur

Source: MS original at Rabindra Bhavan, Shantiniketan; letter published in *CP*, VIII, pp. 127–8.

1 *My Rem*, p. 12/*RR*, XVII, pp. 394–9.
2 See Kshitish Roy, 'Rabindranath Tagore and Priyanath Sen', *VBN*, Dec. 1966, pp. 77–80.
3 Chunder & Brothers was at 98 Radha Bazar, not far from the Tagore house in Jorasanko.
4 Thacker Spink & Co. was a book importing and selling business, which also printed and published (in 1918 it published RT's fable *The Parrot's Training*). It was started in 1819 by W. Thacker; when he died in 1872, his nephew W. Spink took over; later, Indians became partners. The company wound up after Independence. See Biren Roy, *Marshes to Metropolis: Calcutta (1481–1981)* (Calcutta, 1982).
5 Presumably, RT had been praising Sen to Vidyarnava, who had told Sen. Pandit Shivadhan Vidyarnava (1860–1914): Sanskrit scholar; his commentary on the *Tantras* was edited by Arthur Avalon (Sir John Woodroffe) and published in 1915. Vidyanarva was a member of the Adi Brahmo Samaj, and among the first batch of teachers at the Shantiniketan school.
6 Chandranath Bose (1844–1910): librarian, Bengal Library. A friend of RT since 1884, Basu reviewed a number of his books, though not always favourably. In this case he had praised *Kshanika*, *Katha* and *Kalpana* in a letter to RT (Paul, *Rabijibani*, IV, p. 265). Pramatha Chaudhuri was a litterateur and close associate of RT, who married his niece Indira in 1899 (see letter 89).
7 RT's dating is indeed often faulty, as he remarked to various correspondents over the years.
8 Suren: Surendranath Tagore.

27

To (Sir) Jagadish Chandra Bose[1]

J. C. Bose was India's first modern scientist to achieve international acclaim. In 1920, he became a fellow of the Royal Society, the second Indian to be so honoured and the first Indian scientist (the mathematician Srinivasa Ramanujan was the first Indian FRS).

Scientifically, Bose had two distinct careers. Before 1900 he was a physicist, whose pioneering work in Bengal on the effects of electromagnetic radiation on metals received invaluable early recognition from British and other physicists such as Kelvin and Rayleigh. Bose's work contributed to the development of wireless telegraphy and radio but he refused, unlike Marconi, to patent his inventions, because he regarded such financial gain as inappropriate for a true scientist.[2] After 1900, Bose extended his study to the effects of radiation on plant and animal tissues, his highly sensitive apparatus revealing striking – and controversial – similarities in the responses to electrical stimulus of living and non-living substances. He thus became more physiologist than physicist, though his work in plant physiology, with its mystical overtones, was never accepted in the way his work in physics was, either during Bose's lifetime or subsequently.[3]

Bose became a close friend and intellectual companion of Tagore after their meeting in 1897, as this diverse and stimulating letter shows (though latterly Bose fell out with him).[4] He visited Rabindranath regularly at Shelidah, and cajoled him into writing a number of important short stories.[5] He even had one of the best known, 'Kabulioala' ('The Kabuliwallah'), translated into English, and submitted it to *Harper's Magazine* a decade before Tagore became famous in the West. It was rejected, because, according to Bose's British biographer (the biologist and sociologist Patrick Geddes), 'the West was not sufficiently interested in Oriental life'.[6] A comparable indifference – but this time from Bose's own countrymen – would dog all his scientific efforts in Bengal until they received recognition in Europe.

Tagore was Bose's greatest Bengali advocate. Though by his own admission he hardly understood Bose's scientific achievements, he raised money from the maharaja of a local state, Tripura, to enable Bose to stay in Europe and carry on his researches, on the strength of the scientist's brilliant reception at the International Congress of Physicists in Paris in August 1900 (where Bose delivered a paper concerning electric currents in frogs' eyes).[7] On 31 August Bose wrote from London (in Bengali) as follows:

> What I saw in Paris has made me happy . . .; at the same time it has filled me with despair about conditions in my own country . . . How eager and alert people are here! The moment a new discovery is made it is put to use; those who first learn to utilise it leave others behind in the field of business and industry . . . Nature is ruthless: how long can races so inert and inactive as ours hope to survive? . . . Who can cure our rooted degeneracy? It is impossible not to feel distressed when I think of all this; tell me how I can control such thoughts.

The rest of the letter is a detailed description of how Bose had won over by experimental demonstration a number of European scientists, including many of the most sceptical, the physiologists. But a light-hearted diagram in the letter indicated how easily, Bose knew, his fellow-scientists might fall back into contentious dismissal of his new ideas. He concluded, 'Your poor champion is almost at his last gasp, but you may be sure he will not run away from the battle.'[8]

Shelidah, [Khulna, Bangladesh]
1 Ashwin [1307] [17 September 1900]

Priya bandhu,

There I was, quietly turning the pages of a French grammar, when your letter arrived and made me palpitate with excitement like a dead frog connected to an electric current. I was itching to show the letter to Loken and Suren, but both of them are far away. I am sending it to them today.[9]

Yes, declare battle! Do not spare anyone – whichever wretches fail to surrender, burn down their outdated dwellings with the fire of your arguments, be merciless like Lord Roberts: from the way you have deployed the stages of your battle strategy so far, I am firmly convinced you will be in Pretoria for Christmas.[10] Then, afterwards, when victory is yours, we too – all of us Bengalis – will share in the honour and the glory. We do not need to understand what it is you have done, or to have given you any thought, time or money; but the moment we hear the chorus of praise in the *Times* from the lips of Englishmen we shall lap it up. Some important newspapers in our country will observe that we are not inferior men; and another paper will observe that we are making discovery after discovery in science. Earlier, we shall not have felt an iota of responsibility for you, but when victory has been won and you return home bearing a crop of awards, then you will be one of us. Sowing and ploughing you will do alone; reaping we shall do together. The victory, you will find, will be more ours than yours.

You say you are up at point A on your diagram, quivering and restless. I am lying down at point B, supremely unbothered, unperturbed, paddy and sugarcane fields waving all around me in the dew-laden breeze of impending autumn.[11] You will be surprised to hear that I am sitting with a sketchbook drawing.[12] Needless to say, the pictures are not intended for any salon in Paris, they cause me not the least suspicion that the National Gallery of any country will decide suddenly to raise taxes to acquire them. But, just as a mother lavishes most affection on her ugliest son, so I feel secretly drawn to the very skill that comes to me least easily. That is why, having resolved to give my mind a period of absolute idleness, after much thought I settled on drawing. There is one great obstacle to my achieving much progress, however; I use the pencil rather less often than the rubber and have thus made myself quite an expert in erasure. So Raphael can rest undisturbed in his grave: my efforts will not decrease his renown.

Loken is doing his best to drag me off as his travelling partner to Shimla, to the mountains, during the coming Puja vacation – but I won't budge. When the rishis of old went to the mountains to practise their austerities, times were different; these days one finds no peace on the tops of those hills – a fact of which you especially can hardly be unconscious. I trust you have not yet forgotten this friend whom you met by the wayside in Darjeeling.[13] I am now back on the banks of the Padma, among the sand spits and cries of the sandpipers, awaiting the auspicious arrival of autumn. I hope you remember your pledge to me: we are going to have a tour together, in Kashmir maybe, or Orissa, or Travancore; that way I shall get my chance to slip slyly into at least one chapter of your autobiography. I hope you won't disappoint me; I have been saving up for this future trip together.[14] But now the lady of the house, who is sitting in a chair nearby, is urgently reminding me about my bath and food – time's getting on.[15] Excuse me for a moment. I won't be away long.

The enthusiasm that Loken felt for compiling an anthology of my poems has somewhat cooled, since he came back from England. Provided he does not mind, I may set my hand to it myself.[16] If the fact of my drawing has already astonished you, you will be no less astonished to hear that Loken is now writing poetry. What a miserable state of affairs for a man – to be reduced to writing poems! He is translating Omar Khayyam into Bengali.[17] A few lines will give you an idea of his state of mind: [Here follow four lines of Bengali verse, a very free rendering of one quatrain by Omar Khayyam of which the third line reads, 'Take this cash and reject that credit.'] From this you can gather that Loken is issuing a prospectus for his business based on squandering all his capital – he cares not about interest or profits, only about the spending of his entire reserves – and so I, for one, am not ready to buy any shares.

Your brother-in-law's wife, the Noble Lady Sarala, has lately taken up the study of Sanskrit with [Pandit] Vidyarnava.[18] They are using my method.[19] She has made swift progress – Pandit Mashai is really delighted to have such an intelligent pupil. I had earlier assured her that if she learnt Sanskrit by following my way, within a year she would attain competence. I am very happy that she is studying the language: there is a real need for our modern educated women to learn Sanskrit, to compensate for their excessive cultivation of English.

Sir, that land in Puri – I am not hopeful I shall be able to hang on to it for you, because the magistrate has cast his gaze upon it. He writes to me that the Puri district board has a great need for my insignificant acres. If might truly is right, then I shall not be able to protect the plot. If only, while you were here last time, you had begun to build on it, then that man would have had no claim.[20]

The weather today is squally. The sky is overcast – there are frequent sudden bursts of rain – and from time to time gusts of wind come up and make the doors and windows rattle. This kind of rainy season atmosphere induces in me a feeling of total holiday freedom that you over there in the workaholic West will be quite unable to conceive. Under normal circumstances I like to laze around seven days a week; now, when the rain comes or the autumn sun shines or the south wind blows, I like even more time off. Just now I am sitting with the wooden doors open and the glass windows closed, while outside a torrent of water beats down.

If you feel the need to be delivered from your promise to write me letters, then resort to your wife: were she to reply on your behalf, I promise I would not appeal against you. Do give her my cordial greetings. Don't forget that I am waiting to snap up every last titbit of news about the work that has taken you abroad. Whatever people are saying about you, whatever they are writing – in fact every detail of your doings – I'm dying to hear.

Apnar
Shri Rabindranath Thakur

Source: MS copy at Rabindra Bhavan, Shantiniketan; letter published in *CP*, VI, pp. 7–12.

1 Sir Jagadish Chandra Bose (1858–1937): physicist and plant physiologist; in 1917 he founded the Bose Institute in Calcutta. See Patrick Geddes, *The Life and Work of Sir Jagadis C. Bose* (London, 1920).
2 See *ibid.*, pp. 62–4. 'In 1901 one of the great manufacturers of wireless apparatus proposed to Bose, just before his Royal Institution lecture of that year, to sign a remunerative agreement as to his new type of receiver; but to the businessman's frank surprise, not to say disgust, he declined the offer' (*ibid.*, p. 63).
3 According to C. V. Raman, India's first Nobel laureate in science, Bose 'did some very clever physics before he started on all his mumbo-jumbo' (Quoted in Dutta and Robinson, *Rabindranath Tagore*, p. 403.) Today, some of the 'mumbo-jumbo' would be more sympathetically received by scientists.
4 RT first met Bose in 1891, but their close friendship began in 1897 and lasted for some ten years. Bose was a touchy, somewhat vain man who found friendships and collaborations difficult. The success of Shantiniketan and the award of the Nobel prize to RT seem to have provoked Bose to jealousy. See Ashis Nandy, *Alternative Sciences: Creativity and Authenticity in Two Indian Scientists* (2nd edn; New Delhi, 1995), pp. 56–7; also letter 36. RT remains silent on these points in the comments he made on Bose after his death. See 'Jagadish Chandra Bose', *MR*, Dec. 1937, p. 706; 'Jagadish Chandra Bose', *MR*, Jan. 1938, pp. 78–9; and 'Jagadish Chandra Bose and his institute', *MR*, Dec. 1938, pp. 745–6.
5 'Every weekend that Jagadish came to Shelidah he would make Father read out to him the short story that he had written the previous week and get a promise from him to have another ready the next weekend' (Rathindranath Tagore, *Edges of Time*, p. 25).
6 Geddes, *Life and Work*, p. 223.
7 See Rabindranath Tagore, *Tripura's Ties with Tagore* (Chiranjiv Kaviraj trans.; Agartala, 1969), pp. 31–3.
8 Jagadish Chaudra Bose, 'One friend to another', *VBQ*, 24, No. 4, Spring 1959, pp. 260, 263/Jagadish Chandra Bose, *Patrabali* (1365 [1958]), pp. 31–2 (reprinted in Dibakar Sen, *Patrabali*; (1401 [1994]), pp. 28–31).
9 Loken: Loken Palit; Suren: Surendranath Tagore.
10 RT's wry joke about Lord Roberts is obviously a response to Bose's comments on the 'Darwinian' nature of western society, but it also refers implicitly to the support for the British in the Boer War among Indians generally (including Gandhi, then in South Africa): in January 1900, a fundraising meeting at the Calcutta Town Hall raised some Rs 65,000 for the war fund. RT was not one of the supporters, as he made clear in his poem 'Sunset of the Century', composed in Shelidah on 31 Dec. 1900. See Dutta and Robinson, *Rabindranath Tagore*, p. 129.
11 According to Bose, the mind could ascend to A and then suddenly slide down to B.

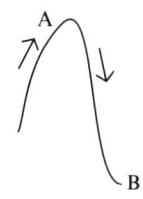

56   *Selected letters of Rabindranath Tagore*

12 RT made occasional references to drawing and painting from the 1890s onwards, but he did not take it up in earnest until about 1928. Ironically, the first exhibition of his paintings did indeed take place in a Paris salon, the Galerie Pigalle, in 1930. See letter 236.
13 RT spent almost a fortnight in Darjeeling in May 1900. Darjeeling was the summer seat of the Bengal Government, which supported Bose's visits to Britain in 1896 and 1900. Bose spent time there in discussion with officials, who, along with wealthy Bengalis escaping the heat of the plains, set the tone of Darjeeling – a tone which RT disliked.
14 In Oct. 1904, RT, Bose and others, including Sister Nivedita, visited Bodhgaya in Bihar. See Barbara Foxe, *Long Journey Home: A Biography of Margaret Noble* (London, 1975), pp. 168–9.
15 Mrinalini Devi spent the major part of 1900 in Shelidah, including Aug.–Dec.
16 Palit's anthology was advertised in *Sahitya*, Kartik 1307 [Oct.–Nov. 1900], but it never appeared. In 1903, Mohit Chandra Sen published his collected edition of RT's poems, *Kavyagrantha*.
17 Palit published a translation of twenty-five quatrains of Omar Khayyam, which has not been traced; it was probably based on the first edition of the famous 1859 version of Edward Fitzgerald. RT quotes No. 12.
18 Sarala Ray (1859?–1940): founder of a school in Calcutta, member of the Calcutta University senate and pioneer of women's emancipation in Bengal, she was well known for her good works (hence RT's gentle mocking tone); sister of Bose's wife Abala, she married P. K. Ray. RT wrote *Mayar Khela* at Sarala Ray's request.
19 Pandit Shivadhan Vidyarnava was presumably using RT's elementary book on Sanskrit, *Sanskrit Siksha* (*RR(AS)*, II, pp. 223–47), which was edited by Hem Chandra Bhattacharya and published in 1896. It avoided the traditional method of rote learning and instead introduced grammar functionally, through the use of the various grammatical forms in the context of actual sentences.
20 The authorities at Puri – RT writes 'magistrate' but the letter to him is signed by the collector – wanted the land in order to extend the European section of Puri, but RT did not agree. In 1903, he offered the land to Bose, who did not accept. It was finally sold to a Bengali in 1905 for Rs 3,000 in aid of Visva-Bharati. (See Paul, *Rabijibani*, IV, p. 296.)

28

To Mrinalini Tagore (Ray Chaudhuri)

Rabindranath continued his attempts to mould his wife by giving her new challenges. By late 1900, she had been living with him at Shelidah for some two years, during which time he had been looking after the scholastic education of their children and she after their practical education (though the responsibilities were not rigid). Rathindranath recorded in his memoirs:

> Father set my mother to prepare an abridged version of the *Ramayana*, keeping to the original but leaving out all superfluous and irrelevant matter so that the main story could be read at a stretch. Father insisted that she should consult the original Sanskrit and not depend upon Bengali translations for preparing her text. This was difficult for Mother, but undaunted she read the *Ramayana* with the help of a pundit, and only then did she start writing, but unfortunately the book was not finished before she died and the MS of the portion she had written got lost. I remember with what avidity we used to read her MS.[1]

[Calcutta, India]
[21 December 1900]

Bhai chhuti[2]

I am very pleased to receive two letters from you today. But I have no leisure to give you an adequate reply . . . I have to go to Bolpur today. I read my piece to Father, who asked me to amplify certain passages – I must get down to it since I have only a few hours.[3] So apart from kissing you in my mind, I can't give you anything else.

Family life 57

To make me happy you need not try very hard – your sincere love is enough. Of course, if you and I could be united in everything we do and think, that would be best – but one cannot will such things. If you could join with me in all that I do and learn, I should be happy; and if I could convey to you all that I wish to know, and you would learn side by side with me – that would be happiness indeed. If we could only manage to move forwards together in all things, progress should be easy. I do not want to leave you behind in anything – but at the same time I am afraid of forcing you. Each of us has his own separate taste, inclination and ability. You do not possess the power to make your own nature correspond wholly with my wishes and inclinations. Therefore, instead of torturing yourself about it, if you sweeten my life with your love and care, and try to protect me from unnecessary pain, your efforts will be precious to me.

Rabi

Source: MS original at Rabindra Bhavan, Shantiniketan; letter published in *CP*, I, pp. 42–3.

1 Rathindranath Tagore, *Edges of Time*, p. 21.
2 See letter 24, n. 4.
3 The piece in question was RT's sermon, which he delivered at Shantiniketan on 7 Paush (22 December), at the annual anniversary celebration of Maharshi Debendranath's initiation as a Brahmo. It appears in *RR(AS)*, II, pp. 181–94.

29

To Mrinalini Tagore (Ray Chaudhuri)

The marriages arranged by Tagore for his daughters Bela and Renuka are controversial. Despite his professed dislike of child marriage and belief in female education before marriage, and despite the lack of mental companionship in his own arranged marriage to a child wife, he married off both girls at young ages – Bela was four months short of fifteen, Renuka a mere ten-and-a-half years old – and to husbands they had never met. In later life, he expressed many guilty feelings about these decisions, and especially about the marriage of his third daughter Mira (see letter 145).

Bela's marriage was negotiated with the help of (amongst others) Priyanath Sen, who knew the family of the bridegroom, Sharat Chandra Chakravarty, the third son of the poet Bihari Lal Chakravarty and a lawyer living in Muzaffarpur, not far from Patna, in the neighbouring state of Bihar. After some difficulties over the matter of dowry, the marriage took place in Jorasanko on 15 June 1901.[1] A month later, on 15 July, RT took Bela to Muzaffarpur by train and, after a few days there, left her with her new family.

This letter was written to his wife on the way back, when he had stopped at Shantiniketan. It shows clearly that Mrinalini Devi was not happy about the marriage. It also suggests that Rabindranath's mind was preoccupied with the idea of Shantiniketan and the institution he was about to found there. Given that he married off Renuka with extraordinary haste in August 1901, both marriages may reasonably be seen as driven by his feeling that he needed to disencumber himself of family commitments, so as to concentrate on his new idea.[2]

[Shantiniketan, West Bengal, India]
[20 July 1901]

Bhai chhuti[3]

I have left Bela and returned here. Things are not as you may imagine from afar – Bela is quite satisfied, and there is no doubt that she likes her new way of life. Now we are no longer necessary to her. I have thought about this and concluded that, at least in the period immediately after marriage, girls need absolute freedom to unite fully with their husbands, away from the influence of their parents. If their mothers and fathers remain in the midst of this union, they will obstruct it. For the habits and tastes of the paternal home and the in-laws' home cannot be the same, there are bound to be differences, in which case the proximity of the parents will prevent a girl from obliterating her old ways from her mind and merging herself in the ways of her husband's home. And since a girl must be given away, why try to keep control of her? In such circumstances, the happiness and welfare of the girl comes first – what is the use of burdening her new ties to her husband's home with other ties, by taking into account the feelings of her parents? Remember that Bela is quite happy and try to console yourself at your separation. I can say with certainty that if we had hemmed her about after marriage, no good would have come of it. Because she is far away, the affection between us will forever remain. At Puja time, when she and her husband will visit us or we them, both sides will find the meeting full of deep and fresh delight. In all loving relationships there should be a degree of separation and independence. Love which tries completely to overwhelm us is never beneficial. If Rani [Renuka] too leaves us after her marriage, it would be good. Of course she will remain with us for the first couple of years – but as soon as she is old enough, it will be necessary for her own good to send her entirely away.[4] Our family has education, tastes, habits, language and attitudes that are different from those of all other Bengali families – hence the particular necessity of our daughters removing themselves from us after marriage. Otherwise, every trifling detail of their new lives will irritate them and tend to undermine their respect for and reliance on their husbands. Rani's character is such that if she is detached from her parental home, her faults will be corrected, but if she keeps close to us, these old associations will never go. Think of your own case. If, after marrying you, I had lived in Fultala, your nature and behaviour would have been something else altogether.[5] As far as one's children are concerned, one should entirely dismiss one's own happiness and sadness. They were not born for our benefit. Their happiness and their success is our sole reward. All day yesterday I kept dwelling on Bela's childhood. I thought of how I reared her with my own hands: how mischievous she was when lying penned in by dumpy bolsters; how as soon as she saw a small boy of her own age she went for him with a yell; how greedy she was, yet how good-natured; and how I used to bathe her myself at the Park Street house and how I used to wake up at night in Darjeeling to give her warm milk.[6] All those moments when I felt the stirring of love for her kept recurring in my mind. But she does not know of them – and that is good. Let her involve herself in her new household duties without regret; let her give herself wholly to this new life with faith and affection; and let us not lament over it.

Reaching Shantiniketan today, I was immersed in the ocean of peace. Looking from afar, one cannot grasp the importance of getting away like this from time to time. Here

I am alone, wrapt only in the endless sky and breezes and light; I feel as if I am being suckled in the arms of the primal Mother.

Tomar
[Rabi]

Source: MS original at Rabindra Bhavan, Shantiniketan; letter published in *CP*, I, pp. 61–3.

1 Sharat Chandra Chakravarty (1870–1942); Bihari Lal Chakravarty (1834–94) was a boyhood literary hero of RT and favourite author of Kadambari Devi. On the dowry question, see Paul, *Rabijibani*, V (1397 [1990]), pp. 2, 9.
2 See Dutta and Robinson, *Rabindranath Tagore*, pp. 130–2.
3 See letter 24, no. 4.
4 The husband chosen for Renuka was sent abroad for training immediately after marriage; a common habit in Bengal at this time.
5 Fultala, Mrinalini's home village, was in Jessore district, East Bengal.
6 Just after Bela's birth in Oct. 1886, RT's sister-in-law Jnanadanandini invited RT and Mrinalini to live with her for a while at her house in Park Street, in the European part of Calcutta. In Sept. 1887, RT, his wife and daughters and other Tagores stayed in Darjeeling. A letter to his niece Indira contains an affectionate reference to Bela's behaviour as a baby at that time (*CPB*, pp. 9–11).

30

To Rathindranath Tagore[1]

In November 1902, Tagore's wife, Mrinalini, died. At the same time Renuka, their second daughter, contracted tuberculosis. The condition worsened, and in May 1903 he took her away from Bengal to the hill-station of Almora. His eldest son Rathindranath, aged fourteen, he left at Shantiniketan in the care of a brilliant and passionate young poet-teacher, Shatish Chandra Roy.[2]

According to Rathindranath, the two of them got on very well in each other's company during the school's summer vacation, when Shantiniketan frazzles in baking heat. Rathindranath's memoirs contain vivid descriptions of hearing Roy reciting screeds of literature (western and Indian) from memory, of lying out all night under the stars and of being attacked by a ferocious storm that grabbed Roy and carried him off.

These were all experiences in which the young school-hating Rabindranath too would have revelled. But writing in this letter as an absent father to his wayward son, Rabindranath lectures Rathindranath in his most solemn (and somewhat sanctimonious) manner. Perhaps the tone was partly the result of his anxiety about his dying daughter, but it is also typical of a certain formality that would always subsist between father and son. Rabindranath expected a great deal from Rathindranath, who was unable to conform to his father's ideal, either as a young man or in later life, despite having many admirable qualities.

Thomson House, Almora, [Uttar Pradesh, India]
[17 May 1903]

Rathi

I hope your work is going well and you are obeying the various rules and engaging yourself in a disciplined course of study. Word is yet to reach me about the precise nature of these rules and the method you are following. My wish is that you board full-time at the school. If you keep going to the Shantiniketan house your mind will be distracted. Never forget that you are a pupil of the school. If you tell yourself that because you have no examination in the offing you can live as you please and let your studies go, you will do yourself a lot of harm. You must continue with your studies just as you did before. Practise English composition with Shatish. If you do not practise, whatever you have learnt so far will be undone. You have a very well-versed teacher of literature – if this opportunity does not serve to foster your own writing ability and your appreciation of literature, then all such efforts will be in vain. You have reached the age when of your own accord you must endeavour to improve yourself and build up your resistance to all kinds of evils: I want to see you assume responsibility for yourself now. My time to retire from such matters has come; and the family's welfare will now be chiefly up to you. Your example and learning, your strength of character and devotion to duty must now shelter and protect my family. Let the concepts of good and evil be steadfast in your mind, and let the words and actions of others not distract you from this understanding. Let modern-day babudom – with all its foppishness and high living – not lure you and contaminate you. Let your way of living be simple and straight, so that you feel no embarrassment to accept any invitation, whether from the rich man in his palace or the poor man in his hut. Poor outside but rich within – that is the ideal of India, and you should strive to embrace it.

Do not make yourself light-weight. Trifling matters and insignificant people must not upset you, and be careful not to resemble whomever you happen to be with – preserve your individuality.

Until today, the ideal of greatness has been present in our family in many forms; but it seems to be vanishing from the sons of the present generation. I cannot see any boy capable of maintaining our family's prestige. No one seems to possess the will-power, stamina and training to initiate our country into greatness. Our family must be saved from this deterioration. And so you, keeping yourself aloof from current crazes, holding high ideals in your heart, must prepare yourself in every respect to take up this noble duty. For this you need training, stamina and discipline, and also self-denial – and you need to remain unwavering and unbothered in the face of external pressures. Our country is a great one, the family in which you have been born is great too, and so were your noble ancestors. Keep these thoughts in mind and try to make yourself worthy of them – God will be your resource.

[Shri Rabindranath Thakur]

Source: MS original at Rabindra Bhavan, Shantiniketan; letter published in *CP*, I, pp. 1–4.

1 Rathindranath Tagore (1888–1961): son of RT; having trained in agricultural science in the USA, he helped to manage the Tagore estates, and after the founding of Visva-Bharati, he became its administrator. He also accompanied RT on many of his overseas tours. See his memoirs, *On the Edges of Time* and *Pitrismriti* (Reminiscences of My Father; 1373 [1966]).
2 Shatish Chandra Roy (1882–1904): teacher at Shantiniketan, 1901–4; he died of smallpox.

Shantiniketan and Swadeshi (1905–1911)

Introduction

Tagore's founding of a school at Shantiniketan in late 1901 was part of an upsurge of *swadeshi* (nationalist) activity in Bengal (and other parts of India) around the turn of the century. His aim was to establish a modern version of the *tapoban* (forest hermitage) of ancient India, apart from Calcutta and its flesh-pots and away from the lure of the West.

The first five pupils came from the city, among them, of course, the founder's son Rathindranath. The first teachers too were chiefly Bengalis, drawn to the place by Rabindranath's personal magnetism and the school's high educational ideals; one of them, who arrived in 1908, was the gifted scholar Kshiti Mohan Sen.

In 1905, the Government announced the Partition of Bengal: the province was divided into its western and its eastern parts (roughly as it would be in 1947), with Calcutta, the capital, severed from East Bengal. Bengalis, particularly the Bengali Hindu *bhadralok* of Calcutta, were incensed, and their feelings of indignation gave rise to the Swadeshi Movement, the forerunner of Gandhi's Noncooperation Movement in the 1920s.

Rabindranath was at first in absolute sympathy with this movement and became one of its leaders, turning his attention away from the Brahmo Samaj and pouring his energies into building up Bengal educationally, artistically and economically (his patriotic songs were his most famous contribution). But by 1907, the movement had degenerated into violence between Hindus and Muslims and bomb attacks against British officials. A disillusioned Tagore withdrew from it and concentrated his efforts on establishing his school and improving the condition of the peasants on his estates. To help in this work, he sent his son and son-in-law to the University of Illinois to train in agricultural science.

31

To Dinesh Chandra Sen[1]

One month after the official government declaration that Bengal had been partitioned into two provinces on 16 October 1905, thus provoking the rise of the Swadeshi Movement, Tagore wrote this brief history of the build-up to the movement in the form of a letter to a scholar who intended to write an article on the subject for *Bangadarshan*.

His main concern was to explain why boycott of the Government in all spheres – which was the passion in late 1905 and would later be the crux of the Noncooperation Movement under Gandhi – was wrong. Tagore was anti-noncooperation from the beginning; and his letter argues that throughout the decades of quiet *swadeshi* work prior to 1905, the motive had been constructive not destructive: to take the best of the West and assimilate it with the best of Bengal so as to create a self-reliant country, able ultimately to dispense with its dependence on alien rule. In the later words of his son Rathindranath, 'It was impossible for [Father] to accept what he called "the passion for rejection" as an ideal.'[2]

Bolpur, [West Bengal, India]
1 Agrahayan 1312 [17 November 1905]

Pritishambhashanametat –

The initial intoxication of English education gave rise to anti-*swadeshi* feelings in the minds of Bengali students. Educated Bengalis of that time out of shame imagined that our art, literature, history and religion were worthless, and they decided to imitate the West in every way as a model of progressive culture.

Owing to their ignorance of and contempt for the ancient scriptures many of them became atheists while many others drew closer to Christianity.

At that time Debendranath, the disciple of Rammohun Roy, felt a keen urge to begin investigating the ancient shastras. Although Debendranath rejected the prevailing religious rituals, he accepted the shastras as authentic and as the foundation for religious advancement.

It was he who first introduced discussions of the *Vedas* and *Upanishads* and foreign scientific writings, publishing them in Bengali in the *Tattvabodhini Patrika*. The Adi Brahmo Samaj tried to draw the attention of educated society away from alien religion towards its own religion and away from a foreign language towards its own language.[3]

When Keshub Babu joined the Brahmo Samaj and endeavoured to split Brahmoism from Hindu society, Debendranath did not reject Hinduism – he considered Brahmoism to be part of Hinduism. This was his method of moving the educated mind of the time towards *swadeshi*.[4]

In Debendranath's family there was a sustained effort to synthesise modern education with *swadeshi* feeling. The Hindu Mela was an example of this. Dwijendranath and Gunendranath assisted Naba Gopal Mitra to found the Mela.[5] It involved displays of *swadeshi* art, *swadeshi* wrestling and *swadeshi* games; *swadeshi* songs were sung and *swadeshi* poems were recited. After that Bankim's *Bangadarshan* nurtured Bengali literature and inspired the educated class to compose literature in the mother tongue.[6] Soon afterwards the appearance of Shashadhar should be mentioned.[7] Meanwhile, away from the public gaze, old Raj Narain Bose was cultivating a special form of *swadeshi* fervour in our family.[8] Secretly we tried to manufacture *swadeshi* matchsticks and improved weaving looms. Jyotirindranath, in a burst of patriotic zeal, established a steamer service from Khulna to Barisal and began an intense rivalry with a British company – you can just imagine the reaction now, under the regime of Fuller, if we were to adopt the same overenthusiastic methods of procuring passengers as were used at that time by the supporters of Swadeshi in Barisal.[9]

4 Rabindranath as patriot, Swadeshi Movement, 1905/6

Congress induced the educated section of society to believe in the policy of petitioning Government.

Sadhana[10] and some other journals advised people to abandon petitioning and concentrate on developing self-reliance – and so Balendranath and other members of our family got together and set up the Swadeshi Stores.[11]

From the ruins of the Swadeshi Stores arose the Indian Stores.

Shortly after that, at the Provincial Conference in Rajshahi, under the leadership of Satyendranath, the first attempt was made to discuss the needs of the country in Bengali, so that our duties to the motherland might not cease with mere petitions to the king in English; and in Dhaka the following year this effort continued.[12]

These ventures were all intimately part of the Swadeshi 'Movement'. Just as in religion the Brahmo Samaj directed people's minds towards the ancient shastras, so in politics the various efforts mentioned above have focussed people's attention on the country. And equally, just as educated people of those days did not easily embrace their indigenous religion and customs, so today's 'agitation'-wallahs do not easily abandon the method of petitioning and face squarely the basic problems of our country.

In the new series of *Bangadarshan*,[13] suggestions were put forward for the cultivation of self-reliance and *swadeshi* sentiment; and the foundation of the Bolpur school has been an effort to take education into our own hands.[14] Here Pandit Vidyasagar was the pioneer. He initiated the process of education with an English-style school run by Bengali teachers – my ideal is to make my entire educational effort as indigenous as possible.[15]

While such movements were quietly working away in the country, Jogesh Chaudhuri started an art exhibition at the Congress, so as to inspire *swadeshi* sentiment among the congressmen, who mainly supported the politics of petition. And this exhibition has been run each year since then.[16]

In the meantime, Ashu Chaudhuri, speaking at the Barddhaman [Burdwan] conference, was reviled for starting a debate about our propensity for mendicant politics.[17] But all the while the country had been gradually coming round to *swadeshi* feelings. When the matter of Partition arose, it was merely a convenient trigger for the full blossoming of the Swadeshi Movement. So the fact is, that the childishness of boycott is not the life force of the movement.

Apnar
Shri Rabindranath Thakur

Source: MS original at Rabindra Bhavan, Shantiniketan; letter published in *CP*, X, pp. 30–2.

1 Dinesh Chandra Sen (1866–1939): literary scholar; author of *A History of Bengali Language and Literature*. On Sen's attitude to RT, see E. P. Thompson, *Alien Homage: Edward Thompson and Rabindranath Tagore* (New Delhi, 1993), pp. 53–4, and E. J. Thompson, *Rabindranath Tagore: Poet and Dramatist* (New Delhi, 1991), pp. 315–16 (where Sen is quoted without attribution).
2 Rathindranath Tagore, *Edges of Time*, p. 62. See also letter 165.
3 See Debendranath Tagore, *The Autobiography of Maharshi Devendranath Tagore* (Satyendranath Tagore and Indira Devi trans.; Calcutta, 1909); also David Kopf, *The Brahmo Samaj and the Shaping of the Modern Indian Mind* (Princeton, 1979).
4 See Debendranath's letter to Keshub printed as an appendix to the 1909 edition of Debendranath's *Autobiography*; also RT's view of the same problem in letter 40.
5 Dwijendranath Tagore (1840–1926): eldest brother of RT. Gunendranath Tagore (1847–81): cousin of RT. Naba Gopal Mitra (1840?–94): editor and patriot, known as 'National' Mitra. On the Hindu Mela,

see *My Rem*, p. 105/*RR*, XVII, p. 348; also Mitter, *Art and Nationalism*, p. 222.
6. Bankim Chandra Chatterji [Chattopadhyay] (1838–94) published *Bangadarshan* from 1872 to 1876, in which he serialised some of his highly popular novels. See *My Rem*, p. 89/*RR*, XVII, p. 333; also Chaudhuri, *Thy Hand*, p. 612.
7. Shashadhar Tarkachudamani (1851?–1928): Hindu revivalist. See *My Rem*, pp. 174–5/*RR*, XVII, pp. 418–19.
8. Raj Narain Bose (1826–99): patriot. See *My Rem*, pp. 109–10/*RR*, XVII, pp. 352–3.
9. On Jyotirindranath's escapade with the steamer service, see *My Rem*, pp. 175–7/*RR*, XVII, pp. 419–21; also Sumit Sarkar, *The Swadeshi Movement in Bengal, 1903–1908* (Calcutta, 1973), pp. 109–10. Sir Bampfylde Fuller was lieutenant governor of Eastern Bengal and Assam at the time of the Partition of Bengal; he had a reputation for impulsive repression, which led to his being forced to resign.
10. *Sadhana*, to which RT was the major contributor, published a series of his articles in 1894–5 on the contemporary political situation in Bengal. See *RR*, X.
11. Balendranath Tagore and other Tagores set up a short-lived Swadeshi Bhandar at 82 Harrison Road, Calcutta, in 1897. See Sarkar, *Swadeshi Movement*, for an account of early *swadeshi* enterprises.
12. On the 1897 conference at Natore (district Rajshahi), see Rathindranath Tagore, *Edges of Time*, p. 17. RT offered a running translation into Bengali of all the speeches made in English; and at Dhaka, in 1898, he read a Bengali summary of the presidential address as it was delivered in English.
13. RT revived *Bangadarshan* after twenty-five years in 1901, and edited it for five years.
14. The Bolpur school at Shantiniketan was founded on 7 Paush 1308 (22 Dec. 1901).
15. RT published two major articles on Vidyasagar, written in 1895 and 1898 (*RR*, IV, pp. 477–502, pp. 502–11); see also Dutta and Robinson, *Rabindranath Tagore*, p. 122. Despite RT's statement about 'indigenousness', three of the first five teachers at Shantiniketan were Christians, and one of them was an Englishman. RT's views on this question of nationality altered within a few years, though he always adhered to the importance of teaching children in Bengali rather than English.
16. Jogesh Chaudhuri (1864–1951): barrister, who organised the first *swadeshi* exhibition at the Calcutta Congress in 1896; brother of Pramatha Chaudhuri.
17. Sir Ashutosh Chaudhuri (1860–1924): judge of the Calcutta High Court from 1912–20, afterwards a member of the Bengal Legislative Council; brother of Pramatha Chaudhuri and husband of RT's niece Pratibha. At the Barddhaman [Burdwan] conference in 1904, 'Chaudhuri's dictum "A subject nation has no politics" and his plea for constructive self-help in place of mendicancy aroused a lot of interest, and was welcomed by Tagore in his "Swadeshi samaj" address' (Sarkar, *Swadeshi Movement*, p. 56).

32

To Mira Gangulee (Tagore)[1]

In the later nineteenth century, as Rabindranath was growing to maturity, English had practically ousted Bengali as the language of a section of the Bengali elite. In response, Tagore's father, the Maharshi, had established a tradition in the family that no Bengali should write to the Tagores in English; if he himself received a letter from a Bengali written in English, he returned it to the writer. His son Rabindranath was less rigid in this respect, but he wrote very few letters in English until he began to make English and American friends in 1912–13.[2] He was bashful about his ability to write in English (see his remarks in letters 37, 40 and 65). Nevertheless, as this English letter to his daughter Mira proves, his English was good, apart from occasional grammatical slips (the most frequent being trouble with the plural 's' and the articles 'a' and 'the').

Mira was then twelve years old and living in Calcutta. The following year, 1907, she married Nagendranath Gangulee.

Bolpur, [West Bengal, India]
10 November 1906

Dear Mirie

I was agreeably surprised to receive your letter in English. Now that the ice is broken, let me hope you will continue to write to me such letters, and I will follow your example. I know one feels ill at ease to write in a language which is not his mother tongue and exercises in English composition can never take the place of a genuine letter but still I must put up with it. All the same, I am not going to be altogether deprived of the sight of your Bengali handwriting and the quaint spellings which betray your East Bengal origin through Mother's side.[3] So, occasional Bengali letters will be most welcome.

Boys are all coming back to our school and in a thousand ways their presence is being felt all over here. As the school works has not begun yet they are having a very jolly time of it. Kusumoto surprised me last night by suddenly making his appearance.[4] There is some hope of his getting an appointment in the National Technical Institute and he wants a recommendation letter from me to Mr Palit.[5] He made enquiries after Mirasan [i.e. Mira] and was disappointed not to find her here. I am glad that you have got a baby in the house to keep you company and I never doubt that you will be able to win her heart at last. I have completely recovered from the bad cold and I am glad you are well. With love.

Your affectionate
father

Source: MS original at Rabindra Bhavan, Shantiniketan; letter published in Sharadiya *Desh*, 1397 [Autumn 1990], p. 17.

1 Mira Gangulee (1894–1969): third daughter of RT; after separating from her husband Nagendranath in the early 1920s, she lived in Shantiniketan.
2 RT's first extant letter in English, an application to the Government to obtain a certificate proving his age (required if he was to compete in the Indian Civil Service examination in England), was dated 12 March 1878 (*Rabindra-Biksha*, Shraban 1396 [July–Aug. 1989], p. 7).
3 Mrinalini, RT's wife, came from a village in East Bengal. East Bengal pronunciation of certain words differed greatly from Calcutta pronunciation, and so, consequently, did some spellings; the three letters for *s* and *sh* were particularly affected. Calcutta Bengalis looked upon the East Bengal ('Bangal') pronunciation as quaintly rustic, as they still tend to do.
4 S. Kusumoto was a Japanese carpenter sent to RT in 1905 by the Japanese artist Okakura Kakuzo, following his visit to India. Kusumoto worked in Shantiniketan, Tripura and Calcutta, where he was appointed professor of carpentry at the Bengal Technical Institute.
5 Sir Taraknath Palit (1831–1914): father of RT's friend Loken Palit. On 25 July 1906, Palit and others founded the Bengal Technical Institute in Calcutta, with a course of studies emphasising training in ceramics, dyeing, soap making, tanning, and candle and match manufacture. Gaganendranath Tagore was one of two treasurers. See Sarkar, *Swadeshi Movement*, p. 166.

33

To Nagendranath Gangulee[1]

In 1906, Tagore sent his son Rathindranath and one other student to study agricultural science in the USA. The following year he met and liked Nagendranath Gangulee, the son of a well-known Brahmo, arranged his marriage to his daughter Mira in June, and agreed to pay for Nagen too to study agriculture in Illinois. Within three weeks of the marriage, Gangulee was on his way to the USA.

Nagen turned out to be a disastrous choice of husband, as subsequent letters reveal. Though not devoid of talent, he had a certain arrogance combined with the Brahmo haughtiness that has given Brahmos their reputation – even among Bengalis – of being stand-offish. As Tagore himself admitted:

> It is a sign of national provincialism . . . to associate natural differences in others with inherent inferiority and disagreeableness. Of all peoples in India, we in Bengal suffer from this imperfect adaptability of imagination which causes arrogance. It is owing to our provincialism, for we have been accustomed for centuries to live in a remote corner developing our race mannerism. The Bengali people are prone to keep themselves isolated when in unaccustomed surroundings, and they have an unenviable talent of making themselves unpopular with the people of other provinces of India.[2]

This letter, written to the eighteen-year-old Nagen in Illinois, warns him of these dangers.

Bolpur, [West Bengal, India]
14 Ashwin 1314 [1 October 1907]

Kalyaniyeshu

I was relieved to get your letter from America. Consult with Rathi and select an area of study which you will be able to apply on your return to India. And there is another area you should pay heed to. If you three Bengali students stick together in a group and hug your corner, you will do yourself a disservice.[3] If you constantly avoid mixing with local students and staff, your command of English will never be reliable. It is vital that in addition to the principles of agriculture you discuss English literature and so on – otherwise your education will become narrow. Do you have any American students at your lodging place? If so, make a special effort to be friendly with them. You need to mix socially with local people as much as possible. So far, judging from Rathi's letters, I have the impression that Rathi and companions have not made much effort to be friends with the local people – you only like each other's company. If that is really so, it is not good. To get on familiar terms with the local people is a part of your education. To know only agriculture is not enough; you must know America too. Of course if, in the process of knowing America, one begins to lose one's identity and falls into the trap of becoming an Americanised person contemptuous of everything Indian, it is preferable to stay in a locked room. Those who are immature and weak-minded tend to lose their own identity when they go abroad and become spoilt – better for such people if they keep to their own home environment. From childhood all of you have displayed a typical Brahmo repugnance for other people's social customs and historical traditions. I know of no worse superstition and prejudice – unless you drive it from your mind, your foreign education will never benefit you fully. Rammohun Roy was a pioneer of the Brahmo Samaj and the first to travel to England, but he preserved his patriotism intact. Unlike modern Brahmos, he never looked down his nose at other country's customs and labelled them superstitions. I have not yet had a meeting with your elder brother.[4] He is still in Barisal. I shall try to procure a job for him there. It is going to be difficult.

Mira is better now after a prolonged bout of illness. She is out of bed but she cannot walk very far.

The school vacation is upon us at Bolpur. I have come here to make the necessary arrangements.

I occasionally receive news of your father. His old aches frequently trouble him. May God keep you well.

Shubhanudhyayi
Shri Rabindranath Thakur

Source: MS original at Rabindra Bhavan, Shantiniketan; letter published in Sharadiya *Desh*, 1398 [Autumn 1991], pp. 19–20.

1 Nagendranath Gangulee (1889–1954): agricultural scientist and writer; husband of RT's daughter Mira. After obtaining a degree in agricultural science from Illinois and then working as a manager on the Tagore estates, Gangulee eventually became professor of agriculture and rural economics, University of Calcutta, 1921–31, during which period he obtained a doctorate in soil biology from the University of London and served on the Royal Commission on Indian Agriculture, 1926–8, and as a member of the Imperial Advisory Council of Agricultural Research, 1929–31. After 1932 he settled in England and published a number of books with major publishers, concerning Indian agriculture and politics, European politics and also religion and literature; they included anthologies prefaced by H. G. Wells and T. S. Eliot (twice). None, however, was of lasting significance, all were essentially derivative works, demonstrating professional ability to assemble the ideas of others, but little originality or deep personal commitment. Judging from stray references to Gangulee in the works of British contemporaries such as Vera Brittain – who called him a 'vital, intelligent man' (Vera Brittain, *Search after Sunrise* (London, 1951), p. 172) – he had a degree of intelligence, charm and plausibility reminiscent of the male characters in certain of RT's satirical short stories. A brief London *Times* obituary (3 Feb. 1954) noted that Gangulee was 'a man of energy and intensity, [who] sponsored one crusade after another in his later years, but failed to fulfil the promise of his early manhood'.
2 'The colour bar', *Spectator*, 9 May 1931, p. 737.
3 The third student, apart from Rathindranath and Nagendranath, was Santosh Chandra Majumdar (1886–1926), son of Shrish Chandra Majumdar.
4 Upendranath, brother of Nagendranath, was the father of the nationalist politician Aruna Asaf Ali.

34

To Kshiti Mohan Sen[1]

The school at Shantiniketan attracted a number of talented teachers in its first few years, most notably Shatish Chandra Roy (see letter 30), who died tragically young in 1904. But it lacked a true scholar who was more than a traditional Sanskritist – until the arrival of Kshiti Mohan Sen in July 1908.

Rabindranath heard about Sen from two of his co-workers[2] and sent a letter of invitation to him at Chamba, the small hill state at the foot of the Himalayas between Punjab and Kashmir, where Sen was then acting as educational adviser to the ruler. Though Kshiti Mohan had never met Rabindranath, he was keenly interested in him both as a man and as a writer – even so, he refused the offer. This letter is Tagore's second, successful, attempt at persuasion.

Rabindranath's instinct was extremely accurate. Sen was perfectly in tune with Tagore's ideas and personality. According to a Bengali writer in 1960:

> When he joined the then small community at Santiniketan over 50 years ago he cast an immediate spell over all its members including the Poet, the king of spell-binders. The relationship between Kshiti Mohan Sen and Rabindranath may be described as a two-way traffic that lasted as long as the Poet lived. Kshiti Mohan Sen found in the Poet the fulfilment of his life's quest. 'Many a sacred place in India have I visited in my time', he once observed, 'but none that is comparable to Santiniketan.' The Poet in his turn

drew freely upon Kshiti Mohan Sen's seemingly endless store of knowledge about Indian culture and religion, particularly his unrivalled knowledge of folklore and obscure byways of the people's life.[3]

Shelidah, [Khulna, Bangladesh]
12 Phalgun 1314 [24 February 1908]

Binayshambhashanpurbbak nibedan –

Your letter disappointed me, but I am not yet ready to abandon hope. I have a great need of an ally suited to the task of putting this school on a firm foundation, which I have been pursuing for the past six years. That is why, having come to hear of you, despite your objections I am persisting with my request. In this school you will have the opportunity to apply your talents in every direction – here you will feel delight in your creations and, by the grace of God, something of permanent benefit to the country will be established. In this task I not only pray for your assistance – I demand it. Our country is much in need of genuine education, and if one receives a call to fulfil this need one should on no account disregard it. I have prepared the ground, which you will now cultivate and make fructuous – you must not let these efforts of mine go to waste. You must once more consider my words deeply and sincerely – and if they do not meet with the approval of your heart, only then shall I endeavour to search elsewhere.

Bhabadiya
Shri Rabindranath Thakur

Source: MS copy at Rabindra Bhavan, Shantiniketan; letter published in *Desh*, 1 Nov. 1986, p. 57.

1 Kshiti Mohan Sen (1880?–1960): scholar and teacher; he wrote many books in Bengali, principally on the religious traditions of medieval India, two of which were translated into English, *Medieval Mysticism of India* and *Hinduism* (which has been in print since publication in 1961). Sen's ancestral home was in East Bengal but he was born in Varanasi, and brought up as an orthodox Hindu, before becoming deeply interested in the syncretic religious traditions (such as the Sants) that were a challenge to orthodoxy; as a young man he travelled all over northern and western India in search of these traditions. On the details of his life, see Kshiti Mohan Sen, 'In remembrance of Kali Mohan Ghosh', *VBN*, April 1971, pp. 298–300; 'Rabindranath and the ashram of early days', *VBN*, June 1939, pp. 91–4; and *VBN*, July 1939, pp. 4–7; also Hiran Kumar Sanyal, 'Kshiti Mohan Sen Sastri', *VBN*, Feb. 1960, pp. 127–9.
2 The two co-workers were Kali Mohan Ghosh (1884–1940) and Vidhu Shekhar Bhattacharya (1878–1959), according to Sen ('In remembrance of Kali Mohan Ghosh', p. 299).
3 Hiran Kumar Sanyal, 'Kshiti Mohan Sen Sastri', *VBN*, Feb. 1960, p. 129.

35

To Nagendranath Gangulee

In 1907, Tagore withdrew abruptly from nationalist politics and the Swadeshi Movement he had helped to lead in 1905–6. He wanted to concentrate his attention on building up his school and on rural reconstruction work on his estates; also he did not want to be part of the violent turn taken by the movement. His ideas were revolutionary, but his methods had nothing to do with bomb throwing: for the rest of his life, he tried to maintain his distance from India's political revolutionaries, not always successfully (see letters 122–4, 126–8).

As already mentioned (letter 33), in that year he sent his son-in-law Nagendranath Gangulee to the USA so that he could be trained in methods applicable for rural reconstruction work in Bengal. But while he was in America, Nagendranath had been influenced by revolutionary propaganda: a number of Indians, including Bengalis, were living in the USA and using the country as a base from which to try to organise the overthrow of British rule in India. In this letter, Tagore issues another warning to Nagendranath that he should keep a clear head while living abroad.

[Calcutta, India]
15 Baishakh 1315 [24 April 1908]

Kalyaniyeshu

Nagendra – your article has appeared in *Prabashi*.[1] By now you must have received it. I had to cut it quite a bit for two reasons. First because it was too long to be published in one instalment, and to print more than one would have spoilt it. Secondly, in some places it contained [gimmicks].[2] These are the trademark of second-rank American authors. One never comes across such melodramatic elements in literary writing by superior authors. Balance and restraint are the hallmarks of the finest literary expression. The explicit and violent expression of strong emotion is inappropriate. I have noticed that you often use two or three exclamation marks in your writing. Have you ever seen such signs of excess in the work of any really good writer? They are found only in advertisements – where writers need to shout – but in literature they are completely out of place. I remember a while ago ticking off the editor of *Nabyabharat* for using excessive and redundant punctuation to express feelings as strenuously as possible.[3] The results of this are usually adverse: when style is overemphasised, emotional impact is actually diminished. Your 'Vera Sazanova' has however gone down well with readers.[4] One of them copied the piece in his own hand and sent it to his village for circulation among the people there. At the same time there is a rumour that a group of Indians in America is secretly sending arms to India for revolutionary purposes. Your article may unexpectedly convey the impression that you too belong to that group. Given the work we are starting in the villages, the Government may conclude that our chief aim is to stir up a Russian-style revolution. That is why I felt obliged to add a comment to your article.[5]

1000 rupees has been sent to Jagadish in England to purchase equipment for the technical departments at Bolpur; he will select, buy and despatch.[6] Obviously this is a fairly small sum – just to get things going – and then little by little I will try to expand. Meanwhile, during this summer vacation, one of our staff teachers is learning tanning at the factory of Nil Ratan Babu.[7] When he has learnt this skill he will be able to establish it at Bolpur, and those boys who do not object to handling leather may learn it too. I hope to establish umbrella making as well.

Shri Rabindranath Thakur

Source: MS original at Rabindra Bhavan, Shantiniketan; letter published in Sharadiya *Desh*, 1398 [Autumn 1991], p. 24.

1 *Prabashi*, Baishakh 1315 [April–May 1908], pp. 24–32.
2 The word is incorrectly spelt but is almost certainly 'gimmick', even though, according to the *Oxford English Dictionary*, 'gimmick' did not come into use in the USA until the 1920s.
3 The editor was Debi Prashanna Ray Chaudhuri (1854–1920), editor of *Nabyabharat* from 1883.
4 The spelling of 'Vera Sazanova' is taken from A. P. Gnatyuk-Danil'chuk, *Tagore, India and the Soviet Union: A Dream Fulfilled* (Calcutta, 1986), p. 193. According to Gangulee's article, this Russian revolutionary was the daughter of a Jewish doctor, and was killed by the forces of the czar. Gangulee appears to have taken the story from a report by Leroy Scott, an American journalist and writer. (See Paul, *Rabijibani*, VI (1399 [1993]), p. 3).
5 RT's signed comment appears on pp. 32–4 of *Prabashi*, after Nagen's article. He observed that most of the methods of the Russian revolutionaries would not be of benefit to Bengalis.
6 Bose later informed RT that he had not bought any equipment because there was no one yet at Bolpur who could make use of it.
7 Sir Nil Ratan Sircar (1861–1943): physician and *swadeshi* enthusiast; he founded the National Tannery at Beliaghata in 1905, and the National Soap Factory, from which RT bought soap for his daughter Bela. He was 'a kind of latter-day Jyotirindranath [Tagore], spending his professional savings with an utterly liberal if quixotic hand in scheme after dubious scheme' (Sarkar, *Swadeshi Movement*, p. 135).

36

To Aurobindo Mohan Bose[1]

Rabindranath aroused much resentment among Bengali nationalists by his withdrawal from the Swadeshi Movement and his subsequent criticisms of the 'patriots'. In 1908 he published a series of articles setting out his arguments.[2] The last of these, 'Deshahit' (National welfare), published in the Ashwin (September–October) issue of *Bangadarshan*, was particularly provocative, it seems, to Abala Bose, the strong-willed wife of Jagadish Chandra Bose. She wrote an angry letter to her nephew Aurobindo Mohan Bose, who sent it to Rabindranath. This letter, explaining his attitude to nationalism, is his response to the young man.

The young Bose had recently left Shantiniketan and was studying science at Calcutta University, before moving on to Cambridge University, with Tagore's help, in 1912. He had been sent to Shantiniketan in 1902 by his uncle and aunt, at the height of Jagadish Chandra's friendship with Rabindranath; now he was to become a bone of contention between J. C. Bose and Tagore, leading to a permanent breach in their friendship.[3] For Aurobindo Mohan, the 'adopted son' of the childless Boses, had fallen for Rabindranath and his school and was seriously considering returning there to teach.[4] Bose and his wife felt that Tagore was threatening to destroy a bond precious to them, while Tagore felt that they were unsympathetic to his school.[5] This conflict, as much as Abala Bose's conventional patriotic beliefs, lay behind her outburst to her nephew.

Bolpur, [West Bengal, India]
4 Agrahayan 1315 [19 November 1908]

Kalyaniyeshu

I have read your aunt's letter. She is so annoyed with me that she has not really read what I wrote. Nowhere in my article did I say that the boycott should stop. Nowhere did I so much as hint that all the races in India should convert to one religion – I uttered not a single word on the merits and demerits of idolatry. All I said was that whatever we may do, such as boycotting, if we resort to unjust, untruthful and unrighteous methods, ultimately we shall not benefit. I shall never attempt to boost my own work by deprecating the highest truth and the greatest good for the sake of some immediate need, however grand a name it may have.

Without first deciding to consecrate worship of country as our religion, enthroning it as our deity, we shall never be able to emulate the example of Europe. There, in the name of 'manliness', they have the habit of dismissing religion by calling it 'weak sentimentalism', which we have started to ape – but surely the concept we in India know as humanity is far greater than this manliness. Let us not, out of shame at our lack of European-style manliness, allow ourselves rapidly to sacrifice this humanity. We have a saying in Sanskrit, which means that one must strive to attain knowledge of Him who is above all – one should not lower Him to the level of lesser ideas.[6] If we downgrade the Almighty and make patriotism our highest ideal, our patriotism will become the blindest of superstitions, similar to the belief in omens about sneezing and lizards croaking, or the worship of goddesses to ward off cholera and skin diseases.[7] The only difference would be that the new superstition would bear the seal of approval of civilised countries – and a big name is a bewitching thing. We must firmly remember that our country is not a god and therefore we cannot substitute it for God. You have read in the *Creed of Buddha* Lord Buddha's saying, 'Conduct moulds character and character is destiny.'[8] If a body – be it an individual or a whole race – defiles its own character in pursuit of short-term goals, it thereby consumes its capital and puts itself on the path to bankruptcy. This is not a matter of debate, it is a fundamental fact. I believe that amidst all the doubts and disputations of this world, all the excitement, desire and blandishment, one must steadfastly hold the helm, irrespective of one's gain or loss, life or death. This is my faith, which I keep with all my heart, believing it to be the greatest truth and the noblest good. Though I may stray from it out of weakness, let me never have the temerity to tell my faith to go to hell and instead come to regard my country as supreme, as a cause worthy of my stealing, robbing and doing wrong. Patriotism cannot be our final spiritual shelter; my refuge is humanity. I will not buy glass for the price of diamonds, and I will never allow patriotism to triumph over humanity as long as I live. I took a few steps down that road and stopped: for when I cannot retain my faith in universal man standing over and above my country, when patriotic prejudices overshadow my God, I feel inwardly starved.

Your aunt is aggrieved because of the spirit of unrest of the time. Many people are averse to me for the same reason. I must put up with it all. Over and over I pray to God that I may surrender my load to Him and make my burden light. If He snatches away my fame and I am scornfully rebuked, even by my friends, that will benefit me – for I have yet to break my inborn habit of depending upon others. When He allows me to face Him entirely on my own, my life will be fulfilled; when that auspicious day arrives, I shall be blessed. You must not feel in the least hurt by the hostile reactions to me. God will recompense me for all my troubles, bringing me closer to Him each time – I will never let Him go.

Shubhanudhyayi
Shri Rabindranath Thakur

Source: MS copy at Rabindra Bhavan, Shantiniketan; letter published in *VBP*, Shraban–Ashwin 1362 [July–Oct. 1955], pp. 1–2.

1 Aurobindo Mohan Bose (1892–1977): translator of RT; he published a series of translations of RT's poetry from 1955 onwards. Bose studied at Shantiniketan (1902–07), Calcutta University (1907–12) and Cambridge University (1912–14, 1919–20 – he was interned in Germany during the war). He then pursued a parallel career as a freelance journalist in Europe, and academic researcher and lecturer at various universities, including Visva-Bharati. His interests ranged widely over science, literature, philosophy and politics.
2 See *RR*, X.
3 See Nandy, *Alternative Sciences*, pp. 56–7. When J. C. Bose's letters to RT were published in *Prabashi*, Asharh 1333 [June–July 1926], pp. 406–8, all the passages concerning Aurobindo Mohan Bose were deleted.
4 The phrase 'adopted son' is A. M. Bose's own. (Quoted in Martin Kämpchen, *Rabindranath Tagore and Germany: A Documentation* (Calcutta, 1991), p. 98.)
5 Abala Bose (1864–1951) wrote to RT on 11 April 1911 (in Bengali): 'You have not invited us to go to Bolpur, which suggests that you don't want us there . . . From now on we shall keep him [Aurobindo Mohan] with us.' RT replied on 13 April: 'it is unbearable to me that you should come here with the slightest negative feeling and just to satisfy your curiosity'. (Quoted in Paul, *Rabijibani*, VI, pp. 199–200.)
6 *Chandogya Upanishad*, 7:23.
7 If one hears a sneeze when one is about to set out on a journey, one is supposed to delay the journey. If a lizard croaks when one is speaking, one's words are held to be true.
8
    We may safely affirm, what Buddha would not have denied, that Right Conduct is the aspect of Righteousness which concerns us most. What we do, besides being the outward and visible sign of our inward and spiritual state, reacts, naturally and necessarily, on what we are, and so moulds our character and controls our destiny – for 'character is destiny' – both in this and in future earth-lives. (Edmund Holmes, *The Creed of Buddha* (London, 1908), p. 82)

37

To Myron H. Phelps[1]

This letter, Tagore's first major one written in English, marks a shift in his thinking from his turn-of-the-century belief that Bengal could be self-sufficient without the help of the West towards a conviction that Bengal needed to absorb the best of western thought and art in order to resuscitate herself. It was written in reply to a New York lawyer, Myron H. Phelps, with a public sympathy for the Indian cause. Phelps had written a series of 'Letters to the Indian people', printed in the *Hindu* of Madras, and in September 1907 had started an Indo-American National Association, followed in March 1908 by an India House, which was intended as a lodging house and meeting place for Indian students in New York. India House fell foul of dissensions between the students and between Phelps and the students, and Phelps closed it at the end of February 1909. Soon afterwards he left America for Europe and eventually reached India via Sri Lanka in June 1910.[2] Wandering the subcontinent for well over a year, he visited Shantiniketan and Shelidah and had discussions with Tagore, though he seems to have been drawn more to theosophy than Brahmoism and to other areas of India more than Bengal.[3]

Tagore's letter to Phelps is noteworthy for its frankness about the causes of the contemporary Indian 'unrest' (i.e. the Swadeshi Movement and its aftermath), presumably because Phelps, besides being sympathetic to Indians, was an American, and therefore not instinctively pro-British. The letter's analysis of caste is particularly interesting; and here Tagore does not hesitate to draw parallels with racial conflict in the USA. Although Phelps' original letter is lost, Tagore's answer suggests that it contained a statement from Phelps of his own disillusionment with the Indians in New York, and a request for advice. Tagore's words, which Phelps should have received within a month, may even have been the trigger that finally persuaded Phelps to close his India House in February and travel East to see India for himself.

Shantiniketan, [West Bengal, India]
4 January 1909

My dear Sir,

I am exceedingly gratified to receive your very kind letter and to know of your desire for our welfare.

In regard to the assistance you expect from me, I am afraid that as I have never been used to express myself in the English language I shall not be able to give an adequate or effective idea of what I feel to be the truth about our country. However, I shall attempt as best I may to give you an outline of my views, more as a response to your message of goodwill than with the hope of rendering any help in your friendly endeavours.

One need not dive deep, it seems to me, to discover the problem of India; it is so plainly evident on the surface. Our country is divided by numberless differences – physical, social, linguistic, religious; and this obvious fact must be taken into account in any course which is destined to lead us into our own place among the nations who are building up the history of man. The trite maxim 'History repeats itself' is like most other sayings but half the truth. The conditions which have prevailed in India from a remote antiquity have guided its history along a particular channel, which does not and cannot coincide with the lines of evolution taken by other countries under different sets of influences. It would be a sad misreading of the lessons of the past to apply our energies to tread too closely in the footsteps of any other nation, however successful in its own career. I feel strongly that our country has been entrusted with a message which is not a mere echo of the living voices that resound from western shores, and to be true to her trust she must realise the divine purpose that has been manifest throughout her history; she must become conscious of the situation she has been instrumental in creating – of its meaning and possibilities.

It has never been India's lot to accept alien races as factors in her civilisation. You know very well how the caste that proceeds from colour takes elsewhere a most virulent form. I need not cite modern instances of the animosity which divides white men from negroes in your own country, and excludes Asiatics from European colonies. When, however, the white-skinned Aryans on encountering the dark aboriginal races of India found themselves face to face with the same problem, the solution of which was either extermination, as has happened in America and Australia, or a modification in the social system of the superior race calculated to accommodate the inferior without the possibility of either friction or fusion, they chose the latter. Now the principle underlying this choice obviously involves mechanical arrangement and juxtaposition, not cohesion and amalgamation. By making very careful provision for the differences, it keeps them ever alive. Unfortunately, the principle once accepted inevitably grows deeper and deeper into the constitution of the race even after the stress of the original necessity ceases to exist.

Thus secure in her rigid system of seclusion, in the very process of inclusion, India in different periods of her history received with open arms the medley of races that poured in on her without any attempt at shutting out undesirable elements. I need not dwell at length on the evils of the resulting caste system. It cannot be denied, and this is a fact which foreign onlookers too often overlook, that it served a very useful purpose in its day and has been even up to a late age, of immense protective benefit to India. It has largely contributed to the freedom from narrowness and intolerance which distinguishes the Hindu religion and has enabled races with widely different culture and even antagonistic social and religious usages and ideals to settle down peaceably side by side – a phenomenon which cannot fail to astonish Europeans, who, with comparatively less jarring elements, have struggled for ages to establish peace and harmony among themselves. But this very absence of struggle, developing into a ready acquiescence in any position assigned by the social system, has crushed individual manhood and has accustomed us for centuries not only to submit to every form of domination, but sometimes actually to venerate the power that holds us down. The assignment of the business of government almost entirely to the military class reacted upon the whole social organism by permanently excluding the rest of the people from all political cooperation, so that now it is hardly surprising to find the almost entire absence of any feeling of common interest, any sense of national responsibility, in the general consciousness of a people of whom as a whole it has seldom been any part of their pride, their honour, their dharma, to take thought or stand up for their country. This completeness of stratification, this utter submergence of the lower by the higher, this immutable and all-pervading system, has no doubt imposed a mechanical uniformity upon the people but has at the same time kept their different sections inflexibly and unalterably separate, with the consequent loss of all power of adaptation and readjustment to new conditions and forces. The regeneration of the Indian people, to my mind, directly and perhaps solely depends upon the removal of this condition. Whenever I realise the hypnotic hold which this gigantic system of cold-blooded repression has taken on the minds of our people whose social body it has so completely entwined in its endless coils that the free expression of manhood even under the direst necessity has become almost an impossibility, the only remedy that suggests itself to me and which even at the risk of uttering a truism I cannot but repeat, is – to educate them out of their trance.

I know I shall be told that foreign dominion is also one of the things not conducive to the free growth of manhood. But it must be remembered that with us foreign dominion is not an excrescence the forcible extirpation of which will restore a condition of normal health and vigour. It has manifested itself as a political symptom of our social disease, and at present it has become necessary to us for effecting the dispersal of all internal obstructive agencies. For we have now come under the domination not of a dead system, but of a living power, which, while holding us under subjection, cannot fail to impart to us some of its own life. This vivifying warmth from outside is gradually making us conscious of our own vitality and the newly awakened life is making its way slowly, but surely, even through the barriers of caste.

The mechanical incompatibility and consequent friction between the American colonies and the parent country was completely done away with by means of a forcible severance. The external force which in eighteenth-century France stood to divide class from class [could] only be overcome by *vis major* to bring emancipation to a homogeneous people. But here in India are working deep-seated social forces, complex internal reactions, for in no other country under the sun has such a juxtaposition of races, ideas and religions occurred; and the great problem which from time immemorial India has undertaken to solve is what in the absence of a better name may be called the race problem. At the sacrifice of her own political welfare she has through long ages borne this great burden of heterogeneity, patiently working all the time to evolve out of these warring contradictions a great synthesis. Her first effort was spent in the arrangement of vast materials, and in this she had attained a perhaps somewhat dearly bought success. Now has come the time when she must begin to build, and dead arrangement must gradually give way to living construction, organic growth. If at this stage vital help has come from the West even in the guise of an alien rule, India must submit – nay welcome it, for above all she must achieve her life's work.

She must take it as a significant fact in her history that when on the point of being overcome with a torpor that well nigh caused her to forget the purpose of what she had accomplished, a rude shock of life should have thus burst in upon her reminding her of her mission and giving her strength to carry it on. It is now manifestly her destiny that East and West should find their meeting place in her ever-hospitable bosom. The unification of the East which has been her splendid if unconscious achievement must now be consciously realised in order that the process may be continued with equal success and England's contribution thereto utilised to full advantage.

For us, there can be no question of blind revolution, but of steady and purposeful education. If to break up the feudal system and the tyrannical conventionalism of the Latin church which had outraged the healthier instincts of humanity, Europe needed the thought impetus of the Renaissance and the fierce struggle of the Reformation, do we not in a greater degree need an overwhelming influx of higher social ideals before a place can be found for true political thinking? Must we not have that greater vision of humanity which will impel us to shake off the fetters that shackle our individual life before we begin to dream of national freedom?

It must be kept in mind, however, that there never has been a time when India completely lost sight of the need of such reformation. In fact she had no other history but the history of this social education. In the earliest dawn of her civilisation there appeared amidst the fiercest conflict of races, factions and creeds, the genius of Ramachandra and Krishna introducing a new epoch of unification and tolerance and allaying the endless struggle of antagonism. India has ever since accepted them as the divine will incarnate, because in their life and teachings her innermost truth has taken an immortal shape. Since then all the illustrious names of our country have been of those who came to bridge over the differences of colours and scriptures and to recognise all that is highest and best as the common heritage of humanity. Such have been our emperors Asoka and Akbar, our philosophers Shankara and Ramanuja, our spiritual masters Kabir, Nanak, Chaitanya and others not less glorious because knit closer to us in time and perspective.[4] They belong to various sects and castes, some of them of the very 'lowest', but still they occupy the ever-sacred seat of the guru, which is the greatest honour that India confers on her children. This shows that even in the darkest of her days the consciousness of her true power and purpose has never forsaken her.

The present unrest in India of which various accounts must have reached you, is to me one of the most hopeful signs of the times.[5] Different causes are assigned and remedies proposed by those whose spheres of activity necessarily lead them to a narrow and one-sided view of the situation. From my seclusion it seems to me clear, that it is not this or that measure, this or that instance of injustice or oppression, which is at the bottom. We have been on the whole comfortable with a comfort unknown for a long time, we have peace and protection and many of the opportunities for prosperity which these imply. Why then this anguish at heart? Because the contact of East and West has done its work and quickened the dormant life of our soul. We have begun to be dimly conscious of the value of the time we have allowed to slip by, of the weight of the clogging effete matter which we have allowed to accumulate, and are angry with ourselves. We have also begun vaguely to realise the failure of England to rise to the great occasion, and to miss more and more the invaluable cooperation which it was so clearly England's mission to offer. And so we are troubled with a trouble which we know not yet how to name. How England can best be made to perceive that the mere establishment of the *Pax Britannica* cannot either justify or make possible her continued dominion, I have no idea; but of this I am sure that the sooner we come to our senses, and take up the broken thread of our appointed task, the earlier will come the final consummation.

With kindest regards,

Yours sincerely,
Rabindranath Tagore

Source: *MR*, Aug. 1910, pp. 184–7.

1 Myron H. Phelps (1856–1916): lawyer; born in Illinois, he graduated from Yale University and law school in California and practised in New York; he also had a farm in New Jersey.
2 Information from *Indian Agitators Abroad*, Shimla, Nov. 1911, pp. 137–40 [IOL] (report compiled in the Criminal Intelligence Office), which comments: 'There is some reason to doubt whether he [Phelps] is quite sane, especially on religious subjects.' An open letter to Phelps signed by six Bengalis in New York, dated 10 March 1908, appeared in *Bande Mataram*, Calcutta, on 11 April 1908, attacking him for 'the arbitrary manner in which you have been working for your Society without desiring the active cooperation of any of our representative Indian gentlemen'.
3 Phelps told Rathindranath Tagore that at Shelidah 'he had discovered a genuinely successful American farm' (Rathindranath Tagore, *Edges of Time*, p. 74).
4 Asoka: emperor of India, *c.* 270–*c.* 232 BC; Akbar, Mughal emperor of India, 1556–1605; Shankara 700?–750?; Ramanuja, 1017?–1137; Kabir, 1440–1518; Nanak, 1469–1539; Chaitanya, 1485–1533. In 1937, RT quoted some lines of Kabir as the conclusion of an address to the Sri Ramakrishna Centenary Parliament of Religions, which summarise his view of India's spiritual genius:

> The jewel is lost in the mud,
>   and all are seeking for it;
> some look for it in the east, and some in the west;
>   some in the water and some amongst stones.
> But the servant Kabir has appraised it at its true value
>   and has wrapped it with care,
> in a corner of the mantle of his own heart.
>   ('Religion of the spirit and sectarianism', *MR*, April 1937, p. 381)

5 In 1910, (Sir) Valentine Chirol looked at the 'unrest' from a British perspective in his book *Indian Unrest* (London, 1910).

38

To Pratima Tagore[1]

Rathindranath Tagore returned from his agricultural studies abroad in 1909 and was immediately put in charge of the Tagore estates. He settled at Shelidah and began to lay out a farm on the American model, with a small laboratory for soil testing. 'As I was engaged in this pleasant occupation Father sent for me and proposed that I should marry Pratima, the niece of my cousin Gaganendranath.'[2] On 27 January 1910, the wedding took place at Jorasanko.

Rathindranath was then twenty-one years old, a year or so younger than Rabindranath at the time of his marriage, while his bride was sixteen, about five years older than Mrinalini Devi in 1883. Pratima had, however, been a child bride like Mrinalini; she had married at the age of about ten in 1903/4, her husband had drowned and she had become a widow; thus her marriage to Rathindranath was the first widow marriage in the Tagore family. Another rule was broken too, since she was not a Brahmo (Gaganendranath's side of the family were relatively orthodox Hindus) – but caste was observed.

Having grown up in the Tagore family house, rather than in a village in East Bengal, Pratima was better educated than Mrinalini. Nevertheless, Rabindranath was keen that she should study and not simply play housewife. A teacher from the University of Illinois (where Rathindranath had recently been), Miss Bourdette, came to live at Shelidah.[3] In this letter, apparently written nine or ten months after the wedding, Tagore encourages Pratima (who was by nature somewhat lazy) to understand and look after her foreign teacher's needs. Shelidah must have been quite a shock to anyone brought up in the American Midwest.

Bolpur, [West Bengal, India]
[late 1910][4]

Kalyaniyashu

Bouma, I was pleased to have received your letter.[5] But just liking Miss Bourdette won't do, you must learn from her. If she is good at sewing then have her teach you how to sew well – but not just embroidery, you need to know how to cut cloth too, and so on. And as you sew together you will begin to practise English conversation. However little English you know, try to use it when speaking to her, don't feel shy. What arrangements have you made for her meals? What do you give her for lunch? Make quite sure she gets her food on time – these people are punctual in all matters while we are just the opposite. Tell Rathi he should see that she is taught a little Bengali: the Bengali letters and pronunciation will tax her quite enough to begin with. Mira can take charge of it.[6] How are you spending your evenings now? Do you play games with her? When I come again I expect to find you all chattering away in fluent English. Looking ahead to Christmas, you must obtain for her some greetings cards and on the day itself have some feasting and fun – you could even take the boat and roam around on the sandbanks. Ask Rathi to obtain some illustrated magazines, Christmas numbers, from Thacker's, and order a Christmas cake from Calcutta at the appropriate time.[7] She plays the piano well and she likes to play, so it is up to Rathi to get a piano for her; right now it's the season in Calcutta and pianos will be costly, but in three or four months' time the price will fall. She is bound to feel a bit lonely being on her own and unless we find some means of entertaining her a little, she will suffer.

I asked Rathi to send Dwipu some palm molasses, but there's no sign of it yet. Dwipu is eagerly looking forward to it.[8]

How is Rathi getting on with his gardening and farming? How's the garden of Mira's uncle-in-law? Perhaps you are importing turnips and carrots from him?

Any news of Nagen's return?[9]

Tell Rathi I have written a letter to *Pishima* asking her to go elsewhere but I've had no reply.[10] Are you all keeping well?

Shubhanudhyayi
Shri Rabindranath Thakur

Source: MS original at Rabindra Bhavan, Shantiniketan; letter published in *CP*, III, pp. 8–9.

1 Pratima Tagore (1893–1969): daughter of Binayini, sister of Gaganendranath and Abanindranath Tagore; she married Rathindranath Tagore in 1910. The marriage was not a success; after RT's death, the couple separated. There were no children. Pratima Devi assisted RT in the staging of his dance dramas.
2 Rathindranath Tagore, *Edges of Time*, p. 74.
3 Miss Bourdette was chosen by Nagendranath Gangulee, who remained in Illinois during 1910. One wonders what he told her about life in Bengal, for she did not stick very long at Shelidah. On 20 Feb. 1911, RT told his daughter Mira that he had heard that Miss Bourdette had become 'inflexible' in her attitudes (Sharadiya *Desh* 1397 [Autumn 1990], p. 32). By March, she had gone back to America, at considerable expense to the Tagores: 'How can we deal with the Yankees?' RT joked to Mira (*CP*, IV, p. 24).
4 The probable period of this letter is Oct./Nov., i.e. the beginning of the cold weather in Calcutta and the social season.
5 *Bouma*: literally, 'Bride-mother'.
6 Mira Gangulee: daughter of RT, sister-in-law of Pratima.
7 On Thacker's, see letter 26, n. 4.
8 Dwipu: Dwipendranath Tagore (1862–1922): nephew of RT, eldest son of Dwijendranath Tagore.
9 Nagen: Nagendranath Gangulee, husband of Mira, returned from the USA in Feb. 1911.
10 *Pishima*: Raj Lakshmi Devi, an aunt of Mrinalini Devi (*pishima* means 'paternal aunt'), had taken charge of RT's children after his wife's death, at her express request. Presumably she was now a member of the married household at Shelidah, which was not altogether convenient.

39

To Ramananda Chatterji [Chattopadhyay][1]

The earliest published translations of Tagore's work into English were short stories published in Calcutta in 1901–2.[2] In December 1909, the *Modern Review* published the first of a series of translations of Tagore short stories, to which was added, in 1911, translations of his poetry. This was at the initiative of the editor, Rabindranath's friend Ramananda Chatterji [Chattopadhyay], the greatest magazine editor of pre-Independence India.

The translators were almost all Bengalis. One of the exceptions was Sister Nivedita, another was Ananda Coomaraswamy, the pioneering historian of Indian art, then at the outset of his career, who was assisted by a Bengali.[3] Rabindranath himself had little involvement, believing his command of English to be insufficient for the task of translation. The quality of the translations was on the whole inadequate – and yet some of them played a role in arousing the interest of William Rothenstein and others in Tagore's work, prior to his visit to Britain in June 1912 and the rapturous reception of his own translations in London.[4] As Coomaraswamy noted in his *Art and Swadeshi* (Madras, 1912), while introducing his versions of Tagore's poetry to a readership which had yet to hear of Tagore:

> The translations convey only a shadow of the original poetry, they give only the meaning, that in the songs themselves is inseparable from their music . . . Some of them

may perhaps convey a hint of the delicate charm of the originals and the perfect unity of thought with emotion that is expressed in them; but those who would really know them, must understand their language – best of all if they hear the poet himself recite them.[5]

Judging from this letter about translation, Coomaraswamy was here reflecting Tagore's own reservations to a great extent.

[Shantiniketan, West Bengal, India]
20 February 1911/8 Phalgun 1317

Shraddhashpadeshu

Coomaraswamy was here in the ashram. He desires to translate some of my poems, so I hastily rendered three or four of them into the plainest of prose in order to help him. If Coomaraswamy writes something based on these, you may publish it in *Modern Review*.[6] I have no objection provided it passes through his hands. Ajit translated a few – these are with Coomaraswamy too, and whatever he considers worth printing, you may publish.[7] But it would not be proper for my name to be given as translator after Coomaraswamy has scrubbed and polished my mockery of a translation.

Doctor Bose told me that Sister Nivedita has translated two of my short stories ('Kabuliwallah' and 'Chhuti') into English, with presentable results, and I gather she has no objection to their being published in your journal.[8]

Bhabadiya
Shri Rabindranath Thakur

Source: MS original at Rabindra Bhavan, Shantiniketan; letter published in *CP*, XII, pp. 4–5.

1 Ramananda Chatterji [Chattopadhyay] (1865–1943): magazine editor; founded *Prabashi* (1901) and *Modern Review* (1907). See Nirad C. Chaudhuri, 'Ramananda Chatterji: a tribute', *MR*, Aug. 1965, pp. 168–71, a brilliant, funny and touching piece by a former assistant editor of *MR*.
2 The Calcutta-based *New India* published several short stories in translation in 1901–2.
3 Ananda Kentish Coomaraswamy (1877–1947): historian of Indian art; in 1917, he joined the Museum of Fine Arts, Boston, as a research fellow and remained there till his death. Around 1911–12, Coomaraswamy was quite intimate with the Tagores.
4 See Dutta and Robinson, *Rabindranath Tagore*, p. 160 and notes.
5 Coomaraswamy, *Art and Swadeshi*, p. 126.
6 'Biday (Farewell)', trans. by the author and A. K. Coomaraswamy, *MR*, April 1911, p. 371.
7 'Janmakatha', trans. by A. K. Chakravarty and A. K. Coomaraswamy, *MR*, March 1911, p. 296. Ajit Kumar Chakravarty (1886–1918) was a teacher at Shantiniketan; a notebook containing his translations of RT's poetry was sent to Rothenstein in 1911 and made a distinct impression. But RT had no high regard for Chakravarty as a translator or literary critic in Bengali. See letter 175.
8 'The Kabuliwallah', trans. by Sister Nivedita, was published in *MR*, Jan. 1912. J. C. Bose had tried to get this translation published in the West in 1900 (see letter 27).

40

To Thanwardas Lilaram Vaswani[1]

During 1911, Rabindranath took the office of secretary of the Adi Brahmo Samaj – the original Brahmo Samaj founded by his father – and made a determined effort to revitalise it. He appointed some new people with less conservative views, persuaded

Kshiti Mohan Sen to visit Calcutta once a week from Shantiniketan in order to conduct divine service, and made himself editor of *Tattvabodhini Patrika*, the organ of the Adi Brahmo Samaj. In its pages he began a sustained attack on Brahmo factionalism and argued for Brahmoism as being 'inner Hinduism', a movement within Hindu society, not something alien to that society produced by the western impact on India.[2] He saw himself as acting in the same spirit as the great Indian reformers and bridge-builders he had praised in his letter to Myron Phelps (letter 37). In this letter to a prominent Brahmo in Karachi seeking advice on the history of the Samaj, Tagore expresses the same vision in a different way.

Shilida, [Shelidah, Khulna, Bangladesh]
24 June 1911

Dear Brother

There are hardly any English books which will be of any help to you in your study of the Adi Brahmo Samaj. Some pamphlets were written by Babu R. N. Bose during the early stormy period of our Samaj.[3] I have never read them myself because I do not expect any deeply comprehensive view of our Samaj from these writings. However, I will send these books to your address when I go to Calcutta.

To my mind the *raison d'être* of the Adi Brahmo Samaj is to show that the Brahmo movement is not a mere episode, much less a break, in the history of the Indian religious consciousness. It is not a violent introduction of an alien matter into our racial constitution. India being rudely shaken in its lethargic sleep by the contact of the West has either had to assert itself or let itself be borne away by the tidal wave. In [the] Brahmo Samaj India tried to find her own solid ground where she could stand firm and make herself recognised. Through this fearful stress and strain our country has been forced to discover anew the abiding purpose, the undying truth in her, which is national, as well as universal. And Adi Samaj says, this is Brahmo Samaj.

As I can very feebly and with difficulty express myself in English I ask your pardon and stop here.

Very sincerely yours
Rabindranath Tagore

Source: MS copy at Rabindra Bhavan, Shantiniketan.

1 Thanwardas Lilaram Vaswani (1879–1966): religious leader, known as Sadhu Vaswani. Apart from a brief spell as a professor in Calcutta from 1903–6 and various travels, Vaswani lived all his life in Sind. In 1911, he was the leader of the New Dispensation, the branch of the Brahmo Samaj founded by Keshub Chandra Sen. Within a matter of years he left the Samaj, resigned his job and became an early supporter of Gandhi and noncooperation. A footnote in the *Collected Works of Mahatma Gandhi* describes Vaswani as the 'seer from Sind' (*CWMG*, XX, p. 57).
2 On RT's work with the Brahmo Samaj in 1911, see the summary in P. C. Mahalanobis, 'The growth of the Visva-Bharati, 1901–1921', *VBQ*, 6, No. 1, p. 89. There is a much fuller discussion in Kopf, *Brahmo Samaj*, p. 299ff.
3 Raj Narain Bose's pamphlets are listed in Kopf, *Brahmo Samaj*, p. 371.

41

To Mira Gangulee (Tagore)

During 1911, Rathindranath Tagore and his wife Pratima (*Bouma*) continued to live in Shelidah, along with his sister Mira and her husband Nagendranath Gangulee, who returned from his studies abroad in February. Rabindranath, living mainly at Shantiniketan, continued to direct his family's education.

[Shantiniketan, West Bengal, India]
Postmark 1 August 1911

Miru

I was glad to receive a letter from you after many days. Is Rathi reading Ball's *Astronomy* to you?[1] When I first read that book I liked it so much that I gave up eating and sleeping. Possibly *Bouma* is enjoying it also. Has she been given some of the *Fairy Land of Science* to read? She will learn a lot from that book too. I have noticed that she has a natural attraction for science. I hope her studies are not too much affected by her teacher rushing off to Kalka?[2] Why don't you teach her? Is your health better now? Your *Mejama* has suggested to me that you go and stay with her at Ranchi. It is a good place – you will like it – and your health will also be good there. You can learn music and musical notation from Jyoti *Dada*. I don't know whether *Meja Dada* has discussed the idea with Nagen or not.[3] Nagen must surely be back in Shelidah.[4] But since you are all roaming the waterways, how will he get in touch with you? How is your uncle getting on?[5] He must be having a problem now that I've gone away – we conversed a lot on serious subjects – he won't find anyone else to listen to him.

Your piece on religion and science is out in *Prabashi* – have you seen?[6] Perhaps your pen is currently still. I hope the boat has not been too knocked about by the rain and wind. Now the dark phase of the moon is here, the weather will be wet.

Father

Source: MS original at Rabindra Bhavan, Shantiniketan; letter published in *CP*, IV, pp. 25–6.

1 Sir Robert Stawell Ball published a series of books on astronomy, beginning with *Elements of Astronomy* (London, 1880).
2 Kalka: town in the foothills of the Himalayas, near Shimla.
3 Jyotirindranath Tagore (Jyoti *Dada*) had moved in 1908 from Jorasanko to Ranchi, a relatively healthy town in the hills of southern Bihar, then the summer capital of the Government of Bihar. Satyendranath Tagore (*Meja Dada*) and his wife Jnanadanandini (*Mejama*) were living in a delightful house in Ballygunj, an up-and-coming professional area of south Calcutta, and used to visit Ranchi. RT himself never went there.
4 Nagendranath Gangulee spent some of his time visiting the Tagore estates, as Rabindranath had done in the 1890s.
5 Uncle: Nagendranath Ray Chaudhuri, brother of Mrinalini Devi.
6 *Prabashi*, Shraban 1318 [July–Aug. 1911]. Mira had translated an article from the *Hibbert Journal*.

42

To Pratima Tagore

Tagore saw much of death during the course of his long life, and he wrote frequently about death.[1] Elisabeth Kübler-Ross, author of the classic study, *On Death and Dying* (New York, 1969), believed that no one had thought more deeply on death than Tagore; she printed Tagore quotations at the head of each chapter in the book.[2] Perhaps his attitude to death comes out most clearly in the description in his memoirs, written at the age of fifty, of losing his beloved sister-in-law Kadambari when he was in his mid-twenties:

> All around, the trees, the soil, the water, the sun, the moon, the stars, remained as immovably true as before, and yet the person who was as truly there, who, through a thousand points of contact with life, mind and heart, was so very much more true for me, had vanished in an instant like a dream. What a perplexing contradiction! How was I ever to reconcile what remained with that which had gone? ...
>
> Yet amid unbearable grief, flashes of joy sparkled in my mind on and off in a way which quite surprised me. The idea that life is not a fixture came as tidings that helped to lighten my mind. That we are not forever prisoners behind a wall of stony-hearted facts was the thought that kept unconsciously rising uppermost in rushes of gladness. What I had possessed I was made to let go – and it distressed me – but when in the same moment I viewed it as a freedom gained, a great peace fell upon me.[3]

This letter was written to condole his daughter-in-law Pratima, on the death of her grandmother, Saudamini Devi, on 19 August 1911.

[Bengal]
[August? 1911]

Kalyaniyashu

Ma, unless we see death as conjoined with life, we cannot see truly. In our perception of everyday life we do not see death's role and we clutch at the world with all our might. Our desires become a terrible shackle. If we can only see death's true place then the burden of the world becomes lighter. But if we persist in seeing death as being quite separate from life then the pangs of bereavement will be severe. Death is the bearer of life, life flows forward in death's current: once this idea is properly grasped, our mind becomes free to see truth – within which there is no conflict. But as long as we persist in seeing life and death as fundamentally opposed, we feel attachment to the world. And attachment binds us, and makes us shed tears. All sins, fears and griefs spring from this.

Shubhanudhyayi
Shri Rabindranath Thakur

Source: MS original at Rabindra Bhavan, Shantiniketan; letter published in *CP*, III, pp. 13–14.

1 Letters 10, 42, 121, 258, 276, 294, 311, 312 and 346 are directly concerned with death.
2 *On Death and Dying* has quotations from *Fruit-Gathering*, *Stray Birds*, *Gitanjali* and *The Fugitive*. The comment on RT by Kübler-Ross is taken from a report in the Calcutta *Statesman*, 29 May 1993.
3 *My Rem*, pp. 179–80/*RR*, XVII, p. 424.

43

To Jnanadanandini Tagore (Mukherji [Mukhopadhyay])[1]

Mira, Rabindranath's daughter, did go to stay with her aunt Jnanadanandini – but in south Calcutta rather than in Ranchi. Rabindranath clearly felt that she would be happier away from Shelidah, probably partly because of the strain that was already starting to develop between her and her husband Nagendranath. He also had in mind his own happy youth as a member of Jnanadanandini's circle in the 1880s, around the time of his marriage. In the words of his favourite niece Indira (daughter of Jnanadanandini), 'my mother had . . . the quality of centrality, that is the power of attracting people around her, owing to her hospitable and hearty nature'.[2]

Bolpur, [West Bengal, India]
Postmark 3 September 1911

Bhai Meja Bouthan –

It's a relief to hear that Mira is fully recovered.[3] I can never believe in the idea that meat eating is good for Mira. The sick diet you have planned for her is the proper one. The food at Rathi's is not satisfactory I agree – that's why Pratima is often unwell, she frequently takes purgatives.[4] Something in our blood from Jessore makes Mira very sociable – when she mixes with people, laughs and gossips, she is at her best.[5] As a circle of female companions gradually congregates in your locality in Ballygunj, Mira will be much happier.

I am somehow managing. When the holidays begin I shall give some time to looking after my own health. Our vacation begins on the 8th Ashwin.[6]

Tomar sneher
Rabi

Source: MS original at Rabindra Bhavan, Shantiniketan; letter published in *CP*, V, p. 8.

1 Jnanadanandini Tagore (1850–1941): pioneer of women's emancipation in Bengal; wife of Satyendranath Tagore, elder brother of RT. She was the first Tagore woman to accompany her husband to Government House in Calcutta; she rode a horse when this was unheard of among Indian women; she designed a blouse and sari so that women could appear in public that eventually became universal among Bengali Hindu women; and she started the first children's magazine in Bengali, *Balak* (1885), to which RT contributed. See Ela Sen, 'Prominent women of India: Sm. Jnanadanandini Devi', *Statesman*, Calcutta, 1 Nov. 1936. In later life, she was the only female Tagore of whom RT was perhaps slightly afraid. He was unable to convince her of the importance of his educational experiments at Shantiniketan. See Leonard K. Elmhirst, *Poet and Plowman* (Calcutta, 1975), pp. 24–5.
2 'Uncle Rabindranath', Sahitya Akademi, *Rabindranath Tagore: A Centenary Volume*, 1861–1961 (New Delhi, 1961), pp. 5–6.
3 Mira was then some six months pregnant.
4 Pratima's health was never strong, and after a severe attack of influenza in 1919, she was a changed person.
5 Most of the Tagore wives came from Jessore, for example Jnanadanandini herself, Kadambari Devi (wife of Jyotirindranath) and Mrinalini Devi (wife of RT).
6 Ashwin: Bengali month corresponding to mid-Sept.–mid-Oct.

44

To Ramananda Chatterji [Chattopadhyay]

In late 1911, the director of public instruction of the Government of East Bengal and Assam issued a draconian confidential circular stating that the school at Shantiniketan was 'altogether unsuitable for the education of the sons of government servants' and advising any such 'well-disposed' servant to remove his son from the school; 'any connection with this institution . . . is likely to prejudice the future of the boys who remain pupils of it after the issue of the present warning'.[1] The effect was disastrous, as this letter shows: parents began to take their sons away from Shantiniketan immediately.

Tagore and his institutions attracted the suspicion of lower British officials, especially the police, from 1905 onwards. At one time he was recorded in the Bolpur police files as suspect 'C class number 12'.[2] But the highest officials generally quashed the urges of their subordinates. 'Just fancy, they wanted to proscribe a school like that: but I soon put a stop to it when I heard about it,' Lord Hardinge, the viceroy, told C. F. Andrews in March 1913;[3] and in 1915 Shantiniketan received its first courtesy visit from the governor of Bengal.

The pervasive antagonism depressed Tagore, who in 1917 wrote that 'when at a sign from the CID, institutions representing the patriotic labour of years crumble to the dust, that makes no difference to the appetite for dinner, or the soundness of sleep, of the ruling power, nor does it even affect his zest for his game of bridge' – but it did not surprise him.[4] 'The conditions being what they are, it is but natural. Bureaucracy always implies dealings, not with the real world as a whole, but with that part of it which is a product of its own regulations.'[5]

[Shantiniketan, West Bengal, India]
9 November 1911/23 Kartik 1318

Shraddhashpadeshu

I like the translation of 'Jay-parajay'. In one or two places on the margin of the proof I have made a suggestion which it is up to you to decide what to do with. One or two sentences sound weak to my ear but I am incapable of improving them.[6]

Nivedita's 'Kabuliwallah' reached me yesterday evening.[7] Although sent by registered post the envelope had been slit open and resealed. I have received three letters similarly opened and resealed. It would appear that the grim and suspicious gaze of our rulers has been turned upon us keenly. Chanakya wrote that one should never trust the rulers and it does indeed seem that a relation of trust between rulers and ruled is a forlorn hope.[8]

Even our school has finally fallen under the official edict. All of a sudden the boys belonging to the families of civil servants are being withdrawn; some are even being instructed by telegram. In our Shantiniketan I have adhered steadfastly to the aims of the ashram, never permitting political debate even at this time of great excitement. Indeed I have been able to divert our pupils' minds away from it – for which I have had to put up with adverse comment.[9] But it is evident that whatever beneficial idea one promotes, religious or otherwise – if one is trying to build something new, one will encounter only obstruction from the rulers of the country. And there is no way to reach a compromise through open debate – because like Meghnad of legend the ruling power hides behind a cloud and unleashes weapons against which one can neither retaliate nor protect oneself.[10] What a mean and wretched attitude it is to trample all efforts to do good with these cowardly methods. By doing so, the ruler drags himself down below the ruled. These spies are like clowns who have got the ear of the ruler and are manipulating it to produce devilish laughter: where will this cruel farce end!

Whatever happens, it will run its course, this unfair contest between unequals. Through sorrow and defeat the charioteer will take us to our destiny, and in the meantime we must do our duty. Even if we lose, dharma will be on our side – that will be our victory.

Within a few days we shall know how much blood the government's secret weapon has drawn. But the injustice is like a knife without a haft: it can wound but it cannot protect itself.

Apnader
Shri Rabindranath Thakur

Source: MS original at Rabindra Bhavan, Shantiniketan; letter published in *CP*, XII, pp. 13–15.

1 The circular was printed in the *Bengalee*, 26 Jan. 1912; it appears in Chinmohan Sehanobis, *Rabindranath o Biplabi Samaj* (1392 [1985]), pp. 28–9.
2 Thompson, *Alien Homage*, p. 154, n. 6.
3 Andrews to RT, 8 March 1913 [RB].
4 'The small and the great', *MR*, Dec. 1917, p. 602/*RR*, XXIV, pp. 290–1.
5 *Ibid*.
6 'Victorious in Defeat', trans. by Jadunath Sarkar, was published in *MR*, Dec. 1911/*RR*, XVII, pp. 210–19. Ramananda Chatterji [Chattopadhyay] may have improved the translation; he had been a professor of English in Calcutta, and his English was certainly more grammatically correct than RT's.
7 See letter 39, n. 8.
8 Chanakya (Kautilya)'s *sloka* in fact says: 'One should never trust women or rajas' (John Haeberlin, *Kavyasangraha: A Sanscrit Anthology* (Calcutta, 1847), *sloka* 27, p. 314).
9 See letter 36, for instance.
10 Meghnad, son of Ravana in the *Ramayana*, won many battles through his magical power of creating illusory reality. RT had used a similar image in an essay in 1905:

> If the thunderbolt is at all to be diverted that cannot be done by making a counterdemonstration of feeble thundering, but only by using the proper scientific appliances. The lightning conductor does not fall from the skies, like the lightning itself; it has to be manufactured patiently, laboriously and skilfully down below, by our own efforts. ('The way to get it done', *MR*, May 1921, p. 598/*RR*, III, p. 565)

45

To Rathindranath Tagore

During 1911 and early 1912, after the return of Rathindranath Tagore and Nagendranath Ganguleefrom training abroad and before his own extended visit to Europe and the USA, Tagore continued to try to develop rural reconstruction work on the Tagore estates. This letter shows how he kept up a flow of suggestions. Both the young men showed some initial enthusiasm, but both seem to have come to the conclusion – probably enhanced by their exposure to the prosperity of American agriculture – that the problems of Indian rural reconstruction were too big for them to tackle in the way that Rabindranath hoped, without government help. In 1912, Nagendranath wrote from Shelidah to a professor at the University of Illinois:

> There is great scope for the improvement of the indigenous ploughs. Tagore has, as you know, imported one planter junior and one disc plough but our plough cattle cannot draw them! The poor quality of our livestock is one of the main causes of agricultural backwardness, and yet animal husbandry as a subject of research has not received adequate attention from the Government. There cannot be any reasonable excuse for this gross neglect of animal husbandry in a country where milk and milk products constitute a large part in the people's dietary.[1]

[Patisar?, Rajshahi, Bangladesh]
[1911 or early 1912]

Kalyaniyeshu

A paddy husking machine is in operation at Bolpur – if a similar machine could be brought here it would be useful. This is paddy-growing country; there is more paddy here than in Bolpur.

My hope is that the farmers here could together take five- or ten-rupee shares in such a machine; it would give them a real opening for cooperation. With a loan from our bank a paddy husking business could easily be got going here – Nagendra and Janaki both believe the project to be suitable for this place and beneficial to the ryots.[2]

Do look into this idea of a machine.

I have also been thinking of what kind of industry could be introduced to the farmers. Apart from paddy nothing else grows here – all they have is stiff clayey soil. I need to know if pottery can be reckoned to be a cottage industry. Will you look into it – whether, say, a small furnace can be brought in and feasibly run by the people of a village. The sort of clay objects that the Mussulmans use – if plates, bowls and so on of similar type could be made, it would be of real service.

Another idea is to start umbrella making. If someone could be found to teach it, such a venture could be launched at Shelidah.

Nagendra was saying that if we bring a potter here who knows how to manufacture roof tiles, it would be immensely beneficial. People like to have a tin roof but they cannot afford it – hence they need clay tiles.

So enquire about a paddy husking machine, a pottery wheel and a teacher of umbrella making – don't forget.[3]

Tomorrow I shall visit Ratwal division, from there I go to Kamta division, and possibly on Thursday I shall head for Shelidah.[4]

Shri Rabindranath Thakur

Source: MS original at Rabindra Bhavan, Shantiniketan; letter published in *CP*, I, pp. 19–20.

1 Nagendranath Gangulee, *The Indian Peasant and his Environment (The Linlithgow Commission and After)* (Oxford, 1935), pp. 43–4.
2 In a journal entry written after a visit to Patisar in 1912, Gangulee writes of his attempt to persuade some

of RT's tenants to start up cooperative societies that might be given loans by the agricultural bank founded by RT. There was some interest as well as much scepticism (*ibid.*, pp. 40–2). Janaki: Janakinath Roy (1856–1929): official on the Tagore estates.
3 Judging from RT's letter, Rathindranath appears to have been away from the estates, probably in Calcutta, where he would have been in a position to look into the feasibility of these ideas.
4 The Kaligram division of the Tagore estates had three subdivisions, Patisar, Kamta and Ratwal, hence the probability that RT's letter was written from Patisar.

Voyage to the West (1912–1913)

Introduction

When Tagore set off for Britain in May 1912, it was the first time he had left India for over twenty years. He undertook the trip partly for medical treatment and partly because he felt a need to get in touch with western artists and intellectuals. Though he was now accepted as the greatest living writer in Bengal, he was dissatisfied with his countrymen and they with him, as a result of his outspoken criticisms of Bengali religious, social and educational orthodoxy.

In London, William Rothenstein read Tagore's poems in his own English translation, was highly impressed and introduced them and their author to a wide range of creative people, beginning with W. B. Yeats. Tagore rapidly became a literary sensation and in November 1912, his collection of poems, *Gitanjali*, with Yeats' introduction, was published by the India Society. Such was their success that Macmillan began publishing *Gitanjali* in March 1913 and became the chief publisher of Tagore's works in English translation.

Meanwhile, Tagore travelled to the United States in October 1912. He established himself in Illinois, where his son had earlier studied, but also visited Chicago and the East Coast, giving acclaimed lectures at Harvard University. In Chicago, Harriet Monroe, encouraged from London by Ezra Pound, published some Tagore poems in her new magazine, *Poetry*.

Returning to Britain in April 1913, he found himself a celebrity. *Gitanjali* was reprinted ten times by Macmillan during that year, before the award of the Nobel prize in November. His play, *The Post Office*, was performed, at the behest of Yeats, by the Irish Players. He also repeated and expanded his Harvard lectures before large and distinguished audiences, and these were published as *Sadhana: The Realisation of Life*. By the time he left for Bengal in September, Tagore had a wide circle of British literary and other admirers.

46

To Kshiti Mohan Sen

Tagore and companions arrived in London on 16 June 1912 and booked into a hotel in Bloomsbury. The following day he contacted William Rothenstein, who was expecting him, and immediately gave him a notebook containing translations of his poetry.[1] Rothenstein promptly settled his guests into a rented house in Hampstead, enthused about the poems and sent typescripts to friends including W. B. Yeats. When Yeats exulted over them, Rothenstein arranged a dinner for him to meet Tagore. The next day Tagore gave an account to Kshiti Mohan Sen, his perceptive scholar friend in Shantiniketan, a letter that is a vivid insight into Rabindranath's lifelong ambivalence about success – western success, on this occasion, but it might have been any success. 'I have this paradox in my nature that when I begin to enjoy my success I grow weary of it in the depth of my mind,' as Tagore remarks in letter 174.

[3 Villas on the Heath, Vale of Health, Hampstead, London, UK]
14 Asharh 1319 [28 June 1912]

Pratinamashkar nibedan –

Kshiti Mohan Babu, last night I dined with one of the poets here, Yeats.[2] He read aloud the prose translations of some of my poems. It was a very beautiful reading in the right tone. I do not have much confidence in my own English – but he remarked that if someone were to say he could improve this piece of writing, that person did not understand literature. People here have taken to my work with such excessive enthusiasm that I cannot really accept it. My impression is that when a place from which nothing is expected somehow produces something, even an ordinary thing, people are amazed – that is the state of mind here. Anyway Yeats himself, after editing my poems and writing an introduction, will see to their publication.[3] As usual, the prospect elates me and wearies me at one and the same time. To have come all the way here and then to find myself again staring at myself and fiddling with my work, is so unpalatable that I want to flee to Germany. But then I reflect that perhaps it was for this that my God dragged me to this country at my age – for it is literature, art and suchlike that are the real bridges uniting one country with another. Maybe from all this I should totally eliminate my personal self and humbly acknowledge the best in my writing without hesitation. What He likes, He makes others like: we appreciate the beauty of the lotus we offer Him in worship because He himself appreciates it. I feel as if God is expressing His own gladness through others' praise of my work; it is as if He has brought me from East to West in order to make me aware of the fact of his gladness. His grace cannot be accepted in a state of infatuation, which is why I am preparing myself to submit to the honour with my forehead touching the dust.

Shri Rabindranath Thakur

Source: MS original at Rabindra Bhavan, Shantiniketan; letter published in *Desh*, 6 Dec. 1986, pp. 15–16.

1 William Rothenstein, *Men and Memories: Recollections, 1900–1922* (London, 1932), p. 262. Rothenstein's and RT's accounts differ significantly. See Dutta and Robinson, *Rabindranath Tagore*, pp. 164–5 and notes.
2 W. B. Yeats to Florence Farr, 27 June [1912]: 'at 7.30 I dine with Rothenstein to meet Tagore the Hindu poet' (W. B. Yeats, *The Letters of W. B. Yeats* (Allan Wade ed.; New York, 1955), p. 569).
3 *Gitanjali (Song Offerings)*, with an introduction by Yeats and a frontispiece drawing of RT by Rothenstein, was published on 1 Nov. 1912 by the India Society in London: 500 copies for members, 250 for general sale. Rothenstein and others supervised its printing.

Voyage to the West

5 Tagore in Hampstead, London, 1912: with Somendra Chandra Dev Burman, D. N. Maitra, John and William Rothenstein, Rathindranath Tagore

47

To (Sir) William Rothenstein[1]

It is exquisitely appropriate that one of the briefest English letters in this book should be freighted with the greatest possible significance. For it was of course the translations of *Gitanjali* that Tagore handed to William Rothenstein in June 1912 that won him the Nobel prize and world fame. In referring here to their 'faded meanings' in English, Rabindranath showed acumen: the phrase perfectly captures how a sympathetic modern reader must feel about even the best of the old translations of Tagore into English. He was also being consistent, as witness his caution about translating his poetry shown in letter 39 (to Ramananda Chatterji) and letter 55 (to Ezra Pound), and his numerous later remarks on the perils of translating Bengali into English (such as letter 286).

3 Villas on the Heath, Vale of Health,
Ham[p]stead, [London, UK][2]
[?7 July] 1912[3]

Dear Mr Rothenstein

I send you some more of my poems rendered into English. They are far too simple to bear the strain of translation but I know you will understand them through their faded meanings.

Very sincerely yours
Rabindranath Tagore

Source: MS original in Rothenstein Papers [Harvard]; letter published in Lago (ed.), *Imperfect Encounter*, p. 49.

1 Sir William Rothenstein (1872–1945): portrait and landscape artist; principal, Royal College of Art, 1920–35. His three-volume autobiography was described by a recent critic as 'one of the indispensable texts of this gregarious generation' (John Hatcher, *Laurence Binyon: Poet, Scholar of East and West* (Oxford, 1995), p. 49). The correspondence of Rothenstein and RT appears in Lago (ed.), *Imperfect Encounter*.
2 RT and companions moved to this address between 21 and 28 June; previously they stayed at nearby Holford Road.
3 RT writes 7 June 1912, which cannot be correct, since he did not reach London until 16 June (Lago (ed.), *Imperfect Encounter*, p. 49). A month later, 7 July, is more likely, because by then an initially sceptical RT would have begun to grasp the degree of interest in the translations and would have had enough time to make some new translations. On 7 July a soirée was held at Rothenstein's house, where Yeats read out some of the translations before an entranced audience. This letter was perhaps a covering note for the new batch of translations that RT took to the soirée in person.

48

To Mira Gangulee (Tagore)

After being fêted by literary London in June and July, an exhausted Tagore, accompanied by his daughter-in-law Pratima, spent a quiet August in the English countryside, first in Staffordshire, near Newcastle-under-Lyme, afterwards with William Rothenstein and family in a village near Stroud in Gloucestershire.[1] This was the first time he had seen English villages since his idyllic stay at Torquay over thirty years earlier (see letter 2), but they do not seem to have exerted the same appeal as before, perhaps partly because it rained constantly during this particular visit. The weather in England was never really to Tagore's taste: sometimes he bemoaned it, other times, as in this letter to his monsoon-bound daughter in Bengal, he made a joke of it.

Oakridge Lynch, Stroud, Gloucestershire, [UK]
[August 1912]

Miru

After hearing the latest chronicle of your small son, I feel very tempted to take a look at him.[2] But the salty ocean between us is like a screen. Give him kisses from me.

You must have heard all our doings from *Bouma* and others.[3] We are moving around a lot. Right now we are staying in a proper village in the house of a well-off farmer. His wife and daughter are looking after us well. The country is really beautiful here – only the weather is atrocious. The other major drawback is the lamentable arrangement for bathing and related activities. If instead something had been cut from my food rations, I would not have complained. But when in the morning there appears in my bedroom a bathtub like a large-size teacup and a container of water the size of a large teapot, I feel like making up for the lack of water with my tears. This must be quite the slimmest volume ever to call itself a bath – I shall omit to describe other essential facilities because that would not be at all sweet to hear.

Having Shanjna and family to stay must have been enjoyable, and when they leave, the house will seem rather desolate at this midmonsoon time.[4] The present season in this country is known as summer, i.e. the time of hot weather – but when the thermometer rises here, it does not even top 60°, so this summer cannot be compared with our summer. But regarding rainfall, it puts our monsoon month of Shraban to shame.[5] This year has been particularly rainy – maybe because I so often sing the praises of the monsoon, the monsoon does not want to desert me. Shraban, having crossed the oceans, has turned up in England: if it has a short-stay return ticket then perhaps the poet, once he has blessed it, may soon bid it adieu. In a cold country there can be no worse companion than rain. What's the monsoon like over there? How are the crops looking? What's the state of the ponds? Has your uncle fled back home yet? If he stayed there and worked, he could save all his travelling expenses.

Father

Source: MS original at Rabindra Bhavan, Shantiniketan; letter published in Sharadiya *Desh*, 1397 [Autumn 1990], pp. 35–6.

1 RT's impressions of England in 1912 are found in *Pather Shanchay*, *RR*, XXVI, pp. 457–582.
2 Nitindranath Gangulee (1911–32): son of Mira and Nagendranath; he was born on 5 Dec. 1911.
3 *Bouma*: Pratima Tagore, RT's daughter-in-law. She accompanied him in Aug. 1912, while his son Rathindranath stayed in London.
4 Shanjna Tagore: wife of Surendranath Tagore, nephew of RT.
5 Shraban: Bengali month corresponding to mid-July–mid-Aug.

49

To William Butler Yeats[1]

While Tagore was staying with Rothenstein in Gloucestershire, translating more of his poems and also plays, Rothenstein wrote to Yeats in London about the need for his introduction to *Gitanjali* and the way in which the book should be published by the India Society.[2] Yeats replied with a warm tribute to Tagore ('I find Tagore as you do a great inspiration in my own art'), which Rothenstein read to his guest.[3] Two weeks later, on his return to London, Tagore wrote this appreciative letter to Yeats, and also a substantial tribute to Yeats in Bengali.[4] Finally, on 10 September, Yeats, who was by then in Ireland, sent his introduction to Rothenstein.[5]

Tagore's letter continues the theme of his letter to Kshiti Mohan Sen (letter 46): that his unexpected success in England is part of God's purpose, to be humbly accepted by him.

21 Cromwell Road, South Kensington, [London, UK]
2 September 1912

Dear Mr Yeats

It has been such a great joy to me to think that things that I wrote in a tongue not known to you should at last fall in your hands and that you should accept them with so much enjoyment and love. When, in spite of all obstacles, something seemed to impel me to come to this country I never dreamt that it was for this that I was taking my voyage. What my soul offered to my master in the solitude of an obscure corner of the world must be brought before the altar of man where hearts come together and tongues mingle like the right and the left palms of hands joined in the act of adoration. My heart fills with gratitude and I write to you this letter to say the appreciation from a man like you comes to me not only as a reward for my lifelong devotion to literature but as a token that my songs have been acceptable to Him, and He has led me over the sea to this country to speak to me His approval of my works through your precious friendship.[6]

We intend to leave England in the beginning of November.[7] I do hope I shall be able to see you before that, and, if possible, to have a sight of my translations published with your introduction.

I hope you will kindly accept from me a copy of the English translation of my father's *Autobiography* which I left with Mr Rothenstein to be sent to your address.[8]

Very sincerely yours
Rabindranath Tagore

Source: MS original in collection of Michael Yeats; letter published in Richard J. Finneran et al. (eds.), *Letters to W. B. Yeats*, II (London, 1977), pp. 251–2.

1 William Butler Yeats (1865–1939): poet and dramatist; awarded Nobel prize for literature, 1923. His letters to RT appear in *VBQ*, 30, No. 3, 1964–5, pp. 159–76.
2 Rothenstein to Yeats, 18 Aug. 1912, in Finneran et al., *Letters*, pp. 248–9.
3 Yeats to Rothenstein [19 Aug. 1912] [Harvard]; Rothenstein to Yeats, 24 Aug. 1912, in Finneran et al., *Letters*, pp. 249–51.
4 'Kabi Yeats', *Prabashi*, Kartik 1319 [Oct.–Nov. 1912]/*RR*, XXVI, pp. 21–8 (dated 19 Bhadra 1319 [4 Sept. 1912]. This is from the opening paragraphs in our translation:

> Yeats can never be one of the crowd, his uniqueness is obvious to all. Just as his height sets him physically above almost everyone, so one notices in his personality a certain affluence which, like a fountain, wells up from the ordinary rut surrounding him, as if propelled by the power of divine creativity. One feels that his esse is inexhaustible.
>
> When I read today's English poets I am often struck by the thought that they are not poets of the world as a whole, but rather poets of the world of letters. Here in England poets have a long literary tradition, with a plentiful supply of similes, metaphors and other stylistic devices. The result is that they do not have to go to the springs of poetic inspiration to make poetry. Instead they emulate those *ustads* in music who no longer feel the call to sing from the heart and thereby reduce music to a series of phrases and tunes, however complex and adroit their technique may be. When passion does not come from deep sensitivity, it becomes just a series of well-crafted words. Then it has to make up for its lack of candour and inner assurance with exaggeration; since it cannot be natural, it resorts to artifice in order to prove its originality.
>
> My meaning will become clearer if we compare Wordsworth with Swinburne. Swinburne is the principal poet of poetry as opposed to life. He is so extraordinarily adroit at verbal music that he is besotted by his skill. Out of suggestive sounds he fashions a gorgeously variegated tapestry of images. His is a striking achievement, no doubt; but it has not established him as a world poet.
>
> The poetry of Wordsworth arose from the direct touch of the world upon his heart. Hence its simplicity – which is not the same thing as being easy of understanding by the reader. Whenever a poet writes out of a direct response to life, his poetry blooms like the flowers and fruits on a tree. It is not conscious of itself, nor does it feel obliged to present itself as being beautiful or deeply felt. Whatever it appears to be, it is: to appreciate and enjoy it is the onus upon the reader.
>
> Certain individuals are born with a need for direct experience, and they do not permit any barrier to come between that experience and its inner realisation. With absolute self-confidence and sincerity, they express the essence of the natural and human worlds in their own idiom. They have the courage to break all the conventions of contemporary poetry.
>
> Burns was born in an age of literary artifice. His feelings sprang straight from the heart and he

could express them in words. And so he was able to pierce through the bonds of literary usage and give unrestrained expression to the soul of Scotland.

In our own time, the poetry of Yeats has been received very warmly for the same basic reason. His poetry does not echo contemporary poetry, it is an expression of his own soul. When I say 'his own soul', I ought to make the idea a bit clearer. Like a cut diamond that needs the light of the sky to show itself, the human soul on its own cannot express its essence, and remains dark. Only when it reflects the light from something greater than itself, does it come into its own. In Yeats' poetry, the soul of Ireland is manifest. ('Poet Yeats', in Krishna Dutta and Andrew Robinson (eds.), *Rabindranath Tagore: An Anthology* (London, 1997), pp. 215–21)

Nowhere, however, in RT's tribute to Yeats did he choose to quote any of Yeats's poetry.

5 Yeats wrote to Rothenstein about the introduction on 7 Sept., and sent it on 10 Sept. with a further letter. See Rothenstein, *Men and Memories*, p. 267, and Yeats to Rothenstein, 10 Sept. [1912] [Harvard].
6 When the poet Thomas Sturge Moore, after hearing Yeats read from *Gitanjali* at Rothenstein's soirée on 7 July, told Yeats he found the poetry 'preposterously optimistic', Yeats said 'Ah, you see, he is absorbed in God' (Moore to Robert Trevelyan, n.d., in Lago (ed.), *Imperfect Encounter*, pp. 17–18).
7 RT sailed for New York on 19 Oct. 1912.
8 See Debendranath Tagore, *Autobiography*.

50

To Bertrand Russell[1]

William Rothenstein recalled, at a memorial meeting for Tagore in 1941, that Tagore had once joked to him after a meeting with Bertrand Russell and Goldsworthy Lowes Dickinson in 1912: 'Such nice men; and they would so much like to believe in God, but they want a receipt first!'[2] Russell and Tagore personified two antithetical conceptions of what constitutes wisdom and the true philosopher. Russell believed in striving through the exercise of human reason to escape the human world – while Tagore believed that 'we can never go beyond man in all that we know and feel'.[3]

Russell's essay, 'The essence of religion', published in October 1912 just before *Gitanjali*, did however appeal to Tagore, with its argument that 'the essence of religion ... lies in subordination of the finite part of our life to the infinite part'.[4] He was struck by the parallel with his own thinking, rooted in the *Upanishads*, and he wrote this letter to Russell.[5]

37 Alfred Place W., South Kensington, [London, UK]
13 October 1912

Dear Mr Russell

Thanks for your kind letter. I will ask Dr Seal to pay you a visit at Cambridge, when you will have an opportunity to know him.[6]

I read your article on the Essence of Religion in the last issue of the *Hibbert Journal* with very great interest. It reminded me of a verse in the *Upanishad* which runs thus –

Yato veiche nivartante aprapya manasa saha
Anandam Brahmano Vidvan na vibheti Kutushchama.

'From him words, as well as mind, come back baffled. Yet he who knows the joy of Brahman (the Infinite) is free from all fear.'[7]

Through knowledge you cannot apprehend him; yet when you live the life of the Infinite and are not bound within the limits of the finite self you realise that great joy which is above all the pleasures and pains of our selfish life and so you are free from all fear.

This joy itself is the positive perception of Brahman. It is not a creed which authority imposes on us but an absolute realisation of the Infinite which we can only attain by breaking through the bonds of the narrow self and setting our will and love free.

Yours sincerely
Rabindranath Tagore

Source: MS original in Bertrand Russell archives [McMaster]; letter published in Bertrand Russell, *The Autobiography of Bertrand Russell, 1872–1914*, (London, 1967), p. 221.

1 Bertrand Arthur William Russell, 3rd Earl Russell (1872–1970): philosopher, mathematician and social reformer. On his ambivalent relationship with RT, see Dutta and Robinson, *Rabindranath Tagore*, pp. 176–8, to which may be added the fact that it was Russell, not RT, who initiated their final meeting, in Cornwall in 1926: 'I hear that you are at Carbis Bay and I should greatly like to see you' (Russell to RT, 9 Aug. 1926 [Dartington]).
2 'Rabindranath Tagore memorial meeting', *Indian Art and Letters*, London, second issue for 1941, p. 67. The meeting took place in Cambridge in July 1912. Lowes Dickinson's description of the meeting is discussed in Dutta and Robinson, *Rabindranath Tagore*, p. 176. See also letter 160.
3 *Religion of Man* (London, 1931), p. 114. Russell told Ottoline Morrell on 9 March 1912: 'I like mathematics largely because it is *not* human and has nothing particular to do with this planet or with the whole accidental universe – because, like Spinoza's God, it won't love us in return.' (Bertrand Russell, *The Selected Letters of Bertrand Russell: I, The Private Years (1884–1914)* (Nicholas Griffin ed.; London, 1992), p. 417).
4 'The essence of religion', *Hibbert Journal*, Oct. 1912, p. 60.
5 Tagore's letter and Russell's essay have a curious history. Russell regretted his rare foray into religious writing almost as soon as it was published, and never allowed it to be reprinted. He knew that Ludwig Wittgenstein, for instance, then an admired colleague in Cambridge, 'detested' the essay, telling him that 'I had been a traitor to the gospel of exactness, and wantonly used words vaguely; also that such things are too intimate for print' (Russell to Ottoline Morrell, 11 Oct. 1912, in *Selected Letters*, pp. 437–8). But in 1967, aged ninety-five, Russell chose to print Tagore's letter praising the essay in his *Autobiography*, without comment. Then, when asked his opinion of it by a Bengali, he wrote: 'I regret I cannot agree with Tagore. His talk about the infinite is vague nonsense. The sort of language admired by many Indians unfortunately does not, in fact, mean anything at all' (Russell to N. Chatterji, 26 April 1967 [copy at McMaster University]).
Russell's definition of the infinite in 'The essence of religion' seems to invite almost the same criticism. Wittgenstein was undoubtedly right to dislike the essay. On Wittgenstein's (later) favourable response to RT, see Ray Monk, 'Seeing in the dark: Wittgenstein and Tagore', in Dutta and Robinson (eds.), *Purabi*, pp. 142–4; also various references in Ray Monk, *Ludwig Wittgenstein: The Duty of Genius* (London, 1990).
6 RT wrote to Russell on 10 Oct. 1912 to introduce (Sir) Brajendranath Seal, 'the most distinguished scholar and thinker we have in India at present', who had just arrived in England. 'He is the only man I know who will be able to present the development of eastern thought to [a] European audience in an adequate manner' [copy at RB]. See also letter 179.
7 *Taittiriya Upanishad*, 2:9.

51

To (Sir) William Rothenstein

From 1912 to 1914 was the halcyon period of the Tagore–Rothenstein friendship, during which letters flowed freely and intimately. According to Rothenstein's biographer Robert Speaight, 'William's conception of friendship was almost oriental in its serious intensity, and Tagore was among the few who shared it.'[1] In Rothenstein's own words to Yeats that first summer, before *Gitanjali* had reached its English public:

What the poems are he is. For years I have believed this to be a necessary relation between the artist and the work of art, and have suffered greatly both in my own struggles and because it has been difficult for me to accept much that is admired by many good men. When I first met Rabindranath it was like a personal reward, and the renewal of intimacy has been one of the prizes of my life. Above all, the poems have nothing in them which any man must feel it necessary to reject, as is the case with so much of the great mystical poetry of the world, where here and there are stated things which offend that perfect balance of visions which great art must show.[2]

This letter was the first from Tagore to Rothenstein after reaching the USA.

Herald Square Hotel, New York, [USA]
27 October 1912

Dear Friend

The first half of our voyage was frightfully rough. I promised a sonnet to the sea god if he behaved decently but I suppose he had not faith in human nature and knew I would forget all about it directly I reached land safely. However he made amends at last and we had some very beautiful days. Altogether our voyage across the Atlantic was as unsatisfactory and uninteresting outwardly as it possibly could be, still I had some moments of most profound peace and sweetness which my physical sufferings seemed to intensify [rather] than otherwise. Misery has the effect of creating a sort of night of intense loneliness through which shine all the true lights which have been gathered in the depths of one's life. One should have occasions to know them.

We have landed in New York this morning and passed through the ordeals of the custom house. My turban attracted the notice of a newspaper interviewer and he attacked me with questions but I was almost as silent as my turban. This was my first taste of America – the custom house and the interviewer.[3]

Each time I come to a city like New York or London I discover afresh that in my veins courses the blood of my ancestors who were forest dwellers. The thick solitude of the crowd is oppressive to me. In London your friendship was the only refuge I had, and I clung to you with all my heart. If I had not known you I should have gone back to India not knowing Europe. It fills me with wonder when I think how by a merest chance I came to know you and in what a short time your friendship has become a part of my life.

Give our love to [the] dear children and our warmest regards to Mrs Rothenstein.[4]

Ever yours
Rabindranath Tagore

[PS] Mr Chapman is not in town.[5] Dr Flexner is on his way to Europe.[6]

Source: MS original in Rothenstein Papers [Harvard]; letter published in Lago (ed.), *Imperfect Encounter*, p. 56.

1 Robert Speaight, *William Rothenstein: The Portrait of an Artist in his Time* (London, 1962), p. 253.
2 18 Aug. 1912, in Finneran et al., *Letters*, p. 249.
3 Unlike Oscar Wilde, RT would never get used to the questions of either port officials or reporters in the USA. In 1929, he cut short his visit to the country after an incident over his passport (see Dutta and Robinson, *Rabindranath Tagore*, pp. 284–5). In 1930, he was furious with the newspapers who misinterpreted his views on Indian politics (see letter 244).

4 Alice Rothenstein (1870–1958): actress; married William Rothenstein in 1899.
5 On John Jay Chapman, see letter 59.
6 Simon Flexner (1863–1946): pathologist; director of laboratories for the Rockefeller Institute for Medical Research.

52

To Jyotirindranath Tagore

William Rothenstein thought Jyotirindranath Tagore, Rabindranath's elder brother, to be India's finest living artist. Since the 1880s, Jyotirindranath had been drawing hundreds of pencil portraits of his family, friends and other Bengalis. 'The drawings of Indian ladies are especially remarkable', wrote Rothenstein in a foreword to the drawings, 'one has almost to go back to Dürer and Holbein to find such frank and sincere portraits as these.'[1] High praise indeed, coming from one of the leading English portraitists of his time; nor was it unmerited.

Rothenstein had first seen some of the drawings in reproduction in a Bengali review. During Rabindranath's visit to England in 1912, his English friend offered to make a portfolio from them, if the Tagores would pay the publishing costs; in addition to making the selection, said Rothenstein, he would also write a foreword. Rabindranath was keen – as this letter shows – and after considerable delays, the book appeared as *Twenty-Five Collotypes From the Original Drawings by Jyotirindra Nath Tagore* (London, 1914). All the copies appear to have been sent to Calcutta, and regrettably the book was never made available beyond a small circle in Bengal.[2]

508 High Street, Urbana, Illinois, USA
7 November 1912

Bhai Jyoti *Dada*

We have moved to America and that is why your letter reached us late. If you will send a hundred pounds, that is 1500 rupees, to Mr Rothenstein, he will make a selection of your drawings and arrange for its printing. If you borrow 1000 rupees from Suren and pay it back at the rate of a hundred a month, there should be no problem.[3] Rothenstein said that with this kind of portrait book one cannot hope for much of a sale – even in England subscribers will be few. The effort of selecting and printing is worthwhile simply for the sake of permanent preservation. Rothenstein himself will write a foreword. He is among England's famous artists – a French professor of sculpture at the South Kensington art college who is a talented artist told me, 'Rothenstein is not an ordinary artist, he is a personality.' I will write to him about the publishing of the drawings.

The place in which we are now staying is a small community within the campus of the university where most of the professors and students reside; as a result it is peaceful, a place after my own heart. Another advantage is that unlike England in winter, which is shrouded in darkness and fog, this place, though cold, has plentiful sunshine. I like that.

We are renting a house and *Bouma* is its mistress – which means that she herself cooks and cleans.[4] In this country everyone is his own boss; servants are almost impossible to find. Most people are of the householding class, and both men and women are used to working with their hands. Only this afternoon I came across a senior professor doing his own laundry. He has no choice. The less well-off students manage to earn their keep or some wages by cooking, cleaning and sweeping. Many of our Indian students are employed in this way. *Bouma* is finding it an educational experience.[5] They all like her here. The wife of a professor is tutoring her in English, and everyone takes great trouble over her.[6] If she could spend a year here it would stand her in good stead. In England there is no such scope. The university staff really like Rathi and as a result we have most friendly relations with everyone.

Apnar sneher
Rabi

Source: MS original at Rabindra Bhavan, Shantiniketan; letter published in *CP*, V, pp. 11–12.

1 Rothenstein concluded the foreword as follows:

> It is not art which produces art, but passion. Art is the cultivation of passion, which like all cultivation, demands infinite labour, skill and patience, as well as infinite will, if it is to bear ripe and wholesome fruit. Something of this passion I feel in the drawings of Mr Jyotirindranath Tagore. It is of a simple and modest kind, but in each of the drawings one feels he was absorbed by the unique desire to express something of the delicacy of form and gravity of character of his sitter.
> We are so used to seeing portraits of maharajahs in their state apparel, or photographs of unusual types in books of travel, that this straightforward portraiture of cultured Indian ladies and gentlemen, of whom we in England hear and know so little, is a new and delightful thing ... I believe these [drawings] will give to many of us the human and intimate picture of Bengali character we get from the novels of Bankim Chandra Chatterji.
> I know of few modern portrait drawings which show greater beauty and insight.

Jyotirindranath himself told Rothenstein, long before this foreword was written, 'Your generous appreciation of my poor sketches is indeed gratifying. I myself thought nothing of their artistic merits. Not having had any training in art it is difficult for me to judge of my own productions by any art standard' (9 Oct. 1912 [IOL]).
2 According to its title page, the portfolio was 'made and printed by Emery Walker Limited' in Hammersmith, 1914. There is a copy of this book in the Rabindra Bhavan library, Shantiniketan, but none in the major libraries in London. Extraordinarily, not even Rothenstein seems to have seen a copy (Jyotirindranath to Rothenstein, 21 April 1920 [IOL]). The original drawings are kept by the Rabindra Bharati Society in Calcutta; no catalogue has been published.
3 Payment proved more complicated than RT thought (see Lago, *Imperfect Encounter*, pp. 192, 194 and 215).
4 On arrival, RT stayed with Morgan Brooks (1861–1955), professor of electrical engineering at the University of Illinois, while Rathindranath and Pratima were guests of Arthur Seymour (1872–1955), professor of Spanish and French, whose wife Mayce was Rathindranath's closest friend at Illinois. Then they moved into 508 W. High Street, a rented house.
5 'It is not easy to set up house in America and my wife who had never been there before had a difficult time' (Rathindranath Tagore, *Edges of Time*, p. 108). Being always accustomed to servants and a slow pace of life, Pratima must have found the Illinois experience something of a shock. There is sometimes a whiff of hypocrisy in RT when writing of such practical matters; it is hard to imagine *him* regularly doing his own laundry.
6 Mayce Seymour assisted Pratima with her English.

53

To (Sir) William Rothenstein

William Rothenstein wrote to Tagore on publication of *Gitanjali* that 'The book is out, & looks very pure and virginal in its covering of white and gold.'[1] The next day he wrote again with further enthusiasm, announcing publication of a review in the *Times Literary Supplement* and commenting, 'It is a great delight to us to feel that what we felt at once is shared by others, and that you have once and for all gained the ear of the West for your literature. I wonder whether Bengal will realise what your simple visit has done for its history.'[2] Tagore's reply is warm but still cautious about the enthusiasm for his translations.

508 W. High Street, Urbana, [Illinois, USA]
19 November 1912

My dear Mr Rothenstein

Your two letters of the same date amply made up for the long delay and eager waiting. They are delightful. I thought I had come to that age when doors to my inner theatre must be closed and no more new admission could be possible. But the impossible has happened and you have made my life larger by your friendship. I feel its truth and its preciousness all the more because it came to me so unexpectedly and in a surrounding not familiar to me at all. That I should, while travelling in a foreign land, meet with some experience of life which is not temporary and superficial fills me with wonder and gratitude. It is to me a gift from the divine source and I shall know how to value it.

I am so glad to learn from your letter that my book has been favourably criticised [by] the *Times Literary Supplement*. I hope the paper has been forwarded to me and I shall see it in a day or two. My happiness is all the more great because I know such appreciations will bring joy to your heart. In fact, I feel that the success of my book is your own success. But for your assurance I never could have dreamt that my translations were worth anything and up to the last moment I was fearful lest you should be mistaken in your estimation of them and all the pains you have taken over them should be thrown away. I am extremely glad that your choice has been vindicated and you will have the right to take pride in your friend, supported by the best judges in your literature. Remember me kindly to Mrs Rothenstein and give our love to the children.

Ever your affectionate friend
Rabindranath Tagore

Source: MS original in Rothenstein Papers [Harvard]; letter published in Lago (ed.), *Imperfect Encounter*, pp. 64–5.

1 6 Nov. 1912, in Lago (ed.), *Imperfect Encounter*, p. 59.
2 7 Nov. 1912, in *ibid.*, p. 61. While Rothenstein's comment was certainly true and perceptive, the review itself mixed some equivocation with its praise of the poems:

> In reading them one feels, not that they are the curiosities of an alien mind, but that they are prophetic of the poetry that might be written in England if our poets could attain the same harmony of emotion and idea . . .
> We seem to be reading the Psalms of a David of our own time who addresses a God realized by his own act of faith and conceived according to his own experience of life . . . If we cannot share the Indian poet's faith, we must at least acknowledge that he has not sacrificed his reason to it. He plays neither an artistic nor an intellectual game. As a poet should be, he is so simple that anyone can understand him; yet this does not mean that there is little to understand. (*Times Literary Supplement*, 7 Nov. 1912)

54

To (Sir) William Rothenstein

Having received several favourable reviews of *Gitanjali*, Tagore now read a review in the *Athenaeum*[1] (not sent by Rothenstein) which was more typical of what he had anticipated when writing to Kshiti Mohan Sen in late June (letter 46). It echoed what Bertrand Russell wrote to him on 16 November:

> About a fortnight ago I received from the publishers your *Gitanjali*, for which please accept my warmest thanks. I waited to write to you until I had read them, which I have now done with the very greatest interest. They have some quality different from that of any English poetry – if I knew India perhaps I could find words to describe it, but as it is I can only say that I feel it has a value of its own, which English literature does not give. I wish I could read them in their original language.[2]

Tagore now wrote to Rothenstein to explain his state of mind about his English reception. His analysis is acute.

508 W. High Street, Urbana, [Illinois, USA]
15 December 1912

My dear Friend,

I have got the manuscripts you sent to me. Last night I read *The Post Office* before a friendly audience here and it was heartily appreciated.[3] My reputation as a poet is fast spreading here but it has not made my stay here impossible as yet. I am left pretty much to myself. People connected with papers came to me to ask for my portrait and materials [on] my life but I held them at bay – but I believe they had better satisfaction from Rathi.[4] Rathi has a natural affection for the people here and he does not like to disappoint them.

I have read the review of my book that appeared in the *Athenaeum*. Do you know, that is the kind of criticism I expected all along. It is not hostile, you can even call it appreciative, but you feel that the reviewer is at a loss how to estimate these poems. He has not got a standard by which to judge these productions, quite strange to him. He sees some beauty in them but they arouse no real emotion in him, so he imagines them as cold – he thinks they have no real life blood in them. He cannot believe that they are quiet and simple, not because there is lack of enthusiasm in them but because they are absolutely real. I can assure you they are not literary productions at all they are life productions.

My writings have met with a very generous appreciation in your country. I never could believe it to be possible. So much so that sometimes it oppresses me. That his works should be accepted by men is the highest reward that can come to an artist. Yet we should be strong enough not to have to depend upon it. Reward should not be made a necessity to us. This fame in a foreign land has a strange fascination and I am afraid it was growing upon me; I was unconsciously getting into the habit of expecting it more and more. But I must get out of it. It is like using your own best works as chains to shackle you. I have a poem which I translated when I was in London. I do not know if it is in your collection. I give it below. –

Free me from bonds of praise and blame of men and guide me only by the beckons of your right hand, my lord. Let all the forces of my life take the one great course, made irresistible by one supreme love, even as the river that ever flows through its boundaries yet ever loses its limits in the sea, led by the hidden call and the inmost impulse of its own.[5]

I send you herewith the translation of a poem, story of which is based upon an episode of the *Ramayana*.[6]

Ever your friend
Rabindranath Tagore

Source: MS original in Rothenstein Papers [Harvard]; letter published in Lago (ed.), *Imperfect Encounter*, pp. 74–5.

1 16 Nov. 1912.
2 [RB]. Russell's letter, written from Cambridge, England, was presumably not sent direct to RT in Illinois but should have reached him before he wrote to Rothenstein on 15 Dec.
3 Rothenstein had returned the manuscripts of two plays, *Malini* and *The King of the Dark Chamber*, with the comment: 'Yeats thinks *The Post Office* a masterpiece, and would like the Dublin theatre people to produce it . . . he thinks the other plays need more knowledge and understanding than an English or Irish audience is likely to possess' (Rothenstein to RT, 2 Dec. 1912, in Lago (ed.), *Imperfect Encounter*, p. 71). *The Post Office* was a translation by Devabrata Mukerjea revised by RT; it was produced by the Irish Players in 1913 and published in 1914 with Yeats' preface.
4 Rathindranath Tagore, as his father's frequent travelling companion, would in due course gain considerable experience of dealing with journalists.
5 *Naibedya* (Offerings), *RR*, VIII, p. 64.
6 RT wrote several poems on themes taken from the *Ramayana*. Two famous ones are 'Ahalyar Prati' (To Ahalya), *Manashi*, *RR*, II, pp. 263–5, and 'Patita' (The Fallen Woman), *Kahini*, *RR*, V, pp. 84–93.

55

To Ezra Pound[1]

Ezra Pound first became drawn to Tagore as a result of Yeats' enthusiasm for *Gitanjali*. After spending an afternoon with Rabindranath, Pound told a friend (Dorothy Shakespear) that he felt 'like a painted pict with a stone war-club'.[2] When he reviewed Tagore's poetry, he compared its piety with 'the poetic piety of Dante', and boldly asserted: 'Briefly, I find in these poems a sort of ultimate common sense, a reminder of one thing and forty things of which we are over likely to lose sight in the confusion of our western life, in the racket of our cities, in the jabber of manufactured literature, in the vortex of advertisement.'[3] At the same time he alerted Harriet Monroe, the editor of *Poetry* in Chicago, and she published six poems by Tagore in December – the first Tagore poetry to be published in the USA – with a brief appreciation by Pound.[4]

Both Pound and *Poetry* now asked for more. During January and February 1913, with Tagore now in Pound's native land and Pound back in London with Yeats, a brief but interesting correspondence about translation developed. It revealed a gap in sensibility between the two poets that would soon become a gulf.

508 W. High Street, Urbana, Illinois, [USA]
5 January 1913

Dear Mr Ezra Pound

I send you the recent translations that I made here.[5] I am not at all strong in my English grammar – please do not hesitate to make corrections when necessary. Then again I do not know the exact value of your English words. Some of them may have their souls worn out by constant use and some others may not have acquired their souls yet.[6] So in my use of words there must be lack of proportion and appropriateness perhaps, that also could be amended by friendly hands.

Yours very sincerely
Rabindranath Tagore

Source: MS original in Pound Papers [Yale]; letter published in Noel Stock, *The Life of Ezra Pound* (London, 1970), p. 110.

1 Ezra Weston Loomis Pound (1885–1972): poet, translator and editor. For Pound's relationship with RT, see Sujit Mukherjee, *Passage to America: The Reception of Rabindranath Tagore in the United States, 1912–1941* (Calcutta, 1964), pp. 8–16; Bikash Chakravarty, 'Incomplete dialogue: Tagore and Ezra Pound', *VBN*, May–June 1986, pp. 307–13; and various references in Dutta and Robinson, *Rabindranath Tagore*.
2 4 Oct. 1912, in Omar Pound and A. Walton Litz (eds.), *Ezra Pound and Dorothy Shakespear: Their Letters: 1909–1914* (London, 1985), p. 163.
3 *Fortnightly Review*, March 1913, p. 575.
4 *Poetry*, Dec. 1912, pp. 84–6 (poems), pp. 92–4 (Pound's appreciation).
5 The precise content of these translations is not clear; they were probably poems that appeared in *The Gardener* later in 1913, and they most likely included copies of the love poems that RT sent separately to Harriet Monroe (see letter 56). Pound used the translations – twenty-five in all – to illustrate a lecture on RT he gave in London on 23 Jan. 1913.
6 This sentence made an impression on Yeats, to whom Pound must have shown RT's letter; Yeats to RT, 25 April 1913: 'I found some words to be changed. It is again the old difficulty "the words that have not got their souls yet and the words that have lost their souls"' (*VBQ*, 30, No. 3, 1964–5, p. 164).

56

To (Sir) William Rothenstein

Though Tagore was in correspondence with Ezra Pound about his English translations, William Rothenstein (and through him W. B. Yeats) remained his chief literary adviser. As a result of Rothenstein's efforts and those of Arthur Fox Strangways, another member of the India Society who admired Tagore, Macmillan & Company began to publish Tagore in March 1913. Meanwhile Tagore, having abused the English winter in previous letters, was at loggerheads with an American winter in the Midwest, as this self-mocking letter reveals.

508 W. High Street, Urbana, [Illinois, USA]
13 January 1913

My dear friend

I send you some more of my translations of which Nos 6, 7, 8, 9 and 13 have been sent to *Poetry* in Chicago for publication.[1] They specially requested me to send them some of my love lyrics and that made me translate these from my earlier writings. I hope these will be enough for this paper and Mr Ezra Pound need not supply them with more of my things.

Last week after a heavy fall of rain at night the roads have become coated with ice and they have become quite impassable for me. Even for those who are accustomed to such things walking is not altogether safe on these roads. So I have been keeping indoors last few days which is not a very great calamity for me. But I have got to sign a document before the notary public empowering Mr Fox Strangways to negotiate with Messrs Macmillan on my behalf.[2] His office is not nearby, cabs or motor cars are not available and as I must take care of my limbs with which I have to sign I don't know what I am to do. Day or two ago I did make a sortie but I am sorry to say the progress I made was not considerable and the fall I had was hardly dignified for a man of my age. Fortunately there was only one other pedestrian in the street and he was not in a mood to enjoy the misfortune of a fellow being, being himself anxiously concerned about his own safety.

I had the curiosity to try the forbidden path, ate the fruit of knowledge and had the fall. But Satan has not left off tempting me and it is urging me that with better caution I am sure to evade consequences. But from the little experience I had I could see that caution is hardly a help [on] a slippery path, where dashing recklessness is a much better guide. Unfortunately caution is within one's means but recklessness is a divine gift not to be had for the asking. So I will have to wait till the ice melts. But the sky is clear, the sun is bright and the colourless white of widowhood of the wintry nature is beautiful to me.

I have an invitation to Rochester to some congress of liberal religious bodies where I am requested to read a paper on Race Conflicts.[3] I have accepted the invitation and I must be ready with my paper before the end of this month. But, as the time allotted for reading it is not more than thirty minutes the paper is not going to be a formidable one.

Ever yours
Rabindranath Tagore

Source: MS original in the Rothenstein Papers [Harvard]; letter published in Lago (ed.), *Imperfect Encounter*, pp. 86–7.

1 RT to Harriet Monroe, 13 Jan. 1913 [Chicago]. *Poetry* published fourteen love poems by RT in June 1913, pp. 81–91; most of them later appeared in a revised form in *The Gardener*.
2 Arthur H. Fox Strangways (1859–1948): music critic, founder of *Music and Letters* and author of *The Music of Hindostan* (1914); he had been RT's unofficial literary agent since July 1912. 'This [agreement with Macmillan] is the result of a long and somewhat intricate correspondence which began on 16 Dec. ... The royalty was all they would give – not so much I think as the book is worth, but I am told the terms would be considered very good indeed for an ordinary book of poems, so I think you may be satisfied' (Fox Strangways to RT, 15 Jan. 1913 [RB]).
3 RT addressed the congress of the National Federation of Religious Liberals at Rochester, N.Y., on 30 Jan. 1913.

57

To William Butler Yeats

As soon as Tagore's reputation as a poet in English began to be established in late 1912, his lack of confidence in the language gave rise to disputes between his English admirers about how best to translate his work, disputes which have continued ever since. Yeats had already clashed with Arthur Fox Strangways as early as September, now he was irritated to discover that small changes had been made to the India Society edition without his approval.[1] C. F. Andrews, a missionary who was to become one of Tagore's closest English friends, had persuaded Tagore to make the changes in October, just before Tagore sailed for America.[2] Having tackled Rothenstein, who defended Andrews, Yeats wrote direct to Tagore, asking his leave to have the text restored to its original form in time for the forthcoming Macmillan edition. 'The Amateur is never to be trusted,' said Yeats sternly.[3] This is Tagore's slightly shame-faced reply.

[508] W. High Street, Urbana, Illinois, [USA]
26 January 1913

Dear Mr Yeats

I am very sorry for some corrections made at the instance of Mr Andrews in *Gitanjali* when it was too late to submit them to you. I am so absolutely ignorant of the proprieties of your language and Mr Andrews was so insistent that my nervousness drove me to those corrections. I do hope you will take the trouble of once going over the proofs of the second edition and make all the restorations you think necessary.

I met Lady Gregory in this town and was present at some of the performances of [the] Irish Theatre.[4] I cannot tell you how deeply moved I was, particularly by *Cathleen Ni Houlihan*. Its effect is still haunting me.

Most sincerely yours
Rabindranath Tagore

Source: MS original in collection of Michael Yeats.

1 See Yeats to Rothenstein, 7 Sept. 1912, in Lago (ed.), *Imperfect Encounter*, p. 41.
2 See Hugh Tinker, *The Ordeal of Love: C. F. Andrews and India* (New Delhi, 1979), p. 62. Andrews disliked Yeats introduction to *Gitanjali*, as being 'altogether unsatisfying and very superficial'.
3 Yeats to RT, 9 Jan. 1913, *VBQ, 30*, No. 3, 1964–5, p. 163.
4 Lady Gregory (1852–1932): Irish writer and playwright; she was a friend and patron of Yeats. From Dec. 1912 to May 1913 she toured the Abbey Players in the USA in a programme including Yeats' play *Cathleen Ni Houlihan*. This is one of the rare occasions when RT mentions a Yeats work by name.

58

To Ezra Pound

This letter is the first indication of a decline in Ezra Pound's enthusiasm for Tagore's poems. By the end of 1913, the time of Tagore's Nobel prize, Pound had become actively critical. The major reason was the inadequacy of Tagore's translations – of which Rabindranath here shows himself to be acutely aware – but there was also a divergence of sensibility which is perhaps best captured by Pound's remark to Harriet Monroe, *Poetry*'s editor, in April 1913, that 'Tagore's philosophy hasn't much in it for a man who has "felt the pangs" and been pestered with western civilisation'.[1] When Pound sent *Personae* (1909), his first successful book of poems, to Tagore, he responded:

> Your *Personae*... has given me genuine pleasure. It is extremely difficult for me to judge poems written in [the] English language and perhaps I do not quite understand them but your modern poetical literature has always seemed to me to have eaten the forbidden fruit, lost her simplicity and shamefully become conscious of her nakedness trying to hide herself in all manner of elaborate garbs woven of dead and decaying leaves. Your muse (pardon me for using this phrase) has come out, clothed in her own youthful body, full of life vigour, and suggestive of incalculable possibilities of growth.[2]

Where Tagore would continue to reject the 'elaborate garbs', Pound would increasingly savour them. One can see why neither poet was interested in the work of the other after their brief honeymoon.

1000 Massachuset[t]s Avenue, Cambridge,
[Massachusetts, USA]
5 February 1913

Dear Mr Ezra Pound

I am so glad that I sent you some of my later translations.[3] When the meaning and music of [the] original haunts you it is difficult for you to know how much has been realised in the translation.

I had my misgivings about the narrative poems myself.[4] But I must say they have not been purposely made moral, they are not to guide people to right path. They merely express the enjoyment of some aspects of life which happen to be morally good. They give you some outlook upon life which has a vastness that transcends all ordinary purposes of life and stirs imagination. I am sure in the original there is nothing that savours of pulpit. Perhaps you miss that sense of enjoyment in the English rendering and bereft of their music and suggestiveness of language they appear as merely didactic. Of course I am not going to include in my next book anything that you think should be left out. I will send you all the translations that I have made lately and I should be thankful to you to have your advice about them. As for the possible sale of my book I should dismiss all thoughts of it altogether from my mind, which is not at all difficult for me to do as I never had any financial success from my books.[5]

Very sincerely yours
Rabindranath Tagore

[P.S.] I am in Boston for a few days, shall be back to Urbana next week.

Source: MS original in Pound Papers [Yale].

1 22 April 1913, in Ezra Pound, *The Letters of Ezra Pound 1907–1941* (D. D. Paige ed.; London, 1951), p. 55.
2 RT to Pound, Feb. 1913 [Yale]. No day of writing is given by RT, but the changed address indicates that this letter postdates his letter of 5 Feb. 1913.
3 See letter 55.
4 Some of these narrative poems were probably included in *The Gardener*, published in Oct. 1913 after revision by Yeats.
5 This remained true in Bengal virtually as long as RT lived: a typical first printing of a new work of his in Bengali was 1,000 copies.

59

To (Sir) William Rothenstein

Through giving lectures, Tagore was becoming a minor celebrity in the USA – a hint of the sensation he would cause in America during his 1916–17 lecture tour. At the same time, encouraged by Yeats and Pound, he was deeply sensitive to the need to maintain a high literary standard in his translations. The complex Bengali artist in him was in conflict with the simple messenger of universal values. Even if he had the linguistic ability to present the former personality, he knew it would have small appeal in the West; but the latter personality, though likely to attract far more western attention, he knew to be at best an oversimplification, at worst a self-falsification. These sharpening dilemmas are implicit in this letter to Rothenstein.

Felton Hall, Cambridge, [Massachusetts, USA]
14 February 1913

Dear friend

I have been rushing through this vast land for the last few weeks going from town to town reading lectures and shaking hands with new acquaintances. I was in New York last week and came to Boston last evening. I am invited to read two lectures in the university here and two others in clubs connected with it.[1] As my lectures were appreciated in Chicago I hope they will be received here with attention.[2] Other invitations have come to me but I do not think I will be able to accept them. I am longing to go back to Urbana and settle down with my quiet work.

I met Mr Chapman in New York and was at once struck with his personality.[3] It was his vigorous sincerity which attracted me to him and I wish I could have the opportunity to see him more. It was entirely my fault that I did not have it. You know very well that exploration of new places is not in my power, and the idea of going about visiting people, however estimable they may be, scares me. But I still have the desire in my heart to know him better, but I doubt very much if it will ever be realised.

In Chicago I was the guest of Mrs Moody.[4] She is the widow of William Vaughan Moody, one of the most famous of modern American poets. Mrs Moody has been extremely kind to me. She has volunteered to pilot me safe through my tour in American cities and I was living under her protection in New York. She has sheltered me from all kinds of intrusion and publicity and within a very short time she has been able to make me feel quite at ease with her which is a difficult feat [as] you know. Had it not been for her I could not have come out of my shell at all as long as I remained in this country. I feel I have been of some help to her – for she was gradually drifting towards the vague region of Christian Science and its allied cults which are in vogue here and which are so destructive of spiritual sanity and health.

I have been experimenting with translation of various kinds of my poems – some, and perhaps most of them, have to be rejected. Only those that can sustain the spirit of the *Gitanjali* poems should be retained. You will have to maintain a severely critical attitude towards them and be uncompromisingly fastidious in your selection for the next publication. Place do not for a moment think that it will hurt me at all. I am going to have typewritten all the translations I have done, in some kind of order, and then send them to you.

Mr Yeats is not satisfied with some of the corrections that have been made without his knowledge. I have promised him to submit to him the proofs of the second edition of *Gitanjali*, for him to make necessary restorations. Will you ask Macmillan to arrange it?[5]

With my love to you all

I am your affectionate friend
Rabindranath Tagore

[PS] Yesterday I read my paper on the Problem of Evil in the Emerson Hall before the university people.[6] You will be glad to learn that it was enthusiastically received. Prof. Woods has been urging me to have all these papers published here in a book form and he thinks he can arrange with some publishers who are reliable.[7] He is sure of having a fairly good sale. What do you advise me to do?

Source: MS original in Rothenstein Papers [Harvard]; letter published in Lago (ed.), *Imperfect Encounter*, pp. 98–9.

1 At Harvard, RT gave three lectures to the philosophy class of James Houghton Woods, a lecture to the Philosophical Club and a lecture to the Divinity Club. One of those present was T. S. Eliot (see letter 339).
2 At Chicago, RT spoke three times, one of them being at the university, on 'Ideals of the ancient civilisation of India' and 'The problem of evil'.
3 John Jay Chapman (1862–1933): poet, dramatist and social critic. Chapman found RT to be 'a little unhealthy . . . and his moral being, *hot house*' (Chapman to Rothenstein, 8 March 1913, quoted in Lago (ed.), *Imperfect Encounter*, p. 100, n. 2.). This was one of many instances of RT's rejecting the more vigorous aspects of American spirituality.
4 On Harriet Moody and her relationship with RT, see Olivia Howard Dunbar, *A House in Chicago* (Chicago, 1947), pp. 93–106; also letter 69.
5 See letter 57.
6 'The problem of evil' appears in *Sadhana*, pp. 47–65.
7 James Houghton Woods (1864–1935): professor of Indian philosophy at Harvard University. 'I am still exhilarated by the influence of your visit. And on your return very many of us hope that you will consent to give the remaining three of your lectures . . . It seems to me that you have penetrated deeper and more resolutely in the evil of life than any of us' (Woods to RT, n.d. [RB]).

60

To Madhurilata Chakravarty (Tagore)[1]

In this letter to his daughter Bela in Bengal, Rabindranath's ambivalence about his western success is again obvious – and perhaps more pointed than in his letter (59) to William Rothenstein. One clearly senses his eagerness for western appreciation, but there is an undercurrent of concern that he is out of touch with home and all those Bengali customs and problems that he knows will never be understood by his American audiences. Furthermore, Rabindranath knew that all was not well with his daughter, who did not answer his letters. The reason for her behaviour is obscure but seems to have been connected with the overbearing behaviour of her brother-in-law Nagendranath Gangulee, whom Tagore had left in charge of the family house at Jorasanko while he and Rathindranath were abroad. This seems to have caused Bela and her husband Sharat Chandra to leave Jorasanko.[2]

[Felton Hall, Cambridge, Massachusetts, USA]
[15 or 16 February 1913]
Postmark Cambridge, 19 February 1913

Bel,

It makes me very anxious to hear that you are not keeping well.[3] My letters to you do not receive replies, and it is not convenient to get news of you from others. Do send me a postcard occasionally with your news. Let me know how Sharat is keeping these days.

For a long time after arriving in America I kept quietly to a corner of a room in a small town called Urbana, unavailable to anyone. But the people of this country have a mania for listening to lectures. Those around me were constantly insisting on my giving a lecture. To begin with I remained firm, because I was absolutely certain that if I were to lecture in the English language, I could not possibly keep my dignity. So I took heed of old Chanakya's advice, and sat solemnly with my mouth firmly shut.[4] In the end I could not refuse a request to say something to an Urbana club called the Unity Club. It is a small kind of place, not very formidable and with a limited membership, and I somehow accepted. Then, after writing out my talk and going there, I found the hall packed with people. Escape was impossible. When my reading was over everyone congratulated me. That gave me courage and I went on to read five papers to that group, one after the other.[5] Since then, invitations to speak have not stopped. After giving a lecture at Chicago University my fears really vanished. I spoke for twenty minutes at Rochester on Race Conflict at the invitation of the annual congress of Religious Liberals.[6] Rochester is near the city of Boston. I thought that having come thus far I should visit Boston. The biggest university in this country is Harvard University in Boston. That is where I have now reached. I lectured here yesterday, and will give three more lectures.[7] After these are done, where I shall go and what I shall do are not yet fixed.

Aside from all this, I have noticed a definite advantage of this country, that even in winter the sun shines frequently. This could never happen in England. Although we were there in summer, almost every day of those few months was rainy. Here the winter is far colder – almost everything is covered in snow – but when the sun comes out, it is a beautiful sight; the whole world sparkles. When we were in Urbana it rained heavily one night and the rainwater turned to ice. The trees beside the road looked as if they were encased in glass; from time to time great branches would crack under the weight of ice and fall crashing to the ground. The roads were solid ice, and it was hard to move on them without one's feet slipping; many people took a tumble. I lacked the courage to leave the house for fear of falling over. But eventually, after two or three days of feeling like a prisoner, I ventured out. I did not get far before I fell. The street was practically empty, with only one pedestrian walking behind me. His attention was entirely focused on keeping his own balance, so he had no time to laugh. But after that I lost all enthusiasm to take even one more step. I retreated inside the house and did not stir again from my corner until the stony heart of the ice was completely softened.

Since leaving Urbana we have slowly acquired a varied group of friends and acquaintances. The widow of a well-known local poet, Mrs Moody, was our hostess in

Chicago. She looked after us with great care, in fact she was so taken with us that she would not let us go. When we went to New York for a week, she made us stay in her place. She has come to Boston too. There is a natural motherliness in her.[8]

One thing here I like very much. In this country, at least in western America, women of almost all conditions must do the entire housework themselves, for it is virtually impossible to get servants. Cooking, bed making, floor sweeping, dish washing are almost everywhere done by the mistress of the house – very often joined by the master. But there are so many convenient devices to lighten the burden as much as possible. Cooking is done by gas oven – without much bother – and a lot of work is carried out with electricity. It should not be inconceivable to introduce these conveniences in our country nowadays. If this were done, it would potentially free us from our dependence on the servants to a large extent. For quite a while here *Bouma* did all the housework, until at last two Indian students agreed to take charge of it in return for board and wages.[9] The poorer students in this country do not feel the least shame or humiliation in doing such commonplace jobs. They work as waiters in hotels and manage their studies at the same time. Often they serve the very students with whom they are studying, in order to meet their expenses. Were they to do this in our country, they would be too ashamed to lift their faces. What news of your own helpers? Is your cook still with you? How is his son keeping? Have you been able to find a maid? We've had no news of the Eleventh Magh celebrations yet – we should receive reports after about a fortnight, in the middle of Phalgun. Here we spent the eleventh on the road. For the first time in a while, I was away at Eleventh Magh.[10] On 7 Paush, early in the morning, we five Bengalis celebrated the festival in a corner of my bedroom at Urbana.[11] There was no crowd – but we enjoyed it.

Father

Source: MS original at Rabindra Bhavan, Shantiniketan; letter published in *CP*, IV, pp. 5–9.

1. Madhurilata Chakravarty (1886–1918): eldest daughter of RT. See letter 29.
2. See Paul, *Rabijibani*, VI, p. 379.
3. Bela was pregnant. RT knew this, since it was mentioned by Rathindranath in a letter written to another member of the family on 27 March (*ibid*.). She later miscarried.
4. See *sloka* 15 of Chanakya in Haeberlin, *Kavyasangraha*, p. 313. RT's account does not totally square with that of Mayce Seymour, one of his devoted hosts in Urbana:

   > It was our good fortune that as soon as he had finished an essay, he permitted us to invite to our home any of our friends whom we thought would be interested in hearing the essay read. He wished to try out what he had written on an American audience, and we were more than willing to assist in the experiment . . . He must have felt at home with this group of listeners, finding them responsive to his thought, for he was happy to greet them again and again. In this way we heard all the *Sadhana* lectures, which he later delivered at a number of universities. (Mayce Seymour, 'That golden time', *VBQ*, 25, No. 1, Summer 1959, pp. 9, 10)

5. Sujit Mukherjee (*Passage to America*) lists four lectures at Urbana: 'World realisation' (10 Nov.), 'Self realisation' (17 Nov.), 'Realisation of Brahma' (24 Nov.), 'The way of action' (1 Dec.). Obviously RT did not wait all that long before giving in to the requests for lectures.
6. 'Race conflict', *MR*, April 1913, pp. 423–6.
7. See letter 59, n. 1.
8. See letter 59, n. 4.
9. See letter 52, n. 5.
10. On 11 Magh, see letter 4.
11. On 7 Paush, see letter 28, n. 3.

61

To Madhurilata Chakravarty (Tagore)

By early March 1913, Tagore knew that Macmillan would publish his English translations in Britain, and probably in the USA too.[1] He was already anticipating the royalties as a source of income for his school. Letters from Shantiniketan had made him think of returning to India soon, rather than staying in Europe for two or three years as he had hoped: and yet he was now possessed by the urge to travel – evident in this letter to his daughter – that would grip him for the rest of his life.[2] Western appreciation of him, his improved financial resources and his own curiosity about other cultures had formed a fortunate conjunction.

[2970 Groveland Avenue, Chicago, USA][3]
Postmark 3 March 1913

Bel,

We have been on the move for just over a month. After numerous readings, lectures, meetings and whatnot we catch a train this afternoon and retreat to our den in Urbana. But we will not serve a long term there. I expect to reach England from America on 17 April.[4] There arrangements will be made to publish my books. Many new translations are ready. People here seem to like them, and so the published books should not do badly. The Macmillan Company in England want to be my publishers and negotiations are in hand. How long it will take to see all these books through the press I cannot guess. Perhaps I shall be occupied until next autumn. Then at the beginning of the cold weather I shall be ready to return home. I have a yen to come full circle to India via Japan, China, Java and Burma – I do not hope to be able to come this way again. But it is not going to happen on this trip. If somehow I can find the time and money I shall go to Japan via the Siberian railway and from there travel to India – at least I am toying with this idea, which will probably not come off, however tempting I may find it. If it does, good, and if it does not, imagining it is still rather pleasant.

Until recently the winter has not been too severe – we have enjoyed sunshine throughout. March has come and the spring is about to begin, yet it looks as if the winter will not depart without one final fling of its weapons. For the past three or four days the weather has been very cold, snowing almost continually, with a biting wind. But one of the advantages of America is that no matter how much it snows and how cold it is, there is no lack of sunshine – which is why I find the winter enjoyable. Last summer in England we had constant rain; I hope that this summer will look upon us more favourably. If you write, do not send it here – our English address is:

C/o W. Rothenstein Esq., 11 Oak Hill Park, Hampstead, London N. W.

Father

Source: MS original at Rabindra Bhavan, Shantiniketan; letter published in *CP*, IV, pp. 10–12.

1 See Rothenstein to RT, 6 Feb. 1913, in Lago (ed.), *Imperfect Encounter*, pp. 97–8.
2 Writing to Rothenstein on 16 Jan. 1913, RT mentioned the possibility of using income from his books to pay off the debts of his school, and added: 'I was planning [on] staying on in Europe for two or three years.

But this will not be possible. I hope I shall be able to spend my summer in England and then I will leave for India' (*ibid.*, p. 88).
3 RT was then staying with Harriet Moody.
4 He reached England on 19 April 1913.

62

To (Sir) William Rothenstein

Ideal and reality were perpetually at war in Tagore's personality, perhaps never more so than in his contact with the USA. In 1940, in his last significant comment on America (addressed to its president), he called it 'the last refuge of spiritual man' (letter 341); mostly, however, he was appalled by America's blatant materialism. He was never able to see how these two aspects might be related, rather than totally distinct. Just before leaving the country after this first visit, he summarised his conflict in this letter to Rothenstein (who had many American friends).

[2970 Groveland Avenue, Chicago, USA]
[1 April? 1913]

Dear friend

Our date of departure has been fixed. Our steamer *Olympic* will start from New York on 12 April, so we shall reach London by the middle of this month. I cannot tell you how glad I feel to be once again near you, for which I always had a longing since I came to this country. But for the dread of the cold weather I should have been back to your place long before this. Except for lapses of very short durations I passed my time like a recluse in the little town of Urbana. I have had my ample compensation for this life of seclusion and I am glad that I have been able to protect myself from the dissipations of social success. I have gone through a series of public engagements but I have been deaf to the alluring calls of drawing-rooms. I have refused to be handled and passed on from one show to the other by the connoisseurs of genius. The people in this country are hearty in their kindness but there is a rudeness in their touch, it is vigorous but not careful. Their admiration is not convincing therefore I could not take any delight in it as I did in your country. However, I have met with some sincere friends in America and I am deeply grateful to them. I feel sure if I had courage to come out and know the people here I should have loved them with all my heart. But I did not have the opportunity and I am certain I have not the right to judge them at all excepting through those few friends of mine whose deep earnestness and transparent simplicity have won my love. Somehow, I have an impression that America has a great mission in the history of western civilisation; for it is rich enough not to concern itself in the greedy exploitation of weaker nations. Its hands are free and perhaps it will hold up the torch of freedom before the world.

Affectionately yours
Rabindranath Tagore

Source: MS original in Rothenstein Papers [Harvard]; letter published in Lago (ed.), *Imperfect Encounter*, pp. 106–7.

63

To Nagendranath Gangulee

Ever since the 1890s, rural reconstruction work had been under way on the Tagore estates, managed first by Rabindranath alone, then by Rabindranath and a volunteer group, and most recently by Rathindranath Tagore and Nagendranath Gangulee. There were some significant achievements but overall, to quote Sumit Sarkar, Rabindranath's programme suffered from an 'inability to integrate the nationalist cause with the economic demands and aspirations of the common people'.[1]

In 1905, for instance, he established an agricultural bank at Patisar, in which he later invested his Nobel prize money (and lost the principal entirely when the debts owed to the bank were written off as a result of new legislation in the 1930s).[2] The idea, a good one in theory, was to lend money at reasonable rates to establish new agricultural techniques and new industries (see letter 45). But almost all the tenants and estate officers were sceptical. Nagendranath wrote from Shelidah to an American professor in Illinois:

> While we are thinking of improving agriculture by laying out an experimental farm here, the village elders think in terms of fixed rent, facile credit, better marketing facilities and so on. I am perplexed. Tagore's idea of an agricultural bank has caught my imagination, and I am trying to grasp the intricacies of a credit system such as could be applied to the existing rural conditions.[3]

That was written in 1911. By 1913 Nagendranath was ready to give up. To what extent he was the victim of Tagore's impossible dream rather than his own inadequacies is debatable, but undoubtedly he made little progress. At the same time his marriage to Mira, Rabindranath's daughter, was heading for disaster. In this letter written just after his return to London, Tagore gives rein to his anxieties on both estate and marital matters.

C/o Messrs Thomas Cook & Son,
Ludgate Circus, London, [UK]
29 April 1913

Kalyaniyeshu

Nagen your letter has reached me via America. I am worried about you all. But it is impossible to work out a suitable arrangement for you at this distance. My return is not so far off now: when I come a solution must be found. But you must certainly keep in mind that neither the *zamindari* nor the bank belongs personally to us; we are accountable to others. If you overlook this fact there is sure to be trouble, and it is wrong to forget it. In my father's day, when I looked after the *zamindari*, I had to take orders in every tiny matter and frequently put up with his rebukes.[4] That is the rule in matters of work. If you had experience of work elsewhere your training would have been strict in this regard and you would know that there is no disrespect in it; on the contrary, it promotes self-respect.

Should you wish to concentrate your mind entirely on the bank and conduct a meticulous survey of its operations so as to promote its progress, then I can say with some confidence that there is real hope for your own progress too. We can give you our word that we will not withdraw money from it, and if for some reason we had to, we would pay proper interest on it. Furthermore, we can formalise this agreement if need be. But you will have to agree to work with due caution – which means that you will not withdraw money at will for your own needs – and to accept that you cannot incur extra expenditure without special sanction; in other words you will have to work in exactly the same way as you would if you were employed by another bank. Something you particularly need to grasp is that in business and property affairs, if one ignores the rules and acts carelessly, the consequences may be both embarrassing and risky. But if you work within the accepted rules, you will not be hampered in anything you do and you will make progress. If you react petulantly to this suggestion, that would be childish. When I used to work, I received plenty of kicks and scratches – and why should I not have? Whatever one's job may be, one cannot expect total freedom, not even in self-employment. Because you work with Rathi you seem to have forgotten that it is not he who is boss.

But discussions of this kind cannot be conducted over a great distance. For a long time my biggest worry about you has been that I clearly see you have no judgement about your expenditure in relation to your income, which is why you are constantly falling into debt; and the more unmanageable the debt becomes, the more restless your mind feels and the more discontented you become with your present job and salary. And yet I know very well that if I increase your income, your expenses will increase still more. Bearing all this in mind I made an arrangement for Mira to receive a hundred rupees monthly.[5] I thought that if, over ten years, at least fifteen thousand rupees could be saved, my worries about her would be to some extent relieved – but this money, instead of being saved, has been frittered away by you on all sorts of futile ventures, and I can no longer feel unconcerned about Mira. Anyway, on my return we must come up with a sensible way out of all this.

Regarding the Brahmo Samaj, when I get back I will do the needful. Meanwhile it can carry on as it is.[6]

Ashirbbadak
Shri Rabindranath Thakur

Source: MS original at Rabindra Bhavan, Shantiniketan; letter published in Sharadiya *Desh*, 1398 [Autumn 1991], pp. 38–9.

1 Sarkar, *Swadeshi Movement*, p. 286.
2 See Rathindranath Tagore, *Pitrismriti*, p. 217. The Nobel prize money was equivalent to Rs 108,000. For as long as the bank lasted, interest on this sum was paid to the Shantiniketan school (about Rs 8,000 per annum).
3 Gangulee, *The Indian Peasant*, p. 40.
4 *My Rem*, p. 70/*RR*, XVII, p. 314.
5 The first payment was made in Dec. 1911, just after the birth of Mira's son Nitindranath. (See Paul, *Rabijibani*, VI, pp. 253–4.) The same sum was mentioned in RT's will.
6 Nagendranath was made secretary of the Adi Brahmo Samaj in RT's absence abroad.

64

To Ramananda Chatterji [Chattopadhyay]

The Tagore who returned to London in April 1913 had a substantial literary reputation. Ezra Pound's weighty review of *Gitanjali* had appeared in the March *Fortnightly Review*; *Gitanjali* had already been reprinted by Macmillan; and the *Times* now referred to Tagore as 'the eminent Bengali poet'.[1] The extraordinary and (to Tagore) unexpected level of English sympathy for himself and his poetry was a glaring reminder to him of the *lack* of English sympathy for the majority of his educated countrymen in England, and vice versa. In 1879, in London, he had laughed at this situation, as well as feeling indignant (see letter 1); four decades later, it chiefly pained him. In 1907, he had lectured his son-in-law Nagendranath on the subject of Bengali insularity, while he was a student in Illinois (letter 33), now he took up the same theme in a letter to his friend Ramananda Chatterji, who as editor of the *Modern Review* was publishing a stream of articles on racial friction and whose son Kedarnath (Buba) was now in England.

37 Alfred Place West, South Kensington,
London, [UK]
1 May 1913/18 Baishakh 1320

Shraddhashpadeshu

Since my return to London I have spent time with both Buba and Prashanta.[2] Buba lives close to our lodgings and before long Prashanta too may find a place in this locality. I will try to introduce Buba to some decent people here. Our students here in London, because they are not in the habit of mixing with strangers, find it almost impossible to get to know English people. They just stay at home in their lodgings and get their study texts by heart, never knowing either the country or its inhabitants. By contrast our Kali Mohan, despite his poor knowledge of English, has mingled here with a group of decent people and has benefited from his contact with them in every way.[3]

I am glad to know that my essay on 'Race conflict' meets with your approval.[4] Out of the six I have prepared I have sent one to the *Hibbert Journal*, and one to the journal *Quest*. Both these journals are quarterly and so the pieces will appear in July.[5] No one here has seen these essays yet. From 19 May I have been invited to give a series of weekly lectures to the Quest Society.[6] The lure of money and fame stops me from declining – and so I am sending only the first lecture for publication in *Modern Review*. This I first read at Chicago University.[7] Please keep an eye out for errors in its English – I write the language without knowing it, almost by guesswork. I wrote the essays with some attention to their sound, and people who have listened to them have liked them – but no one has yet cast a schoolmaster's eye over them. An Englishman did glance through them, and he merely removed a surfeit of definite articles, supplied some missing ones and corrected some misapplied prepositions.[8] So I suppose they contain no really alarming mistakes.

I have not yet received the Chaitra issue of *Prabashi* – perhaps it was purloined while

I was on my travels.⁹ I have had a long break from writing in Bengali. Not that I am writing a great deal in English either: I have been overtaken by a bout of laziness. But I sense that it is more than just lethargy.

Please give Shanta and Sita my New Year's blessings.¹⁰

Apnader
Shri Rabindranath Thakur

Source: MS original at Rabindra Bhavan, Shantiniketan; letter published in *CP*, XII, pp. 38–40.

1 10 May 1913.
2 Kedarnath Chatterji [Chattopadhyay] ('Buba') (1891–1965) had come to England to study geology; RT helped him to get admittance to Imperial College. Prashanta Chandra Mahalanobis (see letter 175) had come to study for a B.Sc. in London; in Oct. 1913 he went instead to Cambridge University to study physics and mathematics.
3 Kali Mohan Ghosh (1884–1940): village development worker. From 1906 he worked devotedly in rural reconstruction on the Tagore estates, as a teacher at Shantiniketan and finally as a key figure at Shriniketan. His particular gift was to inspire trust in uneducated villagers. RT enabled him to visit Britain to study the methods of primary education and adult literacy work. He got on well with William Rothenstein, W. B. Yeats and especially Ezra Pound, who collaborated with him on some translations of Kabir. See Kshiti Mohan Sen, 'In remembrance of Kali Mohan Ghosh', *VBN*, April 1971, pp. 298–300; also Abhra Bose, 'They also served: Kali Mohan Ghosh and Santosh Chandra Majumdar', in Manjula Bose (ed.), *Leonard Elmhirst* (Calcutta, 1994).
4 'Race conflict', *MR*, April 1913, pp. 423–6.
5 'The problem of evil', *Hibbert Journal*, July 1913, pp. 705–16; 'The realisation of Brahma', *Quest*, July 1913, pp. 601–13.
6 These well-attended lectures were published, after revision by Ernest Rhys, as *Sadhana* in autumn 1913. They were: 'The Relation of the universe to the individual' (Caxton Hall, London, 19 May); 'Realisation in love' (Manchester College, Oxford, 23 May); 'Soul consciousness' (Caxton Hall, 26 May); 'The problem of evil' (Caxton Hall, 2 June); 'The problem of self' (Caxton Hall, 9 June); 'Realisation in love' (Caxton Hall, 17 June); 'The realisation of Brahma' (Kensington Town Hall, London, 19 June). RT also lectured on 'The ancient religious ideals of India' (Majlis Society, Cambridge, 18 May).
7 'The relation of the universe to the individual', *MR*, July 1913, pp. 1–6 (same lecture as 'Ideals of the ancient civilisation of India', delivered in Chicago).
8 The Englishman was probably R. F. Rattray, who looked after RT at Harvard in Feb. 1913. See his 'With Tagore in 1913', *Inquirer*, London, 16 March 1940, p. 82; also letter 339.
9 Chaitra: Bengali month corresponding to mid-March–mid-April.
10 Shanta (1893–1984) and Sita (1895–1974): daughters of Ramananda Chatterji [Chattopadhyay]; both became writers. Shanta married the scholar Kalidas Nag.

65

To Indira Devi Chaudhurani

Given the accolades showered upon Tagore by Yeats and Pound, the award of the Nobel prize and the many powerful Tagore works (and letters) either written by him in English or translated by him into English, it is hard to understand that in mid-1913, the vast majority of Bengalis did not believe Rabindranath to be capable of writing proper English. Yet before he went to England in 1912, he had published practically nothing in English – his letter to Myron Phelps (37), published in the *Modern Review* in 1910, was the one prominent exception – and when he did have to write the language he made regular slips. His success in English therefore incensed those many Bengalis whose command of English grammar and syntax was flawless; within a year or so it would be widely believed in Bengal that Yeats had rewritten *Gitanjali* and made it acceptable English (see letter 81). Even Rabindranath's immediate family was somewhat surprised that he had taken to translating his work. When his favourite niece, Indira, hinted at this in a letter from home, Rabindranath let all his thoughts and feelings pour out (of course in Bengali) in one of his richest and most fascinating letters.

C/o Messrs Thomas Cook & Sons,
Ludgate Circus, London, [UK]
6 May 1913

Kalyaniyashu

Bibi, I am delighted to receive your letter. Since crossing the ocean I have yet to receive such detailed news of relations and friends. The reason is, my own letters chiefly deal with the Bolpur school – moreover when our people do occasionally write to me, they cannot think what sort of events would be news to me. And so I live a life in which at home no one seems bothered to wind his watch, while abroad every passing second strikes me like the loud tick-tock of a swinging pendulum.

You mention the English translation of *Gitanjali*. Even today I cannot grasp how I wrote it and how people have liked it so much. That I cannot write English is so plain a fact that I have never felt enough pride in my English to be embarrassed by it. If someone wrote me a note in English asking me to tea, I lacked the confidence to reply. You apparently believe that by now my delusion of modesty has been exposed – far from it: the real delusion is the belief that I have actually managed to write in English.

What happened is that when I was about to leave and get on board the ship for England I had a dizzy spell as a result of my frantic round of goodbyes, and my voyage had to be cancelled; I went off to Shelidah to get some rest.[1] But unless one's brain is kept active one lacks the energy to relax properly, and so I felt obliged to take up some superfluous task, just to keep my mind calm. It was then the month of Chaitra, and the air was saturated with the fragrance of mango blossoms and fervid with the chatter and warble of birds. A small boy, when he is feeling fresh, forgets about his mother, but when he tires, he wants to snuggle up to her. This was my condition. With all my being I opened my arms to Chaitra – her sunshine, breezes, fragrance and music; nothing escaped me. But in such a state of mind I cannot remain mute: when I feel the breeze on my bones, they always stir, as you know of old. Yet I did not feel the strength to gird my loins and compose something new. So instead I took up the poems of *Gitanjali* and began translating them into English. You may wonder why such a demanding task occurred to me in my enfeebled state – but I assure you it was not done out of some crazy bravado. It was just that I knew I had started a festival of poetic delight in my mind once before, fanned by the zephyr of my emotions, and so now I felt an urge to rekindle it through the medium of a foreign language. A small notebook was soon filled. I slipped it into my pocket when I boarded the ship. I wanted to keep it to hand because I had a notion that whenever I felt restless on the high seas, I would lie back in my deckchair and translate a few more poems. And that is what happened. The contents of the notebook spilled over into a second notebook.

Rothenstein had already received word of my poetic tendency from an Indian. When in the course of conversation he expressed interest in reading some of my poetry, I diffidently presented my notebook to him.[2] The opinion he uttered I did not really credit. Then he sent my notebook to the poet Yeats – and from there on you know the story. So you can see, I hope, from the above account, that I am not the guilty party in this tale – chiefly, one thing just led to another.

After all that, when I arrived in America, I expected a period of peace and quiet. But America is not the place for keeping quiet. Even the tight-lipped turn talkative there; and anyone coming from abroad is expected to give lectures. I had no sooner settled in Urbana than I was cajoled into speaking.[3] I told them I did not know English, but when they listened to my statement they did not believe it and said that I spoke excellent English. I have never mastered the knack of dodging requests; and I do not find constant excuses any easier to deliver than lectures. So that is how America came to squeeze my throat and produce these lectures. Though I have been given the credit for them, I still feel they got written almost miraculously. The English language has many pitfalls – think of the definite and indefinite articles, the prepositions, the use of 'shall' and 'will' – which cannot be avoided by intuition, only by tuition. I have reached the conclusion that these elements are like insects that have burrowed into my subliminal consciousness. When I blindly set sail with my pen, these little creatures creep silently out of their dark holes and perform their appointed tasks – but as soon as I consciously focus upon them they go higgledy-piggledy. And so I never feel confident of controlling them, and even now I say I do not know the English language. In stating this I perhaps exaggerate a little – actually I know English well enough to say that I do not know it. This is the truth: and the fact that I have written a few essays in English makes me anxious – will I be able to maintain their standard? Those who achieve something without the necessary training, who succeed by accident, become burdened by their success.

A week before we returned here from America, Suren arrived.[4] We have settled into our former familiar house. There is no vacent room for Suren, however. So every morning he comes over here from his hotel and spends the day with us. He has managed to sort out some of his business, and probably he will get ready to head back within a week or two. Rathi and *Bouma* may go back with him but I am stuck here.[5] I am tied up with lecturing until at least the end of June.[6] Then there's the Irish Theatre, which is preparing a production of my *Post Office*: Yeats and his group seem to like it a good deal.[7] And then too I have filled another exercise book with translations; these have passed the test of Rothenstein and friends, who are keen to see them published. Macmillan are my publishers. The second printing of *Gitanjali* sold out in a short time, and so Macmillan are enthusiastic. Discussions are underway about publishing my latest writings. All this will take some time. In the meantime one of the professors at Harvard University is requesting me to let him publish the lectures I gave there.[8] They will print them at no cost to me, and the entire profit will be given to our Bolpur school. But I am holding back on publication until the lectures have been heard by the cognoscenti here. I sent one of them to the editor of the *Hibbert Journal*, who received it very warmly, and so perhaps they will go down well.[9]

I have read Pramatha's *Sonnet Panchashat*, and it has astonished me. It reminds me of the descriptions of the *yakshis* in the *Meghduta* – his poetry is as slim as a *yakshi*, with two rows of pointed teeth, not a single one blunt; the two lines beginning 'slender in the middle' suggest the firmness of the *yakshi*'s waist and 'the look of a startled deer'. In all, the fourteen lines are like a sparkling necklace, closely strung, with the emotions as liquid as dewdrops but as solid as jewels. I expect that gradually this sharpness of poetic expression will mellow into the mature feeling of adulthood, and the present tendency of each line to make the reader's mind effervesce will instead make it blossom – but then of course the poetry will not be as fiercely flawless as it is now. Pramatha likes to present the goddess of art with a falchion in her hands, rather than the traditional musical *vina*. In his handling of language, rhythm and emotion, extraordinary power and dexterity are revealed.[10]

My elder sister has sent me her translation of her novel *The Flower Garland*. If she could see the literary marketplace here, she would understand why such writing will never work here.[11] What people here call 'reality' is essential in writing. We in Bengal deal very little in this particular commodity – and so we neither recognise its presence nor feel its absence. My problem is that if I say anything about this, people will misunderstand me because my own compositions have been appreciated. If you ask me why they have been, my reply is that in *Gitanjali* I never told myself that I was writing poems – they are simply expressions of my inner life, sincere and humble prayers, my ardent *sadhana*, which has melted all my joy and sorrow into its own form. That it can inspire emotion in other minds I have now finally grasped, but the insight is hard to communicate. For people cannot perceive the artifice in their own work, especially when they have taken much trouble over it and so perhaps feel an especially strong attachment to it. One of our writers at home sent a translation of his own work to someone here.[12] He was told that the work would not do unless it was totally rewritten. His response was, why? – if Rabindranath Thakur's language is alright, why not mine? He made the big mistake of assuming that everything depends on language. In my own case there are undoubtedly no grounds for vanity regarding my command of the English language, but for some reason my perception of the world is unusually candid and my urge to express this perception unusually strong. That is why, though I have given schoolmasters the slip, I have never given life itself the slip; and though I have sinned against English grammar, I have never committed the crime of disgracing English literature. But I can clearly see that by securing a place in English literature despite my being much weaker in the language than the portion of my countrymen who are educated in English, I shall not easily be forgiven or be generously accepted by those I have offended.

The month of May has arrived and today is 22 Baishakh, but here the sky is murky, the light is dim and the sun god's gold is firmly locked away in the treasury.[13] On and off the sky spits with rain, and today there is a fire burning in my room to drive away the damp draughts. I am not very happy because I yearn for light; my heart thirsts for the light that pours down from the endless sky over the fields of Bolpur. But when I consider what will greet me on my return – petty talk on all sides, antipathies, animosities and wearying calumnies – I feel like staying here longer, so as to avoid all that low sweet babel. But unpleasantness cannot be forever bypassed, one must push it aside: that is the proper path. To get across a river by following the bank is impossible, one must plunge in, tackle the waves with both arms and reach dry land. I must not shy away in dread from what is not good, I must try to crush it with all my strength – this is the best vow to hold on to. And so, let the lectures be over and the arrangements for publication be concluded, and I shall set off towards the East.

I have yet to meet Jyotsna; he lives outside London somewhere.[14] Today Mabel invited us for tea.[15] The word has yet to get round that we are back from America, so things have been quiet thus far, but slowly there are signs of a crowd gathering. I do not take very well to all this to-ing and fro-ing – as soon as I receive an invitation to go somewhere I immediately start to feel tired; but after spending some time there my tiredness seems to go.

It is getting late. With my blessing for the New Year, I close my letter.[16]

Shubhanudhyayi
Shri Rabindranath Thakur

Source: MS original at Rabindra Bhavan, Shantiniketan; letter published in *CP*, V, pp. 19–28.

1 RT was to have left for Europe on 19 March 1912.
2 See letter 46, n. 1.
3 See letter 60, n. 4.
4 Suren: Surendranath Tagore. He was secretary of Hindustan Cooperative Insurance, a co-operative society founded in the period of the Swadeshi Movement. He came to London to consult actuaries; see Rathindranath Tagore, 'Surendranath Tagore', *VBQ*, 4, No. 2, Aug.–Oct. 1940, p. 176.
5 Rathindranath and Pratima Tagore returned to Bengal with RT in Sept. 1913.
6 See letter 64 and notes.
7 *The Post Office* was performed in Dublin in May and in London in July. See various letters from Yeats to RT in *VBQ*, 30, No. 3, 1964–5, pp. 164–9; also Thomas Sturge Moore's reaction to the London performance in Dutta and Robinson, *Rabindranath Tagore*, p. 179.
8 The lectures were published by Macmillan as *Sadhana*, not through James Houghton Woods, who organised them at Harvard.
9 L. P. Jacks, editor of the *Hibbert Journal*, to RT, 16 March 1913: 'I shall not alter your expressions in any way' [RB].
10 *Sonnet Panchashat*: fifty Bengali sonnets by Pramatha Chaudhuri in the style of Petrarch, published in 1914.
11 See letter 82, n. 5.
12 The writer was most probably Dinesh Chandra Sen. He had sent some of his work to James Drummond Anderson, lecturer in Bengali at Cambridge University, who asked RT (17 March 1913) to inform Sen, gently, that '*corrections* will not improve his English style. The translation requires to be *rewritten* by someone who knows and enjoys the original' [RB].
13 RT was perhaps alluding to the coming of his birthday on 25 Baishakh.
14 Jyotsnanath Ghoshal (1870–1962): nephew of RT, son of Swarna Kumari Ghoshal, sister of RT.
15 Mabel Palit: wife of Loken Palit, whom she married in 1902; she was the daughter of Kshetra Mohan Dutta.
16 The Bengali New Year falls on 1 Baishakh, i.e. mid-April.

66

To Mira Gangulee (Tagore)

Despite his strong constitution Tagore's health had begun to break down in 1911, as a result of years of overwork and the stress of his involvement in the Swadeshi Movement.[1] He had been suffering for some time from haemorrhoids, indeed the need for medical advice and treatment had been a crucial reason for his original decision to come to Britain.[2] He had hoped to avoid surgery, but finally, in late June 1913, after completing his course of lectures, he entered a London nursing home and underwent an operation.[3] From there, after recovery, he wrote to his daughter Mira.

> [Duchess Nursing Home, 2 Beaumont Street,
> London, UK]
> [July 1913]

Kalyaniyashu

Miru, the photo of your baby son gaping guilelessly is resting on the mantlepiece, where it often catches my eye and makes me impatient to see him.[4] You write that his eczema has been cured but he still feels unwell. If you consult medical books you will find that after a bout of eczema the body is weakened; it becomes ill over nothing. Hence one should not try to cure eczema too rapidly. Get hold of some Sulphur 260 and give Khoka two tablets. Then wait a month and give him two more. If the eczema is lying dormant, the sulphur will see to it.

My operation is over. For the first few days I suffered a good deal. If the illness was painful, the treatment was by no means comfortable. But after a week the nursing home was not too bad. I was spared the constant interruption of visitors for a few days, so I could rest. As I lay there receiving food at two-hourly intervals I was able to read and write a bit.[5] The nursing arrangements were quite good. Close friends occasionally dropped in to see me. There are still some lingering problems, for which I went to see the doctor today. It was very unpleasant. When I was unconscious I was not aware of the doctor's doings – when one is conscious the experience is excruciating. However, it appears that I have been released from the grip of piles. Whether permanently or not is uncertain – some people suffer from piles even after the operation. But at least I should have a respite for four or five months.

At some point I shall take your route via Kharagpur, but I am not sure when. It looks as if I will reach home by the middle of Agrahayan. I do not have the courage to leave before the end of Kartik. So I shall be here up to three months more.[6] During that time I shall be able to conclude the arrangements for printing my books. A book of poems and some lectures are being printed. Both are due out in October.[7] After that the translation of *Shishu* will appear as a Christmas publication.[8]

You must have heard that *Bouma* had her tonsils and adenoids surgically removed.[9] She is well now.

Father

Source: MS original at Rabindra Bhavan, Shantiniketan; letter published in *CP*, IV, pp. 56–7.

1 See Rathindranath Tagore, *Edges of Time*, p. 97: 'After the passing away of my mother in 1902 Father took very little care of his health.'
2 'This voyage is being taken mostly on account of Father's health, and also because he wants to come in closer contact with present-day Europe and America' (Rathindranath Tagore to Mayce Seymour, 10 Oct. 1911 [RB]).
3 RT hoped to get treatment from homeopathic doctors. (See Lago, *Imperfect Encounter*, p. 55.)
4 Nitindranath, grandson of RT, was then just over eighteen months old.
5 From the nursing home RT wrote a letter to Thomas Sturge Moore on 12 July about *The Post Office*, which had just been performed in London [RB]. He also wrote on 6 July to William Rothenstein, who visited him. (See Lago, *Imperfect Encounter*, pp. 116–17.)

6 Kartik and Agrahayan: Bengali months corresponding to mid-Oct.–mid-Nov. and mid-Nov.–mid-Dec., respectively. RT actually departed for India on 4 Sept., less than two months after writing to Mira.
7 *The Gardener* (poems) and *Sadhana* (lectures) were published in Oct. by Macmillan.
8 *The Crescent Moon*, poems from *Shishu* (Infant), was published in late 1913, with a beautiful cover design in gold by Thomas Sturge Moore.
9 *Bouma*: Pratima, wife of Rathindranath Tagore.

67

To Frederik van Eeden[1]

With the publication of the Macmillan edition of *Gitanjali* in March 1913, Tagore began to be read in Europe too, and soon there were plans to translate his work from English into various European languages. His translator into Dutch was a well-known writer, Frederik van Eeden, a physician who had founded an agricultural colony in 1898 based on the ideas of Thoreau. Tagore had hardly any physical contact with van Eeden, though he did visit him at his colony in 1920, but considerable correspondence. The tone of van Eeden's letters was from the first demanding, obsessive, slightly unhinged (towards the end of his life he became insane). While this did not fail to strike Rabindranath as odd, it also called forth from him some profound remarks, such as in this letter.[2]

16 More's Garden, Cheyne Walk,
[London, UK][3]
4 August 1913

Dear friend

I have not yet got my release from my doctor's hands and also I am engaged in making arrangements to publish my next book of poems, and my lectures in book form.[4] This detains me in England. I have a great desire to travel through the Continent and visit countries of which I have read in books. But I am not quite sure whether I shall ever be able to accomplish it as I have my son and daughter-in-law with me, and travelling in your countries is too expensive for my resources.

Believe me, my friend, my heart goes out to you but I am inarticulate. I have to speak to you in a language not my own. The best that I have in me I give out in songs – no, I cannot even say that I give it out – it comes out of itself. The superconscious self of mine which has its expression in beauty is beyond my control – and my ordinary self is stupid and awkward before men. Very often I think and feel that I am like a flute – the flute that cannot talk but when the breath is upon it, can sing. I am sure you have seen me in my book and I shall never be able to make myself seen to you when we meet – for the body of the lamp is dark, it has no expression, only its flame has language.

I find I have made many friends whom I am not likely to meet – but I meet and receive them in my God – I offer to them my gratitude and love through my daily worship.

Very sincerely yours
Rabindranath Tagore

Source: MS copy at Rabindra Bhavan, Shantiniketan.

1 Frederik Willem van Eeden (1860–1932): writer and physician; in 1922 he became a Roman Catholic. From 1913, he translated about ten of RT's books. See 'Tagore in Holland', in Sahitya Akademi, *Rabindranath Tagore*, pp. 309–12.)
2 In a letter of 26 Jan. 1921, RT told Macmillan (UK) that van Eeden was 'an unpractical man, very likely with a vague sense of responsibility' [BL]. According to Rathindranath Tagore, who accompanied his father to van Eeden's colony in Holland,

> Van Eeden was a disillusioned idealist and as a reaction to the inhumanity of the war he was trying to establish a colony where plain living and high thinking would be strictly followed. The difficulty arose when his disciples preferred easy living on the plea of high thinking. Van Eeden's colony met the same fate as all previous attempts by unpractical idealists at establishing utopias in this selfish material world of ours. (*Edges of Time*, p. 130)

3 RT was then staying in a flat lent to him by Harriet Moody.
4 See letter 65, n. 8.

68

To (Sir) William Rothenstein

By mid-August 1913, with his health improved, Tagore was anxious to be on his way to Bengal. Most of his literary friends were away at this time and it appears that William Rothenstein persuaded Rabindranath to stay a little longer, so there could be a farewell dinner for him.[1] This was attended by Rothenstein, Yeats and Ernest Rhys, amongst others.[2] Shortly after, on 4 September, Tagore and his party sailed from Liverpool for India. From on board ship, Rabindranath sent this farewell message to his friend.

SS *City of Lahore* [en route to India]
7 September 1913[3]

Beloved friend, this is just to let you know that it is an uninterrupted delight to me, these days on the sea, full of the sunlight and leisure. The first two days were grey but now that the curtain has been raised I am listening to the duet of the gold and blue, of the silence and sound, of the sky and the sea. This dancing sea seems like a maiden heartfree laughing at the lavish gold of love offered to her feet by the pale sky. My heart is like a greedy bee wallowing in the honey-cells of a gorgeous cluster of forget-me-nots – its wings have grown languid and silent. Kali Mohan[4] and myself, two solitary souls, take our chairs in the loneliest corner of the deck and pass our days in silence while our fellow passengers are busy with their endless schemes of amusements. They do not molest us in any way except a missionary who takes every opportunity of impressing upon my mind the superiority of Christianity over Hinduism. He is after my immortal soul, lying in wait for it, like a cat for a bird. I can see from this window poor Kali Mohan is caught; I should come to his rescue but that would only add to the number of victims.[5]

We are just passing through Gibraltar – the rock looks like a dozing sentry, in the early morning light. My love to you all.

Ever yours
Rabindranath Tagore

124   *Selected letters of Rabindranath Tagore*

[PS] Have you asked for Macmillan's consent for publishing *The King* in the *Nation*?[6] I do not know where Mrs Moody is – I am sending a letter to her addressing it to your care.[7]

Source: MS original in Rothenstein Papers [Harvard]; letter published in Lago (ed.), *Imperfect Encounter*, pp. 119–20.

1 See Lago (ed.), *Imperfect Encounter*, pp. 119 and 120, n. 1.
2 See Rothenstein, *Men and Memories*, p. 269.
3 The date should probably be 8 Sept. (Lago (ed.), *Imperfect Encounter*, p. 120, n. 1).
4 Kali Mohan: Kali Mohan Ghosh.
5 See letter 69.
6 Macmillan did not consent to the *Nation*'s publishing RT's play, *The King of the Dark Chamber*; in 1914 it was published by Macmillan as a book. See Lago (ed.), *Imperfect Encounter*, pp. 170–3.
7 Harriet Moody was staying at Rothenstein's house in Hampstead, until she was well enough to return to the USA early in October.

69

To Harriet Moody[1]

Harriet Moody, Tagore's closest American friend, had been a generous hostess to Tagore, first in Chicago and New York, subsequently in London, where she invited him to stay in her flat. He, for his part, had been of great solace to her (see letter 59). On 7 September, after parting from Rabindranath, she told him in a letter: 'Think of me as one you have blessed beyond belief.'[2] Tagore replied from his steamer, which was now well over half way to India.

SS *City of Lahore* [en route to India]
15 September 1913

My friend, your letter was an unexpected pleasure to me – it was our final handshake on the shore of Europe, at least, for this voyage. The sea is perfectly smooth, the sky is gracious, and our days seem to drop from some heavenly orchard, ripe and soft and full to the core with golden nectar.

The passengers had their fancy-dress ball last night; and this morning – it being Sunday – they had their divine service. I was not present, but my good friend Kali Mohan was. The minister in his sermon made a most violent attack against our society and religion. Kali Mohan could not endure it and he gave a spirited answer when the service was over. Of all the amusements we had on board the steamer this was by far the best. For we could never imagine people's using God's service as a fancy dress while paying compliment to the devil.

Perhaps you are on the sea this moment, if not I hope the generous sunshine that we are enjoying is being lavished on you in that shady corner of the balcony at Hampstead.

At every meal we have here we miss the kind presence of Miss Kellogg, the Guardian Angel of our dining table at More's Garden.[3] Break the news to her gently that we are suffering from an unmitigated famine of icecream and there is not the faintest shadow of hope of lemon pie to relieve the severity of our privation.

Our love to you,

Ever yours
Rabindranath Tagore

[PS] I send a list of the names of our American friends whose photos I should be glad to have in a portfolio as a souvenir.[4]

Source: MS original at Rabindra Bhavan, Shantiniketan.

1 Harriet Converse Moody (1857–1932): literary patron; widow of William Vaughn Moody (1869–1910), whom she married in 1909. In an obituary note on her, Harriet Monroe wrote:

> I shall always remember with gratitude her generous hospitality to Rabindranath Tagore, when, at my suggestion, he came to Chicago from Urbana, with his student son and lovely daughter-in-law, for a brief visit in January 1913. He was then unknown except for *Poetry*'s first English printing of some of his *Gitanjali* in December, and Mrs Moody could have had no idea whether her three guests from Bengal would fit into the daily scheme of an American household. That she found them most adaptable and companionable, and formed a lasting friendship with the distinguished poet of the East, was her well-deserved reward. (*Poetry*, April 1932, p. 53)

Moody shared what she called RT's 'belief in art as the one influence for creating a consciousness of human brotherhood' (Moody to RT, 24 Jan. 1924 [RB]).

2 Moody to RT, 7 Sept. 1913 [RB]. This must be the letter to which RT refers, though it seems to have reached RT on board ship surprisingly fast.
3 Edith Kellogg 'had been a member of [Harriet Moody's] household in the undergraduate days at the University of Chicago and returned in 1912 to be her secretary' (Dunbar, *A House in Chicago*, p. 74).
4 RT wrote the list on a bridge scorecard!

6 Rabindranath in Calcutta, 1914

The Nobel prize (1913–1914)

Introduction

The Nobel prize for literature was awarded to Tagore in late 1913 largely on the strength of his translations of *Gitanjali*, which had been revised by W. B. Yeats. The diverse body of his work written in Bengali, of which *Gitanjali* was by no means typical, played little or no part in the decision of the Swedish Academy. Thus, at the outset, Tagore's western literary fame was based on a misapprehension.

Outside India, the award was greeted with surprise and, particularly in Britain, a degree of hostility, especially from those who felt that Thomas Hardy should have won – though Tagore's admirers, such as William Rothenstein, Yeats and Thomas Sturge Moore, were delighted. In Bengal, there was rejoicing, even by Rabindranath's many detractors. About a week after the announcement, some five hundred Calcutta citizens went by special train to Shantiniketan to felicitate Rabindranath.

He delivered a stinging rebuke to this deputation. He was unable to accept praise from people who did not appreciate his work, and the fact that the praise was offered simply because a foreign readership had shown its appreciation struck him as doubly insincere. Indeed, from the moment he heard about the award on 14 November, he was filled with a mixture of pleasure and regret. All great artists wish to be appreciated with genuine discrimination; they are keenly sensitive to both criticism (of course) and also to praise given for the wrong reasons. In Tagore's case, his sensitivity was accentuated by the political dominance of Bengal by a European power.

70

To Charles Freer Andrews[1]

Tagore landed at Bombay on 27 September 1913, and arrived in Calcutta two days later. In both places he was effusively welcomed. He had been away from Bengal for well over a year. C. F. Andrews, whom he had first befriended in London in July 1912, had returned to India in late 1912, where he had begun to speak enthusiastically about Rabindranath to the viceroy, Lord Hardinge, and many others; he also spent his first extended period in Shantiniketan, in mid-1913, in Tagore's absence. Andrews' mind was in turmoil, as he contemplated leaving his missionary life in Delhi and joining Tagore in Shantiniketan, which he would finally do in 1914.[2] On 1 September, he wrote to Rabindranath: 'All the anxieties, about which I have written to you, are passing away.

128   Selected letters of Rabindranath Tagore

I can quietly leave them all now in God's hands and enter into His peace.'³ Rabindranath's reply is in a similar spirit, thus establishing the confessional tone of their entire prolific correspondence until Andrews' death in 1940 (leavened in Tagore's case by an affectionate teasing of Andrews not evident in this particular letter).

Calcutta, [India]
11 October 1913

Dear Friend

I am sending you in a separate registered cover the manuscript of *Gitanjali* second series so that we may be able to discuss them when we meet next.⁴ I have gone through a period of difficulty. My life had appeared to me lonely and burdened with responsibilities too heavy for a single man to bear. Evidently my mind has got into a habit of leaning too much upon my friends whom I had acquired in England, and letting most of its current flow outward. Therefore, coming to my own country, where the contact of humanity is not so close as in the West, I felt suddenly stranded and in a desolation, wherein every individual has to struggle through his own problem unaided. For some length of time, solitariness weighed upon my heart like a heavy load, till I gained my former mental adjustment and felt again the current turn inward from the world outside. Now I feel the flood-tide of life and companionship. It sweeps the burden from off my shoulders and carries me along with it on its joyous course.

Please let me know how is Mr Rudra and give him my love and *namashkar*.⁵

Ever yours
Rabindranath Tagore

Source: MS copy at Rabindra Bhavan, Shantiniketan.

1 Charles Freer Andrews (1871–1940): Christian missionary and 'friend of India'. Andrews, a fellow of Pembroke College, Cambridge, joined the Cambridge Mission at St Stephen's College, Delhi, in 1904. After 1914, he ceased to think of himself as a missionary and identified wholeheartedly with Indians, in particular Tagore and Gandhi. Though he travelled a great deal, he regarded India as his home for the rest of his life. See Tinker, *Ordeal of Love*; also RT's obituary 'Charlie Andrews', *VBQ*, 6, No. 1, May 1940, pp. 1–6.
2 See Tinker, *Ordeal of Love*, pp. 69–76.
3 Andrews to RT, 1 Sept. 1913 [RB].
4 Despite RT's apology to W. B. Yeats for allowing Andrews to interfere with the translation of *Gitanjali* (see letter 57), he continued to place some faith in Andrews' literary judgement almost until the end; generally, however, he allowed the judgement of others in England to take final precedence. Still, Andrews must bear some responsibility for the poor quality of most translations of Tagore poetry published by Macmillan from 1914 onwards.
5 Susil Rudra (1861–1925): Bengali Christian missionary and father figure to Andrews; he was principal, St Stephen's College, Delhi, from 1907 to 1923.

71

To (Sir) William Rothenstein

After a short period in Calcutta, Tagore returned to Shantiniketan, where the process of readjustment to Bengal continued. Calcutta always agitated his mind, while the landscape of Shantiniketan almost always worked a calming magic. This letter to

The Nobel prize

William Rothenstein (who never visited him there) expresses Rabindranath's feeling for Shantiniketan beautifully, partly through the contrast he draws with the English landscape in autumn and winter.

Shantiniketan, [West Bengal, India]
20 October 1913

My dear friend

I wish I had not to write to you letters but could have you by my side – for I know you would have enjoyed everything I have here around me. It has already become difficult for me to bring before my mind your October landscape dim with mist and numb with creeping cold.[1] As I sit writing to you all the doors of my room are wide open and the stainless golden light of this late autumn is pouring in from all sides flooding my brain with its quivering stream of radiance. The glistening green of the heavy foliage of the tall *shal* trees soaring in the clear blue sky seems to me like an outburst of music from the heart of the earth. I can assure you this is the most beautiful spot of land that I can ever hope to find anywhere. I do not expect every stranger to share my enthusiasm for this place, for until one's life is in harmony with his surroundings one can never see nature in her truth. The life I have been living here for years has helped me to understand the language of the spirit of this place. In spite of the admiration I have for your civilisation I cannot but wish from the depth of my heart that you could come to us in our ashram and share our simple lives filling your leisure with utmost peace and beauty. Of all the friends I have in the West I think of you as the one who ought to have been born as my brother in this country, knowing that you have the power to utilise to their best purposes the opportunities that India, of all countries in the world, offers to men. But with all my attractions for India in its various aspects I cannot but marvel at the fact that my best friends are in England and it took some weeks for me to adjust my mind to my old familiar surroundings where you were absent. With my best love to you

I am

Ever yours
Rabindranath Tagore

Source: MS original in Rothenstein Papers [Harvard]; letter published in Lago (ed.), *Imperfect Encounter*, pp. 127–8.

1 In his reply, Rothenstein remarked: 'Your year with us must seem like a dream to you' (11 Nov. 1913, in Lago (ed.), *Imperfect Encounter*, p. 130).

72

To Edward John Thompson[1]

On Tagore's return to India, he struck up a relationship with Edward J. Thompson, who in the 1920s wrote the first major biography of Tagore in English. Thompson was a missionary, like C. F. Andrews, but the two men were of very different background and temperament. At the time of his first meeting with Tagore, at Jorasanko, in late

October 1913, Thompson had been for three years the principal of the high school attached to the Wesleyan college in Bankura, some fifty miles from Shantiniketan. He was keen to capture Tagore for a visit there – but Rabindranath blew hot and cold and finally never came to see Thompson at his college. This initial note of awkwardness is present throughout the long and significant correspondence of Tagore and Thompson.

Shantiniketan, [West Bengal, India]
2 November 1913

Dear Mr Thompson

Many thanks for your very kind letter. I do not think I shall be free to visit your institution before the last week of January, next year. But I must not have any public reception given to me while I am there. I shall be happy to meet your boys quietly but I hope I shall not be asked to take part in any public function.

Mr Palit's London address is as follows: 2 Fitzallan Road, Church End, Finchley.[2]

Very sincerely yours
Rabindranath Tagore

Source: MS original in Thompson Papers [Bodleian].

1 Edward John Thompson (1886–1946): biographer of RT, poet, novelist, translator and publicist of the cause of Indian independence. His relationship with Tagore and more generally with India was brilliantly analysed by his son E. P. Thompson in *Alien Homage*. See also Harish Trivedi's introduction to the 1991 edition of E. J. Thompson's biography, *Rabindranath Tagore*.
2 Thompson's letter to RT does not survive, but it appears that he had discussed a visit to Bankura when he met RT at Jorasanko and then followed up his talk with a written invitation. Thompson told his mother in a letter that RT had said: 'I shd like to . . . If Lakshman were there, I wd. But I know no one there' (Thompson to Elizabeth Thompson, 30 Oct. 1913 [Thompson Papers, Bodleian]). Lakshman was RT's friend Loken Palit (Thompson must have misheard the name), who had been stationed as a judge in Bankura from 1912 to April 1913, before retirement from the ICS. Thompson knew Palit and may have been introduced to RT's poetry by Palit (see E. P. Thompson, *Alien Homage*, p. 26). Later in 1913, Palit joined his wife, Mabel, in England (see letter 65, n. 15).

73

To (Sir) William Rothenstein

Tagore heard that he had been awarded the Nobel prize on 14 November 1913. Reactions to the news varied wildly. His closest friends in England, such as William Rothenstein, were thrilled,[1] but English literary circles as a whole were sceptical and even hostile, especially as Thomas Hardy had been passed over. In Bengal, and in other parts of India, the prize was a signal for national celebration, though few of those celebrating had read much, if any, of Tagore's work, even among Bengalis; indeed many of the celebrators in Bengal were detractors of Rabindranath. In Shantiniketan, the boys in the school were thrilled. Rabindranath's own initial reaction, as quoted by E. J. Thompson, who happened to be visiting Shantiniketan on 14 November, was: 'I shall get no peace now, Mr Thompson. I shall be worried with appeals, all kinds of people will be writing to me. Do you know, Mr Thompson, sometimes I feel as if it were too much for me, as if I could bear it no longer.'² In this letter written to Rothenstein four days later, Tagore gives vent to his mixed feelings.

Shantiniketan, [West Bengal, India]
18 November 1913

My dear friend

The very first moment I received the message of the great honour conferred on me by the award of the Nobel prize my heart turned towards you with love and gratitude. I felt certain that of all my friends none would be more glad at this news than you. Honour's crown of honour is to know that it will rejoice the hearts of those whom we hold the most dear. But, all the same, it is a very great trial for me. The perfect whirlwind of public excitement it has given rise to is frightful. It is almost as bad as tying a tin can to a dog's tail making it impossible for him to move without creating noise and collecting crowds all along.[3] I am being smothered with telegrams and letters for the last few days and the people who have never had any friendly feelings towards me nor ever read a line of my works are loudest in their protestations of joy. I cannot tell you how tired I am of all this shouting, the stupendous amount of its unreality being something appalling. Really these people honour the honour in me and not myself. The only thing that compensates for this is the unfeigned joy and pride that the boys of my school feel at this occasion. They are having festivities and making the most of me.[4]

I know how glad Mrs Rothenstein must have been at my great good fortune – please give her my kindest remembrances and love to the children.

Yours
Rabindranath Tagore

Source: MS original in Rothenstein Papers [Harvard]; letter published in Lago (ed.), *Imperfect Encounter*, p. 140.

1 Rothenstein wrote to RT on 15 Nov. 1913: 'Never I think did ampler reward fit ampler merit; your pilgrimage is one of the romances of literature' (Lago (ed.), *Imperfect Encounter*, p. 139).
2 E. P. Thompson, *Alien Homage*, p. 115.
3 RT used this image of dog and tin can more than once at this time, but he later modified it diplomatically to reduce the offence felt by Bengalis. (See Dutta and Robinson, *Rabindranath Tagore*, pp. 183, 415.)
4 See E. J. Thompson's description in E. P. Thompson, *Alien Homage*, pp. 114–15.

74

To Edward John Thompson

E. J. Thompson spent some hours with Tagore during his visit to Shantiniketan on 14–15 November 1913, discussing emendations made by Thompson to Tagore's unpublished translations of his poetry. Rabindranath encouraged him to use his pencil, according to a private account of the meeting written by Thompson on 17 November. 'I should be greatly obliged if you would run a pencil over them and improve their diction and rhythm,' Tagore is quoted as saying. 'I demurred, but he meant what he said.' A little later, Thompson told Tagore, 'You know, the English of

Gitanjali astonished us.' 'It surprised *me*. They tell me it is very good, but I did not know it was. You know, Mr Thompson, I am not really at home in English. I can't tell which is the better rhythm of the two.'[1]

While there is no reason to doubt this part of the account, as far as it goes, Thompson appears to have failed to perceive Tagore's subtler signals. Rabindranath wanted corrections to his grammar and perhaps to other aspects of his translations, but his pride rebelled against accepting extensive corrections, especially from someone of low literary standing, as compared to W. B. Yeats and others in England. The letter he now wrote Thompson – disrupted by the immediate effects of winning the Nobel prize – reflects his well-established ambivalence about translation, as well as Thompson.

Shantiniketan, [West Bengal, India]
18 November 1913

Dear Mr Thompson

I hope we are friends and you will not misunderstand me. I have done a wrong to you and I must ask your pardon for it. While you were minutely going over my MSS your very kindness embarrassed me and prevented me from being frank with you – which was foolish on my part and absurdly oriental – and for which I have been feeling ashamed ever since. The *Gitanjali* poems are intimately personal to me and the pleasure I have of polishing their English versions is of a different nature [from] that of an author revising his works for publication.[2] Every line of these should be as closely my own as possible though I must labour under the disadvantage of not being born to your language. In such a case I have to be guided by my instinct, allowing it to work almost unconsciously without being hindered by more than casual suggestions from outside. I think the method that Yeats followed while editing my book was the right one in selecting those poems that required least alterations and rejecting others in spite of their merits. There is a grave risk of my overlooking crudities of language – the evidence of which you will find in *The Gardener* – but still I must go on with my work unaided till I have done what is in my power to do.[3]

20 Nov. Thursday

There has been an immense deal of interruption since I began writing this letter and in the meanwhile I have got your letter with your book of poems, confirming my suspicion that you were a poet.[4] This accounts for the way you attracted my confidence almost before I was aware of it. I hope it will ripen into intimacy.

My complaint against most of the missionaries of all creeds – including Brahmos – is that they lack imagination. You cannot preach love of God unless you are immersed in it heart and soul. There is no 'ought' about it – you can only give the best things of life not because you should but because you have [to]. The preaching of the message of God can never be made into a profession – God sends his own messengers. As poets cannot be made to order [neither can] missionaries. However, this is my opinion and this, I am sure, will never act as a barrier against my making friends with individuals who happen to be missionaries.[5]

Yours
Rabindranath Tagore

Source: MS original in Thompson Papers [Bodleian].

1 Quoted in E. P. Thompson, *Alien Homage*, pp. 110–11.
2 The content of these MSS is not clear; presumably they included some translations from the Bengali *Gitanjali* and other similar devotional poetry which had not been included in the English *Gitanjali* and in *The Gardener*.
3 *The Gardener* was published in Oct. 1913. RT had received copies, but Thompson had yet to receive the book; he therefore borrowed a copy from RT.
4 By 1913, Thompson had published three volumes of his own verse, probably at his own expense.
5 For RT's reaction to missionaries at his meeting with Thompson in Shantiniketan, see E. P. Thompson, *Alien Homage*, p. 117.

75

To Gopal Krishna Gokhale[1]

The second half of 1913 was a turbulent period for Indians living in South Africa, led by Mohandas Karamchand Gandhi, a name then virtually unknown in India. Their non-violent protests against the racist government were brutally repressed. G. K. Gokhale, the leading Indian moderate nationalist of the time (later Gandhi's mentor), was stirred and decided to campaign in India for money to help the cause in South Africa.[2] The amount raised was less than he hoped, but it included a donation from C. F. Andrews; and in late November, following a public statement by the viceroy, Lord Hardinge, in support of the Indians in South Africa, Gokhale asked Andrews to travel to South Africa as his representative.[3] Tagore, as a friend of Andrews, was kept fully informed by him of Gokhale's efforts to raise funds. He tried to collect some money himself at Shantiniketan, and it is this which forms the subject of his letter to Gokhale.

Shilida, [Shelidah, Khulna, Bangladesh]
9 December 1913

Dear Mr Gokhale

I have been feeling much concerned since I learnt from Mr Andrews about your poor state of health. I wish I could feel assured that you would be persuaded to give yourself the necessary rest. You must remember that for men like you to live is itself a service to your country – for your life is not merely useful, it is a light to others. We cannot spare you.

I am ashamed to own that the response has been feeble in Bengal to the call of our countrymen in trouble in South Africa. But I can assure you that my boys' hearts were moved to genuine sympathy when appealed to and little though these children were able to raise for the fund it was not the less valuable in its moral worth. I am sure they will be delighted at the message of encouragement coming from you. I am at present away from them but hope to be shortly back in Bolpur, and if I can manage to be in Calcutta when you are there, it will be a great pleasure to see you once more.

Believe me

Very sincerely yours
Rabindranath Tagore

Source: MS copy at Rabindra Bhavan, Shantiniketan.

134   Selected letters of Rabindranath Tagore

1 Gopal Krishna Gokhale (1866–1915): social reformer and leader of the moderate Indian nationalists; he was among the first Indians to recognise Gandhi's future role in India.
2 See B. R. Nanda, *Gokhale* (New Delhi, 1977), pp. 426ff.
3 See Tinker, *Ordeal of Love*, pp. 76–9.

76

To (Sir) William Rothenstein

All of Tagore's letters to William Rothenstein written in the immediate aftermath of the Nobel prize (letters 73, 76 and 77) harp on the same theme: his dislike of the sudden publicity thrust upon him by the award. On 23 November 1913, a crowd of about five hundred Calcutta citizens hired a special train and descended on the ashram at Shantiniketan to felicitate the poet. A few were his close friends, but the majority were strangers; and not a few had maligned him in print and by word of mouth. (Conversation on the train turned around the financial, rather than the literary value of the Nobel prize.[1]) Rabindranath, in his reply to the speeches in his honour, let fly with his contempt for those who had waited for the western seal of approval before showing any appreciation of him. 'No literary work can have its quality or appeal enhanced by the Nobel prize.' Employing the dog-and-tin-can analogy he had used to Rothenstein (letter 73), he concluded: 'This day of mine will not last forever. The ebbtide will set in again. Then all the squalor of the muddy bottom will be exposed in bank after bank.'[2] The Bengali press in Calcutta responded to his rebuke with predictable hostility. Rabindranath refused to withdraw his comments, but thereafter kept his peace.

After seeing off C. F. Andrews from Calcutta on his way to South Africa, on 6 December Tagore retreated to Shelidah for a few days, and then returned to the city. There he was obliged to attend a number of receptions in his honour; and, after returning to Shantiniketan for the 7 Paush festival, he went back to Calcutta to receive an honorary doctorate from the viceroy, Lord Hardinge, on behalf of the University of Calcutta, on 26 December.

[Shelidah, Khulna, Bangladesh]
10 December 1913

My friend, my days are riddled all over with interruptions, they are becoming perfectly useless to me. I am worn out writing letters, distributing thanks by handfuls and receiving visitors. I cannot tell you how unsuitable this sudden eruption of honour is to a man of my temperament. The winter sun is sweet, the green is luxuriant all around me – I want to be gloriously idle and let my thoughts melt and mingle in the blue of the space. I am beginning to envy the birds that sing and gladly go without honour. I was watching a calf this morning, tired of browsing, basking in the sun on the grass, supinely happy and placid; it made my heart ache with the desire to be one with the great life that surrounds this earth and to be able to be peacefully joyous in the simple enjoyment of the wealth lavished everywhere without being asked. But my mind is invaded and my time is wasted with things that are of the least significance to the inner

The Nobel prize 135

[life]. Perhaps you will smile and think this mood of mine absurdly oriental – but still it has its truth which must not be overlooked.

With love I am

Ever yours
Rabindranath Tagore

Source: MS original in Rothenstein Papers [Harvard]; letter published in Lago (ed.), *Imperfect Encounter*, p. 143.

1 Paul, *Rabijibani*, VI, p. 448.
2 Quoted in Chaudhuri, *Thy Hand*, p. 623 (trans. by Chaudhuri)/*CMG*, 13 Sept. 1941, p. 80.

77

To (Sir) William Rothenstein

[Calcutta, India]
16 December 1913

My dear Friend, . . .

My ordeal is not yet over. I still have dinners to attend to, and listen to speeches in praise of my genius, and to answer them in a becoming spirit of modesty.[1] This has brought me to Calcutta and kept me in our Jorasanko lane, while the mustard fields are in bloom in Shilida [Shelidah] and wild ducks have set up their noisy households in the sandbanks of the Padma. I have already raised a howl of protests and vilifications in our papers by saying in plain words what was in my mind to a deputation who had come to Bolpur to offer me congratulations. This has been a relief to me – for honour is a heavy enough burden even when it is real but intolerable when meaningless and devoid of sincerity. However, I must not complain. Let me patiently wait for the time when all this tumult will be a thing of the past and truth will shine and peace will come even to a man whom West has thought fit to honour.

Ever yours
Rabindranath Tagore

Source: MS original in Rothenstein Papers [Harvard]; letter published in Lago (ed.), *Imperfect Encounter*, pp. 143–4.

1 One such dinner was given by the Orient Club, Calcutta, and was attended by Ramsay MacDonald (then in India as a member of the Royal Commission on Public Services in India). An evocative photograph of the diners, almost all Bengalis dressed in either dinner jackets or Bengali dress, appears in the *CMG*.

78

To Harriet Monroe[1]

Poetry magazine in Chicago published two batches of verse by Tagore, in December 1912 and June 1913. After the Nobel prize, Harriet Monroe wrote to congratulate

136   Selected letters of Rabindranath Tagore

Rabindranath and to request more of his work.[2] His reply shows that, regardless of the prize, he remained acutely aware of the defects in his translations.

Shantiniketan, [West Bengal, India]
31 December 1913

Dear Miss Monroe

My destiny is furiously amusing herself [by] showering upon me dry leaves of correspondence thick and fast – and when, hidden among them, come down by chance a few stray flowers of friendship I have very little breath left to receive them with any show of welcome. Your last letter is of such a kind lying on my table in apparent neglect. I know you will pardon me and will have some sympathy for a poet whose latest acquisition in the shape of honour can, by no means, be described as a feather in his cap, judged by its weight. But still I must bear it proudly, rejoicing in the fact that the East and the West ever touch each other like twin gems in the circlet of humanity, that they had met long before Kipling was born and will meet long after his name is forgotten.[3]

I have been polishing the English versions of some of my narrative poems since we last met. I find it difficult to impart to them the natural vigour of the original poems. Simplicity appears anaemic and spectre-like when she lacks her ruddy bloom of life, which is the case with these translations of mine. Some of these, with my latest revisions, have already appeared in the *Nation* in England, and as for the remaining ones are they worth the trouble of publishing?[4]

I am, dear friend,

Most sincerely yours
Rabindranath Tagore

Source: MS original in Monroe Papers [Chicago].

1 Harriet Monroe (1860–1936): founder and long-time editor of *Poetry: A Magazine of Verse*.
2 Monroe to RT, 23 Nov. 1913 [RB].
3 RT never showed any liking for Kipling's work in his occasional references to it, though he made a respectful comment when Kipling died in 1936.
4 The *Nation* published a series of poems and 'short studies' by RT from 28 June 1913 onwards. The editor, H. W. Massingham, told William Rothenstein, who had suggested the idea, 'His teaching is of the utmost importance to our time and people . . . Nothing like *Gitanjali* has ever appeared in an English dress since Wordsworth.' (Quoted in Alfred F. Havighurst, *Radical Journalist: H. W. Massingham* (Cambridge, 1974), p. 171.)

79

To Harriet Moody

The award of the Nobel prize began to attract foreign visitors to Tagore's school immediately; among them, in December 1913, were Ramsay MacDonald and Will Lawrence, brother of T. E. Lawrence. The stream would continue for the rest of Tagore's life. Gradually, Shantiniketan would become less of a shelter for Rabindranath and more of a show-place. His initial reaction emerges clearly in this letter to Harriet Moody, who had sheltered him in both Chicago and London.

The Nobel prize *137*

Shantiniketan, [West Bengal, India]
22 January 1914

My dear Friend,

I am still suffering from Nobel prize notoriety and I do not know what nursing home there is where I can go and get rid of this my latest and greatest trouble. To deprive me of my seclusion is like shelling an oyster – the rude touch of the curious world is all over me. – I am pining for the shade of obscurity. I hope you have not already tired of my name being discussed in every newspaper and you do not despise me who has been dragged from his nest of dreams into the most crowded market of public applause. Why do I not have a word of sympathy from you in my time of distress?[1]

I hope you have completely recovered from your illness.

Your affectionate friend
Rabindranath Tagore

Source: MS original in Moody Papers [Chicago].

1 Moody wrote to congratulate RT on 19 Nov. 1913 and again on 27 Dec., mentioning that everyone in Chicago was buying RT's books as gifts: 'parsimonious' Chicago booksellers could not get enough of them, she said [RB].

80

To Edward John Thompson

This letter establishes what would become a pattern in Tagore's behaviour after 1913. Shantiniketan and its concerns would hold him for a while, then he would become restless to escape its demands and its parochiality. In the early years after the Nobel award, Shelidah provided a convenient bolt-hole, later he went to other places.

Calcutta, [India]
15 February 1914

Dear Thompson

To the open road! I have fled away from my school and am going to take my shelter with the wild ducks, the belated stragglers who are still lingering in the sandbanks of the Padma. I fully agree with you that our people have no pity for men who have their works to do or their leisure to enjoy. That is why in India you must shun human habitation if *mukti* be your object.[1]

Please apply to Babu Santosh Ch. Majumdar of our school for photos of the Shantiniketan.[2]

Yours
Rabindranath Tagore

Source: MS original in Thompson Papers [Bodleian].

1 *mukti*: freedom. RT was responding to a comment by E. J. Thompson that his time was seldom his own at Bankura (Thompson to RT, 10 Feb. 1914 [RB]). Writing from Shelidah on 16 Feb. 1914 to another

foreigner, who had just visited Shantiniketan, RT said: 'Do not imagine me among the quivering shadows of our *shal* trees busy shedding old leaves and putting on new ones. I am floating down the Ganges in a boat while the post office is waving its letter bags in vain from the bank' (RT to Mr Young [Patrick Geddes Papers, Edinburgh]).
2 Santosh Chandra Majumdar (1886–1926): staff member at Shantiniketan; he trained in agricultural science at the University of Illinois with Rathindranath Tagore. Thompson had requested a photograph in his letter.

81

To Thomas Sturge Moore[1]

While Tagore fretted about the Bengali reaction to the Nobel prize, in Britain a somewhat similar spirit of criticism was abroad, complicated by the long-standing tension between Britons and Bengalis. For instance, in mid-December, the *New Statesman*, commenting on the prize and the sensational sale of Tagore's books as Christmas gifts, said waspishly: 'The unjustified boom we have always with us.'[2] In January, Thomas Sturge Moore, the poet who had nominated Tagore for the prize, remarked to him:

> I am often angered when references to you catch my eye in the papers now for there is an itch about them to treat you as unjustly as before they were fulsome in praise. Your having the Nobel prize when Hardy had been the official candidate of the Royal Society of Literature ... has made you a certain number of enemies whose ill will is not solely due to the fickleness of their minds.[3]

In another letter, Sturge Moore added: 'To be praised is sufficient reason why someone else should run you down ... As Flaubert used to say, "Fleas always jump onto clean linen". Your reputation is as tempting to the many human fleas as a clean sheet just home from the wash.'[4]

Rabindranath, replying to Sturge Moore's January letter, gives another instance of the complex feelings aroused in Bengal.

Shilida, [Shelidah, Khulna, Bangladesh]
17 February 1914

Dear Sturge Moore,

An incident will show you how the award of the Nobel prize has roused up antipathy and suspicion against me in certain quarters. A report has reached me from a barrister friend of mine who was present on the occasion when in a meeting of the leading Mohammedan gentlemen of Bengal Valentine Chirol told the audience that the English *Gitanjali* was practically a production of Yeats.[5] It is very likely he did not believe it himself, it being merely a political move on his part to minimise the significance of this Nobel prize affair which our people naturally consider to be a matter for national rejoicing. It is not possible for him to relish the idea of Mohammedans sharing this honour with Hindus. Unfortunately for me there are signs of this antagonism in England itself which may be partly due to the natural reaction following the chorus of praise that *Gitanjali* evoked and partly, as you have said in your letter, to the bitterness of disappointment in the minds of the partisans of the candidates for the Nobel prize. You know it had been the source of a rare great pleasure for me while

The Nobel prize

in England to be able to admire your manly power of appreciation which was without a tinge of meanness or jealousy. I could have gladly sacrificed my Nobel prize if I could be left to the enjoyment of this strong friendliness and true-hearted admiration.

I had forgotten to tell you how greatly we all admire your beautiful design on the cover of the *Crescent Moon*. It is perfect in its simplicity and grace.

You must have read in the papers that in Paris they are holding an exhibition of pictures by our modern Indian artists. I hope you will find time to go and see it and realise the stir of new life in Bengal that is breaking out in manifold expressions. The head of this art movement in our country is my nephew Abanindranath who is sure to receive recognition one day in Europe. I hear that Havell will try to exhibit these pictures in the South Kensington museum some time later on.[6]

I have got a copy of *Chitra* sent to me last week.[7] Its get-up is attractive and I hope it will not be deprived of its due because my books have been coming out in too quick a succession jostling each other. I am sure my publishers are not giving enough intervals to my readers for their appetite to be revived. However this must be said to my credit that the four poetical works of mine closely following each other are different in character – and by this time critics must be thinking of modifying their classification of my poems as mystic.[8] All poets have the sense of the infinite in some shape or other but it is their own keen sense of the finite that truly individualises them. It is not according to what they contemplate but what they definitely see that poets have to be classified.

It was difficult to believe when I saw Miss Cooper that she was dying.[9] She was so serenely radiant that she seemed less mortal than most other human beings. In fact, I felt an impulse of deeper life in my soul when I met her that evening. I must thank you for giving me the opportunity of knowing this woman in whom life triumphed so beautifully in the face of death.

Kindly remember me to Mrs Moore.[10]

Ever yours,
Rabindranath Tagore

Source: MS copy in Sturge Moore Papers [London]; letter published in *A Tagore Reader* (ed. Amiya Chakravarty; New York, 1961), pp. 21–3. The original MS was sold in London in 1959, and privately purchased. See *A Tagore Reader*, p. 378, n. 6.

1 Thomas Sturge Moore (1870–1944): poet and artist; he was a close friend of W. B. Yeats and the brother of the philosopher G. E. Moore.
2 13 Dec. 1913.
3 Sturge Moore to RT, 22 Jan. 1914 [RB].
4 Sturge Moore to RT, 7 April 1914 [RB].
5 The barrister friend was S. P. Sinha, later Lord Sinha (1863–1928), the first Indian advocate general of Bengal. He attended a party at the Calcutta Club on 16 Jan. 1914 in honour of Syed Shamsul Huda, a judge at the Calcutta High Court, at which Sir Valentine Chirol (1852–1929) was present. On Yeats' role in *Gitanjali*, see Dutta and Robinson, *Rabindranath Tagore*, pp. 183–4.
6 The Paris exhibition was opened by the president of France on 8 Feb. 1914. Afterwards, it toured Belgium and Holland and then came to London, where it was shown at the Imperial Institute in April–May 1914, under the aegis of the India Society. Despite the advocacy of Ernest Binfield Havell (1861–1934), retired principal of the Calcutta School of Art, English art critics were not enthusiastic. See Mitter, *Art and Nationalism*, pp. 324–6. RT's initial enthusiasm for the Bengal School cooled after his visit to Japan in 1916, and he came to share the response of the English critics (see letters 108, 109).
7 *Chitra* was published by the India Society in late 1913, and then by Macmillan in 1914. Writing to RT

on 7 Jan., William Rothenstein commented: 'Now the exquisite *Chitra* has appeared, in sable sari ornamented with the splendid red of an angry sunset' (Lago, *Imperfect Encounter*, p. 144).
8 *Gitanjali*, *The Gardener* and *The Crescent Moon* were published by Macmillan in 1913; the fourth book was presumably *Chitra*, a poetic drama.
9 Sturge Moore introduced RT to Edith Emma Cooper (1862–1913) in the summer of 1913. She described the meeting in her journal, *Works and Days*, which Sturge Moore edited and published in 1933 (see Michael Field, *Works and Days: From the Journal of Michael Field* (T. and D. C. Sturge Moore eds.; London, 1933), pp. 318–21). Cooper and Katharine Bradley were poets and dramatists who published jointly under the pseudonym Michael Field.
10 Mrs Moore: Marie Sturge Moore (1872–1957).

82

To (Sir) William Rothenstein

(incomplete)

This letter to William Rothenstein raises the same subject as the previous letter to Thomas Sturge Moore: the rumour that Yeats had been chiefly responsible for the success of the English *Gitanjali*. Tagore was understandably offended and perhaps wanted to forestall Rothenstein's hearing the rumour from some other source. A miasma of doubt had been created that was never entirely dispelled; it resurfaced between Tagore and Rothenstein in 1932 (see letter 263).

[Shelidah, Khulna, Bangladesh]
[February 1914][1]

... speeding across wild regions, making it impossible for me to guess his whereabouts. Pratima is in Ranchi and our Calcutta house is deserted.[2]

Suren has been translating one of my novels for the *Modern Review*.[3] Do you read it?

It will amuse you to learn that at a semi-public conference of the Mohammedan leaders of Bengal Valentine Chirol gave his audience to understand that the English *Gitanjali* was practically written by Yeats. Naturally such rumours get easy credence among our people who can believe in all kinds of miracles except genuine worth in their own men. It is annoyingly insulting for me to be constantly suspected of being capable of enjoying a reputation by fraud and it makes me wish that the chance had never been given to me to come out of the quiet corner of my obscurity. In your society the admiration that a poet or an artist can get is sometimes so alarmingly great that it is hardly pleasant for the recipient or healthy for the public. Too great [an] uprush of praise makes the atmosphere thick with the dust of envy and antagonism and of what avail can be the honour to a poet when his readers' minds become clouded and simple enjoyment of his works becomes difficult. When there was no printing press and people had to copy their favourite poems in their own hand admiration was genuine. There should be some difficulty in securing things you truly love and they should not be thrust upon you before you are ready to receive them. However it matters very little whoever is the author of a particular work so long as it is good. We do not know who painted the Ajanta pictures or who were the architects who built the Konarak temple. You have read my poem about the man whose harvest had been taken in the golden boat of time but he himself could not secure a place in it.[4] Our names can be spared but not our true works.

One thing is troubling my mind which I must tell you. You know my sister Mrs Ghosal who is an author. She is one of those unfortunate beings who has more ambition than abilities but just enough talent to keep her mediocrity alive for a short period of time. Her weakness has been taken advantage of by some unscrupulous literary agents in London and she has had her stories translated and published. I have given her no encouragement but I have not been successful in making her see things in their proper light. It is likely that she may go to England and use my name and you may meet her but be merciful to her and never let her harbour in her mind any illusion about her worth and her chance. I am afraid she will be a source of trouble to my friends who I hope will be candid to her for my sake and will not allow her to mistake ordinary politeness for encouragement.[5]

Arya Chaudhuri, my grand-nephew, has asked me to give him an introduction letter to you which I have gladly given.[6] He was in England for some years studying architecture and he is going back there to finish his course. He has not any particular talent or ambition so he is pleasant and companionable. I should be glad if you speak to him kindly and introduce him to some people worth knowing.

I am sure you are getting more and more surprised at the length of my letter. My letters to my English friends are usually short, not because of the shortness of my memory or thinness of my love or paucity of subjects. I know you will have no sympathy for me, for it is difficult for you to realise it, when I tell you your language is not easy for me to use. I know I am apt to make a mess of your prepositions and in my blissful ignorance I go on dropping your articles in wrong places or dropping them out altogether. Then I do not know set phrases which greatly economise trouble in sentence making and very often I do not know how to write simple matter-of-fact things in English. No wonder people can hardly believe that I had any hand in translating the poems of *Gitanjali*. You have the unfair advantage over me in not allowing me to answer your letters in Bengali – that would be returning tit for tat. This is the principle of vicarious punishment and I have to suffer for your ignorance of my language and I do not know if you do not have to suffer for my ignorance of yours – for, as your poet says, little learning is a dangerous thing.

I wonder if Mrs Rothenstein occasionally remembers the traveller from the far eastern shore who one day sat dreamily in her balcony under the shadow of the blossoming rose tree. I must not be forgotten because I was quiet and gave her far too little trouble to leave a lasting impression in her memory. She must know that there is a chance, however remote, of my visiting her again when it will be shameful if she cannot recognise me. But I must keep her supplied with my latest photographs. Give my love to her and to the children. When I promised you to send you dolls I did not realise that our people have grown old unawares and dolls have become scarce in our country. But do not despair; dolls are immortal and children. They are somewhere in hiding just now and they will come forth.[7]

Yours
Rabindranath Tagore

Source: MS original in Rothenstein Papers [Harvard]; letter published in Lago (ed.), *Imperfect Encounter*, pp. 146–8, 150.

1 A page (or pages) is missing from this letter. The missing bit must have dealt partly with publishing matters (India Society versus Macmillan), since Rothenstein responded on these points in his letter of 9 March (Lago (ed.), *Imperfect Encounter*, pp. 153–5). RT's letter was almost certainly written in Shelidah and at the same time as his letter to Thomas Sturge Moore of 17 February (letter 81) – perhaps even on the same day – judging by its content and time of arrival in Britain.
2 Rathindranath Tagore started a motor engineering business at this time. It was a failure commercially, but it gave Rathindranath the excuse to try out various new models of cars by touring them in Bengal and neighbouring areas. See Rathindranath Tagore, *Edges of Time*, p. 92. On this occasion his wife Pratima seems to have stopped off at Ranchi to see the family (see letter 41 and note); but sometimes she accompanied her husband. On 10 March, RT told Harriet Moody, 'After a long wild career in their motor car Rathi and Pratima have at last joined me in my school' [Moody Papers, Chicago].
3 Novel: 'Eyesore', *MR*, Jan.–Dec. 1914/*Chokher Bali*, *RR*, III, pp. 281–512 (trans. Surendranath Tagore). Krishna Kripalani translated the novel as *Binodini* (New Delhi, 1959).
4 'The Golden Boat', *Selected Poems* (trans. William Radice; rev. edn, London, 1987), p. 53/'Shonar Tari', *RR*, III, pp. 7–8.
5 Swarna Kumari Ghoshal (Tagore) (1856?–1932): writer of novels and short stories, editor of *Bharati* (1885–1905, 1909–15); she was the first Bengali female novelist. Her first book was published in Bengali in 1870. Two of her novels were published in London, both by T. Werner Laurie: *An Unfinished Song*, in late 1913 (translation of *Kahake*), and *The Fatal Garland*, in 1915 (translation of *Phuler Mala*). The press notices for the first book printed at the front of the second book suggest that *An Unfinished Song* made little impression in Britain, except perhaps as an indication of the social progress of Indian women. It seems probable that both books were published at their author's expense, as suggested by RT in his letter with regard to the first book. Certainly Rothenstein's reaction to the first book, before he received RT's letter, was tepid: 'As it stands it cannot arouse much interest. The peep into a girl's heart is touching enough, but its psychology is a little too unsearching for an European audience' (Rothenstein to RT, 2 March 1914, in Lago (ed.), *Imperfect Encounter*, p. 152). Two chapters of the book in a modern translation appear in Susie Tharu and K. Lalita, (eds.), *Women Writing in India: 600 BC to the Present: I, 600 BC to the Early 20th Century* (New York, 1991), pp. 239–43. RT's criticism seems fair enough, if unnecessarily caustic in its phrasing.
6 Arya Chaudhuri: son of Ashutosh Chaudhuri, who married Pratibha, daughter of RT's elder brother Hemendranath.
7 The dolls were despatched on 1 March. See Lago (ed.), *Imperfect Encounter*, pp. 150–1.

83

To Edward John Thompson

E. J. Thompson thought there was 'no greater short story writer in the world's literature' than Tagore – yet he entirely omitted the short stories from his major study of Tagore.[1] E. P. Thompson, in his detailed analysis of the reasons for this, concluded that his father had probably been 'too much wounded' by his own role in translating the stories to 'commit himself in public'.[2] For some eight years from 1914 E. J. Thompson had been 'alternately discouraged and encouraged' to help in translating the stories, with almost no public recognition of his hard work from either Tagore or Macmillan.[3] 'Those who feed the fires of genius can expect no reward but burnt fingers' (E. P. Thompson).[4]

While this is absolutely true, it must also be said that Tagore was virtually bound to be disappointed by *any* translation of his short stories, including his own. So nuanced is their psychology and their irony, and so deeply rooted are they in Bengali life of Tagore's time, that they require a translator who is equally fluent in Bengali and English, and of considerable creativity, to do them full justice. Tagore understood this from the beginning; E. J. Thompson never fully grasped it.

The Nobel prize

This letter shows Rabindranath's early attempt to grapple with this virtually insoluble difficulty.

Shilida, [Shelidah, Khulna, Bangladesh]
18 February 1914

Dear Thompson

The weather proving unfavourable I had to leave my boat and take shelter in our Shilida house. So your letter was able to catch me without much delay. Now to the business.

Your proposal of translating my stories is a little premature. If you had read at least a dozen of them and felt that they must be translated then I should consider your proposal seriously.

There is another side of the question. You know all the proceeds from my books go to my school. The only right that I have kept to myself about my books is to write them and to receive praise and blame from critics and doctor's degree from the Calcutta University.

When I translate my own books the whole profit goes to the Shantiniketan. That is the only inducement I have for trying to do it myself. But any sustained work in prose, especially translating Bengali stories keeping something of their original flavour, I cannot hope to achieve. Anyhow, I never made any attempt in that direction and I feel a great hesitation in making a trial of it. The next best thing for me is to work with some Englishman who has literary abilities. I have every hope that Andrews will be willing to help me in this work when he comes back from England in April.[5] It is his intention to make a long stay with me in Bolpur. He knows very little Bengali but I know Bengali well enough to supply this deficiency. In fact, the less he knows Bengali [the more considerable] my share of the work will have to be. This arrangement will help Andrews to learn Bengali and help me to learn handling English prose with more freedom than I dare do now.

The Swedish prince has give an account of an interview with me in his recent book of travels. But the beauty of it is that I never met him and the flashes of fire in my eyes which he considered dangerous for the British Government were under observation of the detectives of the Criminal Investigation Department somewhere behind his back. We are not allowed firearms and if any little fire is left playing in our eyes it should not be brought before the notice of our authorities.[6]

Yours
Rabindranath Tagore

Source: MS original in Thompson Papers [Bodleian].

1 Thompson to RT, 28 April 1935, in E. P. Thompson, *Alien Homage*, p. 24.
2 *Ibid.*
3 *Ibid.*, p. 17. In the preface to *The Hungry Stones and Other Stories*, E. J. Thompson was baldly listed, along with others, as having given 'assistance' with translation.
4 *Ibid.*, p. 22.
5 C. F. Andrews returned to India in April 1914 but did not settle at Shantiniketan until June.
6 In late 1913, Prince William of Sweden published an account of a visit to Calcutta in a book in Swedish, which was soon partly translated into English, and gave rise to a rumour that the Swedish Academy had

awarded the Nobel prize to Tagore under pressure from the prince. The account included a vivid description of a meeting with Rabindranath Tagore and family at Jorasanko, in which the prince noticed how their eyes blazed with patriotism and hatred of British rule. 'In all my life, I never spent moments so poignant as at the house of the Hindoo poet Rabindranath Tagore.' (See Dutta and Robinson, *Rabindranath Tagore*, p. 184.) RT may have felt that this misunderstanding would appeal to Thompson's sense of humour; or perhaps Thompson had mentioned the rumour in his letter to RT.

84

To Edward John Thompson

Thompson's reply to letter 83 is lost but this letter from Tagore, written a week later, suggests that Thompson apologised for his importunity in proposing to translate the short stories.

Shilida, [Shelidah, Khulna, Bangladesh]
25 February 1914

Dear Thompson

It pains me to see you needlessly torturing your mind. As an author I have my share of vanity in full measure and I can assure you that it has been a matter of pure delight to me to be approached by a poet having a strong critical faculty for permission to translate my writings. I do not see what makes you think I need any explanation or apology from you. You cannot imagine what a financial mess I have made with my school and [the] debts I have incurred. I have to be careful and strain all my resources to extricate myself from this tangle. That is the reason why I do not consider my books as my own property and I never feel myself at liberty to make any arrangements with regard to them without considering the best interest of my school.

However, I feel I must see you, for these explanations read too stiff and formal in writing. I will leave this place next Saturday and if you get any letter in time and can arrange it will you see me at Jorasanko any time on Sunday?[1]

Yours
Rabindranath Tagore

Source: MS original in Thompson Papers [Bodleian].

1 Thompson went to Jorasanko on 1 March, as requested, despite the short notice and the cost of travelling from Bankura to Calcutta and back (E. P. Thompson, *Alien Homage*, pp. 16–17).

85

To Edward John Thompson

Meeting Thompson in Calcutta on 1 March, RT seems to have given him encouragement to try his hand at translating a short story. Thompson duly did so, and Tagore gave this ambivalent response.

The Nobel prize

Shantiniketan, [West Bengal, India]
24 March 1914

Dear Thompson

I am no judge of English. All I can say [is] I have thoroughly enjoyed reading your translation of my story, for which I must thank you.[1] I will seriously consider what course I should follow about publishing my stories in English when I am a little better and when I am in a mood for it. I hope it will be before long and I will let you know my decision. Just at present I have freed myself from all kinds of plans and have set up at the portal of my mind the announcement – 'No admittance except on no-business.'

Yours
Rabindranath Tagore

Source: MS original in Thompson Papers [Bodleian].

1 The identity of this story is unknown; presumably it was included in *The Hungry Stones and Other Stories*, published in London in 1916.

86

To Thomas Sturge Moore

W. B. Yeats thought Thomas Sturge Moore 'one of the most exquisite poets writing in England'. In 1914, he published *The Sea is Kind*, a collection of sixty-nine poems, which included 'To Rabindranath Tagore'.[1] This is the first half of the poem:

> I cannot mock thy 'Yes' with 'No';
> For what is hidden may be of such worth
> As beggars all we know:
> Yet how mine wonders at thy mind! –
> To see schooled man so easy on this earth
> And yet not blind!
> Is it true thy candour weighs
> Long June Days,
> Deep clear nights,
> Full tenderness on self-forgetful face,
> All-probing knowledge, art perfection-nigh,
> And aught else that delights
> Poor man's goodwill,
> As being really like a trace
> Left on fingers that have touched, –
> Perhaps half-tried to kill –
> Some lustrous butterfly?

Rabindranath read the book and replied with this letter, wonderfully redolent of Shantiniketan in summer.

Santiniketan, [West Bengal, India]
1 May 1914

My dear Sturge Moore,

Our school is closed, and after a long interval of busy time a full day has been given to me to spend as I like. I took up your book, *The Sea is Kind*, finishing it at one sitting. It will be difficult for you to imagine this blazing summer sky of ours with hot blasts of air repeatedly troubling the fresh leaves of a tree whose name will be of no use to you. This is as unlike the climate and the country where your poems were written as anything could be. I feel your environments in your poems. There is in them the reticence of your sky, the compactness of your indoor life and the general consciousness of strength ready to defy fate. Here in the East the transparent stillness of our dark nights, the glare of the noonday sun melting into a tender haze in the blue distance, the plaintive music of the life that feels itself afloat in the Endless, seem to whisper into our hearts some great secret of existence which is uncommunicable.

All the same, nay, all the more, your literature is precious to us. The untiring hold upon life which you never lose, the definiteness of your aims and the positive reliance you have upon things present before you, inspire us with a strong sense of reality which is so much needed both for the purposes of art and of life. Literature of a country is not chiefly for home consumption. Its value lies in the fact that it is imperatively necessary for the lands where it is foreign. I think it has been the good fortune of the West to have the opportunity of absorbing the spirit of the East through the medium of the Bible. It has added to the richness of your life because it is alien to your temperament. In course of time you may discard some of its doctrines and teachings but it has done its work – it has created a bifurcation in your mental system which is so needful for all life growth. The western literature is doing the same with us, bringing into our life elements some of which supplement and some contradict our tendencies. This is what we need.

It is not enough to charm or surprise us – we must receive shocks and be hurt. Therefore we seek in your writings not simply what is artistic but what is vivid and forceful. That is why Byron had such an immense influence over our youths of the last generation. Shelley, in spite of his vague idealism, roused our minds because of his fanatic impetuosity which is born of a faith in life. What I say here is from the point of view of a foreigner. We cannot but miss a great deal of the purely artistic element in your literature but whatever is broadly human and deeply true can be safely shipped for distant times and remote countries. We look for your literature to bring to us the thundering life flood of the West, even though it carries with it all the debris of the passing moments.[2]

I am getting ready to go off to the hills to spend my vacation there.

Ever yours,
Rabindranath Tagore

Source: MS copy in Sturge Moore Papers [London]; letter published in *A Tagore Reader*, pp. 23–4. The original MS was sold in London in 1959, and privately purchased. See *A Tagore Reader*, p. 378, n. 6.

1 Thomas Sturge Moore, *The Sea is Kind* (London, 1914), p. 91.
2 See RT's discussion of the effect of western literature on Bengal in *My Rem*, pp. 130–2/*RR*, XVII, pp. 374–5.

87

To Robert Bridges[1]

Robert Bridges, the poet laureate from 1913, appears to have met Tagore for the first time in May that year, when Tagore gave a lecture at Manchester College, Oxford. He invited him to his secluded house on Boars Hill above the city. In 1926, they met there once again; otherwise their relationship was entirely through correspondence and mutual friends such as Rothenstein, W. B. Yeats and E. J. Thompson, whose enthusiasm for Tagore's work infected Bridges. (Thompson admired the work of both poets, and published a study of Bridges in 1944.)

Their acquaintance – it was never a friendship – was an uneasy one almost from the start. Bridges knew nothing of India or Indian culture, and there is little evidence that Tagore was seriously interested in Bridges' poetry. What drew them together was religion. Bridges, once a 'devoted churchman' (as he informed Tagore), now hoped, with due caution, to share his 'nest of home-made psychological and metaphysical convictions' with Tagore. He admitted to being worried, though, by the frank atheism of his gardener at Boars Hill.[2]

Tagore's reply reaches out in similar generous spirit, tempered with an equal, if not greater, awareness of the cultural divide on the very eve of war. Tagore seems to have had an acute sense of the judicious, precise turn of Bridges' mind, which both attracted and repelled him. He admired the English literary world's pursuit of poetic excellence, but not its calculating, almost mercenary mentality. The gulf between the two men was best described by a mutual friend mentioned by Tagore in this letter, the cosmopolitan Shahid Suhrawardy, a Bengali student at Oxford in 1913. A quarter of a century later, Suhrawardy wrote:

> [They] were the two most beautiful old men I have ever seen . . . Tagore in my eyes represented the melody, the abundance, the grace of the East; to him Beauty came as she flowed down streams or awoke on the sprays of breeze-tossed corn. She came to him naturally as the cherished one to her lover. Whereas to Bridges she was a burden; with him there was a constant struggle to reduce the conflict between language and mood to the counterpoints of harmony, to force Beauty into the fierce shackles of tone and rhythm.[3]

Shantiniketan, [West Bengal, India]
8 July 1914

My dear Dr Bridges

I take this opportunity to tell you how touched I was by the kind welcome you gave me when I met you in Oxford.[4] Although for a poet neglect is hard to bear yet appreciation always come to him as a surprise. Because a poet's work is really no work – it is an outcome of his life. It is like the expression of love by a lover for which he never expects praise simply because it is so vital to him. Life is not self-conscious in my country where there is no such world as a literary world where poets' works are given a conventional value by appraisers expert in their trade. We have our share of praise, no doubt, but it is simple like the warmth of the sun, it gives you pleasure but it has no market value. The reputation I earned in the West was sudden, as well as great – but being brought up in a different atmosphere my mind was not trained to imbibe it and be filled with it to a saturation point. That is why every piece of genuine kindness I had from a man like yourself came to me unexpected and I received it every time with a fresh feeling of wonder and gratefulness. The letter that I have just got from you is precious to me for the hearty goodwill and gift of friendship it brings to me from you. Next time I go to England I should like nothing better than to take shelter in your home for a while and be protected from the whirlwind of the Nobel prize notoriety.

My religion is my life – it is growing with my growth – it has never been grafted on me from outside. I had denied God when I was younger just as the flower in its pride of blossoming youth completely ignores the fruit which is its perfection. But now that the fruit is here with the mystery of the immortal life hidden in the core of its seed I accept it simply as I accept the reality of my own person though I have no logic to explain its existence. Therefore I am not at all anxious about the godlessness of your gardener. For all growth is a rhythm and all true irreligion is a part of true religion – it is [only] hopeless when it is an absolute negation, when it has no seed of life in it, when it is a sign of decay and of death.

I am glad you speak so well of Suhrawardy for whom I felt a very great attraction when I came to know him in Oxford, and the memory of my meeting with him still gives me pleasure.

Yours most sincerely
Rabindranath Tagore

Source: MS original in Bridges Papers [Bodleian].

1 Robert Seymour Bridges (1844–1930): poet and sponsor of the poetry of his friend Gerard Manley Hopkins; he was poet laureate from 1913 until his death.
2 Bridges to RT, 7 June 1914 [RB].
3 'Tagore at Oxford', *CMG*, pp. 39, 40. Hasan Shahid Suhrawardy (1890–1965): Bagiswari professor of fine art, Calcutta University, 1932–43 (visiting lecturer, Visva-Bharati, 1932); in 1947 he went to Pakistan, where he was appointed ambassador to Spain in the late 1950s. Suhrawardy gave major assistance to Bridges in his selection of oriental verse for *The Spirit of Man* (see letter 100).
4 Referring to RT's Oxford visit in May 1913, Bridges told him: 'Your presence there gave reality to the honest but vain profession of the university to be a home for all creeds and nations' (7 June 1914 [RB]).

The crest of a wave (1914–1916)

Introduction

Tagore's western visit, and the award of the Nobel prize, had given him a taste for travel. Though he remained in India in 1914–15, he was restless, constantly on the move, particularly in the last three months of 1914. He made several attempts to visit Japan, before finally going there in May 1916 and then sailing across the Pacific in autumn 1916, for a sensational nationwide speaking tour of the USA.

The outbreak of the First World War greatly disturbed him, but it did not, initially, affect his literary or personal standing in the West. In fact the crest of his western literary success was reached in the first three years of the war, during which he received a knighthood for literary services. After 1916, partly as a consequence of the poor translations of his poetry now being published, partly as a result of his American lectures attacking nationalism and also because of the change in English literary taste during the war, Tagore began to fall from western view as a writer.

His fame accounts for his literary contretemps during 1915 with Robert Bridges, the poet laureate. Bridges wanted to refine the English of one of the *Gitanjali* poems so as to include it in his wartime anthology of great poetry, *The Spirit of Man* (London, 1916). But Tagore refused. Only when Yeats intervened, at the request of Bridges, did Tagore yield. The issue was a literary one, but it also involved, unavoidably, the larger relation of India to Britain.

Though Indian nationalism played a comparatively small role in Tagore's life at this time, it was during 1915 that Tagore first met Gandhi (who was not yet a Mahatma). Early that year, Gandhi visited Shantiniketan, in order to collect the boys he had sent there from South Africa in 1914. Tagore welcomed him, but not without reservations.

88

To Ernest Rhys[1]

Ernest Rhys, founder-editor of Everyman's Library, was one of Tagore's most loyal literary friends in England. During 1913, he helped Rabindranath to revise *Sadhana* for publication; in 1936, he edited (anonymously) Tagore's *Collected Poems and Plays*. During 1914, after Tagore had won the Nobel prize and was back in Bengal, Rhys wrote *Rabindranath Tagore: A Biographical Study*, which was published in 1915 by Macmillan, the first biography of Tagore in English.[2]

Both author and subject were aware that there was an enormous amount of Tagore's work, not to speak of his life, that was unavailable to a western writer in 1915: after all, Rhys knew no Bengali and had never been to Bengal. The book was thus hopelessly inadequate as a biography or critical study, even in its time. Nevertheless it contains some happy phrases – Rhys was a fluent and appealing critic – and it was redeemed by a sure instinct for certain aspects of Tagore's personality that eluded E. J. Thompson in his 1926 study of Tagore. As Rabindranath told Rhys, upon receiving the book: 'Thank you so much for the book you have written about myself – not for your estimate of my life and work but for your love that beams out of its every page.'[3]

This letter refers both to the research for the biography and to the publication of Tagore's play, *The King of the Dark Chamber*, which was attended by some confusion.

Shantiniketan, [West Bengal, India]
23 July 1914

My dear Ernest Rhys,

You may have got long before this some information about my life from Mr Andrews which may be of use to you. He has joined me in my school work and is just now engaged in translating some of my short stories with my help.[4] He is in an excited state of mind and is very sanguine of their success. But the proper way of dealing with success is to let it surprise you when it comes and never to wait at the gate expecting its arrival every moment.

Macmillan in their eagerness to publish my works never waited for my final permission or for the MS which I have with me containing corrections and alterations.[5] They got hold of an earlier MS which I had left with Rothenstein. What is worse, they did not know that the translation was done by Kshitish Chandra Sen – an Indian student studying in Cambridge when I was in England.[6] In fact, it was the draft, hurriedly done in the hope of its being thoroughly revised by myself. I cabled to Macmillan, as soon as I got the copies of this book, to make correct announcement. I do not know what they have done. Can you advise me and help me in this matter? I was under the impression that this drama was going to be published in the winter season and I had the MSS in my hand and never thought of the one left with Rothenstein. I was doing things in my usual leisurely manner.

Can't you persuade your publishers to allow you to come and make a regular scientific study of me, closely observing me in my environment and in all my different moods and manners? Do leave your British Museum and come to us.[7] It will have the effect of expanding my heart when I see you and is the most favourable condition for studying a man. Don't say it is impossible. Take a short holiday and if you can spend even three weeks with me I shall try to be content.

With love to you all.

Yours
Rabindranath Tagore

Source: *Desh*, 12 Sept. 1992, p. 17. The MS was sold in London in 1992 to a Japanese bidder. See 'Discovery of a Tagore letter', *India Weekly*, London, 18–31 Dec. 1992.

7 Tagore in Japan, 1916, at the villa of Okakura Kakuzo

152   Selected letters of Rabindranath Tagore

1 Ernest Percival Rhys (1859–1946): founder-editor of Everyman's Library (whose name he chose), critic and poet.
2 It was followed the same year by a (bad) biography written by Basanta Koomar Roy (*Rabindranath Tagore: The Man and his Poetry* (New York, 1915)), published in the USA.
3 RT to Ernest Rhys, 19 May 1915, in Ernest Rhys, *Letters from Limbo* (London, 1936), p. 168. Rhys himself had written to RT on 27 June 1914: 'That it will quite satisfy you is too much to hope; but you will credit it with more than [that which] lies in the printed page' (Lago (ed.), *Imperfect Encounter*, p. 169). He told Rothenstein on 18 June 1914: 'My task is to get at the reality, and not to minister to any cult: but it is, as you surmise, hard for an outsider to penetrate the Indian confines, and get home there' (*ibid.*). C. F. Andrews, predictably, admired the book; E. J. Thompson, equally predictably, did not (Andrews to RT, 6 June 1915 [RB]; Thompson to RT, 12 Dec. 1920, in E. P. Thompson, *Alien Homage*, p. 47). The British reviews were mixed. The *Manchester Guardian* remarked (7 Sept. 1915):

> Mr Ernest Rhys is, apparently, at the same disadvantage with regard to Tagore's writings as most of the rest of us. He knows these writings only in so far as they have been translated; he has, that is to say, a very partial knowledge of a small portion of them. On the other hand, he knows Tagore personally, and has been at pains to acquire some knowledge of the conditions which have governed the poet's creative development. The book is, largely, a compilation; but it is a compilation managed and informed by acute sympathy with the man and his work.

4 See letter 83.
5 The MS in question was the translation of RT's play *Raja*, which Macmillan published in 1914 as *The King of the Dark Chamber*, without consulting RT and without making it clear that the translation was not his. See Lago (ed.), *Imperfect Encounter*, pp. 170–3.
6 Kshitish Chandra Sen was educated at Cambridge University, sat the ICS exam in 1912, and began his service in Nov. 1913. He had little subsequent literary career.
7 Rhys was never on the staff of the British Museum, but he spent much time in its reading room, as his autobiography (*Everyman Remembers* (London, 1931)) makes clear.

89

To Pramathanath Chaudhuri[1]

The contrast between Rabindranath's English friendships and his relations with his family circle is an illuminating one. As he once admitted to William Rothenstein, 'We in India ... live secluded among a crowd of relations. Things are done and said within the family circle which would not be tolerated outside.'[2] Of course, as in any family, there were certain members from whom Rabindranath expected the same high standards of behaviour as he applied to himself. They included his niece Indira and her husband Pramatha Chaudhuri, editor and writer, to whom this letter, dealing partly with literary and partly with domestic matters, was written. It touches on the freedom from orthodoxy that Rabindranath enjoyed in Shantiniketan, as opposed to the family house in Calcutta.

Postmark Shantiniketan, [West Bengal, India]
5 September 1914

Kalyaniyeshu

The essay you have written on the war is not required to be a piece of literature. Such writings should aim at clarity and simplicity: your piece does this, but it includes one or two clever passages that would have been better avoided. The teachers in the school who have read it are praising it – people feel that the article was needed.[3]

When Mahendra comes, I plan to employ him as my personal servant. Much of my time is spent away from home, during which I depend on my servant Uma Charan for my food, clothing and comforts.[4] That is alright. But as I grow older I am getting lonely and feeling the need of a helper here, and so for some time I have been on the lookout for a companion who would be able to look after me a bit, spare me the bother of having to worry about my personal needs. If Mahendra fits in well, he would answer a major lack.[5] And his wife could certainly join him at Surul. How fussy is she about Hindu practices? You know what infidels we are – of course your people are the same – but in a Calcutta family house such as yours one can, if need be, set aside a corner where Great Manu's injunctions are obeyed: not so in our Surul house.[6] Let me know Bibi's advice about this.[7]

I am keeping events in Belgium very much in mind – the other day I spoke to the boys about them – and perhaps a poem will emerge.[8] Are you planning to publish a double issue for Ashwin/Kartik?[9]

Do get the bank papers formalised – give Suren a serious prod about it.[10]

Shri Rabindranath Thakur

Source: MS original at Rabindra Bhavan, Shantiniketan; letter published in *CP*, V, pp. 185–6.

1 Pramathanath Chaudhuri (1868–1946): editor of *Shabuj Patra*, essayist, short-story writer; he married Indira Devi Chaudhurani and in 1941 moved from Calcutta to Shantiniketan. In many ways he was the antithesis of RT – something of a Bengali Oscar Wilde, in fact – but their relationship was close. He was 'a friend, yes; an admirer, certainly; but not a disciple. In Rabindranath, Pramatha Chaudhuri saw a genius, a greater master, but not The Master' (Buddhadeva Bose, *An Acre of Green Grass: A Review of Modern Bengali Literature* (Calcutta, 1948), p. 15).
2 Quoted in Rothenstein, *Men and Memories*, p. 264.
3 'Bartaman sabhyata banam bartaman sabhyata' (Modern civilisation versus itself), *Shabuj Patra*, Agrahayan 1321 [Nov.–Dec. 1914].
4 Writing of Uma Charan, Kshiti Mohan Sen recalled: 'The master treated him with a degree of familiarity which the servant fully reciprocated. Uma Charan had a keen sense of humour and fully appreciated his master's jokes' (Sen, 'Rabindranath and the ashram of early days', *VBN*, July 1939, p. 4). Uma Charan died in 1916, while RT was in the USA.
5 Mahendra never joined RT. His personal servants were, in succession, Uma Charan, Shadhu Charan and Banamali, who outlived RT. See Chitta Ranjan Dev, 'In memoriam: Banamali', *VBN*, April–May 1954, pp. 109–10.
6 Manu: ancient author of a code of laws in Sanskrit, revered by orthodox Hindus. RT was well aware that despite his father Maharshi Debendranath's aversion for idol worship, many of his own immediate family, including his mother, had not abandoned it altogether. At Jorasanko, it was accepted that each branch of the family would 'do its own thing' religiously speaking; but at Shantiniketan the ethos was basically Brahmo and an orthodox Hindu would have felt out of place in RT's house. On a similar subject, see RT's article, 'The Saraswati Puja in the City College hostel', *MR*, May 1928, pp. 594–7/*Prabashi*, Jaishtha 1335 [May–June 1928], pp. 174–5.
7 Bibi: Indira Devi Chaudhurani.
8 The German army invaded Belgium on 4 Aug. 1914 and took Brussels on 20 Aug. RT does not appear to have written a poem specifically related to events in Belgium.
9 Ashwin/Kartik: Bengali months corresponding to mid-Sept.–mid-Nov. *Shabuj Patra* appeared irregularly, despite regular prodding of its editor by RT.
10 Suren: Surendranath Tagore.

90

To Edward John Thompson

During September 1914, Rabindranath escaped the demands of the ashram at Shantiniketan by moving to his house in the village of Surul, about two miles away.[1]

154   Selected letters of Rabindranath Tagore

He had bought this in 1912, and had it renovated as a residence for his son and daughter-in-law, including the addition of a laboratory; later it became the nucleus of Shriniketan, his 'institute for rural reconstruction'. This brief note to E. J. Thompson, who was eager to see him again about translating, was presumably written from Surul, not Shantiniketan.

> Shantiniketan, [West Bengal, India]
> 18 September 1914

Dear Thompson

I have arranged to be perfectly alone during the holidays and I am afraid you won't find me in Shantiniketan for some time. I shall don the magic garment which will make me invisible.

Yours
Rabindranath Tagore

Source: MS original in Thompson Papers [Bodleian].

1 RT returned to the ashram in early Oct. 'We have all come to Santiniketan from Surul; and this change has done me good' (RT to C. F. Andrews, 4 Oct. 1914 [RB]).

91

To William Butler Yeats

Yeats and Tagore were not in touch for over a year after Tagore left London. In September 1914, urged by Maud Gonne, Yeats wrote to Tagore recommending the claims of Maud Gonne's young daughter Iseult as a suitable translator of *The Gardener* into French, in collaboration with Devabrata Mukerjea (the translator of *The Post Office* into English). He also remarked that he had planned to visit India in the winter, in order to hear Rabindranath's poems sung 'and to study the world out of which you have made them' – but the war had made such a journey impossible. He added: 'Your poetry remains to me as beautiful as when I first read it.'[1]

> Shantiniketan, [West Bengal, India]
> 10 November 1914

My dear Mr Yeats

It has been a great delight to me to have your letter, specially when this war has thinned my correspondence to a comfortable proportion. – Certainly, I can depend on your discretion and allow Miss Gonne to publish her French translations of *The Gardener* when you have satisfied yourself about their merit.[2] I am going to write to Messrs Macmillan, who are also my business agents, to withhold giving permission to anybody else before you decide about Miss Gonne's translations.

I should like nothing better than to have you among us for a time and I do hope you will be able to pay us a visit when this war is over. I have a great mind myself to come to England when the passage is a little safer. However, you have my invitation to stay in our house whenever you choose to come to India. I am sure Calcutta University would be glad to ask you to deliver a course of lectures to the students on literature. If I have your permission I can have a talk with our present vice-chancellor on this matter.[3]

Yours
Rabindranath Tagore

Source: MS original in collection of Michael Yeats.

1 Yeats to RT, 12 Sept. [1914], *VBQ*, 30, No. 3, 1964–5, p. 171.
2 Iseult Stuart (Gonne) (1895–1954): daughter of Maud Gonne. During 1914, Iseult and Mukerjea, together in France, translated some of *The Gardener* direct from Bengali into French. Though Iseult had learnt some Bengali from Mukerjea, she did not persist with the work and the translations were never published. How good they really were is doubtful; Yeats, by his own admission to Tagore, was not sufficiently bilingual to judge their style. In late July 1914, however, the translating was going well and, furthermore, a French woman competitor had appeared on the scene: 'there is danger that she may get from Mr Tagore permission to translate his works before Iseult does', Maud Gonne told Yeats excitedly. Matters were complicated by the fact that both Mukerjea and Yeats were fascinated by Iseult Gonne (Yeats proposed to her in 1916). See Anna MacBride White and A. Norman Jeffares, *The Gonne–Yeats Letters* (London, 1992), esp. pp. 339–56.
3 Yeats never visited India, but unlike, say, André Gide, the French translator of *Gitanjali*, Yeats was interested in Tagore's social and cultural milieu. See Dutta and Robinson, *Rabindranath Tagore*, p. 5.

92

To Charles Freer Andrews

Tagore was deeply affected by the devotion of C. F. Andrews, both to himself and to Shantiniketan. At the same time he retained a clear sense of Andrews' emotionalism and flawed literary judgement. In his letters to Andrews, he opened his mind – and on a wide range of subjects besides 'spiritual' ones. In this letter, for instance, he deals with literature (his play, *The King of the Dark Chamber*, which some English critics thought to be abstract and lifeless), with his periodic need to escape the ashram (which was particularly powerful during 1914, as a result of his western odyssey), and with the influence of Gandhi (the boys from whose Phoenix Settlement in South Africa had been lodged at Shantiniketan, ahead of Gandhi's own return to India). It was Andrews who first brought Tagore and Gandhi together (see letter 94). In the years to come, Andrews would receive many letters from Tagore critical of the Mahatma.

Calcutta, [India]
15 November 1914

My dear Friend

Critics and detectives are naturally suspicious. They scent allegories and bombs where there are no such abominations. It is difficult to convince them of our innocence. [The] human soul has its inner drama which is just as human as anything else that concerns man – and Shudarshana [in *The King of the Dark Chamber*] is no more an abstraction than Lady Macbeth (who could be described as an allegory representing criminal ambition in man's nature).[1] However it does not matter what [things] are what according to the rules of criticism – they are what they are, and therefore difficult of classification.

The geographical position of Ramgarh is said to be not unfavourable for wintering, and this it is that has induced me to try to go there for the next few months till it becomes decently warm and comfortable.[2] But it is a secret of mine and you must not let it out. Our people at Bolpur, including Nagen,[3] will be kept in the dark, and whatever may happen I must remain beyond the reach of correspondence. I shall start from Bolpur, where I am going tonight, on the 18th of November Wednesday by Bombay Mail.[4] Rathi will accompany me and possibly *Bouma*.[5] I shall escape 7 Paush, 11 Magh, the invitation to Theistic Conference and such other evils that the flesh is *not* heir to, but which, all the same, fasten upon it without ceremony. It is wicked of me to be away when you are in the ashram, but I feel you will have better opportunity to come closer to the boys and teachers when I am not there, and that will compensate you for my absence.

What little I have seen of the Phoenix boys they are very nice, but it is a pity to be so completely nice. They have discipline where they should have ideals. They are trained to obey which is bad for a human being, for obedience is good, not because it is good in itself but because it is a sacrifice. These boys are in danger of forgetting to wish for anything, and wishing is the best part of attainment. However they are happy, though they have no business to be happy.[6]

I hope you will not strain your strength too much when you are in Shantiniketan and remain content with doing very much less than your utmost.

Give my kindest regards to Mr Rudra and Sudhir and remember me kindly to my friends in Delhi.[7]

With love.

Yours
Rabindranath Tagore

Source: MS copy at Rabindra Bhavan, Shantiniketan.

1 Andrews had mentioned the English critical reaction to *The King of the Dark Chamber* in his letter to RT of 13 Nov., written from Delhi. It included an unfavourable review in the *Manchester Guardian* (16 Oct. 1914):

> He [RT] writes plays (we have read only this and *Chitra*) to expound and not at the bidding of his gift of inspiration. So he does not build, does not let ideas fill people and things until they become symbolic, but merely chooses symbols so that there may be no mistake as to his meaning . . . Drama the play is not: poem it is not: true allegory it is not. It lives only by the lyric flames which destroy it.

> As a general comment on RT's plays, there is much truth in this. In the case of this play a poor translation, unrevised by RT (see letter 88), had compounded the problem. Nevertheless, though *The King of the Dark Chamber* failed to grip Ludwig Wittgenstein on a first reading ('I do not feel for a single moment that here is a drama taking place. I merely understand the allegory in an abstract way'), a second attempt convinced him that 'there is *indeed* something grand here'. Many years later, Wittgenstein and a friend prepared their own English translation of part of the play. According to Ray Monk, 'it is a reasonable conjecture that the character in the play with whom [Wittgenstein] most identified is that of the king's wife, Shudarshana.' See Monk, 'Seeing in the dark: Wittgenstein and Tagore', in Dutta and Robinson (eds.), *Purabi*, pp. 142–4.

2 Ramgarh, near Naini Tal, in the Kumaon Hills, was where RT had recently acquired a house. He stayed there in May–June 1914.

3 Nagen: Nagendranath Gangulee.
4 RT, as so often with him, changed his mind. He did go back to Shantiniketan, but he returned to Calcutta on 17 Nov., left on 18 Nov. from Calcutta, and, rather than wintering in Ramgarth, spent some weeks travelling in the plains before returning to Shantiniketan in late Dec. As he told Andrews on 18 Nov., just before setting out: 'The enjoyment of my visit to Ramgarh is in the potential mood with me, which, very often, is the happiest mood' [RB].
5 *Bouma*: Pratima Tagore.
6 Three days later, on 18 Nov., RT told Andrews: 'I had been somewhat unfair to the Phoenix boys in my letter to you. Since then I have been able to come closer to them and I think they are very lovable, though I cannot get rid of my misgivings about their system of training' [RB].
7 Sudhir Rudra: son of Sushil Rudra, Andrews' close friend in Delhi.

93

To Macmillan & Co. [UK]

Soon after the outbreak of war in August 1914, Tagore wrote to Macmillan in London enquiring whether this would mean a delay in publishing the volume of his short stories they had requested. 'In that case, would you very kindly let me know immediately, as in that case I should be able to work at more leisure.'[1] He had been struggling with the translation problem since the beginning of that year (see letter 83), a struggle which would continue throughout 1915, until he eventually surrendered the task to Macmillan, who published the book in 1916. He could clearly see that the translations of others, whether Englishmen or Bengalis, were inadequate; and yet he lacked the confidence to tackle the task himself.[2]

Santiniketan, [West Bengal, India]
13 January 1915

Dear Sirs

I am sending you some more of my stories done by various hands.[3] They are of unequal merits and do not satisfy me. I shall depend upon you for their selection, and also for corrections. I am collecting some more of these translations and they will be sent by instalments each mail.

Yours sincerely
Rabindranath Tagore

Source: MS original in Macmillan Company Papers [BL].

1 RT to Macmillan, 20 Aug. 1914 [BL].
2 On 15 Nov. 1915, RT told Macmillan, 'Translating my prose stories into English is a difficult task for me but having them translated by others is hardly satisfactory. I am waiting to take up this work when I shall be able to leave India for a while and be comparatively free from demands of my own countrymen for original Bengali works.' Thus it was not the case that 'Tagore did not wish to be bothered with the translations. Macmillan were bothering him, and he needed money for his school' (E. P. Thompson, *Alien Homage*, p. 20).
3 The exact content of the stories sent by RT is unknown, but it must have included work translated by some of those who had already published translations of RT's short stories in the *MR*, from 1909 onwards; it would probably not have included work translated by E. J. Thompson, who began work later in 1915 at RT's request.

158   Selected letters of Rabindranath Tagore

94

To Mahatma Gandhi[1]

In early 1915, Gandhi returned to India after more than two decades in South Africa. Though he was not yet known as Mahatma Gandhi, his reception at Bombay on 9 January was of a kind given to returning heroes. He spent about a month in Kathiawad with his relatives, and then came to Shantiniketan, where the boys from his Phoenix Settlement had been living since October 1914. Tagore was away in Calcutta, but C. F. Andrews (who had originally suggested Shantiniketan as suitable accommodation for the boys) fulsomely welcomed Gandhi and his wife, as did the rest of the staff and students.[2]

Rabindranath, as we know from his November letter to Andrews (92), took a more ambivalent attitude to the Phoenix boys, and, indeed, to Gandhi himself. He was fond of them, but he distrusted the austerity of their training. He hints, very gently, at his feeling in this letter to Gandhi about the boys.

[Calcutta?, India]
[February? 1915][3]

Dear Mr Gandhi

That you could think of my school as the right and the likely place where your Phoenix boys could take shelter when they are in India has given me real pleasure – and that pleasure has been greatly enhanced when I saw those dear boys in that place. We all feel that their influence will be of great value to our boys and I hope that they in their turn will gain something which will make their stay in Shantiniketan fruitful. I write this letter to thank you for allowing your boys to become our boys as well and thus form a living link in the *sadhana* of both of our lives.[4]

Very sincerely yours
Rabindranath Tagore

Source: MS copy at Rabindra Bhavan, Shantiniketan; letter published in *VBQ, 35*, Nos. 1–4 (Gandhi Number), May 1969–April 1970, p. 237.

1 Mohandas Karamchand Gandhi (1869–1948): leader of India's struggle for freedom from British rule; RT first popularised the title Mahatma for Gandhi.
2 Gandhi replied to the address of welcome:

> The delight I feel today, I have never experienced before. Though Rabindranath, the Gurudev is not present here, yet we feel his presence in our hearts. I am particularly happy to find that you have arranged for the reception in the Indian manner. We were received with great pomp in Bombay, but there was nothing in it to make us happy. (Quoted in D. G. Tendulkar, *Mahatma: Life of Mohandas Karamchand Gandhi*, I–VIII (Bombay, 1951–4): I, p. 197)

From Calcutta, RT wrote to Andrews on 18 Feb. 1915: 'I hope Mr and Mrs Gandhi have arrived in Bolpur, and Shantiniketan has accorded them welcome as befits her and them. I shall convey my love to them personally when we meet.' (Andrews changed 'Mr' to 'Mahatma', when he published this letter in the 1920s.)

One wonders why RT was not present when Gandhi arrived. There was no compelling reason for him to stay in Calcutta at this time. Gandhi had sent a cable to Andrews on 15 Feb. saying to expect him at Shantiniketan on 17 Feb., and no doubt Andrews promptly informed RT of this fact. Yet RT did not return to Shantiniketan until 22 Feb., when, as he knew, Gandhi had already departed for Pune (after hearing of the death of his mentor Gokhale on 19 Feb.); and, having returned, RT settled not in Shantiniketan but at his house in nearby Surul. He did not finally meet Gandhi until 6 March. Probably,

for his own complex reasons, RT deliberately avoided welcoming Gandhi to Shantiniketan on first arrival. See Dutta and Robinson, *Rabindranath Tagore*, pp. 196–7.
3 There is no date and no address on this letter. It could have been written in mid-Jan., soon after Gandhi arrived in India, but a more likely date is mid-Feb., immediately after RT heard that Gandhi was soon to arrive in Shantiniketan.
4 *sadhana*: realisation. The subtitle of RT's essays *Sadhana* is *The Realisation of Life*. The word has connotations of austere endeavour; obviously RT's *sadhana* and Gandhi's *sadhana* differed greatly in attitude to the virtues of austerity.

95

To (Sir) William Rothenstein

On 29 Dec. 1914, Tagore told William Rothenstein hopefully, 'When this reaches you I shall be sailing for Japan . . . following the track of the rising sun.'[1] Instead he stayed in India until May 1916. The period 1914–15 marked the peak of his fame in English literary circles, and the high tide of his friendships with English men and women. It was therefore particularly painful for him now to read a short book by Goldsworthy Lowes Dickinson, the classical scholar, whom he had met and liked in England in 1912 (and who had introduced him to Bertrand Russell in Cambridge). Some ten years before they met, Tagore had admired Lowes Dickinson's (pseudonymous) *Letters from John Chinaman*, an attack on British imperialism in China: Dickinson's distaste for India in his 1914 *Essay on the Civilisations of India, China and Japan*, based on his eastern travels in 1912–13, was therefore a shock to Tagore. Here he writes about it to William Rothenstein, who of course had a sympathetic response to India on his 1910–11 visit.

Calcutta, [India]
18 February 1915

My dear Friend

My visit to Japan has been postponed a few months longer. In the meanwhile I am thinking of spending my summer in Kashmere. I need rest, and going into a new country is rather disconcerting. Lowes Dickinson's *Essay on the Civilisations of India, China and Japan* has made me feel sad.[2] Not only he is entirely out of sympathy with India but has tried to make out that there is something inherent in [an] Englishman which makes him incapable of appreciating India – and to him India by her very nature will be a source of eternal irritation. Of all countries in the world India is *the* East to him – that is to say an abstraction. Possibly he is right in his observations – but then it is a hopeless misery for India till the end of this chapter of her history and it is utterly bad for those who have come merely to govern her from across the sea. I only hope Dickinson is not right and that it was heat and hurry and dyspepsia that blotted out the human India from his sight leading him into the blank of a monotonous mist of classification.[3]

I am sending you another translation of my poem.[4] I hope this may be instrumental in bringing to our soldiers some little comfort to remind them of the anxious love of their countrymen in the distant home.

With my best love

Yours ever
Rabindranath Tagore

Source: MS original in Rothenstein Papers [Harvard]; letter published in Lago (ed.), *Imperfect Encounter*, pp. 190–1.

1 Lago (ed.), *Imperfect Encounter*, p. 175.
2 Goldsworthy Lowes Dickinson (1862–1932): classical scholar, fellow of King's College, Cambridge; E. M. Forster was a close friend of Dickinson, accompanied him in India and later wrote a biography of him. Dickinson's *Essay* was certainly more sympathetic to China than to India, and its central argument remains of interest. In his view, the 'real point of distinction' between the West, China and Japan, on the one hand, and India, on the other, is that they believe that

> all effort ought to centre upon the process of living in time; that the process has reality and significance; and that the business of religion is not to deliver us from effort by convincing us of its futility, but to sanctify and justify it. No modern western man would regard as an admirable type at all – still less as the highest type – a man who withdraws from the world to meditate and come into direct contact with the Universal. But an Indian who is uncontaminated by western culture still regards that as the true ideal of conduct; and views all activities in the world as lower and inferior, though, for an undeveloped man, they are necessary and pardonable . . .
> I believe that the renewal of art, of contemplation, of religion, will arise in the West of its own impulse; and that the East will lose what remains of its achievement in these directions and become as 'materialistic' . . . as the West, before it can recover a new and genuine spiritual life. (Goldsworthy Lowes Dickinson, *An Essay on the Civilisations of India, China and Japan* (London, 1914), pp. 13, 85)

3 Dickinson did fall ill in India. Dyspepsia was a source of chronic irritability for the British in India. For example, Malcolm Muggeridge, despite being drawn to spiritual India and despite having close Bengali friends who profoundly admired RT, wrote about him in the most jaundiced terms after a visit to Shantiniketan – probably partly as a result of chronic illness while in Bengal (Richard Ingrams, *Muggeridge: The Biography* (London, 1995), p. 89).
4 See RT to William Rothenstein, 9 Feb. 1915, in Lago (ed.), *Imperfect Encounter*, pp. 189–90.

96

To Rathindranath Tagore

In 1915, Tagore's relationship with senior British officials in India was closer than with Indian nationalists such as Gandhi. He found Lord Carmichael, the governor of Bengal, particularly sympathetic, and a special effort to honour him was made when he visited the ashram on 20 March, as implied by this letter to Rathindranath. The viceroy, Lord Hardinge, was also sincerely interested in Tagore's work (encouraged by C. F. Andrews). In June that year, a knighthood was conferred upon Tagore.

[Shantiniketan, West Bengal, India]
[March 1915]

Kalyaniyeshu

I cannot find my white notebook containing poems. Have a look and see if I have left it in Calcutta. It contains a number of new poems which I have not yet copied.

For Lord Carmichael[1] we will probably need a large umbrella. It will be hot then. If he chooses to visit the school, an umbrella will need to be held over him.

The letter that Sylvain Lévi has written to Professor Anderson of Cambridge, I am copying an extract from.[2] Let Pramatha and Mani Lal have a look[3] –

> I have not yet, I think, thanked you for your paper translated from Tagore's Bengali.[4] I perused it with great pleasure. I am telling only the plain truth when I say that I have never seen anything about metrics that can compare with it. It is full of original and

The crest of a wave 161

deep thoughts and if ever we enjoy peace again, I shall try to write a note on it, as the subject is peculiarly interesting to me.

Those things have not yet reached me.

[Shri Rabindranath Thakur]

Source: MS original at Rabindra Bhavan, Shantiniketan; letter published in *CP*, I, pp. 25–6.

1 Thomas David Gibson-Carmichael, 1st baron of Skirling (1859–1926): governor of Bengal, 1912–17. Carmichael was pleased by his visit: 'Both my wife and I will always look back to that morning as one of the happiest we have spent in India' (Carmichael to RT, 5 May 1915 [RB]).
2 Sylvain Lévi: French orientalist, who received an honorary doctorate from Calcutta University in Dec. 1913, at the same time as RT. In the early 1920s, he lectured at Visva-Bharati. See letter 221. James Drummond Anderson: lecturer in Bengali, University of Cambridge; he and RT corresponded at length on Bengali philology. See letter 120.
3 Pramatha Chaudhuri: editor of *Shabuj Patra*. Mani Lal Ganguli [Gangopadhyay] (1888–1929): writer and editor; husband of Abanindranath Tagore's daughter.
4 Two letters from RT to Anderson were printed in *Shabuj Patra* during 1914; Anderson presumably translated one or both of them into English (or French?) and sent it to Lévi. See *Chhanda* (rev. edn, 1369 [1962]) (Prosody), pp. 1–20.

97

To (Sir) William Rothenstein

In early 1915, Robert Bridges approached Tagore with a request to alter one of the poems in the English *Gitanjali*, which he wished to include in his popular wartime anthology, *The Spirit of Man*. Rabindranath was unwilling. Bridges assiduously persisted and eventually, after many months and supporting requests from William Rothenstein and W. B. Yeats (the original reviser of the poem), Tagore yielded. The revised version was printed in the anthology between extracts from Plato and Aristotle,[1] and subsequently reprinted by Yeats as editor of *The Oxford Book of Modern Verse, 1892–1935*. As this powerful letter, and letters 100–2 and 104, suggest, Tagore's reluctance was perfectly reasonable, even though the revised poem was a distinct improvement. Taken as a whole, the episode was a microcosm of the intricate nature of Tagore's English literary reputation.[2]

Shantiniketan, [West Bengal, India]
4 April 1915

My dear Friend

I give up Japan, at least, for the present. Not for any sudden failure in courage or enthusiasm but for the same blessed reason that brings a modern war to its halt. My finance is hopeless, mainly owing to the European complications.

I got a letter from Dr Bridges with his own version of a *Gitanjali* poem. I cannot judge it.[3] But since I have got my fame as an English writer I feel extreme reluctance in accepting alterations in my English poems by any of your writers. I must not give men any reasonable ground for accusing me – which they do – of reaping advantage [from] other men's genius and skill. There are people who suspect that I owe in a large measure to Andrews' help for my literary success, which is so false I can afford to laugh at it. But it is different about Yeats. I think Yeats was sparing in his suggestions – moreover, I was with him during the revisions. But one is apt to delude himself, and it is very easy for me to gradually forget the share Yeats had in making my things passable. Though you have the first draft of my translations with you I have unfortunately allowed the revised typed pages to get lost in which Yeats pencilled his corrections. Of course, at that time I could never imagine that anything that I could write would find its place in your literature. But the situation is changed now. And if it be true that Yeats's touches have made it possible for *Gitanjali* to occupy the place it does then that must be confessed.[4] At least by my subsequent unadulterated writing my true level should be found out and the faintest speck of lie should be wiped out from the fame I enjoy now. It does not matter what people think of me but it does matter all the world to me to be true to myself. This is the reason why I cannot accept any help from Bridges excepting where the grammar is wrong or wrong words have been used. My translations are frankly prose – my aim is to make them simple with just a suggestion of rhythm to give them a touch of the lyric, avoiding all archaisms and poetical conventions.

I am sending you some more of my translations – keep them with you till we meet, if you have any doubts about their fitness. I still cherish the hope of seeing you and the dear children in your green solitude and bury there under the fallen leaves all the artificial laurels lurking in my wreath.

With love

Yours affectionately
Rabindranath Tagore

[PS] Andrews does not admire the alterations made by Bridges but that does not affect me.[5] In fact I am not so much anxious about mutilations as about added beauties which I cannot claim as mine.

Source: MS original in Rothenstein Papers [Harvard]; letter published in Lago (ed.), *Imperfect Encounter*, pp. 194–6.

1 *Spirit of Man* (38). Bridges noted:

> I have to thank him [RT] and his English publisher for allowing me to quote from this book [*Gitanjali*], and in the particular instance of this very beautiful poem, for the author's friendliness in permitting me to shift a few words for the sake of what I considered more effective rhythm or grammar.

2 The episode is discussed at length in Lago (ed.), *Imperfect Encounter*, pp. 177–86.
3 'The sample you have sent me, I feel, is beautiful. But with things one has grown to love one does not tolerate any change even for the better. That is my experience' (RT to Bridges, 22 March 1915 [copy at RB]).
4 On the beginning of this rumour, which understandably rankled with RT, see letters 81 and 82.
5 RT's English friends, such as Rothenstein, Thompson and Yeats, thought that C. F. Andrews was behind his initial refusal of Bridges, and scholars have tended to accept their belief as fact. But the balance of the evidence, and particularly this letter, suggests that RT was far more concerned here with his own integrity than with literary excellence. His key statement is surely that 'it does not matter what people think of me but it does matter all the world to me to be true to myself'; and the second sentence of the postscript confirms the strength of his feeling.

98

To William Winstanley Pearson[1]

C. F. Andrews was one of two Englishmen who were closely associated with Shantiniketan in its early days; the other was W. W. Pearson. Like Andrews, he was a Christian missionary in India who lost faith in orthodox mission work. Meeting Tagore in London while on sick leave in the summer of 1912 – the same time as Andrews met Rabindranath – he felt an immediate attraction and impulsively touched Tagore's feet in the Indian manner.[2] Within a couple of years he left the London Missionary Society in Calcutta and moved to Shantiniketan to become a teacher. Though he would spend long periods away from the place, sometimes travelling with Tagore as his secretary, Pearson regarded Shantiniketan as his home for the rest of his tragically brief life.

His attitude to it was almost as complex as Rabindranath's. Emotionally, he was profoundly drawn to the Bengali ethos, especially its affectionate family relationships, its sensitivity to literature and its indifference to commerce; but his critical intelligence (sharpened, unlike that of Andrews, by his science degree from Cambridge) saw and condemned the parochiality, mental passivity and social injustices that were also an integral part of that ethos. 'Willie Pearson had in him something of a volcano, which he found difficult beyond words to control,' Andrews wrote after Pearson's death. 'At times, it would break out and get beyond him.'[3]

In May 1915, with the ashram closed for the holidays, Pearson wrote to Tagore (who was then in Calcutta) from Ramgarh, to protest at the ashram letting go one of its good teachers. 'No teacher was so devoted to the ideals of the ashram . . . To acquiesce in losing him would I fear mean much more than the mere loss of a good man, it would be a confession that the ashram is provincial and narrow.'[4] This is Rabindranath's response.

Shantiniketan, [West Bengal, India]
16 May 1915

My dear Pearson,

The day I was about to leave for Calcutta for a course of wandering life I got the news that Andrews had been attacked with cholera.[5] So I have come to Bolpur and I am glad to say that the worst is over and he is fairly convalescent. Dr Maitra is with me and he assures me that there is no more cause for anxiety for Andrews.[6]

I have got your letter about Dattatreya.[7] Do not for a moment doubt that it was financial difficulty which was at the root of his leaving the ashram. Though I do not interfere in the management of the school, I should have made an exception in the case of Dattatreya, if I were not convinced that the school would not be able to meet his requirements, the details of which he set before us. I know, as I was in one of the meetings, that the school authorities racked their brains to make some provision for him in the ashram and with extreme reluctance they came upon the decision. They went so far as to suggest that Sharat Babu should be removed from the school to make room for Dattatreya and the suggestion was rejected not on the ground of sentiment, but of necessity.[8]

You know how deeply I love you and I earnestly hope you will not take it amiss when I say that the growing feeling of distrust towards your colleagues in the ashram is leading you astray from the paths of charity and love. Though I am a poet and foolish in most things, I have some insight [into] human nature, and I know these people, with whom I have been working for years, are sincere. We become cruel, and our ideals become mere abstractions when we look upon our friends and human beings as mere agents for carrying out the ideas which we consider as the best. I hate falsehood and treachery, for it is treason against God, but I have infinite patience for differences of ideals and outlooks upon life. Thank God that Jagadananda Babu, Nepal Babu and others were not cut out in my own pattern and that is one of the reasons why they are truly helping me in realising my own life.[9] If I began to despise them for some advantage I imagine I have over them, I should hold myself utterly unworthy to enjoy that advantage. Of course, Shantiniketan school has its ideals, which, though not rigidly definite, are definite enough to guide us. But differences of readings they permit, and divergences of methods to a great extent they allow. If they did not they would turn men into machines and goodness would attain its symmetry at the cost of its life. We are quite at liberty to disapprove some of the actions of our friends but it should be the very last thing to distrust their good faith. With very great pain I have been noticing for some time past Andrews also drifting into this hopeless mood of contemptuous mistrust which is strong because vague and which will never lead to the *shantam, shivam, advaitam*.[10] But I shall wait and trust God to remove this mist of misunderstanding and lead us to the clarity of truth and light of love. He has brought us together and before he calls us back we shall know that we are one though we are different.

With best love,

Yours affectionately,
Rabindranath Tagore

Source: MS original at Rabindra Bhavan, Shantiniketan; letter published in *VBQ*, 9, No. 1, May–July 1943, pp. 72–3.

1 William Winstanley Pearson (1881–1923): Christian missionary and teacher at Shantiniketan; he left the London Missionary Society, based at Bhowanipur in Calcutta, and joined Shantiniketan in 1914. Pearson acted as RT's secretary in Japan and the USA in 1916–17 and again in the USA in 1920–1. He published *Shantiniketan: The Bolpur School of Rabindranath Tagore* in 1917, and translated some of RT's writings from Bengali, including *Gora*.
2 Pearson's gesture, something almost unheard of in 1912, occurred on 19 June in his own house, where a paper about RT was read out by Sukumar Ray to a small group of Bengalis. RT mentioned it (describing the sahib erroneously as a retired official of the ICS) in a letter to Ajit Kumar Chakravarty at Shantiniketan, who reported it to the editor of the *MR*. In Aug. 1912, the *MR* carried an article stating that 'Enthusiasm [for RT] in certain circles runs so high that a retired English member of the ICS on meeting the poet made obeisance to him in Indian fashion, "taking the dust of his feet"' ('Rabindranath in England', p. 222). Although RT corrected the mistake in a further letter to Chakravarty (still without naming Pearson), the *MR* did not correct the error in print. It was not until Dec. 1923, at a memorial meeting for Pearson at Shantiniketan, that RT revealed the sahib to have been Pearson (Paul, *Rabijibani*, VI, pp. 311–12).
3 'W. W. Pearson', *Congregational Quarterly*, July 1924, p. 284.
4 'W. W. Pearson and Santiniketan', *VBQ*, 48, Nos. 1–4, May 1982–April 1983, p. 112.
5 Andrews contracted cholera from a slice of water-melon bought from a railway platform vendor (Tinker, *Ordeal of Love*, p. 106).
6 Dwijendranath Maitra (1878–1950): resident surgeon, Mayo Hospital, Calcutta; he is the 'distinguished Bengali doctor of medicine' quoted by W. B. Yeats in his introduction to *Gitanjali* (pp. vii–x).

7 Kakasaheb Karlekar Dattatreya (1885–1981). Dattatreya's attraction to Gandhi may also have been a factor in his departure.
8 Sharat Babu: Sharat Kumar Roy, teacher at Shantiniketan school.
9 Jagadananda Ray (1869–1933) and Nepal Chandra Ray (1866–1944): long-time teachers at RT's school, in science and history respectively.
10 *Mandukya Upanishad*, 7. 'He is the end of evolution, He is nonduality. He is peace and love' (Juan Mascaró (trans.), *The Upanishads* (London, 1965), p. 83). RT explained the significance to himself of this favourite trinity in 'Shantam, shivam, advaitam', *RR*, XIII, pp. 410–16. It may be attained only by *brahmacharya*, self-control.

99

To Nagendranath Gangulee

The financial condition of Nagendranath Gangulee, Tagore's son-in-law, detailed in letter 63, deteriorated steadily. He was unable to stick at *zamindari* work or to control his taste for luxury which he indulged at Tagore's expense. No doubt the award of the Nobel prize encouraged him to think that he would be able to sponge on his father-in-law with impunity. But this letter shows that Rabindranath, though still sympathetic to Nagen and aware of his talents, could be stern about money.

Shantiniketan, [West Bengal, India]
12 Asharh 1322 [27 June 1915]

Kalyaniyeshu

It is now nine months since the last payment from the Berahimpur estate and this year again the *aush* and *jali* paddy has been flooded, so there is no revenue.[1] I am scraping the bottom of my bank loan – and we have stopped our monthly allowance to *Bara Dada*.[2] I had a plan to travel but I lack the means, so I am stuck here.[3] The building and repairing work on the school dining room and hospital has started, and has been delayed for lack of funds – I am in real difficulty with my pupils. I have already borrowed 500 rupees and I have no courage to borrow more because I do not know when I shall receive my own maintenance allowance from the estate.

The money you have requested in order to pay the premium I shall ask Rathi to lend you – but I will have to deduct twenty-five rupees per month from your allowance towards repayment.[4] To do more than this is beyond me.

You have remarked that your requests for money displease me. The reason is that I have been brought up in a certain way. I used to receive two hundred rupees a month, and I never dared ask for more. The entire burden of Balu's business debts fell on my shoulders; my father did not allow any portion of it to be repaid from the estate. I had to pawn my household goods and somehow stave off the creditors – only I know what I had to face there – and even today that debt remains undischarged.[5] I have never indulged myself in the notion that I should receive more than my due. As long as my father was alive, I lived very humbly, and benefited from it. While I have done my utmost to live within my means, you have never kept within yours; you have simply passed your debts on to me, debts that were not even necessary to incur. At no period of my life have I had the audacity to do this. So when you tell me that you cannot make ends meet, I fail to understand. For people must live within their means, otherwise there will be chaos: that is the rule everywhere in the world. If you go on requesting and receiving money without effort it will eventually harm you more than me. Therefore, though it is most disagreeable for me not to comply with your requests in all matters, I must remain firm.

Shubhanudhyayi
Shri Rabindranath Thakur

Source: MS original at Rabindra Bhavan, Shantiniketan; letter published in Sharadiya *Desh*, 1398 [Autumn 1991], p. 39.

1 In Nadia district, location of the Berahimpur *zamindari*, *aush* or autumn rice, sown on comparatively high land, was planted in May (Baishakh) and reaped in Aug. and Sept. (Bhadra); *jali* rice was planted in April or May and reaped in Oct. or Nov. (Kartik) (George Watt, *Dictionary of the Economic Products of India*: V, *Linium to Oyster* (Calcutta and London, 1891), p. 553).
2 *Bara Dada*: 'eldest brother': Dwijendranath Tagore. In 1912, he agreed to lease his portion of the Tagore estates to RT and Satyendranath in exchange for a fixed annual sum of Rs 45,000, to be paid monthly.
3 On 24 June, RT told C. F. Andrews there was a financial crisis in the school. Shortly after, he cancelled his proposed trip to Japan, telling Andrews on 16 July 1915, 'Last year the rent we realised was small and it was largely supplemented by borrowed money. So this year our capacity for raising loans will be limited, so I must not launch myself into an expensive scheme of travels till I have a better prospect before me than now' [RB].
4 Rathi: Rathindranath Tagore. The premium was probably for life insurance.
5 In 1895, Balendranath (Balu) and Surendranath, two nephews of RT, started Tagore and Co. in Kushtia, not far from Shelidah; the company was registered with the two nephews and RT as partners. It engaged in grain storage, jute baling and sugarcane crushing. Competition from an Englishman's company and dishonesty by the Tagore and Co. manager, and the premature death of Balendranath in 1899, bankrupted the business and left RT with large debts. See Rathindranath Tagore, *Edges of Time*, p. 30. RT eventually borrowed Rs 50,000 from Taraknath Palit in 1902, which he could not repay until 1917, after Palit's death, as mentioned in letter 110.

100

To Macmillan & Co. (UK)

The disagreement over translation between Tagore and Robert Bridges, which began in March 1915 (see letter 97), rumbled on through the year, during which Tagore was honoured with a knighthood. By August, William Rothenstein, C. F. Andrews, E. J. Thompson, W. B. Yeats, the Society of Authors and of course the publishers Macmillan, were all involved in the issue. Macmillan, as Tagore's agent as well as his publisher, was inclined to refuse to cooperate with Bridges.[1] This suited Rabindranath, who wanted Macmillan to take the matter out of his hands. As he told Bridges on 19 June, 'being unpractical and ignorant in business matters I have absolutely surrendered my affairs relating to my English books into the hands of my publishers'.[2] In this letter to Macmillan he reinforces this comment.

Shantiniketan, [West Bengal, India]
13 August 1915

Dear Sirs,
The problems that arise out of my English publications in England are quite new to me and I am not competent to deal with them.

If my instinct is right then I think the versions of translations that are already before the public should never be published in altered forms – otherwise they would lose all idea of finality and many a reader's mind would be exercised in trying to improve them. But as I was not quite sure whether Dr Bridges' taking liberty with only one of my poems would matter, I wanted to depend upon your discretion.

I can assure you it would greatly relieve my mind if you can take the responsibility upon yourselves with regard to questions of this kind. I know you will understand my interest far better than I can hope to do myself therefore I trouble you with these things, hoping to be excused.

Though I have ventured to write English, and so far have had the good luck to be appreciated by your readers it is a subconscious process with me – and when a poet like Dr Bridges insists that my prose versions of *Gitanjali* could be greatly improved upon in rhythm and suggestiveness with a little manipulation and sends me a specimen himself I am at a loss what to think of it.[3] This has been the reason of my hesitation and of my wish to leave the final decision in your hands. I think it can be suggested to Dr Bridges that with the help of some of the Indian students he knows at Oxford he can translate some one or two of my poems from the original Bengali, which has not yet been attempted.[4]

Yours truly
Rabindranath Tagore

Source: MS original in Macmillan Company Papers [BL].

1 'We cannot understand how such a proposal could have been made' (Macmillan to RT, 19 April 1915 [copy at BL]).
2 RT to Bridges [typed copy at Bodleian].
3 On 25 June, Bridges sent RT his version of *Gitanjali* (67), annotated line by line with his reasons for changing the original. 'My version of it uses all your own diction, but gets rid of all the little faults of English which otherwise destroy its effect.' He added: 'What immense trouble, my dear poet, you are causing to a well-wisher and friend of your Muse!' [copy at Bodleian].
4 RT obviously had in mind Hasan Shahid Suhrawardy (see letter 87).

101

To Robert Bridges

Writing to Robert Bridges a few days after his letter to Macmillan, Tagore reiterated his desire to rely on Macmillan's judgement of his best interests, and also his earlier comment to Bridges to the effect that one should not tamper with works that people have come to love. (Unsurprisingly, he avoided any reference to his wish not to give further currency to the rumour about English revisers being responsible for the success of his English works, which he had cited at length to William Rothenstein (letter 97).) This letter clearly demonstrates the gulf in sensibility between Tagore and Bridges: for the former, life, with its inevitable imperfections, was pre-eminent in the creation of literature, while for the latter, technique, with its possibilities of perfection, was dominant.

Shantiniketan, [West Bengal, India]
19 August 1915

Dear Dr Bridges,

Perhaps you do not quite realise my helplessness in matters connected with my English publications. As I am living ten thousand miles away from the place and am unfamiliar with conditions prevailing in England I was advised by my friends to choose somebody as my literary agent, leaving my affairs entirely in their hands. So I have entrusted my publishers to act [on] my behalf according to whatever they think proper – and, so far, I have never interfered with their decisions or done anything to lessen their full sense of responsibility. Being confident that they will give their best attention to everything pertaining to my English writings I have asked them to exercise their judgement in the present matter as they have been doing in other cases about my books.

As for my own opinion I think there is a stage in all writings where they must have a finality in spite of their shortcomings. Authors have their limitations and we have to put up with them if they give us something positively good. If we begin to think of improvement there is no end to it and differences of opinion are sure to arise.

Please do not think I have the least conceit about my English. Being not born to it I have no standard of judgement in my mind about this language – at least, I cannot consciously use it. Therefore I am all the more helpless in deciding whether certain alterations add to the value of a poem with which my readers' minds have already become familiar. I know, habit gives a poem its true living character, making it seem inevitable like a flower or a fruit. Flaws are there but life makes up for all its flaws.

Please accept my heartiest thanks for your exquisite book of poems.[1]

Yours sincerely,
Rabindranath Tagore

Source: MS copy in Bridges Papers [Bodleian].

1 The book was probably *Poems Written in the Year MCMXIII*, published in 1914.

102

To William Butler Yeats

In addition to the reasons for not altering *Gitanjali* mentioned in letters 97, 100 and 101, Tagore had also told Robert Bridges that he did not want to offend W. B. Yeats.[1] Bridges took the matter up with Yeats and encouraged him to write to Tagore about it himself. In his letter, dated 31 July 1915, Yeats wrote:

> I should be sorry to prevent Robert Bridges from making the slight changes he wishes. He is at moments a most admirable poet and always the chief scholar in English style now living. His creative power is not great though very exquisite but no living man is so well fitted to measure and amend a detail of speech. I have the same mother tongue as he has, but I would be grateful should he care to revise a poem of mine, and certainly I would be ashamed if consideration for my revision should keep you from accepting

his. I feel that he is the head of my craft in England and have felt so since the death of Swinburne, or from before it, for Swinburne's abundant genius repelled me.[2]

Yeats' letter clinched the matter in Bridges' favour, as this letter shows.[3]

Calcutta, [India]
31 August 1915

My dear Mr Yeats

It is very nice to get your letter when I least expected it. I had a correspondence with Robert Bridges about the subject you mentioned in your letter. I feel now I ought to allow him to make use of my poem as he wished – especially after your recommendation – but Macmillan being my literary agents in England I have to entirely depend upon them for everything concerning my English books. I have asked them to exercise their judgement and do whatever they consider proper in the matter in question. Of course, I am sure, your advice will be valuable to them if offered and they will give every consideration to it.

I am arranging to send you typescript copies of two of my books of translations for your criticism, one of them belonging to the *Gitanjali* series of poems to be named *Fruit-Gathering*, and the other *Lover's Gift* containing lyrics of love and other subjects. I think you will find in them better mastery of your language which I owe to your guidance.[4] I hope to go to England when this war is over and see these books through the press.

I have often thought of the beautiful girl I had the happiness to meet in Chelsea and I shall try to induce and, if possible, to help her to resume her Bengali studies and do some more translations when I meet her.[5]

The Bengali book on the reminiscences of my early days is a difficult piece of writing to translate into English.[6] The atmosphere and everything in this book is so foreign for an Englishman that very few readers, I am afraid, will be able to enter into its spirit. However I shall try to take up the task myself when I am in England.

Kindly remember me to Lady Gregory.

Yours
Rabindranath Tagore

Source: MS original in collection of Michael Yeats; letter published in Finneran et al. (eds.), *Letters*, pp. 315–16.

1 RT mentioned Yeats' possible objection in his letters to Bridges of 22 March [copy at RB] and 25 June [copy at Bodleian], in which he stated, 'At least I ought to be quite certain that he [Yeats] approves of it.'
2 *VBQ*, *30*, No. 3, 1964–5, p. 172.
3 According to Mary Lago, 'Bridges' request was ultimately judged on sentimental, not literary grounds' (Lago (ed.), *Imperfect Encounter*, p. 186). Yeats' letter, and RT's response, show that RT's regard for Yeats' literary judgement was as important as his gratitude to Yeats for his work on *Gitanjali*.
4 Yeats' letters to Macmillan in 1916–17 show that he did think RT's English had improved, but he was not satisfied with the translations. On *Fruit-Gathering*, he commented, 'I have made rather less changes than I did in *The Gardener* or *Gitanjali* for I have not now got the author near to ask him for a more literal translation when [the?] English is vague' (Yeats to Macmillan, 14 April 1916 [BL]). On *Lover's Gift*, he remarked, 'It is rather an embarrassment' (Yeats to Macmillan, 28 Jan. 1917, in Simon Nowell-Smith (ed.), *Letters to Macmillan* (London, 1967), p. 291). RT himself was not satisfied with Yeats' changes to *Fruit-Gathering*; he told George Brett of Macmillan (New York) on 10 Jan. 1917 that 'one or two of the corrections made by Mr W. B. Yeats . . . have altogether changed the meaning' [New York].

5 The girl was Iseult Gonne (see letter 91). Yeats had told RT of his disappointment at her giving up her translating from Bengali.
6 Yeats had a keen interest in *My Reminiscences*, which he described as 'a most valuable and rich work' (Yeats to Macmillan, 28 Jan. 1917, in Nowell-Smith (ed.), *Letters*, p. 291). In his letter to RT of 31 July, he asked:

> Is there any likelihood of your autobiography being published in English? I believe it would be very successful if it came out at the close of the war and thus it would help your fame more just now than any other book you could publish. Your readers know your poetry and your philosophy to some extent, and they are curious to understand its relation to your country and history. To judge too by what I heard of the book it might have political importance.

(See letter 105.)

103

To William Winstanley Pearson

The deeply emotional bond between Rabindranath and W. W. Pearson was apparent in the previous letter to Pearson (98). In October 1915, Tagore received a letter from Pearson, then on a ship to Australia with C. F. Andrews, announcing that his best friend had just been killed in the Dardanelles campaign:

> I knew long ago that the meaning of this war could never be fully clear to me until I had experienced a personal sorrow and so it has come . . . I need your sympathy and strength . . . I am so weak and easily – so easily – forget and say these things must be. But that is no answer and it deadens and cannot inspire the mind.[1]

Rabindranath's answer shows why he and his work had such a powerful impact on people of sensitivity and imagination.

Srinagar, Kashmir, [India]
11 October 1915

My dear Pearson,

A few nights ago I dreamt that I met you somewhere in some battlefield. You were standing on high land with a soldier by your side. Your face was deathly pale, full of profoundest sorrow. I did not know the reason but it seemed to me quite natural. I raised my hand to touch you but I found that you were wounded in your right arm – I said to myself that death had pierced his soul and a prolonged and loud wail came from my heart. It was an intense suffering for me – I suppose it was your pain which was transferred to my heart. Then I woke up. I [have] never had such a vivid dream before. You were silent, your eyes lowered, the whole world of sorrow seemed concentrated in you in its immense stillness. Since then my mind was anxious about you till I got your letter day before yesterday. The dream had affected me so deeply that I had been discussing it with several persons trying to probe the mystery of psychology that could create such vivid vision and intense feeling out of nothing, never suspecting that this dream came to me through the medium of infinite mind that lies between individuals. It gave me the truth for a moment that in reality your suffering was mine.

The barrier of self is a *maya*, and when it is dispelled then we know that in our suffering we have tasted the draught of sorrow that wells up from the heart of creation, flowing out to merge and be transformed into the sea of Endless Joy. When we do not see ourselves in the infinite, when we imagine our sorrow to be our very own then it becomes untrue, and its burden becomes heavy. I realise more and more the truth of Buddha's teaching that the root of all our miseries is in this consciousness of self, which must be translated into the consciousness of All before we can solve the mystery of pain and be free. Our emancipation lies through the path of suffering, we must unlock the gate of joy by the key of pain. Our heart is like a fountain and so long as it is driven through the narrow pipe of self it is full of fear and doubt and sorrow, for then it is in the dark and does not know its end, but when it comes out in the open, in the bosom of the All, then it glistens in the light and sings in the joy of freedom. The narrowness of the self is a blessing when the fountain plays in full force, for then its bondage is being translated every moment into emancipation and its pain into love.

Yours with love,
Rabindranath Tagore

Source: MS original at Rabindra Bhavan, Shantiniketan; letter published in *VBQ*, 9, No. 1, May–July 1943, pp. 75–6.

1 Pearson to RT, 27 Sept. 1915 [RB].

104

To Robert Bridges

On 31 August, Tagore wrote to Macmillan about Robert Bridges' request to alter *Gitanjali*: 'As I feel I cannot refuse Yeats I shall be happy if you see your way to granting [the] request and send your permission to Dr Bridges.'[1] A couple of months later he closed the affair by writing the following letter to Bridges.[2]

Calcutta, [India]
18 November 1915

Dear Dr Bridges,

I am painfully diffident about my English writings and the advices I get from my friends are so conflicting that I think it wise to leave it to my publishers to decide for me when any question arises concerning my English works. Please never think that I have any exaggerated notion of my English style, knowing for certain that it must have blemishes which I am not competent even to detect and much less to remove. I never had the advantage of university training and analytically studying your language. Therefore in my attempts at English writing it is difficult for me to know where I fail or dare to be sure that I have caught the right expression. If there be any excellence in my translations it is unconscious, it is like correctly walking in dreams in places which it is not safe to attempt when wakeful. Indeed I should consider myself fortunate to be able to secure any help from a poet like yourself who is a master of all intimate secrets of the musical capacity of your language. Only thing that makes me hesitate is not being sure [where] the line is beyond which it is dishonest for a man of my position [to go]. In pure literature it is very often that the mode of expression is of greater value than richness of thought. Therefore I feel that in my translations I should be loath to borrow from my brother artists any thing of real splendour and appropriate its value for myself. I must appear before the public with all my natural and accidental limitations excepting about mistakes in grammar and idiom. Henceforth I shall be great deal more careful than before not merely to keep up my reputation, but to attain my true place, if there is any chance for me, in your literature. I believe I have had what is more than enough for me in my own language and I never should be greedy in trying to scramble for that which is not my true position in yours.

I know what this war is to you and I bow my head in awe before your people who are vindicating the divine in man by boundless suffering and heroism. Please let Mrs Bridges accept my heartfelt sympathy and reverence whose son is fighting for the cause of liberty in one of the greatest wars in the history of mankind.[3]

Yours very sincerely
Rabindranath Tagore

Source: MS copy in Bridges Papers [Bodleian].

1 RT to Macmillan, 31 Aug. 1915 [BL]. Bridges' anthology, *The Spirit of Man*, was published in 1916 and reprinted three times during that year. It fulfilled its intention of appealing to the men in the trenches. Their opinion about RT's poetry was divided: Wilfred Owen admired some of it, but Ivor Gurney wrote to a friend that 'one of the best signs of healthy taste at present, is the significant fact that though Rabindranath Tagore has been knighted, the critics I read did not pretend to be transported by his work – not so much, indeed, as before the war' (Ivor Gurney, *Ivor Gurney: War Letters* (R. K. R. Thornton ed.; Manchester, 1983), p. 31).
2 RT's letter appears to have been a response to a letter of thanks from Bridges, which is missing.
3 Edward Bridges joined up in Aug. 1915 and served in France. Wounded on the Somme in Feb. 1917, he survived the war.

105

To William Butler Yeats

During 1916, W. B. Yeats became concerned that Tagore's writing was being dismissed in literary circles as merely mystical and monotonous. Yeats was particularly keen that Tagore's autobiography, which in January 1916 began to be serialised in English as *My Reminiscences* in the Calcutta *Modern Review*, should be published in London by Macmillan. He told Macmillan:

> If that work is as good as I hope, it would I believe be of great value to his reputation if published in full in English. It is important that we should again see him as an Oriental personality speaking to his own people and once more understand that these poems in English are translations of poems which have very intricate and precise form in his own language... I hope you will forgive my unasked advice. But I care very much for Tagore's work and have spent much time and thought upon it.[1]

Yeats had already requested Tagore to prepare a translation in an earlier letter.[2] Now he repeated the request.[3] Rabindranath, in his response, accedes but repeats his earlier doubts (see letter 102).

The crest of a wave

Calcutta, [India]
5 March 1916

Dear Yeats

I would very gladly indeed fall in with your suggestion since few things would give me greater pleasure than to have a part, however remote, in the revival of Irish national culture. But there are certain difficulties which I anticipate. The greatest is this, that my nephew, Suren, will not have finished translating the 'Memoirs' for some months and this may be too late for your plans. A second difficulty arises out of the character of the 'Memoirs'. They deal only with my early days and stop short at about the age of twenty-five, so these reminiscences are more narrowly personal than anything else. Perhaps the best thing for me to do [is] as you suggest and send you the 'Memoirs' as they near completion and then leave you to judge for yourself. My anxiety is that I may not give you any false expectations. If you think that a delay would be fatal to the plan altogether then would you let me know. My nephew could probably advance a little faster with his translation work, but he is a busy man and he could not make much more speed.[4]

I have already sent to my publishers two MSS of my poems asking them to send copies to you. I hope you have got them by this time. I am getting ready to send you a copy of some translations I have done from our folk songs and Vaishnava poems – I think you will get it by the next mail if it is not torpedoed on the way.[5]

Yours
Rabindranath Tagore

Source: MS original in collection of Michael Yeats.

1 Yeats to Macmillan, 14 April 1916 [BL]. Later in the year, Yeats suggested in two letters to Macmillan that they commission a short essay on RT's prosody to preface his next volume of verse, in order to 'remind reviewers that Tagore is not a writer of facile English for English religious readers, but a master of very arduous measures whom they read in a tongue that is not his' (9 July 1916, in Nowell-Smith (ed.), *Letters*, p. 290). Yeats suggested that Ezra Pound might do this, but added: 'I fear however that it may now be too late' (1 July [1916], [BL]). No essay appeared.
2 See letter 102, n. 6.
3 Yeats' letter with its 'plan', to which RT refers, is missing.
4 See 'My reminiscences', *MR*, Jan.–Dec. 1916, trans. by Surendranath Tagore. Macmillan published *My Reminiscences* the following year, with illustrations by Gaganendranath Tagore and other artists.
5 The two MSS became *Fruit-Gathering* (London, 1916) and *Lover's Gift* (London, 1918). Some folk (Baul) songs and Vaishnava poems appeared in *The Fugitive* (London, 1921).

106

To James H. Cousins[1]

Ever since he began reading English literature, Tagore had been drawn to its passion. In 1914 he had told Thomas Sturge Moore (see letter 86) that 'we look for your literature to bring to us the thundering life flood of the West, even though it carries with it all the debris of the passing moments'. In this letter to a poet acquaintance of W. B. Yeats living in India, he reiterates this thought, though now more darkly.

174   Selected letters of Rabindranath Tagore

Shantiniketan, [West Bengal, India]
8 April 1916

Dear Mr Cousins

I greatly enjoyed reading your paper on 'Literary Ideals', for which I thank you.[2] Literature reflects the writer's outlook on life. Generally speaking, an Indian's outlook is philosophical, therefore philosophy naturally assumes a living form in Indian literature. When a European says he fully wants to live he does not mean to say that he wants to live the life of truth but that it is his wish to live the life of passion – and his literature reflects his desire. It is not light that he wants but conflagration. He consumes himself and his world – and the present war is the best illustration of that.

Very sincerely yours
Rabindranath Tagore

[PS] I am very much touched by Mr Bain's letter to me – I shall write to him.

Source: MS original at Rabindra Bhavan, Shantiniketan.

1 James Henry Sproull Cousins (1873–1956): poet and educator, associated with the Irish National Theatre; he and his wife left Ireland in late 1915 – their passages paid by Annie Besant – and settled in south India at the Theosophical College founded by Besant at Madanapalle, birthplace of Krishnamurti.
2 This paper does not appear in Cousins' collection, *New Ways in English Literature* (Madras, 1917), unless it was an early version of the title essay. RT was indulgent towards Cousins but had no high regard for his writing.

107

To Edward John Thompson

From September 1915, at Rabindranath's request, Edward Thompson began assisting in the translation of Tagore's short stories. In the same year, having published an anthology of English verse for Indian students with Tagore's encouragement, Thompson began to work at translations of other Bengali writers, such as Ramprasad Sen, the great song-writer of the eighteenth century. Rabindranath again encouraged him, though he would always be cautious about the likely reception of Bengali literature in English literary circles, as he makes clear in this letter.

Shantiniketan, [West Bengal, India]
13 April 1916

Dear Thompson

Your anthology is excellent; it is the best of its kind for Indian boys.[1]

I am glad to learn that you are translating Ramprasad's songs.[2] These must be done in very simple English prose, as you have discovered yourself. They are so utterly bold and unconventional that any attempt to dress them in respectable English verse forms would only make them look grotesque.

The day after tomorrow I go to Calcutta – and then to the south, and then – I know not where, possibly, across the Pacific.[3] For some time past I have been feeling restless.

It is the migratory instinct in me. I have a nesting place on the other side of the sea and I feel homesick for the wide world.

Yours
Rabindranath Tagore

Source: MS original in Thompson Papers [Bodleian].

1 *An Anthology of Verse for Indian Students* was published in 1915 by Macmillan. Thompson requested RT in Nov. 1913 to act as an editor. Though RT apparently agreed, nothing came of it. Thompson's preface stated: 'Originally I hoped to have compiled this anthology with the cooperation of Sir Rabindranath Tagore, but pressure of other tasks and ill-health have prevented this assistance.' (Quoted in E. P. Thompson, *Alien Homage*, p. 118.)
2 Ramprasad was a devotee of the goddess Kali. His songs remain extremely popular at all levels of Bengali society, with an appeal broader than that of Rabindranath's songs. See J. C. Ghosh, *Bengali Literature* (London, 1976), pp. 87–8, and Sumanta Banerjee, *The Parlour and the Streets: Elite and Popular Culture in Nineteenth Century Calcutta* (Calcutta, 1989), pp. 80–3; there are two wonderful songs in the style of Ramprasad, composed by Satyajit Ray, in his film *Devi* (*The Goddess*).
3 RT did not go south; he left Calcutta by ship on 3 May, heading for Japan, from where he eventually travelled to the USA on a lecture tour.

108

To Gaganendranath Tagore

Japan appealed profoundly to Tagore during his first visit there in 1916. In one of his speeches he said: 'It is the responsibility which every nation has to reveal itself before the world . . . [Japan] has given rise to a civilisation which is perfect in its form, and has evolved a sense of sight which clearly sees truth in beauty and beauty in truth.'[1] It appalled him to see the Japanese embracing the uglier aspects of western civilisation and abandoning their own traditions.

The clash was a sharp reminder of the confused and imperfect situation in Bengal. His nephews, Gaganendranath and Abanindranath, were now leading artists, but Rabindranath was not fully satisfied with their work; he felt that it lacked something. Although it drew upon Indian miniatures and Japanese techniques (introduced to the Tagores by Okakura Kakuzo), it did so more imitatively than creatively. Being in Japan revealed this to Rabindranath and also stimulated him in his own quest to paint. The immediate impact of the country, however, as explained in this letter, was that Rabindranath arranged for two Japanese artists to visit Bengal and for a Shantiniketan art student to stay in Japan.

[Japan]
8 August 1916

Kalyaniyeshu

When will you all leave your corner and go out into the wide world? You ought to make your name properly known. But it is useless to chide you. Finally, after a great deal of deliberation and on the advice of Taikan, I am sending you an artist named Arai.[2] He and his companion will live in India for a couple of years, buying Indian art and painting pictures of India. If he can stay even six months in our house and provide you with some training that would be good. A new stimulus from outside reawakens our mind – the company of these artists will benefit you in this way. Rathi can look after their needs but they must receive at least a hundred rupees a month – they asked for a hundred and fifty but can manage on a hundred.[3] Your boys must gain proficiency in the skills of Japanese brushwork. This man is gentle and of good character – though he is not as good an artist as Taikan, he is by no means inferior. As a teacher he has much to offer. Had you come here, one thing would have made you very happy and could be applicable in your work: utilitarian objects here are very beautiful and also thoroughly suited to our country. If I had been returning home direct from Japan I would have cleared the shops and taken everything back with me. Every aspect of every thing has been made beautiful – not even the tiniest detail has been neglected – which is where these people differ entirely from us. In their houses I do not see refuse anywhere – I don't know where they hide it all. The children learn to take care of everything and do not behave with lack of restraint. Women carry out all tasks with grace and precision that is a pleasure to behold. I spent a couple of days at Okakura's garden house.[4] Today I go to Tokyo via Yokohama. After that America.

Uncle Rabi

Source: MS original at Rabindra Bhavan, Shantiniketan; letter published in *VBP*, Magh–Chaitra 1353 [Jan.–April 1947], pp. 134–5.

1 Quoted in Yasunari Kawabata, *The Existence and Discovery of Beauty* (V. H. Viglielmo trans.; Tokyo, 1969), pp. 53, 54. Kawabata, Japan's first Nobel laureate in literature, commented: 'We may rejoice, and yet at the same time be saddened, by the thought that [our] very ancient *The Tale of Genji* fulfils the "responsibility of a nation" to which Tagore referred, much more brilliantly than any of us can do today, and will very likely continue to do so in the future.'
2 Yokoyama Taikan (1868–1958): artist, who helped to revitalise traditional Japanese painting; in 1914 he revived the Japan Fine Arts Academy, after the death of Okakura Kakuzo. RT stayed at Taikan's house on arrival in Tokyo. Kampo Arai (1878–1945): artist; he taught Japanese painting to Vichitra Club, Jorasanko from Dec. 1916 to May 1917.
3 RT repeated this in a letter to Rathindranath on 22 Aug. (*CP*, II, pp. 48–9).
4 Okakura's house was on the coast at Izura, some 110 miles north of Tokyo. W. W. Pearson accompanied RT and described the visit lyrically: 'In front of the house, overlooking the sea, is a small summer house which was the favourite room of the late Mr Okakura. There Rabi Babu sat during the day, and wrote, or watched the fishing boats as they passed out of the bay into the open sea' ('To the memory of Mr K. Okakura', *MR*, Nov. 1916, pp. 541–2).

109

To Abanindranath Tagore[1]

To Abanindranath, leader of the Bengal School, Rabindranath was more emphatic about the need to visit Japan than to Gaganendranath (letter 108), because he knew that Abanindranath was too often contented to draw upon art at second hand; he never, for instance, stirred himself from Calcutta to visit the great cave-paintings at Ajanta (unlike his Japanese mentor Okakura). Rabindranath could clearly perceive the vitality of Gaganendranath's work compared to his brother's work. This letter is an indication of his own growing indifference to the Bengal School, which would have almost no influence on him when he himself took up painting in the late 1920s – except as a warning of how not to paint.[2]

[Japan]
8 Bhadra 1323 [24 August 1916]

Kalyaniyeshu

Aban, since coming here I've not written to you. Main reason is laziness, second reason is busyness. When you come abroad it is better to cut the ties with home. To be constantly looking over your shoulder hinders your contact with new people. The Almighty is shaking me and gradually shifting me from my old foundations – He wants me not to be confined any longer. So on this trip I have not received many letters from home, nor have I written many. Now Andrews is returning, so I am sending these few hurriedly written lines to you – after I cross the Pacific I probably won't get time to write letters.[3]

The more I travel and see Japan, the more it has struck me that you people should have come with me. How vital it is to get into close contact with the living art of this country in order to infuse life into our own art – this you will never realise if you remain ensconced in your south verandah. Our country has no artistic atmosphere, there is no arterial link between our social life and our art – for us art is a superficial thing, neither here nor there; which is why you people can never derive your full nourishment from indigenous sources.[4] If you came here, you would see how the Japanese race lives in the lap of art – every aspect of its life is artistic. Had you come, the scales would have fallen from your eyes, and the goddess of art in your innermost being would have received her proper homage. Being here has made me realise for the first time that your art is not the twenty-four-carat genuine article. But what can I do, since you will not come out? – except leave Mukul here: everyone's hoping that he will become a real artist.[5] I wonder how your Vichitra is getting on.[6] Perhaps it's better not to ask now – when I return home after a long time I shall see for myself whether the concept is there, nowhere or somewhere in between.

Uncle Rabi

Source: MS original at Rabindra Bhavan, Shantiniketan; letter published in *VBP*, Magh–Chaitra 1353 [Jan.–April 1947], pp. 135–6.

1 Abanindranath Tagore (1871–1951): artist, who inaugurated the Bengal School; his first paintings date from the early 1890s. In 1896, he met E. B. Havell, the new principal of the Calcutta Art School, and became his *chela*; from 1905 to 1915 he was on the staff of the school, latterly as its acting principal. Almost all his life was spent in Calcutta, chiefly in the Jorasanko house. See Mitter, *Art and Nationalism*; also Jaya Appasamy, *Abanindranath Tagore and the Art of his Times* (New Delhi, 1968). He served as the head of Visva-Bharati immediately after RT's death.
2 There is a parallel between RT's dislike of the Bengal School and the young Satyajit Ray's dislike of conventional Bengali cinema. As Ray remarked, '[There was] nothing that I learnt from it . . . In fact, the reason why I was bold enough to come without experience, was that I had a feeling that I could do nothing worse than what was being done' (unpublished interview with Folke Isaksson, 1968).
3 C. F. Andrews parted from RT on 1 Sept., under somewhat unhappy circumstances, and reached India in early Oct. See Tinker, *Ordeal of Love*, pp. 128–31.
4 These comments recall those of W. G. Archer on Abanindranath in his *India and Modern Art*:

> As [Abanindranath's style] developed over a period of thirty years, it became identified with certain qualities – hesitant, indecisive line, misty vagueness of form, sombre murkiness of colour, likings for wistful girlish stances, dainty wanness, anaemic sentimentality . . . due, in part, to the mystical nature of Havell's teaching . . . In essence, however, they derive from the contemporary [cultural] situation. They are the qualities that go with tepid shrinkage from reality, faltering distrust, a failure in courage. (W. G. Archer, *India and Modern Art* (London, 1959), p. 37)

178   *Selected letters of Rabindranath Tagore*

5 Mukul Dey (1895–1989): artist, who specialised in etching; a pupil of Abanindranath from 1911 to 1915, Dey became principal of the Government School of Art, Calcutta, 1928–43. He did not fulful his promise.
6 The Vichitra ('variety') Club was set up in 1915 at Jorasanko, around the time that Abanindranath left the Calcutta Art School, and was periodically active for four years or so. Among its many cultural activities was a daytime art school, which in 1919 shifted to Shantiniketan with the founding of Visva-Bharati. Vichitra's moving spirits were RT, Abanindranath and Gaganendranath, who were organised by Rathindranath and (rather less) Surendranath; but Vichitra seems to have depended to a large extent on RT for its direction. See Rathindranath Tagore, *Edges of Time*, pp. 79–81. A week after writing this letter to Abanindranath, RT told Pratima Devi in a letter from Japan that he was disappointed to hear of a lack of seriousness about Vichitra, as compared to its equivalent in Japan (*CP*, III, p. 26).

110

To Rathindranath Tagore

Tagore's lecture tour of the USA in 1916–17 was a sensational success. It not only made him a celebrity there, it made him, or rather his school at Shantiniketan, a substantial sum of money, which he badly needed. He landed at Seattle on 18 September and worked his way down the West Coast. By the time he reached Los Angeles, where he spent some hours sitting in meditation under fragrant groves of orange trees, he was in a particularly good mood. This letter to his son is the earliest recorded glimmering of Visva-Bharati, his world university-to-be.[1]

Hotel Alexandria, Los Angeles, [USA]
11 October 1916

Kalyaniyeshu

Please forward this letter to Ajit.[2] His own letter had the address 'May Cottage Kurseong' but when this letter reaches him the time will be mid-November. By then perhaps he will no longer be in Kurseong. Dr Maitra may know his permanent address – if you ask him he may forward the letter.[3]

Whirled along by lectures, I reel from city to city. My agent has been involved in this work for two generations: he says he has organised lectures for many speakers but has never seen such a large crowd.[4] People are being turned away for lack of space. My intuition is that the Almighty has brought me here at this time for a particular purpose. My ideas seem to work deeply, especially among the students. When I see their enthusiasm I feel delighted.

Somendra is returning.[5] Possibly he will reach home by the month of Paush.[6] I have given him a thousand rupees. He needs the money for his travelling expenses. The idea is that on his return he will repay one thousand of the three thousand rupees I owe to Andrews.[7] Don't forget to remind him.

My expenses apart, as soon as I have thirty thousand rupees in hand I shall send them to you. The loan I took from Tarak Babu, which was transferred to Calcutta University, falls due in 1917 – and by next year you should repay the money so as to release us from the monthly interest payment.[8] Apart from settling this debt, all other income can be used for the school. I want to open a good hospital and technical department. The rooms will need proper roofs, otherwise there is a risk from fire. I think it will be possible to raise enough money here to cover these costs.

Reeling from place to place is extremely tiring. I put up with it, believing that the Almighty has ordained that I bear messages to these people. I have it in mind to make Shantiniketan the connecting thread between India and the world. I have to found a world centre for the study of humanity there. The days of petty nationalism are numbered – let the first step towards universal union occur in the fields of Bolpur. I want to make that place somewhere beyond the limits of nation and geography – the first flag of victorious universal humanism will be planted there. To rid the world of the suffocating coils of national pride will be the task of my remaining years. That is why, without any prior intimation, God has moored my boat to the western shore; and however unexpected the events of my life may be, I must accept his purpose.

I often feel a longing to see Mira's daughter.[9] Do keep sending me her photos. Did you receive all the things I sent with Andrews? God bless you all.

Shri Rabindranath Thakur

Source: MS original at Rabindra Bhavan, Shantiniketan; letter published in *CP*, I, pp. 54–6.

1 In a conversation in Japan in July, RT spoke of his 'world university' to Paul Richard, who mentioned it to Romain Rolland (Romain Rolland, *Inde: Journal (1915–1943), Tagore Gandhi Nehru et les Problèmes Indiens* (Paris, 1951), pp. 48–9).
2 Ajit Kumar Chakravarty was staying at Kurseong, near Darjeeling, which is cold in mid-Nov.
3 D. N. Maitra.
4 On the details of this tour, see Dutta and Robinson, *Rabindranath Tagore*, pp. 203–6.
5 Somendra Chandra Dev Burman: member of Tripura royal family; a student at Shantiniketan 1908–11, Burman studied at the University of Illinois, Urbana, 1912–16, and scraped a degree. 'He is cheerful and lazy, always humming songs out of tune in perfect unconcern' (RT to Rothenstein, 8 Dec. 1912, in Lago (ed.), *Imperfect Encounter*, p. 74).
6 Paush: Bengali month corresponding to mid-Dec.–mid-Jan.
7 C. F. Andrews.
8 After Sir Taraknath Palit died in 1914, RT's debt was transferred to Calcutta University. See letter 99, n. 5.
9 RT's daughter Mira gave birth to Nandita on 13 July 1916.

8 In *Dak Ghar* (*The Post Office*), Jorasanko, Calcutta, 1917: Gaganendranath Tagore as 'Father', Ashamukul as Amal, Rabindranath as Fakir

The ebbing of faith (1917–1918)

Introduction

Following his triumph in America, Tagore returned to India via Japan in March 1917. There the political situation increasingly came to preoccupy him. The internment of Annie Besant in mid-1917 provoked him to a statement in support of her, which diminished his standing with the Government. The internment of young Bengalis brought him into direct confrontation with the governor of Bengal, Lord Ronaldshay. Neither man was able to convince the other of the fairness of the procedures.

Then, in early 1918, at a trial in San Francisco of Indian revolutionaries in America charged with conspiring with German agents to foment trouble against the Government in India, Tagore's name was mentioned as a sympathiser of the cause. Although this was quite untrue, he felt obliged to write to the authorities in India, the USA and Japan, in order to clear his name. He was unable to do so, particularly in America, where the allegations virtually killed the sales of his books. As a result, he cancelled a second planned tour of America, and came to regard the whole affair with bitterness and disgust.

Although all these episodes did not harm his existing friendships with Englishmen, they damaged his faith in the good faith of the British in India. He had long held to the view that whatever might be the failings of the Government, it held India in 'sacred trust' on behalf of Indians. After 1918, he progressively abandoned this belief.

111

To Sarojini Naidu (Chattopadhyay)[1]

Sarojini Naidu is today remembered chiefly as the first Indian woman to be president of the Indian National Congress, rather than for her poetry. This enjoyed a brief vogue in the Edwardian period, with the support of Arthur Symons and Edmund Gosse. In 1914, Naidu was even elected a fellow of the Royal Society of Literature (who had failed to honour Tagore in 1912 despite the recommendation of W. B. Yeats).[2] It is not hard to see why: Naidu's mellifluous platitudes, written in English unlike Tagore's poems, chimed with long-standing English literary stereotypes of India. But as Naidu herself knew – self-criticism being her saving grace – she was 'not a poet really'. She told Symons, 'I have the vision and the desire, but not the voice. If I could write just one poem full of beauty and the spirit of greatness, I should be exultantly silent for ever; but I sing just as the birds do, and my songs are as ephemeral.'[3] After publishing *The Broken Wing* in 1917 (with its best-known poem headed by a quotation from Tagore), Naidu devoted herself to politics rather than literature.

Although Rabindranath praises her language extravagantly in this letter, there is no evidence that he took her poetry seriously. The praise is, rather, a courtly response to the great charm of the poetess herself, which also enchanted Gandhi and many others who knew her.

Santiniketan, [West Bengal, India]
August 1917

Dear Mrs Naidu,

Shall I make a confession to you? Once again while reading your poems in your last book I became only too conscious of my own broken wing in my flight in the alien sky of English diction.[4] You make me feel jealous of your lyric ease and grace in every movement of your thought among foreign words that are so friendly to you. However, it fills my heart with pride to know that you have gained by your own right your seat among the renowned of the West, thus mitigating the insult that broods over our Motherland.

Your poems in *The Broken Wing* seem to be made of tears and fire like the clouds of a July evening glowing with the muffled passion of the sunset.

Yours
Rabindranath Tagore

Source: MS copy at Rabindra Bhavan, Shantiniketan; letter published in *VBN*, April 1949, p. 100.

1 Sarojini Naidu (Chattopadhyay) (1879–1949): politician and poet; though a Bengali, she could not read Bengali, having been born and brought up in Hyderabad, and she wrote entirely in English. She became president of the Congress in 1925.
2 Gosse may have stymied Yeats' proposal (Lago (ed.), *Imperfect Encounter*, p. 44).
3 Quoted in Padmini Sengupta, *Sarojini Naidu: A Biography* (London, 1966), p. 55.
4 Since English was her first language, Naidu undoubtedly had a surer grasp of its grammar and syntax than Tagore, but there is little evidence in her poetry of her 'movement of thought'.

112

To Moti Lal Ghosh[1]

After his withdrawal from the Swadeshi Movement in 1907, Rabindranath remained aloof from Indian politics until the late 1930s, when he gave his support to Subhash Chandra Bose – with the exception of a brief and unrewarding incident in 1917, when he was cajoled into accepting the chairmanship of the Congress reception committee formed to welcome the Congress to Calcutta for its annual session, held in December 1917. He agreed in early September and withdrew at the end of that month, after various factions had patched up a compromise and Annie Besant had been elected president of the Congress.

The ebbing of faith

Her election was controversial. She was supported by, amongst others, C. R. Das and Moti Lal Ghosh, and opposed by Ghosh's long-time rival, Surendranath Banerji. At a meeting of the Congress reception committee on 30 August, there was a split; the Besant supporters carried the day, and the other party angrily left the hall, accompanied by the chairman of the committee. The Besant supporters, led by Ghosh, now desired to elect their own chairman, in the person of Tagore, whom they knew had earlier given public support to Besant following her internment by the Government. On 8 September, they had a meeting with Rabindranath at Jorasanko, after which he wrote the following letter to Ghosh.[2]

Calcutta, [India]
10 September 1917

Dear Moti Babu

With reference to our conversation when you and other friends kindly came and saw me on the morning of the 8th instant it should be clearly understood that I am willing to be the chairman of the reception committee of the Calcutta Congress only in the event of the seat being vacant and subject to the sanction of the All India Congress Committee being given to the holding of the Congress in Calcutta and to Mrs Besant being its president. Please do not use my name in any way as a rival candidate standing against the present chairman, or as leading any party [to act] counter to the final decision arrived at by the All India Congress Committee.

Yours sincerely
Rabindranath Tagore

Source: *CMG*, 13 Sept. 1941, p. 83.

1 Moti Lal Ghosh (1847–1922): journalist and nationalist; Ghosh and his brother founded the *Amrita Bazar Patrika* in 1868, which Ghosh edited alone from 1911 until his death. His rivalry with Surendranath Banerji, editor of the *Bengalee*, began in the 1870s.
2 On this incident, see the brief discussion in J. H. Broomfield, *Elite Conflict in a Plural Society: Twentieth-century Bengal* (Berkeley, 1968), pp. 135–6; also the full contemporary report, covering RT's role, in *MR*, Oct. 1917, pp. 441–3. RT resigned from the chairmanship in a letter to Surendranath Banerji, to which Surendranath replied on 1 Oct. and published his reply in the *Bengalee*: 'This act of yours is worthy of a sincere well-wisher of the country and an ardent advocate of its political progress.'

113

To George Robert Stour Mead[1]

The second half of 1917 marked a distinct shift in Rabindranath's attitude towards British rule in India. He distrusted theosophy and had not supported Annie Besant's Home Rule League, founded in 1916; but when she was interned in June 1917, Tagore wrote, 'Kindly convey my heartfelt sympathy and gratitude to Mrs Besant, and tell her that the martyrdom for the cause of suffering humanity will produce more good than any small favour that might have been thrown to us to silence our clamour.'[2] This was printed in Besant's paper, *New India*, and quoted in Britain by the Labour politician

George Lansbury. One of Tagore's British admirers, the editor G. R. S. Mead, a former assistant to Besant, now wrote to him, saying that he hoped 'sincerely' that Tagore had been misreported: the poet of *Gitanjali* was not expected to turn political.[3] Rabindranath's reply shows his courageous stand against imperial repression, at a time when even his most radical countrymen proved cowardly.

Calcutta, [India]
18 September 1917

Dear Mr Mead

In your letter you seem puzzled at my conduct in sending a message of sympathy to Mrs Besant who has been interned for her public utterances. I am afraid, compared with yours our troubles may appear to you too small, but yet sufferings have not lost their keenness for us and moral problems still remain as the gravest of all problems in all parts of the world.

The constant conflict between the growing demand of the educated community in India for a substantial share in the administration of their country and the spirit of hostility [on] the part of the Government has given rise among a considerable number of our young men [to] secret methods of violence bred of despair and distrust. This has been met by the Government by a thorough policy of repression. In Bengal itself hundreds of men are interned without trial – a great number of them in unhealthy surroundings, in jails, in solitary cells, in a few cases driving them to insanity or suicide.[4] The misery this has caused in numerous households is deep and widespread, the greatest sufferers being the women and children who are stricken at heart and rendered helpless. I do not wish to go into details but as a general proposition I can safely say that while evidence against them is not publicly sifted by a proper tribunal giving them opportunity to defend themselves we are justified in thinking that a large number of those punished are innocent, many of whom were specially selected as victims by secret spies only because they had made themselves generally conspicuous in some noble mission of self-sacrifice. What I consider to be the worst outcome of this irresponsible policy of panic is the spread of the contagion of hatred against everything western in minds which were free from it.

In this crisis the only European who has shared our sorrow, incurring the anger and derision of her countrymen, is Mrs Besant. This was what led me to express my grateful admiration for her noble courage in this present time when it is particularly dangerous to be on the side of humanity against blind expediency. Possibly there is such a thing as political exigency, just as there may be place for utter ruthlessness in war, but, as a man, I pay my homage to those who have faith in ideals and therefore are willing to take all other risks except that of weakening the foundation of moral responsibility.

Yours sincerely
Rabindranath Tagore

Source: MS copy at Rabindra Bhavan, Shantiniketan.

1 George Robert Stour Mead (1863–1933): theosophist and editor; formerly secretary to Madame Blavatsky, afterwards a close associate of Annie Besant, Mead resigned from the Theosophical Society in

1909, founded an association for mystical research and began publishing the *Quest*. RT published in the *Quest* in 1913; and Mead gave the concluding speech after RT's Caxton Hall Lectures (*Sadhana*) in 1913. W. B. Yeats thought Mead a somewhat over-righteous individual, with the 'intellect of a good size whelp'. (Quoted in Arthur Nethercot, *The First Five Lives of Annie Besant* (London, 1961), p. 317.)
2 RT to Jinarajadasa (aide to Besant), 4 July 1917 [Adyar].
3 Mead to RT, 29 July 1917 [RB], which mentions Lansbury.
4 Lord Ronaldshay, governor of Bengal, denied this charge, when RT's letter to Mead was published in the Indian press, and RT was attacked as an extremist by the British-run newspapers. He responded with a bitter speech ('The small and the great', *MR*, Dec. 1917, pp. 593–604/*RR*, XXIV, pp. 272–93).

114

To William Winstanley Pearson

The attempt to turn Rabindranath into a politician, by making him chairman of the Congress reception committee (see letter 112), farcical as it was, reflected his renewed public status in Bengal in late 1917, partly as a result of a lecture he gave in Calcutta in August, 'Kartar ichchhay karma' ('The Master's will be done').[1] Here he launched a coruscating attack on both goverment repression and Bengali supineness. So excited was the public that when the lecture was repeated in a large theatre hall, mounted police had to be called to disperse the crowd. In a crucial passage, Tagore told his Bengali audience:

> We give the Master a thousand names, such as father, elder brother, police inspector, priest, pundit, Sitala [goddess of smallpox], Manasa [goddess of snakes], Olabibi [goddess of cholera], Dakshin Ray [tiger-god], and the heavenly bodies, Sani, Mangal, Rahu and Ketu. We smash our own power into a thousand bits and cast them to the winds . . .
> National self-respect is making us turn our faces forwards to the world and demand political authority, but it is also making us turn our faces backwards to our country and demand that in all religious, social, and even personal matters we do not move one step against the Master's will. This is what I call the revival of Hinduism. National self-respect is ordering us to perform an impossible task: to keep one of our eyes wide open and the other one closed in sleep.[2]

But, as ever with Tagore, success provoked in him acutely mixed feelings. Had he wanted, he could have been Bengal's political leader, but he knew that this would mean sacrificing both his art and his solitude, as well as a large measure of his integrity. Two months after the lecture, he gave vent to his inner conflict with typical humour, in this letter to W. W. Pearson.

Santiniketan, [West Bengal, India]
25 October 1917

My dear Pearson,

Can you possibly imagine that I was nearly made the chairman of the Congress reception committee this year? It is distractingly comic to think that there was a great fight for the chair – both parties looking so fiercely earnest about it that the gods as spectators in the upper region were in danger of bursting their sides with laughter – particularly in wartime when the czar of all Russia [has] lost his throne without a word and kaiser's crown looks terribly insecure. That I should be drawn into politics does not in the least degree prove that politics of late has developed undreamt-of poetical qualities – it only shows that at present in India things have come to such a tangle that even a poet had to be requisitioned for the purpose of a mock fight in a political playground. I do not know to what tragedy or more possibly to a screaming farce it would have led us on if my fate had persisted in its practical joke to the end.[3]

My continuous stay in Calcutta for the last few months was not a particularly exhilarating experience for me. Yet for all I know, it was necessary, not for my peace of mind, but for realising, rightly or wrongly, that my mission of life was not exclusively [for] turning out verses difficult of comprehension. I was too long out of touch with our Calcutta people – especially with our students. In fact, as far as the Bengali public outside our Santiniketan was concerned, I had been living in a phantom world of a vanished generation. The present generation of our youth merely knows me as a man who has achieved his reputation. But an assured sense of reputation gives a sense of finality to one's career. It no longer appears like a flame but like a splendid snuffer to the candle of life. It was like a railway train which had accomplished its end and reached its terminus, therefore no longer of interest to the passengers who were [after] beginning or continuing their journey. But this time I had the opportunity to prove to them that I was on the running line and that the signal was down. Our students were rather surprised to find that I still had in me most of the properties of solid matter – weight, penetrability and the power of occupying space. So, like Dada of *Phalguni*, I am in danger of being surrounded by the crowd, made use of and even praised.[4] I am feeling excessively nervous because I am beginning to be flattered by my countrymen, to which experience, you know, I am not at all accustomed. When misunderstanding lands one upon the Alpine height of praise it is more perilous for him than when it hurls him into the depth of calumny. I am waiting every moment for the downward push to roll [me] back again into my normal position of unambiguous revilement.

However, I am tired. I wish I were in some Japanese monastery with you practising Zen.[5] I have come to the conclusion that a poet ought to be a poet and nothing else. The combination of a *sitar* and a fishing rod in one may be convenient but such ingenious monstrosities should be discouraged.

But please do not imagine that my clouds had no gold lining whatever. We staged *Dak Ghar* in our Vichitra Hall, gave five performances and felt happier each time we did it. I took the part of Thakurda, Gagan that of Madhav, and Aban personated Morhal to perfection. The boy who personated Amal was glorious.[6] He is a new acquisition to our school whom you do not know. We did miss you so much! I know if Andrews were among the audience he would have created a tremendous scene.

I had a letter from Andrews some time ago saying that he was coming back in November.[7] I hope he will not change his plan. The absence of both of you is a sore trial to me.

I have just come to Santiniketan. The ashram is basking in the beautiful sunshine of Puja holidays. One feels certain that [things are] all right with this great world when year after year such beautiful days find their way back to this earth without interruption.

I am requested to get ready an important lecture for the Congress occasion.[8] But I sit quiet in my upper room and gaze on the ineffable blue of the sunlit sky of October and ask myself if it is absolutely required of me to coin political platitudes to buy cheap applause from a big townhall audience?

My love to you.

Ever yours,
Rabindranath Tagore

Source: MS original in Rabindra Bhavan, Shantiniketan; letter published in *VBQ*, 9, No. 2, Aug.–Oct. 1943, pp. 163–5.

1 *TUM*, pp. 175–201/*RR*, XVIII, pp. 543–65.
2 *Ibid.*, pp. 181, 186–7 (trans. slightly modified)/pp. 549, 553.
3 In the *MR*, the editor, Ramananda Chatterji [Chattopadhyay], commented on the election of RT as chairman of the Congress reception committee as follows:

> That he has acted from a compelling sense of duty can also be presumed from the fact that the party which has elected him contains among its more prominent and vocal members some men with whose aims and ideals the Poet has little in common and some of whom have been among his worst detractors [a reference to Moti Lal Ghosh and C. R. Das, amongst others] . . .
> The *Bengalee* has characterised him as a novice in politics. If by politics is meant the alternate cajoling and bluffing, the childish brag and the hollow declamation to be found in many newspapers, or if politics mean unworthy electioneering tactics, loyalty-mongering, journalistic quibbling, party strategems, and things of that sort – if such be the meaning of politics, Rabindranath Tagore is not even a novice in politics; for he has never practised or sought to practise such arts. Indeed, it is no disparagement to him to say that he is unfit for political life; as, for one thing, he lacks the caution, the astuteness and the suspiciousness which characterise successful politicians. A political career is not necessarily ignoble; it may be and often is honourable and useful. But Rabindranath Tagore was meant for something higher and finer. (*MR*, Oct. 1917, p. 441)

4 *Phalguni*, *MR*, XII, pp. 81–145. This drama was translated as *The Cycle of Spring* and published by Macmillan, London, in 1917. When it was performed at Jorasanko in 1916, Pearson had a role.
5 Pearson had returned from the USA with RT in early 1917 to Japan and stayed there, leading an ascetic existence. Someone who knew him at this time described his condition in a letter to RT, who replied on 24 Oct. 1917, 'I [have] known only one other man among my countrymen – it was Satish Chandra Roy – who, like Pearson, combined in his person the rare power of enjoying beauty with a passion for renunciation' (RT to E. E. Speight, 24 Oct. 1917 [copy at RB]).
6 Under the auspices of the Vichitra Club, *Dak Ghar* (*The Post Office*) was performed seven times altogether, according to Rathindranath Tagore, who provides a fine description of the preparations and performance (*Edges of Time*, p. 90). Amal was played by Ashamukul Das (1902–70), his 'father' Madhav by Gaganendranath Tagore, the doctor and the headman (*morhal*) by Abanindranath Tagore, whose youngest daughter played Shudha, Amal's friend. The final performance was arranged for the delegates of the Indian National Congress in Calcutta, after the session closed on 31 Dec. Gandhi told a friend:

> I had a very nice time of it in Calcutta, but not in the Congress *pandal*. It was all outside the *pandal*. I was enraptured to witness *The Post Office* performed by the Poet and his company. Even as I dictate this, I seem to hear the exquisitely sweet voice of the Poet and the equally exquisite acting on the part of the sick boy. Bengali music has for me a charm all its own. I did not have enough of it, but what I did have had a most soothing effect upon my nerves which are otherwise always on trial. (Gandhi to S. K. Rudra, 16 Jan. 1918, *CWMG*, XIV, p. 153)

7 C. F. Andrews was then lingering in Fiji in a depressed state of mind; he did not return to India until March 1918. See Tinker, *Ordeal of Love*, pp. 135–6. RT's comments to others on Andrews are often accompanied by expressions of slightly exasperated affection, echoing the difference in temperament between himself and the rather neurotic Andrews.
8 In the event, RT read a poem, 'India's Prayer', not a lecture, on the opening day of the Congress, and received a tremendous ovation. See *CMG*, p. 83. Gaganendranath Tagore depicted the scene in a dramatic painting.

115

To (Sir) William Rothenstein

On 19 September 1917, William Rothenstein told Tagore in a letter:

> I was delighted with your book on nationalism. You have said, nobly and wisely, many things which need saying and I found myself in sympathy with you throughout. And your task was no easy one . . . dealing as you do with an Indian, a Japanese and a European public you have been courageous in speaking what is in your heart. Nations respond to flattery always, even when it is flattery of themselves, but at a time like the present this self-flattery becomes so tiresome and ludicrous that to one's surprise, a book like yours is welcomed in quite unexpected quarters. I think it admirable from every point of view.[1]

Tagore's reply shows that he was relieved. He was already under attack in Bengal for his criticism of Indian nationalism (see letter 114), and he clearly feared that his attack on nationalism of all kinds, published in September 1917 as *Nationalism*, would lose him the sympathy of his friends in wartime England.

Shantiniketan, [West Bengal, India]
26 October 1917

My dearest Friend,

It has given me a deep pleasure to know that my last three books you like. I had my fear that my American lectures, especially those about nationalism, might give offence to my readers in England. Possibly to some extent they have done so. But most of the reviews that I have seen in your papers are extremely mild. Some critics have taxed me with having misunderstood the meaning of the word 'nation'.[2] I suppose it is one of those words whose meaning is still in its process of formation. If you really mean by that word the peoples who have the consciousness of a common tradition and aspiration then why do you exclude us Bengalis from its category? for you are never tired of reminding us that we do not belong to a nation. When we try to understand you we find that our tradition and aspiration are of a different character from yours – it is more religious and social than political. Therefore it seems to me that the word nation in its meaning carries a special emphasis upon its political character. Politics becomes aggressively self-conscious when it sets itself in antagonism against other peoples, specially when it extends its dominion among alien races. This convulsive intensity of consciousness is productive of strength but not of health. The rapid growth of nationalism in Europe begins with her period of foreign exploration and exploitation. Its brilliance shines in contrast upon the dark background of the subjection of other peoples. Certainly it is based upon the idea of competition, conflict and conquest and not that of cooperation. In human language there are very few words that have an absolute meaning. The unselfish people have not completely lost their self, only the selfish ones put stronger emphasis upon it and thus have a special designation. And the people with an aggressively emphatic politics is a nation. The [professional man] has very often a special attitude of mind. There he feels an intense satisfaction if he can sell a lame horse at a price which is dear even for a sound one. Because in [his] profession [a] man has

The ebbing of faith 189

no other object before him but success. He may have an exalted standard of life in his private capacity and yet as a professional man his conduct may go entirely against that standard, without disturbing his appetite for dinner. Therefore it is not unusual to find rapacious landlords who are extravagant in their generosity. That grasping professional attitude of mind makes a nation of a people when it furiously pursues success and takes it to be a sign of sentimentalism to budge an inch from its reckless path of power at the dictates of humanity. What I have said in my lectures is that such an attitude of mind in a whole people of a country, such constant self-idolatry by all kinds of ritualism and human sacrifice must go against moral providence of the world ending at last in a catastrophe.[3]

By some unexpected freak of fate I was caught in a dust storm of our politics. I have just come out of it nearly choked to death. I am more convinced than ever that a poet might do worse than write mere verses. Try to be true to yourself by all means but not to be truer which is a hollow temptation set in our path by moral teachers.

Give my love to [your] dear children and tell them not to grow too fast before I come to see them. Because that will be unfair to me who can only grow older without growing at all.

Ever yours
Rabindranath Tagore

Source: MS original in Rothenstein Papers [Harvard]; letter published in Lago (ed.), *Imperfect Encounter*, pp. 244–5.

1 Rothenstein to RT, 19 Sept. 1917, in Lago (ed.), *Imperfect Encounter*, p. 242.
2 RT was probably referring to the lengthy, intelligent and ambivalent review, 'The protest of a seer', in the *Times Literary Supplement*, 13 Sept. 1917, which remarked:

> In Sir Rabindranath's arraignment of the idea of 'the nation' some misapprehension may be caused by his using the term nation instead of the term state. It is the state which, according to the German definition, is an organisation for the purposes of power, and we may allow that the German definition expresses part of the truth. What constitutes a nation is not organisation as a single state (although in certain cases nation and state coincide), but a single tradition expressed in a common language, a common literature, a common body of customs and memories of things done or suffered together . . . And when Sir Rabindranath attacks the state, calling it the nation, it is not merely an idiosyncrasy in the use of words. Whilst a great deal of what he says applies only to the state, and not the nation, he also has in mind things which apply to the nation rather than to the state.

In E. P. Thompson's view, expressed in his introduction to the 1991 edition of *Nationalism* (pp. 8–9):

> [Tagore's] definition of a nation is the political and economic union of a people 'in that aspect which a whole population assumes when organised for a mechanical purpose'. The emphasis falls upon *organised* and *mechanical*. The western nation is coterminous with the nation-state, the mechanical organisation of peoples in pursuit of material aggrandisement and hence necessarily aggressive and imperialist in character; in fact, for 'nationalism' we might often read 'imperialism'.

3 See letter 112. RT's tone here may be an echo of an earlier remark by Rothenstein: 'If politicians could only fall in love with a tree, or a hayrick or an old cart resting under the shadow of a thatched shed, I believe they would be unable to face their tasks any more' (Rothenstein to RT, 25 Aug. 1917, in Lago (ed.), *Imperfect Encounter*, p. 241).

116

To Robert Gourlay[1]

During 1917, under the governorship of Lord Ronaldshay, the Government of Bengal made a determined effort to suppress terrorism and 'sedition' by interning (mainly young) politically active Bengalis. Between 1906 and 1917, eighty-two persons in Bengal, including twenty-one police officers, had been killed by the revolutionaries. Rabindranath, though no supporter of violence, spoke out against injustices under the new policy, notably in September (see letter 113); and his charge was publicly rebutted by Ronaldshay. A powerful lecture by Tagore in Bengali, inspired by the same subject, was translated and published in the *Modern Review* in December 1917, in which he stated:

> Any tender shoot once bitten by the police thrives no longer, for there is poison in their touch. I know a boy whose intelligence was as keen as his diligence in study, and equally noble was his character. He managed to get let off after having been mauled by the police, it is true; but he is now, in the first bloom of his youth, the inmate for life of a madhouse in Berhampur. I can swear that the British Government never had anything to fear, but our country much to gain, from him.

And he concluded with a postscript written in response to Ronaldshay's rebuttal:

> The policy of secret condemnation and punishment hitherto pursued has naturally led a very large number of my countrymen to conclude that a great many of those punished are innocent. Imprisonment in jails, in some cases in solitary cells, savours to the public at large more of vengeance than of prosecution. Moreover the harassment to which a detenu is subjected, even after his release, by reason of continued shadowing by the police, may not be admitted by those who are responsible, but is too painfully patent to those who share the suffering.[2]

This article may have been one of the reasons for Edwin Montagu, the liberal secretary of state for India then on tour in India researching his proposed reforms, to suggest that Tagore's concerns over internment should be examined sympathetically.[3] Robert Gourlay, Ronaldshay's private secretary, took the matter up with Tagore, and during the early months of 1918 the two men had considerable contact in person and by letter: among all the British officials in India Tagore encountered, Gourlay was probably the closest to him in spirit.[4] This letter refers to one of several cases that Tagore brought to the attention of the Government.

Santiniketan, [West Bengal, India]
18 February 1918

Dear Mr Gourlay,

When I wrote to you last I thought it would be of no loss to anybody in the world if I gave up my attempts at rectifying wrongs and stick to literature. But occasions come when to remain in the shelter of one's special vocation becomes a crying shame. And a particularly harrowing account of the helpless condition of a state prisoner having come my notice from a trustworthy source, I am compelled to write to you again. The case is that of Jyotish Chandra Ghosh of Hooghly who is in the Berhampur Lunatic Asylum.[5]

I am informed that he lies motionless on his back day and night in an unconscious condition, jaws firmly set, legs rigid and crooked, probably paralysed. He can neither open his mouth nor speak and does not respond to any outside stimulus however strong. It is said that he has been in this condition for the last six months or so, and that during that period, or longer, he has been artificially fed. The force applied for this purpose does not rouse him to a least sign of consciousness and the only thing which shows that he is alive is that he breathes.

After repeated and unaccountable refusals one of his relatives was given permission to see Jyotish at last. I do not wish to discuss what suspicions our people entertain about such cases as this, though these suspicions, whether legitimate or not, should never be ignored. But in the name of humanity I would appeal to His Excellency the governor of Bengal to look into this case personally and not be satisfied with any report from subordinate functionaries, medical or ordinary. For the sake of humanity I would also urge that the prisoner's mother should now have the consolation of nursing her son in her own home, or if that cannot be, in any other place chosen by Govt where he can have the best possible medical treatment.

I hope you kindly excuse me for this rather long letter.

Yours very sincerely
Rabindranath Tagore

Source: MS copy at Rabindra Bhavan, Shantiniketan.

1 William Robert Gourlay (1874–1938): private secretary to two governors of Bengal (Carmichael and Ronaldshay), 1912–22.
2 'The small and the great' ('Chhoto o baro'), *MR*, Dec. 1917, pp. 601, 604/*RR*, XXIV, p. 287.
3 Gourlay to RT, 12 Dec. 1917 [RB].
4 On 9 Feb. 1918, RT informed Gourlay:

> I am still feeling tired. I suppose it is time for me to husband my energies and strictly fall back upon my own role as poet. Therefore I give up my futile struggle to be useful in order to have time and strength to employ the remainder of my days in something in which I can give and receive satisfaction. [copy at RB]

To which Gourlay, then on holiday in northern India, replied on 20 Feb.:

> I feel like you. I want to give up the struggle to be helpful – when I fail so often: and get away to a quiet spot to rest and think. This life is such a little thing compared with the great eternity beyond: and then I shake myself and say: but after all I was sent into the world not to be useful but to try to be useful – it is for me to go on trying, to go on striving and to leave the results – failure or success – to God [RB].

In 1921, Gourlay told Leonard Elmhirst with a chuckle:

> Tagore is not a Bengali, he is an Internationalist, and we can't afford to have him disturbed at all, he's much too valuable a person . . . I must have spent nearly half my time out here looking after the Tagore family and pulling first one and then another out of a hole. (Elmhirst to Dorothy Straight, 17 Dec. 1921 [Dartington])

5 The case of Ghosh was extensively discussed in the *MR*, Feb. 1918, pp. 224–7, which RT would certainly have read. There was more in the *MR*, March 1918, pp. 336–7. RT's role was not mentioned in either article.

117

To Lord Ronaldshay[1]

Tagore's letter (116) to Robert Gourlay was read, in Gourlay's absence, by the governor of Bengal, Lord Ronaldshay, who replied on 23 February 1918 with an account of the steps taken by himself and various medical officers to treat Jyotish Chandra Ghosh, the young internee described by Rabindranath. Ronaldshay then took Tagore to task for suggesting that Ghosh might have been maltreated in detention:

> I feel obliged to call your attention to the following sentence in your letter. 'I do not wish to discuss what suspicions our people entertain about such cases as this, though these suspicions, whether legitimate or not, should never be ignored.' These words seem to me to contain a very grave insinuation. They seem in fact to convey a scarcely veiled charge of foul play of a most horrible description against some person or persons unnamed. I cannot possibly ignore such a charge, and I must ask you to be good enough to state in perfectly plain language what the suspicions to which you refer are, by whom they are entertained and against whom they are directed [RB].

Tagore's reply takes up this challenge.

Calcutta, [India]
[1] March 1918

Your Excellency,

It greatly relieves my mind to know from Your Excellency's letter that you have personally looked into the case of Jyotish Ghosh. The statement containing the description of his present condition was not directly communicated to me.

I gratefully appreciate Your Excellency's frankness in replying to my letter, and welcome the opportunity it gives me to be equally frank.

Let me first state emphatically and with all sincerity that in writing the sentence which you quote in your letter I was simply alluding to the widespread suspicions of which we hear hints in the course of conversation, or read between the lines of newspaper comments and which, I took it, must have reached Mr Gourlay in some way or other. I expressed my opinion, which I still hold, that it is not wise state policy to ignore the fact of the existence of such suspicions, meaning further to imply that the public should have no excuse for thinking that the true facts have not been furnished to them or to the interested parties in the beginning in cases where later something has admittedly been found to have been really wrong.

As Your Excellency is certainly entitled to insist on my making myself unmistakably plain, let me first repeat that I have no particular person in mind as being the entertainer of the suspicions referred to. They are, however, obviously directed to the lower officials in whose hands the preliminary secret investigations and the drawing up of the case against those who are 'suspects', lie, and who (this is the general impression in which I confess I cannot but share) have the power to give to the superior officials such impression as they may choose.

The words 'foul play of a horrible description' do not, I beg leave to say, accurately describe the charge which I have said [the] above amounts to, as against the lower officials. The charge is this: among the many cases with which they have had to deal, they may be and are mistaken in regard to a certain proportion, though differences of opinion are likely as to how small or large such proportion may be. And yet if the treatment ordinarily reserved for the worst kinds of criminals, be accorded to such an innocent person, [it] is obviously bound to have deleterious effects on his mental or physical constitution or both. The charge is that when the underlings discover their mistake and in the meantime also find that such deleterious effects have already begun to manifest themselves, they become afraid of reporting, or even admitting, the true facts to their more responsible superiors, leading the Govt, unwittingly, to take what must seem to the public, who know the other side, to be a perverse attitude.

As further explanatory of the state of my own mind, it may be of some use to Your Excellency if I inform you that in the case of the boy Anath belonging to my Shantiniketan school, knowing him as I have done for the last 8 years and also all the circumstances of his daily environment, as well as of his last escapade, I have not the least doubt in my mind that he could not have had anything to do with the anarchists, however plausible a case the police may have made against him, and whatever so-called confession he may have been reported to have made. I will not trouble Your Excellency with the detailed reasons for this belief of mine in this letter, I am simply placing before you the fact of my belief in the hope that it may lead Your Excellency to make more searching investigations for yourself as to how these mistakes arise than you might otherwise have thought necessary.[2]

Thanking Your Excellency for your letter. I am

Yours truly,
Rabindranath Tagore

Source: MS copy at Rabindra Bhavan, Shantiniketan.

1 Lawrence Dundas, 2nd marquess of Zetland, earl of Ronaldshay (1876–1961): governor of Bengal, 1917–22. See Lord Ronaldshay, *The Heart of Aryavarta* (London, 1925), especially chapter 8 ('Perverted patriotism').
2 RT had raised the condition of the sixteen-year-old Anath Bandhu Chaudhuri, who was arrested on 22 Dec. 1917, in a letter to Robert Gourlay on 29 Jan. 1918: 'Being a boy of weak mentality the longer he remains in police custody the more will his statements go on multiplying, leading to endless anxiety to his parents and harassment to himself' [copy at RB]. See also *MR*, Feb. 1918, pp. 228–9.

118

To Lord Ronaldshay

In his further reply to Tagore, Lord Ronaldshay was positive but refused to accept Rabindranath's criticism of the method of police investigation of *détenus*. 'I think you hardly realise the large part which the superior police officer takes in these investigations. The matter is not left in the hands of the underlings in the way you suggest.'[1] In this he was either being less than frank or was ignorant of the true situation. Corruption and maltreatment of suspects were endemic in the lower ranks of the police, as Rabindranath well knew from his estate work and reports brought to him at Shantiniketan.[2] In his second letter to the governor, far from retreating from his original position, he goes further.

Calcutta, [India]
4 March 1918

Your Excellency,

Your kind letter in reply to mine, further reassures me as to Your Excellency's personal anxiety to do the best that may yet be possible in the case of Jyotish Ghosh. This emboldens me to suggest that the best way to allay the dissatisfaction and sense of oppression which is undoubtedly troubling the public mind would be for Your Excellency to take the trouble personally to find out and express disapproval of the action or person responsible for the series of incidents which led to Jyotish's present condition, and ignoring of it at a stage when it might have been more effectively dealt with. It would also be an immense relief if Your Excellency could take the country into your confidence as to the steps that have been taken to ensure the exercise of greater caution and more sympathetic discretion in such cases in future.

As to the question of medical help for Jyotish Ghosh, as far as I know, our people have every faith [in] the professional ability of the medical officers of Govt, and there is no desire in this case to supplement their services with that of any non-official practitioner.[3] I have not been, as I said, in direct communication with Jyotish's family, but I have reason to believe that they would greatly value the permission if it could be given, for some nominee of theirs to attend and minister to him, subject of course to the direction of the attending medical officers.

I sincerely thank Your Excellency for the very kind permission to bring other cases should the necessity arise, to Your Excellency's notice.

Yours sincerely,
Rabindranath Tagore

Source: MS copy at Rabindra Bhavan, Shantiniketan.

1 Ronaldshay to RT, 1 March 1918 [RB].
2 Robert Gourlay, secretary to Ronaldshay, admitted privately to Leonard Elmhirst that the police often behaved with a mixture of ignorance and duplicity. Elmhirst himself came to the same conclusion after a discussion with a senior police officer about whether or not Shantiniketan was being watched by police spies; it undoubtedly was, but the chief of police either did not know this or would not admit it (Elmhirst to Dorothy Straight, 17 Dec. 1921 [Dartington]). Ronaldshay's patrician unwillingness to accept such allegations is somewhat reminiscent of the debate about Ronald Merrick, the fictional senior police officer in Paul Scott's novels *The Raj Quartet*, who supervises torture of an Indian *détenu*: was such an incident plausible or not? Ronaldshay would probably have said no; Tagore would probably have said yes.
3 In his letter of 23 Feb., Ronaldshay had offered RT the opportunity to suggest a non-official medical practitioner who might examine Ghosh, independently of the Government.

119

To William Winstanley Pearson

The atmosphere of repression in Bengal from 1917, and his own unsatisfactory attempts to mediate with British officials such as Lord Ronaldshay, the governor (letters 116–18), put Rabindranath into a bitter mood. A change in his attitude towards British rule is evident at this time, epitomised by this letter to W. W. Pearson and a much longer letter he was requested to write to Edwin Montagu, secretary of state for India,

The ebbing of faith

on 6 April 1918, in which he offered his advice on reforming the system of government in India. His concluding paragraph stated:

> The psychology of the question is of more importance than any particular system or method, and unless your people are fully awake to the great moral responsibility and realise the sufferings and humiliation with which the millions of India are burdened – their joyless existence dark, because bereft of all expectation of a great future – you shall never be able to give us anything in that true spirit which will bring more blessings upon yourself than upon the people whom you help.[1]

Calcutta, [India]
6 March 1918

Dear Pearson,

I have asked Macmillan to pay off the money which I owe to the Omaha people. The printing press is still rusting in Shantiniketan. I have not yet received permission to use it. I shall wait a few more weeks and then I shall ask the good citizens of Lincoln, who made a present of it to my school, to take it back.[2] Each one of us in this unfortunate country is looked upon with suspicion – and our authorities cannot see us clearly through the dust which they themselves raise. Humiliation follows us at every step, in every good work we try to do. All blind methods are easy methods in the beginning, they save a lot of thinking and expenditure of sympathy, but such cheap methods do not pay in the end. For after all, bullyism is stupidity, it assumes frightfulness only because it does not know its way. What is radically wrong with our rulers is this – they are fully aware that they do not know us, and yet they do not care to know us. And in consequence, in our penny-dreadful administration, thorny hedges are springing up of unscrupulous intermediaries between the rulers and the ruled, giving rise to a condition which is not only miserable, but unspeakably vulgar. Our people are intimidated, no doubt, but they are losing their respect for the Government which is the only moral and therefore sure foundation of foreign rule. I have just received a letter from Thadani,[3] complaining of the insult and harassment which only Indian British subjects have to go through in all British ports, and which have the effect of making them ashamed of the Government under which they live. Such treatments are sinking deep in the memory of the people, and the moral providence of history cannot altogether ignore such accumulated burden of indignities loaded upon humanity.

I got a telegram from Andrews about three days ago from Singapore.[4] So he will be here within a week. I feel very tired and when he comes he will be of great help to me.

With love

Yours
Rabindranath Tagore

Source: MS original at Rabindra Bhavan, Shantiniketan; letter published in *VBQ*, 9, No. 1, May–July 1943, pp. 79–80.

1 RT wrote this letter with the encouragement of Robert Gourlay (Gourlay to RT, 29 March 1918 [RB]). Montagu replied respectfully, but there is little evidence that he took note of RT's ideas; RT is not even mentioned in S. D. Waley's *Edwin Montagu: A Memoir and an Account of his Visits to India* (London, 1964), and is mentioned only in passing in Montagu's *An Indian Diary* (London, 1930).

2 RT visited Lincoln and Omaha, Nebraska, in Jan. 1917, during his tour of the USA, accompanied by W. W. Pearson, his secretary. The printing press was donated to him for his school, on condition that he paid the cost of transporting it back to Bengal. Presumably officialdom feared that the press would be used for printing 'seditious' materials. But eventually permission was granted, and the first book was printed on it in Ashvin 1325 (Sept.–Oct. 1918).
3 N. V. Thadani: college principal.
4 C. F. Andrews.

120

To James Drummond Anderson[1]

Among Tagore's many friendships with individual Britons, that with J. D. Anderson was unique in being concerned with the minutiae of Bengali philology. Anderson, having been born in Calcutta and served in the ICS in Bengal for twenty-five years, had retired to England, where he became lecturer in Bengali at Cambridge University. He first met Tagore on his visit to Cambridge in July 1912; a correspondence started immediately and continued right up to Anderson's death eight years later.[2]

Though keenly interested in Tagore's writings, and those of other Bengali writers such as Sarat Chandra Chatterji [Chattopadhyay], Anderson did little sustained translating of Bengali.[3] With regard to Tagore translation, he was too wise and sensitive not to perceive the pitfalls, telling Rabindranath in 1918, 'One needs an odd mixture of humility and audacity. One must be humble enough to acknowledge the difficulty of the task; one must have the audacity to believe that the difficulties can be surmounted.'[4] Living in Britain, away from Bengali, and now in his sixties, Anderson lacked the confidence in his powers: 'I am only a dabbler in Bengali, and my teaching of the language only deals with very elementary matters. I rarely hear Bengali spoken nowadays, and have quite forgotten how to talk Bengali from sheer want of practice.'[5]

Rabindranath was of course even more sensitive to his lack of command of English. This letter is part of the gradual process of his understanding of the weakness in his approach to translating his own work into English.

Calcutta, [India]
14 April 1918

Dear Mr Anderson

I have greatly enjoyed reading two of my *Gitanjali* poems done into verse by your friend and thank you for sending them to me.[6] It was the want of mastery in your language that originally prevented me from trying English metres in my translations. But now I have grown reconciled to my limitations through which I have come to know the wonderful power of English prose. The clearness, strength and the suggestive music of well-balanced English sentences make it a delightful task for me to mould my Bengali poems into English prose form. I think one should frankly give up the attempt at reproducing in a translation the lyrical suggestions of the original verse and substitute in their place some new quality inherent in the new vehicle of expression. In English prose there is a magic which seems to transmute my Bengali verses into something which is

The ebbing of faith

original again in a different manner. Therefore it not only satisfies but gives me delight to assist my poems in their English rebirth though I am far from being confident in the success of my task.

I have asked the editor to send you the Chaitra number of *Shabuj Patra* which contains my lecture on Bengali prosody.[7]

With kindest regards, I am

Yours very sincerely
Rabindranath Tagore

Source: MS copy at Rabindra Bhavan, Shantiniketan.

1 James Drummond Anderson (1852–1920): lecturer in Bengali, University of Cambridge, 1909–20; he served in the ICS from 1875 to 1900, retiring as magistrate and collector of Chittagong; he was a regular contributor to the *Times* and the *Spectator*.
2 RT's letters to Anderson were unfortunately not preserved, but Anderson's replies show that they discussed Bengali prosody in far more detail than RT did with E. J. Thompson.
3 Anderson published a short grammar of Bengali, *A Manual of the Bengali Language* (Cambridge, 1920), containing short extracts from various Bengali writers, including RT (*Naukadubi* and *Gitanjali*). They are readable but not notably inspired.
4 Anderson to RT, 15 Sept. 1918 [RB].
5 Anderson to RT, 12 May 1913 [RB].
6 On 3 Sept. 1914, with the outbreak of war, Anderson wrote to RT that he, S. N. Maitra and a 'very learned little lady' were reading *Gitanjali* together. She was most probably Suzanne Karpelès ('Charpetis' in MacBride White and Jeffares (eds.), *Gonne–Yeats Letters*, p. 345), a pupil of Sylvain Lévi. Possibly the translations sent to RT in 1918 were her work.
7 'Chhander artha', *Shabuj Patra*, Chaitra 1324 [March–April 1918]/*RR*, XXI, pp. 295–312.

121

To Rathindranath Tagore

In early 1918, in addition to all his other burdens, Rabindranath (who had already lost two of his children) was worried about his eldest child, Bela, who had contracted tuberculosis. She was his favourite child but their relationship had been difficult for years (see letter 60), and they had hardly seen each other since Rabindranath's departure for the West in 1912. This letter to Rathi was probably written in March, or more likely April 1918. Bela died on 16 May in Calcutta.

[Shantiniketan, West Bengal, India]
[April? 1918]

Kalyaniyeshu

Since yesterday I have been wondering whether to go to Calcutta. But today my mind is lacking in strength. I know that Bela's time of departure is nigh. I do not have the courage to go and look her in the face. Here I am able to keep my mind free of life and death matters, but in Calcutta I have no such refuge. I can only wish Bela well as she goes hence. I know there is nothing more for me to do.[1]

Shri Rabindranath Thakur

Source: MS original at Rabindra Bhavan, Shantiniketan; letter published in *CP*, I, p. 68.

1 In fact, RT was in Calcutta when Bela died. See Dutta and Robinson, *Rabindranath Tagore*, p. 213.

122

To Woodrow Wilson[1]

Extraordinary as it may seem, in April 1918, as his daughter lay dying and the Great War continued to rage, Rabindranath made hurried plans to leave Calcutta for a lecturing tour of the United States. On 11 April, he cabled George Brett, his New York publisher, 'Could you arrange my lecturing this autumn' – and received the cautious response: 'Yes Pond [lecture agent] offers some arrangements doubts possibility any large success.'[2] Immediately, ignoring his own reference to 'autumn', Tagore booked a passage for himself, his son and daughter-in-law from Calcutta on 8 May. So impulsive a decision suggests a desperate desire to escape his commitments in Bengal, perhaps especially the expected death of Bela. But Rabindranath, characteristically, convinced himself that his reasons were high-minded. Writing on 16 April to someone suffering from a depression, he exhorted him to throw off his feelings of personal inadequacy and follow his own example: he was going to America, he said, because 'the fires of destruction are burning throughout the world. History is to be made anew – at this moment I too have some deeds to do, I can no longer remain here in my little corner.'[3]

But events in America intervened. While in Calcutta, preparing to depart, Tagore was shown foreign newspaper reports of the long-running and sensational trial of various Indians, Germans and others in San Francisco on charges of conspiracy to foment revolution in India with German money. Tagore was cited as having been supportive during his 1916–17 tour of the USA; it was even suggested that he had tried to enlist the help of Count Okuma, the Japanese prime minister, when he met him in Japan in 1916.

There was not a shred of genuine evidence for these accusations, nor was there any truth in them. But in the wartime atmosphere prevalent in the USA, they were given considerable credence, bolstered, no doubt, by Tagore's public and passionate condemnation of nationalism, which had attracted strong criticism in parts of the American press in 1916.

Rabindranath, sitting in faraway Calcutta, idealist though he was, was realistic enough to appreciate the likely response of the American public to the press reports. Reacting with a mixture of disgust, anger, pain and disappointment, he cancelled his visit and, over the next week or so, wrote scathing letters (122–4, 126–8) to a range of people concerned with the incident, beginning with President Woodrow Wilson.[4]

Calcutta, [India]
9 May 1918

Dear President Wilson

When I was about to embark for America only a few days ago some newspaper cuttings from Japan came to my hand containing information about a prosecution of some Hindus in San Francisco for revolutionary intrigue against the British

The ebbing of faith 199

Government. I find that the prosecution counsel mentions my name implicating me in this charge of conspiracy assuring the court that he has documentary evidence to support it. It is also stated that my last tour to America was undertaken at the indication of some German agents to whom I gave to understand that Count Terauchi was favourable to my secret proposals and Count Okuma sympathetic.[5]

Though I feel certain that my friends in America and my readers there who have studied my writings at all carefully can never believe such an audacious piece of fabrication, yet the indignity of my name being dragged into the mire of such calumny has given me great pain. It is needless to tell you, that I do not believe in patriotism which can ride roughshod over higher ideals of humanity, and I consider it to be an act of impiety against one's own country when any service is offered to her which is loaded with secret lies and dishonest deeds of violence. I have been outspoken enough in my utterances when my country needed them, and I have taken upon myself the risk of telling unwelcome truths to my own countrymen, as well as to the rulers of my country. But I despise those tortuous methods adopted by some government or other groups of individuals, in which the devil is taken into partnership in the name of duty. I have received great kindness from the hands of your countrymen, and I entertain great admiration for yourself, who are not afraid of incurring the charge of anachronism for introducing idealism in the domain of politics, and therefore I owe it to myself and to you and your people to make this avowal of my faith and to assure your countrymen that their hospitality was not bestowed upon one who was ready to accept it while wallowing in the subsoil sewerage of treason.[6]

Yours sincerely
Rabindranath Tagore

Source: MS copy at Rabindra Bhavan, Shantiniketan.

1 Thomas Woodrow Wilson (1856–1924): 28th president of the USA, 1913–21.
2 RT to Brett, 11 April 1918; Brett to RT, 12 April 1918 [New York]. George Platt Brett (1858–1936): publisher; on the staff of Macmillan in New York from 1874, he later became chairman.
3 RT to Amiya Chakravarty, 3 Baishakh 1325 [16 April 1918], *CP*, XI, p. 15.
4 On this entire incident, see Dutta and Robinson, *Rabindranath Tagore*, pp. 211–15 and notes. RT never met Woodrow Wilson but he requested him, through Macmillan, to allow *Nationalism* to be dedicated to him; Wilson, on British advice, declined.
5 Count Terauchi Masatake (1852–1919): prime minister of Japan, 1916–18. Marquess Okuma Shigenobu (1838–1922): prime minister of Japan, 1914–16.
6 RT's remark about idealism was presumably a reference, in part, to the Fourteen Points announced by Wilson on 8 Jan. 1918, the first of which was a renunciation of all secret diplomacy ('Open covenants openly arrived at').

123

To Macmillan & Co. (USA)

[Calcutta, India]
[9? May 1918]

[Dear Mr Brett]

When I was about to sail for America concerning which I had cabled to you I came to learn that a case had been brought against some Indians in San Francisco in which

I was charged with having conspired with the Germans in a revolutionary design against the British Government. At the first shock of disgust I cancelled my voyage at once. The indignity of ever having to contradict such an accusation was painful to me. It had been inconceivable to me that I should ever have an occasion to assert that conspiracy and all forms of lying ambuscades, followed in the name of patriotism and political exigency, are loathed by me, especially as they claim extolment when successful. It was a cruel irony of fate that I should be accused in an American law court of duplicity and stealthy machinations and that it should find the least credence among your countrymen. On further consideration I have resolved once more, as you know, to visit America and not to shrink from facing the calumny, though it takes away all pleasure from my mind at the intended trip.[1] I send you herewith a copy of the letter which I sent to President Wilson about this matter.[2] I ask you as my friend and publisher, at whose suggestion I accepted the offer of the Lyceum Bureau to lecture in America and who knows my movements while there, to give the lie to the rumours against me floating in your atmosphere.[3]

[Yours sincerely]
Rabindranath Tagore

Source: MS copy at Rabindra Bhavan, Shantiniketan.

1 It appears that RT cabled Brett again that he had decided to visit America after all. He had not yet received Brett's letter of 15 April, in which he wrote:

> Mr Pond and I are very much upset indeed because you have been accused in the press in this country of being what they called disloyal, a good many paragraphs have appeared from time to time indicating that you have had some connection with German agents or with certain disloyal elements in India . . .
> I shall rejoice if you decide to come over because I believe that such a lecture tour at this time will tend wholly to remove the unpleasant and utterly wrong impression which prevails. ([copy at New York])

By July, however, RT had altogether abandoned the idea of an American visit.
2 See letter 122.
3 C. F. Andrews, on behalf of RT, sent a copy to Brett of the viceroy's letter to RT about this matter (see letter 126).

124

To Marquess Okuma Shigenobu

Calcutta, [India]
9 May 1918

Dear Count Okuma

I have been greatly pained to find that your name and Count Terauchi's name have been brought into the prosecution evidence of a conspiracy case in San Francisco in connection with my own. I have never met Count Terauchi in my life and I shall esteem it a kindness if you will convey to him the pain which this canard has caused me.

If you think it necessary you are at liberty to contradict in my name the whole evidence that was reported concerning me, and to state that as far as yourself, Count

The ebbing of faith

Terauchi and myself are concerned, it is one tissue of falsehood from beginning to end. You are at liberty to publish this letter.[1]

Yours sincerely
Rabindranath Tagore

Source: MS copy at Rabindra Bhavan, Shantiniketan.

1 Okuma circulated a translation of RT's letter to the leading Japanese newspapers, and also showed it to Terauchi (Okuma to RT, 10 July 1918 [RB]).

125

To (Sir) Sarvepalli Radhakrishnan[1]

Throughout his life Tagore denied that he should be treated as a philosopher because, he said, he had created no system of thought. But others took a different view, most notably the philosopher Sarvepalli Radhakrishnan, who in 1918 published *The Philosophy of Rabindranath Tagore*. This book, based entirely on the published translations of Tagore's works (Radhakrishnan knew no Bengali and treated Tagore in effect as a writer in English), sank almost without trace and has never resurfaced.[2] Radhakrishnan had very much hoped that Tagore would write an introduction but, as this witty letter makes clear, Rabindranath felt unqualified for the job.[3]

Calcutta, [India]
9 May 1918

Dear Mr Radhakrishnan

It is difficult for me to write an introduction to your book, for I do not know what my duties are in writing it. If they are to make the path easy for the readers I am the last person who is competent to undertake such a task. For about my philosophy I am like M. Jourdain who had been talking prose all his life without knowing it.[4] It may tickle my vanity to be told that my writings carry dissolved in their stream pure gold of philosophical speculation and that gold bricks can be made by washing its sands and melting the precious fragments – but yet it is for the readers to find it out and it would be a perilous responsibility on my part to give assurance to the seekers and stand guarantee for its realisation. If a doctor writes a scientific paper on some disease which I harbour in my constitution it would be ludicrously presumptuous on my part to vouch for its truth, for only sufferings are for me and their pathology is for the doctor.

However your proofsheets are in the hands of Mr Andrews who is in Shantiniketan.[5] He has my instructions to correct some obvious inaccuracies which are in your book. I think he will personally write to you about it and send you back your proofs when he has gone through them.

[Sincerely yours]
Rabindranath Tagore

Source: MS copy at Rabindra Bhavan, Shantiniketan; letter published in *VBQ*, *1*, Nos 1–2, May–Nov. 1990, pp. 16–17.

1 Sir Sarvepalli Radhakrishnan (1888–1975): philosopher; he held chairs at Mysore and Calcutta and was professor of Eastern religions and ethics, University of Oxford, 1936–52; later he became president of India.
2 It was republished in India in 1961, the centenary of RT's birth, with a new preface by Radhakrishnan, but has always been virtually ignored by Tagore scholars. Krishna Kripalani did not refer to it in his biography of RT. E. J. Thompson cited the book once: '[RT] does not love beauty for its own sake, but because he views it as an attribute of the divine' (Radhakrishnan, *Philosophy*, p. 142). Thompson commented: 'This is quite mistaken; no poet ever had a more intimate feeling for natural beauty' (*Rabindranath Tagore*, p. 306). In a letter to RT, written after Radhakrishnan's arrival as a lecturer in Oxford, Thompson wrote: 'You stand for a new kind of man, neither eastern nor western but a reconciler of the best of both. This kind of man is parodied by many charlatans – for example, your Radhakrishnan, who seems to me a blatant and empty humbug. And parodies now get as much esteem as the realities' (14 Jan. 1934 [RB]).
3 Radhakrishnan to RT, 27 April 1918, *VBQ*, *1*, Nos 1 and 2, 1990, p. 32. RT did, however, express his approval of the book after publication.
4 Molière, *Le Bourgeois Gentilhomme*, II:iv.
5 Radhakrishnan received the proofs back from Andrews and returned them to Macmillan on 27 May 1918 with the remark: 'As Sir R. N. Tagore was ill, Mr Andrews revised the proofs' [Reading]. Later, on receiving the finished book, RT told Radhakrishnan: 'When you sent me its proofs, I felt greatly reluctant in going over them and I asked Mr Andrews to do it for me' (28 Dec. 1918, *VBQ*, *1*, Nos 1 and 2, 1990, p. 17).

126

To Lord Chelmsford[1]

Tagore felt obliged to inform the viceroy, Lord Chelmsford, of his actions to clear his name of the allegations made against him in San Francisco (see letter 122). In this letter he also takes the opportunity to plead the case of W. W. Pearson, who, it was reported in the Indian press, had recently been arrested in Peking. The cause was his anti-British pamphlet, 'For India', which he had published in Japan in August 1917 and which had been translated into Russian by the new Bolshevik Government and used as anti-British propaganda; it urged Asians to unite with the Indian nationalists against British rule in India. The pamphlet was proscribed in India and the British authorities in Japan warned Pearson he was liable to penalties under British law. When he happened to come to Peking, he was arrested under special wartime powers and deported to Britain, where he spent the rest of the war.[2]

[Calcutta, India]
[12 May 1918]

Your Excellency

Will you kindly allow me to send you herewith the copies of letters one of which I wrote to President Wilson and the other to Marquess Okuma?[3] These will explain themselves and Your Excellency will know from them what I have to say about the unscrupulous manufacture of lies employed against myself.[4]

Since I posted these letters there has appeared information in the newspapers that Mr W. W. Pearson has been arrested in Peking charged with some political offence. I know Mr Pearson intimately. He is one of those Englishmen whose chivalrous love of humanity has drawn my heart to the English people revealing to me where its true greatness lies. His connection with my school in Bolpur has ever appeared to me as providential, for I hold it firmly that until in India we have institutions in which Englishmen can join Indians in collaboration of love for higher purposes of humanity the object of our history will remain unfulfilled and the spiritual untruth of our situation will be a source of trouble for both parties. Pearson was able completely to win the hearts of our teachers and boys by his selflessness and extraordinary power of sympathy, and I feel certain that mostly owing to his presence my school escaped in great measure the occasional outbreaks of irritation and excitement that passed over Bengal in recent times. So long as he was with me the patchwork of miserly politics had no attraction for him and he solely devoted his life to the fundamental service of education and moral regeneration of men through love and righteousness. A man of his type, full of generous impulses is liable to lend himself to misunderstandings and to come to grief in troublous times like the present one.[5] I am not aware what is the nature of the offence with which he is charged but I am sure that he is incapable of doing anything underhand and dishonourable. I know that I have no power to help him and that he has resources in himself manfully to bear his sufferings, but I feel it my duty to bear testimony to his nobleness and express my faith in his absolute probity whatever appearance his present situation may have for the public.

Your obedient servant
Rabindranath Tagore

Source: MS copy at Rabindra Bhavan, Shantiniketan.

1 Lord Chelmsford, 3rd baron (1868–1933): viceroy of India, 1916–21.
2 See Sanat Bagchi, 'The poet and the Raj', *VBQ*, 50, May 1984–April 1985, pp. 98–9.
3 See letters 122 (to Wilson) and 124 (to Okuma).
4 Sir John Maffey, private secretary to Chelmsford, told RT on 17 June that the viceroy wished 'to express his sympathy with you on finding your name dragged into such unwarrantable prominence in the American press. His Excellency is well aware that there is no foundation whatever for the suggestions made and he is willing that you should make any use of this letter you think fit' [RB]. It was copied and sent to George Brett of Macmillan, who circulated it in the American press to considerable effect.
5 RT was aware that Pearson had mixed feelings about the pamphlet because Pearson had written to him on 27 Sept. 1917 that, when writing it, 'I seemed under a compulsion directly contrary to my real nature which is interested not in political questions or national problems so much as personal relationships' [RB].

127

To Harriet Moody

After writing to President Wilson, Count Okuma, Macmillan and Lord Chelmsford, Tagore finally wrote letters to two American friends, Harriet Moody and Mayce Seymour, explaining why he had cancelled his planned visit to America with his son Rathindranath and daughter-in-law Pratima. Neither friend was convinced that the allegations against Tagore had been taken as seriously by the American public as Rabindranath thought. But they were wrong: when James B. Pond, Tagore's lecture agent, tried to book a tour for Tagore in the USA in 1920, he found it impossible to get sufficient dates as a direct result of the allegations. Americans were much more conformist in their attitude to 'disloyalty' than Tagore's American friends cared to admit.[1]

204 *Selected letters of Rabindranath Tagore*

Calcutta, [India]
13 May 1918

My dear Friend,

I thought I would startle you one fine morning in June by presenting myself at your door and quite naturally taking my seat at your breakfast table. I had engaged my passage, packing was done, Rathi and Pratima were ready to accompany me, when some newspaper cuttings from Japan informed me that there was a prosecution of some Hindus in San Francisco in which the prosecution counsel implicated me, saying that my last tour to America was undertaken at the instigation of the German Conspiration [*sic*] and my real motive was to join the revolutionist party. Such a sublime piece of invention took my breath away, the more so as the counsel said he had documentary evidence to support the charge. Evidently documents can be manufactured in the devil's own factory to support any charge whatever, and therefore for honest truth documents are naturally rare. What I can say against each incrimination can only be oral, which can have effect on people who already trust me. Unfortunately this is the time when people's minds are unsettled and their moods are unreliable. So after due deliberation I came to the conclusion that it was best for me to give up my visit to your country. For it is sure to be very unpleasant for me if there is the least possibility of misunderstanding which is so undignified in this affair that it fills me with disgust. However, this unnatural state of things, prolific of monstrosities of all forms of untruth and injustice, cannot last forever. Therefore I still entertain hope of one day finding my way to your table, enjoying a generous portion of your icecream and your warm-hearted friendliness.

Your affectionate friend
Rabindranath Tagore

Source: MS original in Moody Papers [Chicago].

1 Moody wrote to RT on 12 Sept. 1918, 'I don't think the slightest credence was given by anyone whose judgement could count for a moment, to that sensational newspaper story' [RB]. She repeated her belief in a letter to Rathindranath on 22 Sept. 1924 [RB]. Mayce Seymour's attitude is not on record but may be guessed from her other writings on RT.

128

To Mayce Seymour[1]

Calcutta, [India]
14 May 1918

Dear Mrs Seymour

Our berths were secured and I was to have sailed for America on the 8th last accompanied by Rathi and Pratima when the news came that the prosecution counsel in a revolutionary conspiracy case against some Hindus in San Francisco mentioned my name as that of one of the guilty party. It was especially disgusting to me because I hate to be put in the same category with politicians and diplomats who deal with secret lies and found their schemes upon filth pits of iniquity. I should be proud openly to suffer for truth or my country, but I never can persuade [myself] to believe that lying intrigue can be the proper price to pay for anything of abiding value. With man the end is not the only object, but the means also; and however absurdly paradoxical it may sound yet it is true that for us most often the means of attainment is a truer object than the attainment of object itself and that defeat is not always with the vanquished, but with the victor. For man's world of being far transcends his world of gaining, and though it cannot be proved by the logic of the ledger book yet truly it is a foolish bargain for him in which individuals or nations offer their souls in exchange for success. Everybody should know by this time that I am not an apostle of success and I do not believe in a freedom which is merely political. For this false ideal of freedom has overrun the whole world with narrow patches of national preserves surrounded by thorny hedges of slavery, giving rise to mutual hatred, suspicion and lying diplomacy. The time has come when man must know that true freedom is moral freedom and for it we must fight with moral weapons.

However I postpone my visit to America for the present, for I feel it would be extremely unpleasant for me to have my relationships with your countrymen marred by the least shadow of distrust and to incur the chance of my words being misinterpreted and my movements watched with suspicion.

With my love to you all,

Yours affectionately
Rabindranath Tagore

Source: MS copy at Rabindra Bhavan, Shantiniketan.

1 Mayce Seymour: wife of Arthur Seymour, professor of Spanish and French, University of Illinois, Urbana; she wrote 'That golden time', *VBQ*, 25, No. 1, Summer 1959, pp. 1–15 (an account of RT's 1912–13 visit to Urbana).

129

To (Sir) William Rothenstein

Despite his disgust at being linked with revolutionary conspiracies in America, and his decision to cancel his visit to the United States, Tagore found it very difficult to abandon his plan to travel. This letter to William Rothenstein about his 'homesickness for the far away' indicates his mercurial state of mind in mid-1918.

Shantiniketan, [West Bengal, India]
1 June 1918

Dear Friend, I have not written to you for long. Possibly it is because I find the channel of my correspondence clogged with crowds of letters that do not move – they are [a] mere burden that has to be forcibly disposed of. They need dredgers to clear them up, and in the meanwhile they choke the living stream. Possibly I am growing lethargic like men living in an overcrowded room – my mind being crammed in a dense surrounding of small social claims that are inimical both to real work and to honest leisure. I have got into the habit of putting off writing letters to my friends till my mind regains its window and its easy chair; but the lengthening intervals of such inactivity produces the habit of nonwriting making the joints of my letter writing personality [stiff]. – For some time past I have been pining to go somewhere – it was like a homesickness for the far away. I planned all sorts of excursions in my mind – to the hills, to southern India, to Ceylon – but one by one I gave them up like nuts whose kernels had perished. But I fear it was not the need of [a] change of place which I felt, but for me it was more like [a] strange case of an oyster trying to run away from its own shell.[1] A crust has been formed round me, a crust of reputation and publicity which I can no longer shake off and find my freedom in the world of quiet delights. However, I have decided to start for America next autumn – it is but to take a desperate plunge into a violent change of surroundings. I hope this hateful war will be over some time when I am there and I shall be able to come to England and see you.

Something has happened to me lately which I find difficult even to mention. I very seldom speak about it to anybody. It is the death of my eldest daughter Bela.[2] She was exceptionally beautiful in body and mind, and I cannot but think that all things that are real in this world cannot afford to lose the intense reality of her life and yet remain the same. We can only see the one side of truth from the point where we live and miss the meaning of death, but there must be another side where it is in harmony with life, like the setting sun whose meaning is not in its disappearance but in the sunrise in the new morning outside our ken.

I have met Dr Sadler and was greatly attracted by him.[3] I do not know how much he will be able to accomplish, but he is one of those men who have rare power of vision and who can impart it to others. I believe he will be able to give a shock of life to our inert organisation and make people think. Along with much that is crude and inane he has come to know some of our best men like Dr Seal and I feel sure that will compensate him.[4] I am sending you by this mail a small book of mine named *The Parrot's Training* which has more meaning than words and a great deal more illustration than letterpress.[5]

Your affectionate friend
Rabindranath Tagore

Source: MS original in Rothenstein Papers [Harvard]; letter published in Lago (ed.), *Imperfect Encounter*, pp. 247–8.

1 Compare RT's remark to Harriet Moody about the effect of the Nobel prize: 'To deprive me of my seclusion is like shelling an oyster – the rude touch of the curious world is all over me.' (Letter 79.)
2 See letter 121. Rothenstein replied hauntingly on 20 Aug. 1918:

> Death seems to have become a familiar of men. Not that he has ever stayed far from our haunts, but he has stayed among the shadows of the trees. But now he walks ever openly among men, taking the young by handfuls and putting them, as in the old children's stories, into his bottomless sack. It is we who invited him, so it would not be fair to call him shameless. (Lago (ed.), *Imperfect Encounter*, p. 251)

3 (Sir) Michael Sadler had come to Bengal as chairman of the Calcutta University Commission.

Rothenstein had recommended him to RT: 'I wish we sent many such ambassadors from West to East' (23 Sept. 1917, in *ibid.*, p. 243). See letter 132.
4 (Sir) Brajendranath Seal. See letter 50, n. 6 and letter 179.
5 *The Parrot's Training* was published in 1918 by Thacker Spink & Co. in Calcutta, with illustrations by Abanindranath Tagore and others; the Bengali original, *Tota Kahini*, appeared in *Shabuj Patra*, Magh 1324 [Jan.–Feb. 1918]. It was written partly in response to the Calcutta University Commission, as it is a satire on the futility of education through book-learning. RT sent a copy to Edwin Montagu, secretary of state for India, who responded: 'The story is delightfully told in your own inimitable style, and your brother's drawings add even a further grace to a perfect volume' (Montagu to RT, 16 Aug. 1918 [RB]).

130

To Rachel Rothenstein[1]

Rachel Rothenstein, daughter of William, was nine years old when Tagore first met her in London in 1912. They exchanged several letters over the next few years. This one, written just a fortnight after the death of Rabindranath's daughter Bela, is rather poignant: not only must Bela have hovered in his mind when he wrote it but, with his acute sensitivity to mood, he could sense that the war years had changed the young English girl he had known only a short while before.

Santiniketan, [West Bengal, India]
2 June 1918

My dear little friend

Though often enough I think of you, the writing of letters has become difficult for me because interesting news [has] grown so scarce nowadays. I suppose things *do* happen even now that are fully worth writing to you about, but they are hidden behind the dust raised by the passing events. Even in India our minds have been disturbed to such an extent, that I forget to notice a wonderful yellow bird – a stranger to this garden which came here this morning. It flashed by me like a sudden joyous thought across the heart of the blue sky while I was solemnly reading my newspaper, but when its image developed in my mind through the swarm of the printed letters, the bird had disappeared. I wish I had known the secret of the fairyland, for then I could catch my message from this winged beauty. Possibly it came to remind me of some fair-haired princess dwelling in the island of misty hills across the sea. But dark floods of newspapers are abroad to kill all other messages but they themselves carry.

Rathi[2] writes me to say that he has a pair of peacocks which he will bring here and set free. I should like to know about what you can write to me in answer to match this. Certainly not about beetles, caterpillars. Do you know any creature in your country house whose tail is gorgeously bigger than its entire body? Of course it will not do to seek for instances among human beings.

We had a pet deer. It would tamely take its food from our hands and graze free in our lawn. We never believed that she could ever leave us. But when the springtime came and our *shal* avenue was in blossom the call of the forest came upon her and one afternoon she ran and ran crossing field after field and never came back. I would be glad to know that she had reached some forest at last. But I have reasons to believe that she was killed by men, and it makes me feel ashamed of human beings. Can you believe that foreign sportsmen come and decoy peacocks by the lure of food from some river island where they are protected by our people, to neighbouring land, only to enjoy killing these magnificent birds? Is it not of the same nature as the brutal joy and pride in the power of wanton destruction which so hideously comes out in the time of war?[3] But I am afraid, I am too serious – possibly I am growing hopelessly old, [yet] but I believe you have also grown older than you were only a few years ago. My love to you.

Yours affectionately
Rabindranath Tagore

Source: MS copy at Rabindra Bhavan, Shantiniketan.

1 Rachel Rothenstein (1903–89).
2 Rathindranath Tagore.
3 Rachel Rothenstein replied on 17 Nov. 1918, a week after the armistice, 'I quite agree with you about war, it is the most terrible and brutal thing. But we are all ever so proud of the brave men that have given their lives for their country, and of them who will return victorious!' [RB].

131

To William Butler Yeats

Though disappointed by the poor quality of the recent translations of Tagore's poetry, W. B. Yeats remained receptive to his prose writings, especially *My Reminiscences*, which he had read in 1917, when it was published by Macmillan.[1] To his eternal credit, Yeats wanted Tagore to present to the world his full Bengali personality – not merely the simple image projected by *Gitanjali*. On 24 April 1918, he informed Rabindranath:

> It is a long while since I have written to you but you have not been out of my thoughts. Your 'Autobiography' especially has been a great pleasure. I wish you could give us the latter half – your thoughts on your own life work, and on the different movements of modern Bengal. The more is now written for Bengal, the more it would interest Europe.[2]

In his reply, Rabindranath mentions his lovely letters to his niece (such as letters 5 and 7–23), written in the 1890s, which had recently been published in English translation in Bengal.

Santiniketan, [West Bengal, India]
17 June 1918

Dear Yeats

The rumour of your marriage came to me from Mr Cousins, though he was not quite certain of its truth.[3] Your letter dispels all doubt and you have my best wishes. I do hope I shall be able to come to England once again after this war is over, and meet you both.

What you have heard about Devabrata is true.[4] He has completely lost his mind, and there is hardly any hope of his recovery. I tried my utmost to help him, giving my guarantee to keep him with me which was agreed to. But the mischief had already been

The ebbing of faith

done, and the poor boy became worse and worse till he had to be lodged in a public asylum where he is still detained. His mind was of a most delicate texture, extremely sensitive, and we feel for him more than I can tell you.

A number of my Bengali letters written in my young days had been collected some years ago. I gave my permission to publish them when I was convinced that they could be of great help to explain my writings which appeared unintelligible to some part of my readers.[5] My nephew Suren has translated these letters into English.[6] They cover those very years which were most productive for me and therefore they act like a footpath in my life history, unconsciously laid by the treading of my own thoughts. I feel sure these letters, when published, will present to you pictures and ideas concerning me and my surroundings more vividly and truly than anything that I have yet written.[7]

Yours
Rabindranath Tagore

Source: MS original in collection of Michael Yeats.

1 See letter 105.
2 W. B. Yeats to RT, 24 April [1918], *VBQ, 30*, No. 3, 1964–5, p. 174.
3 Yeats mentioned his marriage, which took place in Oct. 1917. James H. Cousins, never close to Yeats, had been living in India for more than two years.
4 Devabrata Mukerjea, translator of *The Post Office*, had shown signs of mental instability while in Europe in 1914. See MacBride White and Jeffares (eds.), *Gonne–Yeats Letters*, pp. 340–1. He returned to Calcutta, where he got into trouble with the British authorities and had to be rescued by RT, with the help of Lord Carmichael, the governor: the condition was that Mukerjea should stay at Shantiniketan. See Carmichael to RT, 5 May 1915 [RB].
5 The letters stop at 1895, when RT was in his mid-thirties. He never tackled a second volume of autobiography, being no doubt aware of how the requirements of truth and tact would conflict if he wrote about living and recently dead people. The letters, originally written mainly to Indira Devi, were copied out by her in two bound volumes; among these were letters 5 and 7–23. Rathindranath read them as a teenager and was thrilled by them: 'Never have I read any book with more enjoyment.' (*Edges of Time*, p. 54.) In 1912, he and Nagendranath Gangulee published some of the letters, with various portions deleted by Rabindranath, as *Chhinnapatra* (Torn Leaves). Nirad C. Chaudhuri reckoned them to be 'great works of literature', which 'also reveal [RT's] character and personality with unadorned truth' (*Thy Hand*, p. 602).
6 Surendranath Tagore translated a number of RT's works into English, and also assisted in the translation of others. His work was generally revised by RT, but it lacked literary flair.
7 Surendranath's translation was published serially as 'Extracts from old letters of Rabindranath Tagore', *MR*, Jan.–Aug. 1917. In 1921, these extracts were published as a short book, *Glimpses of Bengal*. In 1991, this selection was retranslated and slightly modified by the present authors. There is no record of Yeats' reaction to *Glimpses of Bengal*, unlike *My Reminiscences*, perhaps because the former translation was inferior to the latter and the book was altogether slighter.

132

To (Sir) Michael Sadler[1]

As already mentioned (letter 129), (Sir) Michael Sadler, chairman of the Calcutta University Commission (1917–19), had been recommended to Tagore by William Rothenstein. He visited Rabindranath several times, in both Calcutta and Shantiniketan, and they formed a deep respect and liking for each other. After the first meeting, at Jorasanko, Sadler wrote to Tagore, 'I shall always associate with my thoughts of India what we heard and saw yesterday at your home. You have given colour and melody to our impressions.'[2] Tagore remarked to Sadler in a letter two years later, 'I always feel deeply thankful when I have the occasion to learn to love an Englishman.'[3]

Of course both men were aware that the other members of the commission (who visited Shantiniketan) were less susceptible to this empathy. As Tagore wrote in 1916, following an incident between Bengali students and a British lecturer at Presidency College, Calcutta, 'We sometimes quote the instance of the relations of Oxford and Cambridge dons with their undergraduates. But the cases are not parallel. There, the relationship is natural. Here, it is not. So it appears as if this vacuum in nature has to be filled up with brickbats of "discipline".'[4] This letter, reacting to Sadler's draft of the section of his report dealing with Shantiniketan, which he had sent to Tagore for his comment, deals with the same problem.

Santiniketan, [West Bengal, India]
27 June 1918

Dear Dr Sadler

Please allow me to express my gratitude to you for the appreciation with which you speak of my institute at Bolpur. The summary which you give of my conversation with you about the education in India is accurate in every detail excepting in one point which has to be made more clear to avoid misunderstanding. I have always tried to introduce Englishmen as teachers and helpers in my school, but it must be noted that it was not for the sake of efficiency. My school, as you know, is not a mere teaching institution – it is my intention to bring up in this place our boys in an atmosphere of human brotherhood. For the carrying out of this object, I always welcome help from my English friends when its source is true love for man and a genuine sympathy for our boys. Before I came across such friends I had tried the experiment with an Englishman who was an efficient teacher having a wide experience in teaching Indian boys.[5] But it had the opposite effect to what I aimed at because of his lack of sympathy for Bengali boys. Being naturally sensitive the minds of Bengali boys are sure to be poisoned by the feeling of hatred against the western peoples, if placed under foreign teachers who do not love them and therefore do not care to understand them. The bonds of human relationship of love and sympathy are more needed for our students from their western teachers than a mere official dutifulness and efficiency.

I would wish some such addition as this to be made to the sentence about English teachers: 'But he would refuse such help, at all costs – as being educationally harmful – where lack of sympathy prevented a true human relation between the English teacher and his Bengali pupils.'[6]

Yours very sincerely
Rabindranath Tagore

Source: MS copy at Rabindra Bhavan, Shantiniketan.

1 Sir Michael Ernest Sadler (1861–1943): educationist, who almost singlehandedly created the study of comparative education; vice-chancellor of the University of Leeds, 1911–23, he became master of University College, Oxford until his retirement in 1934. He was also a pioneering collector of modern art.

2 Sadler to RT, 27 Nov. 1917 [RB]. Sadler met RT on 19 Nov. 1917; see his account quoted in Michael Sadleir, *Michael Ernest Sadler: A Memoir by his Son* (London, 1949), p. 287–8.
3 RT to Sadler, 26 Jan. 1920 [copy at RB]. RT intended to dedicate his *Centre of Indian Culture* (Madras, 1919), a kind of prospectus for Visva-Bharati, to Sadler, but the publisher overlooked his request.
4 'Indian students and western teachers', *MR*, April 1916, p. 419.
5 Englishman: probably Capt. J. W. Petavel, a retired military engineer. RT invited him to set up a technical section at Shantiniketan, in 1914. See Paul, *Rabijibani*, VI, p. 487.
6 Sadler incorporated this statement verbatim into his report, which noted, among other detailed comments on the Shantiniketan school:

> No one who has seen the poet, sitting bare-headed in a long robe in the open veranda of a low-roofed house – the wide hedgeless fields stretching to the distant horizon beyond – with a class of little boys, each on his carpet, in a circle before him on the ground, can ever forget the impression, or be insensible to the service which Sir Rabindranath Tagore renders to his country by offering to the younger generation the best that he has to give . . .
> It is Sir Rabindranath's strong conviction that, while English should be skilfully and thoroughly taught as a second language, the chief medium of instruction in schools (and even in colleges up to the stage of the university degree) should be the mother tongue. He has four reasons for this belief; first, because it is through his mother tongue that every man learns the deepest lessons of life; second, because some of those pupils who have a just claim to higher education cannot master the English language; third, because many of those who do acquire English fail to achieve true proficiency in it and yet, in the attempt to learn a language so difficult to a Bengali, spend too large a part of the energy which is indispensable to the growth of the power of independent thought and observation; and, fourth, because a training conducted chiefly through the mother tongue would lighten the load of education for girls, whose deeper culture is of high importance to India. (*Report of the Calcutta University Commission* (Calcutta, 1919), I, pt 1, 'Analysis of present conditions', pp. 226–7)

133

To Annie Besant[1]

Tagore was beset with requests for assistance throughout his adult life, and his instinctive desire to help often led him into unfortunate liaisons. His relationship with Annie Besant and her entourage (such as James Cousins) is a good example: Tagore had a healthy distrust for theosophy, but he was touched by Besant's sympathy for India and Indians.[2] In December 1917, at the time of the annual Congress session, held that year in Calcutta, he allowed himself to be elected chancellor of Besant's proposed National University – even though he was already contemplating the founding of his own university, Visva-Bharati. But he shrank from much further involvement with the project (which never took off), or indeed from getting involved with Besant in other ways, as the next two letters make clear.

Pithapuram, [Andhra Pradesh, India]
15 October 1918

Dear Mrs Besant,

I have just received your letter requesting me to preside over the next congress.[3] Believe me, it is painfully difficult for me to refuse any invitation coming from you concerning our country. But one of the very few things that I know for certain about myself is that I am wholly unfit for politics. Whenever, urged by some necessity of special circumstances, I have tried to dabble in it I have injured myself, consequently injuring those works which it is my mission to perform.[4] Also I believe in our shastric injunction to retire from all activities of public life after a certain period, not to be arbitrarily fixed, but whenever an individual receives inner warnings combined with sure hints from his waning physical powers. This is an excuse which I never could offer to anybody else but yourself, knowing that you will understand me and help me in keeping myself free from all responsibilities that are sure to disturb me in my final adjustment of life.[5]

I started to go to Madras to visit Adyar, and also to meet Mr Cousins in Vijayanagar – but in the midway fatigue overcame me and I felt that I was not strong enough to bear the strain of a long railway journey and of social duties involved in meeting all known and unknown friends in a town where I go for the first time.[6] It is a real disappointment for me but unavoidable, and I have arranged to start on Friday next for Calcutta from this place where I am taking rest.[7]

Very sincerely yours,
Rabindranath Tagore

Source: MS original at Theosophical Society archives [Adyar].

1 Annie Besant (1847–1933): social reformer, theosophist and Indian independence leader; having launched the Indian Home Rule League in 1916, she became president of the Indian National Congress in 1917. She based herself in India from around 1895, living at Adyar near Madras, the headquarters of the Theosophical Society.
2 In Nov. 1913, E. J. Thompson asked RT whether he had met Besant and he 'shuddered: "No, and I never want to."' He agreed with Thompson that she had 'never done any good' in India. (Quoted in E. P. Thompson, *Alien Homage*, p. 110.) While this may have been a slight overstatement of his real feelings, there is plentiful evidence that RT avoided Besant where possible. It is noteworthy that Krishnamurti never refers to RT in his discourses, neither do the majority of Krishnamurti's admirers in their writings about him.
3 The next annual session of the Congress was held at Delhi in Dec. 1918.
4 RT was clearly referring to the muddle over the Calcutta Congress reception committee in 1917 (see letters 112 and 113). Earlier in 1918, he had declined an offer from the Home Rule League to fund his proposed lecture tour of the USA, on the grounds that 'I can only speak my own message as I feel it, and not in accordance with the views of any political party' (RT to S. R. Bomanji, 7 April 1918 [copy at RB]).
5 Besant replied on 18 Oct. from Adyar: 'I quite understand . . . You would have liked the peace at Adyar, the river and the sea and trees . . . I had chosen a room for you where you looked straight into the heart of a great banyan tree . . . Some day, perchance' [RB].
6 In early 1919, RT accepted James H. Cousins' invitation and visited south India on tour (see letter 136).
7 RT left Pithapuram for Calcutta on 18 Oct. 1918.

134

To Charles Freer Andrews

Having travelled half way down the Indian peninsula on his way to Madras and the south, Tagore turned round and went back to Shantiniketan. He gave one explanation to Annie Besant (see letter 133), and another to C. F. Andrews (who was then with Gandhi) in this letter – quite a curious one coming from an indefatigable traveller like Tagore to Andrews, an even more indefatigable traveller. Both reasons were genuine; and Tagore had the extra concern on his mind that his daughter and grandson were ill in Hyderabad (where Nagendranath Gangulee was then living). He considered going from Pithapuram to Hyderabad, but the doctors at Hyderabad advised him by telegram not to come. After returning to Shantiniketan, he explained his state of mind more fully to Andrews (letter 135).

The ebbing of faith

Pithapuram, [Andhra Pradesh, India][1]
18 October 1918

Dear Friend

I am returning to Calcutta, and from there to the ashram. It is not for me to travel about – to dissipate my attention – my mind sets forth on its true pilgrimage when it is at rest.[2] Give my love to Mahatma.[3]

Affectionately yours
Rabindranath Tagore

Source: MS original at Rabindra Bhavan, Shantiniketan.

1 The raja of Pithapuram supported RT's school and university financially.
2 Compare his remark to William Rothenstein in letter 129 that his desire to travel was 'like a homesickness for the far away'.
3 During 1918, RT began to call Gandhi 'Mahatma', thus pioneering the trend.

135

To Charles Freer Andrews

Santiniketan, [West Bengal, India]
[23?] October 1918

Dear Friend,

Our vacation has nearly come to its end. But these days neither brought to me leisure nor work, for I have been going through great anxiety on account of Mira and Nitu's illness.[1] The crisis has been over and doctors have pronounced them out of danger. I knew that you were helping Mahatmaji and therefore I did not like to trouble your mind, though I was sorely tempted to wire you to come.[2] But now I think I need have no compunction to hasten you to come to the ashram, for it is nearly the time for us to resume our work. I have many things to ask your advice about – about myself, our ashram and about Nagen. Nagen writes me a letter with a piteous appeal to you to help him in procuring for him some decent employment in Hyderabad or any other place.[3] I had the idea of asking Cousins for a professorship; but to enter into any relationship of obligation with Mrs Besant and her crew may cost me my freedom, and this is why I hesitate, though the situation for Nagen is getting more and more cruel everyday.[4] However, please come back to the ashram if you have nothing better to do. I have important news about myself which I shall hold back till we meet. Give my *pranam* and love to Mahatmaji.

Your affectionate friend
Rabindranath Tagore

Source: MS original at Rabindra Bhavan, Shantiniketan.

1 Having lost his daughter, Bela, in May, RT must have been desperately anxious.
2 Andrews became close to Gandhi during 1918, particularly from June onwards. See Tinker, *Ordeal of Love*, pp. 140–1.

3 Nagendranath Gangulee, RT's son-in-law, had been at a loose end since losing interest in the rural development work on the Tagore estates. Andrews tried to get him a job without success. In 1921, Gangulee became professor of agriculture and rural economics, University of Calcutta.
4 James H. Cousins was now established at the Theosophical College at Madanapalle in south India, and would no doubt have agreed to help Gangulee. But RT knew that he would then be obliged to lecture at the college and help Cousins in other ways. In 1935, he even, farcically (as he himself admitted), allowed Cousins to cajole him into putting him (Cousins) forward as a candidate for the Nobel prize! (See RT to Bhagawan Das, 20 June 1935 [RB].)

136

To James H. Cousins

In early 1919 Tagore eventually reached south India and spent two months touring and lecturing there. He began at Bangalore, where he had been invited by James Cousins to preside over an art exhibition, including paintings of the Bengal School. His reception was tumultuous. According to Cousins, at the railway station, 'the tall, bearded, long-robed poet had to pick his way along the edge of the platform among the cheerings and peerings and reverent touchings of the ecstatic multitude'.[1] This continued as he visited some of the famous temple towns and finally lectured in Madras under the auspices of Annie Besant's National University. As ever, Rabindranath could not make up his mind whether he liked or disliked all the attention. His initial letter to Cousins sets the tone.

Shantiniketan, [West Bengal, India]
29 December 1918

Dear Mr Cousins

Certainly this time I shall never fail to see you at Madanapalle.[2] But my heart quakes to imagine what is awaiting me at your presidency, and I hope I shall be able to keep up my courage up to the last moment and take the final desperate step towards the south. Death's door is called the southern door in Bengal and I hope it won't claim me as a duly consecrated victim sacrificed to the myriad-tongued divinity of the Public Meeting. However, it will not be possible for me to be present at your art exhibition and I shall not be free to move before the last week of January.[3] But should I not warn you not to put too implicit a faith upon my promises? Chanakya advises never to trust women and kings, but I think poets should top the list of all unreliables.[4]

Very sincerely yours
Rabindranath Tagore

Source: MS original at Rabindra Bhavan, Shantiniketan.

1 J. H. and M. E. Cousins, *We Two Together* (Madras, 1950), p. 340.
2 RT reached Madanapalle in Feb. 1919 and stayed about a week.
3 In fact RT arrived in Bangalore on 12 Jan. 1919 and did attend the art exhibition. See *ibid.*, pp. 340–1.
4 See *sloka* 27 of Chanakya in Haeberlin, *Kavyasangraha*, p. 314.

Anti-imperialist (1919–1920)

Introduction

Visva-Bharati, Tagore's university at Shantiniketan, conceived in 1916, when he was in America, was formally founded in December 1918. The Amritsar massacre took place four months later, on 13 April 1919. Thus Rabindranath started his new institution, dedicated to the mutual understanding of East and West, at the nadir of the relationship between India and the colonial power. This contradiction dogged all his efforts on behalf of Visva-Bharati at this time.

He was the first Indian to make a public protest against the massacre, by repudiating his knighthood in a celebrated letter to the viceroy. That was at the end of May 1919. For the next year, as Gandhi's movement gathered pace, Tagore vacillated about whether or not to pursue the dream of his university by once more visiting the West. He had warned Gandhi, just before the massacre, that he was running a great risk in stirring up mass feeling against the imperial power. Tagore always favoured a positive rather than a negative attitude to the West (as he had shown during the Swadeshi Movement), cooperation rather than noncooperation – but in this attitude he found himself increasingly out of step with both Gandhi and the national mood of Indians.

Eventually, in May 1920, Tagore sailed again for Europe, believing that he would not be away from India for very long. In fact, he did not return for more than a year.

137

To Mahatma Gandhi

The year 1919 was a turning point in the colonial history of India. It was the year of the Amritsar massacre, the year of the emergence of Gandhi as a national leader, and the Rubicon in Tagore's loss of faith in British rule, symbolised by his repudiation of his knighthood.

The trigger for all this was the repressive government legislation recommended by the 1918 Rowlatt report – a recommendation to carry the emergency powers of wartime into peacetime. It became law on 21 March 1919, having been forced through the Imperial Legislative Council on a vote split along purely racial lines. This caused Gandhi to launch an all-India campaign of passive resistance, which immediately led to loss of life, culminating in the shooting of nearly four hundred people and the wounding of two thousand more – all of them unarmed – at Amritsar's Jallianwala

Bagh on 13 April. Gandhi called off the campaign, believing that he had made a 'Himalayan miscalculation' in judging Indians to be sufficiently trained to wage non-violent passive resistance.[1]

In launching satyagraha, Gandhi wanted Tagore's support. On 5 April, six days after disturbances in Delhi in which ten people died, he wrote to him, requesting

> a message from you for publication in the national struggle which, though in form it is only directed against a single piece of legislation, is in reality a struggle for liberty worthy of a self-respecting nation ... The forces arrayed against me are, as you know, enormous. I do not dread them, for I have an unquenchable belief that they are supporting untruth and that if we have sufficient faith in [truth], it will enable us to overpower the former. But all forces work through human agency. I am therefore anxious to gather round this mighty struggle the ennobling assistance of those who approve it. I will not be happy until I have received your considered opinion on this endeavour to purify the political life of the country. If you have seen anything to alter your first opinion of it, I hope you will not hesitate to make it known. I value even adverse opinions from friends, for though they may not make me change my course, they serve the purpose of so many lighthouses to give out warnings of dangers lying in the stormy paths of life.[2]

Rabindranath's reply, written the day before the shootings at Amritsar, is a prescient response which, as ever with his warnings to Gandhi, had almost no effect.

Shantiniketan, [West Bengal, India]
12 April 1919

Dear Mahatmaji

Power in all its forms is irrational – it is like the horse that drags the carriage blindfolded. The moral element in it is only represented in the man who drives the horse. Passive resistance is a force which is not necessarily moral in itself; it can be used against truth as well as for it. The danger inherent in all force grows stronger when it is likely to gain success, for then it becomes temptation.

I know your teaching is to fight against evil by the help of the good. But such a fight is for heroes and not for men led by impulses of the moment. Evil on one side naturally begets evil on the other, injustice leading to violence and insult to vengefulness. Unfortunately such a force has already been started, and either through panic or through wrath our authorities have shown us their claws whose sure effect is to drive some of us into the secret path of resentment and others into utter demoralisation. In this crisis you, as a great leader of men, have stood among us to proclaim your faith in the ideal which you know to be that of India – the ideal which is both against the cowardliness of hidden revenge and the cowed submissiveness of the terror-stricken. You have said, as Lord Buddha has done in his time and for all time to come –

'Akkodhena jine kodham asadhum sadhuna jine' – 'Conquer anger by the power of non-anger and evil by the power of good.'[3]

This power of good must prove its truth and strength by its fearlessness, by its refusal to accept any imposition which depends for its success upon its power to produce frightfulness and is not ashamed to use its machines of destruction to terrorise a population completely disarmed. We must know that moral conquest does not consist

9 Tagore with Buddha

in success, that failure does not deprive it of its dignity and worth. Those who believe in spiritual life know that to stand against wrong which has overwhelming material power behind it is victory itself – it is the victory of the active faith in the ideal in the teeth of evident defeat.

I have always felt, and said accordingly, that the great gift of freedom can never come to a people through charity. We must win it before we own it. And India's opportunity for winning it will come to her when she can prove that she is morally superior to the people who rule her by their right of conquest. She must willingly accept her penance of suffering – the suffering which is the crown of the great. Armed with her utter faith in goodness she must stand unabashed before the arrogance that scoffs at the power of spirit.

And you have come to your motherland in the time of her need to remind her of her mission, to lead her in the true path of conquest, to purge her present-day politics of its feebleness which imagines that it has gained its purpose when it struts in the borrowed feathers of diplomatic dishonesty.

This is why I pray most fervently that nothing that tends to weaken our spiritual freedom may intrude into your marching line, that martyrdom for the cause of truth may never degenerate into fanaticism for mere verbal forms, descending into the self-deception that hides itself behind sacred names.

With these few words for an introduction allow me to offer the following as a poet's contribution to your noble work:

> I
> Let me hold my head high in this faith that thou art our shelter, that all fear is mean distrust of thee.
> Fear of man? But what man is there in this world, what king, O King of Kings, who is thy rival, who has hold of me for all time and in all truth?
> What power is there in this world to rob me of my freedom? For do not thy arms reach the captive through the dungeon walls, bringing unfettered release to the soul?
> And must I cling to this body in fear of death, as a miser to his barren treasure? Has not this spirit of mine the eternal call to thy feast of everlasting life?
> Let me know that all pain and death are shadows of the moment; that the dark force which sweeps between me and my truth is but the mist before the sunrise; that thou alone art mine for ever and greater than all pride of strength that dares to mock my manhood with its menace.[4]
>
> II
> Give me the supreme courage of love, this is my prayer – the courage to speak, to do, to suffer at thy will, to leave all things or be left alone.
> Give me the supreme faith of love, this is my prayer – the faith of the life in death, of the victory in defeat, of the power hidden in the frailness of beauty, of the dignity of pain that accepts hurt but disdains to return it.[5]

Very sincerely yours
Rabindranath Tagore

Source: MS copy at Rabindra Bhavan, Shantiniketan; letter published in *MR*, May 1919, pp. 539–40.

1 Mohandas Karamchand Gandhi, *The Story of my Experiments with Truth*, II (Mahadev Desai trans.; New Delhi, 1930), pp. 508–13. On the Rowlatt satyagraha, see Judith M. Brown, *Gandhi's Rise to Power: Indian Politics 1915–1922* (Cambridge, 1972), chap. 5.
2 *CWMG*, XV, pp. 179–80.
3 *Mahabharata*, 5:39:73. RT quotes it in Pali, not Sanskrit.
4 This is probably an original composition in English, like the second poem. It does not appear in any of RT's works in English translation.
5 This poem, composed in English, was later published in *The Fugitive*, pp. 193–4, with modifications.

138

To Charles Freer Andrews

News of the violent events in the Punjab, where martial law was declared in some areas in mid-April, was suppressed. In the Calcutta *Statesman*, for instance, in late April, the reports were chiefly about atrocities against Europeans in the Punjab; the news from Amritsar was released only in instalments, 200 casualties initially, later amended to 200 deaths.[1] But eyewitness reports reached Susil Rudra, the principal of St Stephen's College in Delhi via his students, and he wrote of them to C. F. Andrews in Shantiniketan. Andrews came to Delhi, heard the reports at first hand, and spent the next month putting pressure on the viceroy, Lord Chelmsford (who was in Shimla) and the British authorities in Delhi to mitigate the repression, with some small success; but he was officially blocked from visiting the Punjab. At his final interview with Chelmsford, Andrews informed Tagore on 14 May, the viceroy was

> cold as ice with me and full of racial bitterness – referring again and again to the murders of English people at Amritsar, but resenting it when I spoke of the intolerable wrongs from which Indians had suffered . . . I had my duty as an Englishman to make this last effort – I think that was needed – but now I have had my lesson.[2]

Tagore himself was so agitated by the meagreness of the press reports and the alarming nature of the rumours that, before hearing a word from Andrews, he wrote him an unprecedented four letters in three days on the subject. They appear here without further comment.

Shantiniketan, [West Bengal, India]
24 April 1919

Dear Friend,

I do not know whom I should pity more – our people or our Government. The utter demoralisation of the latter is becoming so ugly in its enormity that the very success which it may breed will be monstrous, imposing a long-lasting and terrible burden upon its present power.[3] Of one thing our authorities seem to be unconscious – it is that they have completely lost their moral prestige. I can recall the time when our people had great faith in justice and truthfulness of British government. But I am positive that now there are very few individuals in the whole of India who sincerely believe in its promises, its communiques, avowed motives and decisions of its commissions. It was almost ludicrous to find how our masses during the late war refused to accept as true every news of success of the allies that came to them from the English source. This loss of faith in their rulers may or may not be justified, but it is a significant fact, and if our rulers have any statesmanship left in them they ought seriously to consider it.[4] They have far too much been taken up with keeping up their prestige of power which is the biggest rift in their armour. For the mere sight of power in itself is insufferable to man and God alike unless it stands upon the truth of moral law.

Yours
Rabindranath Tagore

Source: MS original at Rabindra Bhavan, Shantiniketan.

1 See Tinker, *Ordeal of Love*, p. 174, n. 5. Sir Michael O'Dwyer, the governor of the Punjab, was informed that about two hundred people had been killed at Amritsar, early on 14 April, but he chose not to inform Lord Chelmsford. The *Statesman*'s figure of 200 casualties may have been taken from a brief report in the (London) *Times* on 19 April. British press reporting of the massacre was practically nil.
2 Andrews to RT, 14 May 1919 [RB].
3 RT meant 'demoralisation' in its less common sense of 'moral corruption', rather than 'loss of morale' – though he would have maintained that the first implies the second.
4 Andrews told the viceroy's secretary, Sir John Maffey, that 'never in this century had the moral prestige of the Indian Government been lower'. Maffey replied the next day: 'I thought over what you said and I would wager a considerable sum that it has never been *higher*.' Andrews commented to RT: 'He simply did not know what moral prestige meant' (Andrews to RT, 1 May 1919 [RB]).

139

To Charles Freer Andrews

Shantiniketan, [West Bengal, India]
25 April 1919

Dear Friend,

When I received the accompanying letter this morning my first impulse was to send it to the viceroy.[1] But then I remembered that the viceroy is not a human being, he is part of a machine, and therefore Lord Chelmsford can enjoy fairly good appetite for his dinner while the Machine is spreading unspeakable miseries over thousands of homes. And then again these people are sure to express their contempt for the anonymity of this letter. At the same time they themselves take every care to keep their own doings dark by suppressing truth and repressing criticism. We are compelled to accept all reports from the very men against whom complaints are being brought and not from other witnesses. Our authorities justify their action by some special necessity of the case while it becomes dangerous to remind them that all crimes are committed, including the atrocities done by the Germans in the late war, when other necessities are considered as more urgent and important than the moral necessity. It is held to be wrong for the people who are helpless to take shelter behind secrecy when they try to remedy their grievances, but the Government claims the exclusive right to indulge in the bloodiest form of anarchism forcibly imposing silence upon its victims. We, we cannot but remain silent, but our retaliation will come by the self-poisoning which the English people is bringing upon itself through its decaying morals and exhaustion of human sympathy.

Yours
Rabindranath Tagore

Source: MS original at Rabindra Bhavan, Shantiniketan.

1 This letter, which is not available, unsigned for obvious reasons, was possibly sent to RT by an eyewitness of the Punjab repression.

140

To Charles Freer Andrews

Shantiniketan, [West Bengal, India]
26 April 1919

Dear Friend,

I believe our outcry against the wrongs inflicted upon us by our governing power is becoming more vehement than is good for us. We must not claim sympathy or kind treatment with too great an insistence and intensity. I remember when in my schooldays I used to get blows and insults from a teacher who was particularly foul in his language and unjust in his dealings I refused to complain or to cry. In fact I tried to maintain my dignity by ignoring my punishment, and thus I had my moral victory. This victory possibly had no outer result and very likely it only exasperated my teacher without touching his conscience in the least. But all the same the victory abided with me and I am glad of it.[1] He who causes suffering becomes small when his victims have the power to rise above it by their heroism of fearlessness. This is the lesson which Gandhi has been trying to preach to his countrymen. And now when his attempt to hold the banner of moral power above those of the brute forces has met with an apparent failure, when those of us who desire success without having to pay for it and others who wait interminable days to reap their harvest of comfortable politics from the soil of sycophancy, are hastening to disown him with shrill protestation of innocence, Gandhi's personality shines before us with a greater glory than when his light was blurred by the dust storm of popularity. And this one fact of his presence in our midst reconciles us to whatever sufferings we are passing through and whatever others we have to face. The expression of the best ideal of the age need not grow fat in bulk but let it become immortal with its truth. And the rejection of it by a number of timid people overwhelmed with terror by no means proves its rejection by our history. Please convey my *namashkar* to Mahatmaji in these days of his trial.

Yours
Rabindranath Tagore

[PS] I send you herewith a copy of the letter I wrote to Lieut. Haynes in answer to his request to be allowed to join us in our ashram.

Source: MS original at Rabindra Bhavan, Shantiniketan; letter published in *MR*, May 1919, pp. 556–7.

1 See *My Rem*, p. 37/*RR*, XVII, p. 282.

141

To Charles Freer Andrews

Shantiniketan, [West Bengal, India]
26 April 1919

Dear Friend,

Most of the Anglo-Indian papers are crying for more blood. They are sure that some mischief makers are behind the present disturbances. Certainly there are. But who are they? Serious disturbances have taken place in all three countries where the British have their sway – Ireland, Egypt and India, respectively containing three different peoples widely different in their civilisation, temperament and tradition. Is it unthinkable that the mischief maker may be lurking somewhere in the common element which they all have, namely the one people who govern them? It is not in the system of government or the law, but in the men entrusted with the carrying on of the government, the men who have not the imagination or sympathy truly to know the people whom they rule, the men who think that it is their material power which carries its own permanence in itself and therefore the eternal truths of human nature and moral providence can be ignored in its favour. It is evident that these people in their blind pride will ever go on seeking for the source of mischief outside themselves and easily succeed in catching some stray dog to give it a bad name and hang it. This will only prolong their period of harbouring the mischief in their own person and driving it deeper into their constitution. It is the same kind of ignorance of the eternal laws which primitive peoples show when they hunt for some so-called witch to whom they ascribe their cause of illness while carrying the disease germs in their own blood. It is quite easy for them to torture and burn the witch and dance the devil dance with proper ceremony, but the disease will continue and they will have to make costly provisions for more burning of witches and more orgies of frightfulness.

Yours
Rabindranath Tagore

Source: MS original at Rabindra Bhavan, Shantiniketan; letter published in *MR*, Jan. 1920, p. 100.

142

To Lord Chelmsford

Despite the fact that Gandhi had suspended his campaign of passive resistance on 18 April, shocked by the violence it had provoked, repression in the Punjab continued well into May. Indeed martial law was extended into other areas of the Punjab on 8 May. C. F. Andrews, having been stopped from entering the area, went to see Gandhi at Sabarmati. He found him in no mood to make a public protest against the Government – rather the opposite, in fact.[1] Returning to Shantiniketan in late May, Andrews appraised Tagore of the entire situation on the basis of his talks with British officials, knowledgeable Indian friends in Delhi, and Gandhi.

Rabindranath felt that he had to act. He travelled to Calcutta and attempted to organise a public meeting, presided over by one of the leading Bengal nationalists. But the obvious choice as chairman, C. R. Das, was cagey: he suggested that Tagore himself should preside. Faced by the Rowlatt legislation, no politician was willing to risk his neck. Tagore was left with no option but to make a solitary protest.[2]

His letter to the viceroy, written on 31 May and published in the Indian press on 2 June, repudiating his knighthood, has become the most widely quoted letter written by Tagore. It is both powerfully written and uniquely significant, being the first public protest by a prominent Indian against 'the massacre that ended the Raj'.[3] As C. F. Andrews told Rabindranath four months later, writing from the Punjab, 'your letter to the viceroy seemed to have been prophetic to an extraordinary degree, as though you had *felt* what had happened without any intervening human agency whatever'.[4]

Calcutta, [India]
31 May 1919

Your Excellency,

The enormity of the measures taken by the Government in the Punjab for quelling some local disturbances has, with a rude shock, revealed to our minds the helplessness of our position as British subjects in India. The disproportionate severity of the punishments inflicted upon the unfortunate people and the methods of carrying them out, we are convinced, are without parallel in the history of civilised governments, barring some conspicuous exceptions, recent and remote. Considering that such treatment has been meted out to a population, disarmed and resourceless, by a power which has the most terribly efficient organisation for destruction of human lives, we must strongly assert that it can claim no political expediency, far less moral justification. The accounts of insults and sufferings undergone by our brothers in the Punjab have trickled through the gagged silence, reaching every corner of India, and the universal agony of indignation roused in the hearts of our people has been ignored by our rulers – possibly congratulating themselves for what they imagine as salutary lessons. This callousness has been praised by most of the Anglo-Indian papers, which have in some cases gone to the brutal length of making fun of our sufferings, without receiving the least check from the same authority – relentlessly careful in smothering every cry of pain and expression of judgement from the organs representing the sufferers. Knowing that our appeals have been in vain and that the passion of vengeance is blinding the nobler vision of statesmanship in our Goverment, which could so easily afford to be magnanimous as befitting its physical strength and moral tradition, the very least I can do for my country is to take all consequences upon myself in giving voice to the protest of millions of my countrymen, surprised into a dumb anguish of terror. The time has come when badges of honour make our shame glaring in their incongruous context of humiliation, and I for my part wish to stand, shorn of all special distinctions, by the side of those of my countrymen, who, for their so-called insignificance, are liable to suffer a degradation not fit for human beings.

These are the reasons which have painfully compelled me to ask Your Excellency, with due deference and regret, to relieve me of my title of Knighthood, which I had the honour to accept from His Majesty the King at the hands of your predecessor, for whose nobleness of heart I still entertain great admiration.[5]

Yours faithfully,
Rabindranath Tagore

Source: letter published in *MR*, July 1919, p. 105; also published as No. 554a in official correspondence of Lord Chelmsford [IOL]. The original MS is lost.

1 Gandhi was preoccupied with his 'Himalayan miscalculation' in starting satyagraha. On 10 May, he told the viceroy's secretary: 'The whole of my weight will be thrown absolutely on the side of preserving internal peace. The viceroy has the right to rely upon my doing no less.' (Quoted in Tinker, *Ordeal of Love*, p. 154.)
2 A public meeting finally took place in Calcutta on 26 June, presided over by Byomkesh Chakravarty. It passed a motion of appreciation of RT's protest. See *MR*, July 1919, p. 120.
3 For an account of RT's repudiation of his knighthood and the British and Indian reaction, see Dutta and Robinson, *Rabindranath Tagore*, pp. 216–18 and notes. No leading Indian politician publicly congratulated RT on his gesture. Gandhi did not return his awards to the viceroy until 1 Aug. 19**20**.
'The massacre that ended the Raj' is the subtitle of Alfred Draper's book *Amritsar* (London, 1981).
4 Andrews to RT, 1 Oct. 1919 (from Lahore) [RB]. Satyajit Ray expresses the same idea as that of Andrews – that RT had somehow felt the pain of the Punjab intuitively – in his documentary film *Rabindranath Tagore* (1961).
5 Chelmsford's predecessor was Lord Hardinge (1858–1944), the viceroy in 1915 when RT was knighted. Hardinge and Andrews enjoyed a close relationship, in which RT played a considerable part.

143

To Macmillan & Co. (USA)

About a year after he aborted his trip to the USA (see letters 122 ff.), Tagore received notification from George Brett of Macmillan (New York) of a 'slump' in sales of his books, which Brett attributed entirely to public acceptance of the 1918 allegations that Tagore supported revolution in India.[1] He asked Tagore's permission to sell off stock of certain titles.

Rabindranath's own response is not recorded, but C. F. Andrews, apparently acting on his behalf, asked the Calcutta manager of Macmillan if someone appointed by Tagore could examine the Tagore accounts at Macmillan in New York. The collapse of Tagore's American sales seemed too dramatic to believe, and was also very damaging to the finances of Shantiniketan. An irritated Brett wrote again to Tagore on 11 June 1919, agreeing to this request, provided the cost was borne by Tagore himself.[2] Rabindranath then responded in person with this letter.

Santiniketan, [West Bengal, India]
22 July 1919

Dear Mr Brett

I have no personal interest in the business side of my publications, for the sale proceeds of my books go the maintenance of my institution. I have never for once looked into the accounts myself but made them over to the parties concerned – who are the members of the financial board of our school. However, if they are puzzled over any details I shall ask them to inform you through Mr Andrews and I feel certain that explanations will be furnished to them which will be completely satisfactory.

Sincerely yours
Rabindranath Tagore

Source: MS original in Macmillan Company Records [New York].

1 The slump is mentioned in Brett to RT, 18 April 1919 [copy at New York]. Writing to Macmillan in London on 11 June, Brett remarked: 'Owing to Tagore's alleged activities in this country, and perhaps in India also, the American public made up its mind that he was pro-German, or pacifist, or both, and for a time ceased buying his books.' He expected the position to recover but saw virtually no chance of there being once again the 'furore' for RT's work that had occurred in 1916–17.
2 Brett undoubtedly found RT unsympathetic and may have given some credence to the allegations made against him in 1918. The American East Coast establishment at this time was not yet aware of Indian nationalism and was often more pro-British than the British, as RT would discover to his cost in New York in 1920. The fact that Brett was born in Britain may also have contributed.

144

To (Sir) William Rothenstein

A gap of six years and a great war now separated Tagore from his last meeting with William Rothenstein. But Rothenstein was still deeply drawn to Tagore and his work, especially *The Home and the World*, published in translation in 1919. He was the only one of Tagore's English friends in England to express his approval of the repudiation of the knighthood in 1919: 'How can I not approve of it? You have not put off, but have put on dignity.'[1] Receiving this letter, Rabindranath responded immediately with a surge of his old feeling for Rothenstein and England – British behaviour in India notwithstanding.

Santiniketan, [West Bengal, India]
25 July 1919

Dearest Friend, your letter always gives me a sudden longing to go to England, just to have a few delightful days of quiet talks with you among those wooded downs under the soft grey light of your English sky. But the obstacle I find against realising this is not external. Somehow my mind shrinks and refuses to get ready with enthusiasm. The first time when I went to England and found out my friends there and they found me out things were simple for me. For I was then a mere guest in your literary circle whose recognition of me depended upon the generosity of my hosts. But now unfortunately I have got a sort of sanctioned right and people do not have the freedom to ignore me. The fame that rests upon some public act of approbation carrying an authoritative warranty creates an unnatural situation vitiating the quality of both the praise and dispraise it excites. This makes me intently wish to go back to my former obscurity lighted only with the love of a few friends, and this makes me cling with all my heart to my work here outside the public gaze. One must have ample privacy and leisure to be fully true to oneself. Do you not think that the constant goading of criticism from the crowd to which all the creative souls of the modern age are subjected is demoralising? It is the subconscious mind which is creative – and to invade its silence with ceaseless chatter is to make it sterile. This is the reason why we find in the modern literature a straining after originality which is not true originality but merely novelty. The things that are original are as old as the hills and as simple as the morning breeze. But cheap criticisms originate from cleverness which is cheap and they only stimulate cleverness that has not the bloom of life but the finish of the manufactured article. In our country literature has not to live and grow under a blazing publicity as in the West and the man of letters is not constantly reminded that he is a literary man. This may not be stimulating but restful and I can say that for me restfulness is more important than the stimulant of a noisy public opinion. However, I should give anything to be able to take an Aeroplane flight and drop down at your door this moment. For I so want to talk to you about all manner of things! We have had our trials as you have had, but ours are all the more painful because it is not given to us to be able to take measures to redress our wrongs. We have to wait for a change of mind in others, wait under the menace of machine guns and the gagging act. What makes it intolerable for us is to know that truth will be suppressed scientifically, and those who have suffered injustice will also have to carry the burden of wrong judgement. It comes to me almost with the force of a new discovery that there is one thing which makes life worth living to us, [that] is doing some work, however small it may be, which is truly human, which has the beauty of the eternal about it and which may be safely and contemptuously ignored by the man gloating in the enjoyment of his unhallowed power. So, in order to forget that this life is a nightmare I have to serve these little boys I have gathered round me, teaching them elementary things and telling them stories. Their happiness, however momentary it may be, has an immense worth like the beauty of a flower that fades by the end of the day.

Ever yours
Rabindranath Tagore

Source: MS original in Rothenstein Papers [Harvard]; letter published in Lago (ed.), *Imperfect Encounter*, pp. 257–8.

1 Rothenstein to RT, 11 July 1919, in Lago (ed.), *Imperfect Encounter*, p. 256. Rothenstein learnt about RT's letter to Chelmsford (142) from an Indian newspaper clipping sent by Andrews, not from a British newspaper. The British press barely reported RT's reaction, as it had barely reported the Amritsar massacre, though the *Manchester Guardian* did carry the text of the letter to Chelmsford on 9 July.

145

To Rathindranath Tagore

Tagore's relationship with his son-in-law Nagendranath Gangulee had been difficult for a long time (see letters 63 and 99). At the same time, Nagen's marriage to Mira deteriorated. In order to escape, Mira began to spend periods with her father in Shantiniketan, leaving Nagen at their house in Calcutta; their two children would sometimes come with her, sometimes not. Rabindranath, of course, felt responsible for both Mira and Nagen, since their marriage had been entirely his idea. In this letter he reveals his lacerating guilt feelings to his son Rathindranath.

[Shantiniketan, West Bengal, India]
[August/September? 1919]

Kalyaniyeshu

Nagen has recently written me an irate letter, which I have sent to Mira. Today Mira came and asked me what advice I would give her – should she return to Nagen? Which means that if I tell her to, she is prepared to go back. But how can I deliver such a cruel blow to Mira? I dealt the first blow in her life – without proper thought and consideration, I arranged her marriage. When I was going through with it, I felt a deep anxiety in my mind. On the night of the wedding, when Mira went to the bathroom, a cobra reared up with hood fully blown – today I think that if it had struck her, this would have been for the best.

There is a wild barbarity in Nagen that Mira always dreaded. If, in spite of the lack of love between them, they could have lived together in reasonable understanding, that would have been good. But there is no possibility of this. Mira is incapable of deception, and Nagen cannot control his temper. Those few days they spent with me in Madras I can never forget. How can I ask Mira to return, knowing what she is likely to face? How can she and her children spend their lives amidst insults and antipathy? There would be no keeping any of it secret from servants, from friends or from relatives – and this would harm the children more than her. Moreover, the fact is that if Nagen wants to take away the children by force, we have no right to stop him.[1] I will have to cross that bridge when I come to it – but let Mira not think that we want her to go back. I will not let her burn alive inside a circle of fire. Her life has already been ruined – now it is up to me to try and protect her and make her happy. Whatever suffering is entailed I must take upon myself, for I am its root cause. As for you, do not let Mira be deprived of your affection and support – let her not become any more fearful, anxious and agonised than she already is.

The letter that arrived from Vadodara [Baroda] I am passing to you. Please let me know the asking price of the machine.

Shri Rabindranath Thakur

Source: MS original at Rabindra Bhavan, Shantiniketan; letter published in Sharadiya *Desh*, 1396 [Autumn 1989], p. 24.

1 In late 1928, there was nearly a court case over the marriage, but at the magistrate's suggestion, RT and Nagendranath were persuaded to settle out of court. The details are obscure but presumably concerned the custody of the children. See RT to Sudhakanta Ray Chaudhuri, 2 Dec. 1928, Sharadiya *Desh*, 1394 [Autumn 1987], p. 18. Nagendranath remained in touch with his children; his daughter was present at his death-bed in London in 1954.

146

To Romain Rolland[1]

Romain Rolland, the winner of the Nobel prize for literature in 1915, had been interested in Tagore since 1916. In April 1919 he invited him, along with many other celebrated thinkers (including Albert Einstein), to sign an anti-national 'déclaration pour l'indépendence de l'esprit', which Tagore duly did. The two men struck up a correspondence, and Rolland, pursuing his idea that Europe, 'after the disaster of this shameful world war', was in need of Asia's thought, mentioned that he would like to start 'a review of Asia and Europe . . . which would bring to light the moral wealth of these fraternal and inimical worlds. It would not concern itself with politics, but with the treasures of thought, of art, of science, and of faith.' He asked Tagore whether he reckoned that such a review would find 'effective help' in the 'most important centres of culture' in Asia.[2] In his reply Tagore is welcoming but realistic.

Bengal [exact place not given]
14 October 1919

Dear Romain Rolland

Let me acknowledge with thanks your letter of 26 August. I had been hoping to come over to Europe and meet you, but the atmosphere there is troubled and in our country sufferings have accumulated in various forms making it hard for me to leave her just now.

It hurts me very deeply when I think that there is hardly a corner in the vast continent of Asia where men have come to feel any real love for Europe. The great event of the meeting of the East and the West has been desecrated by the spirit of contempt on the one side and a corresponding hatred on the other. The reason is, it was greed which brought Europe to Asia and threat of physical power which maintains her there. This prevents our mutual relationship from becoming truly human and this makes it degrading for both parties. Parasitism, whether based upon power or upon weakness, must breed degeneracy. We who in our blind pride of caste deprived man of his full dues of rights and respect, are paying the penalty now, and instead of the soul current running through our society we have left to us the dry sand-bed of dead customs. And the time seems fast approaching when the soul will be sucked dry from the civilisation of Europe also by the growing lust [for] gain in her commerce and politics, unless she has the wisdom and power to change her mind and not merely her system.

Your idea of a Review of Asia and Europe, in which writers of the East and West may take part in dealing with the treasures of thought, of art, of science, of faith, is very attractive to me. I am sure it will rouse interest in cultured minds in our part of the world. At the same time, you must know that in the Asia of the present age, intellect and all means of expression remain unorganised. Our minds are disunited and our thoughts scattered. The vocal section of our countrymen is mainly occupied with mendicant politics and petty journalism. The cramping poverty of our life and its narrowness of prospect tend to make most of our efforts feeble and our aims immediate. We greatly need some outside call to make us conscious of our mission. So long proud Europe has only claimed our homage and gained but the least and the worst that man can give. But if your paper comes bearing to us Europe's claim to our best thoughts we may well hope that response will not be found wanting.

Yours
Rabindranath Tagore

Source: MS copy at Rabindra Bhavan, Shantiniketan.

1 Romain Rolland (1866–1944): novelist, dramatist and essayist; from 1915 he became interested in Indian thought, and in due course wrote studies of Gandhi, Ramakrishna and Vivekananda, though without ever visiting India.
2 Rolland to RT, 26 Aug. 1919, in Rolland, *Selected Letters of Romain Rolland* (Francis Doré and Marie-Laure Prévost eds.; New Delhi, 1990), pp. 13–14. Rolland's review never appeared, but in 1923 RT started the *Visva-Bharati Quarterly*, with a similar intention. On Rolland's interest in Indian thought, see David James Fisher, *Romain Rolland and the Politics of Intellectual Engagement* (Berkeley, 1988), pp. 112ff.

147

To John Graham Drummond[1]

In 1906, Tagore published a novel, *Naukadubi*, in Bengali. It was translated into English by J. G. Drummond, an ICS official working in Bengal, and published by Macmillan in 1921 as *The Wreck*.[2] Tagore did not know Drummond personally but attempted to assist him when he was sent the complete typescript. His letter to Drummond gives an intriguing insight into his approach to writing fiction.

Santiniketan, [West Bengal, India]
21 January 1920

Dear Sir

I send you back your copy of *Naukadubi* with my corrections. You will find most of them are for the sake of chronological consistency of the story. *Naukadubi* not only appeared serially in *Bangadarshan* but the writing of it had not even been finished before the publication began. The story went on developing itself as the writing proceeded and I had to wait till I actually sat down to my work before I knew what was going to happen to the characters. This improvident method of writing a story is the only one that suits me at all though evidently it has disadvantages. I need, for keeping up my own interest in writing, fresh shocks of surprises in the growth of my story – and therefore I never think of a plot but only a central situation which has psychological possibilities.

I do not believe in a literal translation, specially when the languages of the original and that of the translation are essentially different. The words of the one language may have their synonyms in the other carrying the same meanings, but their associations are in most cases different. And the suggestions and flavour contained in these associations are more important in literature than mere meanings.

Is it possible to transliterate such expressions as *didi*, *ma* etc, and use them instead of translating them? Of course, you will have to be very sparing in their use, occasionally substituting for them 'dear', 'darling' and such other endearing terms where they are at all suitable.[3]

Yours sincerely
Rabindranath Tagore

Source: MS original in Patrick Geddes Papers [Edinburgh].

1 John Graham Drummond (1884–1958): ICS official in Bengal, 1908–36; author of *Panchayats in India* (Oxford, 1937).
2 *Naukadubi*, *RR*, V, pp. 165–432. Macmillan's edition of *The Wreck* (London, 1921) contains no note on

the translation, nor even any indication that the novel is a translation! For comparison, see the extract from *Naukadubi* translated by J. D. Anderson in Anderson's *A Manual of the Bengali Language* (Cambridge, 1920).
3 *didi*: elder sister; *ma*: mother.
    The proofs of the novel were sent to Thomas Sturge Moore for revision, but he did not have the time (or the expertise) to do a thorough job, as he made clear to Macmillan. RT was not satisfied with the final book (see letter 171).

148

To Edward John Thompson

E. J. Thompson, still teaching in Bengal, was now working hard on a study of Tagore, undertaking various translations as part of his research (and also with an eye to publication). Despite his earlier bad experience with translating Tagore's short stories (see letters 83–5), he had not lost his affection for them. He now sent Rabindranath a new short-story translation. Tagore's response is appreciative.

Santiniketan, [West Bengal, India]
11 May 1920

Dear Thompson

Your translated fragment of 'Megh o Roudra' has given me immense pleasure.[1] Prof. Anderson of Cambridge thinks that the beauty of my Bengali style is too elusive to allow reproduction in English.[2] But it seems to me that this translation of yours retains the delicate bloom of the original to a great extent. I cannot translate my prose stories myself and very few translations done by others have satisfied me.

I shall be leaving my ashram this afternoon for Europe. I am not feeling happy just now, yet I know I shall come back to this place happier and more fit for my vocation of life.

I have received only a few pages of my MS typed and I hope the rest of them will be sent to me in Bombay before I sail.

Yours
Rabindranath Tagore

Source: MS original in Thompson Papers [Bodleian].

1 'Megh o Roudra' (Cloud and Sunshine), *RR*, XIX, pp. 210–35. Thompson's translation was never published. See E. P. Thompson, *Alien Homage*, pp. 23–4.
2 Anderson wrote:

> Perhaps only an English Rabindranath could do it – and where is your English Rabindranath? That, of course, is not to say that it might not be worthwhile to publish a merely competent and workmanlike version of your prose, leaving it to intelligent readers to guess that some perfume has evaporated in the process, and that he is only looking at dried and pressed flowers...
> The ideal plan would be for some competent person to do it at Bolpur, under your eye, and with the inspiration of your own personality and presence. That means, of course, an English disciple, one filled with a real personal affection for you. For, in truth, the problem is one of the heart rather than of the head. You write with a profound love of your own land and its people, and with the comprehension which such a loving intimacy alone can give of Bengali thought and emotion.
> (Anderson to RT, 29 March 1920 [RB])

149

To Charles Freer Andrews

In May 1920, Tagore departed for Europe. He had been vacillating about leaving India for some months: he needed to publicise his plans and raise funds for Visva-Bharati, his international university, and yet India was in turmoil, on the point of embracing the Gandhian gospel of noncooperation which was anathema to Tagore. Just before sailing from Bombay on 15 May, he wrote two letters to C. F. Andrews (who had been left in charge of Shantiniketan). In one he remarked: 'I wish I had not been leaving India just now but I am certain that the call is for me to go.'[1] This is the second letter.

Bombay, [India]
14 May 1920

Dear Andrews

The heat was tolerable and the journey fairly good though the train reached Bombay nearly three hours late. The typist has left the latter half of 'Wayside' incomplete and what is worse has not returned the original manuscripts. I asked Suren to send them to me at once but I am afraid they won't reach me before I reach England.[2]

The cabin accommodation for our party in the steamer is satisfactory. I shall have to share Bomanji's cabin which is not as nice as having a cabin of my own.[3] But things might have been far worse. I feel we shan't be long in Europe – I am not in a mood to face the world and its questions.[4] I am longing to go back to those days of my youth which were not burdened with usefulness, that is to say I want to be born again – in the arms of the eternal. One grows old to discover that spontaneous simplicity of life is true life – but where is the time and the opportunity to realise it? It requires a great deal of courage to demolish the walls that one has [oneself] built with all [one's] resources. This building and breaking down – both are needed. The cocoon becomes a true prison only when it persists beyond its time. I wonder if my soul has its wings developed – but it is pining for freedom.

I hope things are not hopelessly unhappy for Mira.[5]

Goodbye – try to cultivate restfulness and have leisure to woo your true self and gain her for good.

With love

Ever yours
Rabindranath Tagore

Source: MS original at Rabindra Bhavan, Shantiniketan.

1 RT to Andrews, n.d. [RB].
2 'Wayside' was probably the working title of the translation of RT's letters from *Chhinnapatra*, published by Macmillan in 1921 as *Glimpses of Bengal*. The translator was Surendranath Tagore. In mid-1920, while RT was in Britain, the proof was somewhat revised by Thomas Sturge Moore.

3 S. R. Bomanji was a wealthy Parsee businessman, who admired RT (see letter 238). Also on board were the Aga Khan, with whom RT discussed Hafiz and Sufism, and the great cricketer Ranji (Ranjitsinhji, Jam Sahib of Nawanagar), who was 'very genial company', according to Tagore's son Rathindranath (*Edges of Time*, p. 112).
4 In the event, RT was away from India until July 1921.
5 Mira Devi, RT's daughter, was living partly in Shantiniketan, partly in Calcutta with her husband Nagendranath Gangulee. Andrews helped her financially and in other ways over the coming years.

The founding of a university (1920–1921)

Introduction

Tagore's second major visit to Europe, his first to be undertaken as a fundraiser for his new university, began in London. After two months there, he crossed over to the Continent in August and visited France, Holland and Belgium. By contrast with Britain, where his reception was much cooler than in 1912–13, he was enthusiastically welcomed on the Continent, both by the audiences for his lectures and by individuals such as Romain Rolland. He then returned to London.

Despite warnings from the USA that, in contrast to 1916–17, he would not be welcome as a lecturer to American audiences, because many Americans regarded him as 'disloyal' to the Government in India, he persisted in his plan to visit the country. He stayed there, chiefly in New York and Chicago, for almost five months, from late October to mid-March. Although he made great efforts to overcome the distrust of his intentions and American doubts about the philosophy behind Visva-Bharati, his success was very limited (apart from a brief lecture tour in Texas), and he left America with a feeling of angry failure.

Stopping once again in London, he now flew (for the first time) back to Paris, and began a triumphal visit to France, Switzerland, Denmark, Sweden (where he formally accepted his Nobel prize), Germany, Austria and Czechoslovakia. His German reception was perhaps the most sensational he ever received, and his books became bestsellers.

But on return to India in July 1921 he was faced with the reality that he had dreaded while abroad. The Noncooperation Movement had gripped the minds of the majority, including many of his pupils and staff at Shantiniketan. And yet despite his own sympathy for the fight, and a personal appeal from Gandhi, Tagore could not bring himself to join the movement. His heart remained set on building up his university, which was fundamentally opposed in purpose to that of Gandhi's movement.

150

To Mira Gangulee (Tagore)

The two months Tagore spent in London in the summer of 1920 were crowded but unsatisfying. They coincided with the House of Commons debate on the Hunter report following the Amritsar massacre, an occasion which shocked Rabindranath by its display of virulent Conservative antipathy for Montagu, the secretary of state for India who was trying to introduce reforms into the government of India. Even the most liberal-minded English people whom Tagore met were unaware of Indian feeling on the issue.[1] The predominant attitude to Indian affairs remained one of indifference. Tagore's repudiation of his knighthood the previous year was greeted mainly by silence. Rightly or wrongly, Tagore judged that to enlist official British support for his university project, as he had hoped, would stifle it at birth.

He therefore decided to leave London and visit the Continent for the first time. His idea was to go to Sweden and formally accept his Nobel prize, and afterwards to visit the Scandinavian and some other European countries, including, if possible, Germany. With the war still fresh in British minds, such a plan was bound to provoke official suspicion, and Tagore felt obliged to make an abrupt change of plan. This letter to his daughter explains why.

[London, UK]
[4 August 1920]

Miru

Our plans have been slightly changed. We were about to leave for Norway and Sweden when there was a hitch. A Swedish lady had got hold of us, offering to show us those countries and introduce us to people there. At first I thought she was my sincere admirer – she both looked and sounded the part. Gradually we became suspicious that she might be a spy. Finally our doubts were confirmed: she was exposed the day before we were due to leave. By then we had already bought our tickets. We sent word to her that we would go to Sweden via another route.[2] For the time being we are heading for France – we depart on Friday, the day after tomorrow. From there we will visit Switzerland and other places and then proceed to Sweden and Norway. I received the Nobel prize from Sweden, and so they have a special claim on me; they have been inviting me for a long time.

It rained and rained while I was in England, which was really miserable. Yesterday, after a long time, the sun shone and I thought that the sky would at last remain clear. But today it is again cloudy and dull; perhaps we are in for another spell of rain. However, the place we are going should show us the rain god's brighter face. In Bengal it is now Shraban, monsoon – so there must be heavy rain. Downpours in the lanes of Calcutta are a foul business, and perhaps you are not feeling well. Andrews writes that the rain has been intermittent, making the heat very oppressive – he's suffering, poor fellow. His letter gives me news of Khoka. Have you heard how his studies are going and how he is keeping healthwise – and how is Buri?[3] Can she keep well in Calcutta? She must have learnt to speak many more words by now – give her my kisses.

Father

Source: MS original at Rabindra Bhavan, Shantiniketan; letter published in Sharadiya *Desh*, 1397 [1990], pp. 40–1.

1 See, for instance, the description by Beatrice Webb of a meeting with RT on 20 July 1920 in Beatrice Webb, *Diaries 1912–1926* (Margaret I. Cole ed.; London, 1952), pp. 184–5 (discussed in Dutta and Robinson, *Rabindranath Tagore*, pp. 226–7).

10 Tagore in Germany, 1921, with Kurt Wolff

2 Rathindranath Tagore gave a somewhat cryptic account of this incident (*Edges of Time*, p. 121). The 'lady' was introduced to RT 'by a well-known orientalist whom we knew to be connected with politics but never suspected to be a tool in the hands of a government department'. To C. F. Andrews, RT wrote:

> The fact is I was preparing innocently to surrender myself into the hands of a woman spy who was to escort me through my continental tour and take charge of my correspondence. Just imagine the appalling amount of a white woman's burden ... However, the day before we were to start, all of us were instantaneously struck with a sudden suspicion through an indiscreet remark which she chanced to let fall in a moment of self-forgetfulness. (RT to Andrews, 4 Aug. 1920 [RB])

3 Khoka: Nitindranath Gangulee, son of Mira, aged eight. Buri: Nandita Gangulee, daughter of Mira, aged four. The two children and their mother were together with Nagendranath in Calcutta. An over-optimistic Andrews informed RT on 3 Aug.: 'The difficulty about Mira (which was once so large) is solving itself far better than you could ever have expected; and that anxiety has been in a great measure removed' [RB].

151

To Charles Freer Andrews

On 1 August 1920, Gandhi launched another campaign of noncooperation with the Government. At the same time he tried to enlist the support of India's Muslims by himself supporting the Khilafat Movement (which aimed to restore the suzerainty of the sultan of Turkey as caliph). Tagore, reading of these events in Europe, was hostile: he regarded both noncooperation and Khilafat as the antitheses of his ideal of international cooperation between East and West at their best. When letters reached him from C. F. Andrews, containing the sort of strong criticism of Gandhi that he did not expect from Andrews, Tagore's accumulated frustration came pouring out.[1] In his reply, Tagore explains that noncooperation, as proposed by Gandhi, would be 'a wasteful diversion of the best part of our energy to a course which ends in a mere emptiness of negation'. This was his fundamental attitude to noncooperation until his death.

Autour du Monde, 9 Quai du Quatre-Septembre,
[Paris, France]
7 September 1920

Dear friend

Your letters always bring the atmosphere of Santiniketan round my mind, with all its colours and sounds and movements, and my love for my boys, like a migratory bird, crosses back [over] the sea, seeking its own dear nest in the ashram. Your letters are great gifts to me – I have not the power to repay them in kind. For now my mind faces the West, and all that it has to give naturally flows towards it – therefore, for the time being, my direct communication with you has become thin, like the stream of the Kopai in the summer.[2] But I know Santiniketan will not bring forth its fullness of flower and fruit if, through me, it does not send its roots to the western soil. Stung by insult or injustice, we try to repudiate Europe, but by doing it we insult ourselves. Let us have the dignity not to quarrel or retaliate, not to pay back smallness with being small ourselves. What Gandhi is inculcating in his pugnacious spirit of resentment is the withdrawal of service from the Government. It is a wasteful diversion of the best part of our energy to a course which ends in a mere emptiness of negation. This is the time when we should dedicate all our resources of emotion, thought and character to the service of our country in a positive direction of duty. We are suffering because of some offences of ours against *shivam*, against *advaitam* – we spend all our energy in quarrelling with the punishment and nothing of it is left for the reparation of wrongs we have done and are doing.[3] When we have performed our part of the duties, we shall have the fullest right and power and time to bring others to book for their transgressions.

To what futility Gandhi's methods lead we have seen in his withdrawal of evidence before Hunter's commission. It was merely negative both in its procedure and its results. It merely had the effect of giving vent to a petulant spirit of vexation and we neglected the only opportunity we had of effectively bringing the most atrocious facts of a most terrible crime before the great world's tribunal. The non-official report! The printing cost of it was a fine we imposed upon ourselves over and above that which was imposed by the martial law.[4] But let us forget the Punjab affairs – but never forget that we shall go on deserving such humiliation over and over again until we set our house in order. Do not mind the waves of the sea, but mind the leaks in your vessel. Politics in our country is extremely petty. It has a pair of legs, one of which has shrunk and shrivelled and become paralytic and therefore feebly waits for the other one to drag it on. There is no harmony between the two, and our politics, in its hopping and totterings and falls is comic and undignified. The entreaty and anger, which alternately are struggling to find expression in the ludicrously lame member of this tragic partnership, both belong to our abject feebleness. When noncooperation will naturally come as our final moral protest against the unnaturalness of our political situation then it will be glorious, because true; but when it is another form of begging, maybe the best form – then let us reject it.

The establishment of a perfect cooperation of life and mind among ourselves must come first through *tapasya* of sacrifice and self-dedication, and then will come in its natural course the noncooperation.[5] When the fruit completely ripens it finds its freedom through its own fulfilment of truth. Our country is crying to her own children for their cooperation in the removal of obstacles in our social life which for centuries are hampering us in our self-realisation. We need cooperation of the sacrifice of love, more than anything else, to prove to our country that she is ours and then we shall have the moral right to say to others: 'We have nothing to do with you in our own affairs.' And for this, all the moral fervour which the life of Gandhi represents, and which he, of all other men in the world, can call up, is needed. That such a precious treasure of power should be put into the mean and frail vessel of our politics allowing it to sail across endless waves of angry recrimination is terribly unfortunate for our country where our mission is to revive the dead with the fire of soul. The external waste of our resources of life is great owing to external circumstances – but [that] the waste of our spiritual resources should also be allowed to happen on adventures that are wrong from the point of view of moral truth is heartbreaking. It is criminal to turn moral force into a blind force.

Our time to go to Holland is drawing near. I have numerous invitations from there to lecture. I am not yet fully ready. Just now I am busy writing my message. My subject is the Meeting of the East and West. I hope it will be finished before I leave Paris.

With love

Ever yours
Rabindranath Tagore

[PS] Your proposal about the increment of salaries in the ashram has my fullest approval.

Source: MS original at Rabindra Bhavan, Shantiniketan.

1 'The work that Mr Gandhi and the politicians are doing today – the whole political outlook, with its popular clamour and excitement, is almost entirely destructive' (Andrews to RT, 3 Aug. 1920 [RB]). 'The truth is that the "Khilafat" appeals to the very worst side of Islam – that religious arrogance, which is every bit as bad as racial arrogance' (Andrews to RT, 9 Aug. 1920 [RB]).
2 Kopai: local river of Shantiniketan, much loved by RT.
3 On *shantam, advaitam*, see letter 98, n. 10.

4 When the commission of inquiry into the Amritsar massacre under Lord Hunter was announced by Lord Chelmsford in early Sept. 1919, Gandhi was supportive, urging Indians to trust it and bring evidence before it. But when the Government refused to allow prominent leaders of the disturbances then in jail to be released for the period of the inquiry, Gandhi changed his mind, withdrew his support for Hunter's commission and supported instead the establishment in Nov. 1919 of a separate Congress inquiry into events at Amritsar. This inquiry produced a 'non-official' report, mentioned by RT, which was mainly written by Gandhi and published in March 1920 nearly two months ahead of the Hunter report. 'The amateurishness of the Congress enquiry seems to have given Gandhi the opportunity to consolidate the position he gained in the Congress group late in 1919' (Brown, *Gandhi's Rise*, p. 237). Its appearance was virtually ignored by the British press, as RT must have known from his visit to London in mid-1920. He may have also suspected that Gandhi had manipulated the withdrawal of Indian evidence before Hunter for his own political purposes.

5 *tapasya*: practice of austerities.

152

To Nagendranath Gangulee

The marriage of Mira, Tagore's daughter, and Nagendranath Gangulee did not improve (see letter 145), and Mira continued to live for periods at Shantiniketan, leaving Nagen in Calcutta; their two children generally, though not always, went with their mother. Rabindranath continued to reason with his son-in-law, as in this letter.[1]

[Autour du Monde, 9 Quai du Quatre-Septembre,
Paris, France]
8 September 1920

Kalyaniyeshu

Nagen, please do not misunderstand me. I do not pass judgement on you. I know that the threads of our lives become tangled as a result of our mistakes, defects and wrong actions, and thus we become causes of unhappiness to one another. Perhaps you think that I hold you responsible – and pardon Mira. That is not at all the case. The truth is that I have always demanded freedom for myself in life, and for others too. When I find that because of some social custom, some raja's decree or the interference of some particular power, a group of people has been deprived of its right to independence, I feel pained. Especially when the victim is someone I love. I have never shackled any of my children to my own ideas. Often I have suffered for this – inconvenience, loss and anxiety – but I have never imposed my will. If I had forced Mira's mother to follow my set of rules, it would have been convenient for me – but I did not do it.[2] I feel ashamed to use compulsion on those who are such easy victims: bravado of that sort strikes me as a kind of insult to oneself. Even with my servant Shadhu Charan I avoid it. And so the misfortune that pains me most when it befalls any of my loved ones is lack of freedom. But perhaps you will not fully understand all that I am saying. Whatever I have to suffer I shall accept, and shall bear it silently. I have my other work to consider.

Until now I had not realised how high my position in Europe is. It has come as a big surprise. What I hear sounds very exaggerated, and I am very diffident in believing it. For I am really not the giant they call me: and so I feel encumbered by a heavy burden. Preparations for my lecturing in Holland are in hand – they expect me there in the third week of September. I am now writing the lecture, which will be a kind of message. I receive regular invitations from Germany but to get there is fairly difficult, and I will not make it this time. I shall go when I return from America. The Scandinavian countries too have expressed real eagerness, but for a particular reason I cannot go at present.[3] On my return to Paris in October, I am to read an essay at the Sorbonne University; I also have an invitation from a learned society. All this makes me both busy and anxious. Then on 9 October I head for America – where a series of lectures will again grab me.[4] I am eager to go back home, but I cannot refuse all the demands here.

Ekanta shubhanudhyayi
Shri Rabindranath Thakur

Source: MS original at Rabindra Bhavan, Shantiniketan; letter published in Sharadiya *Desh*, 1398 [Autumn 1991], pp. 51–2.

1 RT's letter appears to be a response to a letter from Nagendranath, which is not available.
2 RT refers to his late wife in the traditional manner ('Mira's mother') – one of his rare references to her in his letters to his family circle.
3 Presumably this was a reference to the incident with the Swedish spy (see letter 150).
4 See letter 153.

153

To Charles Freer Andrews

After lecturing in Europe, Tagore's plan was to visit the USA again, in order to raise a large fund for Visva-Bharati. But in late September he encountered a severe setback. James B. Pond, his promoter on the highly successful lecture tour in 1916–17, informed W. W. Pearson in London, who was acting for Tagore (as he had in 1916), that none of the usual lecture organisers in the USA would book Tagore, because he was still tarred with the reputation of being 'an anti-Ally agitator during the war' (see letter 143).[1] Pearson appears to have communicated this fact by cable to Tagore, who was now in Holland.

This was a shock, and Rabindranath's initial reaction was typically emotional, as it had been when he first heard these allegations more than two years before. Writing to C. F. Andrews in Shantiniketan, he adopts the somewhat sanctimonious tone that came easily to him when writing about the USA, especially in a letter to the sometimes even more sanctimonious Andrews. It would be tempting to call it hypocritical, were it not that Tagore appears genuinely to have deluded himself that his destiny had intervened between him and the mighty dollar – and of course he was writing in the midst of the kind of European applause that would have turned the head of almost any man. Still, the tone is amusing, given Tagore's decision, within a week of two of writing this letter, to venture to America after all.

42, Lge Gasthuisstraat, Antwerp, [Holland]
3 October 1920

Dear Friend
You must have heard by this time from different sources that our American tour has been cancelled. The atmosphere of our mind has been cleared, at a sweep, of the dense

fog of the contemplation of five million dollars.² This is deliverance. In the meanwhile I have spent about a fortnight in Holland. This fortnight has been most generous of its gifts to me – it has condensed the love and fellowship of fifteen years into fifteen days and has made it mine. It is so wonderful to think that I had so completely occupied the heart of this people before I had ever known them. Yet, by nature, they are not quick in their mind and not easily moved. They are phlegmatic – but they have their idealism protected and kept pure by this external covering of something insensitive and thick. This you may be sure of, that a communication of heart has been opened up between this little country and Shantiniketan, and it remains with us to widen it and make use of it for the interchange of spiritual wealth. Altogether Europe has come closer to us by this visit of ours. I only wish that all my friends in Shantiniketan could realise how true it is and what a wealth it represents. Now I know more clearly than ever before that Shantiniketan belongs to all the world and we shall have to be worthy of this great fact. It is extremely difficult for us Indians to forget all the irritations that ever keep our consciousness [concentrated on] our own daily annoyances. But emancipation of consciousness is the means and end of spiritual life and therefore Shantiniketan must be saved from the whirlwind of our dusty politics. Our one *mantram* for meditation is *shantam, shivam, advaitam*.³

I am writing this letter from Antwerp where I came yesterday morning and I am getting ready to go to Brussels where I have invitation. And then I go to Paris. However, a flood of gladness comes over my mind with the thought that I have been saved from America. My going there would not have been prevented if my mission had remained pure, if the desire for five million dollars had not assailed my mind – for message and money are not interchangeable.

With love

Ever yours
Rabindranath Tagore

Source: MS original at Rabindra Bhavan, Shantiniketan.

1 Pond to Pearson, 17 Sept. 1920 [RB].
2 'Five million dollars' was the phrase that RT jokingly called his *mantram* in several letters to Andrews during the second half of 1920.
3 See letter 98, n. 10.

154

To Mira Gangulee (Tagore)

Although Tagore's American lecture agent had been unable to book a tour in the usual way, he did not actually advise against this visit. He told W. W. Pearson that the presence of the poet in person in New York, being 'once again . . . interviewed, photographed and [taking] the centre of the stage as is his custom', could swing public opinion in his favour.¹ 'I personally think there is a big battle to fight, and my opinion is that the best way is to have Tagore come and to book the tour . . . en route as you go.'² This advice seems to have changed Tagore's mind about going.

He arrived in New York on 28 October 1920 and booked into the Hotel Algonquin, which had just become one of the most fashionable places in the city for literary people.[3] (The Algonquin Round Table began meeting there in 1919 and in 1920 was moved to the Rose Room so that its members would be more visible to the public.) His first lecture, 'The meeting of the East and the West', took place two weeks later. It was based on an article of the same name he had published in the *Manchester Guardian* in March 1918, as the First World War was nearing its end.[4] This concluded with the following words, which established the keynote of Tagore's five-month stay in the USA:

> Europe is great. She has been dowered by her destiny with a location and climate and race combination producing a history rich with strength, beauty, and tradition of freedom. Nature in her soil challenged man to put forth all his forces, never overwhelming his mind into a passivity of fatalism. It imparted in the character of her children the energy and daring which never acknowledge limits to their claims, and also at the same time an intellectual sanity, a restraint in imagination, a sense of proportion in their creative works, and a sense of reality in all their aspirations. They explored the secrets of existence, measured and mastered them; they discovered the principle of unity in nature not through the help of meditation or abstract logic, but by boldly crossing barriers of diversity and peeping behind the screen. They surprised themselves into nature's great storehouse of powers, and there they had their fill of temptation.
>
> Europe is fully conscious of her greatness, and that itself is the reason why she does not know where her greatness may fail her. There have been periods of history when great races of men forgot their own souls in the pride and enjoyment of their power and possessions. They were not even aware of this lapse, because things and institutions assumed such magnificence that all their attention was drawn outside their true selves. Just as nature in her aspect of bewildering vastness may have the effect of humiliating man, so also his own accumulation may produce the self-abasement which is spiritual apathy by stimulating all his energy towards his wealth and not his welfare. Through this present war has come the warning to Europe that her things have been getting the better of her truth, and in order to be saved she must find her soul and her God and fulfil her purpose by carrying her ideals into all continents of the earth and not sacrifice them to her greed of money and dominion.

In this letter to his daughter, Rabindranath describes his determination to earn enough money in the USA from lecturing to put his idea of his university, Visva-Bharati, on a firm financial footing.

Hotel Algonquin, New York, [USA]
10 November 1920

Miru

Since coming to this side of the Atlantic, I have been unable to write you a letter. It takes a while to get settled in a new place, particularly where one is among a constant crowd. This time I sailed in a good cabin with an attached bathroom. So I did not suffer any discomfort – I spent much of my time inside the cabin writing my lectures. But such cabins are costly. If I did not expect to make money in America, I could not afford one. Now and again the sea was rough. These days, though, I do not suffer much from seasickness; but for those who do, it can be unbearable. Since we got here I have been preoccupied with raising money for Shantiniketan. At present we are in discussion with various people. Judging from their reactions, perhaps we will not come away empty-handed. Shortage of funds has been my trouble all along. There are times when I feel like abandoning ship; I would certainly have an easier life if I went back to the sandbanks of the Padma and wrote poems. This time I am not returning until I have put an end to my financial worries forever.

My first lecture is this evening.[5] If it is successful, a lot of cash will come floating in on the tide of words. My subject is the Meeting of the West and the East [sic]. There are some harsh comments in the lectures – but the people of this country can stomach harsh criticism. One needs a certain strength to be able to listen to the truth, and they have this strength; whereas people in our country have to be constantly flattered.

Many boys from our country are here. Among them is a group loitering with intent to foment revolution. I gather that this group has spread itself from country to country, and the majority of its members are Bengalis.[6] But something else here makes me very happy: the sight of many people from our country setting up major enterprises within a short space of time, and making substantial profits – one of them has even become a millionaire. Many Bengali boys are following their lead.

When I read in your letter of poor Shabi I was extremely saddened. I did not know that the authorities at the Hindu University were so inhuman. It must have been a terrible blow for Shabi's mother.[7] Here the weather is gradually becoming wintry, but it is not like winter in England – there is no dearth of sunshine, and people keep their houses really warm, indeed overwarm.

Father

Source: MS original at Rabindra Bhavan, Shantiniketan; letter published in Sharadiya *Desh*, 1397 [Autumn 1990], pp. 42–3.

1 J. B. Pond to Pearson, 17 Sept. 1920 [RB].
2 J. B. Pond to Pearson, 21 Sept. 1920 [RB]. Pond's advice probably did not reach RT until he returned to Paris/London in mid-Oct. after visiting Holland. Hence his writing to Andrews on 3 Oct. from Holland (letter 153) that the American tour was cancelled, without qualification. Alternatively, he may have received the advice earlier but ignored it in a fit of disgust until he discussed the whole matter with Pearson and others in London.
3 In his memoirs, *Tales of a Wayward Inn* (New York, 1938), Frank Case, who operated the Algonquin from 1907, wrote vividly of Tagore:

> Of all the well-known people who stayed at the hotel at one time or another I think no one has excited more comment and interest than Gertrude Stein. Along with her I should place Rabindranath Tagore and the Indian poet Madame Naidu [Sarojini Naidu]. These two famous people from India were never at the hotel at the same time; there were years between their visits.
> Tagore with his white hair, white beard, and face of a saint, topped with silken turban, looked like a picture of a Christ grown older than we know Him, and seemed as far removed from the material things of our day. It looked incongruous to see him riding in an elevator and I'm quite sure he never used the telephone. I kept a waiter standing at his door from morning till night, so that if he wanted anything he had but to clap his hands. But he never wanted anything, he was not interested in food nor in the hundreds of other things that the rest of us think indispensable for the day's comfort.
> After three or four days the waiters begged to be relieved of this lonely and monotonous vigil, but before discontinuing the idea, I called on Tagore, or, rather, I was given an audience. I found him seated in one of my own chairs which had somehow become a sort of throne, surrounded by three or four of his countrymen, gentlemen in morning coats and formal attire, all standing. Tagore wore a long silken robe, his head bare but covered with abundant white hair and my first impression of him was of extreme cleanliness; his hair, his nails, his teeth, his skin, all were shining. And he had the eyes of a young man, bright, and they were shining too. He reached a friendly, strong, brown hand out from the world in which he lived and thought into the world in

The founding of a university 243

which I lived, took my hand, told me I was very kind and he was very comfortable. I replied that I was honoured to have him in my house; and the audience was over, and I took the waiters back to the restaurant where the atmosphere was more familiar to them. (Frank Case, *Tales of a Wayward Inn*, pp. 77–8)

4 *Manchester Guardian*, 28 March 1918 (reprinted in the *MR*, June 1918, pp. 655–7).
5 The lecture was at the Brooklyn Academy of Music under the auspices of the Brooklyn Institute.
6 On the Indian revolutionary movement against British rule, see Don Dignan, *The Indian Revolutionary Problem in British Diplomacy 1914–1919* (New Delhi, 1983) and, more recently, Richard J. Popplewell, *Intelligence and Imperial Defence: British Intelligence and the Defence of the Indian Empire 1904–1924* (London, 1995).
7 Shabi: Sharbesh Chandra Majumdar, son of RT's old friend Srish Chandra Majumdar. He was a student at the Benares Hindu University, and fell ill there with a brain disease. The university authorities put him on a train home, alone, and he was found to be dead on arrival in Calcutta.

155

To William Winstanley Pearson

(not sent)

Things did not go well for Tagore in New York. The 1918 propaganda against him (see letter 153) made some potential American donors suspicious of him; he hated the administrative effort necessary to raise funds; he disliked the vulgarity of American commerce, big city life, smart society and literary fashion; and, what was probably most damaging of all, the mood of the country had turned away from Wilsonian (and by extension Tagorean) high-mindedness: the Jazz Age was beginning. 'Tagore was no longer the exotic novelty he had been in 1916; the fickle public had already turned to new fads, preferring bobbed hair to long grey beards, and short flapper skirts to flowing Oriental robes.'[1] Cooped up in Manhattan in winter, Tagore became more and more depressed.

W. W. Pearson, his devoted secretary, who had always been highly strung, disappeared to Boston for a while without warning. Rabindranath, deeply upset, wrote the following letter to him on 13 December but did not send it. Four days later, still inwardly churning, he passionately relieved his feelings in a second letter to the far-distant C. F. Andrews in Shantiniketan (letter 156). On 23 December, in a letter that he sent to Pearson, he blamed himself for Pearson's going away.[2] On 26 December Pearson (now spending a few weeks at an experimental college in Michigan) responded calmly enough to Rathindranath, Tagore's son, who seems have calmed his father.[3] By early January, after more letters to Pearson and Andrews, the emotional storm was over: Tagore had come to terms with the mismatch between his mission and American reality.

Hotel Algonquin, New York, [USA]
13 December 1920

Dear Pearson,

'It was not like your great and gracious ways!' But it is evident that you wanted to hurt me and Rathi. Discourtesy or unkindness is not natural to you and therefore it cruelly hurts when it comes from your hands. You have hinted in your letter to Kedar that you want to part company with us.[4] You could have written to me directly, for you know that I love you, and it is better that we should part as friends. It is more hateful to me than anything else to impose my company or my burden upon anybody when it is the least irksome to him. I hope you remember, that before taking our voyage I tried to release you from this responsibility on account of your ill health. However, I shall not blame you, you must have your freedom. I am old, you are young; I have my own ideas, you have your own predilections and if your friendship for me has received a shock for some reasons, let us do our best to save as much as we can from the wreck and at least have respect for one another. I have never deliberately slighted or offended you; I have my shortcomings, which, I find, have been irritating you without my being conscious of it. I am sure it will be easier for you to forgive me and know me better and realise that I do not merit your disesteem and my love for you is true and deep. I know you are gifted with goodness in a generous measure, you have your own mission to humanity and it will be worse than selfish of me to bar in the least your freedom to do what your natural power urges you do. Only one thing I claim of you, do not go out of your way to try to punish us for any unintentional offence we may have been guilty of, for it is doing yourself injustice, for 'it is not like your great and gracious ways'.

Affectionately yours
Rabindranath Tagore

PS You have got into some conventional habits such as calling me 'Gurudev' and making *pranam* to me.[5] Drop them. For I know there are occasions when they hurt you and for that very reason are truly discourteous to me. You know I never care to assume the role of a prophet or a teacher; I do not claim homage from my fellow-beings, I only need love and sympathy and I am merely a poet and nothing else.

Source: MS original at Rabindra Bhavan, Shantiniketan; letter published in *VBQ*, 48, Nos 1–4, May 1982–April 1983, pp. 127–8.

1 Stephen Hay, 'Rabindranath Tagore in America', *American Quarterly*, Fall 1962, p. 453.
2 RT to Pearson, 23 Dec. 1920:

> Please know that the reason why I did not clearly understand your feeling till you ran away to Boston was not my selfishness, but my stupidity. But possibly it was the stupidity of unconscious selfishness which was to be uprooted. One consolation I have in my mind – I had earnestly asked you not to accompany me in this tour before we sailed. I was absolutely serious in my request. But mere good intention is not enough and so the judgement is against me. (*VBQ*, 9, No. 2, Aug.–Oct. 1943, p. 170)

3 Pearson to Rathindranath Tagore, 26 Dec. 1920 [RB]:

> I think he [RT] has exaggerated my desire for freedom to enjoy an occasional opportunity of contact with the young . . . into a longing for complete freedom from the life of serving him . . . all I need is periods of recreation in activity of this kind just as he finds rest and recreation in his writing work. Without such intervals the kind of life we were compelled to live in New York, surrounded by an atmosphere in which so much was unreal and insincere would be too intolerable . . . I seemed to have lost trust in everything and suspected almost everybody who came to see Gurudev of mean and self-interested motives . . . I am devoted to Gurudev as you know and want to serve him and his ideals.

4 Kedarnath Das Gupta accompanied RT to New York from London.
5 See letter 98, n. 2.

156

To Charles Freer Andrews

Hotel Algonquin, New York, [USA]
17 December 1920

Dear Friend

When all my thoughts were furiously revolving, like dead leaves, in a whirlwind of desire for raising funds a picture came to my hand; it was of Sujata offering a cup of milk to Buddha.[1] Its message went deep into my heart. It said to me – 'The cup of milk comes to you unasked when you have gone through your *tapasya*.[2] It is offered to you with love – and only love can bring its homage to truth.' Then your figure at once came to my mind. The milk has been sent to me through you – it is infinitely more than anything that can come from the cheque book of the rich. I would have been famished in the wilderness of solitude for the lack of sympathy and comradeship when you brought your cup of love to me which is the true life-giving food freely offered by life. And as the poet Morris says, 'Love is enough.'[3] And that voice of love everyday calls me away from the lure of dollars – the voice that comes to nestle in my heart from across the sea, from the shady avenue of *shal* trees resonant with the laughter and songs of simple joy. The mischief is, ambition does not fully believe in love, it believes in power. It leaves the limpid and singing water of everlasting life for the wine of success. Everyday I seem to be growing afraid of the very vision of this success. It has been said in the *Upanishad* 'Bhumaiba shukham', 'Happiness is in greatness.'[4] Ambition points out bigness and calls it greatness and our track is hopelessly lost. When I look at the picture of Buddha I cry for the great peace of inner fulfilment. My longing grows painfully intense as my mind becomes distracted at the stupendous unmeaningness of monstrosity of things around me. Every morning I sit by my window and say to myself 'I must now bow my head to this ugly idol worshipped by the western barbarians with daily human sacrifices.' I remember that morning at Shilida [Shelidah] when the Vaishnava woman came to me and said, 'When are you coming down from your three-storied building [to] meet your love under the shade of the trees?' Just now, I am on the top storey of the skyscraper, to which the tallest of trees dare not send its whisper, but love silently comes to me saying 'When are you coming down to meet me on the green grass under the rustling leaves, where you have the freedom of the sky and of sunlight and the tender touch of life's simplicity?' I try to say – 'Wait, till I have five –', but it sounds so ludicrous and yet tragic that my words grow ashamed of themselves and they stop. 'I despise your millions,' such should be my farewell greeting to this country – 'for my love calls.' I should not let my dignity be soiled by the sordid touch of her dollars; mere lack of means should not be allowed to mock the majesty of soul, seeking its crown in the foolscap of the bank cheque. Spirit of India comes to me in the midst of my spurious activities and whispers the immortal *mantram* to my inner spirit – 'Jenahang namritashyam kimahangten kurjam', 'What shall I do with that which will not make me immortal?'[5]

With love

Ever yours
Rabindranath Tagore

Source: MS original at Rabindra Bhavan, Shantiniketan.

1 Sujata, the daughter of a landowner, offered a bowl of milk rice to Gautama while he was seated under a banyan tree one morning. This was his last meal before his Enlightenment.
2 *tapasya*: practice of austerities.
3 William Morris, 'Love is Enough' (1871).
4 *Chandogya Upanishad*, 7:23.
5 *Brihadaranyaka Upanishad*, 2:4:3.

157

To Charles Freer Andrews

Christmas 1920 was the nadir of Tagore's American visit. Longing to escape into the countryside from a hotel room and the big city, Rabindranath agreed to visit a grand log-house in the Catskill Mountains north of New York City, known as Yama Farms. This had just been launched by a New York advertising magnate and a vivacious socialite as a kind of retreat for industrialists, where they could enjoy the company of the outstanding intellects of the day without any of the fuss surrounding their millions. The first guests had been Thomas Edison, Henry Ford, Harvey Firestone and the long-bearded naturalist John Burroughs. Here, it is said, John D. Rockefeller offered Tagore a dime, having mistaken him for 'an old Negro'.[1] And here, predictably enough, a vitriolic Tagore informed C. F. Andrews: 'These people . . . are like drunkards who are afraid of their lucid intervals . . . I feel oppressed . . . by a crowd of cheap personalities that hustle me on every side – they are the people whose valuation of life's treasure is so utterly different from mine.'[2]

This letter, written on his return to New York, expands on this theme. It also contains some scathing criticism of the Noncooperation Movement, of which much more would follow over the next few months. Tagore was too honest a critic to allow his repugnance for aspects of the West to mitigate his repugnance for (different) aspects of the East.

Hotel Algonquin, New York, [USA]
[1 January 1921]

My friend, today is the New Year's Day. But I do not feel it in the air, it brings no message to me. New Year comes to these countries with possibilities of new inventions, new political adjustments and economic revolutions. But the New Year which we know in Shantiniketan comes to our soul bringing to it the expectation of its own blossoming, some inner miracle of renovation. Last night the whole town went mad with a boisterous fury of merriments and this morning it is too tired to open its heart to the beautiful sunlight of the New Year's Day.

All the while my heart is aching to think that our first day of Baishakh will bring its blessings for me in the early morning light of Shantiniketan and find my seat vacant.[3] How precious with truth and peace those days are made we [come to] know when our hearts are wandering in [a] wilderness of things thirsting for a drop of *amrita*, the draught of everlasting life. In [the] geological history of the earth [there were] ages of titanic storms circulating round this globe – but now in the human period of this planet it is the *andhi*, the duststorm of buildings and business, that is sweeping over the face of the earth. In those remote ages of turbulent hot vapour the earth remained shrouded in a suffocating gloom, remained ignorant of its kinship with the starry world – but that pall of blindness has been lifted and the light has brought to the world of life its message of the eternal. The tornado of the present-day towns will also pass off, the dervish dance of dust will be quieted and [the] human mind will find its communication with the infinite unhindered. We do not even have time to realise with what longing the human spirit is waiting to find itself in that unobstructed realm of light. And the light will come to her and reveal the endless beauty of truth.

Occasionally I read in the newspapers the reports of the Non-Co-operative Movement [*sic*] in India. It seems to me that its current is getting muddled with a great amount of unreason. The forces that mould our history are irrational, but our leaders who guide those forces must have sanity and farsightedness. To be in league with the spirit of destruction is dangerous, for its methods are easy, its results are quick and stupendous in wholesale negation – but it obstructs our road with the ruins it causes, raising the barriers of rubbish heaps between us and our vision of the beyond. Sometimes I suspect Mahatmaji has a great deal of alloy of politics mixed with his idealism, giving rise to strange contradictions and unholy combinations.

With love

Ever yours
Rabindranath Tagore

Source: MS original at Rabindra Bhavan, Shantiniketan.

1 See the description of Yama Farms and RT's visit in the *New Yorker*, 3 May 1982, pp. 71–2, 75; also Dutta and Robinson, *Rabindranath Tagore*, p. 429.
2 RT to C. F. Andrews, 25 Dec. 1920 [RB].
3 Baishakh: Bengali month corresponding to mid-April–mid-May. The Bengali New Year falls on 1 Baishakh. RT was in Europe on 1 Baishakh 1328 (1921).

158

To William Winstanley Pearson

W. W. Pearson remained apart from Tagore for some weeks after his sudden disappearance to Boston in mid-December; he spent a period teaching at the Starr Commonwealth, an experimental educational institution in Michigan. But he wrote to Rabindranath reiterating his devotion to him and urging him to visit the institution. Tagore, however, remained preoccupied with the need to raise funds for Shantiniketan, though with more equanimity and good humour than he had shown in December. In this letter and the subsequent letter, both written to Pearson, Tagore gives a glimpse of his capacity as an effective organiser, when circumstances forced him into the role.

[Hotel Algonquin, New York, USA]
1 January 1921

Dear Pearson,

I have anxiously been waiting for your letter which has come and relieved me.[1] I was afraid lest you should misunderstand me and think that I had written to you in a spirit of resentment. I felt that it should be my duty and my pleasure to let you have the fullest opportunity for doing the work that suits you best. You must find out your own vocation and without losing time prepare yourself for it. There should not be the least contradiction between your service of love to me and that to the world. But it is premature and therefore wrong to talk about our joining hands for a common object. The call for it must come and make it inevitable. Our own words may create unnecessary difficulties in [the] choice of our fields of truth. Paths should be kept open and minds passive till the time comes when there can be no doubt about the courses we should take. I strongly feel that your life is precious; for you have rare gifts given to you by providence, therefore it is imperatively necessary for you to find your fulfilment wherever it may be possible – no personal consideration whatever should stand in its way.

Our stay at Chicago will be narrowed by our New York engagements on one side and Texas engagements on the other.[2] Therefore we should devote all the days we have in hand to hunt for lucky chances in that land of gigantic possibilities. This makes me doubtful about my visit to the Starr Commonwealth.

With love,

Affectionately yours,
Rabindranath Tagore

Source: MS original at Rabindra Bhavan, Shantiniketan; letter published in *VBQ*, 9, No. 2, Aug.–Oct. 1943, p. 170–1.

1 Pearson's letter is missing; it was a reply to RT's letter to him of 23 Dec. 1920 (quoted in letter 155, n. 2).
2 RT remained on the East Coast until 9 Feb. 1921, when he left for Chicago. There he met Pearson and together they travelled to Texas, where RT gave a series of lectures arranged by J. B. Pond over a fortnight from 12 Feb., after which he returned to Chicago.

159

To William Winstanley Pearson

[Hotel Algonquin, New York, USA]
[10? January 1921][1]

Dear Pearson,

Since my return from Yama Farms I have had to be very busy with my propaganda work, writing about it, revising these writings, meeting people, struggling to save myself from being inveigled into plans of schemers cleverer than ourselves, keeping engagements and attending to tasks that are of no conceivable use to any rational creature.[2] Last night before going to retire I looked at my watch and found it was 20 minutes to three. I am tired. However, it seems that wheels are set revolving and the results, I hope, are not likely to be blank disappointment. I shall be leaving for Boston this afternoon where my days will be solidly filled with luncheons and dinners, lectures and talks.[3] But I am happy to inform you that I have definitely refused to accept hospitality from that club whose members by some oversight of providence have been allowed to overstay their terms of life and whose servants with their stare make you despair of your ever being able to come up to their standard of respectability. With the thickening of the plot of the farce of the five millions, my movements are becoming more and more uncertain, and I have not the least notion when I shall be at Chicago or anywhere else. I am in the hands of my destiny whose programme is written in invisible ink, which prevents me from filling my own engagement book with dates that cannot be rubbed out at the shortest notice. This makes it doubtful about my going to Starr Commonwealth and yet not hopeless.

Yours with love,
Rabindranath Tagore

Source: MS original at Rabindra Bhavan, Shantiniketan; letter published in *VBQ*, 9, No. 2, Aug.–Oct. 1943, p. 167.

1 There is no date on this letter, but 10 Jan. is likely, since RT's first lecture in Boston was on 11 Jan.
2 On Yama Farms, see letter 157.
3 Around Boston, RT spoke on 'The poet's religion' on 11 Jan. in the Houghton Memorial Chapel under the auspices of the department of philosophy, Wellesley College, on 'The folk poets of Bengal' on 12 Jan. at Harvard University, and on 'The meeting of East and West' on 13 Jan., again at Harvard.

160

To Charles Freer Andrews

In 1915, Tagore read Goldsworthy Lowes Dickinson's *Essay on the Civilisations of India, China and Japan* and wrote about it to William Rothenstein (see letter 95). In 1921, he came across it again and wrote about it, this time to C. F. Andrews. But whereas in 1915, Dickinson's dislike of India had made Tagore sad, six (eventful) years later it made him angry. His differing reactions illuminate his loss of faith in the imperial 'mission'.

When his second letter was published in the *Modern Review* in April 1921, E. M. Forster, then in India and in the process of writing *A Passage to India*, read it and wrote to his friend Goldie: 'There is a grotesque attack on you by Tagore in the April number of the *Modern Review*, Calcutta. I have written a reply which, if it ever meets your eye you will think doubly grotesque. An organ note of pained surprise. – T. has gone to bits since Amritsar, I gather.'[1] Later Forster added: '[Tagore] had been upset by a comprehending reference to the English [in India] and their efforts. "Mr Dickinson ignores the fact that gifts must be conveyed through sympathy and cannot be imposed by force."[2] I wrote to the effect that to write thus is to ignore Mr Dickinson.'

Ramananda Chatterji (editor of the *Modern Review*) refused to publish Forster's response: 'Very polite to Tagore was I, but the editor returned my criticism as irrelevant and informed me that you and T. were friends. I might have pushed the matter further, but thought it wouldn't have been much use and that you wouldn't have wished it anyhow,' Forster concluded.[3]

What was at issue here was nothing less than the central matters of Forster's classic novel; and it would be reasonable to suggest that the vehemence of Tagore's arguments subtly influenced the writing of the novel and even, perhaps, that Tagore's striking language, poetic and emotional, modulated the tone of Doctor Aziz's language in the novel. For the 'grotesqueness' of Tagore's language to Andrews, of which Forster wrote, is echoed in the hyperbolic language of Aziz.

No doubt Tagore's depressed mood in New York was a factor in the writing of this letter, in the way that Dickinson's depression in India as a result of illness marked his *Essay*.[4] Nevertheless, Tagore's underlying arguments and perceptions were true, consistent with his earlier writings and rooted in experience. Tagore had been exposed to the British in India for a lot longer than Forster, and at every level, from district magistrate and missionary to governor and viceroy. Nor had Forster had any real contact with Indians of Tagore's intelligence, refinement and creativity.[5] In virtually dismissing Tagore's reaction to Dickinson's *Essay* as an over-reaction to the Amritsar massacre, Forster demonstrated the shallowness of his knowledge of India, not, as he thought, his maturity of perspective.

Hotel Algonquin, New York, [USA]
17 January 1921

My friend,

When I was staying at Autour du Monde in Paris I chanced to find a copy of Prof. Lowes Dickinson's report of his travels in the East.[6] It made me realise clearly the mentality of the British people in their relation to India. When the author indicates in it [the] utter difference of their temperament from ours, it fills me with despair at the unnaturalness of our relationship which is so humiliating on our side and so demoralising on theirs. In the pamphlet he quotes with approval a remark made to him by an officer in India whom he describes as 'intelligent and enlightened'. It is about the maintaining by Englishmen of an impassable social gulf between themselves and the people of India; and it says: 'An Englishman cannot be expected to lose his own soul for the sake of other people's politics.' Here the author parenthetically explains the word 'soul' by saying that it denotes the habits and traditions of one's race.[7] All this means that, Englishmen feel a sense of irreconcilable contradiction between their nature and ours, and therefore we are like twins who, by some monstrous freak of destiny, have been tied together back to back. He concludes the summary of his report saying: 'But my own opinion is that India has more to gain and less to lose by contact with the West than any other eastern country.'[8] He contemptuously ignores the fact that where no communication of sympathy is possible, gifts can only be hurled and not given; that while counting the number of gains by the receiver, we also have to consider the fracture of his skull, and while thanking the doctor for the rest cure we must hasten to negotiate with the undertaker for the funeral. It is [an] irony of fate for us to be blamed by these people [for] the iniquity of our caste distinctions. And yet, never in the blindness of our pride of birth have we suggested that by coming in contact with any race of men we can lose our souls, although we may lose our caste which is a merely conventional classification. The analogy would be perfect if the division of the railway compartments, with its inequality of privileges, was defended by the railway directors as being necessary for the salvation of the passengers' souls. Only think in this connection of the ideal which the life of Akbar represented. This emperor's soul was not afraid, for its own safety, of the touch of a neighbouring humanity but of the want of touch. Aurangzeb, on the other hand, who was certainly 'intelligent and enlightened', who was meticulously careful about keeping intact what he considered to be his soul, represented a force, insolent and destructive. Such an enormous difference in the ideals of these two most powerful monarchs of Mughal India sprang from fundamentally different interpretations of the word 'soul'.

Lowes Dickinson has mentioned the possibility of India being benefited by her contact with the West. Very likely he meant the contact to be like that of the root of a tree with the water in the soil, a mere impersonal fact of contiguity. I admit that the light of Europe's culture has reached us. But Europe with its corona of culture is a radiant idea, its light permeates the present age. It is not shut up in a single bull's-eye lantern, which is some particular people from Europe come to us in India. Yet we are repeatedly asked to be grateful to this bull's-eye lantern and prostrate ourselves before it with loyalty and reverence. But it is not possible, for it is a mere lantern, it has no soul. Not only that, it circumscribes the light to a narrow circle of barest necessity. The full radiation of European culture has pervaded Japan only because it has not come to her through an unnatural glare of a miserly lens, exaggerating the division between the small shining patch and the vast obscure.

It is our pride which seeks difference, and gloats upon it. But sympathy is a higher faculty being our spiritual organ of sight; it has the natural vision of the *advaitam*.[9] The world is an ever-moving multitude with an eternal unity of movements which must not be retarded in any of its parts by a break of cadence. The world of man is suffering because all movements in its individual parts are not in harmony with one another and therefore with the whole; because the relationship of races has not been established in a balance of truth and goodness. This balance cannot be maintained by an external regulation as in a puppet show. It is a dance which must have music in its heart to regulate it. This great music of love is lacking in the meeting of men which has taken place in the present age; and all its movements in their discongruity are creating complexities of sufferings.

I wish I could write to you simple letters giving our detailed news. But the worldwide agony of pain fills my mind with thoughts that obstruct natural communications of personal life.

With love

Ever yours
Rabindranath Tagore

Source: MS original at Rabindra Bhavan, Shantiniketan; letter published in modified form in *MR*, April 1921, pp. 527–8.

[1] Forster to Dickinson, [10? April] 1921, in E. M. Forster, *Selected Letters of E. M. Forster* (Mary Lago and P. N. Furbank eds.; London, 1985): II (1921–70), p. 5.
[2] Forster softened RT's comment in reporting it to Dickinson by removing RT's 'contemptuously'.

3 Forster to Dickinson, 6 Aug. 1921, in *ibid.*, p. 11.
4 William Rothenstein commented emolliently in *Men and Memories* (p. 284): 'I agreed with Rabindranath; Dickinson was hardly fair to India, not on account of any prejudice, but because he was not at his ease there.'
5 'Certainly the most sensitive novel about India by an Englishman is *A Passage to India*. But even Forster had no access to large areas of the Indian mind.' (Satyajit Ray, 'Under western eyes', *Sight and Sound*, Autumn 1982, p. 270.) See also Robinson, *Satyajit Ray*, pp. 285–7.
6 Lowes Dickinson's *Essay* was the report on his travels in the East funded by the Albert Kahn Foundation, which ran the centre Autour du Monde, where RT stayed on arrival in France in Aug. 1920. In his letter to Andrews RT seems to imply that he saw the *Essay* for the first time in 1920, despite having written about it to Rothenstein in 1915.
7 Dickinson, *Essay*, pp. 19–20. Dickinson wrote 'very intelligent and enlightened'.
8 *Ibid.*, p. 41.
9 *advaitam*: non-duality.

161

To Charles Freer Andrews

Tagore's efforts to raise funds for his university continued. On 23 January he spoke to a dinner reception in Greenwich Village; the following evening at a reception by the Junior League of America; soon after that, at a reception by the Poetry Society of America. All to no immediate avail. This letter to C. F. Andrews gives further nuances of his mood at this time.

Hotel Algonquin, New York, [USA]
[24 January 1921]

Dear friend,

I have just come back from Greenwich – a suburban city of New York – where last night I had a reception and speech and dinner and discussion till I felt empty like a burst balloon with no gas left in it. I have a dinner tonight at the house of a great society woman.[1] I shall be led into the bosom of a multitude of multimillionaires where I shall grope in the dark for some infinitesimal fraction of their millions, possibly knocking my head against their closed cashbox, feeling stunned and bruised. I have to pursue a series of lunches and dinners drawn by the mirage of the same purpose.

At the far-distant end of the wilderness of such trials what do I see? Mist? Is it golden mist? But what matters what it be? Results of our efforts delude us by appearing as final. They raise expectation of fulfilment and thus draw us on. But they are not final. They are roadside inns where we change our horses for a farther journey. But an ideal is different, it carries its own progress within itself – every stage is not a mere approach towards the goal, it is part of the goal itself. Trees proceed on their upward career, not in a railway track constructed by engineers. We who have been dreamers should never employ coolies to build railway lines of social service. We must solely deal with living ideas, have faith in life, otherwise we are punished. Punished not necessarily with bankruptcy, but with success, behind which sits the Mephistopheles of worldliness chuckling at the sight of an idealist dragged through the dust by the chariot of the prosperous. What has made us love Santiniketan so deeply is the ideal of perfection which we have tasted all through its growth. It has not been made by money, but by our love, our life. With it we need not strain for any result, it is fulfilment itself – the life which forms round it, the service which we daily render to it. Now I realise [more] than ever before how precious and beautiful is the simplicity of our ashram which can reveal itself all the more perfectly because of its background of material want. I know I am harping on this one subject in most of my letters lately – because my suffering is continuous and profound, my soul is being choked in this atmosphere turbid with contamination of dollar. But it is my *tapasya*, through it my mind is completely being purged of its faith in money.[2] Let me not bring fetter of gold for my ashram but freedom of spirit with its wedded companion Poverty, the pure, the simple, the tender and yet austere.

With love

Ever yours
Rabindranath Tagore

Source: MS original at Rabindra Bhavan, Shantiniketan.

1 She was Dorothy Whitney Straight, one of the wealthiest women in America, who later in 1921 gave a large sum of money to RT's institution (see letter 187). The January reception did not go well, as may be seen from a caustic letter written by Tagore's son Rathindranath to his American friend in Chicago, Mayce Seymour, from on board ship returning to Britain after the American visit:

> We got to know many of the millionaires, but we expected more help from Mrs Straight than from anyone else. In an interview she promised to [ask] a few persons who are directly in touch with the big foundations to meet Father at her house. So we went to this dinner hoping much from it, expecting to get things started. We had found out by this time, after much experience, that most of the money in America is controlled by a few persons and without some inside wire-pulling it is impossible to get at the large funds. Mrs Straight was undoubtedly in a position to get us in touch with these persons. But we were disappointed. It turned out to be a social function and father was made to read poems from *Gitanjali* much against his inclination. Undoubtedly Mrs Straight had invited Mr Thomas Lamont, the head of Morgan Co., thinking that if he could become interested everything else would be easy. But he was the very person we were afraid of and trying to avoid. The Morgan Co. is intimately connected with the British Govt. We had anticipated opposition from this quarter, as the British Govt would be absolutely against any project of an international organisation in India . . . And that is exactly what happened. Mrs Straight grew cold and tried to keep aloof, so that there was no more prospect of getting anything in New York. We organised committees, held meetings, and did everything that we could possibly do – but the doors were shut against us. (Rathindranath Tagore to Mayce Seymour, 30 March 1921 [copy at RB])

In the same letter, Rathindranath gave an even more scathing account of the reception for RT at the Poetry Society:

> Here [in New York] the small handful of poets or artists are lionised and they display their meagre talents before a crowd of coarse, stupid, fat and bejewelled women, who need to be kept amused and flattered because they have money. Most of the speeches were dull beyond words . . . Poetry, like everything else in America, must also be organised, advertised and boomed.

2 *tapasya*: practice of austerities.

162

To Edward John Thompson

While Tagore was in the West, E. J. Thompson, back teaching in Bengal again after winning a Military Cross in the recent war, was working hard at writing a study of Tagore and making various translations from Bengali. On 12 December 1920 he wrote a letter to Tagore which E. P. Thompson judged seventy years later to be 'deeply interesting but also unforgivably brash'.[1] It began with a paean to one of Tagore's poems that Thompson had just translated, then he wrote:

> I am going to revolutionise the western notion of you as a poet. As I have told you before, you – with great assistance from yr publishers – have been yr own worst enemy. You thoroughly deserved to have [Ernest] Rhys' book written about you. You have been taking the line of least resistance for years, translating from a certain stratum – and that not the [most] striking one – of yr work, and unconsciously mixing the wine of *Gitanjali* with water, till folk have found the draught tasteless . . . had you trusted the West more, had you given a selection of yr most imaginative stuff, you wd have been rewarded. The result is, I – who have hardly a moment to call my own – have to set things right.[2]

Rabindranath takes the criticism well in his reply. Perhaps his recent experiences in America, such as his readings of *Gitanjali* to wealthy Americans, had clarified for him the gulf between his poetic achievement in Bengali and in English, and made him realise that he lacked the command of English necessary to bridge this gulf.

c/o The Macmillan Company, 64 5th Avenue,
New York, [USA]
2 February 1921

Dear Thompson

You know I began to pay court to your language when I was fifty. It was pretty late for me ever to hope to win her heart. Occasional gifts of favour do not delude me with false hopes. Not being a degree-holder of any of our universities I know my limitations – and I fear to rush into the field reserved for angels to tread. In my translations I timidly avoid all difficulties, which has the effect of making them smooth and thin. I know I am misrepresenting myself as a poet to the western readers. But when I began this career of falsifying my own coins I did it in play. Now I am becoming frightened of its enormity and am willing to make a confession of my misdeeds and withdraw into my original vocation as a mere Bengali poet. I hope it is not yet too late to make reparation, and if you ever feel ready to translate my works into English I shall be glad to help you. Copyright difficulties will not be in your way if we allow Macmillan to publish the translations.

I am glad to learn that Sarat Chatterji's stories are going to be translated.[3] But are they not too difficult for rendering in English?

I believe that Macmillan are waiting to have your translation of 'Megh o Raudra' to be able to include it in the collection of my short stories they want to publish.[4] They seem to be particularly jealous of other publishers and I do not definitely know what is the range of their right over my writings published and unpublished.

I am getting ready for a lecturing tour in Texas. After it is over I shall be back to Europe in April.

Yours
Rabindranath Tagore

Source: MS original in Thompson Papers [Bodleian].

1 E. P. Thompson, *Alien Homage*, p. 47.
2 *Ibid.*, pp. 47–8.
3 E. J. Thompson mentioned his friendship with Sarat Chandra Chatterji [Chattopadhyay] in his letter to RT. In 1922, Oxford University Press published Chatterji's *Srikanta*, translated by Kshitish Chandra Sen and Theodosia Thompson, wife of E. J. Thompson; Thompson wrote an introduction to the book.
4 See letter 148.

163

To Charles Freer Andrews

By early February 1921, Tagore had abandoned hope of raising funds in New York and decided to concentrate on his fortnight's lecture tour of Texas, organised by James B. Pond.[1] His mood on the subject of fundraising, in this letter to C. F. Andrews, is more positive than in his letter of 24 January, possibly out of a sense of relief at no longer having to perform for the unknown rich in New York.

Hotel Algonquin, New York, [USA]
2 February 1921

My friend, after a break of three weeks, and sultriness of weary waiting your letters have come in a downpour and I cannot tell you how refreshing they are. I seem to be travelling across a desert and your letters are like weekly provisions dropped by some air service from cloudlands. They are expected and yet they have the element of surprise which belongs to the unexpected. I hungrily attack them and then fall upon extra portions supplied from your letters written to others. Your letters are delightful because you have [an] interest in details that are generally overlooked. The world is made beautiful by the unimportant [things] – they furnish this great picture with all its modulations of shades and tints. The important is like the sunshine, it comes from a great source – but the important composes the atmosphere of our life – it scatters the sun's rays, breaks it into colours and coaxes it into tenderness.

I do not like to raise your expectation too high – but I can say in a whisper that my meditation *mantram* will not be baffled, I can assure you it will bear golden fruit. If you had been with me in my pilgrim's progress it would have awakened in your heart a tremendous shock of respect for me at my persistence and vigour of shameless brutality in my pursuit of success. I have not the thin rag of decency left about my behaviour when I raise my arms towards the skyscrapers on the top floors of which dwell the Luckeswars of this country.[2] I am in grave danger of losing my reputation as a poet supremely worthless, but to compensate it I shall gain something which will satisfy my friends, though I have my doubts if it will ever come up to the towering heights of Nepal Babu's imagination.[3] However the prospect is bright and the birds of good omen are gathering over my head.

I am getting ready for my lectures, one of which is not yet finished. Its title is 'The poet's religion'.[4] I am sure its message will be accepted by my audience with gratitude.

I met some of my countrymen last night who are hatching revolution. There is something in their presence which hurts me and makes me realise more strongly than ever before that I am not for this. I seem to live in a different planet from theirs where the law of attraction is also different in its degree and character. Of one thing I feel sure, that they do not know what India truly is – they try to find their consolation by deluding themselves into thinking that India is exactly like the western countries.[5]

You have asked for my permission to abolish the matriculation class from our school. Let it go. I have no tenderness for it. In our classical literature it was the strict rule to give all dramas a happy ending. Our matriculation class has ever been the fifth act in our institution ending in a tragedy. Let us drop the curtain before that disaster gathers its forces.[6]

With love

Yours ever
Rabindranath Tagore

Source: MS original at Rabindra Bhavan, Shantiniketan.

1 RT appears to have earned $3,425.00 from eleven lecture dates; the maximum fee was $500 at Houston [RB].
2 Luckeswar is a bilingual pun: it means god (*iswar* in Bengali) of luck and also god of lakhs (a lakh equals 100,000 rupees). Luckeswar is also a character in RT's play *Sharadotsav* (Autumn Festival).
3 Nepal Babu: Nepal Chandra Ray, teacher at Shantiniketan. RT's affectionate irony suggests the yawning gap between the founder of Shantiniketan and the majority of his Bengali co-workers.
4 'The poet's religion', *MR*, July 1921, pp. 107–8.
5 See letter 154. It is somewhat surprising that RT was willing to meet any Indian revolutionaries, after the difficulties in which he had been placed through his contact with revolutionaries in the USA in 1916. (See letter 122 ff.)
6 The 1919 *Report of the Calcutta University Commission* noted:

> The boys from Bolpur are entered for the university matriculation examination as 'private students'. Sir Rabindranath Tagore and the members of his staff feel that it is important that this right be retained. Bolpur School, wishing to work out its own methods, has not applied to the university for recognition. (I, pt 1, 'Analysis of present conditions', p. 230)

There was constant tension at Shantiniketan between Tagore's educational ideals and the needs of students and parents for paper qualifications. In 1920, with RT absent, a vote on whether to retain the matriculation exam was taken among the staff, who split ten in favour of abolition and ten against abolition (C. F. Andrews to RT, 28 Dec. 1920 [RB]). Despite RT's lack of enthusiasm, the matriculation exam was retained, and recognition by Calcutta University was in due course applied for and given.

164

To Charles Freer Andrews

After the Texas lectures Tagore rested in Chicago, looked after by Harriet Moody. He was in a reflective mood, having finished with fundraising for the time being. A letter from C. F. Andrews indicating that he was feeling restless in Shantiniketan prompted some typically Tagorean introspection as to why he should harbour such a distracting desire as to found a university. The feelings he expresses in this letter help to explain his ambivalent attitude towards official British help for Visva-Bharati that surfaced in his letters to William Rothenstein in mid-1921 (letters 167 and 169) and disrupted their friendship.

315 East 23rd Street, Chicago, [USA]
26 February 1921

Dear friend,

I feel frightened at the Fuji-tive mood that seems to have come over you.[1] But my mouth is closed, for I have been playing the truant the last few months as I have been doing the best part of my life. But what fatality is this which pursues me, that when I am ready to come back to take my part in the last scene of a happy comedy you ring down the curtain and disappear! It seems that when I land in India Pearson will remain on this side of Atlantic and you on the other side of the Pacific, and the wind from the East and the wind from the West will both bring to my heart the wail of separation. I think I had some kind of premonition in my mind and was trying to secure you for myself for the full festival of my homecoming by inviting you to join us in our tour.[2] But we have all been entangled in the big enterprise of doing good to the world which unfortunately has such a large area that in its field of duty friends need the most powerful telescope to be distantly visible to one another. I have often wondered in my mind whether my path is the path of the good. When I came to this world I had nothing but a reed given to me which was to find its only value in producing music. I left my school, I neglected my work, but I played with the reed and I played on it 'in mere idle sport'. But all along I had my one playmate who also in his play produced music among leaves, in rushing water, in silence of stars, in tears and laughter rippling into lights and shadows in the stream of human life. While my companion was this eternal piper, this spirit of play, I was nearest to the heart of the world, I knew its mother tongue, and what I sang was caught up by the chorus of the wind and water and the dance master of life. But how came the schoolmaster in the midst of my dream world and I was foolish enough to accept his guidance? I laid aside my reed, I left my playground, where the infinite child is spending his eternity 'in mere idle sport'. In a moment I became old and carried the burden of wisdom on my back, hawking truths from door to door. But why have I been made to carry this burden, I ask myself over and over again, shouting myself hoarse in this noisy world where everybody is crying up his own wares? Pushing the wheelbarrow of propaganda from continent to continent, is this going to be the climax of a poet's life? It seems to me like an evil dream, from which I occasionally wake up in the dead of night and grope about in the bed asking myself in consternation, 'Where is my music?' It is lost. But I had no right to lose it, for I did not earn it with the sweat of my brow, it was a gift to me which I could deserve if I knew how to love it. You know I have said somewhere that 'God praises me when I do good but God loves me when I sing.'[3] Praise is a reward, it can be measured against the work you render, but love is above all rewards, it is measureless. The poet who is true to his mission reaps his harvest of love, but the poet who strays into the path of the good is dismissed with applause. So I am to found my International University – a great work! but I lose my little song – which loss can never be made up to me. How I wish I could find back my reed and be contemptuously ignored by the busy and the wise as a hopeless ne'er-do-well! When I know for certain that I shall never be able to go back to that sweet obscurity which is the birthplace of flowers and birdsongs I feel homesick. It is a world which is so near and yet so far away, so easy of access and yet so immensely difficult. Happiness we go on missing in our life because it is so simple.

With love

Ever yours
Rabindranath Tagore

Source: MS original at Rabindra Bhavan, Shantiniketan.

1 In RT's letters to Andrews there are frequent joking references to Andrews' tendency to take off from Shantiniketan for foreign parts at short notice; in 1915 he and W. W. Pearson left for Fiji in this way.
2 RT had earlier invited Andrews to join him and his party in Europe in the summer vacation of 1921 (RT to Andrews, 25 Dec. 1920 [RB]).
3 *Lekhan*, *RR*, XIV, p. 165.

165

To Charles Freer Andrews

By the beginning of 1921, Mahatma Gandhi was firmly in control of the Indian National Congress and was determined upon noncooperation with the Government at all levels of society. His call for students to boycott their schools and colleges was particularly effective. By the end of January 1921 virtually all the colleges in Calcutta had closed. Some of the students turned up at Shantiniketan where C. F. Andrews tried to enlist them and some of the Shantiniketan students in an attempt to apply Gandhi's ideas in Surul, the nearby village. They based themselves in Tagore's large house there (where Rathindranath had lived after first moving from Shelidah), but soon gave up the struggle; most succumbed to a virulent local form of malaria.[1]

On 31 January, Andrews wrote to Tagore in America:

> It will be quite impossible for you to follow the Noncooperation Movement at a distance. Even we, who are close at hand, have been taken by surprise again and again by it. The supreme danger is not so much destruction, as narrowness of aims. Mahatmaji's own mind is like that of an Ignatius Loyola. He is ready to sacrifice every single thing, in heaven and earth, to get the full moral equivalent for war and fight against iniquity in high places. But such concentration of forces has its own nemesis; and we sadly need a whole army of constructive workers.[2]

Andrews was deeply stirred by the emotions of the time, and his letters of late 1920 and early 1921 swing back and forth between support and criticism of Gandhi. 'The atmosphere was electrical and the spirit of sacrifice was in the very air we breathed ... I myself was carried away in the enthusiasm of the moment,' Andrews wrote a few years later, when editing Tagore's letters for publication.[3] His own letters – along with other reports from India, private and public – caused Rabindranath much heart-searching. Eventually, however, he came down against the Noncooperation Movement, on grounds that he gives in this letter to Andrews, commenting memorably, 'What irony of fate is this, that I should be preaching cooperation of cultures between East and West on this side of the sea just at the moment when the doctrine of noncooperation is preached on the other side?'

2970 Ellis Avenue, Chicago, [USA]
5 March 1921

Dear friend, lately I have been receiving more and more news and newspaper cuttings from India giving rise in my mind to a painful struggle that presages a period of suffering which is waiting for me. I am striving with all my power to tune my mood of mind to be in accord with the great feeling of excitement sweeping across my country. But deep in my being why is there this spirit of resistance maintaining its place in spite of my strong desire to remove it? I fail to find a clear answer and through my gloom of dejection breaks out a smile and voice saying, 'Your place is on the seashore of worlds, with children; there is your truth, your peace, and I am with you there.'[4] And this is why lately I have been playing with metres, with merest nothings. These are whims that are content to be borne away by the current of time, dancing in the sun and laughing as they disappear. But while I play, the whole creation is amused, for are not flowers and leaves never-ending experiments in metre, is not my God an eternal waster of time? He flings stars and planets in the whirlwind of changes, he floats paper boats of ages filled with his fancies on the rushing stream of appearance. When I tease him and beg him to allow me to remain his little follower and accept a few trifles of mine as the cargo of his paper boat, he smiles and I trot behind him catching the hem of his robe. But where am I among the crowd, pushed from behind, pressed from all sides? And what is this noise about me? If it is a song then my own *sitar* can catch the tune and I can join in the chorus, for I am a singer. But if it is a shout then my voice is wrecked and I am lost in bewilderment. I have been trying all these days to find a melody, straining my ear, but the idea of noncooperation, with its mighty volume of sound does not sing to me, its congregated menace of negation shouts. And I say to myself, 'If you cannot keep step with your countrymen at this great crisis of their history, never say that you are right and rest of them wrong; only give up your role as a soldier, go back to your corner as a poet, be ready to accept popular derision and disgrace.'

Rathi, in support of the present movement, has often said to me that the passion for rejection is a stronger power in the beginning than the acceptance of an ideal.[5] Though I know it to be a fact, I cannot accept it as a truth. We must choose our allies once for all, for they stick to us even when we might be glad to be rid of them. If we once claim strength from intoxication, then in the time of reaction our normal strength is bankrupt, and we go back again and again to the demon that lends us resources in a vessel whose bottom it takes away.

Brahma-vidya in India has for its object *mukti*, emancipation, while Buddhism has *nirvana*, extinction.[6] It may be argued that both have the same idea [under] different names. But names represent attitudes of mind, emphasise particular aspects of truth. *Mukti* draws our attention to the positive, and *nirvana* to the negative side of truth. Buddha kept silence all through his teachings about the truth of the *Om*, the *everlasting yes*, his implication being that by the negative path of destroying the self we naturally reach that truth. Therefore he emphasised the fact of *dukkha*, misery, which had to be avoided and the *Brahma-vidya* emphasised the fact of *ananda* which had to be attained. The latter cult also needs for its fulfilment the discipline of self-abnegation, but it holds before its view the idea of Brahma, not only at the end but all through the process of realisation. Therefore the idea of life's training was different in the Vedic period from that of the Buddhistic. In the former it was the purification of life's joy, in the latter it was the eradicating of it. The abnormal type of asceticism to which Buddhism gave rise in India revelled in celibacy and mutilation of life in all different forms. But the forest life of the *Brahmanas* was not antagonistic to the social life of man, but harmonious with it. It was like our musical instrument *tambura* whose duty is to supply the fundamental notes to the music to save it from going astray into discordance. It believed in *anadam*, the music of the soul, and its own simplicity was not to kill it but to guide it.

The idea of noncooperation is political asceticism. Our students are bringing their offering of sacrifices to what? Not to a fuller education but to noneducation. It has at its back a fierce joy of annihilation which in its best form is asceticism and in its worst form is that orgy of frightfulness in which human nature, losing faith in basic reality of normal life, finds a disinterested delight in unmeaning devastation, as has been shown in the late war and on other occasions which came nearer home to us. *No* in its passive moral form is asceticism and in its active moral form is violence. The desert is as much a form of *himsa* as is the raging sea in storm, they both are against life.[7]

I remember the day, during the Swadeshi Movement in Bengal, when a crowd of young students came to see me in the first floor of our Vichitra house. They said to me that if I ordered them to leave their schools and colleges they would instantly obey me. I was emphatic in my refusal to do so, and they went away angry, doubting the sincerity of my love for my motherland. Long before this ebullition of excitement, I myself had given a thousand rupees, when I had not five rupees to call my own, to open a *swadeshi* store and courted banter and bankruptcy.[8] The reason for my refusing to advise those students to leave their schools was because the anarchy of a mere emptiness never tempts me, even when it is resorted to as a temporary shelter. I am frightened of an abstraction which is ready to ignore living reality. These students were no mere phantoms to me; their life was a great fact to them and to the All. I could not lightly take upon myself the tremendous responsibility of a mere negative programme for them which would uproot them from their soil, however thin and poor that soil might be. The great injury and injustice which had been done to those boys who were tempted away from their career before any *real* provision was made, could never be made good to them. Of course that is nothing from the point of view of an abstraction which can ignore the infinite value even of the smallest fraction of reality. But the throb of life in the heart of the most insignificant of men beats in the unison of love with the hearthrob of the infinite. I wish I were the little creature Jack whose one mission was to kill the giant abstraction which is claiming the sacrifice of individuals all over the world under highly painted masks of delusion.

I say again and again that I am a poet, that I am not a fighter by nature. I would give everything to be one with my surroundings. I love my fellow beings and I prize their love. Yet I have been chosen by destiny to ply my boat there where the current is against me. What irony of fate is this, that I should be preaching cooperation of cultures between East and West on this side of the sea just at the moment when the doctrine of noncooperation is preached on the other side? You know that I do not believe in the material civilisation of the West, just as I do not believe the physical body. What is needed is the establishment of harmony between the physical and the spiritual nature of man, maintaining of balance between the foundation and superstructure. I believe in the true meeting of the East and the West. Love is the ultimate truth of soul; we should do all we can not to outrage that truth, to carry its banner against all opposition. The idea of noncooperation unnecessarily hurts that truth. It is not our hearth fire, but the fire that burns out our hearth.

While I have been considering the noncooperation idea one thought has come to me over and over again which I must tell you. *Bara Dada* and myself are zamindars, which means collectors of revenue under British Government.[9] Until the time comes when we give up paying revenue and allow our lands to be sold we have not the right to ask students or anybody else to make any sacrifice which may be all they have. My father was about to give up all his property for the sake of truth and honesty.[10] And likewise we may come to that point when we have to give up our means of livelihood. If we do not feel that that point has been reached by us then at least we should at once make ample provision out of our competency for others who are ready to risk their all. When I put to myself this problem the answer which I find is that by temperament and training all the good I am now capable of doing presupposes [a] certain amount of wealth. If I am to begin to earn my living, possibly I shall be able to support myself but nothing better than that. Which will mean not merely sacrificing my money but my mind. I know that my God may claim even that, and by the very reclaiming repay me. Utter privation and death may have to be my ultimate sacrifice for the sake of some ideals which represent immortality. But so long as I do not feel the call or respond to it myself how can I urge others to follow the path which may prove to be the path of utter renunciation? Let the individuals choose their own responsibility of sacrifice, but are we ready to accept that responsibility for them? Do we fully realise what it may mean in suffering or in evil? or is it a mere abstraction for us which leaves us untouched [by] all the concrete possibilities of misery [for] individuals? Let us first of all try to think [of] them as the nearest and dearest to us and then ask them to choose danger and poverty for their share [in] life.

With love,

Ever yours
Rabindranath Tagore

Source: MS original at Rabindra Bhavan, Shantiniketan; an edited version was published in *MR*, May 1921.

1 See Elmhirst, *Poet and Plowman*, p. 20.
2 Andrews to RT, 31 Jan. 1921 [RB].
3 Quoted in *Letters to a Friend* (C. F. Andrews ed.; London, 1928), p. 122.
4 See *Gitanjali* (60).
5 See Rathindranath Tagore, *Edges of Time*, pp. 62–4.
6 *Brahma-vidya*: the branch of learning imparting knowledge of God.
7 On these philosophical and religious concepts as understood by RT, see, for instance, his *Shantiniketan* lectures collected in *RR*, XIII–XVI; 'Dharma', *RR*, XIII, pp. 335–445; 'Brahma mantra', *RR(AS)*, II, pp. 183–94; 'Upanishad Brahma', *RR(AS)*, II, pp. 199–220.
8 See letter 31.
9 *Bara Dada*: Dwijendranath Tagore, eldest brother of RT, who was one of Gandhi's early supporters in Bengal. Aged over eighty in 1921, he was living in Shantiniketan.

10 Debendranath Tagore, father of RT, volunteered to surrender all his property in settlement of his father's debts after the crash of his father's company in the 1840s. See Dutta and Robinson, *Rabindranath Tagore*, pp. 30–1.

166

To (Sir) William Rothenstein

Tagore spent hardly a fortnight in Britain on his return from America; on 16 April he flew (his first flight) from London to Paris and began a tour of the Continent that would continue until he sailed for India in July 1921.

His university, Visva-Bharati, continued to preoccupy him; the issues it raised appear in many of his letters over the next year or two (for example letters 167, 169, 179 and 184), and so it is worth dwelling on their background at some length. On 9 April, while Tagore was in London, an editorial in the *Nation* entitled 'A league of spirit', captured the quality of the whole endeavour to perfection:

> While the whole world is at war, it is some comfort to hear even one voice, however still and small, persistently murmuring of peace. Amid the turmoil and shouting one may still catch the quiet words of an Indian pleading the cause of understanding, friendliness, and forbearance, as though they, and not devastating conflicts, were the most natural thing in the world. In such a spirit it is that Rabindranath Tagore has been moving, almost silently, from country to country, and from hemisphere to hemisphere, insinuating his conception of an International University . . . Suspected as a seditious agitator, dogged by Government spies, impugned by official detraction, or, at the best, scornfully tolerated as an impracticable dreamer, he has trodden the well-worn and dolorous path of the spirit.[1]

In Britain, his scheme had influential well-wishers: William Rothenstein, first and foremost, who was now principal of the Royal College of Art, Lord Carmichael, former governor of Bengal, Sir Michael Sadler, former chairman of the Calcutta University commission, and Edwin Montagu, who was still secretary of state for India. Tagore met Montagu at the House of Commons and discussed the scheme, in particular requesting him to grant permission for European professors from Germany and other former enemy countries to come to Shantiniketan. (The Indian government had recently passed a law forbidding Germans to visit India for five years.) Rabindranath already had in mind a thoroughly non-political German couple, Heinrich Meyer-Benfey and his wife, Helene Meyer-Franck, who had offered themselves and their entire library to Shantiniketan.[2]

The treatment of their case showed British official attitudes to Visva-Bharati in microcosm. Tagore wrote to the couple that '[Montagu] seemed sympathetic and promised me that he would write to the viceroy of India asking him to help me in this matter'.[3] Montagu did write to Lord Reading, but in a lukewarm manner and in terms that suggest he had not grasped the scope of Tagore's idea (he also misspelt the name of the German professor):

> [Tagore] has tried to enlist my sympathy in the establishment of an International University in India for the study of Oriental philosophy . . . A German disciple of his, named Frank Mayer, has promised to come to the university and to bring with him a

valuable philosophical library. He does not know whether he will be admitted because he is an enemy alien. I told Tagore that you had power to make exceptions.[4]

Prompted by the viceroy, officials looked into the matter. Many months later, passports for Meyer-Benfey and Meyer-Franck were refused. Tagore reacted indignantly to the couple in June 1922:

> It is such an utter piece of injustice to you and to ourselves to prevent you and your husband from coming to us that I cannot help believing that the obstacles will be removed before long. When I was in Europe I could not imagine that our mission which was to bring about union of the East with Europe in the field of intellectual cooperation could be thwarted by such an irrational spirit of political suspiciousness.[5]

For the time being, however, the ban remained; the two Germans never came to Shantiniketan, and their library remained in Europe.

Ever since the Swadeshi Movement of 1905, Tagore had known very well – as his friends in London, such as Rothenstein, either did not know or chose to downplay – that he and his institutions were treated with frank suspicion by civil servants, the intelligence service and the police in India.[6] In 1917, the chief of the British intelligence in the USA had warned the American president against Tagore; and during his visit to America in 1920–1 his efforts at fundraising were constantly dogged by allegations that in India he was anti-Government or worse – allegations that British representatives in the USA did nothing to dispel.[7] Apart from all this, Tagore was acutely conscious of the stifling mediocrity of the University of Calcutta and most other government-sponsored universities in India. It is understandable, therefore, that in 1921 Tagore should view the prospect of official sponsorship of his proposed university with his own doubts and suspicions.

Such deep-seated feelings, based on long and sometimes bitter experience, would shortly disrupt his friendship with William Rothenstein. But initially, as in this letter to Rothenstein, Tagore was in favour of official British sponsorship of Visva-Bharati.

Autour du Monde, 9 Quai du 4-Septembre,
Boulogne-sur-Seine, [France]
17 April 1921

Dear friend, my short career in the sky was unobscured by clouds and luminous with the April sunshine.[8] The only thing to which I could take objection was the deafening noise which followed me from shore to shore and made me glad to be back to the earth again where one has the choice of diluting all noise with silence as much as it is available.

Let me remind you of our conversation about the International University. It was decided that a committee should be formed in England which would help the committee in India about the selection of teachers and students belonging to Europe and about other matters which it would be more convenient for them to deal with. I hope it will be possible for you with the help of Mr Montagu, Lord Carmichael and other sympathisers to make a draft of rules and a list of names of those who will be likely to join us. I have reasons to hope that some oriental society in this country can be persuaded to represent us in France and work [on] our behalf. A considerable number of books have been gathered and sent to our library from here and I feel certain that I can count upon the sympathy and cooperation of some influential persons in this country.

I am afraid that I shall have to be extremely busy the few days that I spend in Paris, in fact, all through my tour in the Continent. But I shall be able to bear the strain knowing that my appeal will find response in all countries of Europe.

You will be glad to learn that the French translation of my *Home and the World* has, as I am told, gone through six editions within a very short time.[9]

Affectionately yours
Rabindranath Tagore

Source: MS original in Rothenstein Papers [Harvard]; letter published in Lago (ed.), *Imperfect Encounter*, pp. 279–80.

1 *Nation and Athenaeum*, 9 April 1921.
2 Meyer-Benfey was a philologist; Meyer-Franck translated some of RT's works into German (see letter 285). On 28 Feb. 1921, she wrote to RT:

> I firmly believe that of all the nations of Europe the soul of Germany is most akin to that of India and that these two countries must join in their work. The Germany of Bismarck lies thrown down, but the true Germany is the Germany of Kant and Goethe and Schiller and Kleist, and in this Germany you will find your ally [RB].

3 RT to Meyer-Franck, 20 April 1921 [copy at RB].
4 Montagu to Reading, 20 April 1921, quoted in Sanat Bagchi, 'Montagu, Rabindranath and Visva-Bharati', *VBQ*, *1*, Nos. 3 and 4, Nov. 1990–April 1991, p. 313.
5 RT to Meyer-Franck, 7 June 1922 [copy at RB].
6 See letter 44.
7 On the British intelligence advice, see letter 122. In July 1921, Leonard Elmhirst (who was of course English), while finishing up at Cornell University and preparing to join RT in Bengal, was constantly warned by American friends and colleagues, 'Isn't Tagore rather dangerous, isn't he a traitor, didn't he speak disparagingly of the British Government?' (Elmhirst to Dorothy Straight, 28 July 1921, quoted in Dutta and Robinson, *Rabindranath Tagore*, p. 432). Elmhirst commented wryly, 'Holy, holy, holy, Lord God Almighty.' Rathindranath Tagore, writing to Mayce Seymour about RT's visit to New York and the East Coast, remarked:

> After having been in America we began to realise the immense power that England exercises in that country. The financial control is astonishing. Political and cultural propaganda is constantly at work, very cleverly managed, so subtle and underground that it is difficult to fight against it or even to expose it . . . We found it safer to criticise the English in England than in America. Most of the rich are strongly, blindly pro-British. (30 March 1921 [copy at RB])

8 At the aerodrome, RT was asked, 'Is this your first flight, poet?' and he replied, 'The first of its kind' – which set everyone laughing. This story was told by W. B. Yeats in 1937 to Abinash Chandra Bose (see R. K. Das Gupta (ed.), *Rabindranath Tagore and W. B. Yeats: The Story of a Literary Friendship* (New Delhi, 1965), p. 23).
9 RT obviously meant 'impressions' not 'editions'. *The Home and the World* was also a major success in German translation at this time. It has been translated into the following European languages: Armenian, Czech, Danish, Dutch, English, Finnish, French, German, Greek, Hebrew, Hungarian, Italian, Polish, Portuguese, Rumanian, Russian, Serbo-Croat, Slovak, Slovenian, Spanish and Swedish.

167

To (Sir) William Rothenstein

Just a week after encouraging Rothenstein to form a board of trustees for Visva-Bharati, Tagore wrote again from France asking him not to. Coming to Paris and meeting French scholars seriously interested in his university idea seems to have precipitated his change of mind; and the esteem in which he was held in France restored his pride, bruised by Britain and America, and perhaps subtly encouraged him to speak his mind about British help.[1] For whatever reason, in a letter to C. F. Andrews he was blunt:

> Mr Montagu showed great sympathy and enthusiasm. Rothenstein proposed to form a board of trustees to help me in my work. But I have a suspicion in my mind that they want to kill my work in its infancy with the pelting of their help. At any rate they want to tame it and exhibit it with pride in their own menagerie. But it is needless to assure you that I am not going to allow my institution to be tied to the tow-boat of the India Office or any other influential body . . . The copy of the letter I am sending to Rothenstein will give you my attitude about our university.[2]

This letter is scarcely more diplomatic. Given his long and heartfelt respect for Rothenstein expressed in the past, Tagore must have felt extremely strongly on the subject to write to him in this vein. It is almost as if he thinks Rothenstein and others are planning to tie *him*, rather than his fledging institution, to an ICS-style 'steel frame'.

Autour du Monde, Boulogne-sur-Seine, [France]
24 April 1921

My dear friend, when I sent my appeal to western people for an International Institution in India I made use of the word 'University' for the sake of convenience. But that word not only has an inner meaning but outer associations in minds of those who use it, and that fact tortures my idea into its own rigid shape. It is unfortunate. I should not allow my idea to be pinned to a word like a dead butterfly for a foreign museum. It must be known not by a definition, but by its own life growth. I saved my Santiniketan from being trampled into smoothness by the steam roller of your education department. It is poor in resources and equipment but it has the wealth of truth that no money can ever buy. I am proud of the fact that it is not a machine-made article perfectly modelled in your workshop – it is our very own. If we must have a university it should spring from our own life and be sustained by it. You may say that such freedom is dangerous and that a machine will help to lessen our personal responsibility and make things easy for us. Yes, life has its risks and freedom its responsibility – and yet they are preferable for their own immense value and not for any other ulterior results. Now I am beginning to discover that it was more an ambition than an ideal which dragged me to the gate of the rich West. It must have been the vision of a big undertaking that lured me away from my seclusion in search of big means and big results. And I am being punished deep in my heart. So long I have been able to retain my perfect independence and self-respect because I had faith in my own resources and proudly worked within their sovereign limits. This is the first time in my life when I have come to the foreign door asking for help and cooperation. But such help has to be bought with a price that is ruinous, and the bird has to accept its cage if it must be fed with comfort and regularity. However, my bird must still retain its freedom of wings and not be turned into a sumptuous nonentity by any controlling agency outside its own living organism. I know that the idea of an International University is complex, but I must make it simple in my own way. I shall be content if it attracts round it men who have neither name nor worldly means, but who have the mind and faith, who are to create a great future with their dreams. Very likely I shall never be able to work in harmony with a board of trustees, influential and highly respectable, for I am a vagabond at heart. But the powerful people of the world, the lords of the earth, may make it difficult for me to carry out my work. I know it, and I had experience of it in connection with my Santiniketan and also in my tour in America. But am I afraid of failure? I am only afraid of being tempted away from truth in pursuit of success. The temptation assaults me occasionally I admit, but it comes from the outside atmosphere – my own abiding faith is in light and life and freedom, and my prayer is: 'Lead me from the unreal to Truth.'[3]

This letter of mine is only to let you know that I free myself from the bondage of help and go back to the great Brotherhood of the Tramp, who seem helpless, but who are recruited by God for his own army.

Ever yours
Rabindranath Tagore

Source: MS original in Rothenstein Papers [Harvard]; letter published in Lago (ed.), *Imperfect Encounter*, pp. 283–4.

1 Soon after his arrival, RT had talks with Romain Rolland and Sylvain Lévi, as well as meeting André Gide for the first time (on 24 April). Rolland was keenly interested in Tagore's university, and Lévi became the first foreign lecturer there, arriving at Shantiniketan in late 1921.
2 RT to Andrews, 24 April 1921 [RB].
3 *Brihadaranyaka Upanishad*, 1:3:28.

168

To Charles Freer Andrews

This letter makes an interesting contrast with letter 167 to William Rothenstein. Tagore had known C. F. Andrews and Rothenstein for about the same length of time, but the former friendship had an Indian setting, while the latter belonged to the West. There is a physical intimacy and a sense of personal concern in the relationship with Andrews lacking in the relationship with Rothenstein. There are also many gleams of subtle humour which were entirely typical of Tagore's conversation with friends but which unfortunately evaporated when he recorded his ideas in his essays and other writings in English. It was, in a way, just such human qualities that Rabindranath thought would be crushed if he accepted a conventional structure for his university.

Les Bergues, Geneva, [Switzerland]
2 May 1921

My friend,

It made me very anxious to hear that you fell ill after your strenuous work in Howrah.[1] There is one consolation in the delay in receiving letters owing to distance – it is the hope that the evil tidings have had the time to give place to good ones; and by this time I expect you have got over your illness. I am sure you need rest and change and this was why I had been hoping that you would be able to spend your summer vacation in Europe. I understand why it was not possible for you to accept my invitation and what a great sacrifice it was for you. There are times when one has to be utterly reckless, but it seems to me [that], for you, those times never come to their end. However, it makes me feel eager to come to your rescue and lure you away from your work and drag you into the delicious depth of neglectfulness of duty. I myself am dreaming for such a glorious opportunity and when it does come you may be sure I shall claim your companionship in my path of idleness strewn with unanswered letters, forgotten engagements and books with uncut pages. But we are fast getting into the vicious habit of keeping ourselves busy – before long we shall lose all taste for leisure, for refinements of laziness. Perhaps a day will come when I shall pine for doing my duty and my pious example will be quoted in textbooks on which I shall have to pass my examination in my next birth. Please know that I am serious. I am afraid of trampling down the limits of my arrested twenty-seventh year in sheer haste for keeping appointed time.[2] When one is not compelled to keep count of time one forgets to grow old, but when you must constantly consult your watch you are pushed into the twenty-eighth year directly you complete your twenty-seventh. Do we not have the example of Nepal Babu before our eyes?[3] He never respects time and therefore time fails to exact its taxes from him and he remains young. In this he is an inveterate noncooperative – he has boycotted the government of chronometry. And I want to register my name in the list of his *chelas*.[4] I shall strew my path of triumphant unpunctuality with shattered watch dials and miss my trains that lead to the terminus of mature age. But sir, what about my International University! It will have its time keeper – who is no respecter of the special privilege of some twenty-seventh year which has taken its *satyagraha* never to move forward. I am afraid it will toll me into the haze of hoariness across the grey years of fifty.[5] Friend, pray for my youth if it ever dies of old age brought about by self-imposed responsibility of ambitious altruism.

This is a beautiful country – dwelling place of gods invaded by man. This town is so dainty and clean with her river of limpid water and the sky unpolluted by the belching of smoke. The big towns like New York and London are vulgar because of their pretentious hugeness and perpetual hustle. In the streets here motor cars are few and crowds are leisurely. It is a town that seems to have been created in the atmosphere of vacation. And yet it is not sluggish or somnolent. Life here flows like its own bright river humming a song and breaking into merry peals of laughter.

I fervently hope you will not run away before I reach home. My mind is so full of plans which it must discuss with you or it will burst. The kernel of a plan is for carrying it out, but the most delicious part of it is the pulp which is merely for discussion. I must have you for the game of agreeing and disagreeing, putting down figures and then flinging [them] it into the wastepaper basket.

With love

Yours
Rabindranath Tagore

Source: MS original at Rabindra Bhavan, Shantiniketan.

1 Since March 1921 Andrews had been labouring as a mediator in an industrial dispute on the railways, which had been stoked up by the noncooperators for political purposes. At Howrah, the major rail terminus across the river from Calcutta, he had got the men back to work.

2 In 1887, when he was entering his twenty-seventh year, past 'the meridian of [my] twenties on [my] progress towards thirty', RT wrote to a friend that he felt uneasy because he was now approaching maturity and people would naturally expect from him 'fruits rather than green shoots'. And yet, 'when I shake my head it still feels full of frivolity, without even a kernel of philosophy' (RT to Shrish Chandra Majumdar, 27 July 1887, in *Glimpses of Bengal*, pp. 24–5/*Chhinnapatra*, p. 21).
3 Nepal Babu: Nepal Chandra Ray, teacher at Shantiniketan.
4 *chela*: disciple.
5 RT was about to turn sixty in May 1921.

169

To (Sir) William Rothenstein

William Rothenstein was, unsurprisingly, offended by Tagore's letter (167) asking him not to proceed with forming a board of trustees for his university. He replied with some warmth:

> I am neither a believer in machines, nor an Inspector of Schools, nor an enemy of freedom; yet you write as though I were all those things . . . I do not believe you to be a man of action and of affairs and I foresee many difficulties in your path if you take that dusty road . . . I felt, when you were here, that someone must stand first of all between you and the quick sympathy of your heart. You say you do not want the learned and the powerful; but likewise you do not want the camp-followers – of the arts and of the artists: these last are not the lowly and simple of heart. No, by no means . . .
>
> I still believe you need men of capacity and integrity to take certain responsibilities from your poet's shoulders. But you need not choose Europeans. Further, unpleasant and humiliating though it may be, the fact has to be envisaged that you cannot approach European scholars and leave English people unconsulted . . . That is why I suggested you should return here before actually inviting foreign guests to stay with you in India . . .
>
> But I realise that it is an ignoble thing to be sober when one's fellow guests are intoxicated . . . You must admit you have taken full advantage of your jug of wine! . . . So my blessing on your pilgrimage. No more sensible words shall come from me to irk your spirit.[1]

The remark about 'unconsulted English people' was a reference to the need to obtain visas for enemy aliens to visit India. Implicitly there was more to it than that, however. By turning to the Continent, and especially the just-defeated Germans, Tagore was at risk of alienating sympathy in Britain. As Rothenstein put it to Rathindranath Tagore twenty years later, just after his father's death: 'Only once was [our friendship] disturbed by a passing breeze, when, after the war, yr dear father preferred German to English support for his great scheme for a model university.'[2]

But Tagore's reply, written from the heart of Europe, shows that he was not to be shifted by such arguments.

Geneva, [Switzerland]
8 May 1921

My dear friend, when I was in America the British agency thwarted me in my appeal to the people for the proposed university. An American friend, who is struggling against obstacles to raise funds for this object has lately informed me that the British consul in his town is hindering him.[3] I am not trusted. How can I be certain that this mistrust that has nearly killed my mission by its antagonism will not kill it by its help? But possibly your point is that trying to be independent will not further my cause. That is true. It would be presumptuous for me to imagine that my project can thrive against suspicion lurking in the minds of British authorities. At the same time I feel strongly that it is far better to allow it openly to be strangled by that mistrust than to be fettered by its help. I remember your suggesting to me once in course of conversation that exuberant protestation of friendliness towards me on the part of the continental people of Europe was easy because they had no responsibility with regard to such demonstrations. You were right. For disinterested relationship is the only pure channel through which sympathy and cooperation can have a clear flow. Possibly these very people would also be wisely suspicious in a similar case where they had their own interest to consider. I have often heard that when the French people tried to be hospitable to our Indian soldiers in the late war the British officers in charge of them were alarmed. It was easier for the French to be human and grateful towards those foreigners who came to fight for them than for the British officers who had their own anxieties about these soldiers which were not purely human. Similarly when I, who belong to a subject race under British rule, am too warmly received in America or in other western countries, the British agency may feel uneasy – for their interest in me and my cause is not purely human and simple. Your contention is that the man who is sober in his mind accepts such facts as facts and deals with them accordingly and that it is a sign of moral drunkenness to be able to think that one can ignore them in pride of his self-sufficiency. But of one thing you may be certain, that I have a natural power of resistance in me against intoxication produced by praise, and my mind at the present moment is not in a dazed state of drunkenness. I am not in the least oblivious of the fact that the breath of official suspiciousness can blight in a moment my cherished scheme. But I have already told you in my last letter that I try to follow the teaching of [the *Bhagavad*] *Gita* according to which all idealism should spurn to seek [its] value in success, but only in truth. So long as my motive is true, my method is honest and the process of my work open to the view of all comers from all countries I shall not be ashamed of the meagreness of result, poorness of appearance, or afraid of an utter failure at the hands of a ruling power which would hesitate to allow us freedom for giving expression to our higher nature.

With love to you all

Ever yours
Rabindranath Tagore

Source: MS original in Rothenstein Papers [Harvard]; letter published in Lago (ed.), *Imperfect Encounter*, pp. 285–7.

1 Rothenstein to RT, 28 April 1921, in Lago (ed.), *Imperfect Encounter*, pp. 284–5.
2 Rothenstein to Rathindranath Tagore, 9 Aug. 1941 [RB].
3 The friend was probably Edwin H. Lewis (1866–1938) of the Lewis Institute, Chicago (see Lago (ed.), *Imperfect Encounter*, pp. 78–9). There are letters from Lewis to RT and his son, explaining his inability to persuade the wealthy that Visva-Bharati would be effective and that RT was not anti-British [RB]. A

detailed account of similar hindrance by a British official in New York in 1925 is given in Sanat Bagchi, 'The poet and the Raj', *VBQ, 50*, Nos 1–4, May 1984–April 1985, pp. 96 ff. This article shows a wide range of attitudes to RT and Shantiniketan among British officials, but it is probable that the director of the Indian Government's Intelligence Bureau was offering a typical opinion when he wrote in 1925 that 'it is, of course, well known that ... [RT] resigned his knighthood, becoming to all intents and purposes, a non-cooperator and a consistent opponent of Government'.

170

To Count Hermann Keyserling[1]

Tagore's visit to Germany in June 1921 was a sensation, even a phenomenon; during 1921–2 his books sold in huge numbers, as they had done in the USA in 1916–17 (more than they had ever done in Britain).[2] The high points were his visits to Berlin, Munich and to the School of Wisdom run by Count Hermann Keyserling at Darmstadt.

Keyserling enjoyed a high reputation in post-war Germany as a philosopher. He had first met Tagore in Jorasanko in 1912, while on the world tour that produced his best-known book, *The Travel Diary of a Philosopher* (J. Holroyd Reece trans.; London, 1927). There he wrote of him: 'Never perhaps have I seen so much spiritualised substance of soul condensed into one man.'[3] During the 'Tagore Week' at Darmstadt, Keyserling acted as a very able interpreter between Tagore and the German-speaking crowd come to ask questions of Rabindranath and listen to his discourse.[4]

Keyserling failed, however, in his more general aim: to act as Tagore's conduit to all Germany, and to attract some of the best German writers of the day to Darmstadt. In a letter to Tagore's son, Keyserling claimed: 'Very likely you will feel your Darmstadt time so well employed that you will stay on here much longer than you [have] thought of so far, for most probably most people of importance are going to come here to show their reverence to your great father.'[5] But Tagore did not want to be monopolised, as he makes clear in this letter to Keyserling.

Streit's Hotel, Hamburg, [Germany]
20 May 1921

Dear Count Keyserling,

I have read the letters you wrote to Mr Bomanji and to my son.[6] I fully appreciate your kind wish to spare me the trouble of unnecessary travelling and the strain of meeting strangers. But it cannot be helped, for it is part of my mission. I should never forgive [myself] if I tried to economise my effort and restrict my movement within a too limited range. I have already been in some other countries of Europe where I have received generous welcome and freely given myself to them. I am humble in my estimate of my own worth and the only claim I have upon my fellow beings is the claim of love which I feel for them. My whole heart shrinks from the idea of raising a special platform for myself in order to receive homage from the people and play the part of a teacher to them who have any regard for me; and I implore you not to create a situation which will be against my nature. Though a stranger I have a great admiration and sympathy for your people, and as I am only to be for a short time in this country, all that I can hope to do is freely to make my general feeling known in every place where

The founding of a university 271

I am able to go. It will be wrong for me to be narrowly exclusive in my selection of places, parties or friends, which, to be fair, needs experience of long acquaintance. I give you my idea of the press notice which should go to the papers in the following paragraph.[7] It should have nothing in it in its reference to me which would make me blush or make it appear that I identify myself with only one institution in this country thus giving valid reason for annoyance to others. I am sure you will understand my scruples and help me, in this my first visit to Germany, in establishing my relationship with your people in consonance with my nature.

With my kindest regards to Countess Keyserling and yourself.

Very sincerely yours,
Rabindranath Tagore

Source: MS copy at Rabindra Bhavan, Shantiniketan; letter published in Kämpchen, *Rabindranath Tagore*, pp. 76–7.

1 Count Hermann Alexander Keyserling (1880–1946): social philosopher and writer.
2 By Sept. 1922, 800,000 copies of Tagore's works in German were said to have been sold (Dutta and Robinson, *Rabindranath Tagore*, p. 439). Kurt Wolff, his German publisher, gave a similar figure (Kurt Wolff, *Kurt Wolff: A Portrait in Essays and Letters* (Michael Ermarth ed.; Chicago, 1991), p. 118). Wolff also gave perhaps the most truly sensational report of the visit, given that he was a shrewd and cosmopolitan man, in no sense credulous. After a long talk with RT in Munich, Wolff left the room so that his author might rest, at his request. Then he realised that he had inadvertently left a notebook in the room and he quietly returned to fetch it:

> I saw – although I could not believe what I was seeing – that Tagore had remained in the same position in which he had conversed for hours, with his large, beautiful eyes wide open. I saw *him*, but *he* did not see me, even though I was less than ten yards away. I gazed at him for a long time and grasped the fact that his open eyes were seeing nothing, not the room, nor me, nor the trees ... Here was a man such as you or I, a member of the species *Homo sapiens* and not a ghost or a magician, who could draw energy from mysterious sources inaccessible to westerners. Where was the Rabindranath Tagore of the preceding hours, where had he withdrawn to? Had he descended to the mothers of Goethe's *Faust*, or was he absorbed in the pure contemplation of God? He was in some infinitely remote place, where no one could or should try to follow him. (Wolff, *Kurt Wolff*, p. 120)

3 Keyserling, *Travel Diary*, p. 335.
4 Kurt Wolff attended the Tagore Week at Darmstadt. Much later he wrote:

> A greater contrast in personality than that between Tagore and Keyserling would be hard to imagine. Tagore's stature lay in the complete identity between his teachings and his own self, in the harmonious purity of his personality. Keyserling's importance was based on his high intelligence and rare ability to absorb the ideas of others with immense speed and to explain them to others, frequently in clearer, more precise, and more comprehensible language than that used by their originators. Tagore, although disclaiming to be a philosopher, epitomised in his attitude our ideas of what a philosopher is or should be. Keyserling, the self-declared philosopher, gave precisely the opposite impression to those who knew him and were familiar with his intensely emotional attitudes and alcoholic instability. What most impressed one in contacts with Tagore was his ability to remain silent and to listen, whereas a dialogue with Keyserling was a virtual impossibility; he overwhelmed his partners, who could not get in a word, with a ceaseless cascade of talk. Thus for me, as doubtless for many others present, encounters between the two served as a distressing example of the differences between East and West and were painful to witness. (Wolff, *Kurt Wolff*, p. 123)

5 Keyserling to Rathindranath Tagore, 18 May 1921, in Kämpchen, *Rabindranath Tagore*, p. 75.
6 S. R. Bomanji accompanied the Tagore party. See letter 238.
7 The press notice was as follows:

> At the School of Wisdom a Tagore Week is going to take place between 5–20th (the precise dates will be published later on) where those who have love for his writings and sympathy for his work will have the opportunity to meet the Indian Poet Rabindranath Tagore and listen and talk to him,

for which purpose the quiet rooms of the school and beautiful gardens of the Grand Duke of Hessen will be available. During his period of stay in Darmstadt one or more lectures from him may be expected. (Quoted in Kämpchen, *Rabindranath Tagore*, p. 77)

171

To Thomas Sturge Moore

The translation of Tagore's works and the problems arising from translation were the common theme in Tagore's letters to Thomas Sturge Moore. In 1913, his wife Marie Sturge Moore, with the approval of Tagore and W. B. Yeats, had received permission to translate *The Crescent Moon* into French. This had upset André Gide, who wanted to translate it himself. Gide withdrew but then the war intervened and killed the project. When it revived in 1920, Gide, as the literary adviser of the publisher (Gallimard/Nouvelle Revue Française), pronounced Marie Sturge Moore's translation mediocre and unpublishable, probably partly in the hope of obtaining the right to translate the book himself. It was only at the personal insistence of Tagore, and after some modification of the translation, that it finally appeared, ten years after Marie Sturge Moore did the work, in 1924, under the title *La Jeune Lune*.[1]

In this letter Tagore, basking in the appreciation of several European nations, shows himself only partly aware of the French publishing situation of his book. He does not seem to have understood Gide's desire to take over the translation.

Grand Hotel, Stockholm, [Sweden]
24 May 1921

Dear Sturge Moore

The rate of my pilgrim's progress through the European countries has been very rapid and owing to this I got your letter only this morning.

While trying to negotiate with some publishers in Paris about French translations of my works I came to know from Macmillan that by an agreement they had given to the *Nouvelle Revue* people the sole right to publish the French translations of all my writings. I have been told that André Gide is their advisor and my works are in his hands either for translation or for revision when translated by some other authors. I suppose he is too proud to submit his alterations for final approval of translators. Do you know Gide personally? In that case it would greatly simplify the matter if you write to him direct and come to some understanding with him. I have no freedom whatever about this. My part in the whole affair is the most insignificant one of merely being the author of the original book.

A copy of *The Wreck* has lately been sent to me by my publishers and I glanced through the pages while travelling in the railway train. I felt that the translator, who is an Englishman, not having an intimate acquaintance with Bengali language had missed most of the subtleties of expression and modulations of style of the original and has made his translation somewhat featureless and dull. In places it seems almost childish and blunt and what had the delicacy of grace in Bengali [has] been reduced to anaemic colourlessness. But I suppose I have no right to complain, for I am convinced that I myself in my translations have done grave injustice to my own work. My English is like a frail boat – and to save it from an utter disaster I had to jettison most part of its cargo. But the cargo being a living one it has been mutilated: which is a literary crime that carries its own punishment.[2]

My experience of the continental countries of Europe has been most delightful and I only regret that the seven barren months that I spent in America cannot be refunded to me by my destiny for my use in the present tour.[3]

I should very much like to see you before I leave for India, but I am sure it will not be possible. So I bid you farewell. Give my kindest regards to Mrs Sturge Moore.[4]

Very sincerely yours
Rabindranath Tagore

Source: MS original in Sturge Moore Papers [London].

1 See Michael Tilby, 'Gide et Tagore', in Patrick Pollard (ed.), *André Gide et l'Angleterre* (London, 1986), pp. 71–2.
2 See letter 147, addressed to the translator of *Naukadubi* (*The Wreck*), J. G. Drummond.
3 RT actually spent less than five months in the USA.
4 Marie Sturge Moore (1872–1957). On her relationship with Thomas Sturge Moore, see Sylvia Legge, *Affectionate Cousins: T. Sturge Moore and Marie Appia* (Oxford, 1980).

172

To Charles Freer Andrews

When Tagore lectured at Berlin University in early June 1921, there were 'scenes of frenzied hero worship', a London newspaper reported. 'In the rush for seats many girl students fainted and were trampled on by the crowd.'[1] The wife of the British ambassador in Berlin tried to attend and could hardly get into the street, let alone the hall, so great was the crush.

At Darmstadt, the reaction to the 'Tagore Week' was deeply gratifying to Rabindranath. He wrote to Thomas Sturge Moore from there on 14 June:

> Of one's fame one can never be sure, but homage of love offered in return for some deeper satisfaction of soul can be trusted . . . Such love has been brought to me in generous abundance, and I go back home, my memory laden with the most precious treasure that I could covet. Time is short, and nothing else is of value but the consciousness that one has lived for some deep moments and helped some others to live.[2]

Undoubtedly, Tagore had touched even the most sophisticated Germans, which explains the aura around his name that is still faintly visible in Germany today. In the early 1960s, Kurt Wolff, Tagore's publisher, who knew almost all the major German writers of the time, analysed his feelings about Tagore in a fascinating essay:

> It is difficult to describe my first impressions of him without sounding gushing or overdramatic . . . What I experienced during this first encounter with Tagore had nothing to do with the question of whether his literary work made him a writer of world stature. This was a question to which I gave hardly any thought at all, either on this day or on those that followed. I was overcome instead by the unforgettable and

profound impression which left me convinced that this man was completely and utterly uncorrupted and genuine, a man from a distant world, whose being included a dimension which we westerners lacked.[3]

While it is true that, by contrast, many German writers and intellectuals kept their distance from Tagore and remained indifferent or privately dismissive, the dominant note of this visit and subsequent visits to Germany was one of sincere admiration.[4] On Tagore himself, the homage had the effect of crystallising his suspicions and resentments regarding the British attitude to his university. This letter to C. F. Andrews, written from Darmstadt, pulls no punches.

Neues Palais, Darmstadt, [Germany]
10 June 1921

My friend, in Darmstadt they have a gathering of people from all parts of Germany to meet me. We have our meeting in the archduke of Hesse's garden where my audience bring before me their questions, I give them my monologues in answer and Count Keyserling translates them into German for those who cannot follow my English. Yesterday I reached this place and in the afternoon we had our first meeting. The first question put to me by a Canadian German was, What is the future of this scientific civilisation? After I had answered him he again asked me, How is the problem of over-population to be solved? After my answer, I was asked to give them some idea about the true character of Buddhism. These three subjects fully occupied two hours. It is delightful to feel the earnestness of these people, they have the habit of mind to think [out] the deeper problems of life, they deal seriously with ideas. In India in our modern schools we receive ideas from textbooks for the purpose of passing examinations. Besides that our modern schoolmasters are [Englishmen] and they of all the western nations, are the least susceptible to ideas. They are good, honest and reliable, but they have a vigorous excess of animal spirit that seeks for its exercise in racing, fox hunting, cricket and boxing [matches] and offers stubborn resistance to all contagion of ideas.[5] Therefore our English education does not inspire our minds – we do not realise that ideas are necessary to enable us to live a true life – we do not have a genuine enthusiasm for ideals. We are losing our gift of aspiration, which is the gift of soul. Our principal object and occupation are going to be the dissipations of politics whose goal is success, whose path is the zigzag of compromise; which in every country has lowered the standard of morality, given rise to a perpetual contest of lies and deceptions, cruelty and hypocrisy and national habit of vaingloriousness. Germany today has received a violent check in her political ambition which has produced almost a universal longing in this country to seek for spiritual resources in man in place of external success. Germany seems to have set out on a spiritual voyage to East, to the land of sunrise – and, in spite of her dire poverty, is not merely thinking of the spinning wheel and some new move in the political game of gambling but of the achievement of spiritual freedom which gives us power to soar above vicissitudes of circumstances. The other day I met the British ambassador in Berlin. While alluding to the enormous appreciation of my works in Germany he expressed his feeling of gratification at the possibility of my supplying some philosophy which may bring consolation to these people. He was glad, I am sure, from his British point of view. He thought that philosophy was a drug which would lull the restless activity of the German nation into sleep affording the victors a better security in their enjoyment of material benefits. He would gladly concede the possession of soul and God to these unfortunate people only keeping for the share of his own nation the sole possession of worldly goods. He smiled up his sleeves and thought his people were going to be the gainers in this bargain. Well, let them laugh and grow fat; only let us have the good sense not to envy them.[6]

Two more letters and then we meet – but these last days are slow, they bear on their back the burden of the fourteen months of my exile which they will throw into the water at the landing of Bombay harbour.

With love

Ever yours
Rabindranath Tagore

Source: MS copy at Rabindra Bhavan, Shantiniketan.

1 *Daily News*, 3 June 1921.
2 RT to Sturge Moore, 14 June 1921 [London].
3 Wolff, *Kurt Wolff*, pp. 118, 120.
4 See Dutta and Robinson, *Rabindranath Tagore*, p. 235.
5 This statement, when published, offended E. J. Thompson: 'Though one understands the superficial truth of this judgement, this is the voice of extreme exasperation' (E. J. Thompson, *Rabindranath Tagore*, p. 265). But even Goldsworthy Lowes Dickinson admitted that 'the English in India are of all the English the least intellectual and the least interested in ideas' (*Essay*, p. 28). And Sturge Moore, replying to RT's letter from Darmstadt, said candidly: 'I am glad that you should receive so much encouragement and satisfaction from the European nations; most of them are very much better educated and more open to ideas than we are' (1 July 1921 [RB]). One feels that if E. J. Thompson had himself made such a remark as RT's, as he often did in private letters, he would have considered it fair comment.
6 On the reaction to Tagore of Viscount D'Abernon, the British ambassador in Berlin, see Dutta and Robinson, *Rabindranath Tagore*, p. 234. Since D'Abernon was a friend of Edwin Montagu, the secretary of state for India (who had given RT a letter of introduction to D'Abernon), the encounter must have hardened RT's determination not to take official British support for Shantiniketan.

173

To Edward John Thompson

Tagore returned to Bengal in mid-July. His immediate preoccupation was political: to decide how he should respond to Gandhi's Noncooperation Movement. But of course he remained interested in literary work, both in Bengali and in English translation. This letter to E. J. Thompson repeats, even more firmly than in his February letter to Thompson (162), Tagore's growing conviction that translation into a language should be done by native-speakers of that language.

Santiniketan, [West Bengal, India]
5 August 1921

Dear Thompson

You are right in your diagnosis. I become acutely conscious of cracks and gaps in my translations and try to cover them up with some pretty designs that may give them an appearance of wholeness. The moral is, I should never have handled your language. However, as you are willing we shall try to do some reparation before it is too late. This year is going to be a very busy year for me, but I hope some time in the cold season it will be possible for me to meet you.

Yours
Rabindranath Tagore

Source: MS original in Thompson Papers [Bodleian].

174

To Edward John Thompson

During August and September 1921, as a result of various public speeches he gave in Calcutta on noncooperation, Tagore was subject to strong criticism by Bengalis.[1] His vision of international cooperation was in flagrant contradiction to Gandhi's rousing call. Rabindranath expected the attacks, but they naturally left him in a mood of depression.

In the meantime, E. J. Thompson's short study, *Rabindranath Tagore: His Life and Work*, was published in Calcutta in 1921. (His major study, *Rabindranath Tagore: Poet and Dramatist*, which grew out of this earlier one, appeared in Britain in 1926.) Though Thompson was not satisfied with the book, he sent a copy to its subject, who read it almost immediately and responded with this fascinating letter.

Santiniketan, [West Bengal, India]
20 September 1921

Dear Thompson

I have just received your book dealing with myself. I believe it is my sensitiveness born of my egotism which makes me shrink from attending to any discussions concerning me. But I have read your book all through. I am sure you have tried to be fair in your estimate of my works. About the comparative merits of my individual productions I myself am undecided though I have my preferences with which I never expect my readers always to agree. In fact as a critic of my own writings my ideas do not often coincide with those of Ajit.[2]

All along my literary career I have run against the taste of my countrymen, at least those of them who represent the vocal portion of my province. It has hardly been pleasant to me, but it has had the effect of making me reconciled to my mental loneliness. In the West – for some little while in England and lately in the continental countries of Europe – the recognition which I met with came to me with a shock of surprise. When a poet's life's works are accepted by his fellow beings it gives him a sense of intellectual companionship with his readers which is precious. But it has a great danger of growing into a temptation – and I believe, consciously and unconsciously I have been succumbing to it with regard to my western readers. But I have this paradox in my nature that when I begin to enjoy my success I grow weary of it in the depth of my mind. It is not through any surfeit of it, but through something in it which hurts me. Reputation is the greatest bondage for an artist. I want to emancipate my mind from its grasp not only for the sake of my art, but for the higher purposes of life, for the dignity of soul. What an immense amount of unreality there is in literary reputation, and I am longing – even while appreciating it like a buffalo the luxury of its mud bath – to come out of it as a *sanyasi*, naked and aloof. A gift has been given to me – this great world – which I can truly enjoy when I am simple and natural. I am looking back to those days of my youth when I had easy access into the heart of this universe – and I believe I shall yet again recover my place there when I am able to sever my mind from the attraction of the literary world which with its offer of rewards tries to standardise creative visions according to criterions distractingly varied and variable.

You have spared yourself no trouble in your attempt to understand me, and I am sure your book is the best one that has yet appeared about myself.[3] I must thank you for this – at the same time I wish I could altogether lose the memory of my fame as a poet.

Yours
Rabindranath Tagore

[PS] In answer to your note just arrived: Surul is a village about two miles away from Shantiniketan where I have a garden containing a building.[4]

The metrical forms in *Gitali* are the natural outcome of the structure of music which I follow in my songs.[5] I shall explain it to you when we meet.

Source: MS original in Thompson Papers [Bodleian].

1 The two most important lectures were 'Shikshar milan' (*Shiksha* (rev. edn, 1397 [1990]), pp. 180–98), delivered on 15 and 18 Aug. 1921, and 'Shatyer ahban' (*RR*, XXIV, pp. 320–40), delivered on 29 Aug. They appear in English translation as 'The unity of education' and 'The call of truth', *TUM*, pp. 231–51 and 252–73.
2 Ajit Kumar Chakravarty, Shantiniketan teacher and literary critic, died in 1918. Thompson told RT in his reply: 'You [i.e. Bengalis] have no criticism worth wasting a rushlight on, so far as I can find, after much enquiry, except your own. Only gusts of prejudice . . . I discovered some time back . . . that I overrated Ajit as a critic. He symbolises too much' (Thompson to RT, 22 Sept. 1921 [RB]).
3 To this doubtful compliment, Thompson responded: 'I am nowise elated by your saying that it is the best book about you. It might easily be that, and yet be damned bad' (*ibid.*).
4 That Thompson did not know about Surul by late 1921 indicates his lack of familiarity with both Shantiniketan and one of RT's main non-literary interests. Shortly after this letter was written, Surul became the site of RT's 'institute for rural reconstruction'.
5 '*Gitali*, like so much of [RT's] work, must be judged simply as word-music' (E. J. Thompson, *Rabindranath Tagore*, p. 229).

175

To Prashanta Chandra Mahalanobis[1]

When Rabindranath wrote to E. J. Thompson about his study of Tagore (letter 174), he tried, naturally enough, to be tactful. But when he wrote to his friend Prashanta Chandra Mahalanobis, who was also Thompson's closest Bengali adviser, he was much franker in his criticism.[2] And there is no doubt that Tagore was right: in 1921, Thompson knew neither sufficient Bengali to read all of Tagore's important work properly nor was he sufficiently acquainted with Bengali life (or Tagore's life) to understand the full import of the work he did read. Tagore was particularly perceptive in sensing Thompson's tendency to make the evidence fit his preconceptions, which were often wrong.

This is not to underestimate the sincerity and hard labour of Thompson in unsympathetic conditions, but it is to recognise, now that the protagonists are long dead and half a century has passed since the end of the British Raj, that E. J. Thompson had some crippling limitations both as a literary critic of Bengali and as biographer of Tagore. As a result his major study of Tagore is primarily important as a historical document, for the quality of some of its translations and as a source of quotations from his interviews with Tagore, rather than as an assessment of a literary figure and human being that has stood the test of time.

[Shantiniketan, West Bengal, India]
[September? 1921]

Kalyaniyeshu

I have read Thompson's book now. He has worked hard and read much in order to write it, and so it is better than any other book about me. However that is not such a great thing.[3] Other books should be entirely discarded.

But while reading it I found myself constantly thinking – the way the sahib describes the atmosphere of my life and works is a construct of his own preconceptions and lack of knowledge. And atmosphere is a vital element in a person's life. Unless one is an artist one cannot describe atmosphere properly, for it is something very delicate. The collecting and assembling of a few opinions and available materials produces a structure that hides the real person. And then, in matters of literary judgement Thompson relies heavily on Ajit. Ajit's drawback was that he could not function without a theory – whether an existing theory or one he had invented. He was not a leader in the area of literary perception; hence his inability to grasp *Kshanika*.[4]

All in all, Thompson's book will be a very convenient resort for those of my countrymen wishing to abuse me as foreigner. And yet that idea is essentially not at all accurate. My own conviction is that I was the first to introduce the land of Bengal to Bengalis as a subject fit for literature – neither Michael nor Nabin Sen nor Bankim did that.[5] I could do it because the family I was born into did not detach my mind from my country. I never let myself become entangled in the usual conventions and rituals; and because I remained a loner by nature, I was able to associate freely with everyone. Thompson seems to me to exaggerate my isolation; he does not grasp my associations. This is why he makes too much of my 'unpopularity' and fails to understand that in spite of the opposition to me my country has accepted me almost unawares. He should have seen the crowd at my lectures.[6] The general impression his book leaves on the reader's mind is a superficial one that is to a great extent incorrect. I feel very tired – but work must continue.

Snehashakta
Shri Rabindranath Thakur

Source: MS original at Rabindra Bhavan, Shantiniketan; published in *Desh*, 9 Jaishtha 1382 [24 May 1975], pp. 253–4.

1 Prashanta Chandra Mahalanobis (1893–1972): statistician, who in 1931 founded the Indian Statistical Institute in Calcutta and in 1933 *Sankhya: The Indian Journal of Statistics*; professor of physics (and latterly principal), Presidency College, Calcutta, he was actively involved in post-Independence government planning. From 1921 to 1932, he was general secretary, Visva-Bharati; in 1921 he framed the constitution of Visva-Bharati. He also travelled with RT several times on his foreign tours. Though undoubtedly a clever man, Mahalanobis was not notably original. See the description of his visit to Surul in Elmhirst, *Poet and Plowman*, pp. 158–9.
2 See 'Nationalism: and Prasanta Mahalanobis' in E. P. Thompson, *Alien Homage*, pp. 69–88.
3 This remark may or may not have been an echo of Thompson's own remark to RT (see letter 174, n. 3), depending on whether or not RT received Thompson's letter before writing to Mahalanobis (letter 175 is undated).
4 'In *Kshanika* [The Momentary One], I first found my language,' RT told E. J. Thompson in an interview. 'I first realised the beauty and music of the colloquial speech . . . I felt I could use absolutely any word I chose . . . There had been nothing like it in our literature before. But now we are flooded with it.' Ajit Chakravarty, RT said, 'misunderstood *Kshanika*. He was too metaphysical, like so many of my people. In *Kshanika*, there is merely my enjoyment in the creation of forms – that is what he could not understand. There is no thought, no doctrine, no subject – simply enjoyment' (E. J. Thompson, *Rabindranath Tagore*, p. 175). See Tagore, *Selected Poems* (William Radice trans.), pp. 66–7.
5 Michael Madhusudan Dutta (1824–73) wrote epic poetry based chiefly on the Indian epics; Nabin Sen (1874–1909) followed in the tradition of Michael, but wrote of more recent events such as the battle of Plassey; Bankim Chandra Chatterji [Chattopadhyay] (1838–94) sometimes dealt with the contemporary period, but was basically a writer of romance, the so-called Scott of Bengal. None of these writers used colloquial Bengali speech. See also RT's comment on 'reality' in literature in letter 65.
6 RT presumably meant the lectures against noncooperation he had given in Calcutta in Aug. 1921.

176

To Mahadev Desai[1]

Mahadev Desai, the private secretary and close associate of Mahatma Gandhi, had accompanied him to Calcutta in early September as part of Gandhi's (unsuccessful) effort to draw Tagore into the Noncooperation Movement. There he had talked with Tagore about the meaning of the *Isha Upanishad*. In this letter, at Desai's request, he explicates what he said. It is a brief discourse on what he had concisely described in his autobiography as 'the subject on which all my writings have dwelt: the delight of attaining the infinite within the finite'.[2]

Shantiniketan, [West Bengal, India]
29 September 1921

Dear Mahadeo,

First, let me make a confession – I have lost your letter – or very likely I took such a special care of it that it is not available even to me. However, I remember you asked me in your letter to explain to you the talk I had with you about *Isha Upanishad*. For some time I have been extremely busy and therefore I have no choice but to be brief.

Isha Upanishad has, from human point of view, divided truth into two aspects: one dealing with life and another with immortality. The characteristic note of this *Upanishad* is in the emphasis it lays upon the importance of both these aspects, [neither] of which should be separated from the other. *Avidya*, which is the cult of the finite, deals with life – and according to *Isha Upanishad* man should strive to live his full term of life in order to perform his karma. For human beings, life is not merely a physiological process, but it is fulfilment of his karma. True karma is not a service of activities generated by blind impulse of instincts or appetites. Karma, which gives meaning to our life, cannot be performed in ignorance of laws of truth – physical and moral. When through the help of *avidya*, the science of the finite, our rational and moral life reaches its fulfilment then it is saved. The life lived in pursuance of mere animal needs, guided by a superficial and empirical knowledge of this world, is death for man. On the contrary, the life that has [been] perfected through enlightened karma – which is not fixed forms of ritualism, or unthinking conformity to customs, but which represents in its varied activities man's reason, and will, and power of aesthetic enjoyment – paves the path towards the spiritual realisation of the infinite. For the infinite is nothing negative – it is not an emptiness that can be reached through an absolute elimination of the finite, but in it the finite has its ultimate meaning.[3] And therefore according to the *Isha Upanishad*, *avidya* and *vidya* both have to be perfected and harmonised. The cult of the finite exclusively pursued leads us to no final goal and yet it gives us something which is concrete, but the cult of the infinite excluding the finite is an abstraction, it is an illimitable abyss of nihilism. The East in the modern time has been beaten in the race of life, because it has neglected to cultivate the science of the finite, and the West is being driven into conflict of passions and unmeasuring multiplication of things because it has lost its respect for the cult of the infinite. The salvation of humanity lies in the meeting of the East and West in a perfect harmony of truth.

Yours affectionately,
Rabindranath Tagore

Source: MS copy at Rabindra Bhavan, Shantiniketan.

1 Mahadev Desai (1892–1942): private secretary to Gandhi.
2 *My Rem*, p. 167/*RR*, XVII, p. 410.
3 This definition of the infinite is of the kind that Bertrand Russell labelled 'vague nonsense' (see letter 50).

177

To Edward John Thompson

From letter 174, E. J. Thompson had formed the impression that Tagore would not welcome his visiting Shantiniketan in October, as they had been planning. But when Prashanta Mahalanobis communicated this to Tagore on a visit to Shantiniketan, Rabindranath said, on the contrary, he was waiting for Thompson to come; any coldness in his letter had been due to his depressed mood.[1] In this letter he expresses his own welcome.

Santiniketan, [West Bengal, India]
2 October 1921

Dear Thompson
  Do not misunderstand me and never think that I am angry. I am going through a

period of struggle in my mind desperately seeking my path across things that do not belong to my nature. If I have given expression to the restlessness which has come over me please do not think that I am holding you responsible for this state of things. I have been expecting you for long. Please do not disappoint me if you can help it.

Yours
Rabindranath Tagore

Source: MS original in Thompson Papers [Bodleian].

1 Mahalanobis to Thompson, 2 Oct. 1921 [RB]. Thompson had commented in his letter to RT on 22 Sept. 1921: 'What troubles me is the note of depression in your letter' [RB]. But he had assumed that the cause was his own book, rather than thinking of non-literary factors (i.e. noncooperation and Visva-Bharati) – a typical misunderstanding of RT by Thompson due to his patchy grasp of RT's social context (see letter 175).

178

To Thomas Sturge Moore

In mid-October 1921, Gandhi published 'The great sentinel', his response to Tagore's criticisms of noncooperation in August and September. 'I regard the Poet as a sentinel warning us against the approach of enemies called Bigotry, Lethargy, Intolerance, Ignorance, Inertia and other members of that brood.'[1] In Shantiniketan, Tagore brooded on his inability to join hands with Gandhi, and his failure to raise funds for his university. He felt pulled apart by contrary forces.

A letter came from Thomas Sturge Moore:

> I think your idea of an international university is a fine one, but a university like a nation cannot be better than the average individual that composes it, and the true university is a world in which any soul can if it likes hold communion with those who were lonely and tormented in all ages since the world began, so as to receive influences from and be stirred by their thought as a flowering shrub is by the breeze. And there are now wandering this planet more such influences than even the best of us can find the leisure to respond to . . .
>
> I think that if you bring into a community two or three of the most open minds in Europe with the same number from India you will have achieved a very great thing. And may possibly have done even if the university apparently fails, more for the future of India than the whole English Raj.[2]

Shantiniketan, [West Bengal, India]
20 October 1921

Dear Sturge Moore

Your delightful letter has been of real help to me. The strenuous feeling of opposition struggling within me against the political fanaticism which has been blinding our vision, blurring our perspective of humanity was wearing me out, because it was alien to my own realm of truth. I know, as a poet, my work is not for achieving immediate results in urgent human affairs. Even my idea of the International University, growing into an obsession, is hampering me in my life's work. What have I to do with establishing solid institutions, fixed and firm upon big funds and public approbation.

I clearly feel that it is wasting my life setting up stone idols on costly altars; some day they will all come down with their own weight. Living creations add to the evergrowing links of life, enrich the soil with their touch, transform the dead dust into vital organisms even when they themselves have had their term of individual existence. The spreading of the desert of heartless efficiency in the human world cannot be checked by institutions, but by all [things] that have the sap and rhythm of life in them however small they may be. Lately, I have taken to composing songs, and writing poems about childhood.[3] Each of them taken by itself seems so absurdly insignificant compared to discussions in our newspapers and decisions arrived at in our council sittings – and yet they make me utterly forget my duties, and I feel certain that in producing them I am one with the infinite personality all [of] whose work lies in the activity of manifestation. These poems of mine may not be of superior quality and yet even [if] they are ephemeral, they have their wings that hum, thrilling the air with dance of colours. Somewhere in the heart of all things there is a delight in them, [a] recognition of their harmony with the eternal therefore having [a] value for me which is ultimate.

I wish I could send my poems to you as I wrote them – but translating them is like putting them inside a case which is not their own body.

Yours
Rabindranath Tagore

Source: MS copy at Rabindra Bhavan, Shantiniketan.

1 *CWMG*, XXI, p. 288 (*Young India*, 13 Oct. 1921).
2 Moore to RT, [Oct.? 1921] [RB].
3 These poems, entitled *Shishu Bholanath*, were published in 1922.

179

To (Sir) Brajendranath Seal[1]

The philosopher Brajendranath Seal was among the handful of contemporary Indian scholars whom Tagore genuinely respected.[2] In 1920, Seal left his position at Calcutta University and became vice-chancellor of Mysore University. On 22 December 1921 he presided over the formal foundation of Visva-Bharati at Shantiniketan. Among the many issues on which Tagore and Seal saw eye to eye was the deleterious effect of non-cooperation on education, the growth of the sectarian spirit. Gandhi's idea of education differed irremediably from that of Tagore and Seal.

Shantiniketan, [West Bengal, India]
14 Kartik 1328 [31 October 1921]

Shraddhashpadeshu

The speech you gave at the annual convocation of Mysore University was a great delight and comfort. The partisan spirit in education that has taken over the minds of our countrymen these days is very painful to me. The fragmenting of education should always be discouraged – but it is especially inappropriate now. For today the different peoples of the world are coming within each other's purview: to try to block their vision with a screen of partisanship is to flout God's purpose. In standing for this truth and thus shielding your students from developing a disdain for it, you have done a fine thing. I too have been carrying a burden with similar aims in mind, but against heavy odds. I find myself very much alone. But then I have always had to work single-handed, whatever my task. I do not possess the power to attract supporters. Often this fact helps to retain a certain purity of endeavour, but the dearth of men and resources pains and wearies me. In this state of mind the poet inside me reproaches me, asking, 'Have you been sent here with some charter to found institutions? It is precisely because this is not your role that you receive no real support. By depriving you, your destiny is showing you the true path.' And certainly institutions require the cooperation of many people – which a poet's work does not. Under time's transforming power institutions rise, fall and metamorphose, but the thing called song floats on the ocean of time, undaunted by the swelling and crashing of the waves. I have my invitation to play with the froth in the perpetual flux of creation. So why have I allowed myself to put my flute aside and all of a sudden tried to become an engineer building a lighthouse in time's flow? That the task is meritorious is insufficient justification. To sacrifice the diverse forms of goodness on the altar of mere necessity is not good. But for which form am I particularly responsible? Questions of this kind churn constantly in my mind when I feel weary.

Thompson in his book has firmly detached me from my natural atmosphere.[3] This no doubt simplified his task, for he can present me in sharp outline. But a cutout is an incomplete picture of a man, who is not a mere individual but relates to his milieu; and this relationship is far-reaching and ill-defined. Thompson does not perceive the true nature of my milieu. Talking to him I have noticed he does not quite grasp that Vaishnava literature and the *Upanishads* have mingled to form my mental climate. They have mixed like the nitrogen and oxygen in the air. In my compositions the finite and the infinite are not in conflict, they are in harmony, and the reason is that they pervade not only my personality but my entire environment – something which cannot be grasped from within the prison of the sectarian intellect. In my father's heart Hafiz and the *Upanishads* were in confluence, a union of two opposed elements, as is necessary for the creation of beauty.[4] In the mind of the Creator, male and female principles are both present – how otherwise could creation arise from uniformity? But perhaps such debates are impertinent coming from a poet; please pardon me.

Apnar
Shri Rabindranath Thakur

Source: MS copy at Rabindra Bhavan, Shantiniketan; published in *VBP*, Baishakh–Asharh 1880 [April–July 1958], pp. 263–4.

1 Sir Brajendranath Seal (1864–1938): philosopher; he was George V professor of mental and moral science, Calcutta University, 1914–20, and vice-chancellor, Mysore University, 1920–30. RT made several attempts to boost Seal internationally. In 1916, he proposed to George Brett of Macmillan that Seal be invited to lecture in the USA. 'He could speak with an authority more weighty than that of any other living man on the relation of eastern philosophy to modern thought' (4 July 1916 [New York]). Another passionate admirer of Seal was Sir Michael Sadler (see *MR*, Jan. 1936, pp. 73–4).

2 RT shared Seal's view that 'I do not have much confidence in the more famous of our savants. Many of them are better appreciated from afar rather than from close up' (Seal to RT, 24 Nov. 1921, *VBP*, Baishakh–Asharh 1880 [April–July 1958], p. 264).
3 RT was of course reiterating what he had already told Prashanta Mahalanobis in letter 175. He raised the subject of E. J. Thompson's book with Seal because he knew that Seal was friendly with Thompson and had given him advice on RT and Bengal in general.
4 See references to Hafiz in Debendranath Tagore's autobiography.

Anti-noncooperator (1921–1923)

Introduction

Politically, the latter part of 1921 and the early part of 1922 was a turbulent time in India. Noncooperation was in full swing, until the Chauri Chaura incident of February 1922, after which the movement was called off by Gandhi, who was then arrested and sent to jail. While Tagore continued to admire Gandhi personally, he did not admire the movement in its existing form, indeed he had predicted violence in an open letter just before the incident.

Staying away from politics, Rabindranath applied his energies to Visva-Bharati and to his latest institutional creation, Shriniketan, his 'institute for rural reconstruction' in Surul, a village near Shantiniketan. To Visva-Bharati there came the first of several distinguished foreign lecturers, the orientalist Sylvain Lévi; and to Shriniketan came the young agricultural economist Leonard Elmhirst, whom Tagore had met in New York in 1921 and invited to Bengal. Elmhirst was made director of the new institute. During 1922 he struggled, with money from the American heiress Dorothy Straight and Tagore's enthusiastic support, to establish a farm, village crafts and industries, and other training schemes – everything that Tagore had attempted to start on his estates with his son and son-in-law ten years previously. While the noncooperators – many of them at Shantiniketan, though not with Tagore's encouragement – continued to stand for the rejection of western assistance in the development of India, Tagore welcomed it, as long as it was offered with the aim of understanding rural needs rather than imposing external (and ultimately unworkable) solutions.

180

To Satyendranath Tagore[1]

Late 1921 to early 1922 was an eventful period for Tagore and his fledgling institution. His first foreign lecturer, Sylvain Lévi, arrived from France; Leonard Elmhirst came from Britain, backed by American money, and began the rural development work that became Shriniketan; on 22 December Visva-Bharati was formally founded and a constitution promulgated. Meanwhile, the tension between the noncooperators and the Government mounted in Calcutta. As Prashanta Mahalanobis wrote to E. J. Thompson, 'Outwardly everything is fairly quiet but there is a tremendous undercurrent of indignation and feeling of outraged self-respect. People have been arrested for merely putting on khaddar.'[2] This letter to Tagore's elder brother reflects all this.

[Shantiniketan, West Bengal, India]
26 Paush 1328 [10 January 1922]

Bhai Meja Dada

Since my last trip to Europe I have been so entangled in Visva-Bharati work that there has been no opportunity to get away. Especially now that Prof. Sylvain Lévi is working here and I cannot leave him.[3] He has come at my invitation in response to my appeal – such a great scholar, yet so large-hearted a man, is rare. If I get the chance I hope to bring him once to your place at Ranchi.

I brought Gourlay over to Jorasanko and told him some home truths about the present punishment regime.[4] Such as how the police forced their way into the Mechuabazar mosque and caused mischief, and how this created the impression in the mind of the public that the police were deliberately provoking the NCOs [noncooperators] to break their vows of nonviolence. And I told him that if this was to be the first of a series of such incidents then even impartial fellows like me would be compelled to join forces with the other side. I liked the message you sent to Krishna Kumar Mitra; I've frequently said similar things to our people here.[5]

Visva-Bharati has now been established to some extent: it has been made over to the public charge and a constitution drafted to that effect, which I shall send you a copy of, once it has been revised by the lawyers.[6] Things have turned out well in many respects, except for the lack of funds, which will cause us perpetual anxiety. Shubir and Manju have been admitted here, as perhaps you know. I believe they have settled in well.[7] Lottie[8] is looking after the girls' section, and Pearson has taken charge of Shubir.

Sneher
Rabi

Source: MS original at Rabindra Bhavan, Shantiniketan; letter published in *CP*, V, pp. 5–6.

1 Satyendranath Tagore (1842–1923): elder brother of RT; the first Indian member of the ICS, he served his entire career in the Bombay presidency, 1864–97. A fine scholar in Sanskrit, he also wrote well in Bengali and English. His books included verse translations of the *Bhagavad Gita* and the *Meghduta*, a study of Buddhism, a volume of reminiscences and a translation into English (with his daughter Indira) of his father Debendranath's autobiography. In the Tagore family, Satyendranath was particularly noted for his devotion to the emancipation of women. See obituary in *MR*, Feb. 1923, pp. 277–8.
2 Mahalanobis to Thompson, 15 Dec. 1921 [RB].
3 Sylvain Lévi and his wife Desirée arrived in Shantiniketan on 9 Nov. 1921 and spent about a year there. See her diary, *Dans l'Inde (de Ceylan au Nepal)* (Paris, 1925; extract translated into English by Mira Ghosh as 'Visva-Bharati: early years', *Rabindra Bhavana*, Summer 1990, pp. 18–21).
4 Robert Gourlay, private secretary of the governor of Bengal, had regular contact with RT (see letter 116).
5 Krishna Kumar Mitra (1852–1936): writer, editor of *Sanjibani* and political activist; he supported the Congress but not noncooperation. He was a well-known Brahmo.
6 The constitution was chiefly the work of Prashanta Chandra Mahalanobis.
7 Shubir and Manjushri were the eldest son and daughter of Surendranath Tagore, nephew of RT. Shubir was soon taken away from Shantiniketan by his grandmother, Jnanadanandini, who did not approve of the place. See Elmhirst, *Poet and Plowman*, pp. 24–5.
8 Lottie: Snehalata Sen (1874–1967), daughter of Bihari Lal Gupta.

11 Rabindranath in Shantiniketan, 1920s/30s, with Leonard Elmhirst

181

To Leonard K. Elmhirst[1]

One of the few positive outcomes of Tagore's visit to the USA in 1920–1 was his meeting with Leonard Elmhirst. It took place in New York in March 1921, just before Tagore sailed back to Britain. Elmhirst, then soon to finish a course in agriculture at Cornell University, wanted to return to India, where he had lived for two-and-a-half years from 1915. Tagore had heard of this wish from Sam Higginbottom, a missionary friend of Elmhirst and agricultural expert, then on leave from India.[2] Tagore immediately proposed to Elmhirst that he join him in Bengal:

> Mr Elmhirst, I have established an educational enterprise in India which is almost wholly academic. It is situated well out in the countryside of West Bengal at Santiniketan. We are surrounded by villages, Hindu, Muslim, Santali. Except that we employ a number of these village folk for various menial tasks in my school, we have no intimate contact with them at all inside their own communities. For some reason these villages appear to be in a state of steady decline. In fact they are all in decay. Some years ago I bought from the Sinha family a farm just outside the village of Surul, a little over a mile from my school. I hear that you might be interested in going to live and work on such a farm in order to find out more clearly the causes of this decay.[3]

Having accepted, Leonard told Dorothy Whitney Straight, the heiress (and his future wife), of his enthusiasm for the plan. She had earlier failed to give money to Tagore (see letter 161), being unimpressed by the philosophy of Shantiniketan, but now she too became enthusiastic. 'It would be such fun to work it out in that way – and so much more satisfactory to me than to hand it over bodily to Tagore.'[4]

With Tagore's blessing and Straight's money (and loyalty) behind him – and with India gripped by the Noncooperation Movement and the cry for *swaraj* (self-rule) – Elmhirst arrived in Shantiniketan on 27 November 1921. On 17 February 1922 he and ten students from Shantiniketan moved into the house at Surul with their pots, pans and tools, and began the process of 'rural reconstruction' that Tagore hoped would act as an example to others and even to the whole of India. In his first letter to Elmhirst, Rabindranath tries to explain his idea – with charm but limited success.

Shilida, [Shelidah, Khulna, Bangladesh]
31 March 1922

Dear Elmhirst

Your letter has delighted me. Every day I am getting more and more envious of your *swaraj* at Surul, especially when I hear of your hens contributing their dues to the commonwealth. Plato had no place for poets in his Republic – I hope your Swaraj of Chashas do not cultivate platonic ideals in their election of members.[5] I am proud to be able to remind you of the fact that my poet's contribution reached you weeks earlier than that of the most conscientious and capable of your hens. I do not know what has happened to that poem of mine which I had to copy twice over – please take that to be my petition of candidature for poet-laureateship of your *swaraj* if you have the good sense to acknowledge that the culture of [the] imagination is not altogether superfluous for the purpose of agriculture. Please take it seriously when I say that my whole heart is with you in the great work you have started. I wish I were young enough to be able to join you and perform the meanest work that can be done in your place thus getting rid of that filmy web of respectability that shuts me off from the intimate touch of mother dust. It is something unclean like prudery itself to have to ask a sweeper to serve that deity who is in charge of the primal cradle of life.[6] I wonder if you fully realise how great is your mission and what a future it has before it. But the small beginning which you have made of this institution [in] a remote corner of the world carries in it a truth for which men today are groping in bewilderment. It is the truth of Peace. Real peace comes from a wealth which is living, which has the blessings of nature's direct touch, which is not machine made – let us seek humbly, coming down to the soil dealing with forces of life which are beautiful and bounteous.

Please cable to Mrs Straight to send her friend to us – she will be of immense help to me. Let her start for India some time in October.[7]

Yours affectionately
Rabindranath Tagore

Source: MS original in Dartington Trust archives [Dartington]; letter published in Dutta and Robinson (eds.), *Purabi*, p. 75.

1 Leonard Knight Elmhirst (1893–1974): agricultural economist, who founded the Dartington Trust with his wife, Dorothy, in 1925; he worked with RT at Surul/Shriniketan from late 1921 to early 1923; in 1924 he acted as secretary to RT in the Far East and in Argentina. Dartington Trust money supported Shriniketan until 1947 and Elmhirst retained a strong interest in its welfare, with regular visits almost until his death. See Michael Young, *The Elmhirsts of Dartington: The Creation of an Utopian Community* (Dartington/London, 1982).
2 See *ibid.*, pp. 64–5.
3 Quoted in Elmhirst, *Poet and Plowman*, p. 16.
4 Straight to Elmhirst, 28 June 1921, in Young, *The Elmhirsts of Dartington*, p. 76.
5 Swaraj of Chashas: self-rule by farmers, i.e. a Peasants' Republic.
6 RT is here referring, a bit archly, to Elmhirst's campaign to persuade the students at Surul to empty and clean their own latrine buckets, rather than employing the traditional low-caste sweeper. Elmhirst gives an account of this in his entertaining Surul diary in *Poet and Plowman* (see especially pp. 75–6). On one occasion Tagore quizzed him directly about the sanitation problem, which he himself had never attempted to tackle in the twenty-year history of the ashram. For Gandhi, sanitation and the bowels were matters for constant public discussion – not so for Tagore; this letter to Elmhirst is one of his rare comments on the subject.
7 Dorothy Straight had agreed to send Gretchen Green to Surul to set up a health centre and clinic. See letter 187, n. 6.

182

To Edward John Thompson

E. J. Thompson, having published his short study of Tagore in 1921, was now immersed in research for his major study, *Rabindranath Tagore: Poet and Dramatist*. During late 1921 and 1922 Tagore gave Thompson a considerable amount of help with the book, both in writing and in conversation, including making translations of his work for him. In so doing, the idea that translation of his poetry into English was beyond him (expressed in letters 162 and 173), seems to have hardened into a conviction that it was beyond anyone, as he implies in this letter.

Shantiniketan, [West Bengal, India]
16 April 1922

Dear Thompson
　I send you the translations you asked for. I have come to the conclusion that translating a poem is doing it wrong, specially when the original belongs to a language which is wholly alien to the medium of its translation. Have you a single honest translation in English, from poems written in any other European language, which occupies a decent seat in your literature? Is not Dante in English a dead star which has its heavy load of materials and no light? You know most of the great poets of Europe through the experience of a large number of your countrymen who have read them in the original – their evidence being supplemented by translations which cannot but be inadequate. Can you ever imagine the best passages of Keats, Shelley or Wordsworth in Bengali – and would it not be a pure act of mercy to leave them out if you must translate their poems?[1]

Yours
Rabindranath Tagore

Source: MS original in Thompson Papers [Bodleian]; letter published (minus first sentence) in E. P. Thompson, *Alien Homage*, p. 48.

1 It is interesting that RT compares himself, by implication, to the Romantic poets, rather than to, say, Dante, Goethe or Shakespeare.

183

To Edward John Thompson

In May 1922, while working on his longer study of Tagore, E. J. Thompson published an extract from it in the *Modern Review*. It was a critique of *Balaka* (Wild Geese), poems written by Rabindranath between 1914 and 1916. Tagore responded very favourably, as this letter shows – one of many occasions when he openly encouraged Thompson, despite being dissatisfied with his first book.

Santiniketan, [West Bengal, India]
2 May 1922

Dear Thompson

I must thank you for your paper on *Balaka* which has delighted me. I can assure you that it will help a large number of my countrymen in appreciating those poems which they find difficult to understand. This is the only real piece of literary criticism that has appeared in an Indian journal, showing an imaginative insight into the subject it deals with.[1]

Yours
Rabindranath Tagore

Source: MS original in Thompson Papers [Bodleian].

1 'Rabindranath Tagore's Balaka', *MR*, May 1922, pp. 592–6. Thompson incorporated this paper, with some significant modifications, into *Rabindranath Tagore* (pp. 230–9). RT's praise is intelligible, though somewhat hyperbolic, given that Thompson describes the most famous image in 'Taj Mahal' ('a tear droplet on the cheek of Time') as 'a bad conceit' (*MR*, p. 595). Presumably, though, RT keenly appreciated Thompson's statement that 'a selection from the work of all his periods would show him as a greater poet than he seems either in the pitiless completeness of his Bengali text or the haphazard mutilation of his English one' (p. 593).

184

To (Sir) Patrick Geddes[1]

In *Creative Unity*, a collection of essays published in 1922, just as Visva-Bharati was getting under way, Tagore wrote, 'I do not put my faith in any new institutions, but in the individuals all over the world who think clearly, feel nobly and act rightly.'[2] The strength and the weakness inherent in this conviction are clearly illustrated in his relationship with Patrick Geddes.

Geddes was then professor of sociology and civics at Bombay University. Earlier, he had been a distinguished biologist trained by Darwin's disciple T. H. Huxley and had formed a strong admiration for Sir Jagadish Chandra Bose (whose biography he published in 1920).[3] His twin interests had coalesced into an attempt to harmonise the arts and the sciences in the planning of institutions.

Tagore had appealed for Geddes' help in planning Visva-Bharati during his European visit in 1921, after abandoning William Rothenstein (see letter 167).[4] In April 1922, in a letter to Tagore, Geddes formulated some of his thoughts into a scheme including a diagram using concepts such as 'ethopolity', 'psychorganics' and 'eutechnics' (the last defined as 'life as Activity, i.e. with esthetics and physics, arts and industries at one'). Geddes commented:

> We need to be logical in our statistics and graphics, physical in our construction, biological in our agriculture, horticulture and hygiene, economic in our general undertakings: yet all the sciences and arts, as Ruskin saw before us . . . are ineffective, when not calamitous, while expressing only the sciences and arts of the material and mechanical order, still so predominant, and so characteristic of the West.[5]

It was too much for Tagore. While he sympathised with the essential attitude, the jargon and the avowedly scientific view of human society did not attract him. Indeed, judging from his reply to Geddes, the whole concept of planning an institution seems to have held small appeal to him. Planning involved teamwork, and however much Tagore may in theory have believed in cooperative activity, in practice he was intensely individualistic. It also involved more or less rigid structures, which Tagore had rejected in London in 1921. As he remarks in this letter, 'All my activities have the character of play in them – they are more or less like writing poems only in different mediums of expression.'

Santiniketan, [West Bengal, India]
9 May 1922

Dear Geddes

You ask me for my opinion about the scheme of your department. I find it rather difficult to answer your question because my own work in Santiniketan has been from first to last a growth, which has had to meet all the obstacles and obstructions due to shortage of funds, paucity of workers, obtuseness in those who were called upon to carry out my ideal. But just because it was a living growth it has surmounted these difficulties and taken its own shape. In writing my stories I hardly ever have a distinct plot in my mind. I start with some general emotional motive which goes on creating its story form very often forgetting in the process its own original boundaries. If I had in the commencement a definite outline which I was merely to fill in it would certainly bore me – for I need the constant stimulation of surprises which comes only to a semi-passive medium through some living truth's gradual self-unfoldment. The same thing happened with my Santiniketan institution. I merely started with this one simple idea that education should never be dissociated from life. I had no experience of teaching, no special gift for organisation, and therefore I had no plan which I could put before the public in order to win their confidence. I had not the power to anticipate as to what line my work was going to take. I began anyhow. All that I could do was to offer to the five little boys who were my first students my company. I talked and sang to them, played with them, recited to them our epics, improvised stories serially given to them from evening to evening, took them on excursions to neighbouring villages. It was an incessant lesson to me and the institution grew with the growth of my own mind and life. With the increase of its population and widening of range, elements have constantly been intruding which go against its spirit of freedom and spontaneity. The consequent struggle has been helpful in strengthening and making us realise the fundamental truth which is in the heart of our ashram. But that which keeps up my enthusiasm is the fact that we have not yet come to a conclusion and therefore our task is not a perpetual repetition of a plan perfected once for all.

My first idea was to emancipate children's mind from the dead grip of a mechanical method and a narrow purpose. This idea has gone on developing itself, gradually comprehending all different branches of life's activities from arts to agriculture. Now it has come to a period when we are fully made aware of the absolute necessity of widening across all barriers the human sympathy of our students, thus leading them to the fulfilment of their education. This stage we have reached, as I have said, not through following any reasoned-out system but through an inner life growth in which the subconscious has ever been bursting up into the conscious plane. Lately it has come to us almost like a sudden discovery that our institution represents that creative force which is acting in the bosom of the present age passing through repeated conflicts and reconciliations, failures and readjustments making for the realisation of the spiritual unity of human races. I have often wished for my mission the help of men like yourself who not only have a most comprehensive sympathy and imagination but a wide range of knowledge and critical acumen. It was with a bewilderment of admiration that I have so often followed the architectural immensity of your vision. But at the same moment I had to acknowledge that it was beyond my power to make a practical use of the background of perspective which your vision provides us with. The temperamental characteristics of my own nature require the most part of my work to remain in the subsoil obscurity of mind. All my activities have the character of play in them – they are more or less like writing poems only in different mediums of expression. Your own schemes also in a great measure have the same element which strongly attracts me, but they have a different idiom which I have not the power to use. You will understand from this, my dear friend, that though I always enjoy listening to you when you formulate your ideas and my mind is stimulated by the vastness of their unity I cannot criticise them. I suppose they are stored in my unconscious memory waiting for living assimilation with my own thoughts.

Cordially yours
Rabindranath Tagore

Source: MS original in Geddes Papers [Edinburgh]; letter published in *Rabindra-Bhavana*, Summer 1990, pp. 12–14.

1 Sir Patrick Geddes (1854–1932): biologist and sociologist who was one of the modern pioneers of the concept of town and regional planning; he was professor of sociology and civics at Bombay University, 1920–3 and director, Scots College, Montpellier, after his return from India until his death (RT was the chancellor). In his later years, at the time he knew RT, Geddes suffered from a sense of frustration that his ideas were respected in theory but ignored in practice.
2 *Creative Unity* (London, 1922), p. 153 (translation slightly modified).
3 On Geddes and Bose, see letter 27.

4 RT to Geddes, 5 May 1921 [Edinburgh].
5 Geddes to RT, 15 April 1921, in Philip Boardman, *The Worlds of Patrick Geddes: Biologist, Town Planner, Re-educator, Peace-warrior* (London, 1978), p. 332. Geddes remained a great admirer of RT but he told C. F. Andrews, who reported it to RT: 'The truth is, the Poet does not really know the West' (Andrews to RT, 20 Dec. 1922 [RB]).

185

To Sten Konow[1]

In the 1920s several distinguished European orientalists visited Tagore's new university, spurred by their meetings with Rabindranath in Europe in 1920–1 or by other contacts with him. The Norwegian Sten Konow came in 1924–5 and became a loyal supporter of Tagore's experiment. In 1924, speaking at Shantiniketan, Konow said:

> The outlook in the West seemed hopeless when the Poet came and asked us to seek salvation through faith in new ideals. Wise men of the world smiled, but there were individuals who felt that there was yet hope for humanity. The Poet's vision must some day come true. The nations of the world must join hands in a common endeavour to build anew the history of the world.[2]

And in 1931, on Tagore's seventieth birthday, Konow wrote:

> We do not want to become Indians, and we do not want the Indians to become Europeans in their mind and in other ways. But we want the East to join hands with the West, in a noble contest for the promotion of the highest ideals, which are common to the whole world.[3]

This letter to Konow, written before his visit, shows the intellectual stimulation that Tagore derived from contacts with sensitive European scholars.

Santiniketan, [West Bengal, India]
14 May 1922

Dear Acharyya[4]

Thank you for your kind letter. I fully agree with you in what you have said about the book on Indian images. I have an idea that Buddhism, having to a great extent deprived [the] human heart of its deepest need of communion with a spiritual reality, helped to fill that chasm with innumerable images some of which were allegorical symbols and some fetishes of the aboriginal tribes which found their chance owing to the religious interregnum of that period.[5] It was like a sudden rush of image storms attracted by the rarefaction of the spiritual atmosphere. This fact had been made evident to me when I went to Nara in Japan and saw in the museum there numerous images made by Indian artists revealing our modern image worship in the process of its growth.[6]

Our university – Visva-Bharati – has already been started. Its international character has been emphasised by Prof. Sylvain Lévi's coming here and helping us with his cooperation.[7] If there is any possibility of your visiting India once again we shall be most glad to make every suitable arrangement for the occasion. Prof. Winternitz of Prague University has accepted our invitation for the next winter season and we are earnestly hoping that there will be no prohibition from the Indian Government in his case.[8]

Yours sincerely,
Rabindranath Tagore

Source: MS copy at Rabindra Bhavan, Shantiniketan.

1 Sten Konow (1867–1948): philologist and founder-editor, *Acta Orientalia*; having assisted Sir George Grierson in the editing of the *Linguistic Survey of India*, Konow went to India as government epigraphist, 1906–8; from 1910 until his death he was professor of Indian philology, University of Oslo (Kristiania). In addition to extensive scholarly publication, he wrote books and articles on India and other subjects for the general reader and had a wide circle of friends: in the words of the Swedish poet Karlfeldt, Konow could talk 'with peasants in the peasants' way, and with learned men in Latin'. See Georg Morgenstierne, 'Sten Konow', *Acta Orientalia*, 21, pt 1, 1950, pp. 3–9.
2 *VBQ*, 2, No. 4, Jan. 1925, p. 395.
3 Quoted in Ramananda Chatterjee (ed.), *The Golden Book of Tagore* (Calcutta, 1931), p. 131.
4 Acharyya: teacher.
5 Concerning Buddhist asceticism, RT wrote at this time:

> The religion, which flowed from the comprehensive mind of Buddha, has its negative aspect – the control of passion and renunciation of self – for purifying spiritual ideas and religious phraseology from all narrowness, anthropomorphic, or egotistic; it is the path of discipline through elimination. But this cannot be the whole of it; and that this has not been all, is amply proved by the direction and form which Buddhism has naturally taken in the greater part of the Buddhistic world. (*VBQ*, 1, No. 4, Jan. 1924, p. 383)

6 RT saw the images at Nara in 1916. He appears to have been confused about their production. Urgyen Sangharakshita, an authority, states:

> I am very doubtful if the Buddhist images at Nara were made by Indian artists working on the spot ... Tagore probably assumed that the images were made by Indian artists because they conformed to the Indian iconographic norms and because many of them were, moreover, of Hindu deities that had been incorporated into the Buddhist 'pantheon'. (Letter to authors, 2 June 1996)

7 See letter 180, n. 3.
8 Moriz Winternitz (1863–1937): authority on ancient and medieval Indian literature; he was professor of Indian philology and ethnology, German University, Prague, and a visiting professor at Shantiniketan from Feb. 1923 to Sept. 1924. On RT's problem with getting visas for Central European professors, see letter 166.

186

To William Winstanley Pearson

W. W. Pearson returned to Shantiniketan in November 1921 after a gap of five-and-a-half years.[1] He could not adjust to the changes, especially to the idea of a university attached to the school he loved. Instead of taking up teaching again, he went away from Shantiniketan in order to translate Rabindranath's novel *Gora*, but soon realised the great difficulty of the task.[2] The religious debates integral to the book also prompted troubled personal reflections. Always a rather tortured figure, Pearson turned to Tagore for guidance. Pearson's letter is missing, but its burden is clear from Rabindranath's reply.

Santiniketan, [West Bengal, India]
2 June 1922

Dear Pearson,

I can guess from your letter that some questions are troubling your mind about the best way of self-realisation. There can be no single path for all individuals, for we vastly differ in our nature and habits. But all great masters agree in their teaching on one cardinal point, saying that we must forget our personal self in order to attain our spiritual freedom. Buddha and Christ have both of them said that this self-abnegation is not something which is negative – its positive aspect is love.

We can only love that which is profoundly real to us. The larger number of men have the most intense feeling of reality only for their own self; and they can never get out of the limits of their self-love. The rest of human beings can be divided into two classes – those who have their love for persons, and those who have [their love] for ideas.

Generally speaking, women fall into the first category and men into the second. In India this fact has been recognised and our teachers have pointed out two different paths for [the] different sexes. It has been said that women can attain their emancipation by sublimating their personal relationships into the realm of the ideal. If, in spite of all obvious contradictions, a woman can realise in her husband something which transcends his personal limitations, then through her devotion to him she touches the infinite and thus is freed from the bondage of self. Through the luminous immensity of her love, her husband and her child reveal to her their ultimate truth which is divine. For biological reasons men's nature has had comparative freedom from the attachment to persons and therefore it has become easier for them to find direct access to ideas which lie behind the screen of things and which they ever have been pursuing in their knowledge and creative activities. Once you become conscious of some idea as the inner spirit of reality, as the higher meaning of the time, the joy becomes so unbounded that your self becomes obliterated, and you can easily lay aside all that you have for its sake.

But we must keep in mind that love of persons and love of ideas both can be terribly egotistic and therefore lead to bondage. It is constant sacrifice in service which [alone] can loosen the shackle. We must not merely enjoy our love, whether personal or ideal, by contemplating its beauty and truth but must, by constantly working for it, tune our being in its music and gradually get rid of all discords. We can only attain truth by giving expression to it in our life's work. Our life is the material with which we have to build the image of the ideal of truth which we have in mind. But our life, like all other materials, contains an obstinate antagonism to the idea to which it must give shape. Only through the active process of creation [can] such antagonism be discovered at every step and chiselled away at every stroke.

Look at the Santal women.[3] In them the ideal of physical life finds its perfect development only because they are active in giving it expression in work. Their figure and their movements attain their beautiful harmony because they are always being tuned by life's activities. The one thing which I am never tired of admiring is the vigorous cleanliness of their limbs, which never get soiled even by the constant contact of dirt. Our ladies with their soaps and scents, washings and dressings, and incessant takings of care of their persons, only give an artificial polish to their superficial body; but the cleanliness which is induced by the body's own current of movements, which comes from the blood, muscle and nerves, from the completeness of physical health, our women can never possess. The same thing happens with regard to our spiritual body. It is not by meticulous care in avoiding all contaminations that we can keep it clean and give it grace, but by urging it to give a vigorous expression to its inner life in the very midst of all dirt and dust and heat and hurts.

But I must stop and find out if I have given any answer to the question you have put to me. It may be that I have not, for it is difficult to know exactly what you want of me. You have spoken of impersonal love and impersonal work and you ask me which I consider the greater. To me they appear as one, like the sun and the light – for love's expression is in work. Where [there is] no work, there it is a dead world.

Affectionately yours
Rabindranath Tagore

Source: MS original at Rabindra Bhavan, Shantiniketan; letter published in *VBQ*, 9, No. 2, Aug.–Oct. 1943, pp. 175–7.

1 Pearson had been denied permission to return to India, as a result of his 'seditious' pamphlet, 'For India' (see letter 126). He eventually returned on the same boat as Leonard Elmhirst. (See Elmhirst, *Poet and Plowman*, p. 52.)
2 See letter 196.
3 Pearson had a close relationship with the Santal tribals who lived around Shantiniketan. See C. F. Andrews, 'W. W. Pearson', *VBQ*, 5, No. 1, May–July 1939, pp. 38–40.

187

To Leonard K. Elmhirst

Throughout 1922, Leonard Elmhirst battled to establish Shriniketan, the 'institute for rural reconstruction', at Surul, the village near Shantiniketan. His two mentors, Dorothy Straight (in New York) and Tagore (on his doorstep), backed him in their very different ways. This letter, written from south India, where Tagore had gone lecturing for the second time in order to raise funds for his university, is the first of a number of letters dealing with the staffing of Shriniketan.

State Guest House, Trivandrum, [Kerala, India]
13 November 1922

Dear Elmhirst

Your marriage proposal has my hearty approval and blessing.[1] It will take a huge load off my mind when it happens, for I have discovered that lately you have been paying an alarming amount of attention to a certain Brahmin maiden, diverting her heart from its previous course.[2] You make me feel envious about the cushions and other luxuries that surround you unasked. I only hope that some part of the surplus may find its way towards us to enliven our cheerless land of neglect.

My days have been strenuous and though often I have felt that I am not strong enough to bear the strain I do not repent. I am the sower of seeds, the soil is not barren and I am sure the harvest will be reaped in my time.

You know my heart is with Surul. I feel that it has life in it – it does not deal with abstractions, but has its roots deep in the heart of living reality. You may be absolutely certain that it will be able to weather all storms and spread its branches wide. I shall have a good talk with you about the questions you have raised in your letter when I return some time in the first week of December. In the meanwhile take my advice, never let Gora leave you.[3] He is the only person you have who understands men and knows how to deal with them firmly and yet tactfully. Santosh and Kali Mohan are invaluable in their own respective spheres but both of them lack the qualification to maintain a complex organisation in proper order.[4] I shall feel truly anxious for Surul if Gora is no longer there. As for me you will have my presence in Surul as long as you can tolerate it, only if you can arrange my accommodation on that sunny side of the establishment where cushions are plentiful.

Rathi will give you a detailed account of our adventure when he meets you which will be some time before I come.[5]

Give my kind regards to Miss Green.[6]

Affectionately yours
Rabindranath Tagore

Source: MS original in Dartington Trust archives [Dartington]; letter published in Dutta and Robinson (eds.), *Purabi*, p. 77.

1 Elmhirst first proposed marriage to Dorothy Straight in Jan. 1922, but it was not until 1924 that she agreed to marry him. See Young, *The Elmhirsts of Dartington*, p. 81.
2 The 'Brahmin maiden' was Ranu Adhikari, later Lady Ranu Mookerjee, who was then a teenager. RT too was strongly attracted to her; the following year, 1923, he wrote a play eventually titled *Rakta Karabi* (*Red Oleanders*; London, 1925), based on the triangle between himself, her and Elmhirst. See Elmhirst's own account quoted in Krishna Kripalani, *Rabindranath Tagore: A Biography* (2nd edn; Calcutta, 1980), pp. 322–3.
3 Elmhirst's letter to RT is missing. Gour Gopal Ghosh ('Gora') (1893–1940): teacher at Shantiniketan, later village development worker at Shriniketan; he played football for the Mohun Bagan club in Calcutta.
4 Santosh Chandra Majumdar and Kali Mohan Ghosh: teachers at Shantiniketan, later village development workers at Shriniketan. See letter 33, n. 3 and letter 64, respectively.
5 Rathi: Rathindranath Tagore, who accompanied his father in south India and Ceylon.
6 Gretchen Green was sent by Dorothy Straight (see letter 181), to set up a health centre in Surul and also, it appears, to provide a potential wife for Elmhirst (Young, *The Elmhirsts of Dartington*, p. 81). She landed at Bombay in Sept. 1922 and immediately joined RT's party for part of his visit to south India, after which she went to Surul. See letter 295.

188

To Charles Freer Andrews

During the 1920s and 1930s, Tagore visited many parts of India in the hope of raising funds for Visva-Bharati. Even in 1922, just after the university was founded, he knew it would be a steep uphill task. Ramananda Chatterji [Chattopadhyay], a lifelong supporter of Tagore and his institution, explained some of the reasons for the failure of Indians to give money, in a *Modern Review* article written in 1936:

> Had Tagore been orthodox in his religious, social, political, educational and cultural ideas and ideals – uttering popular catch-phrases, had he been an educational megalomaniac instead of being India's greatest educational genius who thinks independently, he would probably have got plenty of big donations. Probably the fact of his being the grandson of 'Prince' Dwarkanath Tagore has also stood in the way of his being adequately financed by his countrymen, few of whom know that personally he has given unstintedly not only his time and physical and intellectual energy but his material resources also to his university. There may be other causes which it will do no good to state.[1]

This letter, written to C. F. Andrews who accompanied him on his tour of south India (including a visit to Bombay to meet potential Parsi donors, amongst others), gives a glimpse of Tagore's own perception of his lack of financial success. (Andrews had remained behind in Bombay to try to drum up money and members for Visva-Bharati.)

[Santiniketan, West Bengal, India]
14 December 1922

My friend, though I am extremely busy yet the days here are peaceful, the morning sky overflowing with sunshine and evenings full to the starry brim with the deep intimacy of silence. Visitors are coming in a large number but the vastness of the *shanti* here is hardly ruffled by them.

I am sure that in Bombay I have done what I could do. It was mostly a superficial attraction of curiosity which brought people round me and if I had stayed there for long my visit would have grown stale for them. If we could try to utilise for our motive force some passion which is already burning in the heart of the people our effort would have been greeted with an immense outburst of enthusiasm. But ideals have very little chance of success in the field of popularity specially when they have some passion for their rival. Men immensely greater in personality than myself achieved their fulfilment only through the martyrdom of apparent failure – who am I to claim success?

Your letter has come to me this morning and it has had the effect of toning down my expectation to a low pitch which is the healthy pitch for one's mind. Try to have as many associate members as possible – if their number grows larger and spreads over the country then from the moral and material points of view it will give us our best support.

Our first issue of the journal must contain my lectures on Visva-Bharati in order to give our readers a clear notion of our ideal.[2] This is a journal which is not merely for India, and as I claim the cooperation of the West for my work I must prepare the minds of the western people. It can chiefly be done through this journal. It is better that the first appeal should come from you to my countrymen than from me, and I am absolutely certain that it will have a greater chance of response.[3]

With love

Ever yours
Rabindranath Tagore

[PS] The presents given to us by the junior rani of Travancore have not yet reached us. Can you make enquiries? Write to Kumudini Bose for some sample of oil. I hope Travancore people are still active in their wish to help us. We want members in that province.

Source: MS original at Rabindra Bhavan, Shantiniketan.

1 *MR*, April 1936, p. 476.
2 RT launched the *Visva-Bharati Quarterly* in April 1923, with himself as editor.

3 The first article of the first issue of *VBQ* was 'Visva-Bharati', a statement of aims by RT; 'The meaning of Visva-Bharati', an address given by C. F. Andrews to the students of Travancore, appeared in *VBQ*, 2, No. 1, April 1924, pp. 98–103.

189

To Charles Freer Andrews

Despite the atmosphere of conflict and disappointment in which Tagore moved as a public figure in the India of noncooperation, even in Shantiniketan, within the privacy of his mind Tagore retained an astonishing power of detachment that kept him sane and productive. The emotions of which he spoke in *Gitanjali* – which could so easily seem to be a pose – were everyday realities for their author; the *shanti* in Shantiniketan, which sounds faintly embarrassing when translated as 'Abode of Peace', was a living, palpable presence for Rabindranath. However restless his mind, his capacity to still it never failed him.[1]

The truth of this becomes especially vivid in this letter to C. F. Andrews, 'Christ's Faithful Apostle', as his friends called him. Tagore (and Gandhi) had the still centre for which Andrews searched all his life and never found. C.F.A. was too wedded to the world and its all-too-obvious woes to withdraw into himself (at the time of this letter, he had rushed away from Shantiniketan to north Bengal in an effort to help the starving victims of floods): he was courageous and selfless, but his achievements were built on shifting sands.

[Shantiniketan, West Bengal, India]
17 February 1923

Dear friend

Lately you have looked so distracted and seemed unhappy that it has made me anxious for your sake since you left this place. I always earnestly wish that you can have inner peace amidst your multifarious burden of works. But I find you are very cruel to yourself and you never allow any time of the day to remain unoccupied when you can come to your deeper self. Thus weariness grows and your mind's atmosphere is filled with self-torturing thoughts and imaginings. A great part of your mind's burden consists of useless refuse and fragments of daily cares which have to be swept away at least twice a day in order to enable you to maintain the clearness of life's perspective. I am by nature impatient, anxious and often fretful and therefore I never wish to miss the daily opportunity of coming into touch with the truth which is peace. It has saved me so long from utter breakdown, from the tyranny of the insignificant, from the fetters of the fragmentary. The load of immediate needs and the distractions of miscellaneousness at once lose their weight when you can bring them to the eternal. I am perfectly aware that you know all this and therefore in spite of my intense desire to help you I fail to do so. Some cyclonic hurricane of activity drives you from one point to another through a maze of duties. It is your nature, and your mind, because of its amazing amount of vitality, wants all at once to apply its energy to all different directions. But everyday you are wearing yourself out, not because you work too hard, but because you do not concentrate some part of your energy inwardly for the purpose of maintaining a centre of utter calm in the whirlwind of your work. I believe in yoga, not only for attaining spiritual truth but for keeping up the equilibrium of life that helps our energy to sustain its rhythm which is the harmony of work and rest. Yoga is the transmutation of our dynamic self into the static peace for some time, in order to create that lucid serenity which is the mirror of the eternal.

I have been ill for some time. A touch of influenza. I am well now and am preparing for the spring festival in Calcutta. I am leaving for that place next Tuesday. I have been waiting every day [to hear] from you. Possibly no news is good news.

With love

Ever yours
Rabindranath Tagore

Source: MS original in Rabindra Bhavan, Shantiniketan.

1 See Kurt Wolff's description of RT's remarkable power of withdrawal in letter 170, n. 2.

190

To Atul Prashad Sen[1]

At the beginning of March 1923, Tagore presided over a literary conference of Bengalis living outside Bengal held at Varanasi. From there he travelled to Lucknow and spent a few days with his friend and admirer, the song composer Atul Prashad Sen, a successful Bengali barrister settled in Lucknow since the 1890s. Sen was a prominent citizen of Lucknow well known for his hospitality and he invited a number of local grandees to meet Tagore at a musical occasion (a 'durbar', as Tagore called it with gentle irony). It was a good opportunity to raise funds for Visva-Bharati but, as before, Tagore's success was limited. One can see how much he disliked the process from the letter he wrote afterwards to the raja of Mahmudabad, a *talukdari* estate not far from Lucknow, quoted in this letter to Sen.

Mount Petit, Peddar Street, Bombay, [India]
12 March 1923

Kabi bandhu

Saturn is still guiding my destiny – probably it will continue to do so until my sun finally sets. We were half dead when we reached here; for two days I was practically bedridden. When I got up this morning I wrote a letter to the raja of Mahmudabad, which I now quote:

> I must let you know how deeply I was touched by [the] warm expression of sympathy with which you accepted my appeal for the Visva-Bharati. It has specially delighted me because of the rarity of any real understanding of its ideals which I find among my countrymen who almost rudely refuse to realise the true perspective of their country's problems in the largest [perspective] of humanity. Please accept my hearty thanks not only for the ready welcome you accorded to the ideals I beg to represent in my life's

work but also because you had difficult respect [*sic*] for my personality not to hurt my cause with an impatient gesture of indifferent charity made all the more conspicuous by the high position which you and your peers in Oudh hold in India.

If you could from time to time remind the raja of his pledge to me, it would be most helpful. As I recall, he said he would write to the raja of Benares, Madho Lal, about establishing a permanent chair of Sanskrit. And when he goes to Delhi at the end of March he would discuss the matter there. At present we need two things urgently – the enthronement of Brajen Babu as professor of Sanskrit, and secondly, a guesthouse, where Indian visitors can stay for a while independently.[2] Many people want to come, but there is no place for them, which pains me.

That day at your durbar I sang a song just before we parted. When it was over, you made a request. In the train coming here I composed a song for you – here are the first two lines:

> Your song lingers as I go
> But how can anyone know?[3]

You may be sure of this, however, that the rumble of Mister Wheeler[4] does not linger – instead my heart hums with the sweet melody of your hospitality; and I hope your desire for sweet fruit is fulfilled in due time. Here I am particularly reminded of fruit because upon arrival I have been lucky to find the mangoes ripe. Word of my greed has spread quickly among my friends, and I myself have confessed my guilt, without the least embarrassment. Just because I have departed do not surrender yourself to the demands of your clients, spare occasional sighs of sympathy for this unfortunate typhoon-tossed fellow. One such sigh may perhaps reach the ears of the Almighty.

Tomader
Shri Rabindranath Thakur

Source: MS original at Rabindra Bhavan, Shantiniketan; letter published in Manashi Mukherji [Mukhopadhyay], *Atul Prashad*, (1378 [1971]), pp. 33–4.

1 Atul Prashad Sen (1871–1934): song composer; some of his two hundred or so songs, based on Hindustani classical music but with words in Bengali, remain very popular in Bengal.
2 Neither the raja of Mahmudabad nor the raja of Benares donated to Visva-Bharati. Sir Brajendranath Seal never came to Shantiniketan as professor of Sanskrit; money was, however, given by the trustees of Sir Ratan Tata, the Parsi industrialist, for the building of a guest house, named Ratan Kuthi, primarily for the use of visiting foreign scholars. See Dutta and Robinson, *Rabindranath Tagore*, p. 453. The foundation stone was laid on 14 April 1923, the Bengali New Year's Day.
3 *GB*, II, p. 280.
4 The significance of Mister Wheeler is unknown, but perhaps he was a local British dignitary who struck a false note by his behaviour at the 'durbar'.

191

To Nagendranath Gangulee

Tagore's son-in-law Nagendranath Gangulee, after years of failing to find a suitable role in India, finally decided in 1923 to try his luck in Britain. In due course he obtained a doctorate in soil biology from the University of London and returned to India as a member of the royal commission on Indian agriculture in 1926; from 1932 onwards he made Britain his home, leaving his wife, Tagore's daughter Mira, in Bengal. He remained on friendly terms with his father-in-law and made full use of his family connection with Tagore in making new contacts in Europe.[1]

This letter was written just after Tagore's return from a fundraising visit to western India, following his stay in Bombay.

[Shantiniketan, West Bengal, India]
28 Chaitra 1329 [11 April 1923]

Kalyaniyeshu

I have fallen into penury and debt, otherwise I could easily have helped you. However I am giving Pearson 500 rupees to take for you.[2]

My hope was that after I returned and before you set off I would see you. I did not know that you would be parting from us so soon.

From my heart I pray that God will bid you well.

Wherever in the continent of Europe you may travel, once they know that you are related to me, it will not be long before you receive adequate care and assistance.[3]

Shubhanudhyayi
Shri Rabindranath Thakur

Source: MS original at Rabindra Bhavan, Shantiniketan; letter published in Sharadiya *Desh*, 1398 [Autumn 1991], pp. 57–8.

1 Wherever Gangulee's name comes up in British memoirs or biographies of the period, his connection with RT is always mentioned.
2 Pearson left for Britain on 11 April, never to return to Shantiniketan.
3 This was hardly an exaggeration in the 1920s. See the amazing stories of RT's fame in Europe at this time in Rathindranath Tagore, *Edges of Time*, e.g. pp. 142–3.

192

To Sir Ashutosh Mookerjee [Mukhopadhyay][1]

Tagore's relationships with Calcutta University and its best-known vice-chancellor, Sir Ashutosh Mookerjee, was an awkward one from beginning to end, and perhaps especially in regard to the teaching of the Bengali language and literature. In 1861, the university withdrew the right of candidates to sit the entrance examination in Bengali; English became the sole medium of instruction; the study of Bengali formed a minimal part of university courses. This was the situation for the next half-century, during which period, of course, Bengali literature underwent a renaissance and Rabindranath himself rose to prominence and won the Nobel prize. In his view, expressed in 1918, this neglect of Bengali by academe was 'a blessing in disguise',

> for thus our language and literature have had the opportunity of natural growth, unhampered by worldly temptation, or imposition of outside authority. Our literary language is still in a fluid stage, it is continually trying to adapt itself to new accessions of thought and emotion and to the constant progress in our national life.[2]

Though in theory Tagore welcomed Mookerjee's proposal to introduce Bengali as a subject for MA courses at this time, he had deep misgivings about its implementation: 'I have found that the direct influence which the Calcutta University wields over our language is not strengthening and vitalising, but pedantic and narrow.'[3] Nevertheless, under pressure, he agreed to become chief examiner of Bengali at Calcutta University in 1923 – only to find that he could not endure its requirements. This letter to Mookerjee explains why.[4]

Calcutta, [India]
11 Asharh 1330 [26 June 1923]

Bahumanbhajaneshu
I offer this with friendly greetings –
When the proposal was made to me that I accept the position of chief examiner of Bengali in the MA course of the Calcutta University, I demurred. For I am completely without experience in this work, moreover on the whole I do not have much regard for examinations. Nevertheless, knowing that through this offer you yourself were expressing appreciation of me, after due consideration I diffidently agreed.

Now however that Dinesh Babu has presented me with various examination questions, I see that they are based on certain textbooks.[5] Only those who use such books for teaching are qualified to test people on these questions. I have neither read such books carefully nor am I properly informed about their subject matter, in other words I know less about the answers than do the candidates for examination. In view of this it would be improper for me to take on the examiner's task. Therefore I humbly request you to release me from the post, excusing me on grounds of incompetence.

Bhabadiya
Shri Rabindranath Thakur

Source: MS original at Rabindra Bhavan, Shantiniketan; letter published in *CP*, X, pp. 30–2.

1 Sir Ashutosh Mookerjee [Mukhopadyay] (1864–1924): lawyer and educationist; he was vice-chancellor, University of Calcutta, 1906–14 and 1921–3, and in between he had effective control of the growing postgraduate departments of the university.
2 'Vernaculars for the MA degree', *MR*, Nov. 1918, p. 462.
3 *Ibid*.
4 Mookerjee was no doubt hoping to recruit RT in his battle with the chancellor of Calcutta University, Lord Lytton, who refused to renew his vice-chancellorship in 1923. See Broomfield, *Elite Conflict*, pp. 191–4.
5 On Dinesh Chandra Sen, see letter 31. RT expressed his view of textbooks in Bengali in a funny letter to W. W. Hornell, the director of public instruction in Bengal, in 1914. One of the teachers in Shantiniketan, Jagadananda Ray, had written a textbook which RT hoped Hornell would prescribe for schools:

> By dint of perseverance, worthy of a better cause, he has been successful in turning out something that, I am sure, will satisfy the task of the most fastidious of your textbook pedants, in being safe and insipid, profusely loyal, rigidly grammatical, and dull as ditchwater. He has strictly followed in every particular the regulations laid down by wise heads and hopes to be rewarded for the sacrifice he has made of his literary conscience. (RT to Hornell, 23 June 1914 [copy at RB])

193

To Upton Sinclair[1]

In mid-1923, Tagore wrote a letter to the American radical Upton Sinclair, novelist and socialist, enclosing a postal order for twenty shillings and requesting him to send copies of as many of his books as this sum would buy.[2] Sinclair sent all his books and a letter noting that 'One or two of the specially bad ones I will put in a separate package, and send them later, in the hope that those who keep watch on mail going into India will at least let the good books get by!'[3]

Though Tagore could never have adopted socialism as a creed, unlike Sinclair, his reply to him shows how his familiar repugnance for commercialism and the dehumanising effects of machines brought him close to Sinclair's attitudes to these matters. The vehemence of his language here recalls that of his letters to C. F. Andrews from America in 1920–1, when he was trying to raise money for Visva-Bharati (e.g. letter 157). In the 1930s, such feelings drove him to praise the Soviet Union in a profoundly misguided way.

Visva-Bharati Office, Calcutta, [India]
4 September 1923

Dear Mr Sinclair

The box of books [has] arrived with the kind messages of your friendship inscribed in each and every one. It was indeed kind of you to respond so generously to my request. I am glad to have this expression of your interest and glad also of the opportunity to give your ideas to the students of my Visva-Bharati.

You asked me my opinion of your books. I have not as yet had the opportunity to read them all, but it was *The Brass Check*, read when it was first published, that made me feel that I should like to know both the man and his works. Your fearless stand for truth, for the things that are right, your viewpoint of the humiliation that worship of money brings, its stifling quality, its empty arrogance, its insidious undermining of self-respect, its valuelessness, all the attributes which are its curse when dollars own the man; these ideas which you inculcated in this particular book immediately made a bond of sympathy. For years I have thought over these things, this especial phase of our modern civilisation, and only a few weeks ago I have myself finished a drama on the same subject. It will be published shortly in English and I shall hope to have the pleasure of sending you a copy.[4]

I shall see about the translation of some of your books and let you know.

With the most sincere thanks for your courtesy and the hope that we may have a personal chat someday concerning men and books and things in general and those in particular which seem to interest us both,[5] I am

Yours sincerely
Rabindranath Tagore

Source: letter published in Upton Sinclair, *My Lifetime in Letters* (Missouri, 1960), pp. 292–3.

1 Upton Beall Sinclair (1878–1968): novelist and polemicist for socialism and other causes; his best-known book is *The Jungle* (1906). *The Brass Check* was published in 1919.
2 RT to Sinclair (1923), in Sinclair, *My Lifetime*, p. 291.
3 Sinclair to RT, 3 July 1923 [RB].
4 Over the summer of 1923, while staying in Shillong, RT wrote 'Yakshapuri', the first version of what became *Rakta Karabi* (*Red Oleanders*). It was published in English translation as a special autumn number of *VBQ*, Sept. 1924. See letter 187, n. 2.
5 RT never met for a talk, though Sinclair had come to see RT on the station platform in Pasadena, California, in Oct. 1916, when he visited the town to lecture. Apparently those looking after RT at Pasadena, 'carefully kept him sheltered from the city's one socialist author' (Sinclair, *My Lifetime*, p. 291).

194

To Leonard K. Elmhirst

Leonard Elmhirst was away from India from March to November 1923, much of this time being spent in trying to organise money, men and materials for Shriniketan in the USA and in Britain. The moment he returned, he received this summons from Rabindranath, who was again fundraising among the princely states of western India. Elmhirst immediately joined him and they travelled together as a team, the presence of an Englishman symbolising to potential princely donors the seriousness of Tagore's commitment to internationalism at Shantiniketan.

> Retreat, Shahibag, Ahmedabad,
> [Gujarat, India][1]
> 4 November 1923

Dear Deshika[2]

My welcome greetings to you. I am not very far from Bombay, engaged in a wild goose chase of money. Extricate yourself from your engagements or go through them quickly and come to me. Do not let me wait to see you after your long absence till others have had their chance. You know how proud I am by nature. My name must not be put at the end of your list but somewhere about the top, if not on the topmost line. Kathiawar is one of the most interesting corners of India – the land of a magnificent breed of cattle and a people who still love colour and music and do not allow their womenfolk to wear khaddar.[3]

With love

Affectionately yours
Rabindranath Tagore

[PS] Do not bother yourself about your engagement in Benares, they are not at all serious about it – and do not let Gretchen know that I have been trying to entice you away from the shortest route to Surul. I am willing to meet her wrath after the crime has been committed. I am afraid of the thunderbolt of her telegraphic messages.[4]

Source: MS original in Dartington Trust archives [Dartington]; letter published in Dutta and Robinson (eds.), *Purabi*, p. 81.

1 The Shahibag, a seventeenth-century palace built by Prince Khurram (later Emperor Shahjahan), was where RT had stayed in 1878, when his brother Satyendranath was posted to Ahmedabad as a judge (see *My Rem*, chapter 24).
2 Deshika: guide, preceptor. RT conferred this title upon Elmhirst at Shriniketan, shortly before he departed abroad in 1923.
3 The remark about khaddar was a dig at the puritanism of Gandhi, who was born in Kathiawar. 'The poet, I think, was as much upset by Gandhi's insistence that even colour must be cut out of Indian life as by anything else' (Elmhirst to Dorothy Straight, 10 Dec. 1923 [Dartington]).
4 Gretchen Green continued to run the dispensary at Surul, while Elmhirst was away. She also acted as secretary to RT for a while, who found her very efficient, perhaps a little too efficient (see letter 295).

Travels east and west (1924–1926)

Introduction

In 1916, Tagore had visited Japan, but he had not yet been to China. In April–May 1924, despite the country's disturbed condition, he visited Peking and several other cities, accompanied by Leonard Elmhirst and others from Shantiniketan, and was received by large crowds. He saw himself, as did his Chinese hosts, as renewing the contact between India and China begun by the early Buddhist missionaries, and he developed a conviction that Buddhism was the dominant cultural influence in China. His belief in Sino-Indian friendship later influenced Jawaharlal Nehru, with disastrous consequences during the Indo-China war in 1962.

After a second visit to Japan, Tagore returned to India – but not for long. Invited to Peru to attend the centenary celebrations of Peru's defeat of the Spanish colonial power, Tagore sailed for Europe and thence to South America, again with Elmhirst. But he fell ill and had to winter in Buenos Aires, staying at a house put at his disposal by an admirer, Victoria Ocampo.

On the way back to India, he stopped in Italy and was greeted with a mixed reception by the Fascists. Later that year, however, Mussolini sent two scholars to Visva-Bharati and a fine collection of Italian classics for the university's library. Tagore was persuaded, against his better judgement, to accept an official invitation to visit Italy in May–June 1926. Afterwards he realised his mistake, under pressure from Romain Rolland and Italian dissidents, and though he had not endorsed Fascism, he published an open letter condemning it.

From Italy he went on to tour many European countries, finally leaving the Continent in November 1926. Wherever he went, he was accorded an extraordinary welcome at all levels of society, especially, once again, in Germany, where he met Albert Einstein for the first time and formed a friendship with him.

195

To Romain Rolland

W. W. Pearson died in Italy in September 1923 in a tragic and macabre accident; he fell from a moving train with an insecurely fastened door, broke his spine but lingered in agony for several days. Two days before the accident, he had been with Romain Rolland at his house in Villeneuve in Switzerland. Rolland had been struck by his personality and wrote about him later to Tagore:

> From the sorrow I felt, who saw Pearson only twice, for a few hours, casually, I could well appreciate what must have been your own suffering, you who had for fifteen years felt the ardour of his devotion.
>
> Our last talks were almost exclusively about you and Santiniketan. He was distressed to learn that you had to cope with so many difficulties, devoting all your time to tiring duties, for the sake of the institution and its preservation, which interfered with your creative activities . . .
>
> I can only say: Take care of yourself for the sake of us all! Do not sacrifice the 'still small voice' of poetry even at the cost of building up Santiniketan and its university, however great might be its importance for the world![1]

Rabindranath's response distils all the aspects of his friendship with Pearson present in previous letters (especially letters 98, 103, 155, 158 and 186) and also gives clear expression to his own inner struggle – the greatest of his life – between the life of the artist and the life of the idealist wishing to change the world.

Santiniketan, [West Bengal, India]
28? February 1924

My very dear friend, before I sail for China, the time for which is drawing near, I must thank you for the delight that your letter has given me.

Pearson had an abundant gift of friendship which he freely offered to those, who, because of their obscurity, failed to attract notice. They were like night's background against which his love found its light fully revealed. He was sensitively conscious of the immense value of the individual man, irrespective of his special merits and uses, and this made him keenly suffer whenever that individual was ignored or hurt in consequence of social maladjustment or tyranny of organisation. This grew in him to such an extent that he became jealous of all institutions which represented some ideal which had a wide range transcending the limits of the concretely personal. In fact, lately his mind was distracted when Santiniketan outgrew its vocation as a mere educational body belonging to the immediate locality, when it tried to respond in its various efforts to what I consider to be the great call of the present age. He was afraid lest our attention should in the least measure be diverted from the children attending our school into a channel for the communication of ideas and formation of a community. I was feeling anxious about him for some time before he died when he grew restless at the apprehension of encroachment of some adventurous ideal into the happy realm of personal service. No doubt idealism is a disturbing factor in all settled forms of life and therefore prosperous people have a vigorous suspicion against it. There is such a thing as the enjoyment of emotional prosperity where the stimulation to our personal feeling of love is constantly supplied. Pearson found it when he first came here and his own natural instinct of attachment had its full scope among our school children and the neighbouring villagers. Then came the idea of Visva-Bharati like a strong breeze, scattering the petals from our ashram-flower, claiming its fruit. Pearson never was fully reconciled to it to the end of his days. Intellectually he had nothing to say against it, but his heart ached – for his mind was like the bee which has nothing to do with the fruit but only with the flower.

Travels east and west 309

12 Tagore in Villeneuve, Switzerland, 1926: with Madeleine Rolland, Prashanta Chandra and Rani Mahalanobis, Romain Rolland (*seated*), Pratima Tagore

I understand this conflict in his mind because I myself have a kind of civil war constantly going on in my own nature between my personality as a creative artist, who necessarily must be solitary, and that as an idealist who must realise himself through works of a complex character needing a large field of collaboration with a large body of men. My conflict is within myself between the two opposite forces in my character, and not, as in the case of Pearson, between my individual temperament and the surrounding circumstance. Both of the contending forces being equally natural to me I cannot with impunity get rid of one of them in order to simplify my life's problem. I suppose a proper rhythm is possible to be attained in which both may be harmonised, and my work in the heart of the crowd may find its grace through the touch of the breath that comes from the solitude of the creative mind.

But unfortunately at the present moment, the claim of the organisation is rudely asserting itself, and I do not know how to restrain it within bounds. The poet in me is hurt, his atmosphere of leisure dust-laden. I do not wish that my life's sunset should thus be obscured in a murky air of strenuous work, the work which perpetually devours its own infinite background of peace. I earnestly hope that I shall be rescued in time before I die – in the meanwhile I go to China, in what capacity I do not know. Is it as a poet, or as a bearer of good advice and sound commonsense?[2]

With love,
Rabindranath Tagore

Source: MS copy at Rabindra Bhavan, Shantiniketan; letter published in *MR*, Feb. 1943, p. 97.

1 Rolland to RT, 30 Dec. 1923, in Alex Aronson and Krishna Kripalani (eds.), *Rolland and Tagore* (Calcutta, 1945), pp. 45–6.
2 RT left Calcutta for China on 21 March 1924.

196

To Thomas Sturge Moore

Despite his affection and respect for W. W. Pearson, Tagore did not conceal his dissatisfaction with Pearson's translation of his novel, *Gora*, done in 1922 and published by Macmillan, after various revisions, in 1924. Pearson had bitten off more than he could chew and had to be rescued by Surendranath Tagore (translator of *My Reminiscences*, *The Home and the World* and other Tagore books); but before Surendranath could complete his revisions, Macmillan went ahead with publication.

Rabindranath always lacked confidence in the willingness of his western readers to take an interest in the Bengali – as opposed to the universal – elements in his writings. *Gora* provided perhaps the most pointed example of this. Tagore told Pearson in 1922:

> I find that English readers have very little patience for scenes and sentiments which are foreign to them; they feel a sort of grievance for what they do not understand – and they care not to understand whatever is different from their familiar world. This is the reason why you find translations from oriental works in Germany and France and very few in England. This makes me think that after you have done with your translation it will have to be carefully abridged.[1]

Pearson resisted abridgement and *Gora* was published in full (though Pearson did not live to see it).[2] Most English critics found it simply tedious. The translation was partly to blame, but much more important was the foreignness of the subject matter, just as Tagore had predicted.[3] This letter to Thomas Sturge Moore, who was sensitive to such questions (see letter 86), having himself revised some of Tagore's work for publication, touches on the East–West sensibility gap more than once.

Western Hills Hotel, Peking, [China]
20 May 1924

Dear Sturge Moore

Possibly you know by this time that I am in China. I have just completed my engagements here and am going to Japan. I hope I shall be back to my country some time in September.

I am glad that *Gora* has received some attention in England. Pearson did not know enough Bengali to be able to give a correct rendering of the story in English. My nephew Suren revised it comparing it with the original. Macmillan in their haste only had the half of the corrected version and the latter half remains untouched with its ludicrous mistakes and crudities.[4] If you could read the Bengali book you would at once know how extremely unsatisfactory the translation is.

My friend Leonard Elmhirst who has for [the] last two years been connected with my Visva-Bharati work is going to England through Siberian railway. I have asked him to see you and let you know how glad we should be if you could come to our ashram in India. I have also asked him to show you my copies of lectures in China and arrange with my publishers to allow you to edit them. My friends in China want to have them in a book form.[5]

The brother of Mrs Sarojini Naidu has translated in English verse some of my child poems. He wishes me to recommend these to my publishers in England.[6] I do not trust my judgement about anything written in your language – verse or prose, and therefore, I am sending these to you through my friend for your opinion.

I am sorry to learn that you have not been well for some time, and hope that by this time you have completely recovered. I have not heard from or about Mukul for a long time.[7] There was some rumour that he has been preparing to come back to India. I hope it is true. I do not know how far his career as an artist has progressed – I am certain that he will find fresh inspiration if he *does* come to India. However, I feel glad that he has been of service to you when you were ill.

You will find Elmhirst, if you have time to know him, an extremely nice and interesting young man full of ideas and experience. You will know from him some idea of our work in Santiniketan.

Very sincerely yours,
Rabindranath Tagore

Source: MS original in Sturge Moore Papers [London].

1 RT to Pearson (1922), *VBQ*, 9, No. 2, Aug.–Oct. 1943, pp. 178–9.
2 Pearson to RT, 15 June 1922 [RB].
3 See Dutta and Robinson, *Rabindranath Tagore*, pp. 154–5.
4 There are various letters from Pearson to Macmillan, the last written from Geneva on 7 Sept. 1923, asking if the publishers have yet received Surendranath Tagore's final corrections. No translator is credited on the title page of the finished book, instead a note appears on the following page: 'My thanks are due to Mr Surendranath Tagore, who very kindly made the final corrections and revisions for this translation. Any merits it possesses are due to his painstaking efforts to rectify my mistakes. – TRANSLATOR.'
5 *Talks in China: Lectures Delivered in April and May, 1924* was published in Calcutta in 1925 by the Visva-Bharati Book Shop; there was no London edition.
6 The poetry of Harindranath Chatterji [Chattopadhyay] (1898–1990) was of some interest to W. B Yeats. Some of his work was published in India, but there was no British edition.
7 On Mukul Dey, see letter 109, n. 5.

197

To Leonard K. Elmhirst

Instead of returning to Britain by rail across Russia (as indicated by Tagore in letter 196), Leonard Elmhirst accompanied Tagore to Japan. They sailed from Shanghai on

30 May 1924 in a ship specially chartered for Rabindranath by the Japanese textile magnates of Shanghai, and remained together in Japan for almost a month. Then Elmhirst headed for the USA, while Tagore headed homewards, sailing from Kobe and stopping en route at Shanghai again. Here, however, he refused to go ashore, saying he was indisposed.

This Far Eastern tour marked the high point of the Tagore–Elmhirst relationship. During it the two men were in close proximity for over three months. Before, for more than two years, they had worked in harmony but to a great extent separately; afterwards, Elmhirst's thoughts increasingly turned away from Bengal and towards the idea of founding an institution of his own in Britain. This letter, written from Shanghai on the way home, is among the most intimate of Tagore's letters written to non-Bengalis.

[on board ship], Shanghai, [China]
26 June 1924

Dear Leonard

Directly you left the steamer there came two copies of the typescripts of 'City and village'.[1] If you possibly can, try to send me my talk about education given at Mrs Bena's house.[2]

I am glad to say there is no sign of Kadoorie or of Shastri.[3] Our Indian friends came and took away Kshiti Babu and company to their house.[4] They wrestled with me for some time and then gave up. I am the sole monarch of that cabin of mine with my Manchu friend somewhere beyond my reach.[5]

I hope you do not need to be told how much I feel about the service you have done me on this trip. Also you must know that it is not merely a feeling of gratitude that you have won from me, it is something deeper.

I believe you have realised this time what I mean by my Visva-Bharati ideals. There are numerous institutions in this world for all kinds of object – but they are for practical people possessing expert knowledge and trained skill. I have neither the ambition nor talent for such organisations. But I believe I have the power of vision which seeks its realisation in some concrete form. Unless our different works in Visva-Bharati are luminous with the fire of vision I myself can have no place in them. This is why all the time when Sriniketan has been struggling to grow into a form, I was intently wishing that it should not only have a shape, but also light; so that it might transcend its immediate limits of time, space and some special purpose. If Visva-Bharati comes to attain truth through the life of those who serve her then she will illumine the path of pilgrimage and not merely fill the store room of benefits. I hope I may say it with truth that herein lies the difference between America and ourselves.

I carry an infinite space of loneliness around my soul through which the voice of my personal life very often does not reach my friends – for which I suffer more than they do. I have my yearning for the personal world as much as any other mortal, or perhaps more. But my destiny seems to be careful that in my life's experience I should only have the *touch* of personality and not the *ties* of it. All the while she claims my thoughts, my dreams and my voice, and for that detachment of life and mind is needed. In fact, I have constantly been deprived of opportunities for intimate [long-lasting] attachments of companionship. Then again I have such an extreme delicacy of sensitiveness with regard to personal relationship that even when I acknowledge and welcome it I cannot invite it to the immediate closeness of my life. This deficiency I acknowledge with resignation knowing that it is a sacrifice claimed of me by my providence for some purpose which he knows.

A lighted lamp is [at] the end [for] us and not a lump of gold. I could have taken the path of politics or social service and [been] idolised by my people, but I naturally avoided it and incurred [the] bitter displeasure of my countrymen. In the same manner we must avoid trying to do a particular kind of good according to some recipe made by clever learned men who have a technical knowledge and a specialised experience. Let us bring all our power of imagination and create a world. Nanda Lal[6] is there ready for his task, you must also come and join us and let all your dreams shine across the boundaries of practical achievements.

Ever yours
Rabindranath Tagore

Source: MS original in Dartington Trust archives [Dartington]; letter published in Dutta and Robinson (eds.), *Purabi*, pp. 83–4.

1 *VBQ*, 2, No. 3, Oct. 1924, pp. 215–27.
2 In late May, in Shanghai, RT stayed with a prominent businessman, the Italian G. A. Bena. His wife, who was interested in education, persuaded him to speak to some of her European friends in her living room on the evening of his arrival, 28 May.
3 Sir Elly Kadoorie (1867–1944), founder of a business house in his own name in Shanghai and Hong Kong, gave generously to charities. He donated money to Shantiniketan to build an artesian well (RT to Kadoorie, 15 Aug. 1924 [copy at RB]).
4 Kshiti Mohan Sen accompanied RT throughout his Far Eastern tour.
5 According to Elmhirst, the 'Manchu friend' was Hsu Chih-mo, RT's interpreter throughout his Chinese tour in April–May 1924.
6 Nanda Lal Bose (1882–1966): artist; he founded Kala Bhavan, the art school at Shantiniketan. He accompanied RT on his Far Eastern tour.

198

To Victoria Ocampo[1]

While he was in Japan in June 1924, Tagore received an official invitation to visit Peru. The government in Lima was planning a celebration of the centenary of Peru's defeat of the Spanish colonial power. Rabindranath agreed to attend and sailed from Europe, reaching Buenos Aires on 6 November 1924, attended once more by Leonard Elmhirst (the last tour on which Elmhirst acted as Tagore's secretary). But there, in Argentina, he felt too weak to continue to Peru; he also received advice that the Peruvian Government, a dictatorship, was planning to exploit his presence in a way he would not approve. The result was that he stayed in Argentina for nearly two months convalescing, before returning to Europe in early January 1925.

Most of this time was spent in the riverside Villa Miralrío at San Isidro, outside the capital, which was put at his disposal by Victoria Ocampo, a remarkable aristocratic Argentinian woman who was not yet the well-known litterateur she became after the launch of her magazine *Sur* (South Wind) in 1931. She lavished attention on Rabindranath, and he, in his own way, reciprocated. With Elmhirst caught in the

314 *Selected letters of Rabindranath Tagore*

middle, devoted to Tagore and physically attracted to Ocampo, and Ocampo needing Elmhirst as an interpreter of Tagore, a triangle was formed which was a fascinating tangle of mutual attraction and repulsion. All three were strong individuals and yet they were also representatives of their utterly disparate cultures, compelled to communicate the subtlest ideas and emotions in English, a language native to only one of them.

As Elmhirst wrote to Tagore's son Rathindranath in 1956, more than thirty years later, Ocampo 'wanted so badly to be recognised and appreciated' by Tagore 'for all her inner qualities of mind and feeling and scholarship and not just for her outward attractions, but at the same time could not entirely separate the one from the other. She was always jealous of what she regarded as my greater intimacy with Gurudev and for a time tried to insert herself between Gurudev and myself.'[2]

Although Tagore and Ocampo saw little of each other in person after he left Argentina (she never visited India), they remained in each others' minds. The poems Rabindranath wrote during this trip (published as *Purabi* in late 1925) were dedicated to Ocampo, and in the year before his death he wrote a poem that referred to her; some of his paintings also probably refer to her. The two long letters that follow (198 and 199), which he wrote her as he sailed away to Italy, are eloquent testimony to the bond between them.

SS *Giulio Cesare* [en route to Italy]
5 January 1925

Vijaya,[3] under a grey sky my days are repeated in rhymes that are monotonous, like a perpetual telling of beads. I pass most part of my day and a great part of my night deeply buried in your armchair which, at last, has explained to me the lyrical meaning of the poem of Baudelaire that I read with you.[4] I had hoped that I should be able to do some writing while crossing the interval between two shores – but the wind has veered and my manuscript book lies idle, its virgin papers looking like the sandy beach of a distant island unexplored. My day is divided into 2/3rd part of sleep and 1/3rd part of reading. I am completamente[5] surrounded by a deep atmosphere of laziness as befits a human male in an ideal condition of life. In these two days I have been able to understand why Chinamen must smoke opium in order to realise intensely for a few moments the profound dignity of the male, his natural birthright of inutile passiveness of which he is forcibly deprived the rest of his waking hours. The modern human females are never tired of accusing us of violence and tyranny, they do not know that it is a perverse expression of our inherent contemplative placidness repressed and tortured through the compelling necessity for us to be useful members of society. The Spanish Philosopher was right when he said that it was women who civilised us, and thus they have made our life burdensome, have imposed upon us missions which are not ours.[6] We have taken our revenge, made them more decorative than useful, turned them into a hothouse where forced sentiments are cultivated, prized for their ravishing colours and perfume of sickly passion. Life has its necessities, but Mind must have its leisure – women who are the guardian spirits of life are allowed leisure and men who, at their best, are philosophers, lovers of ideas, are made to toil for supplying necessaries of life and overfeeding the race. The modern feminists want to compete with men in an open field of work – but that will have the effect of accelerating men's energy, and their fire of ferocity will rage with a greater intensity. The only satisfactory solution will be to remove them altogether from the region of usefulness, to let the lure of the unnecessary set them free in the realm of the unknown. They are natural savages who love to roam alone in the wilderness of thoughts and dreams. But you want civilisation for your progeny, that they may be secure from all injuries and privations. And therefore you lasso these wild creatures and try to train them for domestic needs which are the needs of society. The antisocial beings are captured by the social beings, but the adjustments are not properly made and most of the works which are yours we are compelled to do with the mistaken notion that you are not fit for them and in return saddle you with a leisure which only makes you restless. I only wish you could see how greatly Leonard has improved since he has got his leisure on this ship (not shiiiiip).[7] He has suddenly turned an astronomer, haunting the upper deck, waiting for the chance of meeting some star of the first magnitude belonging to the southern hemisphere. You know, human males as secretaries are inefficient, but as astronomers they know how to make their opportunities rich and shining. I suppose you know that also for me astronomy has a great attraction, but being a poet I have my chart of stars in my memory which I can study even when I am confined in my cabin. I have been advised never to joke with a woman but I am afraid that some of the observations in this letter show signs of frivolity. You will excuse me when you know that a man who is not a prophet and yet who is treated as a prophet must give vent to his fit of laughter even at the risk of misunderstanding.

Shri Rabindranath Thakur[8]

Source: MS copy at Rabindra Bhavan, Shantiniketan; letter published in Ketaki Kushari Dyson, *In your Blossoming Flower-Garden: Rabindranath Tagore and Victoria Ocampo* (New Delhi, 1988), pp. 384–6.

1 Victoria Ocampo (1890–1979): editor, publisher and writer; her magazine *Sur*, founded in 1931, was notably international in its choice of contributors, among whom was Jorge Luis Borges, then barely known as a writer. On her relationship with RT, see Dyson, *Flower-Garden*, and the essay by Ocampo, 'Tagore on the banks of the River Plate', in Sahitya Akademi, *Rabindranath Tagore*, pp. 27–47.
2 Elmhirst to Rathindranath Tagore, 9 Sept. 1956, in Dyson, *Flower Garden*, p. 277.
3 Vijaya was RT's version of Victoria; in Sanskrit it means 'victory', in Bengali it signifies the goddess Durga.
4 As part of her devotion to RT, Ocampo insisted that an armchair at the Villa Miralrío which he greatly liked was put into his cabin on board ship to Europe (to do this, the cabin door had to be removed from its hinges). See *ibid.*, p. 189. The Baudelaire poem was 'L'Invitation au voyage' from *Les Fleurs du Mal*, to which Ocampo had introduced RT at the villa, translating it herself into English and provoking the comment from RT: 'Vijaya, I don't like your furniture poet' (Sahitya Akademi, *Rabindranath Tagore*, p. 44).
5 'Completamente', Spanish for 'completely', is a joking reference to Ocampo's tendency to exaggerate.
6 According to Ocampo, the Spanish philosopher is Ortega y Gasset, her principal literary influence, of whom she often spoke to RT. See Dyson, *Flower-Garden*, pp. 387–8.
7 Ocampo used to pronounce an English 'i' (as in 'ship') in the elongated manner common among Spanish speakers of English.
8 Signed in Bengali.

199

To Victoria Ocampo

SS *Giulio Cesare* [en route to Italy]
13 January 1925

Dear Vijaya

I am drifting farther and farther away from your shore and now it has become possible for me to set the vision of my everyday surroundings at San Isidro against a background of separation. I am not a born traveller – I have not the energy and strength needed for knowing a strange country and helping the mind to gather materials from a wide area of new experience for building its foreign nest. And therefore when I am away from my own land I seek for some individuals who may represent to me the country to which they belong. For me the spirit of Latin America will ever dwell in my memory incarnated in your person. You rescued me from the organised hospitality of a reception committee and allowed me to receive through yourself the personal touch of your country. Unfortunately there was the barrier of language that prevented a free enough communication of minds between us, for you never felt fully at home in the only European language I happen to know. It was unfortunate because you have a richness of mind which naturally longs to offer its own tribute to those whom you accept as your friends, and I fully understand the pain which you must have suffered for not being able to reveal adequately to me your deeper thoughts and to dissolve the fog that screened off the world of your intellectual life from my vision. I am deeply sorry that it has not been possible for me to have an acquaintance of your complete personality – the difficulty having been enhanced owing to the literary character of your mind. For such a mind has its aristocratic code of honour about its manner of self-expression choosing to remain dumb [rather] than to send out its thoughts dressed in rags. But never for a moment imagine that I failed to recognise that you had a mind. To me it was like a star that was distant and not a planet that was dark. When we were together we mostly played with words and tried to laugh away our best opportunities to see each other clearly. Such laughter often disturbs the atmosphere of our mind, raising dust from its surface which only blurs our view. One thing most of my friends fail to know [is] that where I am real I am profoundly serious. Our reality is like treasure, it is not left exposed in the outer chamber of our personal self. It waits to be explored and only in our serious moments [can it] be approached. You have often found me homesick – it was not so much for India, it was for that abiding reality in me in which I can have my inner freedom. It becomes totally obscured when for some reason or other my attention is too much directed upon my own personal self. My true home is there where from my surroundings comes the call to me to bring out the best that I have, for that inevitably leads me to the touch with the universal. My mind must have a nest to which the voice of the sky can descend freely, the sky that has no other allurements but light and freedom. Whenever there is the least sign of the nest becoming a jealous rival of the sky, my mind, like a migrant bird, tries to take its flight to a distant shore. When my freedom of light is obstructed for some length of time I feel as if I am bearing the burden of a disguise, like the morning in its disguise of a mist. I do not see myself – and this obscurity, like a nightmare, seems to suffocate me with its heavy emptiness. I have often said to you that I am not free to give up my freedom – for this freedom is claimed by my Master for his own service. There have been times when I *did* forget this and allowed myself to drift into some easeful captivity – but every time it ended in catastrophe and I was driven by an angry power to the open, across broken walls.

I tell you all this because I know you love me. I trust my providence. I feel certain – and I say this in all humility – that he has chosen me for some special mission of his own and not merely for the purpose of linking the endless chain of generation. Therefore I believe that your love may, in some way, help me in my fulfilment. It will sound egoistic, only because the voice of our ego has in it the same masterful cry of insistence as the voice of that which infinitely surpasses it. I assure you, that through me a claim comes which is not mine. A child's claim upon its mother has a sublime origin – it is not a claim of an individual, it is that of humanity. Those who come on some special errand of God are like that child, if they ever attract love and service it should be for a higher end than merely their own enjoyment. Not only love, but hurts and insults, neglect and rejection come not to grind them into dust but to kindle their life into a brighter flame.

Your friendship has come to me unexpectedly. It will grow to its fullness of truth when you know and accept my real being and see clearly the deeper meaning of my life. I have lost most of my friends because they asked me for themselves, and when I said I was not free to offer away myself – they thought I was proud. I have deeply suffered from this over and over again – and therefore I always feel nervous whenever a new gift of friendship comes in my way. But I accept my destiny and if you also have the courage fully to accept it we shall ever remain friends.

Shri Rabindranath Thakur[1]

17 Jan. [1925]

Tomorrow we shall reach Barcelona and the day after Genoa. I am about to leave my easy chair in my cabin. That chair has been my real nest for these two weeks giving me rest and privacy and a feeling that my happiness is of value to somebody.[2] I do not know when it will be possible for me to write to you again but I shall always remember you.

Source: MS copy at Rabindra Bhavan, Shantiniketan; letter published in Dyson, *Flower-Garden*, pp. 390–2.

1 Signed in Bengali.
2 See letter 198, n. 4. In Italy, Leonard Elmhirst managed to have Ocampo's chair transferred to the ship that took RT home to India. It now lies at the Rabindra Bhavan, Shantiniketan.

200

To Dorothy Whitney Elmhirst (Straight)[1]

After the Far Eastern tour, Tagore had cherished the hope that Leonard Elmhirst would join him in Bengal and direct the rural reconstruction he had started at Surul on a long-term basis, in the way that C. F. Andrews and W. W. Pearson had made commitments to Shantiniketan. But during their voyage to and sojourn in Argentina, Elmhirst made it clear, first, that he intended to start an institution of his own in England and, later, that he and Dorothy Straight, his sponsor at Surul, were to marry; her fortune was to fund the institution. According to Leonard (who was writing to Dorothy from Buenos Aires), to the first piece of news Tagore responded: 'If only you will start an experiment in England . . . I shall be sure that in one place my ideas will be given a fair trial and I shall not forever be condemned as an impractical poet.'[2] And to the second piece of news: 'You should congratulate yourself, anyhow I congratulate you, you've found something that I find very rarely, a woman's love that is pure gold and you ought to be very happy – I know that this is to be the right and the only thing for you both.'[3]

He undoubtedly meant what he said in both cases – and yet losing Leonard to Dartington and Dorothy was a blow. Tagore's relationship with both Dartington and Dorothy Elmhirst would always be an ambivalent one, and vice versa. He could never feel comfortable with her unique mixture of idealism and vast financial wealth, as he had shown on his first encounter with her during his visit to America in 1920–1 (see letter 161), when he showed small sympathy for American life. She, for her part, could never feel at ease with his egotism and disconnection from worldly affairs, and felt an indifference bordering on distaste for Indian life. As important, they were in a tug of war over Leonard. This letter, wishing Dorothy well in her marriage, hints at the deeper conflict.

Port Said, [Egypt]
7 February 1925

Dear Mrs Straight,

Leonard has a natural wisdom which makes it easy for him to find friends wherever he goes and I also belong to that crowd of admirers to whom he has made himself very dear. He has that rare adaptability of mind and large-heartedness which enable him to understand and respect those who are different from him in race and tradition and to serve those who for him have no other kinship but the kinship of a common humanity. Feeling certain that he has been born with a true mission I cannot help believing that his providence has called you inevitably to him and that your love will give him the wealth of life for which his heart has been in need so long. Opportunities will come to him which will lead him to his fulfilment and I love to think that your union with him is one such with its possibilities of delight and greatness.

Today I feel more grieved than ever before that it has not been possible for you to know me.[4] I do not at all wish that you should ever strain yourself in order to understand my personality or my work. I only hope that you may realise that I have been of help to Leonard and [may] through [that] find it easy to acknowledge me as your friend.

Rabindranath Tagore

Source: MS original in Dartington Trust archives [Dartington]; letter published in Dutta and Robinson (eds.), *Purabi*, p. 88.

1 Dorothy Whitney Elmhirst (Straight) (1887–1968): founder of the Dartington Trust with Leonard Elmhirst, philanthropist and patron of the arts; with her first husband, Willard Straight, she helped found

the *New Republic* and *Asia*. Until her marriage to Elmhirst in April 1925, Dorothy Straight lived in the USA, thereafter she moved to Dartington. See Young, *The Elmhirsts of Dartington*.
2 Elmhirst to Straight, 23 Oct. 1924 [Dartington].
3 Elmhirst to Straight, 26 Dec. 1924 [Dartington].
4 Note RT's construction here: 'you to know me', rather than 'me to know you'. Dorothy Elmhirst never clearly articulated her reservations about RT in writing. A letter she wrote to Leonard in Aug. 1924 probably comes nearest to it, with these shrewd criticisms:

> I have finished reading the Poet's articles . . . I have to admit now to being entirely won over to him! My questions seem rather futile I'm afraid against the background of his greatness, but what I wonder is this – is he perhaps too much an individualist? That must sound like a foolish question in view of what he is trying to do with his school, but here and there he says something that makes me wonder whether he is losing sight of the social values in education as well as in life. You remember what he says about his own education? There he seems to glory in the independent and individualistic line he took, disregarding I think the fact that he must surely have lost something in gaining his own free way . . . Of course one of the problems always is to combine individual freedom with certain group responsibilities and I know you have balanced the two successfully – but I wonder if the Poet has! And I miss in the religious article something that corresponds to the Kingdom of God – the same note of social aspiration. Then the other question in my mind is this – has he the capacity to appreciate western culture? He tries hard to be fair to the West but I think the only western contribution he really admits is science. And I want to ask him about Italian painting, English poetry, German music and the English political genius. Science after all is not the only achievement of the West, is it? But taking the articles by and large, they are quite extraordinary, I think, and they lift life to a pure and high plane. (Straight to Elmhirst, 5 Aug. 1924 [Dartington])

201

To Rathindranath Tagore

On 16 June 1925, Chitta Ranjan Das died, putting Rabindranath in a quandary. C. R. Das had been an extremely popular leader with many Bengalis, mainly the *bhadralok*, but to Tagore he represented much that was not at all admirable in Bengali public life.[1] However a response was expected from him: if he eulogised, he would be perjuring himself; if he criticised, he would attract public odium; if he temporised, he would please hardly anyone.[2] Writing to his son he expresses his familiar dilemma.

Shantiniketan, [West Bengal, India]
4 Asharh 1332 [18 June 1925]

Kalyaniyeshu

With Chitta Ranjan's death, should I go to Calcutta? – my mind is in turmoil about it. You know how I had to fall in with my countrymen and express condolences when Ashu Babu died – should I do so on this occasion too? – give it some thought.[3] Especially given that all along I disagreed with Chitta – [however,] no one must get the impression that I hold a grudge against him. If nothing else, perhaps I ought to pay a visit to his family home in Calcutta. But then I will get dragged into memorial meetings and have to say a few words as well. When you get this letter, send me your advice by urgent wire. I am writing to Prashanta also.[4]

Shri Rabindranath Thakur

Source: MS original at Rabindra Bhavan, Shantiniketan; letter published in *CP*, I, p. 79.

1 Chitta Ranjan Das (1870–1925): nationalist leader. RT's disagreements with Das arose from facts such as the following: in 1905, Das, as an 'ultra-radical' young barrister, enthusiastically supported student boycotts of schools and colleges, despite having no serious alternative educational programme; in 1907–8, Das skilfully defended Bengali terrorists at political trials and made his name as a barrister; in 1917, entering politics in response to the prospect of constitutional reform, Das insinuated that Tagore's knighthood had made him soft on the Government; in 1919, he lacked the courage to accept Tagore's proposal that he chair a meeting to protest against the Amritsar massacre and subsequently Das failed to congratulate him for repudiating his knighthood; in 1920, scenting power, Das swallowed his reservations about Gandhi and became the leader of noncooperation in Bengal, organising strikes and *hartals*; and in 1923, his Swaraj party accepted seats in the legislative council only to wreck the system of diarchy introduced in the recent government reforms. Das was an able politician but had few scruples about exploiting the prejudices of his supporters.
2 In the event, RT composed a very brief and mild eulogy in Bengali and another in English (*VBQ*, *3*, No. 2, July 1925, p. 181).
3 See RT's obituary of Sir Ashutosh Mookerjee [Mukhopadhyay] in *VBQ*, *2*, No. 2, July 1924, pp. 196–7.
4 RT often called upon Prashanta Chandra Mahalanobis for advice on 'political' matters.

202

To Margaret Sanger[1]

In August 1925, Tagore received a letter from Margaret Sanger, the American pioneer of the birth control movement. Mahatma Gandhi had just issued a statement in *Young India* supporting birth control but opposing artificial methods: Sanger hoped that Tagore would counter this with his own statement. 'You have travelled all over this earth, and you have observed the joys and sorrows and miseries of the world, and we take it for granted that with your international outlook on life and human society you cannot but feel friendly towards birth control.'[2] Tagore's reply, which follows, was printed in Sanger's *Birth Control Review*, with her editorial comment: 'Rabindranath Tagore has placed himself on the opposite side from the great ascetic.'

Santiniketan, [West Bengal, India]
30 September 1925

Dear Margaret Sanger

I am of opinion that the birth control movement is a great movement not only because it will save women from enforced and undesirable maternity, but because it will help the cause of peace by lessening the number of surplus population of a country, scrambling for food and space outside its own rightful limits. In a hunger-stricken country like India it is a cruel crime thoughtlessly to bring more children into existence than could properly be taken care of, causing endless sufferings to them and imposing a degrading condition upon the whole family. It is evident that the utter helplessness of a growing poverty very rarely acts as a check controlling the burden of overpopulation. It proves that in this case nature's urging gets the better of the severe warning that comes from the providence of civilised social life. Therefore, I believe, that to wait till the moral sense of man becomes a great deal more powerful than it is now and till then to allow countless generations of children to suffer privations and ultimately death for no fault of their own is a great social injustice which should not be tolerated. I feel grateful for the cause you have made your own and for which you have suffered.[3]

I am eagerly waiting for the literature that has been sent to me according to your letter, and I have asked our secretary to send you our Visva-Bharati journal in exchange for your *Birth Control Review*.[4]

Sincerely yours,
Rabindranath Tagore

Source: MS copy at Rabindra Bhavan, Shantiniketan; letter published in *Birth Control Review*, Dec. 1925.

1 Margaret Sanger (1879–1966): founder of the birth control movement in the USA. She visited RT at Shantiniketan in Dec. 1935.
2 Sanger to RT, 12 Aug. 1925, *VBQ, 1*, 1985, p. 13.
3 Leonard Elmhirst provided RT with books by Havelock Ellis, Marie Stopes and Margaret Sanger in Argentina in 1924. 'He is going to try and introduce the idea [of birth control] in our own dispensary and among his own women folk as a beginning' (Elmhirst to Dorothy Straight, 25 Dec. 1924 [Dartington]).
4 RT meant *Visva-Bharati Quarterly*, which Sanger had requested in her letter.

203

To Romain Rolland

The gap between Tagore and Gandhi widened as the 1920s wore on. In September 1925, Tagore published 'The cult of the *charka*', a devastating attack on Gandhi's notion of spinning as the way to attain *swaraj*. He felt a strong urge to escape from the isolation he had imposed upon himself by his refusal to fall in with noncooperation; his idea was to visit Europe again, but illness (the after-effects of a bout of influenza during his stay in Italy in January) dogged him.

Romain Rolland had been encouraging him to come, for both rest and medical treatment. Having himself been vilified and ostracised in France, for his pacifist writings, Rolland had some conception of Tagore's position in Bengal (though his view was coloured by his huge admiration for Gandhi):

> What a contrast between the immense human society that has been formed in the world round your name, between the resonances which vibrate in thousands of human hearts in all countries and the moral solitude which surrounds you in your own country! . . .
>
> He who wishes to save his people is an enemy of the people, as is said in the beautiful play of Ibsen.[1]

Tagore, for his part, wrote of Rolland at this time:

> Human civilisations have their genesis in individuals, and they also have their protectors in them. One of the few proofs that the present day is not utterly barren of them is the life and work of Romain Rolland. And that the present day needs him most is proved by the scourging he has received from it, which is a true recognition of his greatness by his fellow beings.[2]

This melancholy letter shows the genuine bond of sympathy between these two men. It would be severely tested when they did finally meet again in 1926.

Calcutta, [India]
23 September 1925

My very dear friend

I am sure we shall meet once again and our meeting will not be futile. The beginning of this autumn when I was about to leave India offered me too narrow a margin of time for the renewal of my acquaintance with Europe. On the other hand I shall easily have six months there next summer both for repairing my health and meeting my friends. Personally I do not think that my cautious doctor was wise in holding me back. He does not fully realise how great is the mental strain that my stay in India imposes upon me. It is the moral loneliness which is a constant and invisible burden that oppresses me most.[3] I wish it were possible for me to join hands with Mahatma Gandhi and thus at once surrender myself to the current of popular approbation. But I can no longer hide it from myself that we are radically different in our apprehension and pursuit of truth. Today to disagree with Mahatma and yet to find rest in one's surroundings in India is not possible and therefore I am waiting for my escape next March with an impatient feeling of longing. I know I have friends in Europe who are my real kindred and whose sympathy will act as a true restorative in my present state of weariness.

With love

Ever yours
Rabindranath Tagore

Source: MS copy at Rabindra Bhavan, Shantiniketan.

1 Rolland to RT, 22 Dec. 1925, in Rolland, *Selected Letters*, pp. 65–6.
2 'To Romain Rolland', *MR*, Jan. 1926, p. 49 (dated 5 Oct. 1925).
3 As early as 1922, RT told Rolland, 'I felt the utter loneliness of my position when I came back to India' (30 May 1922 [copy at RB]).

204

To Leonard K. Elmhirst

Having married Dorothy Straight in April 1925, Leonard Elmhirst located and purchased an estate at Dartington in Devon, with a derelict fourteenth-century manor house, and set to work creating his utopia inspired by Tagore's ideals. Rabindranath, back in Shantiniketan, felt somewhat bereft and a little envious of the new experiment; feelings that were exacerbated by his long period of illness. He did not write to Leonard for some five months, partly for these reasons and also because he had hoped to see him in person in Europe. This next letter was prompted by a brief one from Elmhirst, enclosing a pen which Leonard hoped would encourage Rabindranath's desire to draw: in Argentina he had watched this urge manifesting itself as elaborate doodles on manuscripts; from now on drawing and painting would become increasingly important to Tagore. The pen, said Leonard, 'is to encourage you to waste your time, thoroughly, endlessly and yet withal profitably'.[1]

Santiniketan, [West Bengal, India]
4 October 1925

Dear Leonard

My kind providence must have secretly urged you to send me a pen which has not yet had time to form any prejudice against me. I already have three pens conspiring to gain their *swaraj*.[2] They try to make my government of them impossible and have adopted the ink leakage tactics soiling themselves to spite me. Very likely the original sin is within myself, and I hope the newcomer which has a respectable exterior, will not join the ranks of its predecessors.

You have expressed your hope that this pen of yours will help me in the flowering season of my eccentricity which comes from an excess of dream energy. I have hardly enough left of it even for writing poems. Of late I have occasionally been compelled to write prose compositions with tracks across them of scratches – the hasty burial places of errors – but they remain there undisturbed like a maze of deserted trenches in a shell-ravaged battlefield. Pages full of them rebuke me in pathetic silence claiming for some harmony in this anarchy of forms. But my mind is too weary to respond. It has lost its enthusiasm for all kinds of aristocratic works that are supremely useless.

For a long time I have been postponing writing to you, for in my present state of lassitude some extra force has become necessary to push down my inertia. For a business letter or a letter conveying good advice such exertion is commendable, but not for letters to one's friends. Yesterday morning at a fortunate moment of release from some compulsory work came your pen with its inevitable insinuation which spontaneously set me down to write.

I do not like to dwell upon my illness, but this is the great dark background of my life at present and the whole picture upon it is that of a dusky landscape dim and grey. This breakdown of health creates an atmosphere of loneliness isolating one from the world of normal life which gets bored at all the small and mean details of infirmity. I am in a perpetually apologetic mood for my wretched feebleness which is an obstruction in the current of life's activities. It is not at all decent to be ill and make oneself pitifully conspicuous by causing a break in the rhythm of existence. Animals have the instinctive wisdom to realise it and they resignedly retire when overtaken by disease. [The] only thing which gives it dignity [comes] at the end of it – which is death.

Some time ago I got a letter from Vijaya[3] bewailing the evil fate which wrenched me away from her protection and wrecked my health. She wished I had spent South American summer months in San Isidro. Occasionally in weak moments I also indulge in such regrets which are foolish – for nobody can ever have the chance to be sure of the comparative desirability of the have-been and the would-have-been. [The] only thing in this case on which I can dwell with certain joy is the amazing fact that there is someone in this world for whom the mere fact that I exist could have an ultimate value.

Months ago I commissioned Asit Haldar to paint a picture for me, the subject of which I supplied to him.[4] I meant it for your wedding present. But at the last moment I thought of taking it with me to Europe and personally giving it to you. Lately I have discovered the fact that waiting for a chance that is not immediately before me is unreliable – in other words I have discovered at last my own old age. So I have decided to send it by mail. The name of the picture is *Recognition*.

I do not have a definite idea of what you are doing in your new English home. Are you busy translating Shriniketan into English? But the two languages are different – yours is too rich and mature. You have condensed, ready-made phrases that are sure to obtrude and clog the spontaneity of creative outflow; you have helpers who are experts and will render your progress easy and rapid but – I must stop. I do not wish to let you have an impression that I am jealous of your new adventure – and I humbly confess that our Shriniketan has a great disadvantage – it lacks the fullness of the dual stream of inspirations, the personal and the impersonal.

Just when I was about to close my letter another letter came from you.[5]

I have purposely refrained from giving you news. I vaguely know what is happening round me. My ill health has formed a fence of segregation [round me]. Occasionally I do some good deeds which I hope the record keeper at the Paradise gate takes note of. One such was my rescuing Kasahara from the attack of a committee meeting resolution.[6] As for the doctor he deserved deportation long ago and there is no doubt that Lal was comfortably taken in by him from the very beginning.[7]

Though the shadow of uncertainty is deepening everyday yet let me dream of the possibility of my visiting Europe and meeting you next March.[8]

My neighbours have observed a change of personality in me since my attack of illness. They say that the human in me has become more apparent than before. When the seed reaches its final maturity its protective sheath disappears. I hope the same thing is happening to me and the wall of reserve which was insurmountable for me is ready to topple down.

With love
Shri Rabindranath Thakur[9]

I have long been away from English teacher and hope to be excused for lapses.

Source: MS original in Dartington Trust archives [Dartington]; letter published in Dutta and Robinson (eds.), *Purabi*, pp. 94–5.

1 Elmhirst to RT, 3 Sept. 1925, in Dutta and Robinson (eds.), *Purabi*, p. 92.
2 *swaraj*: self-rule. See letter 181.
3 Vijaya: Victoria Ocampo. See letters 198, 199. Ocampo's letter to RT appears in Dyson, *Flower-Garden*, p. 413.
4 Asit Kumar Haldar (1890–1964): Bengal School painter; a pupil of Abanindranath Tagore, Haldar taught art at Shantiniketan and later became principal, Lucknow School of Art. He was a sentimentalist drawn to (Indian) mythology – a most unsuitable combination for the taste of Dorothy Elmhirst!
5 Elmhirst to RT, 10 Sept. 1925, in Dutta and Robinson (eds.), *Purabi*, pp. 92–3.
6 Kim-Taro Kasahara was a Japanese carpenter–gardener at Surul. A committee had attempted to deprive Kasahara of his garden. Elmhirst had already heard this from someone else and commented in his letter to RT on 10 Sept. that 'if ever [Kasahara's] paid job is to be simply that of carpenter may I beg that he be left sufficient land and garden to support his family with and to grow a few of those flowers which were ever our delight'.
7 Prem Chand Lal worked at Shriniketan until 1936. See his book, *Reconstruction and Education in Rural India* (London, 1932), which has an introduction by RT and a dedication to Dorothy Elmhirst, who funded Lal's work. He died in 1954. See obituary in *VBN*, June 1954, p. 12.
8 RT eventually arrived in Europe again in May 1926. He met Elmhirst briefly in Italy and later in Britain.
9 Signed in Bengali.

205

To Victoria Ocampo

Tagore and Victoria Ocampo, his hostess in Argentina, had exchanged several romantic letters since the two long letters he wrote her from on board ship (letters 198 and 199). Then he sent her the book of poems, *Purabi* (Easterner), which he had written partly in the Villa Miralrío. They were dedicated to her, his Vijaya, even though (as he points out in this covering letter), she would never read them.

Calcutta, [India]
29 October 1925

Dear Vijaya

I do not like to talk about my illness which has become a bore in its endless monotony. I am wearily waiting for the summer to come when I shall make another attempt to visit Europe in order to get proper medical treatment.

I am sending to you a Bengali book of poems which I wish I could place in your hand personally. I have dedicated it to you though you will never be able to know what it contains. A large number of poems in this book were written while I was in San Isidro. My readers who will understand these poems will never know who my Vijaya is with whom they are associated. I hope this book will have the chance of a longer time with you than its author had.

Bhalobasa[1]
Shri Rabindranath Thakur

Source: MS copy at Rabindra Bhavan, Shantiniketan; letter published in Dyson, *Flower-Garden*, pp. 416–17.

1 Both *Bhalobasa* and Tagore's signature are in Bengali script. *Bhalobasa* means 'love'. In 1961, Ocampo wrote: 'During his stay at San Isidro, Tagore taught me a few words of Bengali. I have retained only one, which I shall always repeat to India: *Bhalobasa*' (Sahitya Akademi, *Rabindranath Tagore*, p. 47).

206

To Edward John Thompson

Tagore and Edward J. Thompson had fallen out of touch, partly because Tagore did not much like Thompson's short study of him (see letter 174) and also because Thompson left Bengal in 1923 to become lecturer in Bengali at Oxford University. In Britain he began to produce a steady flow of books, including his first work of history, *The Other Side of the Medal* (London, 1925), a revisionist study of the Indian Mutiny which was deliberately intended to provoke 'old India hands' and indeed almost any Englishman associated with the governing of India. In November 1925 he informed Tagore that a copy was on its way to him, inscribed to 'R.T. An individual Englishman's act of atonement', and commented: 'I wish I were still in India. I was very ignorant, ill-informed, and John Bullish when I was there. I see better now.'[1] Tagore replied with a copy of his just-published *Purabi* and remarked: 'I have heard about your latest book which is rumoured to be a disquieting one, but I have not yet had a personal acquaintance with it.'[2]

This letter, written three weeks later, expresses an awkward solidarity with Thompson: both of them, says Tagore, are under attack for standing outside the current of orthodox opinion in their respective countries. But while this was superficially true, Britain's political dominance of India, with the attendant sense of western cultural superiority, still divided the two men. The publication of Thompson's long biography of Tagore the following year would rupture the uneasy truce spectacularly (see letter 218).

Santiniketan, [West Bengal, India]
30 December 1925

Dear Thompson

I am sure you have received a letter of mine before this and also my latest book of poems.

Our annual festival of the 7 Paush is just over, the strain of which has left me exhausted.[3] I am longing to get away to Europe as soon as possible but I am afraid I shall not be able to secure accommodation in any steamer before next May.

You are in disgrace with your people just now for which you have my congratulation – and I am proud to say that my position with my own countrymen is, if anything, worse than yours, the reason being very much the same as it is in your case.[4]

I am not quite certain whether I shall be able to visit England this time as I shall have to be in doctor's hands – and the sanatorium which has been selected for me is in Switzerland. I hope it may be possible for you to meet me before I shall leave Europe.

Yours
Rabindranath Tagore

Source: MS original in Thompson papers [Bodleian].

1 Thompson to RT, 15 Nov. 1925 [RB].
2 RT to Thompson, 7 Dec. 1925 [Bodleian].
3 On the 7 Paush festival, see letter 28, no. 3.
4 Generally, RT meant his flat refusal to join the Noncooperation Movement, specifically he may have meant Mahatma Gandhi's article, 'The poet and the wheel', *CWMG*, XXVIII, p. 427, published on 5 Nov. 1925 in *Young India*, which openly accused RT of living in an ivory tower and insinuated that he was jealous of Gandhi. The reaction to Thompson's book in the British press was by no means all fury and 'disgrace'. Both the *New Statesman* and the *Spectator* reviewed the book favourably, for instance, the latter commenting, 'This little book contains high explosive. The author was advised not to publish. On the whole we think he was right in rejecting that advice . . . Our people have only been asked to hear one-half of the horrible story of the Mutiny. They ought to hear the whole' (*Spectator*, 14 Nov. 1925).

207

To Maria Montessori[1]

Tagore first came in contact with Maria Montessori, the Italian educator, on his American tour in 1916. Ten years later, she wrote to him to enquire of the potential for the Montessori system in India: 'I feel that your people have achieved a higher degree of capability for feeling and sentiment than the Europeans, and I am certain that my ideas which are founded only on love for the children would find a good welcome in the hearts of the Indian people'.²

Rabindranath, a great admirer of Montessori, responds in kind.

Santiniketan, [West Bengal, India]
3 February 1926

Dear Dr Maria Montessori

I read with much pleasure your last letter for which I express to you my sincere thanks. As far as I know, the Montessori method is widely read and studied not only in some of the big cities of India but also in out of the way places; the method is, however, not so extensively followed in practice largely owing to the handicap imposed by the officialised system of education prevalent in the country. The enthusiasm and admiration felt for your work have induced a few private individuals of means to institute small experiments which are conducted with success on lines recommended by you.³

With all good wishes,

Yours very sincerely
Rabindranath Tagore

Source: MS copy at Rabindra Bhavan, Shantiniketan.

1 Maria Montessori (1870–1952): educator of children; she lectured extensively in India. In 1939, she visited Shantiniketan and was warmly welcomed by RT. In Aug. 1941, when RT died, Montessori was at Adyar, near Madras, from where she wrote to Rathindranath Tagore on 16 Aug.:

> There are two kinds of tears, one from the common side of life, and those tears everybody can master. But there are other tears which come from God. Such tears are the expression of one's very heart, one's very soul. These are the tears which come with something that uplifts humanity, and these tears are permitted. Such tears I have at this moment. (*VBN*, Sept. 1941, p. 30)

2 Montessori to RT, 8 Germajo 1926 [RB].
3 For example, a Montessori school was opened at Rajghat, Varanasi, on 2 Dec. 1934. RT gave a speech (see *VBN*, Dec. 1934, pp. 43–4).

208

*To Arthur Geddes*¹

Although (Sir) Patrick Geddes' plans for Shantiniketan never came to fruition (see letter 184), his son Arthur, who worked at Shriniketan in 1923, became fascinated by Rabindranath's songs. In due course, Arthur Geddes devised a programme of songs in which the words were translated into English by Tagore and himself and the musical setting was by Geddes based on Tagore's tunes; and this he presented to audiences in the West for many years. This letter shows the genesis of the programme.²

Comilla, [Chittagong, Bangladesh]
18 February 1926

Dear Arthur

How delighted [I am] to have your letter. Do whatever you like with my songs; only do not ask me to do the impossible. To translate Bengali poems into English verse form reproducing the original rhythm so that the words may fit in with the tune would be foolish for me to attempt. All that I can venture to do is to render them in simple prose making it possible for a worthier person than myself to versify them. Please write the accompaniment yourself. I can trust you, for you are modest and are not likely to smother my tunes with a ruthless display of your own musical talent. I shall be able to give the outline of the play from which the songs are taken in order to give them their proper background. As for the other details, I shall have them discussed when we meet in Europe.

Just now I am busy touring in East Bengal. It is perfectly unwise from a medical point of view but there are other points of view in its favour which it has been difficult for me to ignore.[3]

But I am tired and am longing to give up missions of all kinds and merely to share the life impulse of the trees and birds in this delightful springtime redolent of mango blossoms.

With love

Yours affectionately
Rabindranath Tagore

Source: MS copy at Rabindra Bhavan, Shantiniketan.

1 Arthur Geddes (1895–1968): lecturer in geography, University of Edinburgh; son of Sir Patrick Geddes, whose interest in sociology was shared by his son.
2 Writing in 1961, the Tagore birth centenary, Geddes remembered:

> Only twice in my life, when hearing sustained prose spoken in a language of dialect almost unintelligible to me, have I listened as to music. The second time – when an old crofter was pronouncing a long extempore blessing in the Norse-like Gaelic of the Isle of Lewis – recalled the first, when, one Sunday morning at Santiniketan, we listened in the open to an extempore sermon in Bengali by Tagore. Like some *partita* for violin only by Bach, melody guided by continuously welling thought, it flowed, paused, changed and flowed afresh to the very close. (Arthur Geddes, 'Rabindranath Tagore – bard, musician and seer', *Scotsman*, 13 May 1961)

3 RT was invited by the University of Dhaka to lecture in what was then East Bengal. He spent over three weeks there in various towns.

209

To Romain Rolland

In late May 1926 Tagore finally returned to Europe, beginning with a visit to Italy which he soon came to regret. The Italian Government under Mussolini had recently sent two Italian scholars, Carlo Formichi and Giuseppe Tucci, to Shantiniketan, and had made a handsome gift of Italian classics to the Visva-Bharati library; its invitation to visit Italy completed the offer of intercultural cooperation. Tagore was seduced, despite warnings against Fascism from his friends and despite his own experience of Fascist antipathy in Italy in January 1925.

Romain Rolland, with whom Tagore stayed in Switzerland after being fêted in Italy, felt himself obliged to disillusion Tagore.[1] It proved to be exceedingly difficult. Rolland demonstrated with Italian news clippings how the press had distorted Tagore's statements. He described the experiences of Italian friends who had suffered under the

Fascists. He introduced Tagore to the novelist and essayist Georges Duhamel, who was familiar with the Fascist threat. Eventually, he arranged for his famous visitor to meet the wife of an Italian dissident, Guglielmo Salvadori, who had been badly beaten by Fascist thugs in 1924 and was now living in exile in Switzerland, too ill to travel. The meeting occurred in Zurich, and was followed by a detailed letter from Salvadori himself and further contact with dissidents when Tagore reached Vienna.[2] Though it took Rabindranath some more days to speak publicly about Fascism, by mid-July – the date of this letter to Rolland – he had made up his mind to do so.

Hotel Bristol, Vienna, [Austria]
13 July 1926

My very dear friend

I feel homeless since I have left your neighbourhood. To be always glancing at faces passing by and never to be able to recognise anybody is too tiring for the mind. It is like a bird flying from twig to twig and finding that they cannot bear the burden of its body. Every morning I wake up from sleep I find myself in a world where there are men who have no names, who are a moving mass, like clouds, who can only envelop you but cannot offer you company. I feel myself belonging to a mere stream of facts with no landing place of acknowledgement.

Someone in this place has arranged for me a lecture in a very big hall – such engagements always oppress me – every time I feel frightened to have to turn myself into a megaphone. Unfortunately for me I have a big reputation and people expect from me a big effect, a sensation in a wholesale quantity. What a waste!

I am waiting to consult a doctor, and I have an appointment with him this afternoon. After it is over I do not know what I have to do in Europe. Before I sailed from India I had one fixed aim in my mind, it was to meet you. And we *did* meet and though it was only for a few days, those days were full – the days of feast.[3] In a festival one has the home and a great deal more added to it. I have come out from it into the road with no destination whatever.

In Zurich I had an interview with Madam Salvadori the result of which you will see later on. I have to pass through a purification ceremony for the defilement to which I submitted myself in Italy.

Give my warmest regards to your sister for whom I have realised a deep affection.[4] I am glad that I have been able to leave with her as my gift, at least one of my poems, with its original music.

With love
Rabindranath Tagore

Source: MS copy at Rabindra Bhavan, Shantiniketan.

1 On Rolland's reaction to RT's visit to Italy, see Dutta and Robinson, *Rabindranath Tagore*, pp. 269–70 and Rolland's journal *Inde*, which has a full account. In a later letter to RT, Rolland summed up his attitude:

> Often I have accused myself for having disturbed your rest when I took away from you the confidence you had in your Italian hosts. However, I had no other interest in my mind but your glory, which I value more than your rest. I did not want devils misusing your sacred name in the annals of history. Forgive me if my intervention has caused you some restless hours. The future (the

present already) will show you that I have acted as your faithful and vigilant guide. (Rolland to RT, 11 Nov. 1926, in Aronson and Kripalani (eds.), *Rolland and Tagore*, p. 67)

2 The interview was published as 'A conversation with Tagore', *Manchester Guardian*, 7 Aug. 1926/*VBQ*, 4, No. 3, Oct. 1926, pp. 299–303; the original transcript of this interview, which differs significantly from the published version, is kept at Rabindra Bhavan, Shantiniketan. Salvadori, a lecturer at the University of Rome, was attacked for publishing articles hostile to Fascism in two British journals in March 1924. In a letter to RT written on 16 July 1926, he described in detail how he was assaulted [RB]. The incident was publicised in 1928 by Gaetano Salvemini (Gaetano Salvemini, *The Fascist Dictatorship in Italy*: I, *Origins and Practices* (London, 1928), pp. 244–7) and described by Salvadori's son, Massimo (Max) Salvadori in 1958 (Massimo Salvadori, *The Labour and the Wounds* (London, 1958), pp. 15–17).

3 RT reached Rolland on 22 June and stayed near his house for twelve days. On 8 July Rolland wrote fulsomely to RT about the visit, tactfully not even mentioning the Italian debacle (Rolland, *Selected Letters*, pp. 68–9).

4 Madeleine Rolland (1872–1960): translator and interpreter; sister of Romain Rolland. Her brother's faithful companion for many years, she was present whenever RT met Rolland, who spoke no English.

210

To Leonard K. Elmhirst

Tagore's preferred method of unburdening himself of his considered views on Italian Fascism was to address a long letter to C. F. Andrews in India (letter 211), some of which could be printed in both the Indian and the British press with the editing of his English friends. Andrews was an appropriate choice since he had written to Tagore in alarm on reading reports of his support for Fascism in the Indian press.[1] Leonard Elmhirst too had done what he could to warn Rabindranath, coming to Naples in May 1926 to join his party at his request. 'But realising that I was not at all approved of by the official Italian party of welcome, I explained to Tagore that it would be wiser for me to leave him free to pursue his own plans. He was very much upset by my suggestion, but I left the next day for home.'[2]

There was no further communication between Tagore and Elmhirst for some seven weeks, by which time Tagore was in Vienna. Meanwhile the Fascist press had been busy misrepresenting him.[3] This letter is Tagore's request to Elmhirst to help him clear his name of the Fascist taint.

Hotel Bristol, Vienna, [Austria]
[20 July 1926]

Dear Leonard

Accompanying this you will find a letter which I am sending to Andrews in Santiniketan. I hope in this letter I have clearly been able to explain my opinion about Fascism and that you will agree with me that it should be published in some of the papers in England as well as in India. You can ask Spender's advice about it.[4] Of course my opinion is based upon inadequate data and my mind may still be obsessed with some bias in favour of Mussolini for what he has done for Visva-Bharati. Possibly some day I shall come to the conclusion that it [was] a sinister design on the part of my evil fate to have brought me into any relation [with] this man who may be altogether a fraud and no real personality. Somehow I have the unenviable knack of getting myself entangled in responsibilities that should have been avoided and I regret that I have allowed myself to pay this last visit to Italy.

This evening I shall read my last lecture in Vienna and then I shall have to decide whether I should accept an invitation from Poland that has come to me or another from Switzerland. Some time in August I shall be in your neighbourhood and then through Norway and Sweden come to Germany. We shall leave Europe about the end of September.[5]

It always fills me with wonder when I realise how deep and widespread is the feeling for me in Europe. It is more than admiration, it is love. I have over and over been assured by persons belonging to different stations in life how my words have helped them in their path of self-realisation. It makes me feel truly humble and also desirous to do my best for them who have a pathetic faith in my capacity to render them spiritual assistance. At the same time it is of help to me when the claim comes from outside for the best gift which I may possess in my nature. I am seriously thinking of spending six months every year in Europe choosing a place in a neutral country like Switzerland.

Doctors all declare that physically I am sound – all my internal organs, including my heart, are in perfect condition. But there can be no question that I am excessively tired. This, I am sure, is the cumulative effect of worries connected with my Visva-Bharati work. I often long to go back to my former life of perfect inutility and freedom of response to the call of inaction so much needed for maturing dreams into a shape. But, I am afraid, the path is closed, and I shall have to wait till my next birth when I hope the same chance will come once again.

Have you, by chance, lost the typescript of my story – 'Two Friends'? Have you formed your own opinion about it or do you want to remain discreetly silent?[6]

Can you lend me an Aeroplane, if you have one at your disposal? I want to fly back to Uttarayan immediately.[7] For the rainclouds of July have gathered above our ashram and are wondering where the poet could have gone who was to greet them with his grateful songs in return for the music of rain.

With love

Ever yours
Rabindranath Tagore

Source: MS original in Dartington Trust archives [Dartington]; letter published in Dutta and Robinson (eds.), *Purabi*, p. 98.

1 Andrews to RT, 14 June 1926 [RB].
2 Leonard Elmhirst, 'Personal memories of Tagore' in Sahitya Akademi, *Rabindranath Tagore*, p. 24.
3 The Associated Press put out a message purporting to be from RT, on 31 July (i.e. long after his departure from Italy), which included the ludicrous statement: 'I left Shantiniketan and India for a while to fly from the fierce blaze of world celebrity and seek the shelter of obscurity in Rome, that remote corner of the world, but renown has hounded me, even while I am under the aegis of Mussolini, that gentle hermit, who like myself shuns fame' (*Times of India*, 2 Aug. 1926).
4 There is no record of J. A. Spender advising on the publication of RT's letter on Fascism, but S. K. Ratcliffe, former editor of the Calcutta *Statesman*, was consulted. See Ratcliffe to RT, 1 Aug. 1926 [RB].
5 RT followed this plan, but then stayed in Europe, visiting central and south-eastern Europe, until Nov. 1926.
6 'Two Friends': this title does not match the title of any story published by RT. The typescript given to Elmhirst was probably one of the two copies of a typescript today kept at Rabindra Bhavan, entitled 'Friends'.
7 Uttarayan was RT's chief residence in Shantiniketan.

211

To Charles Freer Andrews[1]

[Hotel Bristol], Vienna, [Austria]
20 July 1926

[Dear Charlie]

My mind is passing through a conflict. I have my love and gratitude for the people of Italy. I deeply appreciate their feeling of admiration for me, which is so genuine and generous. On the other hand, the Italy revealed in Fascism alienates itself from the ideal picture of that great country which I should love to cherish in my heart.

You know I had my first introduction to Italy when I was invited to Milan last year. It takes a long time to study the mind of a people, but not long to feel their heart when that heart opens itself. I was in the city only for a very few days, and in that time I realised that the people loved me. Rightly or wrongly, one can claim praise as one's desert, but love is a surprise every time it comes. I was strongly moved by that surprise when I found loving friends and not merely kind hosts in the people of Italy. It grieved me deeply, and I felt almost ashamed when I suddenly fell ill and had to sail back home before I could fulfil my engagements in all the other towns.

Then followed the magnificent gift from Mussolini, an almost complete library of Italian literature, for my institution.[2] It was a great surprise to me. In this greeting I felt the touch of a personality which could express itself in this direct manner in an appropriate action of unstinted magnificence. This helped me to make up my mind to visit Italy once again, in spite of the misgivings created by the reports reaching us in India about the character of the Fascist movement.

I had neither the qualifications nor any inclination to dabble in the internal political issues of the European countries. For this reason I wanted to keep my mind neutral when I came to Italy. But we live in a whirlwind of talk today, and an individual like myself is compelled to contribute to that universal noise, dragged by the chain of karma, as we say in our country. I allowed myself to fall a victim to this relentless karma, with its ever-lengthening coil of consequence, when I succumbed to the importunity of the interviewers in Italy.

The interview is a dangerous trap in which our unwary opinions are not only captured but mutilated. Words that come out of a moment's mood are meant to be forgotten; but when they are snapshotted, most often our thoughts are presented in a grotesque posture which is chance's irony. The camera in this case being also a living mind, the picture becomes a composite one in which two dissimilar features of mentality have made a *mesalliance* that is likely to be unhappy and undignified. My interviews in Italy were the products of three personalities – the reporter's, the interpreter's, and my own. Over and above that, there evidently was a hum in the atmosphere of another insistent and universal whisper, which, without our knowing it, mingled in all our talks. Being ignorant of Italian I had no means of checking the result of this concoction. The only precaution which I could take was to repeat emphatically to all my listeners that I had had as yet no opportunity to study the history and character of Fascism.

Since then I have had the opportunity of learning the contents of some of these interviews from the newspaper cuttings that my friends have gathered and translated for me. And I was not surprised to find in them what was, perhaps, inevitable. Through misunderstanding, wrong emphasis, natural defects in the mediums of communication, and the preoccupation of the national mind, some of these writings have been made to convey that I have given my deliberate opinion on Fascism, expressing my unqualified admiration.

This time it was not directly the people of Italy whose hospitality I enjoyed, but that of Mussolini himself as the head of the Government. This was, no doubt, an act of kindness, but somewhat unfortunate for me. For always and everywhere official vehicles, though comfortable, move only along a chalked path of programme too restricted to lead to any places of significance, or persons of daring individuality, providing the visitors with specially selected morsels of experience.

The only opinions I could gather in such an atmosphere of distraction were enthusiastically unanimous in praise of Mussolini for having rescued Italy in a most critical moment of her history, from the brink of ruin.

In Rome I came to know a professor, a genuinely spiritual character, a seeker of peace, who was strongly convinced not only of the necessity but of the philosophy of Fascism. About the necessity I am not competent to discuss, but about the philosophy I am doubtful. For it costs very little to fashion a suitable philosophy in order to mitigate the rudeness of facts that secretly hurt one's conscience. One statement which particularly surprised me, coming from the mouths of fervent patriots, was that the Italian people owing to their unreasoning impulsive nature, had proved their incapacity to govern themselves, and that, therefore, in the inevitable logic of things, they lent themselves to government from outside by strong hands.

However, these are facts that immediately and exclusively concern Italy herself, though their validity has sometimes been challenged by European critics. But whatever may be the case as to that, the methods and the principles of Fascism concern all humanity, and it is absurd to imagine that I could ever support a movement which ruthlessly suppresses freedom of expression, enforces observances that are against individual conscience, and walks through a bloodstained path of violence and stealthy crime. I have said over and over again that the aggressive spirit of nationalism and imperialism, religiously cultivated by most of the nations of the West, is a menace to the whole world. The demoralisation which it produces in European politics is sure to have disastrous effects, especially upon the peoples of the East who are helpless to resist the western methods of exploitation. It would be most foolish, if it were not almost criminal, for me to express my admiration for a political ideal which openly declares its loyalty to brute force as the motive power of civilisation. That barbarism is not altogether incompatible with material prosperity may be taken for granted, but the cost is terribly great; indeed it is fatal. The worship of unscrupulous force as the vehicle of nationalism keeps ignited the fire of international jealousy, and makes for universal incendiarism, for a fearful orgy of devastation. The mischief of the infection of this moral aberration is great because today the races of humanity have come close together, and any process of destruction set going does its work on an enormously vast scale. Knowing all this, could it be believed that I should have played my fiddle while an unholy fire was being fed with human sacrifice?

I was greatly amazed when reading a Fascist organ to find a writer vehemently decrying the pantheistic philosophy of the passive and meditative East, and contrasting it with the vigorous self-assertion and fury of efficiency which he acknowledges to have been borrowed by his people from their modern schoolmasters in America. This has suggested to my mind the possibility of the idea of Fascism being actually an infection from across the Atlantic.

The unconscious irony in the article I refer to lies in the fact of the writer's using with unction the name of Christianity in this context – a religion which had its origins in the East. He evidently does not realise that if Christ had been born again in this world he would have been forcibly turned back from New York had he come there from abroad if for no other reason, then certainly for the want of the necessary amount of dollars to be shown to the gate keeper. Or if he had been born in that country, the Ku Klux Klan would have beaten him to death or lynched him. For did he not give utterance to that political blasphemy, 'Blessed are the meek.' thus insulting the Nordic right to rule the world, and to that economic heresy, 'Blessed are the poor.'? Would he not have been put in prison for twenty or more years for saying that it was as easy for the prosperous to reach the Kingdom of Heaven as for the camel to pass through the eye of a needle?

The Fascist professor deals a pen thrust against what he calls our pantheism; but that is a word that has no synonym in our language, nor has the doctrine any place in our philosophy. He does not seem to have realised that the idea of Christian theology, that God remains essentially what he is while manifesting himself in the Son's being, belongs to the same principle as our principle of immanence. According to this doctrine the divinity of God accepts humanity for its purpose of self-revelation and thus bridges the infinite gulf between the two. This idea has glorified all human beings, and has had the effect in the Christian West of emancipating individuals from the thraldom of absolute power. It has trained that attitude of mind which is the origin of the best internal politics of the western peoples. It has helped to distribute the power of government all over the country, and thus has given it a permanent foundation which cannot be tampered with or destroyed by the will of one individual or the whim of a group. This consciousness of the dignity of the individual has encouraged in the West the freedom of conscience and thought. We in the East come to Europe for this inspiration. We are also dreaming of the time when the individuals belonging to the people of India will have courage to think for themselves and express their thoughts, feel their strength, know their rights, and take charge of their own government.

The Fascist writer I have quoted is evidently fascinated by the prospect of the economic self-aggrandisement of the nation at the cost of the moral self-respect of the people. But it is the killing of the goose for the sake of golden eggs. In the olden civilisations the slavery of the people did build up for the time being powers of stupendous splendour. But this spirit of slavishness constantly weakened the foundations till the towers came down into the dust, offering as their contribution to humanity ruins haunted by venerable ghosts.

In bygone days in India the state was only a part of the people. The mass of the population had its own self-government in the village community. Dynasties changed, but the people always possessed the power to manage all that was vital to them. This saved them from sinking into barbarism, this has given our country a continuity through centuries of political vicissitudes.

Our western rulers have destroyed this fundamental structure of our civilisation, the civilisation based upon the obligations of intimate human relationship. And therefore nothing today has been left for the people through which they can express their collective mind, their creative will, or realise the dignity of their soul, except the political instrument, the foreign model of which is always present before their envious gaze. We come to Europe for our lesson in the mastery of this instrument, as Japan has done and has been successful in her purpose. But must our friend the Fascist philosopher come to us to copy our political impotence, the result of the surrender of freedom for centuries to the authority of some exclusive reservoir of concentrated power, while rejecting our great ideal of spiritual freedom, which has its basis in the philosophy that infinite truth is everywhere, that it is for everyone to reach it by removing the obstruction of the self that obscures light?

I am sure you will be interested to know what was the impression that I have carried away from my interview with Mussolini. We met only twice, and our meetings were extremely brief, owing very likely to our difficulty of communication through the slow and interrupted medium of an interpreter.

In a hall of which the great size is accentuated by an unusual bareness of furniture, Mussolini has his seat in a distant corner. I believe this gives him the time and space to observe visitors who approach him, and makes him ready to deal with them. I was not sure of his identity while he was walking towards me to receive me, for he was not tall in proportion to his fame which towers high. But when he came near me I was startled by the massive strength of his head. The lower part of the face, the lips, the smile, revealed a singular contradiction to the upper part, and I have often wondered since then if there was not a secret hesitation in his nature, a timid doubt which was human. Such an admixture of vacillation in a masterful personality makes his power of determination all the more vigilant and strong because of the internecine fight in his own character. But this is a mere surmise.

For an artist it is a great chance to be able to meet a man of personality who walks solitary among those who are mere fragments of a crowd which is always on the move, pressed from behind. He is fully visible in his integrity above the lower horizon obstructed by the dense human undergrowth. Such men are the masters of history, and one cannot but feel anxious lest they miss their eternity by using all their force in taking the present by the throat, leaving it dead for all time. Men have not altogether been rare who furiously created their world by trampling human materials into the shape of their megalomaniac dreams, to burden history at last with the bleached bones of their short-lived glory; while there were others, the serene souls, who with the light of truth and magic of love have made deserts fruitful along endless stretches of grateful years.

But to be honest, I must confess that I cannot fully trust my own impression, caught from a momentary glimpse of Mussolini in which mingled the emphasis of the surroundings in which I was placed. There have been times when history has played tricks with man and through a combination of accidents has magnified the features of essentially small persons into a parody of greatness. Such a distortion of truth often finds its chance not because these men have an extraordinary power in themselves but because they represent some extraordinary weakness of those whom they lead. This produces a mirage that falsifies the real and startles our imagination into a feeling of awe and exaggerated expectation.

To be tortured by tyranny is tolerable; but to be deluded into the worship of a wrong ideal is humiliating for the whole age which has blundered into submission to it. If Italy has made even a temporary gain through ruthless politics she may be excused for such an obsession: but for us, if we believe in idealism, there can be no such excuse. And therefore it would be wise for us to wait before we bring our homage to a person who has suddenly been forced upon our attention by a catastrophe, till through the process of time all the veils are removed that are woven round him by the vivid sensations of the moment.

My letter has run to a great length. But I hope you will bear with it, knowing that it has helped me in making my thoughts clear about my experience in Italy and also in explaining the situation in which I have been placed. This letter which I write you I shall make use of in removing the misunderstanding that has unfortunately been created in the minds of those who are in harmony with my ideals about the problems of the present age.

Rabindranath Tagore

Source: *Manchester Guardian*, 5 Aug. 1926. The original MS is lost.

1 A typed copy of the letter sent to Elmhirst (mentioned in letter 210) exists at Rabindra Bhavan, Shantiniketan. It differs slightly from the version printed in the *Manchester Guardian* and more substantially from that printed in *VBQ, 4*, No. 3, Oct. 1926, pp. 273–9.
2 Guglielmo Salvadori suggested to RT that he return all these books to Mussolini. 'As soon as Italy has recovered her liberty and her place among civilised nations, I promise to you, in the name of all true Italians to make a new gift of the same books and works of art for your school' (Salvadori to RT, 16 July 1926 [RB]).

212

To Carlo Formichi[1]

The day after composing his letter (211) on Fascism and sending it to C. F. Andrews and Leonard Elmhirst, Tagore sent it also to Carlo Formichi, the Italian professor who had been his chief guide and interpreter while in Italy and who was now in charge of gathering Italian support for Visva-Bharati. It cannot have come as too much of a surprise to Formichi, since he had already received two letters from Tagore written in Switzerland, alluding to his unease about his visit.[2] To the first letter Formichi replied on 29 June in a tone of injured innocence:

> You say you are happy in being free 'from the swarming interviews whose ephemeral wings fill the air with the hum, not always of truth'. And yet, you are the man that has heard the least of falsehood in the world, if I have to judge from what has happened in Italy twice: all those that were brought near you were utterly sincere in their admiration of you.[3]

To the second letter, written after Tagore's interview with the wife of Guglielmo Salvadori in Zurich, Formichi kept silent. To Tagore's final letter, he responded 'with infinite sadness', calling it 'a declaration of war'.[4]

Hotel Bristol, Vienna, [Austria]
21 July 1926

Dear friend

I send you a copy of the letter which I have sent to Andrews. This will give you my idea about my attitude towards Fascism. I have been forced to give my explanation, because not only in Europe, but in India the rumour has been circulated that I have advocated the doctrine of Fascism and I have taken up the mission of defending it when I go to India.

In the meanwhile the evidence from the other side is pouring down upon me – and some of the facts are of a disturbing character. I cannot tell you what a great suffering it has caused me – for I have a deep love for your people. Also I realise that my expressed opinion on this political movement will hurt you and this thought is constantly oppressing my mind. Our cause of Visva-Bharati will receive a setback in Italy – which is a matter of very great regret for me. And yet I cannot help taking the step I have taken – for I do represent certain ideals for which I had faced unpopularity in my own country and derision in some parts of the West. The report which appeared in the Italian newspapers last year after my return from Italy contained extracts from the Fascist papers fiercely attacking me for my humanitarian ideals. I feel certain that my espousing the cause of Fascism would be a kind of moral suicide. But exactly that is being widely believed by people of all shades of opinion in Europe and other continents. I find it absolutely impossible to let it go uncontradicted and with a great feeling of pain I have allowed myself to express my opinion about my position with regard to this movement.

I fervently hope that you will understand the situation and forgive me and still consider me as one of your best friends.

With love
Rabindranath Tagore

Source: MS copy at Rabindra Bhavan, Shantiniketan.

1 Carlo Formichi (1871–1943): Indologist; professor of Sanskrit, University of Rome, 1915–41; he was a visiting professor at Shantiniketan for four months in 1925–6. Today he is a forgotten figure in Indology, unlike Sylvain Lévi, Sten Konow and Giuseppe Tucci.
2 RT wrote to Formichi on 25 June and 7 July 1926, according to Formichi's letter published in the *Manchester Guardian*, 25 Aug. 1926. These letters have not been traced.
3 Formichi to RT, 29 June 1926 [RB].
4 Formichi to RT, 30 July 1926 [RB]. Formichi responded to the 'declaration of war' with a defiant letter dated 14 Aug., published in the *Manchester Guardian*, 25 Aug. 1926. Although its tone was respectful to RT, it contained several lies, and made a determined attempt to show RT as having spoken in favour of Mussolini and his policies.

213

To C. P. Scott[1]

The *Manchester Guardian*, under its most famous editor, C. P. Scott, was the first major newspaper in Britain to show serious and sustained comprehension of Indian nationalist aspirations. In 1919, it printed Tagore's letter to the viceroy repudiating his knighthood (letter 142) – uniquely in the British press – and in the 1920s it began to carry reports on Indian affairs from correspondents such as C. F. Andrews. In 1926 it covered Tagore's Italian imbroglio extensively and sympathetically. The paper published his long letter to C. F. Andrews (5 Aug.) and his interview with the wife of the dissident Guglielmo Salvadori (7 Aug.), Carlo Formichi's letter in response (25 Aug.), a further letter from Tagore commenting on Formichi's (20 Sept.), and two leaders (7 and 25 Aug.), in between which Scott had a long talk with Tagore in London (on 19 Aug.) On 23 Sept., Scott informed Tagore in a letter:

> I am sorry for the Italians, a great people, full of generous feeling, but in the welter of the modern world, they will hardly find guidance in the counsel now given them to revive the spirit of the Roman empire. – You have been very kind to them. Some day they may realise it.[2]

Tagore's reply shows his empathy with Scott, coupled with an awareness of the pitfalls of communication even with the most enlightened of Europeans interested in India.

Hotel Inlis, Prague, [Czech Republic]
12 October 1926

Dear Mr Scott,

Thank you for your letter. I am still roving about driven by a cyclonic fury of engagements which still shows no signs of abatement.[3] I have often wondered whether such rapid flashes of communication which are allowed me can leave any impression upon the minds of my hearers, whether the cost is not too great for me and the recompense too meagre. But what urges me to accept this task is the thought that the mere fact of the welcome which I receive from the different peoples of the West is valuable in itself. That they can express such a genuine enthusiasm in their recognition of a poet from the East is something which could never have been possible fifty years ago – and this is one of the signs of the age which has a positive significance.

I had the intention of visiting England once more before I left Europe, but I am afraid it will not be possible, for I have only a few weeks before I sail for India and they are all full with my programme.[4]

I shall try to carry out your suggestion when I go back home. I hope it will not be difficult for me to find out an Indian who is competent to write letters for your paper discussing in an unbiassed manner all problems arising out of the relationship of India with England. Andrews has gone out to South Africa and when I meet him after his return I shall try to persuade him to take up this work himself.[5]

Hoping to have the opportunity to meet you again. I am

Yours very sincerely
Rabindranath Tagore

[PS] May I know if the last letter of mine has been published in *Manchester Guardian*?[6]

Source: MS original in *Manchester Guardian* archives [Manchester].

1 Charles Prestwich Scott (1846–1932): journalist; editor, *Manchester Guardian*, 1872–1929.
2 Scott to RT, 23 Sept. 1926 [RB].
3 According to Prashanta Mahalanobis, who acted as RT's secretary in Europe in 1926, 'We have been going from place to place like gypsies. Poet had a nervous breakdown in Prague . . . there are two different sets in Prague, Czechs and Germans, and everything had to be repeated twice' (Mahalanobis to E. J. Thompson, 12 Dec. 1926 [Bodleian]).
4 RT did not return to Britain after his August visit.
5 Scott and RT discussed the problem of finding an Indian correspondent when they met on 19 Aug. and concluded that it would be difficult to find someone with insight who was above the conflict. Andrews wrote frequently for the *Manchester Guardian* under Scott's editorship.
6 RT's second letter, his reply to Carlo Formichi, was published by Scott on 20 Sept.

214

To Leonard Knight Elmhirst

From Prague Tagore went on to Austria, Hungary, Yugoslavia, Bulgaria, Romania, Greece and Egypt, in a kind of triumphal progress. He travelled in a special saloon placed at his disposal by the various governments, and in each country he was welcomed by all ranks in society. The Balkans, being less industrialised and sophisticated than western Europe, resembled India in many ways (including musically), which appealed to Tagore and his party. He felt an immediate emotional rapport.

But Romain Rolland, writing to one of Tagore's Bengali friends in Calcutta, was disapproving of these peripatetics, particularly in relation to Romania and Bulgaria:

> our great Tagore, after his visit to Mussolini, has once again been ill advised to have himself received and patronised by the criminals who are torturing Bulgaria and Romania. It is no use telling him that now, it is too late. And moreover, I have the impression that if anything to that effect is said to him, it would only pain him, without convincing him. But his guides and advisers are much to blame . . . They have not tried to penetrate, behind the official and officious facade, into the freedom-loving and oppressed conscience of Europe, which has been disappointed and, I am afraid, alienated by their tourist-like attitudes . . . I know only too well how dangerous a ground today's blood-stained Europe is for a foreigner who, without precautions, ventures into it as an observer. Perhaps India would be as dangerous a country for me if I went there. But that is why I am not going there.[1]

Tagore was aware of these criticisms, but less convinced than Rolland of the greater righteousness of western Europe compared to eastern Europe, as this letter shows. And the manifest affection showered on him in his travels simply could not be dismissed as an illusion. To Rabindranath, individuals always meant more than systems, trust was always more honourable than suspicion: these attitudes were his great strengths and at the same time his great weaknesses.

Balatonfüred, [Hungary]
7 November 1926

Dear Leonard

This is a delightful watering place. The bath here is charged with carbonic acid gas which I am told is good for distracted nerves. Doctors advise me to take the shorter eastern route to India through Yugoslavia, Serbia, Constantinople, Greece and Egypt. The prescription is very much like the French wine ordered for me in Milan; it is tempting. The people [in] this eastern corner of Europe are perfectly charming – their personality unshrouded by the grey monotony of a uniform civilisation that has overspread the western world. It is mixed with something primitive and therefore is fresh and vital and warmly human. How naively simple and direct is the expression of their feeling for me. I am the guest of the people here, their one object being to nurse me into health taking real pride in rendering this service.[2] Is there any other individual today in the whole world who is so fortunate as I am in gaining the adoration of such a multitude of peoples in spite of the insuperable obstacles against making himself fully known and dedicating to them what he has in store? They seem to offer me their love on trust without waiting to be sure that they do not deceive themselves. When I had my welcome in Germany and in Norway, the people very often shouting to me 'Come back to us,' it made me wonder how I had deserved it. But in places like Budapest the attitude of the people towards me is so clingingly personal, so full of tender solicitude that I forget to ask myself what price I had ever paid for it. It only reveals a spontaneous attraction of a mysterious feeling of kinship. I cannot help thinking that in spite of my numerous deficiencies my providence has found in me an instrument which he can use for his own great purpose, though it is a matter of perpetual puzzle to the instrument itself. I wish you were with me to realise how human these people are. I am sure they make terrible mistakes and can be frankly cruel to their neighbours – not because they are callous with the callousness of senility with its cold calculating and cautious unscrupulousness but because they have the passionate impetuosity of their youthfulness. They are too often chastised for their delinquencies by their big brothers [with] stronger muscles, but those old sinners themselves are waiting for their doom in God's own hands.

This time I have been able to see the state of things in Europe that has filled my mind with misgivings. There was a time when ideals of justice, love of freedom could find their voice from some corner or other of this continent. But today all the big nations seem to have gone half seas over in their reckless career of political ambition and adventures of greed. None of them has the natural privilege today to stand for the right when any great wrong is done to humanity. The standard of life has become so complex and costly that these people cannot help thinking that righteousness is a luxury that can only be indulged in when all claims [by] their insatiable self [are] fairly satisfied. They are ashamed of the sentiments that help to keep life green and tender and in its place they cultivate the sneering spirit of cynicism brilliant and barren. Europe has got her science not as complimentary to religion but as its substitute. Science is great, but it only affords us knowledge, power, efficiency, but no ideal of unity, no aspiration for the perfect – it is nonhuman, impersonal, and therefore is like things that are inorganic, useful in many ways but useless as our food of life. If it is allowed to go on extending its sole dominion in the human world then the living flesh of man will wither away and his skeleton will reign supreme in the midst of his dead wealth. I have very strongly felt this time that the European countries have found themselves [in] a vicious circle of mutual hatred and suspicion and they do not know how to stop, however much they may wish. Their passion of greed has been ignited to a terrible intensity and magnitude through the immense possibility of power that science has offered to them and they appear like a star suddenly flaring up into rapid and fatal brilliancy through some enormous accession of materials. The present European atmosphere has been very oppressive to me making me think over and over again what a terrible menace man has been for man. – But no more of this – and goodbye.

Ever yours
Rabindranath Tagore

Source: MS original in Dartington Trust and archives [Dartington]; letter published in Dutta and Robinson (eds.), *Purabi*, p. 101.

1 Rolland to Kalidas Nag, 6 Dec. 1926, in Rolland, *Selected Letters*, pp. 80–1.
2 RT was sent to a sanatorium at Lake Balaton in order to recuperate from the strain of his travels. It was a happy experience for him, and today there is a bust of him by the lake, a linden tree which he planted and a plaque in Hungarian and English bearing a short poem which he composed on 8 Nov. 1926:

> When I am no longer on this earth, my tree,
> Let the ever-renewed leaves of thy spring,
> Murmur to the wayfarer:
> 'The poet did love while he lived.'

215

To Giuseppe Tucci[1]

While Tagore was in Europe, the second of the Italian scholars visiting Shantiniketan, Giuseppe Tucci, remained at Shantiniketan. Despite the rift between Tagore and the Fascists that became public in August 1926, Tucci stayed on at the university – and then suddenly left, not long before Tagore's return in December, after eleven months' residence. Though Italian politics played some role in this, the chief reason was Tucci's disenchantment with Tagore's co-workers, excepting one or two excellent scholars (such as Kshiti Mohan Sen). He wrote to Tagore on 29 December to explain himself:

> Speaking of your school you said recently that a poet is like a butterfly and those who have to carry into practice his ideals are like silkworms. I wanted specially to entertain [*sic*] you about those silkworms and the defectiveness of their work . . . The consequence is that there is something in the atmosphere of Shantiniketan which does not agree with your main idea, to make of it a meeting place of the East and the West.[2]

To others connected with Shantiniketan, Tucci was much blunter in his criticism.[3] He told Tagore that it was essential that he find 'somebody who is really conscious of the great responsibility of running an institution as Shantiniketan is', in other words someone such as himself (in 1933 he founded in Rome IsMEO, the Istituto Italiano per il Medio ed Estremo Oriente, a centre for research on oriental cultures).[4] But this was a sensitive point for Rabindranath, who had received similar advice from William Rothenstein (see letters 167 and 169). In replying, he politely but firmly disagrees with Tucci's assessment.

[Shantiniketan, West Bengal, India]
31 December 1926

Dear friend

I felt very much relieved when I received your letter this morning, for I was assured that nothing has happened which could permanently alienate you from me. Though I was given to understand, when I was in Europe, that your attitude towards our ashram had become contemptuously hostile, I never allowed this fact to modify in the least my feeling for you as a friend, and my admiration for you as a richly gifted scholar. I am fully conscious that my own ideals find many obstacles in their realisation in my ashram, but the same thing would have happened in other parts of the world where the great multitude of men has faith in results that have the stamp of orthodox sanction and therefore are easy and useful. I have seen new educational experiments attempted in several institutions in Europe with big funds and efficient organisation, struggling with the same moral difficulties as ours which are inherent in the materials they must use and surroundings they cannot alter.[5] But the most unfortunate factor in our case which created the unfavourable impression in your mind was the scurrilous calumny repeatedly whispered to you behind our back against some of our important members who, at that moment, had no opportunity to defend themselves.[6] However, this has been the usual fate of those who in the service of their cause not only trust their own ideas but also all sorts of men who are allowed to come close to their bosom upon which they can easily inflict cruel hurts.

I earnestly hope that we shall have occasion to meet again and in the meanwhile do not forget that I am

your affectionate friend
Rabindranath Tagore

Source: MS copy at Rabindra Bhavan, Shantiniketan.

1 Giuseppe Tucci (1895–1984): Indologist, specialising in Buddhism; he is best known for his work on Nepal and Tibet, to which country he organised and led eight expeditions. See Mircea Eliade, 'Giuseppe Tucci', *History of Religions*, 24, No. 2, 1984, pp. 157–9. Tucci's founding of IsMEO in 1933 brought him into close contact with the Fascists and he showed much sympathy for Fascism in his writings and behaviour during this period, as shown by Gustavo Benavides:

> Tucci's Orientalism . . . is a peculiar creature in which a deep dissatisfaction with modernity led him to imagine an Orient in which he could always find – constantly contradicting himself in the process – the wholeness no longer available in the West. His Orientalism imagined a timeless realm ready to receive him when he wanted to escape the tyranny of time; but this imaginary realm was also a repository of power and violence, found in its purest form in Japan, where it had blossomed, so he . . . claimed, as the result of the happy conjunction of Shinto and Zen. As a student of the exotic, one of his tasks . . . during the age of Fascism was to bring home that irrational presence to reinforce with it the ideological machinery of the state. ('Giuseppe Tucci, or Buddhology in the age of Fascism', in Donald S. Lopez, Jr (ed.), *Curators of the Buddha: The Study of Buddhism under Colonialism* (Chicago, 1995), p. 182)

2 Tucci to RT, 29 Dec. 1926 [RB]. The butterfly/silkworm image occurs in 'A poet's school', *VBQ*, 4, No. 3, Oct. 1926, p. 197.

3 On Tucci and Shantiniketan, see Dutta and Robinson, *Rabindranath Tagore*, pp. 275–6.
4 Tucci to RT, n.d. [RB]; this letter was written in response to RT's reply. According to Tucci, Prashanta Mahalanobis, one of the general secretaries of Visva-Bharati, suggested that Tucci become director of the institution, but Tucci refused because he thought the proposal was a ruse to show that, if he accepted, he had personal ambition rather than the good of the institution at heart. 'It was very clever,' said Tucci, 'but at the same time it was the best proof that he [Mahalanobis] did not realise – and I am sorry for him – that critiques can very often be moved by some ideal[istic] preoccupations and not by mere ambition or practical interest.' Such a situation was common in the administration of Visva-Bharati (Tucci to unknown friend [probably C. F. Andrews], n.d. [copy at RB]).
5 RT must have had Dartington chiefly in mind, where he stayed for the first time in Aug. 1926.
6 Tucci had fallen out with both Rathindranath Tagore and Prashanta Mahalanobis, concerning the administration of Visva-Bharati and the arrangements for the ship taking RT and his party to Italy in May 1926. They probably fed RT with criticisms of Tucci while they travelled with him in Europe.

13 Tagore at the opening of an exhibition of his paintings, Galerie Pigalle, Paris, 1930: with Countess Anna de Noailles, French minister of fine arts, Victoria Ocampo

Nationalism and internationalism (1927–1930)

Introduction

In the late 1920s, the war within Tagore between his trust in the idea of Indian cooperation with the West and his distrust of western, especially British, intentions towards India reached an acute pitch. He disliked imperial arrogance, but he disliked as much the chauvinism and parochial attitudes of many Indians. He still could not bring himself to align his patriotic efforts with Gandhi and his movement, and he was still less persuaded by the claims of Bengali revolutionaries; but he did now begin to become more attentive to the arguments of Indian nationalists.

His conflict emerged in other ways too, that affected his art. In 1927, he read Edward J. Thompson's biography, *Rabindranath Tagore: Poet and Dramatist*. Despite having encouraged Thompson, and despite Thompson's well-known admiration for him, Tagore vitriolically dismissed the book and accused its author of ignorance and arrogance.

At the same time he began painting and drawing. His untrained art seemed to express the pent-up tensions of his inner struggle. There was a strangeness and savagery about some of the images that seemed to bear little resemblance to most of his literary output. Tagore knew that it bore no resemblance at all to the accepted conventions of Indian painting, such as the Bengal School started by his nephew Abanindranath; and so he deliberately kept his works away from Bengalis, until the paintings had received the approval of European lovers of modern art in 1930.

216

To Sir Ronald Ross[1]

Sir Ronald Ross, famous for his work on malaria, also wrote poetry. He sent some of it to Tagore after watching him perform one of his dramas in Calcutta in early 1927.[2] Tagore's tactful reply is a small gem.

Calcutta, [India]
1 February 1927

Dear Sir Ronald

I appreciate your kindness in sending me your book of poems and take this opportunity to express my admiration for your great gifts.³

With thanks
Rabindranath Tagore

Source: MS original at library of London School of Hygiene and Tropical Medicine.

1 Sir Ronald Ross (1857–1932): bacteriologist who won the Nobel prize in 1902 for his work on malaria (done in Calcutta) and its transmission by the *Anopheles* mosquito. Ross was born in India.
2 The poems were a suite of 'sonnetelles', *In Exile*, privately printed in Liverpool in 1906.
3 'It is a source of wonder to me that Ross had the nerve to send a copy of some of his poems to Tagore' (Assistant librarian, London School of Hygiene and Tropical Medicine, to authors, 29 April 1992).

217

*To Sarat Chandra Chatterji [Chattopadhyay]*¹

There is a story told about Sarat Chandra Chatterji [Chattopadhyay], Bengal's most popular novelist, that he once rebuked one of his worshippers, who told him that he held him far above Rabindranath, with the words: 'Yes sir, I can quite believe it. It is readers like *you* I write for, whereas Rabindranath writes for readers like *me*.'² As the critic Buddhadeva Bose wrote in 1948, when both writers were dead:

> Rabindranath's words were unequivocal, bolder than ever before; he was definitely out to formulate new human values – and make new enemies into the bargain. Sarat Chandra, however, sang the song to another tune. His mildness, his wistful smile, his pathos – these brought him on a level with the average reader who tasted in him all forbidden joys without actually encountering the rebellion he still at heart dreaded . . . Indeed his feebleness of artistic conscience served him well in his popularity; this, really, is why the average Bengali reader is in him much more at home than he can yet be in Rabindranath.³

In 1926 Chatterji published a novel, *Pather Dabi* (The Claims of the Road), which was soon banned by the government, even though it had already appeared as a serial in a magazine during the preceding four years. The plot concerns a militant patriotic secret society with the name of the book's title and draws a contrast between two Bengalis: a mysterious hero, a kind of superman dedicated to obtaining national freedom by violence, and a typical *babu*, a cowardly and vacillating clerk, who fails to live up to 'Pather Dabi' and eventually becomes a police informer. Bose called the novel, accurately enough, 'a melodrama of violent action interspersed with patriotic rant'.⁴

The banning of the book naturally served to increase Chatterji's standing among Bengalis. But it seems that this relatively cheap popularity did not satisfy him and he wanted a favourable opinion from Rabindranath, whose own novel *The Home and the World* had ten years previously attracted severe criticism from the same Bengali readers for its unflattering portrait of a revolutionary.

Rabindranath's reply is pointed: he goes for Sarat Chandra's artistic jugular. By all means speak out against British rule and take a stand, he says – but do not behave like a weak *babu* when the Government hits back, as was only to be expected.

Shantiniketan, [West Bengal, India]
27 Magh 1333 [10 February 1927]

Kalyaniyeshu

I have finished reading your *Pather Dabi*. The book is certainly inflammatory. In other words it aims to incite the minds of its readers against British rule. This is not necessarily a black mark against its author, because if a writer feels British rule to be reprehensible, he cannot remain silent. But he must accept that there are penalties for not remaining silent. There is no manliness in the idea that however much we vilify the British rulers, they will always forgive us. I have travelled in many countries and in my experience no government bar the British Government would tolerate such opposition in both word and deed from its people, whether native born or immigrant, with such patience. If we taunt the foreign rulers while relying on their tolerance rather than our inner strength, we make a mockery of manliness – acts of this kind signify respect for them and not self-respect. They are physically powerful, and if we are to stand up to them honorably, on our own side we need strength of character, which means the strength to endure blows. But we demand this strength of character from the British side, never from ourselves. And so whatever we may say, secretly we are offering the British our admiration – our abusing them and expecting them not to retaliate is part of the whole performance. Looked at from the point of view of those in power, the suppression of your book without punishing you personally is almost like a pardon. No other power, whether oriental or western, would have behaved thus. If we were the rulers we would have acted differently I am sure, judging from the actions of our zamindars and princes. So should our pens then be stilled? I do not say they should be – only that we should put pen to paper with due recognition of the likely penalties. The situation is always the same in any country where there is a real confrontation between the rulers and the people; resistance to one's rulers is never easy or comfortable. Had you expressed anti-British ideas in a newspaper, the effect would have been limited and temporary, but a writer like you, who uses the story form, has a much wider impact, unlimited in space and time, captivating everyone from immature boys and girls to people of the older generation. Knowing this, if the British rulers had failed to ban your book it would have meant either that they did not grasp your literary powers or that they were ignorant of or contemptuous of your fame. In deciding to confront authority, one must be ready for the counterattack – for therein lies the challenge. To lament the severity of the blow will only impair the value of one's action.

Tomader
Shri Rabindranath Thakur

Source: MS original at Rabindra Bhavan, Shantiniketan; letter published in *Visva-Bharati Patrika*, Kartik–Paush 1356 [Oct. 1949–Jan. 1950], pp. 96–7.

1 Sarat Chandra Chattopadhyay (1876–1938): novelist; his best-known novel is *Srikanta* (extract in Dutta and Robinson (eds.), *Noon in Calcutta*, pp. 13–18). His popularity in Bengal has been compared with the popularity of Dickens in Victorian Britain. See Buddadeva Bose, *An Acre of Green Grass*, pp. 27–35.
2 Buddhadeva Bose, *An Acre of Green Grass*, p. 35.
3 *Ibid.*, pp. 30, 31.
4 *Ibid.*, p. 34.

218

To (Sir) William Rothenstein

In late 1926, Oxford University Press published E. J. Thompson's major study of Tagore, on which he had started work after completing his short study published in 1921. Although Tagore had not cared for the short book (see letter 174), he had encouraged Thompson to continue his work (see letter 183) and had given him considerable assistance. Yet when the big book appeared and was admired by William Rothenstein, who mentioned it appreciatively to Tagore in a letter, Rothenstein received a violent reaction. Judging from Rabindranath's reply, he could see no merit of any kind in Thompson's book. He even went so far as to review it himself in *Prabashi* under a pseudonym and in the most vitriolic terms, and to encourage other Bengali members of his circle to criticise the book in print in both the Bengali and the English press of Calcutta. Altogether, from Tagore-lovers in Bengal the unfortunate Thompson received a 'multiple hatchet-job' (in the phrase of Harish Trivedi, who in 1991 introduced an Indian edition of Thompson's biography).[1]

Both Trivedi and, more particularly, E. P. Thompson (in his *Alien Homage*) have delved into the reasons for Tagore's vehemence. E. P. Thompson wrote: 'I must confess that I find something still unexplained, in the violence of Tagore's reaction to the major study as contrasted with his toleration of the *gaucher*, slimmer [1921] volume.'[2]

The full explanation is certainly complex. Perhaps the clearest indication is to be found in a letter written by E. J. Thompson in early 1922, while researching the book, to his closest adviser, Prashanta Chandra Mahalanobis (who was of course himself close to Tagore). Thompson had just received some London reviews of his short study which plainly showed the collapse of Tagore's literary reputation in English translation, of which he (Thompson) had long been conscious. He told Mahalanobis:

> No man ever had such a chance as Tagore. No man ever lost it more absolutely. He might have helped East and West to a new understanding – instead, he has lost the ear of the best folk in the West, and has become the poet of our insincere coteries. On his translations, he cannot be called a great poet, but only a very charming manipulator of words. You don't believe this. Compare the translations and the originals, before you decide I am mistaken. I am not mistaken . . .
>
> There is one hope – one only. Reissue his work, in real translations, and chronologically, with the necessary minimum of notes . . .
>
> I tried to serve him, and you – the Bengalis. I did not expect garlands; but you have, most of you, thrown big stones. If I continue, till I have finished the bigger book . . . it is not because I any longer think you folk are anything but hard taskmasters, who do not understand service, but because I care about the truth. Therefore I shall finish, in spite of everything. When I have had my say, the stones can come. But no one hereafter will be able to write of Tagore, without taking into account what I have said. So I will finish.[3]

Tagore too knew what had happened to his English literary reputation, as many of his letters show, including those to Thompson (letters 162, 173 and 182). He blamed the West for its insensitivity and indifference to Indian culture, which had the effect of making him oversimplify and even falsify his work when translating; and he blamed himself for falling in with this con and for lacking linguistic skills in English sufficient to capture the nuances of his Bengali. At the same time, he hoped that through Thompson, who was both interested in Bengali culture and linguistically gifted, assisted by himself and Bengali friends, the East–West barrier might be bridged – according to the basic ideal of his Shantiniketan experiment. And so when Thompson proved insensitive to Bengal in many vital respects in his book – for most of Tagore's criticisms undoubtedly were merited, though the book had other merits Tagore did not mention – Rabindranath must have felt an emotion compounded of anger at western cultural arrogance and frustration with himself, which would have reminded him, painfully, of the failures of Shantiniketan so recently and bluntly pointed out by another foreign scholar, the Italian Giuseppe Tucci (see letter 215).

Santiniketan, [West Bengal, India]
20 April 1927

Dear friend, I am glad to know that you reached the cause of your illness and that has helped you. I have come back to my institution and am attending to its claims some of which are material in their character and most exhausting. My work being nonpolitical fails to attract help from my countrymen, and this loneliness heavy with a spirit of antipathy is a difficult burden for me to bear. I have not the gift of the moral asceticism which some of my countrymen have, and I have never pretended to say that I can dispense with human sympathy.

From your letter it is evident that you have read Thompson's book about myself.[4] It is one of the most absurd books that I have ever read dealing with a poet's life and writings. All through his pages he has never allowed his readers to guess that he has a very imperfect knowledge of Bengali language which necessarily prevents him from realising the atmosphere of our words and therefore the colour and music and life of them. He cannot make distinction between that which is essential and nonessential and he jumbles together details without any consideration for their significance. For those who know Bengali his presentation of the subject is too often ludicrously disproportionate. He has been a schoolmaster in an Indian school and that comes out in his pages too often in his pompous spirit of self-confidence even in a realm where he ought to have been conscious of his limitations. The book is full of prejudices which have no foundation in facts, as for instance when he insinuates that I lack in my admiration for Shakespeare – or that I have an antipathy against Englishmen.[5] Of course, I have my grievances against the British Government in India, but I have a genuine respect for the English character which has so often been expressed in my writings. Then again, being a Christian missionary, his training makes him incapable of understanding some of the ideas that run all through my writings – like that of the *jiban debata*, the limited aspect of divinity which has its unique place in the individual life, in contrast to that which belongs to the universe.[6] The God of Christianity has his special recognition as the God of humanity – in Hinduism in our everyday meditation we try to realise his cosmic manifestation and thus free our soul from its bondage of the limitedness of the immediate; but for us he is also individual for the individual, working out, through our evolution in time, our ultimate destiny. On the whole, the author is never afraid to be unjust, and that only shows his want of respect. I am certain he would have been much more careful in his treatment if his subject were a continental poet of reputation in Europe. He ought to have realised his responsibility all the more because of the fact that there was hardly anyone in Europe who could judge his book from his own first-hand knowledge. But this has only made him bold and safely dogmatic, affording him impunity when he built his conclusions upon inaccurate data.[7]

How I wish you had known Bengali!

With love

Ever yours
Rabindranath Tagore

Source: MS original in Rothenstein Papers [Harvard]; letter published in Lago (ed.), *Imperfect Encounter*, pp. 320–2.

1 On RT's pseudonymous review, see Trivedi's introduction to E. J. Thompson, *Rabindranath Tagore*, pp. a12–15; 'multiple hatchet-job' appears on p. a14.
2 E. P. Thompson, *Alien Homage*, p. 90.
3 Thompson to Mahalanobis, 15 Feb. 1922 [RB].
4 Rothenstein praised the translations in Thompson's book in his letter to RT, but did not mention the rest of the book (15 March 1927, in Lago (ed.), *Imperfect Encounter*, p. 319). But he was effusive about the book to Thompson himself, whom he did not know personally, calling it 'an illuminating and profound critical work . . . your understanding of Rabindranath's great vision has touched me closely' (13 March 1927, quoted in Introduction to E. J. Thompson, *Rabindranath Tagore*, p. a29).
5 Referring to *Balaka*, Thompson wrote: 'The Englishman finds in its pages a (not very illuminating) tribute to Shakespeare, from this unlikeliest of admirers' (*Rabindranath Tagore*, p. 234). Originally Thompson wrote, 'The Englishman thrills to find in its pages a tribute to Shakespeare, from this unlikeliest of admirers' ('Rabindranath Tagore's Balaka', *MR*, May 1922, p. 594). What was initially a compliment ceased to be one in the published book, and could easily have been read as patronising. Thompson's book is riddled with such uncertainties of literary judgement, which were unquestionably the product of his lack of confidence in his grasp of the language and culture of Bengal.
6 Thompson wrote a whole chapter of his book on the *jiban debata* concept, one of the weaker sections of the biography.
7 It is not clear whether Rothenstein showed RT's devastating letter to Thompson or not. In E. P. Thompson's view, 'I rather think (but can't prove) that my father did see Tagore's letter re the biography' (Thompson to authors, 3 Dec. 1991). At any rate, there was a long period of coolness between Tagore and Thompson after the publication of the biography, though their relationship resumed in the 1930s.

219

To George Bernard Shaw[1]

Tagore met George Bernard Shaw in London in 1913. Neither man was much interested in the other's writing, but they were intrigued by each other's personalities.[2] Tagore made at least two attempts to persuade Shaw to visit Shantiniketan, of which this is the first.[3]

Santiniketan, [West Bengal, India]
1 July 1927

Dear Mr George Bernard Shaw

In consequence of an announcement appearing in all the papers in India that you are coming to us as my guest next winter, I am assailed from all sides with the question if it is true. I hope that it is not an unpardonable sin on my part if I am evasive in my answer and not too callously honest in denying the certainty of this report. In the meanwhile I am enjoying my precarious reputation as a prospective host of George Bernard Shaw incurring the risk of a rude fact shattering the expectation when it is ripe. I am sure, you can easily save me from this dubious situation and allow me proudly to declare that I have a confirmation of the rumour from a source which is reliable. I have for a long time wished to welcome you in our midst, and I shall be truly grateful to the paragraph makers if by their suggestion they help me in the realisation of this desire of mine. Please tell Mrs Shaw how I still remember the occasion when years ago we had our conversation at your house in London and how I shall appreciate the opportunity if it does come again to have it revived in another environment.[4]

Cordially yours
Rabindranath Tagore

Source: MS original in Shaw Papers [BL].

1 George Bernard Shaw (1856–1950): playwright and writer; awarded Nobel prize for literature, 1925.
2 On RT and Shaw, see Dutta and Robinson, *Rabindranath Tagore*, p. 176.
3 The second attempt was in 1933, when Shaw reached India on a world cruise. See Shaw to RT, 10 Jan. 1933, in George Bernard Shaw, *Collected Letters*, (Dan H. Lawrence ed.; London, 1988): IV (1925–1950), p. 321. Shaw had a low opinion of Shantiniketan, judging from a remark to Rothenstein about 'Nitwitiketant idiots'. (Quoted in William Rothenstein, *Since Fifty: Recollections, 1922–1938* (London, 1939), p. 178.)
4 Shaw replied by cable on 31 July: 'Alas a poetic fiction invented by someone who knew our regard for you. Bernard Shaw' [RB]. Shaw's wife, Charlotte, was seriously interested in RT. She met him several times in 1913 and attended his lectures and the performance of *The Post Office*. RT and the Rothensteins came to the Shaw house on 29 May 1913, according to her annuary kept at the British Library.

220

To N. Zwager[1]

During his visit to Java and Bali in August and September 1927, one of Tagore's lectures was heard by a Dutch woman, who wrote him a letter soon afterwards. Her chief concern was the lack of understanding and growing bad blood between the Dutch colonists and the Javanese. She wrote:

> I have tried to be good to my servants and they cheated me, such as they behave to everybody who is not very severe to them . . .
> I think Kipling's saying, 'East is East and West is West and never the twain shall meet' is certainly not meant for such great souls as you are, Mr Tagore, for whom no borders count, but for such humble everyday souls that have not gone far into psychology, it is as real and true as anything. I am sure, Mr Tagore, that in my case the fault is all mine, and I will go on and try as hard as ever to feel their feelings as my own
> . . .
> If only the Javanese and all other Malayan races could be led to believe that we Europeans really mean good to them, if they could only be taught to *appreciate* the western civilisation! Of course I do not allude to the 'movies', it is only the beautiful ideas that count and the wonderful inventions that should be looked to. You will no doubt say, Mr Tagore, that civilisation is not the main thing, but can it be avoided? And

is not it wonderful, how the whole world is being made ready for the close intermingling of all races, now we can fly in so short a time to the other end of the world and we can speak with our antipodes and even photograph them from immense distances?[2]

Tagore's reply is characteristic: he concentrates on the psychological question, just as he always did in considering Indo-British relations, and leaves aside what he always thought of as less essential matters, such as (in this case) western technological advances.

Solo, [Surakarta, Java, Indonesia]
16 September 1927

Dear Madam

Each people has its physical environment given to it, and social surroundings created by itself. Its history is its continual adjustment to them through modification of its inner and outer world. If in the midst of it some alien element is thrust upon it, some human power which has its own distinct evolution, its separate need, its object which is not only not coincident with that of the other but very often hurtfully antagonistic – a confusion results and this people in its perplexity can never show itself to its best advantage. Europe today is the predominant factor in the human world, but unfortunately she has come to the East, not with an ideal, but with an object that primarily concerns her own self-interest. It naturally makes the eastern peoples suspicious and nervously eager in their turn to exploit the circumstances for their own profit; but, not having the power in their hand and being unequally matched, they cannot afford to be frank in their manner and method. They have become accustomed to being misunderstood which helps them to develop, for the sake of self-respect and self-protection, the habit of hiding their thoughts. This makes it difficult for individuals who have natural gift of sympathy and a desire to deal with their fellow beings in the East in a spirit of justice and love. You will surely understand why generally a Chinese may feel constrained to shut his heart and even reveal the worst side of his nature to some European who is the member of a race that for the sake of profit felt no compunction in drugging the whole great people of China and humiliating them because they showed resistance.[3] If the European had come to China to offer to her the best that their own civilisation had produced, China would also in her relationship to them have the opportunity to do herself justice and show to them her best side.

Allow me to assure you that your letter has given me genuine pleasure for which I thank you.

Rabindranath Tagore

Source: MS copy at Rabindra Bhavan, Shantiniketan; letter published in *VBQ*, 7, No. 1, April–July 1929, p. 168.

1 The letter from N. Zwager contains no details about her. On Dutch colonial life in Java during this period, see Frances Gouda, *Dutch Culture Overseas: Colonial Practice in the Netherlands Indies, 1900–1942* (Amsterdam, 1995). RT's views are to be found in his 'Letters from Java', *VBQ*, 5, No. 4, Jan. 1928 and 6, Nos 1–4, April 1928–Jan. 1929/*RR*, XIX, some of which appear in Dutta and Robinson (eds.), *Anthology*, pp. 108–19.

2 Zwager to RT, 12 Sept. 1927. The letter was written from Surabaya, where RT went after his return from Bali.
3 RT first wrote about the opium trade with China as far back as 1881 ('The death traffic', *MR*, May 1925, pp. 504–7).

221

To Sylvain Lévi[1]

Sylvain Lévi, one of the world's great orientalists, had been the first foreign lecturer at Visva-Bharati. He and his wife stayed at Shantiniketan from November 1921 until August 1922 and became really intimate with Tagore and his circle. After accompanying Tagore in south India, they parted from him and visited Nepal, China, Japan and other Far Eastern countries on a tour that eventually produced an important dictionary of Buddhism based on Chinese and Japanese sources.[2]

Over the next few years Lévi wrote occasional letters to Tagore. Though always respectful and affectionate, they contain a critical note, particularly in relation to Tagore's pan-Asian tendency: Lévi had seen war-torn China and crisis-ridden Japan at close quarters and could not accept Tagore's generalisations about the peaceful East.[3] About Shantiniketan, he wrote to Tagore in late 1923:

> I do not know if Santiniketan will ever rank among the most developed institutions of learning in the world, but you can be satisfied that you have built up an abode of unparalleled peace. I long [for] the day when I can sit again in the shade of the mango-trees, walk along the noble alley of *shals*, talk, dream, listen to music, to verses, enjoy your delightful, sweet, dear company together with the beloved friends there.[4]

The consequence was a gradual cooling of the friendship. Lévi was politically a conservative and by temperament a scholar; Tagore was neither. What they shared was a commitment to the primacy of human relationships. But after they had been apart for some five years, their bond had naturally weakened. It became fairly easy for Tagore to believe that Lévi, like Giuseppe Tucci, might have turned against Shantiniketan, as a newspaper had alleged. In this letter he tackles Lévi on the question directly.

Santiniketan, [West Bengal, India]
16 November 1927

Shuhrittameshu

Your very kind letter has to some extent relieved my mind of an intolerable burden which has been troubling it for some time.[5]

When I was in Java some stranger, with evident delight, sent me a report purporting to give your unfavourable criticism about me and my life's work. Needless to say, it hurt me to the quick because so unexpected and I hope unmerited.[6] I am sure you know we lavished upon you our love and admiration in an unstinted measure and were genuinely grateful to you for your inspiration. Nothing can be more terribly cruel to us than to know that while we invited you without hesitation to the most sensitive intimacy of our life both of you were laughing at the homage of our simple hearts and at the inevitable deficiency of our hospitality which certainly could not stand comparison with

354   Selected letters of Rabindranath Tagore

anything to which you are accustomed, specially in the rich circle of officialdom and aristocracy. However, the whole thing has been too intensely painful to me to try [to] humiliate ourselves and you in an undignified controversy.

I assure you, my friend, that still I am tied to you in a bond of comradeship which was established in those winter months rich with the wealth of your companionship. I hope you know and remember how we tried to express in our own way our recognition of your valuable service. I still acknowledge our debt to you and our wounded love struggles to think that it was some nightmare of misunderstanding which certainly could not be truer than the love I felt to have won from you.

I hope this letter of mine will not deviate you from your plan and you will still visit Santiniketan making us forget that we have done anything to alienate your affection for us.[7] You will find the same warm welcome awaiting you as before, and there will not be the least obstacle on our own side against a perfect revival of those beautiful days of overflowing friendliness. There are too many shatterings of dreams in this world for me to allow lightly another contribution to that unsightly pile of ruins in the evening of my life when time is short for losses to be made up and breakages repaired.[8]

Ever yours
Rabindranath Tagore

Source: MS copy at Rabindra Bhavan, Shantiniketan.

1 Sylvain Lévi (1863–1935): orientalist, particularly noted for his dictionary of Buddhism; he was a professor, Collège de France, 1894–1935.
2 *Hobogirin: Dictionnaire du Bouddhisme d'après les sources chinoises et japonaises* (Paris, 1929), produced in collaboration with the Japanese Buddhist scholar Takakusu Junjiro.
3 See Lévi to RT, 7 Feb. 1923, in Dutta and Robinson, *Rabindranath Tagore*, pp. 247–8.
4 Lévi to RT, 17 Oct. 1923 [RB].
5 Lévi to RT, 16 Oct. 1927 [RB]. This letter simply shows Lévi's friendly feelings towards RT; it appears to be the first from him to RT for over two years.
6 Probably Lévi did speak contemptuously of Shantiniketan as an academic institution, perhaps in private, which was then quoted in a newspaper with or without his permission; but his feelings towards RT and some of the scholars there remained warm and respectful to the end.
7 Lévi paid a farewell visit to Shantiniketan in Aug. 1928.
8 Lévi replied to RT from Tokyo with a pained letter: 'I am deeply sorry that you have taken *au sérieux* some miserable reports the author of which I do not even guess... Shall I refer you to the book published by my wife, about which old friends used to tease her as being in love with you?' (Lévi to RT, 16 Dec. 1927 [RB]). RT was mollified but not entirely convinced; he continued to feel wounded and cut himself off from Lévi after 1928. (See Dutta and Robinson, *Rabindranath Tagore*, p. 442.) The book by Desirée Lévi, *Dans l'Inde (de Ceylan au Nepal)*, published in Paris in 1925, was indeed full of affection for RT. The whole episode was a somewhat sad commentary on RT's inability to accept sincere and objective criticism of his institution.

222

To Prashanta Chandra Mahalanobis

The first interracial marriage in Shantiniketan took place in December 1927, when Tagore's secretary Amiya Chakravarty married Hiordis Siggard, a Danish woman whom Tagore renamed Haimanti Devi.[1] It compelled Rabindranath to consider what kind of marriage ceremony would be in keeping with his ideals. He himself had been married according to a Brahmo ceremony, and he had followed Brahmo ceremonies in the marriages of his four children. These would obviously not be appropriate for Chakravarty, who came from a relatively orthodox Hindu family, and his foreign wife-to-be, who wanted to become a Hindu. In this letter to Prashanta Mahalanobis, who had made a slightly unconventional marriage a few years earlier, Rabindranath muses on the nature of the problem.[2]

[Shantiniketan?, West Bengal, India]
8 Agrahayan 1334 [24 November 1927]

Kalyaniyeshu

Prashanta, before I received your letter I somehow came up with a good idea whereby we could avoid purification prior to the marriage ceremony of Amiya.[3] Pramatha[4] has given Amiya advice too, that he should marry according to the Christian Marriage Act, because this leaves the religion and customs of both parties intact. You are the expert in marriage matters, you can surely advise on the pros and cons of these suggestions.

If the marriage takes place without the purification ritual but with the customary Vedic *mantrams*, sincerely spoken, what objection can there be? So far as the ideals of Visva-Bharati are concerned, we must support interracial marriage. But we must do it without hypocrisy. If the usual paraphernalia – the sacred stone of Narayan and suchlike – are done away with, there should not be any objection from any quarter to the rest of the ceremony.[5] The only question that may arise concerns the giving away of the bride. Here again it could be argued that since the girl herself has the right to give herself away, why keep up a superfluous pretence of having someone else give her away? But the real meaning of the giving away is symbolic: it sanctions the marriage. So if Haimanti has someone she reveres as a father, what would be wrong with an initiation ceremony for him to bestow his blessings on the marriage? Of course no giver-away of a bride can generate the true and natural state of marriage except the bride herself through her loving self-sacrifice – but is there anything improper in a well-wisher giving the marriage his seal of approval? If such a condition cannot be met, I would not go on to say that the marriage cannot take place, but if it is easily fulfillable and the bride is able to enter the bridegroom's family after being dedicated by a fatherly hand, the ceremony will acquire a certain charm.[6] Still, the gift that comes from within the girl herself stands above all other gifts, such as any gift involving society's representative. Which raises the question whether 'gift' is a good word or not in the circumstances. Is the bride really a gift object? It seems that social customs have yet to advance beyond this idea. But unless a marriage receives a gift from heaven, it will not work, even though there may be a meeting of minds. This apart, you may also argue that the giving is visibly not just one way, for the bride receives a groom in exchange. Agreed – but for various reasons, both natural and conventional, the tendency is to see only the bride as a gift. It is she who goes to her husband's home, she who changes her name and calls herself Mrs Mahalanobis, she who takes charge of her husband's household, and she who (at least in our country) accepts his relatives as her own. A husband, by contrast, does none of this – the main reason being that he continues to live with his own family and simply includes his wife among them – and he regards it as a social disgrace if he lives in the house of his father-in-law but not if he lives in his father's house. Hence, whatever may be the spiritual meaning of marriage, in practice the bride comes as a gift to her husband's house and acknowledges it as her own: if she does not, society treats her as if she has breached a contract and censures her for being too independent-minded. In time all this will change and marriage will not stay in its present form, but for now, as long as the system endures, not to go along with it creates certain difficulties of adjustment. Anyhow do let me know what you think of adopting the Vedic ritual in a modified form. The basic problem is that modern ways of thinking do not suit ancient rituals.[7]

Tomader
Shri Rabindranath Thakur

Source: MS original at Rabindra Bhavan, Shantiniketan; letter published in *Desh*, 20 Asharh 1382 [5 July 1975], p. 733.

1 The wedding was held at Shantiniketan on 1 Paush 1334 (17 Dec. 1927). The couple had one child, in 1930. Haimanti Devi (1905–91) lived in Shantiniketan for the rest of her life. Their marriage seems to have been the basis for the somewhat similar Bengali–Danish relationship in Rózsa Hajnóczy's novel *Fire of Bengal* (Eva Wimmer and David Grant trans., William Radice ed.; Dhaka, 1993).
2 Mahalanobis married Nirmal Kumari Maitra, the daughter of a prominent Brahmo, Heramba Chandra Maitra, in 1923, in the presence of RT and many other leading Brahmos. The couple refused to marry according to the Brahmo Marriage Act of 1872, because they regarded themselves as part of Hindu society, not as belonging to a non-Hindu, Brahmo community. This led to a split between the bride and her father, who did not attend the wedding.
3 Orthodoxy requires the purification of a *mlechchha*, a foreigner, wishing to become a Hindu, through rituals such as the eating of cow-dung and bathing in Ganges water.
4 Pramatha: Pramathanath Chaudhuri, who married Indira Devi, RT's niece. See letter 89.
5 Those aspects of the orthodox Hindu marriage ceremony that were idolatrous would have offended the founding principles of Shantiniketan, which forbade idolatrous worship in the ashram. The other parts of the Hindu ritual – *baran* (the welcoming of the bride), *shaptapadi* (the seven steps taken together by bridegroom and bride) and the *shubhadristi* (the solemn look exchanged between the two) – were retained in Chakravarty's wedding. Three Tagore songs, with some modifications, were sung.
6 C. F. Andrews performed the *kanya-shampradan*, the giving away of the bride to the groom.
7 In 1925, in 'The Indian ideal of marriage', RT wrote:

> The civilisation of man has not, up to now, loyally recognised the reign of the spirit. Therefore the married state is still one of the most fruitful sources of the unhappiness and downfall of man, of his disgrace and humiliation. But those who believe that society is a manifestation of the spirit, will assuredly not rest in their endeavours till they have rescued human marriage relations from outrage by the brute forces of society – till they have thereby given free play to the force of love in all the concerns of humanity. (*VBQ*, 3, No. 2, July 1925, p. 108)

223

To Dilip Kumar Roy[1]

This letter, like letter 222, deals with marriage. But it makes an interesting contrast with the earlier letter. There, writing to a fairly conventional married friend, Rabindranath was compelled by events (a forthcoming interracial marriage in Shantiniketan) to consider how his social ideals might fit social reality; how his own natural unconventionality might come to terms with other people's social convention. In this letter, written to an unconventional and unmarried friend, he is able to expatiate on his social ideals unconstrained by practical demands.

[Shantiniketan, West Bengal, India]
2 February 1928

[*Kalyaniyeshu*]

In Europe the customary idea of long standing, that in the conjugal relationship the husband and wife have sole rights over each other's body, has been gradually losing its hold. In my view the main reason is that for some time now men have been unwilling to marry. The standard of living has become expensive in Europe, and no one finds it easy to shoulder the burden of a family. Hence many women have been forced to remain unmarried. The convention of keeping the body chaste before marriage can never endure in a society where a large number of women have no hope of finding a bridegroom. In our country, by contrast, the convention about physical chastity is as strictly observed as is the convention that a woman's duty is to marry. And for widows there are endless restrictions on food and behaviour. In Europe, the more daunting the prospect of marriage becomes, the looser become the rules on virginity.

There is another reason too. When women were compelled to remain dependent on men, when they had no other means of livelihood but to get married, they had to try their utmost to protect what was their most valuable possession in the marriage market. In the modern age such restraints on women are slowly eroding. The problem of pregnancy is no longer so great, and preventive methods are simpler now. Generally speaking, because the woman is the one who conceives, the responsibility for looking after the body carefully has fallen more heavily on her. The man, at any rate in our country, has enjoyed both polygamy and promiscuity with little or no public disgrace: that came only quite recently, along with Christianity. Even when we were children, such practices were openly indulged in without shame. Thus the basic fact is, prescriptive rules about bodily chastity among men and especially among women are firmly founded in economic and social reasoning; and when the force of these arguments diminishes and fades away, the rules cannot last as mere commandments. Society has managed to curb people's natural instincts by dint of necessity – and this curbing has required a great deal of contrivance, hindrance and vigilance – but when the necessity is relaxed, these instincts are not so easy to suppress. Consider the example of personal property. If I am hungry and there happens to be no fruit on my tree, I will naturally crave to eat the fruit on your tree. But such eating is stealing, according to society, because the protection of personal property is considered essential to the maintenance of social discipline. Society has implanted this concept of stealing deep in our minds in order to make us easier to manage. If some day, for some scientific or social reason, material objects were collectively to lose their value, the prohibition against theft would also disappear. The commandment against stealing is really not an eternal commandment, but a manmade one: if we disregard it and there is no social upheaval as a result, then the taking of other people's things is not stealing. Thus if you, Dilip Kumar – while I, Rabindranath, happen to be absent from my garden – come and eat some of my lychees, you would not feel remorse for having stolen and I for my part would not brand you a thief. The same applies to sexual misconduct. Since the element in it which is criminal is social, only if it provokes social upheaval must society be on its guard against it; but if such sexual acts have no effect on society, they are not misconduct – the black mask that has been hung over them to deter perpetrators will not, if lifted off, reveal the darkness of hell underneath.

Of course lack of physical restraint is a type of misconduct whatever the circumstances, moreover the suppression of one's physical nature through the practice of certain austerities may have a particular value which cannot be discussed under the category of ethics. Indeed there are two aspects to all enduring principles: that of the heart, and that of the mind. One is without truth, the other is without love. One involves deceit, the other involves ruthlessness. One aims to bewitch, the other aims to kill. Let me say just a little more on this. A certain kind of untruth, for example the poetic imagination, can be on a par with truth, and a certain kind of ruthlessness, such as the punishment of injustice, can be on a par with love. But I have prattled enough – in terms of time wasted, I have committed a misdemeanour, and yet if time were to have little or no value, no blame would attach to my volubility.

Snehashakta
Shri Rabindranath Thakur

Source: MS original at Rabindra Bhavan, Shantiniketan; letter published in Dilip Kumar Roy, *Tirthankar* (rev. edn. 1382 [1975]), pp. 295–6.

1 Dilip Kumar Roy (1897–1980): poet, writer and musician; son of Dwijendra Lal Roy, playwright, poet and composer. Roy was educated at Cambridge University and later studied German and Italian music on the Continent. Of his voice, Mahatma Gandhi said: 'I make bold to claim that very few persons in India – or, rather, in the world – have a voice like his, so rich and sweet and intense.' (Quoted in 'Mystic musician', *Sunday Statesman*, Calcutta, 26 Jan. 1992.) In 1928, Roy joined the Aurobindo ashram, Pondicherry, and stayed there until Aurobindo's death in 1950. He published a series of conversations with RT in the *VBQ*, for example one on marriage ('The function of woman's shakti in society', *VBQ*, 6, No. 1, April 1928, pp. 68–78) and a book, *Among the Great* (4th edn, Pondicherry, 1984), consisting of his conversations with various celebrities, including RT.

224

To Suniti Kumar Chatterji [Chattopadhyay][1]

Rabindranath sometimes gave 'benefit' performances with his Shantiniketan dance, music and acting troupe, in order to raise money for worthy causes other than his university, such as a famine or a flood in Bengal. Fundraising for patriotic causes he generally left to the politicians, but in early 1928 there was a proposal that the Shantiniketan students give performances to raise money for the suffering families of Bengali political prisoners, following the example of a concert given in Calcutta. The idea proved controversial and one of Tagore's younger friends, who shared the objections of the puritans, warned him of the opposition. Rabindranath's reply shows the intelligence and depth of his commitment to the welfare of his countrymen, despite their failure to live up to his expectations.

[Shantiniketan, West Bengal, India]
19 Magh 1334 [2 February 1928]

Kalyaniyeshu

The fundraising drive for the political prisoners has upset many people. But the really deplorable thing is not the drive itself, rather the fact that such an effort was even necessary. It was inevitable that the families of the prisoners would suffer financially, once sentence had been passed. Yet while we could only lament over the situation of those actually detained by the government, it was open to us to relieve the difficulties of their families, which lie outside government control. But even here we merely petitioned the government and did nothing ourselves. If our anguish were genuine, such inaction would be impossible. Were a mere four lakhs of people out of many crores to contribute four annas each in four instalments over a year, the orphaned families would realise that the country they have been addressing as Mother truly is a mother.[2] In some other countries the well-to-do section of the population would have donated of its own volition. The reason this does not happen here is that politics in our country is not the genuine article. And if you ask me why this is so, I shall say it is because our politics is not dedicated to serving the common man, it is restricted to nudging government officials about their duties. Those of us who get worked up about politics are perpetually shouting about the need of the country for self-rule, but I say – which country do you mean? Is it the country for which we ourselves do nothing, and whose desperate people no one yet believes we regard as our own? Every day, before our eyes, we watch them go to rack and ruin for lack of food, lack of water, lack of education and lack of health, and we fail to act: only against lack of self-rule, which we loudly proclaim to be the source of our sorrows, do we really stir ourselves. On the pretext of serving the villages, lakhs of rupees are collected, and before long they simply vanish.

When the people of a country perceive that their country consists of a union with each other in mutual service, their fellow-feeling gives rise to genuine politics. In sum, I believe that the pain felt by our people at the plight of the political prisoners is not sincere enough – hence the fact that even now people do not find it easy to make a small sacrifice for these prisoners. And yet the hardship of the families is genuine enough. Despite a certain shame attached to relief efforts that appeal to pleasure rather than compassion, we know we cannot appeal simply to the patriotism and generosity of our countrymen – to do so would be inadequate, however much we may regret it. Those who pay to see dance and music programmes are not motivated by patriotic appeals. But how else to arrange food for a large number of innocent bereft women, boys and girls, except by making a hole in people's pockets with the burgling tool of entertainment? We cannot relieve the starvation of a starving person by clutching at the bogus belief that our countrymen are ready and willing to make sacrifices to alleviate the country's difficulties. You may say that if this is really the case, then fasting to death by starvation is preferable. We have no right to say such a thing, since we are not the ones who are starving. Where is the heroism in making someone else become a martyr? I have seen that sort of heroism recently, when for want of food and clothing many women were too ashamed to leave their dwellings – meanwhile, foreign cloth was burnt outside their houses. Objections to its burning were overruled by saying that impure cloth could not be used to cover semi-naked women. Not until such women receive enough khaddar to clothe themselves do those who have at least two items of serviceable cloth have the right to speak like that.[3]

The people who paid to hear the music said quite openly – we will pay several rupees for this purpose but not for some other purpose. Only those in need have the right to oppose the idea of money collected in this way being used to relieve their need, because they are the ones who are in jeopardy. Though such a fundraising event should never have been required, at the same time it must be said that the puritanical attitude of scorn for all music is undesirable. The cultivation of taste is an important item in the assets of a country. Of course the problem is that questions of taste always provoke discord. But if taste is a debatable matter, there can be no debate about whether singing for one's country is wrong. If an author chooses to give away the income from his book for some patriotic purpose, there will probably be no objection – it is because we have looked down upon music for so long, that to use music in the same way is controversial. How the particular musical event in question was presented and publicised, I have no idea. On behalf of Art, I can say only that if the pleasure given by the music was indistinguishable from what is commonly called entertainment, then the music stands guilty before goddess Saraswati. In which case, Saraswati's *vina*, given her by sage Narada, may be confiscated by some puritanical *sanyasi* determined to do good to the world. If however a real artist were to choose to commit his art to the service of the country, then let this *sanyasi* not criticise.

I shall bear in mind the other points in your letter.

Tomader
Shri Rabindranath Thakur

Source: MS original at Rabindra Bhavan, Shantiniketan; letter published in *Desh*, 28 July 1990, pp. 41–2.

1 Suniti Kumar Chatterji [Chattopadhyay] (1890–1977): philologist, author of *The Origin and Development of the Bengali Language*; he was Khaira professor of Indian linguistics and phonetics, University of Calcutta, 1922–52. Though closely associated with Visva-Bharati, Chatterji was never on the staff. He travelled to South-east Asia with RT in 1927. See Uma Das Gupta, 'The poet and the linguist', *VBN*, Aug.–Sept. 1977, pp. 35–6.
2 lakh: one hundred thousand; crore: ten million.
3 RT had no patience with the concept of 'impure' foreign cloth, which he regarded as an irresponsible political slogan used by Gandhi to hypnotise his supporters.

225

To Edward John Thompson

After taking a thorough dislike to E. J. Thompson's book about him when it appeared in 1926 (see letter 218), Tagore cut himself off from Thompson – but not absolutely. This letter, the only one written to Thompson between 1926 and 1931, prompted by a minor request from him, has just a hint of the old warmth in its second paragraph. Possibly being back in Shelidah, where Tagore seldom now went, had rekindled old memories of his friendship with Thompson. Within a few years, they were on amicable terms.

Shilida, [Shelidah, Khulna, Bangladesh]
29 March 1928

Dear Thompson

I write this letter from Shilida where I mean to spend a few more days before I return to my work. Letters addressed to me in Bolpur are being opened in my absence by

Morris[1] who informs me that he has the list of my translations you refer to in your note. I do not know why he does not send it to me. I suppose he wants to enjoy the power given to him of doing what he likes with my correspondence by doing what is not proper. I believe the day will come some time when it will be given up to me.

My reputation as a poet will be enhanced in your mind when you know my plans and preparations to visit Nepal have brought me to this place.

Yours
Rabindranath Tagore

Source: MS original in Thompson Papers [Bodleian].

1 Morris: Hirjibhai Pestonji Morriswala, also known as Marichi: RT's secretary during part of the 1920s. He was a Parsi whom C. F. Andrews introduced to RT, who attempted, rather ineffectually, to raise money for Visva-Bharati.

226

To Boyd Tucker[1]

Although Tagore had no liking for Christian missionaries as a group, he became friendly with a number of individuals who were missionaries, notably C. F. Andrews, W. W. Pearson and E. J. Thompson (see letter 74). In 1927, an American Methodist, Boyd W. Tucker, came to Shantiniketan and remained there until 1934. He seems to have become involved in politics, more closely than perhaps Tagore realised, and this brought him into conflict with the Government, which advised him to desist or have his visa withdrawn. Turning to Tagore for advice, Tucker wrote:

> I am vitally interested in the life of India, and want to identify myself as far as possible with her limitations and sufferings. I am not sympathetic with the cult of advice-mongers and soul-savers who fail to realise their responsibilities to this present generation and this present world . . .
> The Government of India like all other present-day governments are now taking us [missionaries] at our word, and are saying in effect that they will not interfere with us in our conduct of the affairs of the future world, but say to us that we must not interfere with them in the conduct of this world.[2]

Rabindranath, ever responsive to such language, is unequivocally supportive in his reply.

Santiniketan, [West Bengal, India]
13 July 1928

Dear Tucker

I am not yet strong enough to be able to attend to my correspondence and therefore I shall be brief. Of course you cannot accept the conditions which our Government imposes on you in return for the permission they give you to do your duty to our people. I am not at all surprised at the suspicion entertained by the Indian Government even against meetings that deal with social questions. They are wise, for every removal of social evils truly leads us to our emancipation. The Congress politics having no foundation in reality can be ignored but all organised efforts that we make in order to rescue us from the bondage of social humiliation are sure to rouse in our national soul the true spirit of freedom.

The best way of keeping a people permanently under foreign subjection is to kill their humanity, to allow them to remain content in a state of social stagnation that breeds rottenness. While admiring the political cleverness of our rulers let us follow our conscience and offer our life and love not for the sake of the British Empire but for man and for God.

Yours affectionately
Rabindranath Tagore

Source: MS copy at Rabindra Bhavan, Shantiniketan.

1 Boyd W. Tucker (1902–72): Methodist missionary. In 1929, Tucker travelled with RT as his secretary in Canada and the USA. During the trip, RT's passport was mislaid, which led to some unpleasant cross-examination by American immigration officials and the subsequent curtailing by an offended RT of his visit to the USA. Tucker seems to have handled the incident maladroitly. In Shantiniketan, he appears as a character in Hajnóczy's novel *Fire of Bengal*, who stirs up the student body to support Gandhi but is unable to control them, all without RT's knowledge. See also letter 264.
2 Tucker to RT, 10 July 1928 [RB].

227

To Amal Home[1]

Some of Tagore's letters, especially those in Bengali, show that he could be extremely practical. Most of these make for dull reading, but this one, written for publication in the fourth anniversary issue of the *Calcutta Municipal Gazette*, is both interesting and practical on a subject of real importance: the state of Calcutta's streets.

Santiniketan, [West Bengal, India]
8 November 1928

My dear Amal,

I am glad that you asked me for a few lines for the anniversary number of the *Municipal Gazette*. Your kind invitation has given me an opportunity of putting forward a suggestion for consideration by our city fathers.

I had the misfortune some time ago to try to discover a house with a street number, which, doubtless for some excellent municipal reason, was occult for a mere citizen like myself. After many journeyings, up and down the road, in desperation I turned for help – to a policeman; I had forgotten that we are unique in the world in the matter of our police force; for, though in other lands the policeman may have grey matter in the brain, our national brand has merely red material on the head – perhaps more decorative, but undoubtedly not quite so useful. The hiatus in the numbering of the houses was apparently unnoticed by even the people in the locality, for, when appealed to, they could make merely large and inutile gestures.

The present system of numbering houses and planning streets may be a splendid way of training the young generation to become future Livingstones. But the course is, perhaps, too difficult, and I sometimes wonder if Livingstone himself would not have found exploration in Darkest Africa easier than fruitful exploration in the City of Palaces. And, for those of us who have little inclination for exploration, this scheme is extravagant both in time (perhaps a slight matter) and in petrol (which, certainly, is a matter for momentous consideration).

It should not be a very difficult task to assist both citizens and strangers to the city, uninitiated into the mysteries of street planning, in their adventurous undertaking of trying to discover places and houses in Calcutta. The lamp posts might be easily utilised for hanging from them plates bearing useful information; and I believe that though the quality of illumination emanating at night from many of the city lamp posts might conveniently be a matter of civic discussion, the utility of these plates pendant from the lamp posts will be freely recognised by all. It would enable even me to discover a house mystically numbered let us say, 99–1–N, Cornwallis Street.[2]

I would suggest that an enamelled or painted board should be attached to each lamp post. On the board should be the following information:

(a) the number of the houses in the street between the lamp post and the next lamp post on either side; an arrow would indicate whether the numbers are in the ascending or in the descending order; e.g.,

48←56   56→64

(b) the name of any street or lane opening out of the street and the number of the house from which such street or lanes begins; e.g.

60, Ram Chandra Dutta Lane.

As there are lamp posts on either side of the street, it is unnecessary to point out whether the street or lane is on the right or the left.

(c) the names of all public buildings or important places, lying between lamp posts, should also be entered; if any private individual or business firm wishes to have his name on the direction plate, it might be a source of income to the corporation. It is quite conceivable that many shops or even private individuals may be willing to pay well for the publicity of the plates.

At the place where each important street begins, there may be put up a large board stating prominently the more important streets opening out from the street and also any important public places to be seen along this street. Here again, a considerable revenue may be acquired by permitting business firms or private individuals to have their names on these boards.

The cost of providing these plates and boards should not be prohibitive; if steps are taken to encourage business firms to have their names on the plates and boards, the cost would, perhaps, be practically nothing. But in any case the assistance to the public would be so great that any expenditure should be considered a legitimate charge on the municipal revenue. A beginning might be made with the more important of the streets.

Wishing your paper all success, I am,

Yours sincerely,
Rabindranath Tagore

Source: letter published as 'The poet wants a street-number', *CMG*, p. 150.

1 Amal Home (1893–1975): editor, *Calcutta Municipal Gazette*, 1924–48; he organised the Calcutta celebration of RT's seventieth birthday in 1931. Home was an admirer of RT but not part of his circle; he was appointed as editor by C. R. Das, the mayor of Calcutta.
2 The address of Amal Home.

228

To Rani Mahalanobis (Maitra)[1]

In 1925, in his most direct hit at Gandhi and the cult of spinning, 'The cult of the *charka*', Tagore wrote:

> There are many who assert and some who believe that *swaraj* can be attained by the *charka*; but I have yet to meet a person who has a clear idea of the process. That is why there is no discussion, but only quarrelling over the question . . . If any true devotee of our motherland should be able to eradicate poverty of only one of her villages, he will have given permanent wealth to the thirty-three crores of his countrymen.[2]

Tagore saw, more clearly than any other Indian, that Gandhi's central ideas, though appealing to many Indians, could never lift India out of her material and intellectual poverty. Spinning was no substitute for thinking. Western ideas, particularly science, were vital to India's regeneration. Unlike the Mahatma, Tagore had travelled extensively in industrially developed countries, talked with the most advanced thinkers in many fields and come into close touch with agricultural scientists such as Leonard Elmhirst. Whatever his reservations about the machine, he was in sympathy with the spirit of rational curiosity driving the development of science. His desperate wish was to inculcate this spirit in the minds of Indians.

This letter expresses his feeling, sharpened by the fact that he was writing to the wife of his scientist friend Prashanta Mahalanobis. Rani Mahalanobis had travelled with Rabindranath throughout Europe for nearly six months in 1926. Together they had seen the affluence and inventiveness of Europeans. Their shared experience forms the background to the letter.

Shantiniketan, [West Bengal, India]
2 Kartik 1336 [16 October 1929]

Kalyaniyashu

Today is Lakshmi Purnima.[3] The ashram is missing out on the festival because of the vacation. People normally embroider these occasions with all sorts of activities, at least they do in our country. For here we have a surfeit of leisure, which we cannot allow to remain entirely vacant. Our quotidian existence is so nearly stagnant that algae accumulate upon its surface, which create a sludge supporting the flotsam of our petty concerns. A rustic country like ours, devoid of serious endeavour, needs to have a superabundance of festivals at which everyone may mingle, hospitality may flow and people may imagine that the particular deities of the moment have an eternal significance transcending the narrowness and paltriness of their setting. In a land of indolence such an emotion lifts people out of their ruts, otherwise there would be nothing to stop them from sinking right up to their topknots in total lethargy. In cold countries people have a profuse abundance of energy, they are perpetually at war with their natural environment, constantly engaged in extracting the wealth concealed in nature's storehouse. The affluence they have created for themselves you have seen with your own eyes – they never cease their efforts to make the impossible possible, whether on land, at sea or in the air. Not for them the idea of sitting in a corner of some room in a shady village with time on their hands and some ceremonial quilt in their laps for decorative stitching. They have elevated the pursuit of their own welfare into a great undertaking, free of pettiness, by dint of their formidable powers of application and far-reaching intelligence. While we, though we are now searching for ways to liberate the country, fail to rise above the ideology of the *charka*.

The *charka* does not require anyone to think: one simply turns the wheel of the antiquated invention endlessly, using the minimum of judgement and stamina. In a more industrious, vital country than ours such a proposition would have stood no chance of acceptance – but in this country anything more strenuous than spinning would be rejected. Just think what would happen if instead of spinning Mahatma were to rule that each cultivator must grow at least two seers of produce per *bigha* of land; that such a target should be his sole aim and a mark of his piety; and that his patriotism would be judged by the extent to which he achieved this aim – then everyone would argue that such a programme would require intelligence, knowledge, drive and commitment to productive agricultural techniques.[4] Indeed it would – and those are precisely the means whereby a country may be liberated; a country cannot be awakened by the inane enthusiasm of ignorant minds. That the cultivators who form three-quarters of this country's population should receive advice on how to spin with a *charka* like an imbecile rather than on how to become better farmers, is an insult to their humanity. Of course to speak of progress in cultivation means to speak of founding a countrywide organisation; and that would be a higher aim than the spreading of the *charka* and khaddar. The cultivators must be introduced to the techniques of cooperative crop production; distribution points for high-quality seeds must be established in every province; and schemes must be started to test soils and supply suitable manures. Once upon a time the *charka* was to be found in homes throughout our country (and abroad too), but it disappeared for quite natural reasons – if today in our excitement it is enjoying something of a revival, this is bound to come to a halt before too long. Because the device in question is thoroughly out of tune with today's times. By contrast, any improvement of farming by cooperative methods that may be introduced on an all-India basis – on however limited a scale – will bear fruit and will gradually spread, because it is in harmony with the age. The chief reason why the cult of khaddar could be proposed at all as being for the good of the country and could receive widespread acceptance, is in my view because our minds are in thrall to an urge to extort concessions from a merchant nation by putting pressure on the looms of Lancashire. Thus we look outside ourselves for ways to liberate the country – which is a symptom of our hidden dependence on others. In Swadeshi Movement days, when the boycott business was at its height, our aims were also external.[5] Now, in the midst of noncooperation, we plan to obtain the other side's cooperation by coercive means. Such worldly goals are merely superficial.

Why I should suddenly have felt the desire to embark on this subject in a letter to you eludes proper explanation. My letter is hardly going to help you recover from your illness. I began with Lakshmi Purnima. That was not accidental. My next idea was to ask why our villages boast a profusion of such festivals. After that I had meant to continue by citing my experience of the island of Bali, because there I noticed a tradition of festivals similar to ours. Bali stands apart from the modern world. It is under extensive cultivation, with a surplus of produce and without a sign of mills and workshops or the kind of jostling for position that accompanies political and other ideologies. Instead the people of that green island while away their days with arts and crafts in the shade of some private forest grove – full of peace and beauty but lacking in drive and utility. Bali seems to me comparable with our ancient Bengal.[6]

In countries where, in contrast, the goddess of wealth is worshipped through hard toil, there is no call for a ritual like our *puja* to Lakshmi, and no one misses it. It is only young girls without experience of housekeeping who like to play Mothers and Fathers – a grown-up woman like you feels no enthusiasm for playing Mothers and Fathers-in-law. The same applies to wealth creation in the modern age: it requires experience and tremendous perseverance, not childish rituals. But how can we in India cope with this fact? Not having the required commitment, we simply carry on as usual with our Lakshmi *puja* and our *charka* spinning, and treat the latter cult as some kind of triumph. Maybe nothing better is to be expected here – and yet I persist in hoping that we *can* derive benefit from the results of hard effort in other countries. My mind is brimming over with such feelings of frustration, which is why they tend to pop out at the least prompting by related thoughts.

I stopped writing at this point last night. In the meanwhile, rain clouds have rolled up with their usual passion. I adore such days of dark shadow and vibrant showers. But on this occasion, with the harvesting of the *aush* paddy imminent, I feel some anxiety.[7] In a country that depends entirely on agriculture for its survival, one's mind is alert to every little sign in the sky. Other countries have many other means of livelihood and these form great highways which girdle the earth. In India we have but a narrow road, with death lurking on either side. Every morning, when I open my newspaper, I look first at the weather report. Europe looks for its wealth underground, in the bowels of the earth, while we look upwards to the sky. Excavations for Europeans – invocations for Indians.

No matter what I do, it seems this letter cannot evade my patriotic obsession. The only way to get rid of it is to stop writing. The rest of this sheet will remain blank – you must not sue me for the missing bit.

The time is about two o'clock. Afternoon. We have obtained some lovely scented Chinese tea and I feel like drinking a cup. I must call Nilmani.[8] If you want to know why I suddenly thought of tea, it is because I am feeling rather drowsy.

Tomader
Shri Rabindranath Thakur

Source: MS original at Rabindra Bhavan, Shantiniketan; letter published in *Desh*, 13 May 1961, pp. 227–8.

1 Nirmal Kumari ('Rani') Mahalanobis (Maitra) (1900–81): wife of Prashanta Chandra Mahalanobis; she and her husband travelled with RT in Europe in 1926. On her marriage, see letter 222, n. 2.
2 crore: ten million.
3 Lakshmi Purnima: annual festival of Lakshmi, goddess of wealth, that takes place at full moon (*purnima*) in October.
4 seer: measure of weight corresponding to about two pounds; *bigha*: measure of land corresponding to about one-third of an acre.
5 See letter 31.
6 RT visited Bali in Aug.–Sept. 1927 (see letter 220, n. 1).
7 On *aush* paddy, see letter 99, n. 1.
8 Nilmani: RT's name for Banamali, his personal servant from 1923 to 1941. See Chitta Ranjan Dev, 'In memoriam: Banamali', *VBN*, April–May 1954, pp. 109–10.

229

To Suniti Kumar Chatterji [Chattopadhyay]

Tagore's painting grew out of his habit of elaborating the erasures on his manuscripts, which he started on his visit to Argentina in 1924 (see letter 204). The doodling continued and in 1928 became a 'mania' for drawing and painting that lasted till the last months of Rabindranath's life.[1]

His art bore little resemblance to the rest of his works, and was little appreciated in Bengal. Tagore decided to keep it to himself: only after the paintings had been appreciated internationally in 1930 did he allow them to be exhibited in Bengal. This letter reveals his attitude.

Santiniketan, [West Bengal, India]
5 Paush 1336 [20 December 1929]

Kalyaniyeshu

Some time ago I drew a picture in your notebook. I am not sure it was a good idea. I did not sign the picture, and I will not.[2] I have no wish to acquaint the people of my province with my work as an artist; but in spite of this they have already begun to pass judgement on it. You came across my pictures by your own initiative and I feel rather uneasy about it. Alive or dead I have no desire to make this creation of mine public here. My pictures will not be allowed to commit the same offence as my other creations. The evidence in your notebook was left there by accident. So my earnest request is that I may tear out the offending page before returning the notebook to you – this will not threaten the storehouse of Indian art in the slightest, but I shall feel secure.

It will be good if you send me a list of names and addresses of our new contacts in Malaya, Java and Siam.[3] On my earlier visits, these were collected by my companions. I am thinking of sending these people an annual gift of some sort for a while. So please let me have your list. I have been very busy of late with urgent pieces of work. That is why I could not send you the list of words I have compiled – as soon as I can breathe a bit, I shall send it.[4]

Shubhakangkshi
Shri Rabindranath Thakur

Source: MS original at Rabindra Bhavan, Shantiniketan; letter published in *Desh*, 28 July 1990, pp. 43–4.

1 In letter 204, written in 1925, RT refers to his 'cult of frenzied drawing', in letter 232, written in 1930, to his 'mania of producing pictures'. On the genesis of his art, see *Rabindranath Tagore on Art and Aesthetics* (Prithwish Neogy ed.; New Delhi, 1961) and also Andrew Robinson, *The Art of Rabindranath Tagore* (London, 1989).
2 RT did not sign his works prior to his European exhibitions in 1930. Later he signed many but not all works.
3 Suniti Kumar Chatterji [Chattopadhyay] visited South-east Asia with RT in 1927. The 'earlier visits' took place in 1916 and 1924, en route to Japan/China.
4 In March 1930, RT gave a paper on Bengali equivalents of English words, in which he acknowledged the help of Chatterji. He may have been referring to this. (See *Desh*, 28 July 1990, p. 48.)

230

To Suniti Kumar Chatterji [Chattopadhyay]

Among Rabindranath's many critics in Bengal, the most malicious were perhaps the writers of *Shanibarer Chithi* (Saturday Squibs), a satirical magazine edited in Calcutta.[1] Although Suniti Kumar Chatterji [Chattopadhyay] never wrote for this magazine, he was friendly with those who did. Rabindranath was perfectly well aware of this, but nevertheless remained on good terms with Chatterji.[2] In fact he hoped to gain an understanding of the grievances of his critics by discussing them with Chatterji, as this letter demonstrates.

[Shantiniketan, West Bengal, India]
11 Paush 1336 [26 December 1929]

Kalyaniyeshu

I had decided to banish my picture from your notebook. You have asked to keep it – alright.[3]

I want to say a bit more about the subject I discussed with you the other day. You told me that those who humiliate me in *Shanibarer Chithi* are really my admirers, that their attacks on me are only for personal reasons, in order to relieve their anguished feelings. But I have noticed that long before they had any personal grievance they relished their barbs against me. I have also noticed that those who have never written a single line in my favour lose no opportunity to criticise me elaborately. There are positive and negative aspects to the work of any writer, but it is not a sign of respect in a critic to keep silent about the positive aspects and proclaim the negative ones at the top of his voice. Generally speaking, we are naturally curious about someone who has been labelled controversial; no one will be censured for such curiosity. And it would be a matter of shame if I expected everyone to admire my works or my character; nor is there any reason in Bengal to entertain such expectations. But the comments against me have been spiteful – to the effect that there is a multitude of flatterers who surround me and sing my praises and deprive me of the capacity to see my own failings. The critics who say this are not part of my circle but they indulge in foolish fantasies about the doings of those who are, thereby demonstrating their hostility towards me. You, who spent quite a long period with me continuously, can vouch for whether or not I tried to use you to gratify some hankering of mine to hear praise of myself. So far as I recall, whenever I came across your good qualities, I sang their praises, whether you were present or not. My basic point is therefore this: the numerous people who enjoy stinging me with their criticisms – while I do not blame them, one cannot say that they do it out of *respect* for me.

It is time I grew able to accept all this equably.[4] There is no profit in complaining and calling for a detailed reckoning of what I am and am not owed by my countrymen. There is no honour in it either. But for my own peace of mind, I need to be aware of the truth. My countrymen have occasionally protested against Chitta Ranjan or Mahatmaji, have even censured them, but, despite their grievances against these two, they have never insulted them in a low and vile way. Not that they would not have enjoyed doing so, but they lacked the courage, because they knew that the public would not stand for it. In my case, however, there is not the slightest reason for hesitation – many people are pleased when I am censured and most of the rest are completely indifferent. My countrymen are not hurt when I am publicly insulted, and therefore those engaged in slandering me have no fear of suffering any rebuke or loss.[5] In a sense they act as representatives of the whole country; they are merely proxies for the rest. And it is pretty obvious to me why those who are supposed to be my blind supporters and those who are counted allies of mine do not seek public redress for my humiliation. They lack the courage and craftiness of the other group chiefly because they know they do not have the support of the public. In no other country are those who have earned their countrymen's respect dragged down by slander of this kind; they are never subjected to helpless humiliation in full public view. That is why, as I say, I feel a need to get at the fundamental truth of this matter – but to keep a calm mind is of course even more necessary. I am approaching seventy and the end of my days is coming. Now I pray with all my power that when I leave this world my inner self will be fully released from the burden of harassment that troubles my mundane self.

In this context, let me briefly speak of something else. To express myself is my dharma – to confine my urge for expression goes against my grain. In my nature there are various fountains of expression: if I neglect any one of them, I shall diminish myself. Expression and enjoyment are not the same thing: expression leads outwards, indeed it releases the inner being, whereas enjoyment is directed inwards, and is absorbed. You have reservations about my acting on the stage.[6] But the urge to act is the same as the urge to express oneself as a playwright. If there is a fault in a play, let it be criticised; and the same goes for acting. But one does not trivialise oneself by the mere act of performing. Each and every creative urge that is in me I am bound to acknowledge. If I were to check my urge and regard it as some fancied lapse – following your conventional belief and tradition – I would be doing myself a grave injustice.

Shubhakangkshi
Shri Rabindranath Thakur

Source: MS original at Rahindra Bhavan, Shantiniketan; letter published in *Desh*, 28 July 1990, pp. 42–3.

1 On *Shanibarer Chithi*, see Chaudhuri, *Thy Hand*, pp. 217 ff. On the animus of Bengali writers and critics against RT, see *ibid.*, pp. 607–8. Chaudhuri quotes a critic and 'writer of no ordinary calibre' who answered

the question of why he and his fellow critics and writers had such a grievance against RT with the words: 'Shall I tell you the plain truth? We thought he and we were playmates in the same team, but suddenly discovered that he was very much above us. That, we could not tolerate' (p. 607). The critic was Suresh Samajpati, editor of *Sahitya*; he made the comment to Amal Home, *c.* 1913, who told Chaudhuri some years later (Chaudhuri to authors, 9 May 1996).
2 RT to Hemanta Bala Devi (20 Sept. 1932) [copy at Rabindra Bharati].
3 See letter 229.
4 'Tagore ... was abnormally sensitive, and did not possess the knack for cool disdain which a man of his social position naturally should have had. He did not have the worldly loftiness of his grandfather, nor the aristocratic and robust self-sufficiency of his father' (Chaudhuri, *Thy Hand*, p. 608).
5 One Bengali newspaper even alleged that RT had syphilis contracted when young. See Dutta and Robinson, *Rabindranath Tagore*, pp. 9, 382. Though pained by these attacks, RT never sued the press. 'One obvious reason for the persistence of such vituperations appearing regularly in a section of the Bengali press, was that the editors had early discovered that slandering Father paid handsomely' (Rathindranath Tagore, *Edges of Time*, pp. 152–3).
6 Chatterji's inhibitions about RT's acting probably referred to *Tapati*, which was performed at Jorasanko in Sept. 1929. RT's plays were hardly ever popular successes, and with their static symbolism they were easy targets for humour.

231

To Lord Irwin[1]

In December 1928, Lord Irwin became the first viceroy to visit Shantiniketan. His sympathy for Indian aspirations encouraged Tagore to approach him for obtaining a grant to develop the work of rural reconstruction at Shriniketan, which since 1921 had been funded entirely by an annual grant given by the Dartington Trust (Leonard and Dorothy Elmhirst). In February 1930, after a visit from the Elmhirsts – Dorothy's first and only visit to Shantiniketan – and from Sir Stanley Jackson, the governor of Bengal, who announced a small grant to Shriniketan – Tagore wrote this letter to Irwin.[2]

In doing so, he was to some extent compromising his own ideal of independence from Government, and also openly inviting yet more public disapproval of himself and his institution. For in February 1930, Mahatma Gandhi was widely known to be considering another campaign of civil disobedience – and here was Tagore soliciting Government assistance. On 12 March, Gandhi launched his historic march to the sea at Dandi in order to defy the Government's salt laws – just as Tagore set off for Europe once more on his final international odyssey. Yet again, Rabindranath was fundamentally out of step with Indian public opinion.

Santiniketan, [West Bengal, India]
14 February 1930

Your Excellency,

On the occasion of your visit to our Visva-Bharati it seemed to us that Your Excellency received a favourable impression of the value of the work that is being done here. This emboldens me to address my appeal for help directly to you.

We have so long had to struggle on almost in isolation, not really understood by either our countrymen or our Government, but nonetheless cheered by the progressive unfolding of our own results, as well as the heartfelt appreciation of thinkers, belonging to widely different parts of the world, who have seen or heard of our work.

The time has come when it will not be much longer possible for me to go on finding the money for the growing needs of our several institutions by my personal efforts, as I have so far been doing. If, therefore, Your Excellency feels that it is for the benefit of the people under your charge that Visva-Bharati should continue to live and grow, then it is for you to consider how adequate and timely help may reach it while I am yet there to guide the working of my idea towards its fulfilment. I am temperamentally unfit to proceed through the regular stages demanded by official routine, and if we are worthy of government help, that can come only through Your Excellency's personal interest and initiative.[3]

If that cannot be, we needs must carry on as we are doing, trusting to such future development as may be inherent in the vitality of the seed.

Our friend and helper, Mr L. K. Elmhirst, is taking this letter to Your Excellency, and is in a position to give authoritative answers to any questions that you may care to ask him about our institution.[4]

Yours very sincerely,
Rabindranath Tagore

Source: MS copy at Rabindra Bhavan, Shantiniketan; letter published as No. 59k in official correspondence of Lord Irwin [IOL].

1 Edward Frederick Lindley Wood, 1st Baron Irwin (1925–34), 3rd Viscount Halifax (1934–44), 1st earl of Halifax (1881–1959): viceroy of India, 1926–31. Irwin became particularly close to Gandhi in 1930.
2 Elmhirst and his wife celebrated the anniversary of the founding of Shriniketan on 6 Feb. 1930. Jackson opened a conference on the cooperative movement there on 10 Feb., and announced a capital grant of Rs 5,000 and an annual grant of Rs 1,000 for three years. Presumably both men encouraged RT to make his approach to Irwin on 14 Feb.
3 Irwin, after talking to Elmhirst in New Delhi, asked the Council of Agricultural Research to look into giving a grant for agricultural research at Shriniketan, an idea which gained the support of Jackson, the governor of Bengal. RT appointed a committee to put forward a scheme, one of whose members was his son-in-law Nagendranath Gangulee, who was also a member of the Council of Agricultural Research. See RT to Irwin, 28 Feb. 1930, letter No 75c in official correspondence of Lord Irwin [IOL]; Irwin to RT, 5 March and 23 March 1930 [RB]; and Gangulee, *The Indian Peasant*, pp. 165–6. Gangulee, as always, was pessimistic of success.
4 Elmhirst later wrote to RT from Dartington: 'I have a letter from Sir Stanley Jackson saying that he will take a personal interest in the research scheme' (7 April 1930, in Dutta and Robinson (eds.), *Purabi*, p. 104).

14 Tagore in New York, 1930, with Albert Einstein

Farewell to the West (1930)

Introduction

As Gandhi prepared for his famous Salt March and the beginning of another phase of noncooperation, Tagore left India on what would be his final visit to the West. Though, as always, he hoped to raise money for Visva-Bharati and also to increase western understanding of Indian needs and intentions, he was also driven by curiosity to see the reaction of western artists and critics to his unorthodox paintings. On this last score, at least, he was not disappointed: exhibitions were held in several European countries, beginning in Paris, and the paintings aroused genuine enthusiasm and respect, especially in Germany.

Tagore's programme was a busy one. Reaching France at the end of March, he stayed there until mid-May, then moved to Britain, where he gave the Hibbert lectures at Oxford University, later published as *The Religion of Man*. During his two-month stay, he was fêted by various groups and held discussions on the Indian political situation, which was now of immediate interest in Britain (unlike on Tagore's previous visits in 1920–1 and 1926), because of Gandhi's movement.

He then travelled to Europe, visiting many countries, including Germany, where he held several long discussions with Albert Einstein. The highlight of the tour was his visit to the Soviet Union in September. He was immensely impressed by the Soviet education system, but doubtful about Communism as a political ideal. The energy and self-respect of the masses made, for him, a painful contrast with their equivalents in India.

From there he moved to the USA, reaching New York in October. Although, as before, he was unhappy with the American atmosphere, this time he was lionised; he even received a private audience with the president. When he spoke at Carnegie Hall, thousands had to be turned away. But his general appeal against imperial arrogance went unheard.

232

To (Sir) William Rothenstein

From letter 229, we already know of Tagore's unwillingness to expose his paintings to the critical gaze of Bengalis. But he did show them to a few foreign artists who visited Shantiniketan, such as the sculptress Marguerite Milward. Reviewing the Paris

374   Selected letters of Rabindranath Tagore

exhibition of Tagore's paintings in May 1930, she recalled the occasion when in Tagore's house she expressed 'deep interest' in seeing the paintings:

> With much diffidence the Poet allowed a large portfolio to be fetched. We spread the contents all over the room. They were large, bold and cubistic in style, for the most part monochrome, but some of the deepest colour obtained with paint or ink mixed to get the richness desired . . .
>
> He was surprised at my eagerness and enthusiasm, and demurred greatly when I said: 'You must exhibit these in Paris, there the artists will understand and appreciate them.'[1]

Tagore was naturally interested in the reaction of William Rothenstein (now principal of the Royal College of Art). In February 1929, he told him, with gingerly caution, 'If I ever have the opportunity I should like to show you some pictures that I have done myself with the hope of once again being startled with your appreciation as in the case of *Gitanjali*.'[2] In this letter written a year later, after receiving the reactions of Milward and others, he is somewhat bolder, and offers an acute analysis of his own art.

> Villa Kahn, Cap Martin, [near Nice, France]
> 30 March 1930

Dear friend

Surviving [a] series of mishaps on the way we have at last arrived in Europe after a prolonged voyage of 26 days. I intend to spend some weeks in south of France till it gets warmer when I am expected in Paris.[3] I suppose you know I have my invitation to lecture in Oxford possibly in the beginning of June when I hope it will be tolerably warm in England.[4]

I find that you already know that of late I have suddenly been seized with the mania of producing pictures. The praise which they had won from our own circle of artists I did not take at all seriously till some of them attracted notice of a Japanese artist of renown whose appreciation came to me as a surprise.[5] Some European painters who lately visited our ashram strongly recommended me to have them exhibited in Berlin and Paris.[6] Thus I have been persuaded to bring them with me, about four hundreds of them. I still feel misgivings and I want your advice. They certainly possess psychological interest being products of untutored fingers and untrained mind. I am sure they do not represent what they call Indian Art, and in one sense they may be original, revealing a strangeness born of my utter inexperience and individual limitations.[7] But I strongly desire to have your opinion before they are judged by others in Europe.[8] I do hope it is not utterly impossible for you to come to this beautiful villa and stay with us for a few days.[9] I shall only be too happy to bear your travelling expenses and shall do my best to make you comfortable.

Ever yours
Rabindranath Tagore

Source: MS original in Rothenstein Papers [Harvard]; letter published in Lago (ed.), *Imperfect Encounter*, pp. 325–6.

1 R. M. Milward, 'Rabindranath Tagore's paintings', *MR*, Nov. 1930, p. 545. Milward, a pupil of the sculptor Emile Bourdelle, had come to Shantiniketan to do a bust of Tagore. This is now kept at India House,

London; a photograph of Milward finishing the bust forms the frontispiece of Milward's *An Artist in Unknown India* (London, 1948). The sensitivity of the bust – which is perhaps the best one of RT there is – is of a piece with Milward's response to RT's paintings.

2 RT to Rothenstein, 22 Feb. 1929, in Lago (ed.), *Imperfect Encounter*, p. 325.
3 When RT arrived in the south of France, he knew that he wanted to exhibit his paintings in Paris, but he had no outlet for doing so. The exhibition was arranged in less than a month with the help of Victoria Ocampo, and opened at the Galerie Pigalle on 2 May 1930. See Dyson, *Flower-Garden*, pp. 230–9.
4 RT's Oxford lecture, the Hibbert lectures, were delivered in Oxford in late May, and later published as *The Religion of Man*.
5 We have been unable to identify the renowned Japanese artist. According to K. G. Subramanyan, he (she?) was likely to be someone from outside the circle of Okakura Kakuzo (Subramanyan to authors, 24 March 1996).
6 One of these 'European painters' was presumably Milward. See also letter 233, in which RT mentions German encouragement.
7 RT's art was totally distinct from that of the Bengal School, as he well knew. In a lecture on 'Art and tradition' delivered in Dhaka in 1926, he commented:

> When in the name of Indian Art we cultivate with deliberate aggressiveness a certain bigotry born of the habit of a past generation, we smother our soul under idiosyncrasies unearthed from buried centuries. These are like masks with exaggerated grimaces that fail to respond to the ever-changing play of life. (*Art and Aesthetics*, pp. 61–2)

8 Rothenstein declined to be drawn in as judge of RT's paintings, suspecting, no doubt, that he would not like them. When he later saw the paintings in London, he was genuinely appreciative, however, though never enthusiastic. See Dutta and Robinson, *Rabindranath Tagore*, pp. 288, 444.
9 The villa belonged to Albert Kahn (1860–1940), a wealthy but ascetic French-Jewish banker who kept a number of houses in France in his Cercle Autour du Monde. RT first stayed in them in 1920 and again in 1921. Today, Kahn's 'international' garden can be seen at Boulogne, along with a museum devoted to his life and works.

233

To Sudhindranath Datta[1]

During his long life Rabindranath helped a great many Bengalis in whom he discerned talent. One such was the philologist Suniti Kumar Chatterji [Chattopadhyay] (see letter 229), another was the poet Sudhindranath Datta. Datta travelled with Tagore to Canada and the USA in early 1929, acting as his secretary; afterwards, when Tagore returned home, Datta stayed abroad and visited Europe, not returning to Bengal until December 1929. He now needed to find a way of supporting himself. From this letter he was evidently considering the possibility of finding some academic position in Europe – but in the event he stayed in Bengal; the 1930s were in fact the most productive period of his life, in which he established his literary reputation in Bengali.

[Villa Dunure, Cap Martin, near Nice, France]
1 April 1930

Kalyaniyeshu

I've just received your letter. I'm now in the south of France, where the sky is full of light and the ground is bountiful with flowers and foliage. I am well and would be even better but for various responsibilities; I have to write my lectures, ignoring the signals of spring.[2] Whenever there is a break, I paint, and this can be compared to the tender green shoots of spring. There's a German gentleman here with his wife – he's a diplomat. Seeing my paintings he became really excited and said I must show them in Berlin – 'absolutely!' I am hoping they will attract the attention of connoisseurs. I vow not to take them back to my dear motherland: no more of this crude handling by unsuitable and unworthy fellows. Your letter to Rothenstein will not be in vain, I hope. When I see him I shall speak to him. But I'm not sure how much influence he has. And when I go to Oxford I will sound things out. If any opportunity arises on the Continent I will also not forget. Today I shall speak to my German friend. Let's hope this letter reaches you alright. If instead it falls into another's hand, my advice to him is that if I had really resolved to poke a hole in the hull of the British Empire, I would not be such a dimwit as to state it in a letter.[3]

Shri Rabindranath Thakur

Source: MS original at Rabindra Bhavan, Shantiniketan; letter published in *CP*, XVI, p. 30.

1 Sudhindranath Datta (1901–60): poet, critic and editor; in 1931 he founded the quarterly *Parichay*. See Sudhindranath Datta, *The World of Twilight: Essays and Poems* (Calcutta, 1970). He married the singer Rajeshwari Datta.
2 See letter 232, n. 4.
3 This was of course a reference to British censorship of the Indian post.

234

To Kostís Palamás[1]

In responding to the work of contemporary European poets, Tagore almost always preferred simplicity and lyricism (see, for example, the introduction to letter 58 to Ezra Pound). The poetry of the Greek poet Kostís Palamás therefore held some appeal for him, as this letter shows. Although he and Palamás never met each other, Palamás agreed to join Romain Rolland (who had introduced Palamás to Tagore's work), Mahatma Gandhi, Albert Einstein and Sir J. C. Bose, as sponsors of *The Golden Book of Tagore* in 1931.

Villa Dunure, Cap Martin, [near Nice, France]
6 April 1930

Dear Poet

I cannot thank you enough for your books of poems that you have sent me. Most of the modern poetry has become like your own lagoon – a shroud weed-woven has wrapped it, the weeds that are wild technique and individual idiosyncrasies. We need world poets today, for the whole world has opened itself to our vision. Such poets must come from those countries which have leisure and light, whose soul is not smothered under the load of prosperity and mental horizon densely misted with political obsessions. And you are such a poet – and it seems natural for you to belong to your own country as well as all countries of the world.[2]

My cordial greetings to you
Rabindranath Tagore

[PS] Your books being redirected from India I am late in acknowledging your kindness.[3]

Source: MS copy at Rabindra Bhavan, Shantiniketan.

1 Kostís Palamás (1859–1943): poet and critic; he was the first poet to express the national sufferings and aspirations of the Greeks. Eastern philosophy had some influence on his poetry.
2 One of the books by Palamás sent to RT would certainly have been the translation by Aristides E. Phoutrides, *Life Immovable* (Cambridge, Mass., 1919), of some poems written in 1904, in which there appears an epigraph to one of his poems ('The Twelve Words of the Gypsy') that is strikingly reminiscent of RT's attitudes:

> And then I saw that I am the poet, surely a poet among many, a mere soldier of the verse, but always the poet who desires to close within his verse the longings and questionings of the universal man, and the cares and fanaticism of the citizen. I may not be a worthy citizen; but it cannot be that I am the poet of myself alone. I am the poet of my age and of my race. And what I hold within me cannot be divided from the world without.

3 This is a puzzling statement, for Romain Rolland sent RT the books of Palamás on 31 March 1930, with the comment that Palamás was 'the greatest living poet of Europe' and the fervent hope that the two poets would meet each other; he also gave RT the address of Palamás in Athens (Aronson and Kripalani (eds.), *Rolland and Tagore*, p. 68). Did Palamás separately send his books to India, or had RT somehow become confused about who had sent him the books?

235

To Dorothy Whitney Elmhirst (Straight)

The unease between Tagore and Dorothy Elmhirst that existed right from their first encounter in America in 1920 (see letters 161, n. 1, and 200) is again evident in this letter, in which Tagore invites her to meet him at the Villa Dunure (she was staying not far away). Leonard Elmhirst being delayed at Dartington, it seems she was unwilling to face Tagore alone.[1] Once he reached Paris in late April, Tagore again asked her to join him at the opening of the exhibition of his pictures on 2 May: 'It is a new turning point in the path of my adventure where I need [the] hand grip of my friends.'[2] Perhaps he sensed, rightly as it turned out, that the pictures might interest her, given her keen interest in modern art.[3] But again she seems to have avoided him.

Villa Dunure, Cap Martin, [near Nice, France]
7 April 1930

Dear Dorothy

We are daily expecting you. But why do you keep yourselves behind the screen of an immeasurable silence? Our fate seems to have been unaccountably adverse. The steamer took 26 weary days to complete its voyage narrowly missing a shipwreck; our box containing passports got stolen; Riviera belied its reputation for fair weather and the worst part of our misfortune was supplied by your awe-inspiring aloofness. The clouds have dispersed from our horizon since last two days, the sunshine is lavish and it brings hope in my mind that the chance of your coming to our neighbourhood is growing brighter. Please do not delay.

I am fairly busy writing my lectures though I have not received any communication from Dr Drummond about the time when I must come to England for my engagement.[4]

With love

Ever yours
Rabindranath Tagore

Source: MS original in Dartington Trust archives [Dartington]; letter published in *VBQ*, *32*, No. 2, 1966–7, p. 113.

1 It is not quite clear whether or not Dorothy Elmhirst visited RT, judging from Leonard Elmhirst's letter to RT of 7 April, i.e. the very same day on which RT wrote to Dorothy: 'I hope that by this time Dorothy has rung you up from the Beau Site Hotel and explained why I am still absent' (Dutta and Robinson (eds.), *Purabi*, p. 104).
2 RT to Dorothy Elmhirst, 26 April 1930, in *ibid.*, p. 105.
3 In 1938, Dorothy Elmhirst visited twice an exhibition of RT's paintings in London and told Leonard (who was in India with RT), 'I hope you will tell him that I enjoyed my second visit even more than the first' (28 Dec. 1938 [Dartington]).
4 William Hamilton Drummond (1863–1945): secretary, Hibbert Trust, 1919–38.

236

To Victoria Ocampo

Leaving Argentina in 1925, Tagore had written to his hostess Victoria Ocampo from on board ship, 'When we were together we mostly played with words and tried to laugh away our best opportunities to see each other clearly. Such laughter often disturbs the atmosphere of our mind, raising dust from its surface which only blurs our view' (letter 199). Now, five years on, having again parted from Ocampo, this time in Paris, after the success of his paintings exhibition which she had organised, Tagore makes a similar comment. Their relationship, though genuine, would always suffer from his hypersensitivity to intimacy, especially in a foreign language, and her urge to romanticise a great poet from India, a land she had never seen.

C/o American Exp[ress] Co., 6 Haymarket,
London, [UK]
14 May 1930

Dear Vijaya

Since coming to this country I have never had a moment of my own; and my mind is distracted.

I do not know what to say to you. About my reputation as an artist it is too sudden for me to take it seriously but your own association with this exhibition and my pictures has a very deep hold upon my mind. I wish I could express to you how I felt – but I joked and jested and trifled away my time possibly because I was serious and because conversation is a medium that feels shy of all earnest thoughts. To be simple, natural and true to one's deeper self is impossible in the daily social life in the West. It is like the dense water of the Dead Sea which keeps everything floating on the surface however weighty it might be. I do not know where you are – but I only hope we shall meet in India.

Bhalobasha[1]
Shri Rabindranath Thakur

Source: MS copy at Rabindra Bhavan, Shantiniketan; letter published in Dyson, *Flower-Garden*, p. 441.

1 *Bhalobasha*: see letter 205, n. 1.

237

To André Gide[1]

André Gide, Tagore's French translator, whom he had first met in Paris in 1921, came to see him on 23 April 1930 at his hotel in Paris. He looked at Tagore's paintings and was enthusiastic about some of them.[2] Either at this meeting or soon after, he presented Tagore with a copy of the English translation of his novel, *Strait is the Gate*.[3] Tagore's appreciative letter was probably written from Paris, but may have been written after he reached Britain on 11 May (the surviving copy is undated). It is noteworthy for being one of Tagore's relatively few letters to a major European writer about a specific work, as opposed to a body of unnamed work. One can see why Gide's novel would have appealed: there is a clear similarity in atmosphere with Tagore's novella *Nashtanirh* (*The Broken Nest*) and his novel *Ghare Baire* (*The Home and the World*), among other works.

[Paris or Britain]
[May? 1930]

Dear Mr Gide

I offer you my heartiest thanks for your book, *Strait is the Gate*.

It has produced a strong impression upon my mind – its transparent simplicity reveals a depth of a subtle truth which is the most difficult of all manners of dealing in literature. I feel intimately familiar with the atmosphere you have created in this story. I hope that we shall meet once again before I leave Europe.

Yours in admiration
Rabindranath Tagore

Source: MS copy at Rabindra Bhavan, Shantiniketan.

1 André Gide (1869–1951): novelist, poet and writer; awarded Nobel prize for literature, 1947. Gide translated *Gitanjali* as *L'Offrande Lyrique (Gitanjali)* (Paris, 1913) and *The Post Office* as *Amal et la Lettre du Roi* (Paris, 1922).
2 According to RT's secretary, Gide liked some of the pictures 'extremely well'; his preference was for the 'masks, animals and landscapes' (E. W. Aryanayakam to Rathindranath Tagore, 23 April 1930 [RB]).
3 *Strait is the Gate* (Dorothy Bussy trans.; London, 1924).

238

To S. R. Bomanji[1]

Ever since he established Visva-Bharati in 1921, Tagore had wanted to include Persian studies in its activities. He hoped that Aga Khan III, whose mother was Persian, would fund a chair of Persian studies, and in February 1930 he wrote to him with the suggestion.[2] They had known each other in person since travelling together to Europe in 1920, when they had had long talks on board ship discussing Sufism and the poet Hafiz (a favourite of Debendranath Tagore).[3]

When Tagore reached Europe in 1930, a mutual friend who was a wealthy Parsi businessman and nationalist, S. R. Bomanji, eventually arranged a meeting with the Aga Khan in London. Though he was not present, Bomanji had prepared the ground in advance and was under the impression that the Aga Khan was willing to give Rs 7,500 per annum for five years.[4] In the event, however, no money was forthcoming. Rabindranath, deeply upset, dashed off this letter to Bomanji, expressing, yet again, his profound dislike of fundraising – whether the potential sponsors were American millionaires or Indian princes.[5]

[London, UK]
[1? June 1930]

Dear Bomanji,

It was most cruel of you not to warn me of the utter futility of my attempt to induce Aga Khan to help me in my cause. I frankly gave him my reason for wishing to see him and when in spite of that fact he invited me I naturally felt sure he had some idea of coming to my aid however meagre might be the result. I was in bed most of the day, my body was aching, my head was heavy, my temperature above normal and the weather beastly. I painfully dragged myself to his door to find that he was not there. However he did turn up after a while and I talked and talked about all kinds of subject, about the other world and this world, about poetry and pictures, about medieval India and India that is yet to be – till at the end of the last chapter it came out that the times were unpropitious and that the whole world was suffering from penury and privation. I was deeply mortified to find that you did not try to save your poor friend from such a beggar's mission knowing that his health was bad and that he needed some consideration at your hand owing to his own position in this world. Andrews repeatedly tried to prevent me from this fool's errand but having more faith in your opinion and mediation I ignored his friendly advice.[6] But I am deservedly punished for I ought to have known that my place is elsewhere. But do you not also know it and should you not have advised me if not for the sake of my dignity at least for my health to get out of this engagement which I myself sought for [while] blissfully ignorant of the true state of things?

I feel miserably tired and humiliated. I have lost my caste.

Yours affectionately
Rabindranath Tagore

Source: MS copy at Rabindra Bhavan, Shantiniketan.

1 Shavaksha Ratanji Bomanji (1868–1951): businessman based in Bombay, who left India in the 1920s and lived in France and the USA; he travelled with RT on more than one occasion in the 1920s. In 1918, he was treasurer of the Home Rule League and donated heavily to this cause; he also gave money to Shantiniketan for the purpose of technical education. Though close to Gandhi, Bomanji seems to have remained a convinced capitalist: the governor of Bombay described him in 1921 as 'completely mad and constantly fluctuating'. (Quoted in A. D. D. Gordon, *Businessmen and Politics: Rising Nationalism and a Modernising Economy in Bombay, 1918–1933* (New Delhi, 1978), p. 162.)
2 RT to Aga Khan, 17 Feb. 1930 [copy at RB].
3 Sahitya Akademi, *Rabindranath Tagore*, p. 476.
4 Bomanji to RT, 4 June 1930 [RB]. But Bomanji admitted that the Aga Khan had not formally agreed to this figure in their discussions.

5 Persian studies at Visva-Bharati were eventually supported by the Persian Government, following RT's visit to Persia in 1932. Earlier, in 1927, the nizam of Hyderabad gave a lakh of rupees to establish a chair of Islamic culture at Shantiniketan.
6 RT's attitude towards advice given him by C. F. Andrews varied a great deal. At this time, Andrews was trying to discourage RT from exhibiting his paintings in Britain, and this fact may have turned RT against his advice on other subjects too.

239

To Sir Daniel Hamilton[1]

In attempting to develop Shriniketan, his 'institute for rural reconstruction', Tagore was naturally interested to explore other similar enterprises in India. One of these was the cooperative movement established by Sir Daniel Hamilton, a partner in a Calcutta business house, on his estate at Gosaba in the swampy Sunderbans region of Bengal. Here, independent of the Government, over more than two decades, a group of nineteen villages on the 22,000-acre estate consisting of 9,000 agriculturists had established cooperative credit societies and then a federated central bank, a cooperative store, a cooperative paddy sale society with boats to transport the paddy to Calcutta's most important paddy mart and a rice mill, in addition to a system of *panchayats* (village councils), such that criminal and civil law cases had virtually been eliminated.[2] When Tagore visited Gosaba in December 1932, he commented, 'My friend Sir Daniel Hamilton comes from a country which is far away, but he has the best interest of the people at heart and it is by this that he has made our people his own. This is the surest way of achieving unity between the East and the West.'[3]

In this letter to Hamilton, Tagore attempts to define his own vision of Indian development. Written in the wake of Gandhi's arrest after his Salt March and in the run-up to the first Round Table Conference in London, the letter expresses what E. P. Thompson called Tagore's 'clear conception of a civil society, as something distinct from and of stronger and more personal texture than political or economic structures . . . Tagore was a founder of "anti-politics".'[4] In the next few years, however, he would feel compelled to move increasingly to a (reluctant) acceptance of the dominant influence of politics in the Indian relationship with Britain.

Dartington Hall, Totnes, [Devon, UK]
20 June 1930

Dear Sir Daniel

Many thanks for your very kind letter. I do not wish to miss this opportunity of coming to your place and [having] a quiet talk with you about the present situation in our country. I shall try my best, though I am not certain if I shall be able to extricate myself from some urgent engagements and find a chance to avail of your kind invitation.

I have not much faith in politicians when the problem is vast needing a complete vision of the future of a country like India entangled in difficulties that are enormous. These specialists have the habit of isolating politics from the large context of national life and the psychology of the people and of the period. They put all their emphasis upon law and order, something which is external and superficial, and ignore the vital needs of the spirit of the nation comprehending its culture, its economics, its social adjustments and potentialities that create perpetual sufferings and mischievous aberrations when continually deprived of their opportunity and expression.

The politicians with their constant preoccupation with what they call settled facts (as if any human fact could be absolutely settled) are unable to look upon India as an entire truth with an atmosphere of sensitive personality. She is studied and dealt with in a narrow cage, made of rigid steel bars of official traditions, meagre prospects and disabilities of a cramped existence. She has been brought before her alien judges deprived of the perspective that life needs and therefore [she] is perpetually misunderstood with plausible excuses that have [an] artificial origin [in] an unnatural situation.

Politicians on our side also seem to think that Indian politics can be detached, like a cap or a coat, from the complete life of the people and repaired or made anew. This is the reason why no serious effort has been made by the political lovers of India for a scientific and an organised knowledge of her condition in all its vital aspects, no proper foundation has been laid for a cooperation on an adequate scale in constructive and comprehensive work of service. We also have become specialists and fondly cherish the pathetic faith that the deep-rooted welfare of a country can be grown chiefly on the surface soil of politics. I have my trust in individuals like yourself who are simple lovers of humanity, whose minds are free from race prejudice and the too-loyal idolatry of the machine. I believe that the cooperative principle is the only civilised principle in commerce and also in politics. We have our respective gifts which can be and should be freely exchanged among nations for their mutual benefit in all departments of life. I never dream of absolute severance [from] the English people as representing the higher stage of our freedom, but the purification of that connection which will cure it of parasitism for one of the parties and poverty and humiliation for the other. And this is the reason why my appeal is to the English nation and not the English Government. For the machine loudly claims that it 'must go on' whatever may be the result, while man only can say that the machine must change its course or its character for the sake of humanity.

With cordial greetings

I am yours sincerely
Rabindranath Tagore

Source: MS copy at Rabindra Bhavan, Shantiniketan; letter published in *Vigil* (Weekly Organ of Sarva Seva Sangh), 13 April 1979, pp. 3–4.

1 Sir Daniel Hamilton (1860–1939): estate owner and pioneer of cooperative movement in India. In Feb. 1929, Hamilton spoke at a conference on the cooperative movement, organised by RT at Shantiniketan. His speech, 'India's best hope', appears in a collection of his speeches and writings, *New India and How to Get There* (London, 1930); see pp. 44–53.
2 On Hamilton, see Nagendranath Gangulee, *India: What Now?* (London, 1933), pp. 129–30.
3 *Amrita Bazar Patrika*, 2 Jan. 1933.
4 Introduction to Rabindranath Tagore, *Nationalism* (London, 1991), p. 14.

240

To Mira Gangulee (Tagore)

In 1934, Tagore received a letter from Arthur Probsthain, the oriental bookseller and publisher in London, suggesting that a young German printer friend of his be invited to Bengal to start printing schools and improve the quality of publishing by the University of Calcutta, 'whose books are published in a manner totally unworthy of a real university'.[1] Tagore's secretary replied that Shantiniketan had no resources for this but that Rabindranath was 'keenly conscious of our deficiency in the line and it is precisely because of this, that he sent his grandson [Nitindranath (Nitu)] over to Germany to study the latest methods of printing in Europe. Unfortunately he died at the early age of 20 of consumption.'[2]

This letter to his daughter, written during Tagore's 1930 German visit, shows how serious Rabindranath was in the matter. It also demonstrates the great respect in which he was held in Germany; an experience which made it very difficult for him to accept the reports of Nazi beastliness that reached him in India after 1933.

[Berlin, Germany]
12 August 1930

Kalyaniyashu

Miru, I did not like the look of Nitu at all before I left for Europe. Everyone knows that in our climate to work in a stuffy printing press is unhealthy. Nitu does not possess a strong constitution, and at this age, when he is growing, the strain is not good for him. You may not be aware that for printing and publishing there is no better place than Germany. The cities of Munich and Leipzig are world famous for it. My friends here have agreed to help Nitu in this field. They say they will be able to arrange something at little expense – say not more than 50/60 rupees per month. If he begins his training in Munich, he can complete it in Leipzig. He can also carry on with his general education here – so that he will become not only a printer but a well-rounded person. He will seriously learn both literature and art and the technical aspects of printing. In addition there is the great skill of publishing – he will master that. Such an opportunity is not available to everyone, it is possible only because of the respect that people here have for me. Moreover there is no lack of local people willing to look after Nitu as if he were part of their own family. If you waste such a chance, you will be doing Nitu a real injustice.

Were you to send him in September when you get this letter of mine, I could myself start him off while I am here. I shall be in Europe until the second week in October – after that I go to America.[3] If he comes here after September, he will face the severe cold of winter, which may not be a good idea. But if sending him so soon is simply not possible, then to wait until March would not be a bad plan. If that is what you jointly decide, then keep Nitu at Shantiniketan and let him have intensive practice in German for a few months. He does not need to learn mathematics, so he need not be anxious about that.[4]

After delivering a lecture in Amiya's father-in-law's country, I have at last reached

Germany.⁵ I am living in great comfort here. This being the house of a doctor, both creature comforts and medical care are treated with equal importance. Whenever I leave the borders of my own country I enter the territory of real intimacy. If you saw how wholeheartedly they love me here, you would be astonished.

Father

Source: MS original at Rabindra Bhavan, Shantiniketan; letter published in Sharadiya *Desh*, 1397 [Autumn 1990], pp. 50–1.

1 Probsthain to RT, 21 Feb. 1934 [RB].
2 Anil Chanda to Probsthain, 18 March 1934 [copy at RB].
3 RT returned from Russia on 25 Sept. and left for the USA on 3 Oct. 1930.
4 Nitindranath left for Germany in April 1931.
5 RT had just returned from Denmark, where he lectured at Elsinore. His secretary Amiya Chakravarty had married a Danish woman (see letter 222).

241

To Nandini Tagore[1]

After staying in Berlin for a week or so, Tagore moved on to Geneva, where he rested. This chatty letter was written to his nine-year-old granddaughter, the adoptive daughter of Rathindranath and Pratima, who was in Shantiniketan. It shows how much he was enjoying being a painter, having received encouragement from European artists and critics.

7, Rue de l'Université, Geneva, [Switzerland]
21 August 1930

Pupumani[2]

Dada Mashai is in a terrible state.[3] Papers are scattered all over his table, inkpots full of coloured ink are all in a jumble – where his pens and pencils are he has no idea. His spectacles are sitting on his nose, still he searches for them. He wears a long loose garment smudged red and blue and yellow. His fingers too are all covered in paint, and when he sits at table to eat, people notice this and secretly smile. Although they see his loose clothes every day, they still smile. Each morning he gets up very early before anyone else is up. Gradually it is six o'clock, then seven o'clock, then eight – Ariam Sahib pops out of his bedroom and enquires, Did you sleep well last night?[4] *Dada Mashai* replies, Yes I slept very well. After that the gong strikes dhong, dhong, dhong – he knows it's time to go for food next door. There he sees one boiled egg, some toasted bread, butter and tea. After eating he stays at the table. He sits and writes. Often Andrews Sahib drops in and makes a racket.[5] Visitors come and go. Soon it reaches ten or eleven o'clock. Suddenly it is time to take a bath. After that he lounges in a chair. Then, lunchtime. Some green vegetables, tomatoes, bread and butter, and so on. Then rest a while, work a while, chit-chat with others a while. That's how the days pass by. At half past four it's time for tea and more talk with people. Then about eight o'clock there's food – similar stuff, green vegetables, potatoes, tomatoes, bread and butter. With all the talking that goes on, it gets pretty late. Then *Dada Mashai* lies down to sleep. What happens during the night he has no notion. No more time today – that's all.

Dada Mashai

Source: MS original at Rabindra Bhavan, Shantiniketan; letter published in *CP*, IV, pp. 215–16.

1 Nandini Tagore (1921–1995): adoptive daughter of Rathindranath Tagore and Pratima Devi, known as La Poupée.
2 Pupumani: Pupu my jewel; Pupu derives from Poupée.
3 *Dada Mashai*: grandfather.
4 Ariam Sahib: E. Ariam Williams, later known as E. W. Aryanayakam (1889–1967): teacher at Shantiniketan 1924–34, who acted as a secretary to RT in 1927 and 1930; he was a Ceylonese Christian of Tamil origin.
5 Andrews Sahib: C. F. Andrews. RT's comments on Andrews, particularly in later years, are usually accompanied by some affectionate criticism of his tendency to create an unnecessary fuss.

242

To Nirmal Kumari Mahalanobis (Maitra)

Tagore had wanted to visit Russia for several years, in order to judge the Soviet system for himself, particularly in relation to its impact on the peasants. He eventually arrived on 11 September 1930 and stayed for two weeks, along with a small group. This letter is the first he wrote from Moscow, and therefore perhaps gives the truest impression of his initial reaction.[1] It was written in the summer villa of his host, L. M. Karakhan, the deputy peoples' commissar of foreign affairs, on the outskirts of Moscow.[2] In 1931, it was published in Bengali as part of *Russiar Chithi* (*Letters from Russia*).

[Moscow, Russia]
19 September 1930

[*Kalyaniyashu?*]

Place – Russia. Scene – a mansion in a suburb of Moscow. Through my window, woodland stretching to the horizon in a billowing wave of greens – dark green, pale green, green mingled with purple, and green with a hint of yellow. At the edge of the trees, in the far distance, a line of cottages forming a village. Time, nearly ten in the morning. The sky banked up with clouds, a grand foregathering of impending rain; the wind blows through the stiffly erect poplars, making their tops sway.

The hotel where I stayed in Moscow was called the Grand Hotel. It is an imposing place, but its condition is very poor, as if it were the bankrupt scion of a wealthy family. The furniture and fittings of former times have been sold off and what remains is torn and unpatched for lack of means, filthy and unlaundered. The entire city looks in a similar state – behind its utter untidiness, glimpses of its former splendour are visible, like gold buttons on a torn shirt or a Dacca muslin dhoti that has been darned. This all-embracing indigence of food and shelter is not seen anywhere else in Europe. And that is chiefly because everywhere else there is maintained a sharp separation between haves and have-nots, creating a picture of concentrated wealth in which the poverty is rendered invisible to the observer by a drop curtain; an invisibility which conceals scenes of chaos, filth and unhealthiness full of dark misery and misdeeds. Yet to outsiders like us, who look from the windows of borrowed dwellings, everything appears ordered, elegant and well nourished. Were it possible to distribute such affluence equally between all, immediately it would be apparent that the national wealth was insufficient to provide everyone with a square meal and a roof over his head. But here, where no such sharp separation exists, wealth is no longer ostentatious, and poverty is more a matter of neediness than ugliness. Such absence of ostentation throughout a whole nation is unheard of, and therefore eye-catching. The people whom in other countries we would call the masses, are here the only class of person.

All sorts of people are out on the streets of Moscow. None of them looks spick and span; the leisured class seems to have completely melted away. Everyone must earn his living by his own efforts; the polish of luxury is nowhere to be seen. I went to call on Dr Petrov, a high official and respected figure here.[3] His office is in a building that once belonged to an aristocrat, but it has meagre furniture and little in the way of spruceness; there is just a kind of table in one corner and the floor is uncarpeted; the overall impression is like one of our houses at the time of a bereavement, when we abandon our usual household routine and undertake no social obligations. The arrangements for looking after me at the Grand Hotel bore no resemblance to the name of that place – but no one was embarrassed about it, because they are all in the same condition.

I am reminded of my childhood days. How negligible was our standard of living and our accumulation of things then, compared with today, but we felt not the least embarrassment. The reason was that in those days there were no sharp discrepancies in people's material expectations. Everyone carried on at roughly the same [economic] level; the differences lay in general culture – in the different cultivation of music, scholarship and so on – and also in language, manners and the observance of family rituals. But as for food and possessions – what we had at that time would provoke scorn among today's middle classes.

This pride in wealth has come to us from the West. With the influx of new money into the homes of our office-going and business classes, came a vogue for foreign luxuries. From then on we began to measure our degree of civilisation by the amount of furniture in our houses. And so today, even in our country, wealth attracts more attention than a good lineage, polished manners or great intellect. To honour someone in this way is really the worst kind of dishonour. We must take care that such baseness does not enter the marrow of our being.

Coming here, what has struck me more than anything else has been the vanishing of this base vanity of wealth. Simply because of this, a feeling of self-respect has suddenly been released in people. The peasants and others have shaken off the burden of humiliation and lifted their heads; and I have been astonished and gladdened to witness this. Human intercourse has become wonderfully easy. There is much more to say on the subject, and I will try to say it; but just now I am in need of rest. So I am going to recline in a big chair beside the window and pull a blanket over my feet – then if my eyes feel the need to close, I shall not try to keep them open by force.

[Shri Rabindranath Thakur]

Source: MS original at Rabindra Bhavan, Shantiniketan; letter published in *RR*, XX, pp. 276–7.

1 On RT's ambivalent reaction to Communisim, see Dutta and Robinson, *Rabindranath Tagore*, pp. 296–8.
2 Gnatyuk-Danil'chuk, *Soviet Union*, p. 241. On RT and Karakhan in China in 1924. see Dutta and Robinson, *Rabindranath Tagore*, p. 434.
3 Fedor Nikolaevich Petrov (1876–1973): president, VOKS (All-Union Society for Cultural Links with Foreign Countries), 1929–33; a member of the Communist Party since 1896, he survived the Purges and received numerous awards, including four Orders of Lenin.

243

To Dorothy Whitney Elmhirst (Straight)

Sailing to the United States from Germany, Tagore's mind remained filled with his new-found enthusiasm for the Soviet Union, especially its educational advances. Several of the letters in his *Russiar Chithi* (*Letters from Russia*) were written from on board ship, as he pondered his latest experiences. In this letter to Dorothy Elmhirst, he tries to persuade her to pay for one of his Indian staff at Shriniketan to visit the Soviet Union, rather than the United States, for agricultural training. But, as always with Dorothy, he encountered resistance: although both of the Elmhirsts had socialist inclinations, neither Dorothy nor Leonard was involved with the Soviet experiment in the way that was common among well-off left-wing intellectuals in Britain and the USA at this time. Tagore's advice was ignored.

SS *Bremen* [en route to the USA]
5 October 1930

Dear Dorothy

Being as lazy in my letter writing enterprises as you are and also Leonard [is], I cannot give you the details of my adventure in Soviet Russia. It has been a most wonderful experience for me and I assure you those people have done miracles in the realm of education. I implore you, do not hesitate to send Leonard to that country which is the only place where all the numerous activities of the people's life are comprehended in a most intensive and intelligent form of education. My mind is humming with a swarm of suggestions for my own work – but my time is short, my resources are meagre. I find that you have sent Lal to the United States for his further training but the proper training needed for India can only be had in Russia where the cultivation of People's Education is being carried on not [in] the soil of unlimited wealth but [by] indomitable energy and resourceful intelligence.[1] I feel proud of the fact that the ideal which is [at] the centre of their effort is very similar to mine, only they have a very vast instrument and an unobstructed perspective for their work. The titanic forces that are tremendously active over this vast country at the creation of a new world have very deeply impressed me, for the background of the manifestation of this great dream is not the limited area of national interest but all humanity.

However, you must allow Lal to study the great educational experiments which they are making in Russia, during the course of the next summer months.

I hear that you have already heard something about my pictures and I shall try to appear modest by not adding my own voice to the rumour that has reached you.[2]

I hope I shall meet you when I come back from America at the end of November.[3] With love to you both

Ever yours
Rabindranath Tagore

Source: MS original in Dartington Trust archives [Dartington]; letter published in *VBQ, 32*, No. 2, 1966–7, pp. 116–17.

1 Lal: Prem Chand Lal. See letter 204, n. 7. In the bibliography of Lal's book on the Shriniketan experiment, there are listed some books on Soviet education among a great number of books on American education; but the Soviet experience does not appear to have influenced him.
2 See letter 235, no. 3.
3 RT reached Britain on 23 Dec. 1930.

244

To Ellery Sedgwick[1]

In February 1912, the *Modern Review* of Calcutta noted that 'whoever has heard [Rabindranath's] extempore sermons and addresses knows what an eloquent speaker he is, though his delivery is often so rapid and his sentences branch out in such bewildering luxuriance as to make him the despair of reporters'.[2] Tagore himself, on his pan-American speaking tour in 1916, when asked which American marvel had impressed him most, replied tersely, 'The American newspaper reporter.'[3] During his western travels in the 1920s, he became reluctant to give interviews, especially to American reporters, because he often found his words misreported, either unintentionally or, in some cases, deliberately.

Yet on arrival in New York in October 1930, he allowed himself to fall victim to publicity once again. Reporters invaded his cabin as soon as the ship docked. His hosts, the American Quakers, put him into a limousine with motor escort which 'squealed its way the full distance from lower Manhattan to the upper Seventies', where, at the apartment at which he was to stay while in New York, reporters and movie cameramen were waiting. 'Tagore was rebellious and wholly unwilling to cooperate,' a leading American Quaker later wrote – but eventually a press conference was arranged.[4]

The following day, 10 October, the *New York Times*, under the headline, 'Tagore, Here, Hails Advance in Russia' with the subheading, 'Scorns Home Rule Theory', announced that 'Sir Rabindranath told of conditions among his people and scorned the theory of home rule or independence in the present state of illiteracy. No country, he said, is capable of governing herself that has so long been in a state of subjugation.'

Two days later, having escaped New York for the peace of Williamstown, Massachusetts (where he met Robert Frost), Tagore wrote this somewhat anguished – though typically witty – private letter to Ellery Sedgwick, editor of the *Atlantic Monthly*, with whom he had long been on friendly terms.[5]

Williamstown, Massachusetts, [USA]
12 October 1930

My dear Mr Ellery Sedgwick

Some time ago while travelling in Europe I got your letter and in a fury of movement I completely forgot that I had not answered that letter. Can you forgive me?

I hope I shall be able to elbow my way to a meeting with you while I am here and shall have the opportunity of a talk. In the meanwhile I ask your friendly advice in my present state of helpless bewilderment. Let me state my case in brief.

Directly my steamer came to the dock in New York my cabin was invaded by a host of strangers before I could guess their intention and adequately prepare myself for the attack. In my own country I am used to such unannounced and unforeseen catastrophe. We are a democratic people and our doors [are] open to all kinds and conditions of men. My position in the world offers no barricade against intrusion into my privacy, interruption of my work, or disturbance of my peace of mind. So with a spirit of resignation which has become habitual to me I silently suffered these unexpected guests of mine to fill up all the available space in my cabin. At first, in my pathetic vanity, I thought it was a deputation from some committee which tried in its own manner to express its obligation to offer me welcome at the moment of my reaching your shore. But their object was made clear to me when they brandished their pencils and notebooks and began to question me about matters that were personal to me or that concerned my own country. I accepted meekly the inevitable decree of my fate and did my best to satisfy their curiosity in as clear a language as was in my ability to use. Let me assure you that I did not court this publicity nor did I appreciate it as a favour. However, the next morning to my painful surprise I found in the first newspaper that came to my hand my words tortured to give a contrary suggestion to what I tried to convey through them. Then I came to know from my friends that several other newspapers have followed the same track of misinterpretation on questions vitally important for my people and for the cause of truth. I am sorely puzzled. I cannot ascribe this to a sudden epidemic of unintelligence among the American reporters and my vanity forbids me to think that I failed to make my meaning clear specially on points which would lead to mischief if vaguely expressed. I fully know that all earlier misinformations have the advantage over the contradictions that may follow later as the wound creates a deeper impression than the bandage. And yet I did send my own original version to one of the most important of those papers and expected that it would appear on the next morning. But I find that they are not as prompt in publishing the correction as they have been in giving currency to the wrong statement.[6]

I am a simple man from the East and I hate to carry in my mind distrust against any section of your community specially those whose duty it is to supply information to the public. I tell you truly it has made me feel afraid, for I do not know the technique of your public life and it tires me to be always on my guard. I am beginning to feel like a pedestrian from my country trying to walk in his own absent-minded manner in some busy street in New York and suddenly finding some necessary portions of his limbs disappearing in the dust. I only wish I could laugh at my misadventure, but that has become impossible even for an oriental philosopher owing to its extremely mischievous nature. I have come to the conclusion that the only place which is safe for the eastern simpleton is his own remote corner of obscurity. Waiting for some advice and consolation from you.

I remain

Very sincerely yours
Rabindranath Tagore

Source: MS copy at Rabindra Bhavan, Shantiniketan.

1 Ellery Sedgwick (1872–1960): editor, *Atlantic Monthly*, 1908–38.
2 *MR*, Feb. 1912, p. 229. Satyajit Ray, recalling Tagore's conversation at Shantiniketan in 1940–1, said, 'He never used a wrong word; I mean if you recorded his normal conversation it would sound like a prepared speech. Everything was so incredibly perfect.' (Interview with Julian Crandall Hollick in 1987, in Robinson, *Satyajit Ray*, p. 48.)
3 *Rocky Mountain News*, 17 Oct. 1916, in Sujit Mukherjee, *Passage to America*, p. 77.
4 Clarence Pickett, *For More than Bread* (Boston, 1953), p. 92. 'It was like handling a piece of delicate glass to take care of this aged saint.'
5 RT and Sedgwick first met at Harvard in 1913. Sedgwick published in *Atlantic Monthly* two pieces by RT, on Shantiniketan (July 1913, pp. 58–61), and a vitriolic attack on America (June 1927, pp. 85–92), which Sedgwick admired though felt obliged to preface with a warning to Americans not to react defensively.
6 RT's correction appeared in the *New York Times* on 13 Oct. 1930; see Dutta and Robinson, *Rabindranath Tagore*, p. 299. Presumably, RT had looked for it in the paper on 12 Oct., before he left New York.

245

To Rathindranath Tagore

Although Tagore's stay in the United States in 1930, which was his last visit to that country, was extensively publicised, it was financially a flop. As in 1920–1, Tagore's principles and personality were rubbing Americans the wrong way.

After the encouraging reception of his paintings in Europe, first in Paris and then especially in Germany, Tagore keenly hoped to sell some of them in America to raise funds for his university. Exhibitions were held in Boston (October), New York (November) and Philadelphia (December) during his stay, but there were almost no sales. Ananda Coomaraswamy wrote, somewhat reluctantly, a sympathetic and perceptive catalogue introduction for the Boston exhibition at the Museum of Fine Arts (where he was a research fellow).[1] But the *New York Times*, reviewing the exhibition in New York, commented:

> Were it not that Sir Rabindranath Tagore has himself expressly stated that his paintings . . . are 'spontaneous creations and must stand by themselves as they are,' the approach to them would be easier. That is to say, it would seem most simple and reasonable to look upon them as spray from the mystic fountain whose major waters have been communicated in words . . .
>
> What are we to make of these curious animal forms, of these hardly less curious human [forms]? Despite Tagore's warning, we cannot help trying to retrace their journey from the subconscious, trying to visualise the mystic concept from which they spring. But the questions are never answered; and in the end we turn aside, not without impatience, though remembering, in the bustle of the street, certain queer, haunting beauties of light, a kind of fugitive translucence, glimpsed and then gone, suggestive, tantalising, never really articulate.[2]

Writing to his son, who had stayed in Europe, from New Haven, Connecticut, Rabindranath gave his own view of the problem in this letter, at the same time shedding a frank light on his own naive tendency to trust his Shantiniketan co-workers (in this case his secretary Ariam Williams) with tasks that were way beyond their capacities.

30 Mansfield, Newhaven, Connecticut, [USA]
26 October 1930

Kalyaniyeshu

Rathi, I had to give responsibility for the paintings to Ariam.[3] You see Harry Timbres is caught up in fundraising – and the people whom Andrews knows well do not care about painting.[4]

The other day Ariam came and said emphatically that the paintings had begun to sell – between Boston and New York, he said, there would not be a single painting left. And much more in that vein.

Today Harry came and told me that although there is interest in the paintings, not one has been sold – Coomaraswamy said to him that there were only two artists in Boston capable of genuinely understanding Rabindranath's paintings. Harry's impression is that there is little hope of selling much. The chief reason is that Ariam, though he travelled to Boston and New York, did not organise any sales. Ariam lacks the intellectual capacity to plan things and yet he is so thin-skinned it is impossible to tell him off. What's more, he has an impetuosity that easily distracts him. However when he came and told me all the paintings were about to be sold, I believed him – trusting people is my disease – if it had been you, you would certainly not have believed him. At any rate you should assume that not many paintings will be sold. I do not fear that this time round no money at all will be raised for Visva-Bharati, but I keep on hearing that there has not been such a widespread economic depression in this country for a long time. This means that the people of moderate wealth have no money to spare – and they are normally most generous givers. So my hopes are not high – then, if I do get something, it will seem like a miracle. Ariam took the Visva-Bharati begging bag to some people in Boston: they told Harry that Ariam's description and appeal were so vague they were not much impressed. I am in great difficulty over my secretary. He cannot achieve much, and yet he will not give up; and he exaggerates so much that one of his rupees is worth barely an anna.[5]

I have finally decided to leave here on 29 November. If I can get a passage on the ship you are sailing on, I will do so, otherwise I shall try for the Japanese liner.[6]

Shri Rabindranath Thakur

Source: MS original at Rabindra Bhavan, Shantiniketan; letter published in Sharadiya *Desh*, 1396 [Autumn 1989], p. 12.

1 See Dutta and Robinson, *Rabindranath Tagore*, pp. 357, 461.
2 *New York Times*, 30 Nov. 1930.
3 On Ariam Williams, see letter 241, n. 4.
4 Harry Garland Timbres (1899–1937): malariologist, who worked at Shantiniketan in the early 1930s; having travelled with RT in Russia in Sept. 1930, he returned to the USA and attempted to raise money

for Shantiniketan during 1930–1 as part of the Quaker effort, before going out to India. In 1934, disease forced him to leave Bengal. He died of typhus in Russia. Though a highly trained and gifted scientist, Timbres was hardly best suited to the task of selling RT's paintings to American lovers of modern art.
5 There were sixteen annas in a rupee.
6 RT sailed from New York on 15 Dec. 1930.

246

To Rathindranath Tagore

In March 1921, at the beginning of Gandhi's Noncooperation Movement, in a letter from New York to C. F. Andrews (165), Tagore had written, 'we may come to that point when we have to give up our means of livelihood' – that is, the income from the Tagore *zamindari* estates. Now, writing to his son from Philadelphia, he raises the question again, and even suggests selling the Jorasanko family house in Calcutta. Nothing came of either proposal, because Rathindranath did not share his father's ascetic attitude, but they show how his Russian experience had stirred Rabindranath.[1] Tagore also clearly saw how Russian educational advances among the peasants had been made possible by a change of political system in 1917 (whatever his doubts about that system); and this too encouraged him to come closer to the political struggle in India during the 1930s, following a long period of estrangement from Gandhi in the 1920s. Education always mattered more to him than politics, but he now recognised that he would have to behave more expediently to attain his real goal.

[Philadelphia, USA]
31 October 1930

Kalyaniyeshu

Rathi, I am now in Philadelphia. Perhaps you have heard this from Miss Green.[2] Meetings and discussions are continuing – with some result, we are hoping. If we can transport the paintings here, perhaps some will be sold. The most hopeful place is however New York. There some good arrangements have been made, fixed up by Govil; this is our best chance of selling some. People there are not traditionalists, they appreciate new art. Not that there was no curiosity about my paintings in Boston but people were puzzled by them – and moreover in Boston they follow the English, not the Continental lead, and are unsympathetic to India.[3] Nevertheless some paintings were sold. I have had no word from Ariam for some time – perhaps he is in New York.[4] I shall go there on Monday. If we can sell some paintings in New York and Philadelphia, we shall have some money in hand.

You have written about the state of our *zamindari*. In the era that is now upon us, we can no longer depend on our *zamindari* for income. My mind has been rebelling against it from way back and the feeling is now definite. The ideas I have been dwelling on for ages have taken shape in Russia today. And so the whole business of *zamindari* makes me ashamed. Today my mind has stepped down from its landlord's seat and taken a seat on the ground. I feel sad to think that from childhood we have been raised as parasites.

If it is not absolutely impossible to sell our Calcutta house, what is the harm in our doing so? It would make us much lighter. My Father comes to mind – one day with total confidence he sold off almost all our property and brought down our standard of living with a jolt. Those were dark days for us children. But though our means had become scanty, inwardly we lacked nothing. Today, once more, I should like to reduce the external trappings of our lives.

Right now a new chapter in our country's history is unfolding. Many things will be altered. At such a time, the more we can shed our loads, the easier our problems will become. It is time to change our lives radically, and I hope I can do so with a contented heart. The more one remains entangled, the more one will suffer. In times of sorrow it is better to welcome the sorrow than to bear it because one has no choice: this mitigates the suffering and avoids a pointless struggle. At certain historical junctures everyone must suffer: indeed everyone is already experiencing this; it is wrong to expect to remain comfortable by evading the crisis. Adjustment to new habits is not so difficult if one is mentally prepared, if one lets old ties slip away rather than clinging to them and making them into nooses.

From my small experience in Europe, I have come to realise that I can trust in my ability to paint. This has made me very happy. The task that you have undertaken is of no less value, even if it brings you no external appreciation.[5] My sole preoccupation now is to make that task a success. I have realised that our greatest challenge lies in Shriniketan. Our mission there is to show how, on a small scale, to revive the whole country. If you had come to Russia you would have gained much experience in this field. However I have collected various materials there which we will talk about when I get home. We have to forget personal matters completely – greater things are beckoning us on.

Shri Rabindranath Thakur

Source: MS original at Rabindra Bhavan, Shantiniketan; letter published in *CP*, I, pp. 102–5.

1 According to Annada Shankar Ray:
> When Tagore visited Russia he said he was ashamed of being a zamindar. He left the administration of his estate to his son as Tolstoy had left it to his wife, washing his own hands of it. But when Amiya Chakravarty suggested he make a gift to the nation of his *zamindari* rights before his death Tagore refused. He refused to deprive his son. ('Tagore as a zamindar', *Statesman* (Tagore Centenary Supplement), 8 May 1961)

2 Miss Green: Gretchen Green. See letters 187, n. 6, and 295.
3 To Andrée Karpelès, a French artist present at the Galerie Pigalle opening in May 1930, RT commented from New York, probably accurately, 'These people are afraid to praise lest they should make a fool of themselves' (RT to Karpelès, 27 Nov. 1930 [copy at RB]).
4 See letter 245.
5 Rathindranath Tagore was in charge of the administration of Shantiniketan and Shriniketan.

247

To Benito Mussolini

(not sent)

There had been no contact between Tagore and Mussolini since their meeting in Rome in 1926, and none between Tagore and Carlo Formichi, his Italian host, since they exchanged critical letters in private and in the *Manchester Guardian* (see letters 209–12) after Tagore's visit to Italy. Now, in November 1930, Tagore and Formichi met again in New York, and the encounter seems to have persuaded Tagore that he should try to mend fences with Mussolini by writing this letter to him. It was not sent, however, probably on the advice of Tagore's son Rathindranath.

1172 Park Avenue, New York, [USA]
21 November 1930

Your Excellency

It often comes to my memory how we were startled by the magnanimous token of your sympathy reaching us through my very dear friend – Professor Formichi. The precious gift, the library of Italian literature, is a treasure to us highly prized by our institution and for which we are deeply grateful to Your Excellency.[1]

I am also personally indebted to you for the lavish generosity you showed to me in your hospitality when I was your guest in Italy and I earnestly hope that the misunderstanding which has unfortunately caused a barrier between me and the great people you represent, the people for whom I have genuine love, will not remain permanent, and that this expression of my gratitude to you and your nation will be accepted. The politics of a country is its own, its culture belongs to all humanity. My mission is to acknowledge all that has eternal value in the self-expression of any country. Your Excellency has nobly offered to our institution on behalf of Italy the opportunity of a festival of spirit which will remain inexhaustible and ever claim our homage of a cordial admiration.

I am, Your Excellency,

Gratefully yours,
Rabindranath Tagore

Source: MS copy at Rabindra Bhavan, Shantiniketan.

1 In 1926, the Italian anti-Fascist Guglielmo Salvadori had suggested that RT should return this entire library to Mussolini (letter 211, n. 2). RT ignored the suggestion.

248

To Pratima Tagore

When Tagore spoke at Carnegie Hall on 1 December 1930, thousands had to be turned away, according to the *New York Times*.[1] A week before this, there was a special fund-raising banquet for him at the Biltmore Hotel in New York, arranged by Henry Morgenthau, in the presence of Franklin Roosevelt, the governor of New York, Sinclair Lewis, the latest Nobel laureate (and the first American to win), and five hundred others. In his speech Tagore said bluntly, 'The age belongs to the West and humanity must be grateful to you for your science. But you have exploited those who are helpless and humiliated those who are unfortunate with this gift. A great portion of the world suffers from your civilisation.'[2]

In this letter to his daughter-in-law (who was in Europe), he expresses his ever-complicated feelings about all the attention and publicity heaped upon him in America, yet with so still genuine understanding.

1172 Park Avenue, [New York, USA]
25 November 1930

Kalyaniyashu

Bouma, tonight there is a banquet. Five hundred people are holding a reception for me. Just what a torture I find this no one seems to appreciate. Fame in this country requires such a load of seasoning – its weight becomes an intolerable burden. Everything here suffers from a frightening addiction to hyperbole; whoever wants to achieve something must keep a megaphone handy, known as 'publicity'. It magnfies all sounds, inflates all ideas and generally shouts out – look at me! There are thousands of people shouting like this. Alas, why am I in the centre of it all? What sin have I committed? Visva-Bharati? If I could only make atonement, say my farewell and escape. With every step I feel I am turning truth into falsity; the burden of untruth scares me. Day and night I look forward to the time when I will float carefree, free of all this paraphernalia, at ease with myself. I will write and read and paint pictures, and pace up and down my pebbled garden any time of day I like; and then I shall lie back in a favourite chair and let the colours of my thoughts mingle with the colours of the clouds in the sky – for as long as I like. Rabindranath Tagore, profound prophet and philosopher – this false idea allows me no means of escape. Letters come from far and wide, parties of visitors turn up, questions of all kinds have to be answered. If I could only clear a little space amongst all this, I would open up a studio. Among the regular visitors would be Pupu – but possibly she would no longer be charmed by my tiger tales, I'll have to change my stories, though at least I'm certain she won't trouble me with demands for philosophy.[3] On the 27th I shall be leaving here on the liner *Bremen*.[4] Before that I will visit Canada.[5] From Europe I am trying to get a passage on a Japanese liner.

Baba Mashai[6]

[PS] Please forward Amita's letter.[7]

Source: MS original at Rabindra Bhavan, Shantiniketan; letter published in *CP*, III, pp. 86–8.

1 *New York Times*, 2 Dec. 1930.
2 Quoted in Stephen N. Hay, 'Rabindranath Tagore in America', *American Quarterly*, Fall 1962, p. 459.
3 Pupu: Nandini Tagore, adoptive daughter of Pratima Devi. See letter 241.
4 RT left New York on 15 Dec. 1930.
5 RT did not visit Canada.
6 *Baba Mashai*: respectful form of 'Father'.
7 Amita: Amita Tagore, wife of Ajindranath Tagore.

15 Rabindranath on the Maidan, Calcutta, 1931, protesting against the shooting of prisoners at Hijli detention camp

Against the Raj (1931–1933)

Introduction

Tagore returned to India in January 1931. Although he continued to travel within India for several years, he did not leave its shores again until he died, except for a visit to Persia by air in 1932 and a visit to Sri Lanka in 1934.

For the rest of his life he identified closely with the freedom struggle in India. Before 1931, he had not emphasised the need for political freedom for India: from 1931 onwards he did. Though he continued to maintain friendships with individual Englishmen such as C. F. Andrews and Leonard Elmhirst, and even revived his ruptured friendship with Edward J. Thompson, he became more and more critical of British rule in India. His old faith in the underlying good intentions of the British Government towards India did not entirely disappear, but it took a severe knock, especially in Bengal, where the governor, Sir John Anderson, introduced a harsh regime on his arrival in 1932, in an attempt to stamp out terrorism.

His change in attitude brought Tagore progressively closer to Gandhi, though they continued to disagree fundamentally about education, science and economics. On the need to wipe out Untouchability, they were as one. In 1932, Tagore wholeheartedly supported Gandhi's fast against the Communal Award. But he was unable to support his further fast in 1933, because he did not share Gandhi's attraction for asceticism as a method of self-purification.

The Poona Pact, concluded with the British Government as a result of Gandhi's 1932 fast, at first received Tagore's endorsement. But he soon came to share the reaction of Bengali Hindus that the Pact would destroy Hindu–Muslim harmony in Bengal. He was unable to persuade Gandhi of this, however, and as the 1930s wore on, Tagore became convinced that Bengal was heading for catastrophe.

249

To Sir William Rothenstein[1]

In Britain, during Tagore's visit in 1930, there had been exhibitions of his paintings in Birmingham (at the City Museum and Art Gallery) and in London (under the auspices of the India Society) but, as in America, there was no great enthusiasm for Tagore's new departure. On the whole, the Anglo-Saxon world's response to Tagore's art was lukewarm, as compared to the Continental countries, especially Germany.

Nevertheless, William Rothenstein, by now an important sponsor of modern art in Britain, told Thomas Sturge Moore that 'the drawings are extraordinarily vital: they show none of the weakness of the revivalist schools which stand for modern Indian art' – i.e. the Bengal School, led by Abanindranath Tagore.[2] Rothenstein made active efforts to have the paintings exhibited in London, but he expected Tagore to bear the gallery and framing charges.[3] This letter gives Rabindranath's reaction.

Santiniketan, [West Bengal, India]
24 March 1931

My dear Friend

The present economic condition in Bengal is severely critical. The jute which is the mainstay of our peasants remains unreaped in the field owing to an abnormally low price. We who mainly depend upon our income from the land are desperately devising curtailment of expenditure to an extreme limit. In such an atmosphere of compulsory self-immolation I do not feel the least enthusiasm about spending money over my picture exhibition. However, let me know the probable cost if I venture to proceed about it. The pictures which are in the American gallery waiting to be brought to you are all mounted and only require framing. I hardly feel sanguine about their sale and my empty pocket cannot afford to be reckless.[4] The money that I had earned in previous exhibitions has vanished like raindrops upon an arid land – and therefore I cannot help asking you to be wisely cautious in your advice . . .

You will be surprised to learn that I hardly know anything about the recent political development in India. I do not read newspapers for I have my own work which I consider to be important and I cannot allow my mind to be waylaid by discussions that are outside my scope.

My love to you all

Ever yours
Rabindranath Tagore

Source: MS original in Rothenstein Papers [Harvard]; letter published in Lago (ed.), *Imperfect Encounter*, p. 334.

1 Rothenstein was knighted in Jan. 1931.
2 Rothenstein to Sturge Moore, 6 June 1930, in Lago (ed.), *Imperfect Encounter*, p. 329.
3 Rothenstein to RT, 5 March 1930 [RB].
4 In May 1931, RT wrote from India to an American friend who had helped to organise the New York paintings exhibition, 'I was not at all sanguine about their sale knowing the present economic depression in America that has been steadily growing worse since I left your country' (RT to Nina Perera, 12 May 1931 [RB]).

250

To Hertha Mendel[1]

In August 1930, and again in September, on his return from Moscow, Tagore stayed in a beautiful villa at Wannsee, a suburb of Berlin. His hosts were friends of Albert

Einstein, Bruno Mendel, a scientist, and his wife Hertha, who was interested in modern art. Tagore arranged for her to receive some of his paintings and requested, in return, some recent publications on modern European art: 'I have a great curiosity to know its tendencies and achievements.'[2]

In her reply to him in India, Hertha Mendel remarked:

> Your pictures have arrived safely, they are dreaming their dreams and allowing us to share them. We love them deeply – most of all the wonderful peace and harmony and the enveloping darkness of 'companions'. Their atmosphere is freedom. I am afraid the books I sent you about modern European art have nothing of that atmosphere of freedom.[3]

In this further letter on art, Tagore makes a shrewd judgement, drawing an implied contrast between the studied primitivism of many European artists and his own spontaneous primitivism as an artist. Though the identity of the artists in the art books sent by Mendel is unfortunately unknown, we can guess that Tagore was referring to painters such as Pablo Picasso.

Santiniketan, [West Bengal, India]
15 April 1931

Dear Hertha

The books on modern art which you so kindly sent me have reached me at last. I feel deeply interested in studying them though a considerable number of them puzzles me sorely. Some of these artists seem to be obsessed with a doctrine and a primitive quality which they try to impart to their work is not naturally their own. Evidently it is a reaction against a certain formal conventionalism, a sort of *cul-de-sac* of artistic respectability that had no spirit of growth in it, but the reaction itself may turn into a convention because of its lack of sincerity. But I cannot trust my own judgement in this matter owing to my utter inexperience.

The departing spring is squandering away its prodigal gift of flowers in a final display of recklessness. My mind feels a deep sympathy with this improvident extravagance and I long to indulge in a last orgy of lavishness. The cycle of my life having nearly come to its end has faced the point from which it started[;] it was a period of time irresponsible in its wilfulness. I feel a homesickness for that original obscurity free of all obligations which gave me the privilege to be nakedly true to my own inner urge of expression and nothing more recommendable than that. I have taken the first step towards attaining this primitive freedom and have given up reading newspapers.

With love to you both,

Yours affectionately
Rabindranath Tagore

Source: MS copy at Rabindra Bhavan, Shantiniketan.

1 We have been unable to find out any details about Bruno or Hertha Mendel, despite the assistance of Einstein scholars.
2 RT to Mendel, 24 Jan. 1931 [copy at RB].
3 Mendel to RT, 28 Feb. 1931 [RB].

251

To Bidhan Chandra Roy[1]

In 1929, during his stop in Japan on the way back from the United States to India, Tagore invited Tokyo Kodokan, the main centre for judo in Japan, to provide a teacher for Shantiniketan. He was already the pioneer of judo in India, having invited a teacher, Sano Jinnosuke, to Shantiniketan in 1905 (at the suggestion of Okakura Kakuzo). The second teacher was Shinzo Takagaki (1893–1977). He reached Shantiniketan in November 1929 and stayed about two years in India, where he wrote the text of his book, *Techniques of Judo*.[2] From India, Takagaki went on to introduce judo in Afghanistan (where he trained the king's army for five years) and Nepal, before returning to Japan. After the Second World War he toured extensively in many countries and contributed more than perhaps any other individual to the growth of interest in judo internationally.[3] At his death, he was 9th-*dan* (9th grade), only one grade short of the maximum grade ever awarded by the Kodokan.

As so often happened, Tagore's new ideas did not catch on in Bengal. He had hoped that Takagaki would be funded out of popular demand; in fact Tagore himself had to bear the costs of his stay in Bengal. This letter is an attempt to persuade the Calcutta Corporation to take up the responsibility. Not unreasonably, Rabindranath thought that martial arts would appeal to the discipline-minded Subhas Chandra Bose, who had been elected mayor in 1930, and possibly also to Bidhan Chandra Roy, his successor. But despite encouraging noises, nothing was done by the corporation and Takagaki left India.

Santiniketan, [West Bengal, India]
25 April 1931

Dear Dr Roy

Please accept my sincere congratulations on your election as the mayor of the Calcutta Corporation.

I wrote some time ago to Shrijukta Subhash Chandra Bose about our jiu-jitsu professor, Mr Takagaki, but apparently he has not been able to reply to it as he is touring about in East Bengal. May I now put before you the case of Prof. Takagaki, whom as you know I brought from Japan specially for the purpose of giving a thorough training in the art of jiu-jitsu to the students of Bengal. Prof. Takagaki comes of a highly distinguished family in Japan and is one of the most well-known experts in jiu-jitsu in that country. When I found out that our countrymen did not properly realise the importance of the visit of Prof. Takagaki to our country I had to take up myself the entire financial responsibility of his travel and stay in this country. I engaged his services for two years and boys and girls of our institution have received instruction from him with remarkable results. Our students gave a demonstration of jiu-jitsu in Calcutta at which several members of the corporation were present, and I was told that they all appreciated it very much.[4] At that time I was also given the assurance that the corporation might retain his services after his term of appointment in Santiniketan is over by the end of September.

It will be a great pity if Prof. Takagaki has to be sent back to Japan without the student community in Calcutta ever getting the opportunity of mastering from him the art of self-defence and physical training which I need hardly point out is specially required for our boys and girls. Prof. Takagaki has to make definite arrangements from now for his future programme, and therefore I am writing to you requesting the corporation to take advantage of his presence in our country and to engage him for giving instructions to the students of Calcutta. Prof. Takagaki is willing to remain in Calcutta for the purpose if suitable arrangements are made for him.

I do hope that my appeal will find response in the Calcutta Corporation and that both yourself and Shrijukta Subhash Chandra Bose will consider the proposal favourably and retain the services of Prof. Takagaki for a cause which concerns the well-being of the students of Bengal.[5]

With kind regards,

Yours sincerely
Rabindranath Tagore

Source: MS copy at Rabindra Bhavan, Shantiniketan.

1 Bidhan Chandra Roy (1882–1962): physician and Congress politician; he was vice chancellor, University of Calcutta, 1942–4, and chief minister, West Bengal, 1948–62.
2 Shinzo Takagaki and Harold E. Sharp, *Techniques of Judo* (Tokyo and Vermont, 1956).
3 This was the judgement in 1956 of the president of the Tokyo Kodokan in his foreword to *Techniques of Judo*. On Takagaki and Shantiniketan, see *VBN*, Jan. 1954, pp. 68–9.
4 The demonstration took place at the Empire Theatre, Calcutta, on 16 March 1931.
5 Satyajit Ray recalled receiving judo lessons as a teenager from Takagaki, in Calcutta in 1934 (Satyajit Ray, *Jakhan Chhoto Chhilam* (1389 [1982]), pp. 37–9). Perhaps this occurred when Takagaki returned from Afghanistan to Japan on leave in Oct. 1934.

252

To Edward John Thompson

As Tagore's seventieth birthday approached, in 1931, some of his admirers, both in Europe and in Bengal, began to consider how best to mark the occasion. *The Golden Book of Tagore*, published in late 1931, was initiated in the autumn of 1930 by Romain Rolland, who was joined as a 'sponsor' by Sir J. C. Bose, Albert Einstein, Mahatma Gandhi and Kostís Palamás. The editor was Ramananda Chatterji [Chattopadhyay], editor of the *Modern Review*. Most of the famous people who had personally known Tagore contributed, though often very briefly. In Bengal, money was collected – which Rabindranath requested be given to Bengali flood victims – and in December 1931/January 1932, a fortnight's festival was arranged in Tagore's honour in Calcutta, at which his paintings were first seen publicly in India. (The festival had to be cut short when Gandhi, returning from London, was arrested.)

Edward J. Thompson was one of the contributors, despite Tagore's violent rejection of his biography (see letter 218). In this letter Tagore thanks Thompson for his tribute with his characteristic diffidence about publicity, and at the same time offers an olive branch.

402   Selected letters of Rabindranath Tagore

Darjeeling, [West Bengal, India]
9 July 1931

Dear Thompson

It is no longer a secret to me that in my country they are making ready for a celebration of my seventieth year in a grand style.

I wish it were for someone else who could truly enjoy it – but I shrink with all my heart from such an ordeal. I cannot deny that I have a healthy appetite for any genuine approbation of my work coming from any source whatever but when they try to make a regular ceremony of it I feel inclined to run away to the other end of the world. I realise from your letter that you have been approached for a contribution to this festival to be held in my honour and whatever may be my feeling about such an attempt at a public acclamation of my merit I must thank you for your very kind words carrying with them a sincere note of appreciation.[1]

Yours
Rabindranath Tagore

Source: MS original in Thompson Papers [Bodleian].

1 Thompson wrote, in part:

> I think most often of you, not as the poet of *Balaka* or *Chitrangada* or *Naivedya* or as the writer whose short stories have so opened up his country's life to us, but as the patriot whose passionate love for 'Banga-Lakshmi' has not prevented him from being just to our 'Inga-Lakshmi' (if Mother Saraswati will forgive such an outrage on Sanskrit rules of union). I never forget that your generosity has been conspicuous under cruel provocation. A great writer, you have been greater still in this magnanimity. (Ramananda Chatterjee (ed.), *Golden Book*, p. 252)

253

To Nitindranath Gangulee[1]

In August 1930, while in Germany, Rabindranath had written to his daughter suggesting that his grandson Nitindranath be sent to Germany to learn printing and publishing (letter 240). The young man arrived nine months later and began his training, helped by German friends and admirers of Tagore.

In the meantime, Germany was in chaos, at the beginning of the great depression. The Nazis and Communists had together substantially increased their vote, polling a third of the votes cast in the Reichstag elections in September 1930. During 1931, the depression deepened and on 13 July, all the banks closed until 5 August, following the collapse of a major bank. The streets of German cities were alive with political agitation, particularly in Bavaria. Nitindranath, studying in Munich, was in the thick of the struggle.

Tagore's letter to him is remarkable chiefly for its very clear grasp of the dark side of both Fascism and Communism. While this is not surprising in relation to Fascism, it is significant in regard to Communism. Despite his praise for the Soviet education programme in 1930 and after, this letter is evidence that Tagore was not taken in by Communism as a system.

[Shantiniketan, West Bengal, India]
31 July 1931

Kalyaniyeshu

Nitu, I was pleased to get your letter. I don't like the attitude of Bavaria towards the rest of Germany. Just as weak people struck by poverty can be gripped by epidemics, so the spread of famine in Europe is enabling Fascism and Bolshevism to get a strong hold. Both are symptoms of unhealthiness. No sane person can regard the suppression of independent thinking as something beneficial to man. It is the sharpening pangs of hunger that provoke this kind of twisted thinking. I dread Bolshevism getting a grip on India as the current famine becomes more acute – when the last gasp draws nigh, these sorts of ideas appear like the Grim Reaper.[2] Man's brutality to man makes me shudder: the whole world seems to be girding its loins for a lethal contest, to decide who will wipe out whom. Man, in order to protect himself from his fellow man, becomes more and more brutal, violence spiralling like some murderous whirlpool with no end in sight.

Whatever you do, do not become part of this cannibal party. Europe today is denying her own greatness. Our own people – Bengalis especially – if they can do nothing else, can imitate; and many of them are busy aping this European malaise. Keep yourself aloof from this contagion of mimicry. There are sure to be many of these Indians with possessed minds where you are. Don't associate with them, carry on working on your own.

I too don't feel much enthusiasm for your learning the violin. But the cello appeals to me quite a lot. I think it is a good instrument for playing our music. But what you say is quite true – to pick up any of these instruments will take up so much time that your other studies will suffer. So better postpone it. The most important thing for your work is to improve your design skills. When you return you will be able to follow this line.

It is monsoon here. All around me is turning green. After a few days in Darjeeling it is good to be back. Trust you are receiving news of this place.

Grandfather

Source: MS original at Rabindra Bhavan, Shantiniketan; letter published in *CP*, IV, pp. 179–80.

1 Nitindranath Gangulee (1911–32): grandson of RT, son of Mira and Nagendranath Gangulee. He died young (see letter 258).
2 On the famine in Bengal, see letter 249.

254

To Hemanta Bala Ray (Ray Chaudhuri)[1]

In the 1920s, there was an increase in communal tension in Bengal between Hindus and Muslims. Rabindranath's attitude to it was complex. He had genuine sympathy for the Muslim tenants of his estates, as is clear from his pioneering rural development work on the estates after 1890, from the letters he wrote to his niece and others while managing the estates (for instance, letter 7) and from his novel *Ghare Baire* (*The Home and the World*); unlike other zamindars in East Bengal, Tagore openly allowed that Hindu arrogance had fanned Muslim fanaticism, and he never supported political or economic actions likely to divide Hindu from Muslim. And yet at the same time, he had a clear conviction that the Muslims of Bengal were culturally backward, he disliked their religious fanaticism and their loyalty to Islam over India, and he had very few friendships with Bengali Muslims comparable to those with Hindus; when, in the mid-1930s, the Poona Pact and the Communal Award divided Hindus and Muslims in Bengal, Tagore sided unequivocally, if reluctantly, with his own community.[2]

On 31 August 1931 and subsequent days, there were severe riots in Chittagong and neighbouring areas, occasioned by the assassination of a Muslim police inspector by a young Hindu revolutionary (though the latter was not, it would appear, acting for communal reasons). Hindus and businesses run by Hindus were attacked by Muslims and looted, and the police refused to intervene, abetted by the local British magistracy, which was hostile to the (mainly Hindu) nationalists and revolutionaries.[3]

Tagore read the reports in the press and wrote a letter to the Calcutta *Statesman* on 5 September:

> The ebullition of atrocities visiting town after town in Bengal in quick succession has caused us not merely sorrow but intolerable shame. It is no doubt [also] a matter of deep regret that it has undermined our confidence in the British Government, whose moral prestige, through easy repetition of such occurrences, has received a fatal stab in the back . . .
>
> It can never be in the nature of things for a people belonging to a far distant island to fix their hold upon India for all time to come; but we Hindus and Mohammedans, the children of the same soil, will ever remain side by side to build up a commonwealth, to share our triumphs and also our shame, whoever may be responsible for it. We cannot afford, in this heart-breaking time of crisis, to indulge in mutual recrimination; but let us appeal to all God-fearing Mohammedans, for the sake of their own great religion and culture and for the sake of our bleeding humanity, to join hands with us in checking the evil which may grow for ourselves into a permanent source of futility bringing upon our unfortunate country the disgust and derision of the whole world.[4]

The following day he wrote in Bengali to a (Hindu) woman friend, the daughter of an orthodox *zamindari* family from Natore in East Bengal, explaining his feelings about the rioting. His Bengali letter makes an interesting contrast with his English letter to the newspaper.

[Shantiniketan, West Bengal, India]
20 Bhadra 1338 [6 September 1931]

Kalyaniyashu

My burden of work increases. I have to comply with so many requests from so many people, though years of practice have made it easier to cope.

But I feel very upset when I hear about outrages. When news of them jangles my nerve ends, I feel almost dizzy with pain, which does not abate. Just now I am in the grip of such an attack, both mentally and physically.

For a long time the sufferings caused by the flood have weighed like a great stone upon the chest of our country; now, on top of that, the incidents at Chattagram [Chittagong] have shaken the very foundations of the country like a cyclone.[5]

When we too become merciless, it gives me no solace. And even if some distant planet is behind all that is happening, to lament the fact will do us no good. We must tell ourselves, 'that's irrelevant'. The greatest harm of all would be for Hindus to become inimical to the Mussulman community. Needless to say – and I know this very well from my personal experience – generally speaking, our relationship with the Mussulmans has been difficult on both sides, for lack of proper contact. And inevitably, when one group among a community commits a heinous act, the stain adheres to the whole community – but we must not fall into making wrong generalisations as a result of this act, despite our suffering.

As far as the country itself is concerned, despite this calamity we cannot deny the fact that the Mussulmans are our close relations. Once, a Mussulman tenant of mine offered me a rupee, for no reason. I told him I had made no demand upon him. He said, If I don't give how will you eat? He spoke truly. I have been living off my Mussulman tenants for ages. I love them from my heart, because they deserve it. If today they were somehow suddenly to attack me, I would be compelled to regard such an act as an aberration resulting from some unexpected provocation – not at all as their natural behaviour. If only people would think in this way in these evil days, such mental perversions would be kept in their proper perspective. But if, instead, we furiously snatch the Mussulmans' weapons and hit them back, these perversions will become permanent – and they will drive us eventually to perdition.

When a Mussulman gets excited and is unafraid to persecute a Hindu, one must remember that such acts are not like missiles that pierce from outside but like inflammations of the heart: by fighting each other we only increase the inflammation. To remain calm and try for a fundamental cure is the only solution. We must take that path without delay.

That a foreign race should treat India as a plateful of morsels, and that it should become cruel in apprehension of its food supply being cut off, should not surprise us; it is simply acting out of self-interest. If their better instincts are subverted by worldly considerations (leave alone spiritual ones), we can understand this fairly easily. But dark deeds that are committed by ourselves go entirely against our interests. They permanently defile the national mind with distrust, and cause us eternal loss. If one of the boatmen of the boat in which we all ply manages to hole it in an argument with a passenger, will this be regarded as his victory? The English once stuffed opium balls down the throats of all China at the point of a sword and insulted their age-old faith, but at least the Chinese derived some material benefit from this sin.[6] Imagine instead, if southern China in a fit of rage had poured poison into the mouths of the northern Chinese – the resultant mayhem would have spread, and southern China would not have escaped it. When relatives fight each other, both victories and defeats are equally fatal. When one community begins hacking enthusiastically at the roots of national integrity, thinking that it is safe among the high branches, its own security will not last long. Sad to say, however, such ideas are not heeded in hard times. Once their passions are aroused by some cause, men do not hesitate to commit a kind of suicide by hurting a close relation. The tragic events that have occurred in history, came about like this. A death wish possesses men: they kill others knowing full well that in the end they will kill themselves. Today it has become difficult to practise *sadhana*, self-restraint. But if we cannot restrain our passions in the face of intolerable blows, we may as well prepare for self-slaughter – and the alien planet will have triumphed.

My mind is full of pain, hence my writing to you like this. My words may not have much relevance to you, but I am heart-broken.

[Shri Rabindranath Thakur]

Source: MS original at Rabindra Bhavan, Shantiniketan; letter published in *CP*, IX, pp. 433–5 (see also pp. 87–90).

1 Hemanta Bala Ray (1894–1975): having admired a Tagore novel, *Yogayog*, she began corresponding with RT under various pseudonyms because she did not wish her orthodox family to know of her contact, then, with the help of her brother, she finally met him on 9 July 1931. Altogether, RT wrote her 264 letters, remarking in one of them that her letters breathed 'the air of a real Bengali household' and admitting that he did not know such Bengali society as intimately as he needed to, in order to capture it in his writing (*CP*, IX, p. 105). Inspired by RT, she became a writer.
2 See Dutta and Robinson, *Rabindranath Tagore*, pp. 274–5, 338–40; also the English report of RT's interview on political matters with Mrinal Kanti Bose, *Ceylon Independent*, 8 Oct. 1923.
3 See Suranjan Das, *Communal Riots in Bengal 1905–1947* (New Delhi, 1991), pp. 133–41.
4 *Statesman*, 6 Sept. 1931. RT made the same point about British 'divide-and-rule' policy during the Dhaka communal riots of 1930, in a letter to the *Spectator*, 30 Aug. 1930: 'This event at Dacca has alienated, more than anything else in Bengal, the sympathies of those who were clinging to their faith in British justice.'
5 The floods were in north Bengal. RT arranged benefit performances for the victims in Calcutta on 14 and 15 Sept.
6 RT had a long-standing revulsion for British opium trafficking in China; see his essay 'The death traffic', *MR*, May 1925, pp. 504–7, first published in Bengali in 1881.

255

To William Butler Yeats

From 1918, there were no letters between Yeats and Tagore for over ten years, though the two men did meet in London in 1920. Yeats was disappointed by the poor quality of Tagore's poetry translations after 1913 – though he remained receptive to some of his prose – and Tagore was aware both of the poor quality of the poetry and, no doubt, of Yeats's reaction.[1] In addition, Tagore seems to have had no interest in Yeats's own poetry of this period.

In 1931, William Rothenstein asked Yeats to contribute to *The Golden Book of Tagore*. Instead of writing a contribution, Yeats wrote a letter to Tagore, which was published in *The Golden Book*. 'I . . . want to tell you that I am still your most loyal student and admirer,' he said. 'Your poems, as you know, came to me as a great excitement; and of recent years I have found wisdom and beauty, or both, in your prose – *The Home and the World*, your short stories and your *Reminiscences*.'[2]

Santiniketan, [West Bengal, India]
4 October 1931

Dear Yeats

Your letter has given me great pleasure and specially reminded me of an intimate evening in the quaint little room you then had in London.[3] Last year while travelling in Europe I tried to find out your address and to see you once again. Ezra Pound, whom I met in Paris, informed me that you were in indifferent health and staying somewhere in Italy.[4] I dared not seek you in that country for, as you may know, I had seriously displeased Mussolini by my criticism of his cruel policy of persecution.

During my last tour in the West I came to discover that I am no longer fit for travelling in distant lands and therefore I am not likely to risk a long voyage to Europe. No more chance [is there] for me personally to meet my friends in England so I can only send you my greetings from across the sea.

Yours sincerely
Rabindranath Tagore

Source: MS original in collection of Michael Yeats.

1 On Yeats and Tagore, see Dutta and Robinson, *Rabindranath Tagore*, pp. 3–4.
2 Ramananda Chatterjee (ed.), *Golden Book*, p. 269. The letter was dated 7 Sept. 1931.
3 In 1912–13, when RT was in London, Yeats lived at 18 Woburn Buildings, Upper Woburn Place, London WC1.
4 RT met Pound in April 1930 just before the Paris exhibition of his paintings. Yeats lived at Rapallo, in Italy, from Nov. 1929 to early July 1930.

256

To Sharashi Lal Sarkar[1]

In 1925, Tagore remarked, 'Science recognises atoms, all of which can be weighed and measured, but never recognises personality, the one thing that lies at the basis of reality.'[2] He was already aware of psychoanalysis, and became more so, but he always treated it with scepticism bordering on suspicion. At Tagore's request, Sigmund Freud called on him in Vienna in October 1926, but the meeting was not a success.[3] When in the 1930s, Tagore wrote some epigrams to accompany his paintings – those open invitations to psychoanalysis – one of the epigrams, which accompanied a mysterious head of a woman, treated psychoanalysis with ironic detachment:

> A strange face, uninvited
> hovers before my brush.
> By psychoanalysis its identity
> May be known to the pundits, but not to me.[4]

In essence, Rabindranath believed that poets were far better guides to the human personality than psychoanalysts could ever be.

This letter to a Bengali psychoanalyst and student of Freud by correspondence begins with Tagore's reservations about psychoanalysis, and then moves onto the nature of consciousness and mystical realisations.

Shantiniketan, [West Bengal, India]
24 Ashwin 1338 [11 October 1931]

Kalyaniyeshu

I have read your letter to Amiya.[5] I do not want to intrude upon the field of psychoanalysis. This is in the early stages of becoming a science, still undeveloped, thus providing a perfect excuse for people to chatter as they please. Furthermore, there can be no better opportunity for giving vent to unhealthy thoughts than this form of scientifically approved scandal. In this so-called branch of science anyone can assume the role of a scientist, there is no need to pass a stiff examination to be selected as a competent practitioner. In Bengal, psychoanalysis opens a further door for throwing insults at people; those with a taste for this will be delighted.

What I say in conversation is seldom accurately reported. The portion of the interview that you quote I do not recall, so it is not clear to me either. One cannot say anything definite about mystical realisations. They are like the nature of our sense perceptions – ineffable. To discuss why our eyes perceive ether waves as visible light is pointless: they just do, and that is a fundamental truth. Consciousness has many facets, just as white light contains many perceptible colours. Some people cannot see red, others cannot see blue; some see one colour more strongly, others another colour. These days I am painting pictures, and my mixing of colours is distinctive, the reason being that my palette expresses the colours as perceived by my consciousness. I do not see all colours with equal intensity, I am partial to some – who can say why?[6] Why do the leaves of a tree strike us as green? and why are its blossoms seen as red? Mystical perceptions, likewise, are not of only one kind but come in many varieties. This diversity cannot be properly described because it cannot all be seen with the eyes. If one calls the perceptions of some poets mystical, that is because they have the language to articulate their perceptions – which is what makes them poets. Kabir and the other old ascetic poets had this gift of language. But in order fully to understand them, one must to some extent share their feelings. Feeling combined with language creates genius. By language I mean more than words: the language of symbols, of logic, of lines, of gestures, of archetypes, and so on.

Tomader
Shri Rabindranath Thakur

Source: MS original [IOL]; letter published in *Bichitra*, Paush 1338 [Dec. 1931–Jan. 1932].

1 Sharashi Lal Sarkar (1874–1944): physician and psychoanalyst; he was a great-nephew of Nil Ratan Sircar [Sarkar].
2 Interview with Duke Gallarati Scotti in Milan, 28 Jan. 1925, noted by Leonard Elmhirst, published in *VBQ*, 29, No. 4, 1963–4, pp. 284–8.
3 The meeting took place on 25 Oct. 1926. 'He [RT] did not seem to have made much of an impression on Freud, because when another Indian, Gupta, a professor of philosophy in Calcutta, visited him a little later Freud commented: "My need for Indians is for the present fully satisfied"' (Ernest Jones, *The Life and Work of Sigmund Freud* (Lionel Trilling and Steven Marcus eds.; London, 1961), p. 462).
4 *Chitralipi*, I (2nd edn, Calcutta, 1962), p. 11. The first two lines of the translation are by RT, the second two by ourselves; curiously, RT's own translation does not include 'psychoanalysis' (even though the word is in the Bengali original):

> A strange face, uninvited
>   hovers before my brush

> making me wonder
> whence does it appear.

Perhaps RT altered the meaning because he had slightly more faith in western psychoanalysis than in its Bengali incarnation?
5 Amiya: Amiya Chakravarty, RT's secretary, who was precisely the kind of Bengali likely to be attracted to psychoanalysis.
6 RT's paintings, with their bold but harmonious colours, could support the thesis that he had a defect of colour vision at this time, though it cannot have been any straightforward colour blindness. See R. W. Pickford and J. Bose, 'Colour vision and aesthetic problems in pictures by Rabindranath Tagore', *British Journal of Aesthetics*, Winter 1987, pp. 70–5.

257

To Charles Freer Andrews

In mid-1932, C. F. Andrews published his spiritual autobiography, *What I Owe to Christ*.[1] 'The title may seem to promise a conventional piety,' wrote Hugh Tinker, the biographer of Andrews, 'but the actual work – simple, yet profound – is a most important key to understanding [Andrews].'[2] Gandhi read the book in jail in Pune, while meditating his greatest fast. He told Andrews that the book gave 'great help to a struggling soul', and that this self-portrait would 'reveal you as nothing else that you have written can do'.[3]

Tagore's reaction, given in this letter, was a deep one. It becomes deeper still when one knows that Rabindranath read the book while expecting imminently news from Germany of the death of his only grandson Nitindranath, who was being attended there by his daughter Mira, son-in-law Nagendranath Gangulee and Andrews. (He died on 7 August.)

Santiniketan, [West Bengal, India]
2 August 1932

Dear Charlie,

I have read your book on Christ. It made me think. The mode of self-expression in a Christian life is in love which works, in that of a Hindu it is in love which contemplates, enjoys the spiritual emotion as an end in itself. The attitude of mind that realises the superhuman in a human setting has rendered a great service to civilisation, just as its perversion has been the cause of an awful and widespread mischief. You know how all through my life, my idea of the divine has concentrated in Man the Eternal and I find that in your own religious experience. You have the same idea centred in a concrete historic personality. Evidently it strongly helps you in the realisation of perfection in your life and it must be a source of unfailing consolation to you to be able to feel in your constant love a divine comradeship in Christ. The mental and physical energy stored up for ages in your western constitution urges you to activities that are saved from aberration when they are related to a living centre of truth. Instances of heroic devotion and unselfish sacrifice springing from that source are most valuable for us in order to keep us firm in the faith in the abiding truth in the immortal. And I know you have been of help to your fellow beings not merely for some individual benefits that you may have rendered them but for a direct inspiration that gives us certainty of the ultimate greatness of man.[4]

With love,

Ever yours
Rabindranath Tagore

Source: MS original at Rabindra Bhavan, Shantiniketan; letter published in *VBN*, March 1933, p. 81.

1 While writing the book, Andrews decided to dedicate all its royalties to Shantiniketan. Since it went through many editions, the income for Shantiniketan was substantial (Tinker, *Ordeal of Love*, p. 267). The royalties also assisted with the funeral and other arrangements for Nitindranath, Mira and Nagendranath in July–Aug. 1932 (Andrews to RT, 30 July 1932 [RB]).
2 Tinker, *Ordeal of Love*, p. xiv.
3 Quoted in *ibid.*, p. 262. The book does indeed reveal Andrews' character: it shows his moral courage– always his strongest suit – and also his capacity for self-delusion and blithe disregard of facts.
4 Cf. Dorothy Elmhirst's reaction to RT's religion (letter 200, n. 4): 'I miss in the religious article something that corresponds to the Kingdom of God – the same note of social aspiration.' Or Dean Inge's comment on 'The realisation of the infinite' in *Sadhana*: 'The Absolute may be perilously close near to zero, if all determinations are denied to it' (W. R. Inge, *Diary of a Dean* (London, 1949), p. 20).

258

To Mira Gangulee (Tagore)

Nitindranath, Tagore's grandson, died of tuberculosis in a Black Forest sanatorium on 7 August 1932. The news reached Rabindranath on 8 August, followed by a letter from C. F. Andrews written on the day of the death: 'And you, my dearest Gurudev, have the very hardest lot of all – to remain behind and wait and know what suffering is going on and yet to be unable to help.'[1] In this letter, written three weeks later, Rabindranath tries to comfort his stricken daughter, Nitindranath's mother, who was by then on her way back to India.

Shantiniketan, [West Bengal, India]
28 August 1932

Miru

We fumble in darkness and hurt those we love without knowing it and without grasping the cause of our own suffering. But this is not the final reality: the great thing is, that despite all our mistakes and distress, we have loved. The external bonds may be severed, but it is when the inner relationship is denied to us that we feel the loss as a great emptiness. We enter this world, encounter each other, and then drift apart on the current of time – thus it was and ever shall be – and in our joys and in our sorrows our life is fulfilled. However many fractures in my own world there may be, the great world continues, flowing onwards – and my own journey must, with an unwavering mind, keep pace. I should feel ashamed if I and my grief withdrew from the world of others even a little, or tried to load the wheels of this world with the least part of my immovable burden. In every home there are intolerable griefs that time effaces day by day; it has left its mark on my life too. Let us not make this worldwide task of recovery more difficult; let the passage of grief be made easier, let it not obstruct our daily routine.

I deeply loved Nitu, and when I thought of you, an intense sorrow oppressed me. But I am ashamed to trivialise my grief before the whole world. When grief upsets our normal activities and draws everyone's attention, it is debased. I can never ask anyone to clear a path on my account: let them carry on as they are, and I shall be with them. Many people have been saying that the monsoon festival should be cancelled – in deference to my mourning – but I say it should not be. I must cope with my grief myself; no outsider can understand its real meaning. But they should at least understand that there is no call for any outward signs of condolence, no need for any ceremony of grieving, which would humiliate me. I was afraid lest everyone came to console me, and that is why for a few days I forbade anyone to come near me. But I went on with my work in the usual way. I did not want to drop any of my duties and so exhibit my feelings. To display one's personal life above all else is the greatest insult to oneself. For many days my earnest prayer was that if my special Friend really does exist, He should show me mercy. I do not know – perhaps he has shown it, perhaps I have been saved from still greater sorrows. But this kind of prayer is a weakness. My mind has become dull when I am able to hope that a special exception to the universal laws will be made for me. I ought to feel ashamed to beg for favours when everyone else has to suffer.

The night Shami departed, I told myself with all my heart that he must have a smooth voyage into the Great Beyond – my grief must not hold him back even a little.[2] In the same way, when I heard that Nitu had left us, for days I repeated to myself that I had no responsibilities left, except to pray that he should find well-being in that Infinite to which he has gone. Our service will not reach him there, but perhaps our love will – why, otherwise, does love endure?

The night after Shami went, I was travelling by train and I saw the sky awash with moonlight, with no sign of anything amiss anywhere. My heart cried out – nothing is missing, everything continues within the All, I too continue. My work for everyone continues also. I must have courage, must not grow weary, must allow no thread to be broken anywhere – I must freely accept what has happened, and must not hesitate to welcome what is to come.

If I sent this letter to Aden, I do not know if you will receive it, so I think I shall send it to Bombay.

Father

Source: MS original at Rabindra Bhavan, Shantiniketan; letter published in *CP*, V, pp. 150–3.

1 Andrews to RT, 7 Aug. 1932 [RB].
2 RT's son Shamindranath died in 1907, aged eleven. See the account of his death in letter 294.

259

To Leonard Knight Elmhirst

At his last speech in Shriniketan during Tagore's lifetime, a visiting Leonard Elmhirst looked back some fifteen years to his inauguration of the 'institute for rural reconstruction' in 1922 and concluded:

> To respect the individual, to treat each day as a new opportunity for some creative experiment, to look upon the whole of life and all its processes as the natural playground for human art and scientific measurement: these habits of mind I learnt to appreciate from our founder-president, and, fail as one is bound to do, lacking that strength and poise that seem to come to him from his inner certainty of vision and of the meaning to life, I can never be too grateful for the opportunity he gave me to draw upon his inspiration.[1]

Elmhirst supported Shriniketan financially with money provided by his wife, Dorothy, from 1922 until Indian Independence in 1947, funding a number of staff positions and schemes for overseas training of those staff in agricultural science and related disciplines. Throughout, there was a fundamental tension between Tagore's and Elmhirst's views of the role of science in development. As Rabindranath makes clear in this letter to Elmhirst, his most eloquent letter on the subject, he was convinced that (to put it at its simplest) science must be subservient to society, and not vice versa. And he was intensely irritated by the standard civil service criticism of Shriniketan, that its methods were 'unscientific'. In late 1932, he responded to one such critique as follows:

> We admit we may lack the full-fledged machinery of science, but we certainly possess the vital gift of sympathy. The latter I consider to be far more indispensable in dealing with one's fellow-beings. You cannot deal with humanity merely through expensive systems . . . Due to their profound concern for the well-being of villagers, whom they do not consider to be a problem but as part of their own social being, our workers are inevitably led to devise means wherewith to mitigate their suffering. This brings in science, which has to stand the test of honest conscience and of daily utility, a harder test surely than that to which theoretical criticisms by an alien superciliousness dare submit.[2]

While he never regarded Leonard Elmhirst in this way, Tagore was disturbed by the vast resources available at Dartington, as compared to Shriniketan, and he constantly warned Elmhirst against importing methods which had worked well there into Shriniketan, Dartington's Bengali progenitor (see letter 204). Elmhirst, out of his deep respect for Tagore, took note of these warnings.

Santiniketan, [West Bengal, India]
3 September 1932

My dear Leonard,

I have just seen the letter which Ali has sent to you.[3] I generally try to remain silent when things become tangled and allow them to find their own solution. But the letter in question has suddenly revealed to me the fact that forces are working [to create] a complete deviation from the path which we pursued when we first began our work. And this is the only reason why I feel impelled in spite of my weak health and mental depression, to enunciate once again the principle which represents the ideal of Sriniketan. It is the principle of life and completeness.

It is true that when Ali first came to us I assured him complete freedom [in] the work which he was going to take in hand. I also had the idea that it should be something comprehensive and not fractional. It may seem foolish of me to anticipate but I am sure you know this is how I always welcome all the workers who come to me expressing their willingness to offer their service for the love of the cause. It does not mean that we have things ready for them like a cage for [a] bird, but that they should have to win themselves [a] seat which [will be] their own, through patience and perseverance, through establishing mutual understanding among their colleagues and firm faith in the institution in spite of obstructions and deficiencies that are often inevitable. If they fail then they should not begin to accuse everybody else but themselves for choosing [a] particular path which must have been foreign to them. You know you had from me the same unstinted welcome yourself when you first came to me as a stranger. Your path was not too smooth and there were factors that were obdurately obstructive. You won your place and justified my trust in you. You won it through your power of vision, through the wisdom that was helped by imagination, that could see things in their totality and would not accept as final whatever was imperfect during [the] process of [becoming].

The ideal, which I cherish in my heart for the work I have been struggling to build up through the best portion of my mature life, [does] need qualifications that are not divided into compartments. It was not the Kingdom of the Expert in the midst of the inept and ignorant which we wanted to establish – although the experts' advice [is] valuable. The villages are waiting for the living touch of creative faith and not for the cold aloofness of science which uses efficient machinery for extracting statistics, the statistics that deal with fragments of dissected life. I remember how you came fresh from your university and you were absurdly young but you were not in the least academic or aridly intellectual. With your instinctive humanity you came into the closest touch with the living being which is the village, and which is not a mere intellectual problem that [can] be solved through the help of arithmetical figures. I have personal experience of such scientists who think they know human facts without taking the trouble to know the man himself. It is not for them to create and not even to construct, they have never done [this], though they help. You had human sympathy in abundance which was the principal motive power that carried you across all the difficulties that stood against you in their congregated might. You rightly named your work Village Reconstruction Work, for it was a living work comprehending village life in all its various activities and not merely productive of analytic knowledge.

One may compare it with other institutions of similar nature in other big countries and be so ashamed of the paltriness of our own efforts [that we may be advised] to abandon them.[4] It is like comparing the mothers of our country to those in the West who possibly carry on their maternal duties more intelligently and with greater efficiency [than we do], and [then] to say that mothers' business should altogether be given up in India. And yet mothers' love *does* work even in the East though not fully supplemented by medical science. The principal element is there and similarly the valuable gift of sympathy in some of our humble workers has worked miracles which must not be contemptuously mentioned because [they have] not been measured [or] accurately recorded.

The immense benefit realised by the surrounding villages through the constant inspiration of sympathy and encouragement of Sriniketan must never be belittled in favour of some impersonal abstractions of science, however valuable they may be. I who am no scientist, set more value upon this human side of our service than upon anything which is academic. I can never believe that specialists are in their proper place at the head of an organisation where constant coordination of human factors [has] to be made through personal contact and wisdom born of sympathy. The function of specialists, with their equipment for detailed analysis and [their] statistics, should be to serve the makers of history, the guides and lovers of men who, possessing the gift of imaginative understanding, can vitalise knowledge and make it acceptable to others.

Possibly you may have heard by this time that [as] I [near] my end I [have been] appointed [by] our university as a lecturer in literature. My fellow professors are likely to look down upon me for not being an expert in accurate measurement [of] literary parallelism and [for] being completely ignorant of the archaeology of literature. But literature is organic to me, it would hurt me to treat it in fragments. I myself have approached it through direct touch and not through logical training and I can only try to help my students [to a] realisation of literature not through pedantry but [through] inner experience. In the same way I shall claim that direct touch of life [for] Sriniketan, that sympathy by which our experience of men is truly formed and enriched. At the same time science must have its place there but not to swamp it and Sriniketan must never be hardened into a scientific laboratory but be a living growth and an active service of love.

You will be glad to know that we have now on our staff for three months a distinguished educator from New Zealand, Mr N. Jacobson who has been highly recommended by Dewey and others and has already proved his ability to inspire our workers with creative ideas of education.[5] Owing to lack of resources we are unfortunately not able to retain his services for a longer period but our teachers are taking full advantage of his cooperation and hope to derive lasting benefit from his experience of educational organisation.

My best love to you and Dorothy.

Ever yours
Rabindranath Tagore

Source: MS original in Dartington Trust archives [Dartington]; letter published in Dutta and Robinson (eds.), *Purabi*, pp. 108–10.

1 L. K. Elmhirst, 'Our work at Shriniketan', *VBN*, Jan. 1939, p. 53.
2 'Rural welfare methods', *MR*, Dec. 1932, pp. 683–4. RT was responding to C. F. Strickland's *Review of Rural Welfare Activities in India 1932* (Calcutta, 1932), pp. 30–1, which remarked that 'the spirit of the institution [Shriniketan], possibly even the institution itself, may not long outlive Dr Tagore', and that 'the work done, with lofty intention and unselfish labour, may be unscientific and superficial'.
3 Ali: Hashim Amir Ali, Elmhirst fellow in economic research at Shriniketan, 1931–4.
4 This was a clear reference to Dartington, among other institutions RT had visited in his European travels.
5 John Dewey (1859–1952): educationist and philosopher.

260

To Mahatma Gandhi

(telegram)

On 4 August 1932, the British Government announced the so-called Communal Award: Hindus, Muslims and some other communities, including Europeans and

Untouchables, were to have separate electorates in the constitutional reform of India. This was the demand of the Untouchable leader B. R. Ambedkar, also supported by many Muslims. But to Gandhi (and to Tagore) it was anathema: Untouchables – Harijans, as Gandhi called them, 'People of God' – were Hindus and must be treated as such. Britain, with the connivance of Indians, must not be permitted to divide the nation. In protest Gandhi announced that from 20 September he would fast 'unto death' if the decision was not revoked.

The announcement was made first in a letter to the British prime minister Ramsay MacDonald and in conversation with Gandhi's fellow prisoners in jail in Pune. In mid-September, the plan became public knowledge. Among the many messages showered on Gandhi was this telegram from Tagore sent on 19 September, which reached him in jail just as he was handing a letter to the jail superintendent asking Rabindranath for his opinion of the planned fast and, if possible, his support. Gandhi had written, 'You have been to me a true friend because you have been a candid friend often speaking your thoughts aloud. I had looked forward to a firm opinion from you one way or the other. But you have refused to criticise . . . If your heart approves of my action I want your blessing.'[1]

Santiniketan, [West Bengal, India]
19 September 1932

It is worth sacrificing precious life for the sake of India's unity and her social integrity. Though we cannot anticipate what effect it may have upon our rulers who may not understand its immense importance for our people we feel certain that the supreme appeal of such self-offering to the conscience of our own countrymen will not be in vain. I fervently hope that we will not callously allow such national tragedy to reach its extreme length. Our sorrowing hearts will follow your sublime penance with reverence and love.[2]

Rabindranath Tagore

Source: MS copy at Rabindra Bhavan, Shantiniketan; telegram published in *VBQ*, 35, Nos. 1–4 (Gandhi Number), May 1969–April 1970, p. 238.

1 *VBQ*, 35, Nos. 1–4 (Gandhi Number), May 1969–April 1970, p. 230–1. The letter was sent, but in the meantime Gandhi wired RT, calling his telegram 'your loving and magnificent wire' which 'will sustain me in the midst of the storm I am about to enter' (*ibid.*, p. 231).
2 On the morning of 20 Sept., in Shantiniketan, RT gave an address in which he spoke of the meaning of the fast (translated in *VBN*, Oct. 1932, pp. 27–9).

261

To Ramsay MacDonald[1]

C. F. Andrews, returning to Britain after the death of Nitindranath Gangulee in Germany in early August (see letter 258), informed Ramsay MacDonald, the prime minister and a political patron of Andrews, of Tagore's great personal loss.

416   *Selected letters of Rabindranath Tagore*

MacDonald wrote a condolence letter on 24 August, mistakenly referring to the death of Rabindranath's 'son', rather than grandson, to which Tagore wrote this reply a month later, adding a PS about the political situation (Gandhi's fast was then in its fifth day).[2]

MacDonald's letter was not a formality. He admired Bengal, and in 1913, just after the award of the Nobel prize, he paid a visit to Shantiniketan and wrote a sensitive article about it for the British press.[3] In his book, *The Awakening of India* (London, 1910), based on an earlier visit to India, MacDonald wrote of hearing the hymns of Rabindranath: 'The music, much of it new and all so unlike our own, clung round our hearts and stole again and again all that day into our ears.'[4]

Santiniketan, [West Bengal, India]
24 September 1932

My dear Mr MacDonald

It was my grandson whom I lost lately; who was young, lovable and promising. My sorrow is for him as well as for his mother who is stricken sore. However, having travelled a long path of life I have learnt the lesson of death and have received the training which enables me to be reconciled to the inevitable. Please accept my thanks for your kind letter of sympathy and my best wishes.

Very sincerely yours,
Rabindranath Tagore

[PS] I must take this opportunity to let you know that though I keep away from politics I cannot help feeling sadly concerned at the turn which our negotiations have taken at last. I appeal to you for the sake of humanity – do nothing to help the alienation of our country [from] yours, to embitter the memory of our relationship for good.

Source: MS copy at Rabindra Bhavan, Shantiniketan.

1 James Ramsay MacDonald (1866–1937): first Labour prime minister of Britain, who was prime minister in 1924, 1929–31, 1931–5; in 1913–14, he visited India as a member of the public services commission.
2 MacDonald to RT, 24 Aug. 1932 [RB].
3 'Mr Rabindranath Tagore's school', *Daily Chronicle*, 12 Jan. 1914.
4 MacDonald, *Awakening*, p. 73. RT had considerable respect for MacDonald up to this period. But in 1936 (after MacDonald had been replaced by Baldwin), in a speech on the 1932 Communal Award and its deleterious influence on Hindu–Muslim relations in Bengal, RT spoke of 'the late premier who betrayed his often-pronounced ideals when they concerned India' ('The communal decision', *MR*, Aug. 1936, p. 186).

262

To Mahatma Gandhi

On 26 September 1932, in the presence of Tagore and many others, Gandhi broke his fast against separate electorates, on receiving word that the British cabinet had accepted the so-called Poona Pact. The initial reaction in India was one of relief at his survival and an outburst of ceremonial breaking of caste taboos: wells and temples were opened to Untouchables, high-caste Hindus embraced Untouchables publicly and intercaste dinners took place.[1] But when the euphoria wore off, the inevitable orthodox Hindu reaction set in, especially in Bengal, where the Poona Pact had been highly damaging to the political power of high-caste Hindus and had greatly strengthened the power of Muslims.[2]

Tagore, now back in Bengal, felt that Gandhi should encourage the leading Hindu communal group, the Hindu Mahasabha, to make a gesture of goodwill to Muslims, as he expresses in this letter. But Gandhi, as so often, ignored Tagore's advice, and concentrated for the next few months and years on a campaign against untouchability.[3]

Calcutta, [West Bengal, India]
30 September 1932

Mahatmaji

Our people are wonder-struck at the impossible being made possible in these few days and there is a universal feeling of immense relief at your being saved for us. Now is the opportune moment when a definite command from you will rouse the Hindu community to make a desperate effort to win over the Mahommedans to our common cause. It is even more difficult of success than your fight against untouchability, for there is a deep rooted antipathy against the Moslems in most of our people and they also have not much love for ourselves. But you know how to move the hearts of those that are obdurate, and only you, I am sure, have the patient love that can conquer the hatred that has accumulated for ages. I do not know how to calculate political consequences but I believe that nothing can be too costly which would enable us to win their confidence and convince them that we understand their difficulties and their own point of view. However, it is not for me to advise you and I shall fully rely upon your own judgement as to the course that should be taken. Only one suggestion I must venture to make to you that you might ask the Hindu Mahasabha to make a conciliatory gesture towards the other party.[4]

I have no doubt that you are gaining strength and inspiring every moment strength and hope around you.

With reverent love I am

Ever yours
Rabindranath Tagore

Source: MS copy at Rabindra Bhavan, Shantiniketan; letter published in *Rabindra-Biksha*, *Paush* 1398 [Dec. 1991], pp. 16–17.

1 At Shantiniketan, during the fast itself, traditional low castes garlanded high-caste Hindus, such as the veteran Sanskrit scholar Vidhu Sekhar Sastri, and were garlanded in return; the high-caste Hindus also accepted food served by the low castes.
2 On the reaction of Bengal to the Poona Pact, see Joya Chatterji, *Bengal Divided: Hindu Communalism and Partition, 1932–1947* (Cambridge, 1994).
3 Gandhi to RT, 9 Oct. 1932: 'I have your beautiful letter. I am daily seeking light. This unity between Hindus and Muslims is also my life's mission' (*CWMG*, LI, p. 215).
4 Gandhi was close to Madan Mohan Malaviya, one of the leaders of the Hindu Mahasabha. The Mahasabha had little influence in Bengal at this time; later, in 1939, it was re-established there by Shyama Prasad Mookerjee [Mukhopadhyay], the son of Sir Ashutosh Mookerjee, and became a significant political force.

263

To Sir William Rothenstein

In April 1932, William Rothenstein published the second volume of his memoirs, *Men and Memories*, covering the period 1900–22, where he wrote about the episode in which Robert Bridges wanted to alter a poem from *Gitanjali* for his anthology, *The Spirit of Man* (see letters 97, 100–2, 104), to which request Tagore was extremely reluctant to agree. Rothenstein reminisced:

> I knew that it was said in India that the success of *Gitanjali* was largely owing to Yeats' rewriting of Tagore's English. That this is false can easily be proved. The original MS of *Gitanjali* in English and in Bengali is in my possession. Yeats did here and there suggest slight changes, but the main text was printed as it came from Tagore's hands. I could readily understand Rabindranath's hesitation, but he respected Bridges' judgement, and the poem was included in *The Spirit of Man*.[1]

Writing to Tagore some months after publication, Rothenstein further remarked, *inter alia*:

> Yeats was in London recently... He thought I had somewhat underestimated the help he and Sturge Moore gave you on your translations: that you could not discern the finer shades between used and unused phrases as they could. But you would be the first to admit that: I only wanted to rebut the malicious suggestions made in India – never here.[2]

Tagore's reply on this point suggests that the accusation still irritated him. He always hated to think of himself as someone courting publicity in the West, whether for his writing or for himself.

Santiniketan, [West Bengal, India]
26 November 1932

My dear friend,

Your letter has given me deep joy. I have suffered much in life and my grandson's death was one more poignant sorrow for me.[3] He was a lovable boy, and that his fresh young life should be taken away from us was hard indeed to bear. I have now recovered from the shock: experience widens our realisation of life which includes death as well.

Persia was a great inspiration to me.[4] It is splendid to find a nation courageously throwing off the stranglehold of inert tradition and relentless foreign exploitation, and emerging with fresh and rebellious life into the sunlight and freedom. I felt a stir of new consciousness in the air of Persia, which harmonised so well with the beauty of the land and the great culture of its people.

Coming back to my country I find things worse in India – a deepening gloom which has been relieved by the vigorous reforms set in motion by Mahatmaji's great fast.[5] Not being a politician I cannot presume to devise means and methods which may bring in better days for our peoples but I suffer with them. As you say there is exaggeration on both sides and I shrink from the aggressiveness inevitably produced by litigants both of whom are to blame for the present condition. The party whose voice is smothered by every means at the command of an efficient scientific power naturally attach too much importance to events which are inconsequential when seen in a wide perspective of truth. It is a pity that Sastri whom you rightly praise has been ruled out from the conference in London.[6]

Your letter has the subtle atmosphere of Art evoking many-coloured images of reality. Who would leave them for the harsh assertiveness of facts that carry no meaning in themselves and must wait for the inner mind to be related to significance?

You remind me of those early days of *Gitanjali*.

Poets are proverbially vain and I am no exception. Therefore if I cherish even an exaggerated notion of the value of my own poems which are in Bengali I am sure you will half humorously tolerate it. But I am no such fool as to claim an exorbitant price for my English which is a borrowed acquisition coming late in my life. I am sure you remember with what reluctant hesitation I gave up to your hand my manuscript of *Gitanjali* feeling sure that my English was of that amorphous kind for whose syntax a schoolboy could be reprimanded.[7] The next day you came rushing to me with assurance which I dared not take seriously and to prove to me the competence of your literary judgement you made three copies of those translations and sent them to Stopford Brooke, Bradley and Yeats.[8] The letter which Bradley sent to you in answer left no room for me to feel diffident about the merit of those poems and Stopford Brooke's opinion also was a corroboration. These were enthusiastic as far as I remember. But even then I had no doubt that it was not the language but the earnest feeling expressed in a simple manner which touched their hearts. That was [ample] enough for a foreigner and the unstinted praise offered to me by those renowned critics was a great deal more than I could ever expect. Then came those delightful days when I worked with Yeats and I am sure the magic of his pen helped my English to attain some quality of permanence. It was not at all necessary for my own reputation that I should find my place in the history of your literature. It was an accident for which you were also responsible and possibly most of all was Yeats. But yet sometimes I feel almost ashamed that I whose undoubted claim has been recognised by my countrymen to a sovereignty in our own world of letters should not have waited till it was discovered by the outside world in its own true majesty and environment, that I should ever go out of my way to court the attention of others having their own language for their enjoyment and use. At least it is never the function of a poet to personally help in the transportation of his poems to an alien form and atmosphere, and be responsible for any unseemly risk that may happen to them. However, you must own that you alone were to blame for this and not myself. To the end of my days I should have felt happy and contented to think that the translations I did were merely for private recreation and never for public display if you did not bring them before your readers. Please thank Yeats once again on my behalf for the help which he rendered to my poems in their perilous adventure of a foreign reincarnation and assure him that I at least never underrate the value of his literary comradeship. Latterly I have written and published both prose and poetry in English, mostly translations, unaided by any friendly help, but this again I have done in order to express my ideas, not for gaining any reputation for my mastery in the use of a language which can never be mine.[9]

It is sad that some of our artists should feel that they have little scope for creative work in our own land.[10] Burman, as far as I know, is still in Tipperah [Tripura] state, and there is a danger of his wasting his talents for want of proper stimulation.[11]

European art, like European literature has its great message for us, and this can be truly realised only when we have developed our own individuality which can react to it and assimilate it into the living texture of its being. What is fatal for our creative workers is to get into the habit of depending upon the approbation of western critics and trying to come up to their expectations. The standard of critical judgement must be in the artists' own realisations and in the atmosphere which surrounds them. I feel that the present ferment in India's social and cultural life should open up new vistas before our artists, giving them abundant material wherewith to enrich their art. Nanda Lal and others have already felt the need of a new orientation in their technique and subject matter and their recent works show a vigorous departure from traditions and that spirit of creative adventure which you speak of so beautifully.[12]

Ever sincerely yours,
Rabindranath Tagore

Source: MS original in Rothenstein Papers [Harvard]; letter published in Lago (ed.), *Imperfect Encounter*, pp. 344–7.

1 Rothenstein, *Men and Memories*, p. 301. RT first mentioned this rumour in Feb. 1914 in letters (81 and 82) to Thomas Sturge Moore and Rothenstein, and it had wide currency in the years after that, especially in Bengal.
2 Rothenstein to RT, 4 Nov. 1932, in Lago (ed.), *Imperfect Encounter*, p. 343. On Yeats' role in RT's translations, see Dutta and Robinson, *Rabindranath Tagore*, pp. 183–4, and letters 55 and 57.
3 On the death of Nitindranath, see letter 258.
4 RT flew to Persia in April 1932 and returned to Calcutta in early June. He was welcomed by many, including Reza Shah Pehlavi and King Feisal of Iraq.
5 On Gandhi's fast, see letters 260 and 262.
6 Sastri: V. S. Srinivasa Sastri (1869–1946): Moderate politician; he was member, viceroy's legislative council, 1916–20. His group, the Indian National Liberal Federation, was unrepresented at the third Round Table Conference in late 1932.
7 According to RT, he was 'reluctant' to show Rothenstein his translations, but according to Rothenstein, Tagore offered the translations the moment they met in London and 'begged that I would accept them' (Rothenstein, *Men and Memories*, p. 262). See Dutta and Robinson, *Rabindranath Tagore*, pp. 164–5. Rothenstein's account seems more probable than RT's.
8 Stopford Brooke (1832–1916): churchman. Bradley: Andrew Cecil Bradley (1851–1935): Shakespeare scholar; he was professor of poetry, University of Oxford. See Rothenstein, *Men and Memories*, pp. 262–3. On the reaction of Yeats, see letters 46 and 49.
9 From the 1920s until his death, RT published many English translations of his poems, in *VBQ* and *MR* especially, but some were published abroad, e.g. in the *Spectator*.
10 Rothenstein was much involved in helping Indian artists find work in Britain, notably in the decoration of India House. But he increasingly felt that they should work in India, deriving their inspiration from Indian, not European life. As he percipiently told RT in his letter, 'Do they really care so much for your mythological tales, and so little for the beauty of everything under the light of the sun?' (Lago (ed.), *Imperfect Encounter*, p. 343).
11 D. K. Dev Burman (1902–95): painter; member of the Tripura royal family. He was a student at the Royal College of Art, 1929–30, and was one of the mural painters at India House.
12 Nanda Lal: Nanda Lal Bose.

264

To Mahatma Gandhi

The barring of temples, with their sacred images, to low-caste Hindus (and of course Muslims and Christians) was a major social and political issue in the period following Gandhi's fast of September 1932. In November, for instance, Tagore wrote a letter about it to the zamorin of Calicut, a leading trustee of the Guruvayur temple, arguing that he must welcome Untouchables in the temple: 'Everlasting shame and ignominy will be our deserved fate if we fail . . . to uphold all that is pure and just in the great religious traditions of our country.'[1]

Tagore himself did not require images for worship, of course, nor did he visit Hindu temples. Worship at Shantiniketan was generally conducted in a *mandir*, built under the aegis of Maharshi Debendranath Tagore in 1890-1; this was an ornamental wrought-iron structure, consisting mainly of glass, some of it multi-coloured, with a fine marble floor – a sort of mini-Crystal Palace.[2]

In March 1933, Boyd Tucker, the American missionary who knew both Tagore and Gandhi (see letter 226), suggested to Gandhi that temple entry for Untouchables was not what he should be fighting for, since it was wrong to enclose God in any kind of structure. Tucker claimed that Tagore was in support of this view, but Gandhi was unconvinced. Citing the existence of the *mandir* at Shantiniketan, Gandhi then referred to his own ashram at Sabarmati where 'we have no building, no walls, but the cardinal points are the walls, the sky is the roof and mother earth is the floor; nevertheless, the spot that has been selected for the morning and the evening prayers has all the essentials of a temple.'[3] He suggested that his letter be shown to Tagore by Tucker, who might then discuss the matter with Rabindranath. Tucker did so, and this letter is Tagore's direct response to Gandhi.

Santiniketan, [West Bengal, India]
[March 1933]

Dear Mahatmaji

It is needless to say that I do not at all relish the idea of divinity being enclosed in a brick and mortar temple for the special purpose of exploitation by a particular group of people. I strongly believe that it is possible for simple-hearted people to realise the presence of God in the open air, in a surrounding free from all artificial obstruction. We know a sect in Bengal, illiterate and not dominated by Brahminical tradition who enjoy a perfect freedom of worship profoundly universal in character. It was the prohibition for them to enter temples that has helped them in their purity of realisation.[4]

The traditional idea of Godhead and conventional forms of worship hardly lay emphasis upon the moral worth of religious practices[;] their essential value lies in the conformity to custom which creates in the minds of the worshippers an abstract sense of sanctity and sanction. When we argue with them in the name of justice and humanity it is contemptuously ignored for as I have said the moral appeal of the cause has no meaning for them and you know that there are practices and legends connected with a number of our sectarian creeds and practices which are ignoble and irrational.

There is a tradition of religion connected with temple worship, and though such traditions can be morally wrong and harmful, yet they cannot merely be ignored. There the question comes of changing them, of widening their range and character. There can be differences of opinion with regard to the methods to be adopted. From the point of view of the trustees of traditions they are acting according to an inherent sense of property in preserving them as they are, in keeping the enjoyment of idol worship in temples for exclusive groups of people. They not only deny the right of such worship to Christians and Mohammedans but to sections of their own community. Particular temples and deities are their own property and they keep them locked up in an iron chest. In this they are acting according to traditional religion which allows them such freedom, rather enjoins them to act in this manner. A reformer in dealing with such morally wrong traditions cannot adopt coercion and yet as in fighting with other wrong and harmful customs he must exert moral force and constantly seek to rectify them. This fight is necessary. I do not think Tucker makes this point clear.

As to the Santiniketan prayer hall it is open to all peoples of every faith. Just as its doors do not shut out anybody so there is nothing in the simple form of worship which excludes people of different religions. Our religious service could as well take place under the trees, its truth and sacredness would not at all be affected but perhaps enhanced by such a natural environment. Difficulties of climate and season intervene, otherwise I do not think separate buildings are really necessary for prayer and communion with the divine.

I have sent a poem for the *Harijan* – translating it from one of my recent Bengali writings.[5] I do hope it is one in spirit with the ideal of the *Harijan* which I read with much pleasure and interest. There can be no more hopeful sign for India than the fact that her repressed humanity is waking up as a result of the great fast.

With loving regards

Yours sincerely
Rabindranath Tagore

Source: MS copy at Rabindra Bhavan, Shantiniketan; letter published in *VBQ*, 35, Nos. 1–4 (Gandhi Number), May 1969–April 1970, pp. 238–40.

1 RT to zamorin of Calicut, 16 Nov. 1932, in *Hindu*, Madras, 6 Dec. 1932; see also Dutta and Robinson, *Rabindranath Tagore*, p. 309.
2 On the *mandir* at Shantiniketan, see Andrew Robinson, 'A poet's vision: the houses of Rabindranath Tagore', in Christopher W. London (ed.), *Architecture in Victorian and Edwardian India* (Bombay, 1994), pp. 119–21.
3 Gandhi to Tucker, 4 March 1933, *CWMG*, LIII, p. 466.
4 The sect was the Bauls, whose songs were of particular interest to RT; see 'Bauler gan' (Baul songs), *RR(AS)*, II, pp. 131–7.
5 'The Sacred Touch', *Harijan*, 25 March 1933/'Snan Shamapan', *Punashcha*, *RR*, XVI, pp. 109–11. The poem was written at the beginning of March 1933. Gandhi had requested a contribution to *Harijan* in a letter to RT on 20 Feb. 1933 (*CWMG*, LIII, p. 363).

265

To Frieda Hauswirth Das[1]

In the 1920s, marriages between Indians and Europeans were rare. Frieda Hauswirth was a Swiss woman who completed her academic studies in California and there married an Indian (Oriya) student of sugar technology, Sarangadhar Das, in 1917. In 1920 she returned with him to India, and lived there for eight years. They eventually parted because she could not cope with the demands of establishing a sugar plantation in the jungles of Orissa.

After ceasing to live in India (though she continued to visit regularly), Frieda

Hauswirth Das began writing vividly about the country.[2] During the 1930s, she published a series of books, beginning with *A Marriage to India* (London, 1931), a lively, passionate personal account that is probably her best book.[3] *Purdah: The Status of Indian Women* (London, 1932) followed a year later. Written partly to rebut *Mother India* (New York, 1927), the notorious shocker by Katherine Mayo ('Maiden-aunt Mayo', as Das called her), *Purdah* derived its strength, once again, from its author's inside knowledge of purdah in many parts of India, but showed some of the defects of partisanry.[4] Tagore, in writing about the book to Das in this letter, singles out her treatment of the Brahmins, with considerable justification. For the book is consistently negative about Brahminism, from its early statement that 'there could be no uncontested or secure supremacy for Brahmins until woman lost her high estate, stood degraded and branded as an inferior being in the eyes of men, and was moulded into a mindless slave to religious dictation', right to its closing page.[5]

[Shantiniketan, West Bengal, India]
27 March 1933

Dear Mrs Das

I read your *Purdah* with keen pleasure and can unhesitatingly recommend it to all those who want a genuine and penetrating picture of Indian womanhood. You have drawn richly upon past literature and history of our country and traced our traditions to their living sources showing how most of our current conventions are the result of decadence and decay of our national vitality. Your presentation of the modern women's movements in India is superb.

I do not quite agree when you make the Brahmins responsible for all the evils existing in our society and run them down from Manu's day to ours. I think there is some overemphasis in your account. The Brahmins in the middle ages reflected the times as much as others did, and often associated themselves with movements which we would not support now not because they diabolically wanted to injure society but simply because they had to represent their own age. As a matter of truth, they belonged to the aristocracy of intellect, and maintained a purity of ideals and an austerity of habit which have done great benefit to our people for generations.

Another point has to be considered. The social aberrations which appear on the surface of a nation's life are not indicative of the essential nature of its peoples. No one would claim that witch-burning, inquisition, and other such social crimes of the West indicate some radical and characteristic traits of the European mind. In India, too, we had and still have our social wrongs but they are on the surface and merely prove that our daily life has yet to be fully harmonised to our ideals. In medieval India great saints and seers took up this great work of social uplift, and had the courage to offer relentless fight to customs which wronged our humanity. They often belonged to the lowest strata of society and yet had the closest cooperation of the high-caste Hindus. In their campaign for social reform they were joined by their own daughter, wife and other women members of their family who were held in great veneration by the public.

I consider your book to be one of the most significant and enduring contributions to the understanding of modern India.

Your book on monkeys is delightful.[6] You go deep into the life of rural India, and show how subtly it is harmonised with the larger life of bird and beast and insect and trees through a cosmic feeling of fellowship and faith characteristic of Indian thought. Your manner of expression is brilliant and your way of presenting the characteristic qualities of Indian life and habit very effective indeed. It is a book which will be enjoyed alike by the young and the old and bring together the western and the eastern peoples in common ties of sympathy.

I do hope you are getting on well with your new book which I will be very much interested to read when it comes out.

With kindest regards,

Sincerely yours
Rabindranath Tagore

Source: MS copy at Rabindra Bhavan, Shantiniketan.

1 Frieda Mathilda Hauswirth Das (1886–1974): writer. Her career, her vigorous combination of sympathy and exasperation with India, and her occasional blindspots are slightly reminiscent of E. J. Thompson, RT's biographer.
2 Besides *A Marriage to India* and the two books mentioned by RT, Das published *Gandhi* (1931) and *Into the Sun* (1933), as well as two novels in German (1937, 1938). Her English books were all published in London.
3 This book contains several interesting passages on Bengal and two on RT, including a description of a performance of *Natir Puja* at Jorasanko (Das, *A Marriage to India*, pp. 159–60).
4 On RT's reaction to *Mother India*, see Dutta and Robinson, *Rabindranath Tagore*, pp. 279–80, 284, 285.
5 Das, *Purdah*, pp. 24–5.
6 *Leap-Home and Gentlebrawn* (London, 1932). Das described this book in the introduction to *Purdah* as 'a series of linked tales' that 'beneath their superstructure of fiction' were 'based on this [same] foundation of actuality and experience' (Das, *Purdah*, p. viii).

266

To Mahatma Gandhi

On 2 May 1933, Gandhi, still in jail in Pune, wrote a note to Tagore: 'It is just now 1.45 a.m. and I think of you and some other friends. If your heart endorses contemplated fast, I want your blessings again.'[1] Tagore replied on 3 May from Calcutta by telegram: 'Pray reconsider decision for the sake of humanity which cannot spare you now.'[2]

Unlike the fast of September 1932, Tagore was instinctively as well as rationally opposed to Gandhi's latest plan to fast for twenty-one days. Few of the Mahatma's friends and associates were in favour, and many, including his wife, were strongly against.

The change of attitude between one fast and the next stems from the different goals of the two fasts, as stated by Gandhi. On 8 May 1933, soon after commencing the fast at noon, he issued a statement, which was printed in the Bombay press on 9 May:

> Every day brings me fresh justification for the ordeal that God the Truth has sent me. The discoveries I am making [about the practice of untouchability] would have paralysed me, but for the fast. Whatever it may mean for the cause, it will certainly be my saving. Whether I survive the fast or not, is a matter of little moment. Without it I would, in all probability, have been useless for further service of Harijans [Untouchables], and for that matter, any other service.
>
> Those friends who have sent me urgent wires dissuading me from the step will, I

hope, appreciate the fact that for a person built as I am, such fasts are indispensable. This I say apart from my claim, by which I stand, that it was God's call . . .

A telegram was received by me from a Harijan Association that my fast was unnecessary, as the Harijans do not stand in need of assistance from the caste Hindus. From its own standpoint, the Association is right. Only it should be clearly understood that the fast is taken not to oblige the Harijans, but for purification of self and associates . . .

Sanatanist [i.e. the most orthodox] Hindus scent further coercion in this fast. When they realise that it cannot be broken before its period, even if every temple was opened and untouchability wholly removed from the heart, they will perhaps admit that it cannot be regarded as in any way coercive. The fast is intended to remove bitterness, to purify hearts and to make it clear that the movement [against untouchability] is wholly moral, to be prosecuted by wholly moral persons. May God bless the ordeal and fulfil its purpose.[3]

Even before he read this statement, Tagore was opposed to the fast, as his letter of 9 May (this letter) makes clear. His letter of 11 May, written after reading the statement, shows that Tagore did not feel 'self-purification' to be a valid goal for a fast that might well end in death; better, Tagore thought, to purify oneself by loving and helping others. In his opinion, Gandhi was putting his own purity before India's crying need of his leadership.

From the beginning of their relationship, the two men had differed fundamentally in their attitude towards life's purpose. Both of them spoke and wrote constantly of joy and of the spirit of renunciation, but they gave opposite emphases to the two emotions. Gandhi, it is said, once delightedly answered a western journalist who had asked for the secret of his life in five words: 'I can give it to you in three, "Tena tyaktena bhunjithah" – renounce and rejoice.'[4] Tagore would have wanted this put the other way around: rejoice and renounce. He, like Gandhi, was deeply influenced by the opening verse of the *Isopanishad*: 'All that is changing in this changeful world, know that it is enveloped by Him who is the Lord of all things. Therefore take your enjoyment in renunciation. Never covet wealth.' But Gandhi translated the verse with a significant difference, as follows: 'This whole world is the garment of the Lord. Renounce it then, and enjoy it, receiving it back as the gift of God.'[5]

As Tagore told Gandhi's disciple Miraben (Madeleine Slade), 'According to the *Upanishad* the reconciliation of the contradiction between *tapasya* [austerity] and *ananda* [joyfulness] is at the root of creation – and Mahatmaji is the prophet of *tapasya* and I am the poet of *ananda*.'[6] Gandhi's May 1933 fast, entirely ascetic in its principle, therefore made little appeal to Tagore's personality: he saw it, at root, as life-denying not life-affirming. And its potentially disastrous consequences for India frightened him.

Nevertheless, once the fast was a fact, Tagore supported it. He sent Gandhi an encouraging telegram (letter 268) on 22 May, the fourteenth day of the fast, and a second telegram on 27 May, to be read as the fast was broken.[7]

Glen Eden, Darjeeling, [West Bengal, India]
9 May 1933

Dear Mahatmaji

Evidently the telegram which I sent to you some days ago has failed to reach its destination though it has appeared in some of the papers.

You must not blame me if I cannot feel a complete agreement with you at the immense responsibility you incur by the step you have taken. I have not before me the entire background of thoughts and facts against which should be placed your own judgement in order to understand its significance. From the beginning of creation there continue things that are ugly and wrong – the negative factors of existence – and the ideals which are positive and eternal ever wait to be represented by messengers of truth who never have the right to leave the field of their work in despair or disgust because of the impurities and imperfections in their surroundings. It is a presumption [on] my part to remind you that when Lord Buddha woke up to the multitude of miseries from which the world suffers he strenuously went on preaching the path of liberation till the last day of his earthly career. Death when it is physically or morally inevitable has to be bravely endured, but we have not the liberty to court it unless there is absolutely no other alternative for the expression of the ultimate purpose of life itself. It is not unlikely that you are mistaken about the imperative necessity of your present vow, and when we realise that there is a grave risk of its fatal termination, we shudder at the possibility of the tremendous mistake never having the opportunity of being rectified. I cannot help beseeching you not to offer such an ultimatum of mortification to God for His scheme of things and almost refuse the great gift of life with all its opportunities to hold up till its last moment the ideal of perfection which justifies humanity.

However I must confess that I have not the vision which you have before your mind, nor can I fully realise the call which has come only to yourself, and therefore whatever may happen I shall try to believe that you are right in your resolve and that my misgivings may be the outcome of a timidity of ignorance.

With love and reverence

Yours
Rabindranath Tagore

Source: MS copy at Rabindra Bhavan, Shantiniketan; letter published in *MR*, June 1933, p.704.

1 Gandhi to RT, 2 May 1933, *CWMG*, LV, p. 92.
2 RT to Gandhi, 3 May 1933, *Rabindra-Biksha*, Paush 1398 [Dec. 1991], p. 36, n. 16.
3 *CWMG*, LIV, pp. 156–7 (published in *Bombay Chronicle*, 9 May 1933).
4 Quoted in Jehangir P. Patel and Marjorie Sykes, *Gandhi: His Gift of the Fight* (Rasulia, 1987), p. 65.
5 RT's translation is quoted in 'Rabindranath Tagore on his father Debendranath Tagore', *VBQ*, 27, No. 1, 1961, p. 1; Gandhi's translation appears in Patel and Sykes, *Gandhi*, p. 65. Juan Mascaró translated the same verse as follows: 'Behold the universe in the glory of God and all that lives and moves on earth. Leaving the transient, find joy in the Eternal: set not your heart on another's possession' (Mascaró, *The Upanishads*, p. 49).
6 RT to Slade, 19 Dec. 1929, *VBQ*, 1, No. 1, 1985, p. 23.
7 RT to Gandhi, 27 May 1933: 'Relieved from poignant anxiety. With thankful heart we welcome this great day when from death's challenge you come out victorious to renew your fight against sacrilegious bigotry simulating piety and moral degeneracy of the powerful' (*Rabindra-Biksha*, Paush 1398 [Dec. 1991], p. 24).

267

To Mahatma Gandhi

Glen Eden, Darjeeling, [West Bengal, India]
11 May 1933

Dear Mahatmaji

I am trying clearly to find out the meaning of this last message of yours which is before the world today. In every important act of his life Buddha preached limitless love for all creatures. Christ said 'Love thine enemies' and that teaching of his found its final expression in the words of forgiveness he uttered for those who killed him. As far as I can understand, the fast that you have started carries in it the idea of expiation for the sins of your countrymen. But I ask to be excused when I say that the expiation can truly and heroically be done only by daily endeavours for the sake of those unfortunate beings who do not know what they do. The fasting which has no direct action upon the conduct of misdoers and which may abruptly terminate one's power further to serve those who need help, cannot be universally accepted and therefore it is all the more unacceptable for any individual who has the responsibility to represent humanity.

The logical consequence of your example, if followed, will be an elimination of all noble souls from the world leaving the morally feeble and down-trodden multitude to sink into the fathomless depth of ignorance and iniquity. You have no right to say that this process of penance can only be efficacious through your own individual endeavour and for others it has no meaning. If that were true you ought to have performed it in absolute secrecy as a special mystic rite which only claims its one sacrifice beginning and ending in yourself. You ask others to actively devote their energy to extirpate the evil which smothers our national life and enjoin only upon yourself an extreme form of sacrifice which is of a passive character. For lesser men than yourself it opens up an easy and futile path of duty by urging them to take a plunge into a dark abyss of self-mortification. You cannot blame them if they follow you in this special method of purification of their country, for all messages must be universal in their application and if not they should never be expressed at all.

The suffering that has been caused to me by the vow you have taken has compelled me to write to you thus – for I cannot bear the sight of a sublimely noble career journeying towards a finality which, to my mind, lacks a perfectly satisfying justification. And once again I appeal to you for the sake of the dignity of our nation which is truly impersonated in you, and for the sake of the millions of my countrymen who need your living touch and help to desist from any act that you think is good only for you and not for the rest of humanity.

With deepest pain and love
Rabindranath Tagore

Source: MS copy at Rabindra Bhavan, Shantiniketan; letter published in *MR*, June 1933, pp. 704–5.

428   *Selected letters of Rabindranath Tagore*

268

To Mahatma Gandhi

(telegram)

Darjeeling, [West Bengal, India]
22 May 1933

May your penance bring you close to the bosom of the Eternal away from the burdensome pressure of life's malignant facts thus freshening your spirit to fight them with vigorous detachment.

Rabindranath

Source: MS copy at Rabindra Bhavan, Shantiniketan; telegram published in *Rabindra-Biksha*, Paush 1398 [Dec. 1991], p. 23.

269

To Ramananda Chatterji [Chattopadhyay]

During his 1916 visit to San Francisco to lecture, Tagore had been provided with an escort after rumours that Indian revolutionaries, the Gahdr party, living in the area, were planning to assassinate him.[1] At the time Tagore scoffed at this, but in July 1933, the Calcutta *Statesman* published a report from an anonymous Sikh informant recently returned from many years living in America. The newspaper stated that, according to the informant,

> when Dr Tagore visited the United States during the war the [Gahdr] party actually deputed two of its members to murder the poet at the hotel in San Francisco where he was staying. The two men fell out in the lobby of the hotel as there was a difference of opinion between them as to whether Dr Tagore should be murdered, and thus the plot was disclosed. The motive for the attempted murder was that the Gahdr party regarded Dr Tagore as an agent of the British Government.[2]

This report prompted Tagore's friend, Ramananda Chatterji [Chattopadhyay], editor of the *Modern Review*, to ask Rabindranath for his considered reaction, which he gives in this letter.

Shantiniketan, [West Bengal, India]
28 Asharh 1340 [12 July 1933]

Shraddhashpadeshu

  When I was invited to lecture in San Francisco – probably in 1916 – secret agents came to my hotel and informed me that the Gahdr party active there was conspiring to murder me, and that for my protection several men would accompany me constantly.

I told them I did not believe it. They said, whether you believe it or not we are responsible for your safety because you are our guest. And they came and occupied the next-door room in the hotel. When I went out to lecture, they came with me and sat with me on the platform when I spoke. At the same time I also heard that some Sikhs got into a scuffle over me in the hotel lobby and the hotel management ejected them. I was told that the cause was that one group wanted to meet me and the opposing group tried to prevent them. There was no way to establish the true facts. When I first came to the city some of these people asked me to lecture. I noticed one thing, that they did not greet me and sat through with a dissatisfied look – I do not know whether they could grasp the spirit of my lecture or not, perhaps not. I discussed their peculiar behaviour with Pearson.[3] At that time my lectures were on the subject of nationalism. I spoke against the prevailing nationalism of the West. Pearson's guess was that the Gadhr party did not approve of my views. Anyway, after that I had no further contact with them – one reason being that my protectors prevented it. But right up to the end I could never believe that any Indian group intended to assassinate me and I regularly expressed my irritation at those who followed me around in the guise of protectors. When I had finished in San Francisco they even followed me to Los Angeles, though more discreetly.

My work entangles me in difficulties more than ever. The load is becoming unbearable, especially as Amiya's out of action.[4] I am trying gradually to divest myself of duties and responsibilities. And now the time has come to divorce my pen too.

Apnader
Shri Rabindranath Thakur

Source: MS original at Rabindra Bhavan, Shantiniketan; letter published in *CP*, XII, pp. 163–5.

1 See Dutta and Robinson, *Rabindranath Tagore*, pp. 204–5.
2 'Gahdr party and Dr Tagore', *Statesman*, 9 July 1933.
3 Pearson: W. W. Pearson, who acted as secretary of RT in America in 1916–17.
4 Amiya: Amiya Chakravarty, secretary to RT; he was feeling ill.

270

To Mahatma Gandhi

In September 1932, at the time of his visit to Pune to see Gandhi on fast, Tagore had supported the Poona Pact (see letter 262). With the passing of time, however, it became increasingly clear to him that the Pact would cause irreparable damage to Hindu–Muslim relations in Bengal. When, therefore, he was approached for his views on the Pact by a leading Bengali Hindu politician, Sir N. N. Sircar,[1] he recanted and issued a statement to Sircar on 24 July 1933, to the effect that out of his 'intolerable anxiety' for the health of Gandhi during the fast, he had agreed to support the Pact, 'which I now realise was a mistake from the point of view of our country's permanent interest'. This was published in the Indian press on 27 July, and Tagore also sent the statement to Gandhi, with this covering letter.[2]

Santiniketan, [West Bengal, India]
28 July 1933

Dear Mahatmaji

This is a copy of the message which, with very great pain and reluctance, I cabled to Sir Nripen and from which you will know how I feel about the Poona Pact. I am fully convinced that if it is accepted without modification it will be a source of perpetual communal jealousy leading to constant disturbance of peace and a fatal break in the spirit of mutual cooperation in our province.

With love and reverence,
Rabindranath Tagore

Source: MS copy at Rabindra Bhavan, Shantiniketan; letter published in *Rabindra-Biksha*, Paush 1398 [Dec. 1991], p. 31.

1 Sir Nripendranath Sircar (1876–1945): barrister and politician; appointed advocate-general of Bengal in 1928, he represented Bengali Hindus at the third Round Table Conference in London in 1932. In July 1933, he appeared before the parliamentary committee sitting in London to consider Indian constitutional reform, where he was able to announce RT's change of mind about the Poona Pact.
2 The statement appears in N. N. Sircar, *Sir N. N. Sircar's Speeches and Pamphlets* (B. N. Dutta Roy ed.; Calcutta, 1934), pp. 207–8, but minus its last paragraph in which RT criticised the British Government's handling of the Communal Award: Sircar clearly thought that to quote these remarks would be unhelpful to his case.

271

To Sarojini Naidu (Chattopadhyay)

In late November 1933, Sarojini Naidu organised a Tagore week in Bombay, with performances of his plays by the students of Shantiniketan and an exhibition of his paintings in the town hall. His previous visits to Bombay had not been particularly fruitful, but this was a success, because of the inimitable charm of his hostess. Although she had long since given up poetry for politics (see letter 111), she remained poetic in her approach to politics, which appealed to Tagore, and was close to many of the Congress leaders; thus she was an ideal conduit for Rabindranath into the public life of Bombay.

This letter was by way of a thank you to Naidu, before Tagore left Bombay.

Esplanade House, Waudby Road, Bombay, [India]
3 December 1933

Dear Sarojini,

You are great. Once I thought that you were as frivolous as I am. I still hope I was not wrong – but there is another side of your character, and I repeat once again that you are great. You have helped me as none else could have done but what is still more important to me is that I have come close to you and known you. You have amazing gifts which would have made me envious but I have loved you and that has saved me. I am afraid my language sounds absurdly sentimental, but I do not care. I expose myself to your delightful laughter, for I know it cannot be unkind to me. Please do not doubt my sincerity when I say that from this trip I carry back the memory of an experience which will be precious to me.

Ever yours,
Rabindranath Tagore

Source: MS copy at Rabindra Bhavan, Shantiniketan; letter published in *VBN*, April 1949, p. 100.

16 Rabindranath in Shantiniketan, with Jawaharlal Nehru, 1939

International nationalist (1934–1936)

Introduction

Though Indian politics continued to preoccupy Tagore in the mid-1930s, he was almost equally concerned at the parlous state of international relations, and the insidious undermining of humanitarian values in the West and in the Far East.

He knew that the growing cynicism about politics in the West, and the trough into which his western literary reputation had fallen, were connected. Literary taste in the 1930s was very different from what it had been before the Great War. And he also knew, but was less willing to accept, that his own feeble translations of his poetry had irretrievably damaged that reputation. During 1934–6, he therefore wavered as to whether to accept an offer from Macmillan to publish his English poetry and plays in a collected edition. Here was an opportunity to retranslate them, which was what most of them required, but Rabindranath felt that he had neither the energy nor the literary skill for this daunting task. Eventually, he gave the go-ahead for an edition based on the existing translations, anonymously edited by Ernest Rhys, the editor of Everyman's Library and one of his most loyal British friends. This appeared in late 1936 and was ignored by the critics, though it sold well and remained in print for decades.

Fundraising for Visva-Bharati remained an imperative challenge. But with advancing age, Tagore was finally forced to admit that he could no longer maintain the institution by touring India with his Shantiniketan troupe. In 1935, he appealed to Gandhi, who, despite their differences, put his mind to fundraising. In 1936, the Mahatma presented Tagore with a cheque, which temporarily solved the institution's cash crisis.

272

To Mahatma Gandhi

On 15 January 1934, a huge earthquake struck Bihar in the area north of Patna. There were high casualties and massive destruction. (Jawaharlal Nehru at Allahabad could hardly keep his balance.) Tagore was in Shantiniketan, Gandhi on tour in south India fighting untouchability. On 24 January, after calm reflection, Gandhi stated publicly that the earthquake and untouchability were linked. 'You may call me superstitious if you like. A man like me cannot but believe that this earthquake is a divine chastisement sent by God for our sins.'[1]

Tagore read a report in the newspapers and immediately wrote an article for publication, which he sent to Gandhi with the following letter.

[Shantiniketan, West Bengal, India]
28 January 1934

Dear Mahatmaji

The press reports that you in a recent speech referring to the recent earthquake in Bihar spoke as follows, 'I want you, the superstitious enough to believe with me that the earthquake is a divine chastisement for the great sin we have committed against those whom we describe as Harijans'. I find it difficult to believe it. But if this be your real view on the matter, I do not think it should go unchallenged. Herewith you will find a rejoinder from me. If you are correctly reported in the press, would you kindly send it to the press? I have not sent it myself for publication, for I would be the last person to criticise you on unreal facts.[2]

I am looking forward to meeting you here.

With deep love,

Yours as ever
Rabindranath Tagore

Source: MS copy at Rabindra Bhavan, Shantiniketan; letter published in *VBQ*, *35*, Nos. 1–4 (Gandhi Number), May 1969–April 1970, p. 242.

1 *CWMG*, LVII, p. 44.
2 RT's article and Gandhi's response appear in appendix 2. On their disagreement, see Dutta and Robinson, *Rabindranath Tagore*, pp. 312–14.

273

To Muriel Lester[1]

During the 1920s and 1930s, a number of westerners were attracted to both Gandhi and Tagore, one of them being Muriel Lester, a pacifist with Christian socialist convictions who had given up a comfortable family income to live and work with the poor in London's East End. In 1931, she became Gandhi's host in London during the second Round Table Conference, when he stayed at Kingsley Hall in Bow, the centre that Lester had founded in 1915. She became very close to Gandhi, but not to Tagore.

Lester's first visit to India was in 1926, when she stayed at Gandhi's ashram and also visited Shantiniketan. This letter to her refers to her 1934 visit, during which she toured with Gandhi and attempted to act as an intermediary with high officials such as the governor of Bengal, Sir John Anderson, and the viceroy, Lord Willingdon. In her letter to Tagore, Lester wrote with typical robustness: 'I am ashamed of the childish behaviour of many of my fellow-countrymen here; a sort of petulant intransigence . . . Barrels of whitewash are splashed sedulously over their underlings, from the policeman to the magistrate; but they use a microscope on their opponents' faults.'[2]

Santiniketan, [West Bengal, India]
26 April 1934

Dear Miss Muriel Lester

Let me thank you for your letter. Your remarks on the enclosed correspondence with the governor were so touched with genuine sympathy for our people that I could not help being moved by them. Yes, I too am an incorrigible idealist. My necessity for believing in others is real and imperative. I have real respect for your countrymen, despite all their doings here; and so long as they protest their good faith I cannot deny them partial credit for it and shall continue to appeal to the best that is in their character, trusting that one day they will wake up and redeem themselves from the disgrace of imperialist heritage which the circumstances of the past have bequeathed to them. We too will wake up and redeem our centuries of [complacent] inactivity and only when we both have redeemed our disgraces will we meet in the dignity of true friendship. In the meanwhile let us cooperate in these activities where cooperation is possible and where the insolence of authority does not defeat our human aspirations.

As regards Sir John Anderson's reply to your letter which you have kindly enclosed, in so far as it justifies the new Anti-Terrorist Bill, I understand it as little as you do; but is so far as it gives the Government's assurance actively to further rural reconstruction in our province, I can only thank him for it.[3]

My best wishes,

Sincerely yours,
Rabindranath Tagore

Source: MS copy at Rabindra Bhavan, Shantiniketan.

1 Muriel Lester (1883–1968): social worker and pacifist; from the mid-1920s she took an active interest in the cause of Indian independence, and became one of Gandhi's closest friends in England. See Jill Wallis, *Mother of World Peace: The Life of Muriel Lester* (London, 1993).
2 Lester to RT, n.d. [RB].
3 See letter 309 to Anderson, concerning the convicted terrorists in the Andaman Islands penal colony. Anderson had been appointed to Bengal with the specific brief of dealing with terrorism there.

274

To Amiya Chakravarty[1]

Tagore found fundraising for Visva-Bharati a wearying and demeaning business, whether he was appealing to westerners or to Indians, as we know from many previous letters. In December 1933, while visiting Hyderabad, he stated that in India, he received 'casual donations collected at the risk of my health and of an utter neglect of my vocation as a literary man'.[2]

His visit to Ceylon in 1934, mentioned in this letter, was a considerable artistic success.[3] But financially, it was a disaster.

Colombo, [Sri Lanka]
15 May 1934

Kalyaniyeshu

These are very hard times. In the first place, my ryots are destitute, the price of their crops being hopelessly low, and so the revenue is almost nil. The interest on the Nobel prize money has ceased.[4] The maharaja of Baroda [Vadodara] has stopped paying his monthly grant of Rs 600.[5] The expenses of my family – both my actual family and my Visva [-Bharati] family – are being met from the dregs of my income and from loans. Hence my having come out on tour with a troupe, in the hope of collecting money by presenting dance and music. Not long back, I raised something from Bombay, otherwise the situation would have been desperate.[6] Now I have reached Ceylon. We seem to have captured their minds but capturing their purses is not so easy – especially given the huge expense in bringing our group this far. With such a large outlay only a small profit can be expected. It is a bit like pouring water into a leaky pitcher – the money I put in does not seal the leak – and I have been importing money from abroad to maintain a steady flow. But I will not live forever.

If we can keep one of our people in Europe so as to stay in touch with the world, that would certainly be of benefit.[7] I have mentioned this to Rathi.[8] He is thinking about how we might find the means to do so. Even though the college entrance school at Shantiniketan is not Visva-Bharati's own offspring – it belongs to the Calcutta University – yet, in order to keep it running, we have driven our own work close to the abyss of bankruptcy; we may still go under. We are, so to speak, in the grip of an obsession – and such delusion is always more alluring than reality. My days of being personally involved in this matter are over. Visva-Bharati now has a constitution: though I must still toil for the institution, I pay my respects to it only from a distance.

Snehanurakta
Rabindranath Thakur

Source: MS original at Rabindra Bhavan, Shantiniketan; letter published in *CP*, XI, pp. 111–12.

1 Amiya Chakravarty (1901–86): secretary to RT, 1927–33; he accompanied RT during part of his European visit in 1930. From 1934 to 1939 he lived in Europe. See letter 287.
2 Letter to *Hyderabad Bulletin*, 15 Dec. 1933.
3 RT was in Ceylon from 9 May to 15 June 1934. On this visit, see Dutta and Robinson, *Rabindranath Tagore*, pp. 318–19.
4 The Nobel prize money was invested in a bank, which ceased to pay interest on it when new land-reform legislation was introduced (see letter 63).
5 RT lectured at Vadodara in Jan. 1930, at the invitation of the gaekwad (maharaja). But the relationship was never a close one (see Rathindranath Tagore, *Edges of Time*, pp. 155–6).
6 On RT's success in Bombay, see letter 271.
7 Chakravarty was in Oxford at this time. Presumably, in his letter to RT, he had suggested that it would be helpful if he could remain in Europe for some time, in order to represent the interests of Visva-Bharati.
8 Rathi: Rathindranath Tagore, then executive secretary of Visva-Bharati.

275

To N. E. B. Ezra[1]

In April 1934, N. E. B. Ezra, a Zionist newspaper editor in Shanghai, who had met Tagore when he visited China in 1924, wrote to him enclosing his article on 'Civilisation's debt to Asia', which included the statement: '[The] modern West gave us a Hitler with his new dispensation of hate and strife and murder; [the] modern East gave us a Tagore with his soulful plea for the union of humanity and the destruction of dark forces.'[2] Ezra requested a message from Tagore for publication.

Tagore's letter to Ezra is one of his very few public comments on the Nazi regime. In publishing it later in 1934, Ezra editorialised that he could not share Tagore's hopes for the Germans while ruled by Hitler: 'History will brand the Hitler regime as the most cowardly and infamous that has ever disfigured the annals of our civilisation.'[3]

Santiniketan, [West Bengal, India]
17 June 1934

Dear friend,

I thank for you for drawing my attention to your address on 'Civilisation's debt to Asia', published in *Israel's Messenger*, April 1934.

To me racial hatred in any form is a creed of barbarism and I cannot recognise the value of any cause in whose name nations and peoples indulge their gluttony of violence. We in India are striving to safeguard our growing spirit of nationalism from this dangerous perversion of racial hatred, and when I see western nations building their faith on this barbarism and making elaborate preparations for a scientific slaughter I cannot help feeling proud of my people who, poor as they are and persecuted, yet are unwilling to win human rights through brutish ways. It revives my faith in the undying spirit of the East.[4]

As regards the Hitler regime in Germany, we read different versions of it. And certainly it cannot be denied that the German people were goaded to many acts of desperate folly by the humiliations imposed on them by the victorious nations of the war. Nevertheless, if the brutalities we read of are authentic, then no civilised conscience can allow compromise with them. The insults offered to my friend Einstein have shocked me to the point of torturing my faith in modern civilisation.[5] I can only draw consolation from the hope that it was an unhappy act done in a drunken mood and not the sober choice of a people so gifted as the Germans.

All my life I have cried against blindness of prejudice that divides men from men and called upon my fellow men all over the globe to stretch their hands in a common endeavour to realise the nobility of the human in each one of us. Today when this most enduring heritage from the truly great ones of all races, is being assaulted by the aggressive communalism of the Blacks and the Browns on the one hand, and the fanatic materialistic idealism of the Reds on the other, I once again raise my humble voice of protest and warning, however feeble it may have grown with age. In our frantic despair to save the community let us not crush the free individual on the steps of whose sublime heresies humanity has ever been rising upwards.

Yours sincerely,
Rabindranath Tagore

Source: MS copy at Rabindra Bhavan, Shantiniketan; letter published in *Israel's Messenger*, Shanghai, 3 Aug. 1934 (copy at Jews' College, Hendon, London).

1 Nissim Ezra Benjamin Ezra (1880–1936): Zionist and newspaper editor; born in Lahore, he settled in Shanghai where in 1904 he founded *Israel's Messenger*, a monthly that described itself as 'a fearless exponent of traditional Judaism and Jewish nationalism; official organ of the Shanghai Zionist Association and the Jewish National Fund Commission for China'. Ezra was a ceaseless worker for the cultural advancement of the Jews in China and elsewhere, and a leading figure in scotching the birth of anti-Semitism in China in the late 1920s.
2 *Israel's Messenger*, 1 April 1934.
3 *Ibid.*, 3 Aug. 1934.
4 But in Dec. 1938, RT remarked in a service held at Shantiniketan:

> Europe by its recent callous attitude to the homeless Jews has proved beyond doubt that she has given up all claims of humanity.
> In our self-righteousness we might think we are above blame, but let me tell you no other country has been guilty of insulting humanity so grossly or for such a long stretch of time as ours. (*Madras Mail*, 24 Dec. 1938)

5 In Dec. 1932, Albert Einstein fled Germany, never to return. A few months after, brownshirt thugs raided Einstein's villa at Caputh where he and RT had talked in 1930, supposedly searching for arms.

276

To Mrs George Engel[1]

Strangers frequently wrote to Tagore asking for advice on how to cope with the death of a loved one. This letter was written to a woman living in Budapest, whose five-year-old daughter had died.

[Shantiniketan, West Bengal, India]
[4 July 1934]

Dear friend

Please accept my heartfelt sympathy for the bereavement which has shadowed your life lately. I have some experience of death myself and I have come to realise that being inevitable it must have as great a meaning as life itself. The suffering which it causes is owing to a sudden interruption in our faith in life's reality, but we must know that every moment that passes carries the footstep of death which walks hand in hand with life as its ceaseless companion. Life, only in its inseparable unity with death, is complete in its reality. Let us accept its mystery and bow to that great truth which we name as death, which comprehends all life as the sea all the running waters which are fulfilled in the depth of its bosom.

With blessings

Affectionately
Rabindranath Tagore

Source: MS original in the estate of the late P. Engel.

1 According to P. Engel, the son of Mrs George Engel, 'my late mother read a great deal of literature and one of her favourite writers was Tagore . . . My parents had four children; the youngest died on 19 March 1934. She was a girl aged five' (P. Engel to authors, 23 July 1992). Possibly Mrs Engel had heard RT speak in Budapest in 1926.

277

To Victoria Ocampo

Tagore did not meet Victoria Ocampo again after 1930. Despite her expressed wish, and his encouragement, she never visited India – as perhaps, in truth, both she and he intended. Like W. B. Yeats and others with whom Tagore had enjoyed a brief but intense personal relationship, Ocampo became for him a fragrant memory, which he preferred not to expose to harsh reality.[1] Hence the somewhat surprising opening of this nostalgic letter.

> Santiniketan, [West Bengal, India]
> [9? July 1934]

Dear Vijaya

Lately I have tried to find your address but failed. Often I have wished to meet you once again, but I am afraid the chance is growing more and more remote. This very morning in my letter to Elmhirst[2] I wrote about one Christmas morning in the beautiful garden in Argentina where you so kindly sheltered me and a shadow of sadness still hangs over my mind to know that those days belong to an irrevocable past. It is a strange coincidence that your card unexpectedly reached me just after I had sent that letter, reminiscent of your loving care, to Leonard.

Last month I had an adventure in Ceylon where I took with me some of our singers and girl students from our institution. We gave some performances which had lyrical appeal and the success was far beyond our expectation.[3] If the expenses were not too heavy for us I could confidently take them over to Paris and I believe that the French audience would have been pleased to see something which is genuinely oriental and full of exotic beauty.

With all my heart I wish you could include India in your extensive programme of travels and visit me in my own place in Santiniketan. Why should it be impossible? From the middle of November to the end of the year you will find the climate delightful and you know I shall do my best to make you comfortable.

I am sending you a latest photograph of mine taken in Ceylon and I hope it will reach your hand.

With my *bhalobasha*[4]
Rabindranath Tagore

Source: MS copy at Rabindra Bhavan, Shantiniketan; published in Dyson, *Flower-Garden*, p. 447.

1 See letter 288 to Yeats.
2 Elmhirst to RT, 9? July 1934, in Dutta and Robinson (eds.), *Purabi*, pp. 106–7. We have misdated this letter in *Purabi*, as a result of following the dating of Leonard Elmhirst. The original letter to Elmhirst (kept at Dartington) is undated, but appears to have been postmarked 10 July 1934, which was misread in Dartington as 10 July 1930 (an impossible date, since RT was then in Europe). RT's letter to Ocampo, also undated, was postmarked 10 July 1934 at Calcutta (see Dyson, *Flower-Garden*, pp. 446–7). Most likely both letters were written in Shantiniketan on 9 July and posted the following day from Calcutta.
3 On the Ceylon visit, see letter 274.
4 *Bhalobasha*: see letter 205, n. 1.

278

To Muriel Lester

After returning from India in 1934, Muriel Lester wrote to Tagore again, this time from London, with some frank but sympathetic criticisms of Shantiniketan, where she had stayed a few days. She described herself as 'a sort of safety-valve, a message taker, from side to side, an interpreter in a small way – longing for our two races each to bring the best out of the other – instead of continually annoying and misunderstanding the other'.

Her main point was the cynicism of the young teaching staff at Shantiniketan, who had asked her to communicate their disillusionment to Tagore himself.

> I gathered that they were by no means nonviolence people – that they did not believe in the principle – that they were wanting a crash to occur, believing that more bloodshed would clear the air – 'another Amritsar would do good' said one.
>
> I accepted and was interested in all this. I know well, here in East London, the British equivalent of these young idealist revolutionaries. But when I asked them what their plans were for building up a new social, economic and national fabric they had nothing in mind, apparently – had no experience of working conditions – proletariat projects – had no political experience. Their talk seemed hot air with nothing realist behind it ...
>
> Actually the students who came to me for a talk had taken up the position that the best way for them to serve India was not by doing quiet constructive work but by journalism. They were rather scornful of the nonviolent program.[1]

Tagore's reply, which he published the following year in the *Visva-Bharati News* – obviously hoping to provoke reflection among the teachers and students Lester had criticised – came from more than thirty years' heart-searching.[2] Unlike most previous criticisms of Shantiniketan by foreigners, he felt obliged to accept those of Lester, because she was so evidently a well-wisher of his institution.[3]

Santiniketan, [West Bengal, India]
15 August 1934

Dear friend,

What you have said in your letter about certain opinions expressed by some of our young professors does, no doubt, represent the mental attitude of some of the young generation of modern India. It is a mentality bred of utter despair, a bitterness generated in a closed atmosphere of a narrow prospect of life. Mostly they are men of keen intellect, confident of their own attainments who find it hard to forget that they have lost their best opportunities and have been deprived of their life's fulfilment. They harbour a futile anger against their destiny and seek an outlet for their brooding vengefulness by hurling defiance at those ideals which men have held as sacred. They have readily accepted the teaching of some modern pundits of the West, that religion offers refuge to the cowards and supplies opiate to the mind that is helplessly compelled to suffer.

You have hinted in your letter about [a] constructive programme, but you must know that those persons are extremely rare who have the genius to construct anything worth building, in an environment where things have to be begun from the very beginning, very often with meagre means and in unsympathetic circumstances. The burden of poverty in our country has been cruelly heavy and widespread, the training to fight it is absent, and on the top of it the depression of spirit that causes inertia finds its shelter in a body whose vitality has been run down owing to the want of nourishment and the consequent series of illnesses amidst surroundings devoid of proper medical help. It hurts me very deeply to find the best of our young minds indulging in a militant form of cynicism borrowed from the West, the cynicism which is all the more virulent because of its blankly negative character, destitute of all true vision. Because they have grown callously incapable of the deeper enjoyment of spiritual life they helplessly become addicted to cheap political sensationalism. I understand them, I suffer for them and I can never keep myself away from their wounded selves. I can only nourish a pathetic hope in my mind that in the end the wisdom which is of our own soil will find its way into their life, and if my own inspiration fails them I shall ever blame my own feeble power.

The boys with whom you had a talk are college students newly come who have not yet been naturalised in our ashram. They are immature in mind; their education imperfect. Like all young men of similar stage they like to talk loud in order to hide their deficiency in language and feign scepticism because they are lacking in all thoughts; and they believe that by denying all time-honoured notions of truth they prove their own superiority. This must be a passing phase which a number of them, I hope, will outgrow and the rest of them will go on flaunting a livery of the smart only because they are incurably foolish.

With kind regards,

Yours sincerely,
Rabindranath Tagore

Source: MS copy at Rabindra Bhavan, Shantiniketan; letter published in *VBN*, Dec. 1935, p. 43–4.

1 Lester to RT, 9 July 1934 [RB].
2 *VBN*, Dec. 1935, p. 43. See also the remarkably frank, anonymous article ('by an inmate'), 'Some problems of Santiniketan', *VBN*, June 1933, pp. 101–2.
3 See, for instance, the criticisms of Giuseppe Tucci (letter 215) and Sylvain Lévi (letter 221). The fact that Lester was in no sense an academic may also, paradoxically, have made her criticisms more acceptable to RT.

279

To Sir Malcolm Hailey[1]

On 16 September 1934, Indira Nehru, now a student at Shantiniketan, wrote to her father Jawaharlal, who was back in the central prison of Allahabad after a brief spell of freedom, 'I get a p.c. daily from Allahabad [from the Nehru house] informing me of Mummie's progress. This is a great relief, and as everyone here is anxious to know I have to learn the content of the card by heart and repeat it to almost every person I come across.'[2]

The health of Kamala Nehru, the wife of Jawaharlal, had deteriorated in the summer of 1934, when Indira arrived in Shantiniketan. In late September, her condition became critical. Jawaharlal was allowed to see her only twice a week, at most, and felt desperate.[3] In early October, Tagore, presumably after talking to Indira, made an appeal to the governor of the United Provinces (in whose jurisdiction the prison fell), first by telegram followed by this letter.[4]

[Shantiniketan?, West Bengal, India]
2 October 1934

Your Excellency,

I ventured in the cause of humanity to send you a telegram pleading for Pandit Jawaharlal Nehru's unconditional release. The news which has come to me this morning shows that his wife has reached the last stage of exhaustion. She has only her husband to look to. Without him she suffers an isolation which aggravates her illness. While the occasional allowance of a visit from her husband has partly relieved matters, he is now needed constantly by her side, since at any moment there may be a tragic collapse. Any act of kindness to Jawaharlal at this time will touch the hearts of our people as nothing else can do.

Yours sincerely
Rabindranath Tagore

Source: MS copy at Rabindra Bhavan, Shantiniketan.

1 Sir Malcolm Hailey (1872–1969): public servant, most of whose career was spent in India; he was governor of the United Provinces (Uttar Pradesh), 1928–34.
2 Indira to Jawaharlal Nehru, 16 Sept. 1934, in Sonia Gandhi (ed.), *Freedom's Daughter: Letters between Indira Gandhi and Jawaharlal Nehru, 1922–1939* (London, 1989), p. 126. Indira arrived in Shantiniketan in early July.
3 See Jawaharlal Nehru, *An Autobiography* (2nd edn; London, 1989), p. 567.
4 Hailey replied that he had referred the matter to the viceroy (Hailey to RT, 5 Oct. 1934 [RB]). Nehru was not released until Sept. 1935, when his wife was thought to be about to die, but he was moved from Allahabad to Almora in late Oct. 1934 so that he could be near her at a sanatorium in the Himalayan foothills. RT's appeal may have influenced this decision.

280

To Edward John Thompson

Just before he left western shores for the last time, in January 1931, Tagore wrote, through his secretary Amiya Chakravarty, to his publishers Macmillan, that he 'appreciated' their suggestion of issuing a 'collected and thoroughly revised edition' of his works. He said he would give further attention to the matter on reaching Shantiniketan.[1]

The *Collected Poems and Plays* was published six years later, and remained in print for many decades, indeed became the main introduction to Tagore for English readers. It contained most of the poetry and plays Tagore had himself translated or revised from 1912 onwards, and a few new translations, but no retranslations.[2] There was no indication of any kind in the book that it consisted of translations from Bengali, nor was there any introduction or notes nor the name of any editor or the name of anyone who had assisted with the translations, such as Yeats. To all intents and purposes, the book appeared to be entirely the work of Rabindranath Tagore, the celebrated Anglo-Indian poet and playwright.[3] Since most of the translations in it were poor, and many of the works, especially the plays, were of limited literary merit even in Bengali, this book lay like a tombstone on Tagore's English literary reputation.

Without doubt, Tagore must bear the lion's share of blame for this travesty of his work. He was acutely aware of the mediocrity of most of the translations of his poetry and plays, and yet he connived in their republishing because, for all his protestations to the contrary, he could not bear to let go of his western literary fame. The rest of the blame lies mainly on the shoulders of his secretary Amiya Chakravarty, then in Britain, who constantly gave Tagore bad and sometimes mendacious advice, and a little on Ernest Rhys, who agreed to make the final selection.

When Chakravarty left Bengal to study English literature in Oxford (see letter 274), he was asked by Tagore to see to the selecting and publishing of an edition of his English writings by Macmillan, in conjunction with Tagore's English literary friends, such as E. J. Thompson, Thomas Sturge Moore and Ernest Rhys. This position as a go-between suited Chakravarty very well, because it gave him a bona fide entree into British literary and publishing circles, which he hoped would help him in his own ambitions as a poet and writer; he probably also hoped that he would be named as editor of the book (as he would be after Tagore's death, when he edited *A Tagore Reader* in 1961).

Thompson was the first to respond to the call to help Tagore. But from the beginning he wanted Rabindranath to revise his work properly, as they had discussed in the early 1920s (see letters 162 and 173). He wrote to Tagore:

> Amiya and I spent an evening, this last week, doing a preliminary look over your books of translated verse. He is sending you our suggestions. I also saw Macmillan, and they tell me they intend to set the whole book up afresh, so that expense need not be considered, i.e., you have a free hand to revise, retranslate, add – do anything you like. Macmillan particularly want some new verses as well.[4]

From Tagore's reply, it is clear that he was only interested in making a selection from his existing translations, not in retranslating his works.

444 Selected letters of Rabindranath Tagore

Santiniketan, [West Bengal, India]
6 January 193[5]

Dear Thompson,

Many thanks for your letter. I am glad Amiya has had the advantage of your cooperation in the sifting of my poems for an authorised collected edition. My own judgement on the matter would not be reliable though I have made an attempt and have already sent my selection to Amiya. Probably he has shown it to you. But I would ask you and Amiya to be absolutely unfettered in your choice and do the thing yourselves.

I quite appreciate the changes you suggest in the translations but today I am afraid the task is beyond me. Twenty years ago with the courage born of inexperience I had rushed on with the work but I am wiser now and realise the inherent difficulties of translating lyrical pieces such as my own into a foreign tongue with anything approaching proper adequacy and poetical justice. I am extremely doubtful if I would have the patience now to go through my translations all over again and effect improvements.

I like the idea of such an experienced film-magnate [as] Korda doing some of my books for the screen.[5] I shall await developments with interest.

With all good wishes for the season,

Yours sincerely
Rabindranath Tagore

Source: MS original in Thompson Papers [Bodleian].

1 Amiya Chakravarty to Macmillan, 7 Jan. 1931 [BL].
2 The book included all the poetry collections translated by RT and published in book form in Britain/USA up to the 1930s, except for *The Child* and *Fireflies*, but certain collections were edited (as indicated by dots). See *The English Writings of Rabindranath Tagore*: I, Poems (Sisir Kumar Das ed.; New Delhi, 1994), pp. 612–13. Of the plays, *The King of the Dark Chamber* and *Red Oleanders* were omitted, as was the name of Devabrata Mukerjea, as translator of *The Post Office*.
3 On RT as an honorary European writer, see Dutta and Robinson, *Rabindranath Tagore*, pp. 5–6.
4 E. J. Thompson to RT, 7 Dec. 1934 [RB].
5 Thompson mentioned in his letter that he was trying to persuade Alexander Korda (1893–1956) to film works by RT such as the dramas *Chitrangada, Biday-Abhishap* (translated by Thompson as *The Curse at Farewell* in 1924) and the short story 'The Hungry Stones'. See letter 281.

281

To Edward John Thompson

In March 1935, E. J. Thompson wrote again to Tagore with renewed enthusiasm for films of his works. His fervour was kindled by a mixture of liking for the cinema, awareness of its potential for showing 'the real India' to western audiences and, probably, his reluctant acceptance (after reading letter 280) that Tagore's purely literary fame in English was doomed, at least until new translations appeared. He wrote:

> The western idea of India is a jumble – rajas, elephants, tigers, cobras, holy men, Untouchables, Brahmins, child marriage, Clive and Nicholson. Literature is now definitely a minor matter, a mere backwater. The only way to do anything effective is through wireless and the films. India must express herself through the films – not as

Malaviya or your extreme enthusiasts would express her, not as our own Hollywood and London occasionally express her now (as in the recent *Lives of a Bengal Lancer*!), but as Art and Truth (I do not often indulge in capitals!) demand.[1]

It is tempting to think that Thompson, had he lived into the 1950s, would have fallen for the work of Satyajit Ray, whose films undoubtedly fit his description. But his respect for Korda's films, his comparatively superficial knowledge of the visual arts and his desire that films should proselytise about India suggest that Thompson would have found Ray's India too subtle for his romantic taste.[2]

Santiniketan, [West Bengal, India]
28 March 1935

Dear Thompson
Your letter of [3] March. Thanks.

I have always appreciated your anxiety that justice should be done to the name of India in foreign countries. But do you know I am getting almost despondent where justice to the poor is concerned! It seems it is the lot of our poor country to be misunderstood and maligned. And even if we stirred up and did propaganda on our behalf through films and the wireless, as you suggest, can our resources ever equal the resources of the organised interests ranged against us? However, I shall be glad to meet the man Korda is sending out to India on his film mission.[3] And, believe me, I am always grateful to you for your interest in international justice.

As regards Barindra Ghosh's book, I am not surprised at your not having received it.[4] Very likely it has been intercepted. It is a pleasant pastime with our police to practise petty annoyances.

Yours sincerely
Rabindranath Tagore

[PS] I am not sure that you will get this letter. The communication between your country and ours is greatly curtailed – I suppose for the sake of law and order.

Source: MS original in Thompson Papers [Bodleian].

1 E. J. Thompson to RT, 3 March 1935 [RB]. Ironically, *Lives of a Bengal Lancer* was based, albeit remotely, on a novel RT admired by Francis Yeats-Brown (see his review, 'India and the "Bengal Lancer"', *Spectator*, 22 Nov. 1930). On Madan Mohan Malaviya (1861–1946), the Hindu Mahasabha politician, see letter 262, no. 4; by 1935, the Indian film industry was churning out Hindu 'mythologicals' of the kind Thompson meant.
2 On Thompson's reaction to the cinema, see his remarks in his anonymous leading article, 'A land made for poetry: new India's hopes and fears', *Times Literary Supplement*, 1 Feb. 1936. On Ray's reaction to western films about India, see his profound and brilliant article, 'Under western eyes', *Sight and Sound*, Autumn 1982, pp. 268–74. Fortunately, nothing came of Thompson's attempt to interest Korda in RT.
3 Thompson wrote in his letter that Korda 'is sending a man out to India to film Kipling's "Toomai of the Elephants"'. This man was Robert Flaherty, and the film was *Elephant Boy*. Flaherty was already renowned for his documentaries, but this film would be mangled by Korda.
4 Barindra Kumar Ghosh (1880–1956): revolutionary; he was the brother of Aurobindo Ghosh. He published *Amar Atmakatha* (My Autobiography) in 1931.

282

To Edward John Thompson

Just as, twenty years before, Rabindranath had found E. J. Thompson's enthusiasm for translating his work hard to handle (see letters 83–5 and 90, for example), now he again gave vent to his ambivalence about his western fame. He wanted to see an edition of his English works, as discussed with Thompson in letter 280, and during the previous few months he had sent various suggestions for inclusions and exclusions to Amiya Chakravarty, but in his heart he knew that the literary quality of even the best of his English translations was inadequate to represent him in an enduring manner as a poet in English, as his remarks on European poets in translation (letter 182) and in this letter make clear.

Santiniketan, [West Bengal, India]
10 April 1935

Dear Thompson,

The editorial responsibility of the Visva-Bharati journal has not been placed upon me as you seem to have imagined.[1] It is high time that I should withdraw myself from all activities and not add to my karma which is already grown enormously burdensome.

It may be difficult for you to realise that I am a shy individual brought up in retirement from my young days. And yet my fate takes every opportunity to drag me into a crowded publicity. I often wish that I had belonged to that noiseless age when artists took their delight in their work and forgot to publish their names. I feel painfully stupid when I am handled by the multitude who by celebrating some particular period of my life indulge in their avidness for some sort of a crowd ritual which is mostly made of unreality.

Amiya has taken charge of arranging for the publication of the collected edition of my translations. While going through them as appearing in different books I was startled with the slipshod character of most of their number and strongly felt the desire for ruthless excision. I have done gross injustice to my original productions partly owing to my incompetence and partly to carelessness. Amiya asks me to come to England for discussing with my literary friends there about final changes that should not be neglected. But unfortunately I do not feel fit for a journey to Europe and do not even think that it is imperatively necessary. In any case I should have to rely upon my English friends for the revision, for I never can trust my own English. As my age advances I find that I am fast losing my hold upon your language, thus proving that it never had truly been naturalised in my mind. It is growing evident to me that it resists my thoughts and refuses to yield to my own idioms of sentiments. And now with this lessening of my power I suffer from the responsibility imposed upon me by my past reputation which, as the saying is in our own language, proves itself as a living bear which originally offered its boon as a blanket.[2]

However I am sure I can depend upon your kindness for taking your own share in this work of emendation.[3] I do not know if you have received my last letter written to you some time back and I can only hope this will reach and not be delayed.[4]

With kind regards,

Cordially yours,
Rabindranath Tagore

Source: MS original in Thompson Papers [Bodleian].

1 Thompson had received a request to contribute to the revived *Visva-Bharati Quarterly* and thought that RT was the editor (Thompson to RT, 22 March 1935 [RB]). The editor was in fact Krishna Kripalani, and the first issue appeared in mid-1935.
2 See our introduction, p. 3.
3 Thompson had no role in the editing of the *Collected Poems and Plays*. In the first place, as always, he favoured retranslation, rather than editing of at least some of the poems, and he knew that RT did not want to do this. Second, he was ill and overworked. Third, he did not much care for Chakravarty. In early April, therefore, Chakravarty approached Thomas Sturge Moore in the hope of interesting him in selection and polishing, rather than retranslation. See letter 286.
4 Letter 281.

283

To Jawaharlal Nehru

Indira Nehru was a student at Shantiniketan for less than a year.[1] She was obliged to leave in order to accompany her ailing mother from a sanatorium in the Himalayas to a sanatorium in Germany. Her father, Jawaharlal, meanwhile remained in jail in Almora (see letter 279).

Santiniketan, [West Bengal, India]
20 April 1935

My dear Jawaharlal,

It is with a heavy heart we bade farewell to Indira, for she was such an asset to our place. I have watched her very closely and have felt admiration for the way you have brought her up. Her teachers, all in one voice, praise her and I know she is extremely popular with the students. I only hope things will turn for the better and she will soon return here and get back to her studies.

I could hardly tell you how sad I feel when I think of your wife's sufferings – but I am sure the sea voyage and the treatment in Europe will do her immense good and she would be her old self again before long.

With my affectionate blessings,

Yours,
Rabindranath Tagore

Source: MS copy at Rabindra Bhavan, Shantiniketan; letter published in *VBQ*, 29, Nos. 2–3, 1963–4, p. 99.

1 She arrived in July 1934, was away for about a month in Oct.–Nov. for the Puja holiday, and left in April 1935. See Sonia Gandhi (ed.), *Freedom's Daughter*, pp. 122–52.

284

To Andrée Karpelès[1]

During his long life, Tagore received the devotion of many women, both Bengalis and foreigners. A few of them, such as Ranu Mookerjee and Victoria Ocampo were remarkable in their own right, but most were not; and the more devoted they were to Rabindranath, the less remarkable they were as individuals.[2] One of the latter was Andrée Karpelès, a minor artist, French Jewish, who spent some time at Shantiniketan in the early 1920s and then returned to France and marriage to a Swede whom she had met at Shantiniketan. In 1930, these two acted as hosts to Tagore in Paris, while Ocampo organised the exhibition of his paintings. Karpelès remained in touch with Rabindranath in his last decade and particularly with his son and daughter-in-law. This letter to Karpelès expresses Tagore's lifelong need for undemanding love from women, though, as he joked in another letter to her, 'women have their god-given gift of flattery which we fools take seriously and complacently believe that their existence is for the sake of our own glorification'.[3]

Santiniketan, [West Bengal, India]
14 May 1935

My dear Andrée

Your letter comes to remind me that somehow you ought to be near us and though I have very great love for your big Scandinavian I cannot forgive him for snatching you away from our neighbourhood. As my age advances the longing in me grows in intensity for the near touch of those very few individuals whose love I can absolutely rely upon. The time has been long enough in my case for the process of elimination to have reached its finality and the few friends who remain as the best gifts of life become immensely precious. That the rapid changes in our environments should miss the association of our dear ones is a sad fact and I cannot help strongly wishing that we should know each other in our respective changing backgrounds with all their differences of aspects which may enrich the reality of our memory visions.

Suren has built for me a mud house – a mud casket beautifully worked, for enshrining in it the last few days of my life.[4] All our dwelling places contain varied partnerships of love but this last one will only offer me a perfect solitude of a final departure which will not have the time to allow life's trespassers to invade its loneliness.

The unusual heat of this summer has driven me from Santiniketan and I am planning to take my refuge in a houseboat on the Ganges until rain sets in.[5] I envy you your south of France and other easily available places where life can be made tolerable all the year round. In this country we have to pay heavy tolls for bare existence and with a pitifully small remnant of our energy have to do our best to justify our tenantry in this world. However, I have already rendered my account and I hope it will be found satisfactory.

With love and blessings
Rabindranath Tagore

Source: MS original at Rabindra Bhavan, Shantiniketan.

1 Andrée Karpelès (1885–1956): artist; some of her paintings hang at Rabindra Bhavan, Shantiniketan. Her family lived in Calcutta in her twenties, where she knew the Tagore family, and then returned to France. She met RT in Paris in 1920 and came to Shantiniketan in the early 1920s. Her sister, Suzanne Karpelès, was a student of Sanskrit, a pupil of Sylvain Lévi, and was given the title Saraswati by Calcutta University; she was less devoted to RT than Andrée.
2 On Mookerjee, see letter 187, n. 2. On Ocampo, see various letters, especially 198 and 199.
3 RT to Karpelès, 4 July 1935 [RB]. On her relationship with RT, see Rathindranath Tagore, *Edges of Time*, pp. 124, 126–7; also Dyson, *Flower-Garden*, pp. 234–9, 279–84.
4 Surendranath Kar (1892–1970) built Shyamali, a mud hut, for RT, which he occupied on 7 May 1935, his birthday. He moved out of it within a year into another small specially built house, well before he was carried out. See Dutta and Robinson, *Rabindranath Tagore*, pp. 330–1.
5 RT went to Chandannagar and lived aboard his house-boat, *Padma*, in late May and June, returning to Shantiniketan in early July.

285

To Helene Meyer-Franck[1]

During the Third Reich, Tagore's contact with German friends practically ceased. But he continued to exchange letters, such as this one, with Helene Meyer-Franck, a devotee and translator of his work whom he had met in Europe in 1920–1. (She and her husband had offered to come to Shantiniketan with their entire library, but had been unable to obtain visas from the Indian Government.[2]) In the 1930s, Meyer-Franck, working from Tagore's original Bengali with the help of a Bengali student from Shantiniketan then in Germany, a Mr Sen, translated some of Tagore's writings into German. Although Rabindranath could not read German, he told her he was 'deeply touched by the tribute you have paid me by learning Bengali only in order to read me in the original'.[3] She wrote to him: 'In this dark present there is no hope for me to see my translations published.'[4]

On houseboat *Padma*, Chandernagore,
[Chandannagar, West Bengal, India]
6 June 1935

My dear Mrs Meyer-Franck

I thank you for your kind letter in which you have sent me your greetings on the occasion of my 75th birthday. These friendly remembrances lighten one's life burden and I am so grateful for them. Let me also send you both my cordial greetings and good wishes. Kindly remember me to Mr Sen, when he comes to spend his summer holidays with you. I am glad he is helping you in translating my books.

Mr Tavadia's surmise was quite correct, as I did not get his letter. Or, I would surely have accorded him a welcome to Santiniketan. Please tell him we shall be happy to have him in our midst if only for a short time. Let him write to me as soon as he starts homewards, giving an approximate idea as to when we can expect him at Santiniketan. The institution will make necessary arrangements for his stay.

The heat has been terrific this summer in this part of the country and soon after my birthday, I sought shelter in my house-boat on the broad expanse of the Ganges. I am now staying at Chandernagore [Chandannagar], a small French possession, about 20 miles up the Ganges from Calcutta. This place is redolent with my childhood memories and though [it] now suffers from the inevitable onrush of steel and coal, I still find it pleasant and inviting.[5] I intend staying here till the rains finally break out in right earnest.

Yours sincerely
Rabindranath Tagore

Source: MS copy at Rabindra Bhavan, Shantiniketan.

1 Helene Meyer-Franck (1873–1946): translator; her husband, Heinrich Meyer-Benfey, was a philologist.
2 See letter 166.
3 RT to Meyer-Franck, 30 April 1936 [copy at RB].
4 Meyer-Franck to RT, 7 April 1936 [RB]. Her translations of poems were published posthumously after the Second World War, in 1947 (see Kämpchen, *Rabindranath Tagore*, pp. 112–13). Some were of high quality.
5 RT stayed at Chandannagar during his childhood and youth, most notably in 1881; there are atmospheric descriptions of the experience in his two memoirs.

286

To Thomas Sturge Moore

Throughout the first half of 1935, the issue of who in Britain would take charge of editing a collected edition of Tagore's poems and plays lay unresolved. When E. J. Thompson was lukewarm, Amiya Chakravarty, at Tagore's suggestion, contacted Thomas Sturge Moore.

Although there had been a long silence between the two poets, Sturge Moore had not lost interest in Tagore, though he had been wondering if he had not overestimated his work.[1] But a recent visit from an intelligent, enthusiastic and passionate Bengali admirer of Tagore's work – not Chakravarty, whom Sturge Moore did not care for – 'convinced me that you are a very much greater poet than the English versions give any idea of', he told Rabindranath on 20 May.[2] He therefore 'could not advise republication without retranslation'. Then he went on to explain part of the reason for the collapse of Tagore's reputation as a poet in English:

> Fear is the worst councillor and every nation is afraid of every other and increasingly so. Immediately after the war there had been a violent reaction towards hope and generosity but it was short-lived and people are no longer thirsty for spirituality and beauty, but relish cynicism, pessimism, and mechanical cruelty. Just as your work fed the first reaction it now seems tasteless to the second . . . But a real estimate of any poet takes a very long while to mature . . . It is in silence and stillness that solitary readers build the future of great poets, the crowds are often as fickle as the wind.[3]

Tagore had earlier fruitfully discussed translation from Bengali in his letters to Sturge Moore (for example, letters 86 and 196), as he had with E. J. Thompson – though of course Sturge Moore knew no Bengali. His response to this particular letter is his most interesting comment of all on the problem.

Santiniketan, [West Bengal, India]
11 June 1935

My dear Sturge Moore

I am no longer young, and I have had ample time to realise the futility of going out of one's own natural sphere for winning recognition. Languages are jealous sovereigns, and passports are rarely allowed for travellers to cross their strictly guarded boundaries. What is the use of my awkwardly knocking my head against their prohibitions, specially when I have the cause to feel sure of having contributed something acceptable to the world literature through my own mother tongue. I ought to remain loyally content with her limitations that are inevitable and yet which afford the only reliable means I have of offering my hospitality to the larger world.

In India circumstances almost compel us to learn English, and this lucky accident has given us the opportunity of an access into the richest of all poetical literatures of the world. Otherwise it would have remained to us like a mine of wealth unknown, unclaimed and unregretted, concealed for all time in an alien planet. Translations, however clever, can only transfigure dancing into acrobatic tricks, in most cases playing treason against the majesty of the original. I often imagine apes to be an attempt by the devil of a translator to render human form in the mould of his outlandish idiom. The case may be to some extent different in European languages which, in spite of their respective individual characteristics, have closely similar temperaments and atmospheres, the western culture being truly a common culture.

As for myself, I ought never to have intruded into your realm of glory with my offerings hastily giving them a foreign shine and certain assumed gestures familiar to you. I have done thereby injustice to myself and the shrine of Muse which proudly claims flowers from its own climate and culture. There is something humiliating in such an indecent hurry of impatience clamouring for one's immediate dues in wrong time and out of the way places. That is why I asked my young friend Chakravarty, who is in Oxford now, not to participate in perpetuating my offence of transgression by arranging a collected edition of my own translations which they [i.e. Chakravarty and Macmillan] had planned. Inadequate though these translations may be in their representation they have helped to introduce me to your people with some success. I was lured to a risky adventure when I submitted my manuscript to my English publishers only because of my great admiration for your literature which tempted me to seek the precious courtesy of its acknowledgement for my own things. But casual visitors must not overstay their welcome and I feel that it is time for them to leave the stage withdrawing themselves from a too-prolonged stare of the critical footlight.

In the meanwhile, let me assure you that I have not taken too much to heart the dying away of the applause and the inattention of my yawning audience, for I know that I had staked a very small portion of my capital in this enterprise. Only I feel like a departing guest at a weary ceremony of farewell, when the railway train which is to take him away makes an unaccountable delay in spite of repeated whistles.

However, once when I was busy launching my literary canoe in strange waters I came upon some very delightful chances of my life and my meeting with you has been one of the most adorable of them. I have hardly ever had occasion to let you know how dearly I prize your friendship full of generous sympathy, so simple and sincere. I cannot hope to take a long and expensive voyage to your country once again, but if ever I do so it is the expectation of your kindly presence which will be one of the very strong incentives.

I have just got out from England the latest edition of your collected works knowing that I shall understand and appreciate them which, as a foreigner, is more than I can say of a large number of the modern poems bearing the aggressive label of postwar literature.[4]

With love

Ever yours
Rabindranath Tagore

Source: MS original in Sturge Moore Papers [London].

1 No letters between RT and Sturge Moore survive from the period 1930–4. Presumably this was partly the result of Sturge Moore's doubts about RT's poetry, to which he confessed in 1935.
2 The Bengali was Sudhanshu K. Sen Gupta (Sturge Moore to RT, 21 Oct. 1935 [RB]).
3 Sturge Moore to RT, 20 May 1935 [RB].
4 *The Poems of T. Sturge Moore* were published in four volumes by Macmillan in 1931–3.

287

To Amiya Chakravarty

There were few relationships between Tagore and members of his inner circle that were more convoluted than that with Amiya Chakravarty, his erstwhile secretary. At one and the same time, Rabindranath represented Chakravarty as his personal ambassador to his western friends, and yet did not trust his reports; he also invested Chakravarty with literary judgement in English which he himself claimed not to possess, while at the same time distrusting this literary judgement.[1] As part of his ideal for Shantiniketan, Tagore felt obliged to give his friends and associates the benefit of the doubt, and more, as he had explained to Muriel Lester (letter 278) – but in Chakravarty's case, the situation got completely out of hand. 'How a person of normal intelligence can fail to see through the patent hypocrisy of Dr Chakravarty is beyond me, but it happened,' Satyajit Ray once told a friend who had been stabbed in the back by Chakravarty.[2] And as Ezra Pound once wrote to Tagore, when suggesting that he help a talented young poet by recommending him to his admirer, the artist Nicholas Roerich, 'there are one or two Roerich vice/wubblebubs who would knife anyone I recommended, so better not mention me'.[3] Amiya Chakravarty was the archetypal Tagore vice/wubblebub.

He was extremely keen to exploit his connection with Tagore when he arrived in Britain in 1934, and his letters to Rabindranath are full of shameless flattery.[4] In late 1934, he took up the translating of Rabindranath's latest novel, *Char Adhyay* (*Four Chapters*), a story of Bengali revolutionaries, with a view to publishing it in London simultaneously with its publication in Bengali in Calcutta. Tagore at first encouraged this, because he believed that the Bengali version might be proscribed by the Government in Bengal (see letter 217). When this did not happen, and the novel was widely read in Bengal (and bitterly attacked by Bengalis for its critique of violence in the service of idealism, even more than they had attacked *Ghare Baire* (*The Home and the World*) in 1916), the need for an English version lost its urgency. Thus, when Chakravarty sent his typescript of *Four Chapters* from Oxford to Shantiniketan for Tagore's approval in early 1935, Tagore took his time over it – and in due course made a completely new translation with his nephew Surendranath.[5] Not only did he find Chakravarty's English unsatisfactory, he was aware that Chakravarty had considerably altered the book, concealing some of its criticisms of the Bengali character from its expected British readers.[6]

Over the collected edition of his poems and plays, which Chakravarty was supposed to set in motion, Tagore also blew hot and cold. This was partly the result of his ambivalence about translations from Bengali into English, partly of his lack of confidence in Chakravarty. Although Tagore told Thomas Sturge Moore in mid-June (see letter 286) that he had asked Chakravarty to desist from arranging the collection, he had written to Macmillan a month earlier, clearly agreeing to the book and putting Chakravarty in charge 'with the help of my English literary friends', but then adding 'I shall of course myself revise the final selection.'[7] All along, it seems, while encouraging Chakravarty, he had been aware that a collaboration between Chakravarty and someone like Thompson or Sturge Moore would founder on Chakravarty's lack of judgement, and he had been hoping that one of his English literary friends alone would offer himself for the task. In the end it was Ernest Rhys, founding editor of Everyman's Library and Tagore's first biographer in English, who obliged him.

This letter to Chakravarty is a uniquely Tagorean mixture of oblique criticism and flattery. By criticising the Bengali reaction to his novel, Rabindranath implicitly criticises Chakravarty's own reaction, and by going out of his way to praise Rhys's character, he aims to exhort Chakravarty to emulate Rhys and avoid malicious behaviour.

[Shantiniketan, West Bengal, India]
11 July 1935

Kalyaniyeshu

The translation of *Char Adhyay* is on its way. You should receive it any day now. It is very close to the original. Some of it may not be acceptable. If, after it is shown to your friends, the book does not seem suitable for readers there, put it aside. The original is now published in Bengali, so if the translation does not appear, there is no great loss.[8] As I grow older, my taste for fame is declining. I would be content if my already-published books could be edited and rendered into as good English as possible. My real duty is to Bengali. I am convinced that most of my Bengali writings will endure. Those who study the Bengali language will read them – though there are many of my countrymen who are not pleased with *Char Adhyay*. I clearly see that unless one mixes an element of flattery into literature, readers do not appreciate the work. One has to woo the present age. In the future, when such elements are no longer needed, the verdict will be purely literary.

The other day I received a letter from Ernest Rhys. I was pleased. I have a natural friendship with him that goes back to the golden time of *Gitanjali*. His wife was a generous and artistically sensitive woman. Their house was in Golders Green, and had a small rose garden at the back – we spent so many afternoons there drinking tea and chatting in the shadow as the light faded. There was a sofa in a corner of the drawing room, over which I had some kind of permanent right of occupancy. Rhys was a busy man, yet whenever I needed him I could call for him and he would absent himself from his work and journey to Kensington from Golders Green: I spent hour after hour with him. Both he and his wife were genuinely discriminating people. When I sought his advice on any of my writing, he was meticulous in his selection of words – I learnt a great deal from him. I have written to him about my collected works.[9] If you consult him, I think that he will give the matter due consideration. I have heard nothing from you about the collection recently. If you are busy and cannot make the time, you can free yourself by relying on the opinion of someone like Rhys.[10]

Rathi and *Bouma* are back – I found them in good health and in an optimistic mood.[11] They are much impressed by the way you have secured yourself a group of friends. In my view it would be an injustice to our country were you unable to attract admiration in the country where you are living now. Most of our modern youth seem to take an approach opposite to yours. They regard it as manly to be disagreeable and discourteous to foreigners. They forget that English forebearance towards their manly behaviour is due not to their courage but to English tolerance. Wherever there is no fear of punishment, people of weak character take pleasure in displaying their arrogance. I have frequently confessed that in intelligence and character the English are superior to us. Whatever their occasional mistakes and injustices towards us, we lack their characteristic faculty of empathy with excellence. The older I get, the more I feel ashamed and despairing about my own race. This thing called 'malice' in English, seems to be spontaneous among our people. They take infinite pleasure in disgracing anyone who excels at anything.

Tomader
Rabindranath Thakur

Source: MS original at Rabindra Bhavan, Shantiniketan; letter published in *CP*, XI, pp. 161–3.

1 'No one else has understood me as intimately as you have' (RT to Chakravarty, 2 April 1934, *CP*, XI, p. 105). In his recommendation letter, given to Chakravarty when he went to Britain, RT wrote:

> I feel sure that with his scholarship, and his brilliant intellectual gifts he will be able to make outstanding contribution to our common task of bringing humanity together . . .
> I take this opportunity of commending my friend to my many friends in Europe and wish for him that same hospitality and inspiration from the West which I have enjoyed so frequently, the remembrance of which abides with me in rare sweetness. (Quoted in Brittain, *Search after Sunrise*, pp. 23–4)

2 Ray to Alex Aronson, 19 Sept. 1945, in Dutta and Robinson, *Rabindranath Tagore*, p. 454.
3 Pound to RT, 28 April (1934) [RB]. The poet was Basil Bunting. RT wrote to Roerich as requested.
4 For example, in one letter Chakravarty wrote that an English edition of *Char Adhyay* would 'shake Europe'! (4 Feb. 1935, in *Desh*, 4 Jan. 1992). In another letter, he claimed that the older generation of literary people in Britain were only superficially interested in RT, while the younger generation 'know you and love you because they are in search of a new and vital voice' (26 April 1935, *Desh*, 18 Feb. 1992). Chakravarty knew very well how untrue this comment was, not least because he was himself much more attracted to modernist poetry than the romantic poets who had influenced RT.
5 RT 'read thoroughly the translation done by Mr Chakravarty and felt that the book deserved to be translated by himself. So, assisted by my cousin Mr Surendranath Tagore . . ., he set himself to the task' (Rathindranath Tagore to Gertrude Emerson Sen, 15 Aug. 1936 [copy at RB]).
6 See RT to Chakravarty, 26 June 1935, *CP*, XI, pp. 159–60.

7 RT to Macmillan, 17 May 1935 [BL].
8 *Char Adhyay* was published by Gertrude Emerson Sen as 'Novelette of Young India – Four Chapters' in four issues of *Asia* (Dec. 1936–Feb. 1937 and April 1937), where the translator was uncredited, to avoid offending Chakravarty; in 1950, it appeared as *Four Chapters*, published by Visva-Bharati, translator Surendranath Tagore.
9 After a long period of silence, Rhys wrote to RT on 13 June 1935 asking for permission to print some of RT's letters in his memoirs, *Everyman Remembers* [RB]. RT replied warmly on 9 July, and asked if Rhys would be willing to help Chakravarty put together the collection of his English writings [copy at RB].
10 Neither E. J. Thompson nor Thomas Sturge Moore was willing to help – since both wanted retranslation – and so Chakravarty was stymied, lacking an English collaborator.
11 Rathindranath Tagore and his wife Pratima (*Bouma*) had recently returned from a European tour.

288

To William Butler Yeats

Despite rejecting most of the English translations of Tagore's poetry, W. B. Yeats remained interested in Tagore, in both his prose (see letter 255) and his personality. In June 1935, in his last letter to Tagore, Yeats wrote, 'I have always so much regretted that no chance has arisen to renew our old friendship. I have heard of you from time to time from English or Indian friends, and I have a book with your remarkable pictures in it.'[1] Tagore's letter in response is perhaps the most concise expression he ever gave of his deepest feelings about the West. When Yeats died in 1939, Rabindranath commented, 'I shall cherish the fact to the end of my days that my life has been linked with the memory of one of the greatest poets of modern Europe.'[2]

Santiniketan, [West Bengal, India]
16 July 1935

Dear Yeats

Your letter seems to come to me from a remote age reminding me of those days of my acquaintance with you intense and intimate. Though I had already left behind one half of a century of my life when I visited your country I felt that I had come to the beginning of a fresh existence young with the surprise of an experience in an atmosphere of kindly personalities. I often remember a meeting with you in that chamber of yours, quaintly unique, that seemed to me, I do not know why, resonant of an old world silence, and though I find it difficult distinctly to recollect the subject of our talk the feeling of it lingers in my mind like the aroma of a rich and rare wine.[3]

I know you have entered into an epoch of life which is vague to me and distant, but I shall always remember the generosity of your simple and sensitive poetic youth which exercised in my mind a profound attraction for your genius.

Ever yours
Rabindranath Tagore

Source: MS original in collection of Michael Yeats.

1 Yeats to RT, 20 June 1935, *VBQ*, 30, No. 3, 1964–5, p. 176. Yeats' last recorded comments on RT appear in Abinash Chandra Bose's interview with Yeats on 1 June 1937, in R. K. Das Gupta (ed.), *Literary Friendship*, pp. 18–24. The book with the 'remarkable pictures' was probably either *Shesh Shaptak* (1935)

"Uttarayan"
Santiniketan, Bengal
July 16, 1935

Dear Yeats

Your letter seems to come to me from a remote age reminding me of those days of my acquaintance with you intense and intimate. Though I had already left behind me half a century of my life when I visited your country I felt that I had come to the beginning of a fresh existence young with the surprise of an experience in an atmosphere of kindly personalities. I often remember a meeting with you in that chamber of yours, quaintly unique, that seemed to me, I don't know why, resonant of an old world silence, and though I find it difficult distinctly to recollect the subject of our talk the feeling of it lingers in my mind like the aroma of a rich and rare wine.

I know you have entered into an epoch of life which is vague to me and distant, but I shall always remember the generosity of your simple and sensitive poetic youth which exercised in my mind a profound attraction for your genius.

Ever yours

Rabindranath Tagore

17 Letter to W. B. Yeats, 1935

or *Bichitrita* (1933), both of them volumes of verse by RT, published by Visva-Bharati, the first with his illustrations alone, the second with illustrations by RT, Abanindranath and Gaganendranath Tagore, and Nandalal Bose.
2 'Rabindranath's message on the passing away of Yeats', *VBQ, 17*, No. 1, May–July 1951, p. 28. Though RT sincerely felt the greatness of Yeats, he did not care for his poetry. It is significant that while Yeats made a comment on RT's work in his letter, RT in his reply made no comment on Yeats' work, only on his personality.
3 See letter 255, n. 3.

289

To Mahatma Gandhi

Now in his mid-seventies and unable to continue travelling much longer in order to raise funds for Visva-Bharati, Tagore was brought face to face with the imminent financial bankruptcy of his institution. Only one person seemed capable of rescuing it. At the insistence of C. F. Andrews, Tagore put his pride in his pocket and wrote almost piteously to Gandhi requesting his help with fundraising; and in a subsequent letter (290), written a month later, he again mentioned the problem, this time to Nehru (who was now in Germany looking after his dying wife, after being released from jail in early September).

Gandhi rose to the occasion, and found enough money in early 1936 to tide Visva-Bharati over.[1] After that he raised further sums, both while Tagore lived and after his death in 1941 (see letter 336).

Santiniketan, [West Bengal, India]
12 September 1935

My dear Mahatmaji

I am glad Suren had an opportunity to discuss with you in detail the financial situation of the ashram during his recent visit to Wardha.[2] I know how busy you are with your various activities and though I have often thought of telling you of my difficulties I have never done so before. But Charlie[3] insisted that you must be informed about the situation and then only I gave permission to discuss it with you. Over thirty years I have practically given my all to this mission of my life and so long as I was comparatively young and active I faced all my difficulties unaided and through my struggles the institution grew its manifold aspects. And now, however, when I am 75 I feel the burden of my responsibility growing too heavy for me, that owing to some deficiency in me my appeals fail to find adequate response in the heart of my people. Though the cause that I have done my utmost to serve is certainly valuable, constant begging excursions with absurdly meagre results added to the strain of my daily anxieties have brought my physical constitution nearly to an extreme verge of exhaustion. Now I know of none else but yourself whose words may help my countrymen to realise that it is their worthwhile [*sic*] to maintain this institution in fullness of its functions and to relieve me of perpetual worry at this last period of my waning life and health.

With deepest love,

Yours sincerely
Rabindranath Tagore

Source: MS copy at Rabindra Bhavan, Shantiniketan; letter published in *VBQ*, 35, Nos. 1–4 (Gandhi Number), May 1969–April 1970, p. 243.

1 Gandhi did not reply for a month, but that was because RT's letter was not given to him until 11 Oct.: RT's secretary, who took it, wanted to deliver it personally, and Gandhi was very busy. He replied almost immediately, 'You may depend upon my straining every nerve to find the required money... It is unthinkable that you should have to undertake another begging mission at your age' (Gandhi to RT, 13 Oct. 1935, *CWMG*, LXII, p. 34). See Nepal Majumdar, 'Visva-Bharati, Rabindranath and Gandhiji', *VBQ*, 35, Nos. 1–4 (Gandhi Number), May 1969–April 1970, pp. 62–80.
2 Suren: Surendranath Kar. He became executive secretary of Visva-Bharati in 1935 and had considerable contact with Gandhi in connection with the All-India Village Industries Association (see *CWMG*, LXI, p. 87). Wardha was the site of Gandhi's Sevagram ashram.
3 Charlie: C. F. Andrews.

290

To Jawaharlal Nehru

Santiniketan, [West Bengal, India]
9 October 1935

My dear Jawaharlal

We have been anxiously following in the daily papers the news of your wife's illness watching for some favourable signs of improvement. I earnestly hope that the amazing strength of mind which she has shown through all the vicissitudes of her life will help her. Please convey to her my kindest regards.

Every winter Visva-Bharati rudely reminds me of the scantiness of her means, for that is the season when I have to stir myself to go out for gathering funds. It is a hateful trial for me – this begging business either in the guise of entertaining people or appealing to the generosity of those who are by no means generous. I try to exult in a sense of martyrdom accepting the thorny crown of humiliation and futility without complaining. Should I not keep in mind for consolation what you are going through yourself for the cause which is dearer to you than your life and your personal freedom? But the question which often troubles my mind is whether it is worth my while to exhaust my energy laboriously picking up minute crumbs of favour from the tables of parsimonious patrons or keep my mind fresh from the indignity of storing up disappointments. But possibly this is my excuse for shirking unpleasantness. I have asked Mahatmaji for lending me his voice which he has kindly consented to.[1] Of course his influence is likely to meet with a greater success than I can ever hope to attain. I must not forget to tell you that Sir Tej Bahadur Sapru also has promised to support me.[2]

Kindly remember me to dear Indira.[3] I hope some day or other she will find opportunity to revisit our ashram and revise[4] her memory of those few months which she spent here making us happy.

With love,

Yours
Rabindranath Tagore

Source: MS copy at Rabindra Bhavan, Shantiniketan.

1 When RT wrote this, Gandhi had not yet replied to his letter of 12 Sept. (see letter 289, n. 1), so RT's mentioning the matter to Nehru may have been done partly in the hope of reminding the Mahatma.

2 Sir Tej Bahadur Sapru (1875–1949): lawyer and politician; he had good connections with the Indian princes. See RT to Sapru, 28 July 1935 and 5 Nov. 1935 [copies at RB].
3 Indira Nehru was then back at school, at Bex in Switzerland, from where she could visit her mother regularly.
4 RT wrote 'revise', not 'revive'.

291

To Edward John Thompson

Although Tagore and E. J. Thompson had been unable to come together on the editing of Tagore's collected works (see letters 280–2), and in spite of their past differences over the Tagore biography, a feeling of mutual regard subsisted between them. So when Thompson announced in a letter that he was to visit India again, Tagore, who had not met him for a long time, responded with this warm letter.

Santiniketan, [West Bengal, India]
16 October 1935

Dear Thompson,

It is welcome news for me that you intend visiting India this winter and I hasten to send you a warm welcome to Santiniketan. I am feeling quite oldish and there is not even the remotest chance of my ever again visiting England and I shall be sorry if you fail to look me up during this trip of yours to India. I am particularly anxious about your coming to Santiniketan as you threaten it's going to be your last visit to this country.[1]

I have very little faith in any Hollywood concern doing justice to my plays and though I have often been approached on the matter I have not shown any warmth. If you of course take interest in this, then it is another matter. For you know the language as well as local conditions and environments. I am hoping you will be able to visit me here this time and we would be able to talk things over.[2]

With kindest regards,

Yours
Rabindranath Tagore

Source: MS original in Thompson papers [Bodleian].

1 Thompson's visit was cancelled, and he did not return to India until late 1936. He made one attempt to visit RT at Shantiniketan, but without success (see E. P. Thompson, *Alien Homage*, p. 99, n. 34). His final visit to India was in Oct. 1939, again without meeting RT.
2 On Thompson and Indian films see letters 280, n. 5 and 281. During his (aborted) visit to India, he was expecting to write a report on Indian cinema for a British and American group of producers. He remarked, 'So far as I can discover, Indian-made films are largely Hollywood with just Indian clothes on. A pity' (Thompson to RT, 19 Sept. 1935 [RB]).

292

Nandita Kripalani (Gangulee)[1]

One of Rabindranath's many services to the social life of India was his introduction of girls and women as actors in his dramas and dance dramas, first in Shantiniketan, then in Calcutta and later on in many parts of India, when he toured with his troupe. The first such public performance was of *Natir Puja* in Calcutta in January 1927. By the 1930s, Tagore's lead was beginning to make respectable the acting roles that had till then been the preserve of nautch girls and prostitutes.

In 1935, he produced a version of *Arup Ratan* (Formless Jewel), based on his play *Raja* (*The King of the Dark Chamber*).[2] It was performed in Shantiniketan on 8 December and at the Empire Theatre, Calcutta, on 11 and 12 December, with himself playing two roles (one of them the invisible Raja). According to a light-hearted letter he wrote to a friend three weeks later, 'the press went into positive hysterics of eulogy over my performance, but then, I had to be in bed for over a week'.[3] It turned out to be his final acting role.

In this letter he cajoles his nineteen-year-old granddaughter to take a part in the play.

[Shantiniketan, West Bengal, India]
23 November 1935

Briddha

The part of Shurangama will not be all that hard, if I am able to coach you. Have a good read of it. We've tried it out with some local girls – with what might be called miserable failure. If I can work with you intensively for a few days, there is no doubt you'll do well. What a fix I'm in. Often I've wanted to play Shurangama myself, but people always vetoed the idea, saying that I wasn't strong enough for such extra strain even though the idea was good.

Queenie[4] has written to me, saying she'll reach Sylhet via Shillong[?] by early December. Which means that she'll be a spectator rather than an actor in our performance. Even if she had been available here at the beginning of December, there would still have been hardly any time.

After much persuasion Amita[5] has agreed to play the part of Shudarshana. I hope she lasts the course.

I don't have much time to think about my own health. Every evening I apply ultra-violet rays to my waist in the hope of stiffening my spine. When you come here I'll shine some rays at your head which may pierce into your brainbox and shed some light into its dense darkness – though I'm not sure about the results. All day I've been rehearsing, attempting to make the impossible possible. With what outcome nobody can yet say.

Grandfather

Source: MS original at Rabindra Bhavan, Shantiniketan; letter published in *CP*, IV, pp. 13–14.

1 Nandita Kripalani (Gangulee) (1916–67): granddaughter of RT; she was the daughter of Mira and Nagendranath Gangulee. She married Krishna Kripalani in 1935.
2 *Raja* was written in 1910; a version of it for the stage, *Arup Ratan*, in 1920; a musical version, *Shapmochan*, in 1931 (revised in 1933); and in 1935 RT completely reworked the original *Arup Ratan* for the Shantiniketan/Calcutta production. See *Three Plays* (Ananda Lal trans.; Calcutta, 1987), pp. 265–8.
3 RT to Schlomith Flaum, 2 Jan. 1936 [copy at RB].
4 Queenie: Kamala Dutta, student at Shantiniketan.
5 Amita: Amita Tagore, wife of Ajindranath Tagore.

293

To Ernest Rhys

As Tagore told Amiya Chakravarty in July (letter 287), he had decided to ask Ernest Rhys to take a hand in editing the collected edition of his poems and plays. He told Rhys, 'You know I fully trust your judgement and shall be relieved if you offer your advice to Amiya.'[1] Rhys promptly agreed, commenting that 'Your lyric best is so good it deserves to be winnowed out and put into a rich Indian vessel.'[2]

Tagore then despatched some further translations of poems with C. F. Andrews, who was on his way back to Britain via Shantiniketan, along with a request that he contact Rhys, Chakravarty and Macmillan, and push the book forward. Since Andrews had always had an unwarrantedly high opinion of his own literary judgement, especially where Tagore's work was concerned (see letters 57 and 97), this could have been a recipe for further muddle and delay. But although Andrews did his best to interject his own selection, the stature of Rhys, as editor of Everyman's Library, was beyond dispute, and eventually Rhys took over the editorial role entirely from Chakravarty and Andrews.[3] In late November 1935, he sent Tagore a list of what he thought should be in the book.[4] This is his reply.

Santiniketan, [West Bengal, India]
18 December 1935

My dear Ernest Rhys

I cannot thank you enough for the trouble you have taken, going over the poems for the purpose of selection. I requested my publishers and also Charlie to entrust you with this task for I have complete reliance on your judgement. The unpublished poems which Charlie Andrews took with him did not represent my choice, they were submitted to you for your own final opinion.[5] As a translator I have not the least faith in my own preferences, simply because the ghosts of the original poems haunt and hover over the translations concealing from their author their deficiencies. I earnestly request you to take up the responsibility without hesitation and leave out all those pieces which are likely to interfere with the harmony of the whole group. I have been wondering if *Chitra* has been excluded from this selection because you think it is out of place in this book owing to its bulk or [for] other reasons.[6] However it won't matter to me in the least if you consider it inappropriate or unnecessary. My only regret is that I am not there by your side working together as was the case when you helped me in going through the MSS of *Sadhana*.[7] Those were delightful days and I shall never forget them.

Yours affectionately
Rabindranath Tagore

Source: MS copy at Rabindra Bhavan, Shantiniketan.

1 RT to Rhys, 9 July 1935 [copy at RB].
2 Rhys to RT, 29 July 1935 [RB].
3 Chakravarty seems to have dropped out of the selection process completely, but Andrews played a role

throughout, airing his disagreement with Rhys in a letter to RT on 20 Jan. 1936 and pontificating on 24 Jan. that 'the great bulk of English readers are tired of the new poetical poems of T. S. Eliot and others and long for something simpler again' [RB].
4 Rhys to RT, 21 Nov. 1935 [RB].
5 Among these 'unpublished poems' were presumably those included in the *Collected Poems and Plays*, pp. 450–8.
6 *Chitra* was included in the published book.
7 *Sadhana* (1913) was dedicated to Ernest Rhys. In his memoirs, Rhys wrote of RT at his home in London in 1913:

> When he arrived, he looked so like an old Hebrew prophet, with so august a presence, that we were overawed, and wondered what we should say to so formidable a personage. However, he proved to be the simplest and most natural of guests, and the easiest to entertain. He did not require to be fed on mangoes and tamarinds, loved a good story, enjoyed a good laugh, and had a graceful way of making light of his own poetry. (Rhys, *Everyman Remembers*, p. 273)

294

To Maharajkumari Vidyavati Devi[1]

Tagore wrote many condolence letters, as already remarked. This one is addressed to a minor princess and well-wisher of Visva-Bharati, who had lost a son. Rabindranath recalls the sudden death from cholera of Shamindranath, his youngest son, in 1907, as he had done three years previously in his letter (258) to his daughter Mira, when her son died.

Santiniketan, [West Bengal, India]
27 December 1935

Dear Vidyavati,

I do not know how adequately to impart my experience to you. I shall simply speak to you of an incident full of the most poignant sorrow of my life. My youngest son, beautiful in appearance and lovable in character, was about sixteen when he was invited to spend his vacation with a boy friend of his in Monghyr [Munger].[2] I hastened to his side when I suddenly received a telegram in Calcutta, informing me of a serious attack of illness causing grave anxiety to his host who was a doctor. The boy lingered for three days after my arrival, trying repeatedly to assure me that he was free from all physical sufferings. When his last moment was about to come I was sitting alone in the dark in an adjoining room, praying intently for his passing away to his next stage of existence in perfect peace and well-being. At a particular point of time my mind seemed to float in a sky where there was neither darkness nor light, but a profound depth of calm, a boundless sea of consciousness without a ripple or murmur. I saw the vision of my son lying in the heart of the infinite and I was about to cry to my friend, who was nursing the boy in the next room, that the child was safe, that he had found his liberation. I felt like a father who had sent his son across the sea, relieved to learn of his safe arrival and success in finding his place. I felt at once that the physical nearness of our dear ones to ourselves is not the final meaning of their protection. It is merely a means of satisfaction to our own selves and not necessarily the best that could be wished for them. I believe that the love which is true can help the departed spirit in crossing the boundaries of earthly life and finding its spiritual destination. And therefore it should be our sacred duty to direct that love of ours, through concentration of will, towards winning for them their best fulfilment and never to waste it in futile desire for our own consolation. Of course, all bereavements naturally bring sufferings, but let us through them find freedom and joy by realising that they are our sacrifices which we dedicated for the salvation of our beloved ones, and that by our own emancipation we bring emancipation to them also.

With heartfelt sympathy and blessings,
Rabindranath Tagore

Source: MS copy at Rabindra Bhavan, Shantiniketan; letter published in *VBN*, Dec. 1942, p. 67.

1 Maharajkumari Vidyavati Devi: she belonged to the princely family of Vizianagaram and became, through marriage, yuvarani of Kasmunda, in Uttar Pradesh. In 1934, she donated Rs 5,000 to Visva-Bharati, for which RT was most grateful (RT to Sarvepalli Radhakrishnan, 21 Nov. 1934, *VBQ, 1*, Nos. 1 and 2, May–Nov. 1990, p. 22).
2 Shamindranath was actually eleven when he died.

295

To Gretchen Green[1]

Among the women who admired Tagore but were not besotted by him was Gretchen Green. She was the daughter of an itinerant American preacher, without much money or education, ordinary looking, but with a determined and adventurous streak. In 1922, she was sent to India by Dorothy Straight to work with Leonard Elmhirst and set up a village clinic for women at Shriniketan, Tagore's 'institute for rural reconstruction' (see letter 187, n. 6). She stayed several years in Bengal, travelled to China in 1924 with Tagore's party (which he dubbed the 'Peripatetic Philistines', according to a self-mocking Green), and then returned to the United States.[2]

In 1936, she published a jaunty autobiography, *The Whole World and Company* (New York, 1936), with a section on her time with Tagore. Some of her stories were quite amusing, including her comment on her role as temporary secretary to Tagore dealing with his large amount of crank mail. She recalled one American woman from Kalamazoo, Michigan, who sent Tagore a stamped addressed envelope in 1926, with an indignant request for the return of three poems she had sent him in 1916 when he was lecturing in the USA.[3] Although Green herself could be a parochial small-town American too, Tagore liked her for her practicality and energy; and she brought out his humorous side. While she was never able to understand much of his personality and work, she was conscious of this and wrote in her book, 'I know I went to India thinking to do the teaching and I have come back from India aware of my own ignorance.'[4]

Santiniketan, [West Bengal, India]
16 January 1936

Dear Gretchen

Thousand thanks for your book in which you have preserved the memory of those days that you spent in Shriniketan and which I shared with you. I often look back to it with a feeling which is akin to nostalgia. You will be surprised to learn that I have almost been able to decipher your script unaided and was delighted to find that you still cherish for me the same devotion and love to which you made me accustomed and with which you almost spoilt me. Your successors in the line of my private secretaries are excellent persons but unfortunately they belong to my own sex and therefore are woefully deficient in the tender tactfulness that knows how beautifully to flatter me and also to create in the minds of my correspondents the illusion that they are of some consequence.

The life here is going on in the usual tempo, work and enjoyment completing the circle. Of late I have been giving a good deal of my time and attention to the development of the music department, where we have quite a few talented students from various parts of India learning the intricacies of oriental dancing. We are proposing to take a group of these students to Delhi and interpret my *Chitra* through songs and dances.[5] I do not sing now and I have never danced but curiously enough I have to go, for my wise advisors tell me if I am not with the party, the box-office attraction will be 75 per cent vanished. Perhaps you too will agree with them![6] And as the chief reason for our invading the imperial capital is to hunt the golden stag, I am afraid I will have to lead the chase.[7]

With affectionate blessings,

Sincerely yours
Rabindranath Tagore

Source: MS copy at Rabindra Bhavan, Shantiniketan.

1 Gretchen Green (????–1971): nurse and social worker. After the Second World War, she was made an MBE (Member of the British Empire) for her work during the war and in its immediate aftermath. See obituary, *New York Times*, 16 Nov. 1971.
2 Green, *Whole World*, p. 177.
3 *Ibid.*, p. 124.
4 *Ibid.*, p. 192.
5 It was on this visit to Delhi that RT met Gandhi, who there and then raised Rs 60,000 from G. D. Birla for Visva-Bharati, on condition that RT stopped straining himself by touring with his troupe.
6 Green's book makes RT's box-office appeal very clear, especially when they travelled together in China.
7 RT liked this image from the *Ramayana*, which he had earlier used in a letter to Ezra Pound on the same subject (RT to Pound, 12 June (1934) [Yale]).

296

To Jawaharlal Nehru

Kamala Nehru, wife of Jawaharlal, died on 28 February 1936 in a sanatorium in Germany, with her husband by her side. On 8 March, in Shantiniketan, Tagore declared a day of mourning for her, and gave an address in Bengali, in the course of which he said:

> Most often condolence meetings as a part of their ceremony use exaggerations to give them an artificial fullness. In the case of Kamala it is not needed, for she was truly great, and that greatness of hers has spontaneously introduced itself into the hearts of

the people and found immediate acceptance. The reticent dignity that she had maintained all through the vicissitudes of her noble life finds its voice today that overwhelms us by its truth.[1]

Jawaharlal, who had flown back to India with his wife's ashes leaving Indira in Switzerland, heard about the tribute from Gandhi, read it and wrote to Indira, 'it moved me greatly . . . Character and dignity and quiet restraint, together with inner fire, have a way of stealing into the hearts of millions.'[2] To Tagore, he wrote, 'I wish to tell you, if I may, how much strengthened I feel by your blessings and by the thought that you are there to keep us, erring ones, on the straight path.'[3]

Santiniketan, [West Bengal, India]
5 April 1936

My dear Jawaharlal,

I have received your letter and it has given me pleasure that you found hope and strength in the few words I said about Kamala to my students in the ashram. Believe me, I do feel, very sincerely, your great loss.

I was myself not satisfied with the few minutes I had with you in the train.[4] Both my body and mind were fagged with the strain of the journey and I could hardly speak. You must come here and spend a few days with me and I can assure you that Santiniketan would not be warmer than Allahabad.

Yours affectionately
Rabindranath Tagore

Source: MS copy at Rabindra Bhavan, Shantiniketan; letter published in *VBQ, 29*, Nos. 2–3, 1963–4, p. 101.

1 'In memory of Mrs Kamala Nehru', *VBN*, April 1936, p. 75.
2 Jawaharlal to Indira, 1 April 1936, in Sonia Gandhi (ed.), *Freedom's Daughter*, p. 252.
3 Nehru to RT, 1 April 1936, *VBQ, 29*, Nos. 2–3, 1963–4, p. 100.
4 RT met Nehru briefly at Delhi railway station on the night of 20 March, as he travelled from Allahabad to Lahore with his troupe (see Sonia Gandhi (ed.), *Freedom's Daughter*, p. 247).

297

To Jawaharlal Nehru

In 1936, Nehru published *An Autobiography*. Tagore read it immediately and wrote him this brief appreciation. The second sentence, a beautiful one, applies equally well to himself.

Santiniketan, [West Bengal, India]
31 May 1936

Dear Jawaharlal,

I have just finished reading your great book and I feel intensely impressed and proud of your achievement. Through all its details there runs a deep current of humanity which overpasses the tangles of facts and leads us to the person who is greater than his deeds and truer than his surroundings.

Yours very sincerely
Rabindranath Tagore

Source: MS copy at Rabindra Bhavan, Shantiniketan; letter published in *VBQ*, 29, Nos. 2–3, 1963–4, p. 101.

298

To Schlomith Flaum[1]

Although Tagore was never able to visit Palestine, he was interested in the Jewish settlement there and even hoped that Jewish settlers would come to Shriniketan, in order to teach and energise the local villagers and his Bengali staff (see letter 310). He also made a number of Jewish friends during his life after 1912, such as Sylvain Lévi, Albert Einstein, Andrée Karpelès – and Schlomith Flaum, whom he called Santi.

Lithuanian by birth, Flaum had settled in Palestine in 1911 when she was eighteen and organised a kindergarten for the Zionist Organisation. Later she studied education at Columbia University, probably met Tagore while in America, in 1920–1, and spent about two years at Shantiniketan, before returning to Palestine to set up a school based on Tagore's educational ideas.

During the 1930s, as violence flared between Jews and Arabs in Palestine, Flaum corresponded with Tagore. In late May 1936, during a particularly bad period of rioting in which she was stoned several times, she wrote to him from Jerusalem:

> The Arabs wish, that Jewish immigration should stop in Palestine, because they fear our superiority and progress of work. We make out of a desert a blooming and prosperous country in every way of which they themselves gain most, as they do nothing, just sit . . . and smoke leisurely and peacefully their pipes![2]

Tagore's reply is sympathetic but avoids the political issue.[3]

Santiniketan, [West Bengal, India]
15 June 1936

My dear Santi

I have just received your letter and it has pained me deeply to read of the bloody conflicts between the Jews and the Arabs in Palestine. Of course, I was somewhat prepared for it, for the newspapers had been giving some prominence to this. We who know of the communal troubles of India, can easily picture the situation – the utter cruelty and senselessness of such mad interracial conflicts. And yet where is the way out? Don't you feel this postwar world of ours is still more gross and brutal than it used to be? We almost seem to be going back to the medieval ages when greatest atrocities were being daily committed in the name of religion and civilisation. I despair of the future.

Nandita is very happy in her marriage.[4] At the moment she is away in far off Karachi with her husband's people. She will return soon and I am holding on[to] the beautiful album you have sent her till she returns.

I am glad there is some chance of your looking us up again. Will you please write to Rathi[5] about this in detail? He will be best able to advise.

With loving blessings,
Rabindranath Tagore

Source: MS copy at Rabindra Bhavan, Shantiniketan.

1 Schlomith Flaum: teacher. She published a memoir in Hebrew (2nd edn, Jerusalem, 1936), the title of which translates as 'The Wanderer: A Jewish Woman Travels the World: Memories of Travels and Encounters', in which she sensitively describes RT's paintings. She spent a period with RT in Berlin in 1930, at the time of his exhibition there.
2 Flaum to RT, 30 May 1936 [RB].
3 On RT's views of the Palestine problem, see Dutta and Robinson, *Rabindranath Tagore*, p. 300.
4 Nandita: Nandita Gangulee, granddaughter of RT, who married Krishna Kripalani in 1935; his family was from Karachi.
5 Rathi: Rathindranath Tagore.

299

To Rafiuddin Ahmed[1]

The recipient of this letter was founder and principal, Calcutta Dental College and Hospital.

Baranagore, [Baranagar, Calcutta, India]
[September 1936]

Dear Dr Ahmed

May I request you kindly to examine my companion Babu Promode Lal Ganguly who may need some help about his decaying teeth.[2] Poor fellow has been suffering for long and is growing quite desperate.

Affectionately,
Rabindranath Tagore

[PS] I have never been troubled with the set of teeth that you made for me, for which please accept my thanks.[3]

Source: MS original at Rabindra Bhavan, Shantiniketan.

1 Rafiuddin Ahmed (1890–1961): dental surgeon; he trained in the United States. In the 1950s, he was minister for agriculture and animal husbandry, Government of West Bengal.
2 There is a handwritten note on the letter, signed by Ganguly and dated 7 Sept. 1936: '4 extractions done today'. The patient's identity is unknown to us.
3 On RT's false teeth, see Dutta and Robinson, *Rabindranth Tagore*, p. 206.

468   *Selected letters of Rabindranath Tagore*

300

To Macmillan & Co. (UK)

In late 1936, after much hesitation and indirection, Tagore's *Collected Poems and Plays* appeared under the anonymous editorship of Ernest Rhys. Its faults have already been remarked upon (see letter 280). This letter of thanks to Macmillan is interesting for two reasons: it confirms that Tagore desired publication, and second it is clear that he had no reservations about the book's lack of critical apparatus, especially its failure to make clear the fact that the poems and plays were translations from Bengali; if he had had any such reservations, he would surely have avoided writing to Macmillan at all, or indeed pointed them out to the publisher.[1]

Santiniketan, [West Bengal, India]
3 December 1936

Dear Mr Daniel Macmillan,

I am writing to tell you how very pleased I am with the new book of my *Collected Poems and Plays*. I am most grateful to you for taking such trouble about it and for giving so much space in print for the collection. It contains what I wished to remain in this collected form and I sincerely hope it will meet with a good reception in your country.[2]

Yours very sincerely,
Rabindranath Tagore

Source: MS original in Macmillan Company Papers [BL].

1 Furthermore, RT said nothing about any reservations in his letter of thanks to Ernest Rhys on 31 Dec. 1936 [copy at RB]. He did, however, avoid sending a copy to Thomas Sturge Moore, because he must have realised that by agreeing to the book he had blatantly contradicted his own views on the weakness of his English translations, as expressed in letter 286. He asked for copies to be sent to E. J. Thompson and W. B. Yeats, however (A. K. Chanda, secretary of RT, to Macmillan, 3 Nov. 1936 [BL]).
2 There was a deafening silence from the British critics; the *Times Literary Supplement*, which had reviewed almost every previous Tagore translation, did not review the *Collected Poems and Plays*. But the book sold well and remained in print for decades.

301

To Jawaharlal Nehru

Jawaharlal Nehru never found it easy to pinpoint what Tagore meant to him, either during his lifetime or after his death; and the same was true of his daughter Indira.[1] In late 1936, she wrote to her father from Britain, where she was now at Badminton school (after leaving Switzerland), commenting that she found it 'difficult to fit in with the usual English schoolgirl', and adding, 'I am afraid a lot of the admiration I had for the English has vanished . . . I was glad of my stay in Santiniketan – chiefly because of Gurudev. In the very atmosphere there, his spirit seemed to roam and hover over one and follow one with a loving though deep watchfulness. And this spirit, I feel, has greatly influenced my life and thought.'[2]

Nehru passed these comments on to Tagore in Shantiniketan, with the remark, 'Of course she did not write them for you and I am sending them to you without her knowledge.'[3] This is Rabindranath's response.

Santiniketan, [West Bengal, India]
21 December 1936

My dear Jawaharlal,

I am indeed deeply touched by Indira's affectionate reference to me in her letter. She is a charming child who has left behind a very pleasant memory in the minds of her teachers and fellow students. She has your strength of character as well as your ideas and I am not surprised she finds herself rather alien to the complacent English society. When you write to her next, kindly give her my blessings.

We are in the midst of our anniversary celebrations and, I am afraid, the crowd and the activity mean now a great strain on my physical resources. But I wisely refrain from comparing my lot with that of yours!![4]

With affectionate blessings,

Yours sincerely
Rabindranath Tagore

Source: MS copy at Rabindra Bhavan, Shantiniketan.

1 On Indira Gandhi and Tagore, see Dutta and Robinson, *Rabindranath Tagore*, pp. 11, 324–6.
2 Indira to Jawaharlal, 15 Nov. 1936, in Sonia Gandhi (ed.), *Freedom's Daughter*, pp. 295–6.
3 Nehru to RT, *VBQ, 29*, Nos. 2–3, 1963–4, p. 104.
4 Though out of jail, Nehru was now president of the Congress.

18 Rabindranath in Shantiniketan, with Mahatma Gandhi, 1940

The Great Sentinel (1937–1939)

Introduction

Back in 1921, at the time of Tagore's first trenchant criticisms of the Noncooperation Movement, Gandhi had dubbed Tagore 'The Great Sentinel'. Though the Mahatma's respect and affection for Rabindranath had strengthened in the intervening period, he continued to ignore almost all his advice.

This was particularly true in regard to the politics of Bengal. In the 1930s, Subhash Chandra Bose emerged as the political leader of Bengal and, potentially, of the Indian National Congress. Though Tagore disagreed with Bose on some issues, particularly his faith in violent struggle, he came openly to support his candidature for the leadership. In 1938–9, this brought him into direct conflict with Gandhi and other Congress leaders, who eventually forced Bose out of Congress politics.

Nevertheless, Tagore's relationship with Jawaharlal Nehru deepened. Not only had Nehru sent his daughter to be educated at Shantiniketan, the two men shared a similar vision of international relations, which were of comparatively little concern to Gandhi. Nehru visited Shantiniketan several times, which laid the basis for his later support of Visva-Bharati as its chancellor from 1951 until his death.

Tagore was horrified by the policy of western appeasement of Hitler and Mussolini. The aggression of the Japanese leaders did not surprise him, as he had become aware of it during his last visit to Japan in 1929. But he still hoped that other traditions in Japanese life, which he had earlier greatly admired, would prevail. Japan's attack on China shattered his hopes. Like Nehru, he placed his faith in Chiang Kai-shek.

Despite the fact that he had never been more famous and revered as a moral beacon, Tagore felt that all the warnings he had uttered, both internationally and nationally, were being ignored in the late 1930s.

302

To Mahadev Desai

The fight to eradicate untouchability, led by Gandhi and fully supported by Tagore (see letter 260), inevitably acquired a strongly political colouring during the 1930s – for the Untouchables (Harijans, to use Gandhi's word) formed a large voting bloc, with separate seats reserved for them within the Hindu community, as defined in the Communal Award of 1932 and the subsequent Poona Pact. When the Untouchables began to convert to Sikhism and Buddhism, in order to escape the oppression of Hindu orthodoxy, the question arose of whether they were still Hindus, politically speaking. Tagore, when approached for an opinion, said:

> Whatever may be the political status of the Sikhs today, I cannot myself look upon them as very far away from the Hindu religion, for the simple reason that the fundamental ethical principles are practically the same . . . If the Sanatani Hindus [i.e. the most orthodox] of the upper classes [are] not prepared to extend the ordinary rights of a civilised existence to the Harijans, they should not also cry against these unfortunate victims seeking shelter in the Sikh fold.[1]

This statement provoked Mahadev Desai, Gandhi's secretary, to contact Tagore for clarification. He wrote:

> A number of people have been quoting your opinion on the question of the conversion of Harijans to Sikhism in support of their own contention that to embrace Sikhism is the only way to retain Hindu culture and yet renounce Hinduism. Bapu [Gandhi] could not believe that you could ever have given your assent to a proposition like this. If Sikhism is a part of Hinduism there is no question of renouncing the latter. One may, though he may be a Hindu, hold Sikh beliefs or Buddhist beliefs, as he does Shaiva or Vaishnava beliefs. That however is not renunciation of Hinduism. If he renounces Hinduism, he renounces Hindu culture and all that goes by that name, for you cannot separate culture from religion. Culture is a reflection of one's religion. And Sikhism at best is no religion or philosophy but an attempt to reform Hindu practices. There can, on this ground too, be no question of conversion to Sikhism![2]

Desai's relative complacency – the typical belief of the mainstream Hindu that all other religions in India (except Islam) are merely offshoots of one *sanatan dharma* (original, pure and everlasting truth) – is matched by the relative radicalism of Tagore's reply.

Santiniketan, [West Bengal, India]
4 January 1937

My dear Mahadeo,

I am not surprised that you should have requested me to explain fully my views with regard to the question of conversion of Harijans to Sikhism. At the very outset, let me tell you that I have not actually advised them to change their religious faith, but pleaded the case of Sikhism if, for reasons well known to all of us, they contemplated such a radical step. I hold the same view with regard to Buddhism as well.

In everyday use, Hinduism is just a way of life, and however great its philosophical and cultural basis may be, that alone will not atone for all the social injustices perpetrated throughout ages, in its name. Our religion divides the society into so many graded groups, and those at the bottom are not only denied bare social justice but are constantly made to feel themselves as less than human. Sanatanists are not very far wrong when they claim that this spirit of division, keeping down a large section of our community, is in the permanent structure of our religion forming the basis of our society, as can be proved by the injunction of our ancient law-givers such as Manu, Parasara and others.

Many of us try to give their texts a civilised gloss but such individual interpretations do not help the victims or touch the social autocrats in their behaviour. There are some modern incidents of their defeat such as had happpened even so late as in the time of Chaitanya[3] which was quickly followed by reaction, and we cannot be certain that the future of the social reform already achieved by our modern pioneers is permanently assured.

I am hardly concerned about the political aspect of the case. Whether they vote as Hindus or Sikhs is, according to me, of much lesser importance than what affects our humanity and forms our mental attitude towards our fellow beings. Long ago, it is now nearly 25 years, in a poem 'Hey Mor Durbhaga Desh' I had uttered my denunciation of the society that has raised itself on the indignity imposed upon the majority of our population in India and made her ready for centuries of defeat and degradation.[4] My cry has been a feeble cry in a wilderness that has obstructed along its history of dense growth the path of light and repeated efforts of those path-makers, who were the predecessors of the present great guide of our nation. Mahatmaji with his phenomenal hold upon the masses has indeed stirred us up but yet I do not know how long we must wait for his teaching to work effectively at the noxious roots in the dark depth of the soil. At the same time we must know that disasters that dog the footsteps of evils do not wait to consult our own time for their mitigation – for medicine which is sluggishly slow in its curative effect is too often overtaken by death.

I do hold the view that Buddhism or Sikhism were attempts from within at the eradication of one of the most intractable social deformities in Hinduism that turns into ridicule our aspiration for freedom. It was indeed a great day not only for the Sikhs but also for the whole of India when Guru Govinda, defying the age-long conventions of the Hindu society, made his followers one, by breaking down all barriers of caste and thereby made them free to inherit the true blessings of a self-respecting manhood.[5] Sikhism has a brave message to the people and it has a noble record. How great would be its effect, if this religion can get out of its geographical provincialism, shed its exclusiveness inevitable in a small community and acquire a nationwide perspective, one can only guess. I do not find anything in [the Sikh] religious practices and creeds which hurts my human dignity. My father often used to offer his worship in Amritsar *gurdwara* where I daily accompanied him but I never could imagine him at the Kali's temple in Calcutta.[6] Yet, in his culture and religion he was a Hindu and in his daily living maintained a purer standard of Hinduism than most of those who profess it by words of mouth and pollute it in their habits. I therefore do not fear that the [Harijans'] conversion to Sikhism or Buddhism will mean also their neglecting or abandoning Hindu culture.

I felt very happy that Nanda Lal proved once again his great worth. But I never had any doubts about his making Faizpur arrangements an unqualified success.[7]

With loving blessings,

Yours sincerely,
Rabindranath Tagore

Source: MS copy at Rabindra Bhavan, Shantiniketan.

1 *MR*, Oct. 1936, p. 479.
2 Desai to RT, 20 Dec. 1936 [copy at RB].

3 Chaitanya (1485–1533): Bengali mystic, who founded Vaishnavism.
4 'O My Unfortunate Country', *Gitanjali*, *RR*, XI, pp. 85–6; the lines were in fact written more than twenty-five years previously, in 1910.
5 Guru Govinda (Gobind Singh) (1666–1708): tenth and last guru of the Sikhs.
6 RT's father would not have tolerated either the idolatry or the animal sacrifice at the great Kali temple in Calcutta. In *My Rem*, RT describes how, as a boy, he accompanied his father to the worship at the Golden Temple in Amritsar: 'My father, seated amidst the throng of worshippers, would sometimes add his voice to the hymn of praise and, finding a stranger joining in their devotions they would welcome him most cordially, and we would return loaded with the sanctified offerings of sugar crystals and other sweets' (*My Rem*, p. 72/*RR*, XVII, p. 316).
7 Nanda Lal: Nanda Lal Bose, who at the express request of Gandhi decorated the exhibition at the annual Congress session in Dec. 1936 held in the village of Faizpur.

303

To Amiya Chakravarty

In October 1936, a year after Mussolini's invasion of Ethiopia, Tagore told C. F. Andrews that Amiya Chakravarty, then studying at Balliol College, Oxford, 'has been inciting me to express my indignation at Italy's expedition of brigandage, but I keenly feel the absurdity of raising my voice against any act of virulence of unscrupulous imperialism when it is pitifully feeble against all cases that vitally concern us'[1] – in other words, imperial oppression nearer home, in India. Rather than making a statement, Tagore eventually wrote a poem, 'Africa', and sent it to Chakravarty with this letter. Though the Italian invasion was the trigger for his writing it, the poem dealt with the exploitation of Africa in the widest sense.[2] Indeed it was remarkable less for what it said about Africa than for its view of modern civilisation as a form of savagery.

[Shantiniketan, West Bengal, India]
27 Magh 1343 [9 February 1937]

Kalyaniyeshu

You have requested me to write a poem on Africa. I have written it. But to what purpose I do not know. The styles of contemporary writers baffle me. And the sensibility I express in my own language cannot please the palates of those who speak another tongue. I lack the confidence to translate it into English. It saddens me to drag a poem in Bengali letters to a foreign marketplace. Moreover I feel mortified to beg for renown from strangers. My time of hankering after fame is almost over. What use is an English poem imprisoned in Bengali?[3]

Tomader
Rabindranath Thakur

Source: MS original at Rabindra Bhavan, Shantiniketan; letter published in *CP*, XI, p. 201.

1 RT to C. F. Andrews, 8 Oct. (1936 – misdated 1935) [RB].
2 'Africa', *Patraput*, *RR*, XX, pp. 49–50. The original poem is untitled. Four published versions exist, three of which are very similar.
3 On the English version of the poem, see letter 306.

304

To Mahatma Gandhi

Tagore's approach to Gandhi for help with the funding of Visva-Bharati (see letter 289), which had been made in desperation, had borne fruit in 1936 when the Mahatma raised some money on condition that Tagore stop his touring, given his weak state of health.[1] It emboldened Rabindranath to write this letter asking for further assistance, a request which had unfortunate repercussions. For Gandhi felt unable to accept Tagore's proposal: 'My shoulders are too weak to bear the burden you wish to impose upon me.' Then he continued, with a touch of sternness:

> I understand that in spite of your promise to me in Delhi you are about to go to Ahmedabad on a begging expedition ... I would ask you on bended knee to forgo the expedition if it is really decided upon. And in any case I would beg of you to recall my appointment as one of the trustees.[2]

This was like a spark to gunpowder. Tagore already felt humiliated by his dependence on Gandhi, now the latter seemed to be implying that his art was worthless, except as a (rather ineffective) way of raising money for worthwhile educational activities – at least that is how his words struck an understandably sensitive Tagore. Recalling years of accumulated frustration at the lack of appreciation of Visva-Bharati by his countrymen, and temporarily forgetting that both he and Gandhi had jokingly used the term begging many times before, Tagore wrote an angry, if dignified letter to the Mahatma (letter 305).[3]

[Shantiniketan, West Bengal, India]
10 February 1937

My dear Mahatmaji

I have taken the liberty of nominating you as a life-trustee of our Visva-Bharati. In these last frail years of my life it will give me great consolation to know that the institution to which I have given the best part and energy of my life will have you as one of its guardians. You will see from the bulletin of statutes and regulations that is being sent under a separate cover that no strain of actual work will be put upon you save what is entailed in occasional advice and decision in regard to matters that touch the financial security of the institution. I feel justified in sharing my responsibilities with you for I know that no difference in our spheres of activity can loosen the bond of mutual love and common aspiration. I hope you will allow me that privilege.

Yours affectionately
Rabindranath Tagore

Source: MS copy at Rabindra Bhavan, Shantiniketan; letter published in *Rabindra-Biksha*, Paush 1398 [Dec. 1991], p. 32.

1 See letter 295, n. 5.
2 Gandhi to RT, *CWMG*, LXIV, p. 381. Ahmedabad was of course Gandhi's home territory, which may have contributed to his reluctance to cooperate with RT.
3 RT spoke of 'begging' in letter 289, for example.

305

To Mahatma Gandhi

[Shantiniketan, West Bengal, India]
[26 February 1937]

Dear Mahatmaji

You have grievously misjudged me on mere suspicion which is so unlike your great and gracious ways that it has startled me into a painful amazement. I feel ashamed to have to assert that it was never my intention financially to exploit you or your name when I asked you to accept the trusteeship of Visva-Bharati. However, if it has been a mistake on my part, be the reason what it may, I readily withdraw my request and ask to be forgiven.

In your letter you have strangely accused me of contemplating to break my promise and go to Ahmedabad for the purpose of raising funds. You were not certain of the facts, and had no justification for hinting such a charge against me.[1] Allow me to be frank in return and to tell you that possibly your own temperament prevents you [from understanding] the dignity of the mission which I am glad to call my own – a mission that is not merely concerned with the economic problems of India, or her sectarian religions, but which comprehends the culture of the human mind in its broadest sense.[2] And when I feel the urge to send abroad some poetical creation of mine, which according to me carries within it a permanent standard of beauty, I expect, not alms or favour, but grateful homage to my art from those who have the sensitiveness of soul to respond to it. And if I have to receive contribution in the shape of admission fees from the audience, I claim it as very much less than what is due to me in return for the rare benefit conferred upon them. Therefore I must refuse to accept the term 'begging expedition' as an accurate or worthy expression coming from your pen.

It is a part of a poet's religion to entertain in his life a solemn faith in his own function, to realise that he is specially called to collaborate with his Creator in adding to the joy of existence. Let me confess that I should like nothing better than proudly to sit by the side of the artists trained by me when they try to give perfect expression to my dreams of beauty in their rhythmic movements and voice, and so be able to tell them that they have done well.

Yours sincerely
Rabindranath Tagore

Source: MS copy at Rabindra Bhavan, Shantiniketan; letter published in *VBQ*, 35, Nos. 1–4 (Gandhi Number), May 1969–April 1970, pp. 244–5.

1 The expedition was actually being planned by RT's son Rathindranath in order to raise money for the music and dance department of Visva-Bharati. The idea was to go *without* RT. See Dutta and Robinson, *Rabindranath Tagore*, pp. 321–2.
2 In 1935, RT said, in an appeal to Gandhi:

> The economic life of a nation is not such an isolated fact as Mahatmaji imagines and, today, side by side with economic poverty, we are faced with a cultural poverty which puts us to shame – shame that is in no way lessened when we consider what we once were . . . Please tell Mahatmaji to consider that art is not a luxury of the well-to-do. The poor man needs it as much and employs it as much in his cottage-building, his pots, his floor decorations, his clay deities, and in many other

ways. (Quoted in K. R. Kripalani, 'Rabindranath appeals to Gandhiji', *VBQ*, *1*, No. 1, May 1935, p. 112)

306

To Prince Akiki Nyabongo[1]

The poem 'Africa', which Tagore sent Amiya Chakravarty in February 1937 (see letter 303), was rendered into English by Chakravarty for the benefit of a Ugandan prince, Akiki Nyabongo, then studying in Oxford, who had just published a controversial novel, *Africa Answers Back*.[2] Nyabongo promptly wrote to Tagore enthusiastically requesting the poet to make his own translation, so that he could publish it 'for our people'.[3] This was enough to overcome Rabindranath's diffidence about his English, as he says in this letter.

In May 1937, 'To Africa' was published in the *Spectator*.[4]

Santiniketan, [West Bengal, India]
22 March 1937

Dear Prince Nyabongo

It has been exceedingly gratifying to me to find my poem on Africa received with such warm approbation by a representative African like yourself and I have found it difficult to resist your request to translate it into English. I must confess however that I have done it with the greatest diffidence, for I know the form of literary expression in English has now changed beyond recognition and I am by no means a modern.[5] Still your request was like a call to duty which could not be denied. I shall feel richly compensated if I know it will reach my friends in Africa and let them realise how an Indian poet feels about the despoliation of a whole continent in the name of civilisation.[6]

I have not yet received your book, it must be on its way. I assure you I shall read it with great interest.

With kind regards,

Yours sincerely
Rabindranath Tagore

Source: MS copy at Rabindra Bhavan, Shantiniketan.

1 Akiki Nyabongo (*c*. 1906–76): Ugandan prince, eldest son of Mukama Daudi Kasagama of Toro; he was educated in Uganda, at Yale and at Queen's College, Oxford, where he obtained a D.Phil. He was 'an eccentric who rebelled against his royal background and against colonial rule' (M. Louise Pirouet, *Historical Dictionary of Uganda* (Metuchen (New Jersey) and London, 1995)). His novel *Africa Answers Back* was banned by the Ugandan government of the time.
2 *Africa Answers Back* (London, 1936).
3 Nyabongo to RT, 3 March 1937 [RB].
4 *Spectator*, 7 May 1937.
5 E. J. Thompson read 'To Africa' and commented to RT, 'It struck me as very powerful in both thought and impression – and every bit as "modern" as any of our admired young lions roaring in the break-up of western civilisation' (Thompson to RT, 8 May 1937 [RB]).
6 Writing on the death centenary of William Wilberforce in 1933, RT commented:

> In the dark corners of civilisation slavery still lurks hiding its name and nourishing its spirit. It is there in our plantations, in factories, in business offices, in the punitive department of government

where the primitive vindictiveness of man claims special privilege to indulge in fierce barbarism. A considerable section of men still seems to have an innate sympathy for the strong seeking victims in [their] chase of profit and power. (*VBN*, Aug. 1933, p. 9)

307

To Sir William Rothenstein

As Tagore and William Rothenstein aged, there were long gaps in their correspondence, with Rothenstein making the main effort to keep it going. In May 1937, he wrote an affectionate, nostalgic letter and remarked:

> I hear that you divide your time between writing and drawing in fruitful production. What a mass of work you have put into the world! but I hear too that there is no one to follow you in creative vitality. Is India too political to have the necessary energy to give; like Ireland too preoccupied with self? . . . I must think of her as of old, though I am told of great changes, not altogether to my own 'visual' taste. But we may say the same of Europe.[1]

Tagore's reply includes a graphic comment on his painting and drawing, which was then fecund.

Almora, [Uttar Pradesh, India]
11 June 1937

My dear Rothenstein,

Your letters invariably bring to me the fragrance of [a] world, the shores of which are fast receding away from us. You, Sturge Moore, and Ernest Rhys are perhaps my only link with that world and I can quite realise that you do not exactly fit in with the modern scheme of things. I myself sometimes feel quite anti-dated [*sic*] in my country even though I try to keep abreast of modern tendencies in our world of thought and action; strange gods have been put on the altar, stranger incantations are being mumbled. But I do not grumble, for each generation has its own problems to face and its own set of values. Only we are out of place.

You must forgive me if I am no longer an assiduous letter writer as I used to be; a strange listlessness envelops me so often and my only shelter then is with my brush and the paints. With the ruthless freedom of an invader, I have been playing havoc in the complacent and stagnant world of Indian art and my people are puzzled for they do not know what judgement to pronounce upon my pictures. But I must say I am enjoying hugely my role as a painter.[2]

The advent of old age I have to admit freely and it is perhaps the first time that I have sought shelter in the hills frightened of the summer heat of the plains. Almora is far away from the beaten tracks of civilisation and here I am comparatively safe from meetings, receptions and interviews.[3] I wish I could have stayed here for an indefinitely long period but Santiniketan has its exorbitant demands and I am afraid I have to go back when the institution reopens [in] early July.

With warmest greetings, as of old,
Rabindranath Tagore

Source: MS original in Rothenstein Papers [Harvard]; letter published in Lago (ed.), *Imperfect Encounter*, p. 363.

1 Rothenstein to RT, 10 May 1937, in Lago (ed.), *Imperfect Encounter*, p. 362.
2 As RT became more and more vital and radical in his painting, the majority of Indian painters, particularly those belonging to the Bengal School, e.g. Asit Kumar Haldar and Kshitindranath Majumdar, became more and more anaemic and saccharine. Not until modern Indian painters threw off their debilitating obsession with mythology (which never much interested Rabindranath the painter) could they begin to develop.
3 RT was then staying with Basiswar Sen and his American wife Gertrude Emerson Sen (see letter 308).

308

To Gertrude Emerson Sen[1]

In the hot weather of 1937, Tagore, feeling his years, escaped to the hills at Almora (see letter 307) and stayed with a Bengali scientist, Boshi Sen, and his American journalist wife, Gertrude Emerson. They had married in 1932, and she had settled in India after many years of wandering as a correspondent for *Asia*, a pioneering magazine founded in the United States by Willard Straight, the first husband of Dorothy Straight. Leonard Elmhirst (who married Dorothy, some years after Willard Straight's death), met Gertrude Emerson in Calcutta in 1921 and described her thus: 'short of stature, angular in face, with penetrating eyes and unkempt hair, but very much alive. Full of common sense and level-headed, I guessed, and well accustomed to take care of herself.'[2] These mental qualities are latent in Tagore's letter to her, written after returning to the plains of Bengal from Almora, following the arrival of the monsoon.

[Baranagar, West Bengal, India]
21 July 1937

My dear Gertrude

I also believed like you that 'Where the heart is, there is Buddha', and in my case, the Buddha has proved thoroughly incompetent to shelter me from the onslaught of our merciless climate and I ever regret that I, in my good faith and impetuosity, ignored your sane advice and made a premature descent from your hill top.[3] I miss your climate and the company and, most decidedly, the icecream. *Bouma* tries to console me of an evening with a cup of a cool viscous substance, which, I understand, is known as icecream in the plains of Bengal.[4]

Boshi is really clever with his suggestion that I should no longer strive and strain myself with the impossible task of benefiting humanity and improving the world.[5] He says I should just keep to my chair and emanate a sort of spiritual electricity of a high voltage which will successfully do the trick. The suggestion has my full approval and would suit admirably my own temperament. I shall try to live up to the ideal.

You should not bother any more about those 'cards'. I found on a closer examination that I had plagiarised myself too well and the Macmillan might raise objections about my purloining their copyright property. I have therefore given up the idea altogether and there is no need of my writing to Miss Weil.[6]

I have come down to Calcutta for a short stay to arrange for the publication of my book on science.[7] I am staying with Rani and Prashanta in their new home near Dakshineswar – I feel rather lost and unnerved in this vast palace, which however does real justice to the royal name of its proprietress.[8]

With my affection and blessings,

Yours sincerely,
Rabindranath Tagore

Source: MS copy at Rabindra Bhavan, Shantiniketan.

1 Gertrude Emerson Sen (1890–1982): journalist and writer; she married Basiswar Sen and settled in India. In 1931, as Gertrude Emerson, she published *Voiceless India*, based on her experiences living in the villages of India, which was favourably reviewed by RT (*MR*, May 1931, pp. 501–2).
2 Elmhirst, *Poet and Plowman*, p. 51. There are many letters from Gertrude Emerson to Elmhirst in the Elmhirst Papers at High Cross House, Dartington.
3 In her letter to RT, Sen wrote, 'Are you really glad to be back at Bolpur? Of course I know that "Where the heart is, there is Buddha." You have your heart at Santiniketan' (Sen to RT, 16 July 1937 [RB]).
4 *Bouma*: Pratima Tagore.
5 Boshi: Basiswar Sen (1887–1971): scientist, who originally worked with Sir J. C. Bose and then founded the Vivekananda Laboratory at Almora, in 1924.
6 Sen had suggested that Miss Weil, associate editor of *Asia* in New York, might approach Woolworth's with the idea of selling cards carrying 'aphorisms' by RT. But RT realised that the best aphorisms had already appeared in English in *Stray Birds* (New York, 1916) and *Fireflies* (New York, 1928) (many of which were anyway unsatisfactory in translation).
7 The book was *Visva-Parichay* (*Our Universe*: Indu Dutt trans.; London, 1958), a science primer, written with the assistance of Basiswar Sen.
8 Baranagar was the home of the Indian Statistical Institute, of which Prashanta Chandra Mahalanobis was the director. RT's joke was about the name of his wife Rani, who had about her something of the air of a maharani.

309

To Sir John Anderson[1]

(marked PERSONAL AND CONFIDENTIAL)

Bengal in the 1930s was a politically troubled land. Among its long-running problems was terrorism and the Government's reaction to terrorism (see letters 116–18). From 1932 onwards, after a period of non-use, the penal settlement in the Andaman Islands was reactivated and by 1937 contained more than three hundred political prisoners living in harsh conditions. In mid-1933 they began a hunger strike against these conditions, as a result of which three of them died.[2] Four years later, in July 1937, another hunger strike began. Tagore, along with the political leaders in Bengal and the Congress leadership including Nehru and Gandhi, appealed to the prisoners to desist while attempts were made to mediate with the Bengal Government, whose ministers were now Indians.

On 2 August, Rabindranath gave a speech to a packed meeting at the Calcutta Town Hall. This letter to the governor of Bengal shows that Tagore, as might be expected, based his appeal to the Government on humanitarian considerations. He disapproved on principle of isolated penal settlements.[3] But in Sir John Anderson, he was dealing with the least sympathetic of the governors he had known. Anderson had been sent to Bengal specifically to take a tough line with terrorism; and during his five-and-a-half-year term of office he narrowly escaped assassination twice. (When Anderson visited Shantiniketan in 1935, so heavy was the security that Tagore, in protest, sent his entire staff and students away to Shriniketan for the day.) He was also, to quote the *Dictionary of National Biography*, 'in the general judgement of Whitehall, the greatest administrator of his time, perhaps of any time in the country's history'.[4] Tagore later condemned Anderson's tenure as governor as a 'vindictive regime': Anderson epitomised almost everything that Rabindranath disliked about British officialdom in India – though he gave Anderson credit for his later policy of arranging useful training for political *détenus* before they were released.[5]

[Shantiniketan, West Bengal, India]
16 August 1937

Dear Sir John Anderson,

I feel greatly relieved to learn from Dr Amiya Chakravarty, who had an interview with you on the 14th inst., that you and your Government are taking the earliest opportunity of bringing about a satisfactory settlement with regard to the Andaman prisoners. It is needless to emphasise that the matter is fraught with grave consequences and I am afraid, if no generous gesture is forthcoming from the Government, the situation might be too embittered for ever restoring normal atmosphere in the province. I have sent just now the following cable to the prisoners,

> Earnestly appeal to you to call off hunger strike. Your case taken up by the whole nation. Feel restoration of atmosphere favourable for discussion will be greatly helpful

and I am also wiring to Mahatma Gandhi and Pandit Nehru, whose words would have great consideration with the prisoners, to issue similar appeal to them. I quite realise that the calling off of the fast would considerably lessen the tension in the country and restore conditions more suitable for a dispassionate discussion. I have every hope that our request would be honoured by the prisoners and the Government will also generously review the whole question.

Dr Chakravarty tells me that a scheme of repatriation has been already accepted by the Government and that you are also considering the question of release of detenus. I feel very strongly on these matters on humanitarian grounds and we should like Great Britain to take the lead in abolishing the system of maintaining penal settlements for political prisoners, entirely cut off from humanising contacts with society and we trust that in India the reform of prisons will follow the advanced technique now being adopted by all progressive countries. You have already shown the way with the detenus' educational camps, a wise humanitarian step for which we all feel grateful to you.

With kind regards,

Yours sincerely
Rabindranath Tagore

Source: MS copy at Rabindra Bhavan, Shantiniketan.

1 Sir John Anderson, 1st Viscount Waverley (1952–8), (1882–1958): governor of Bengal, 1932–7.
2 See *MR*, Oct. 1933, pp. 469–70.

3 'Solitary confinement or banishment in the Andamans I would not advocate for offenders on either side. If our representatives seated in high authority do so, I, standing below, must contradict them' (speech at Shantiniketan on Andaman Day, *MR*, Sept. 1937, p. 316).
4 *Dictionary of National Biography, 1951–1960*, p. 23 (entry for Anderson). During the Second World War, Anderson was in the war cabinet and had 'overall responsibility for the organisation of [Britain's] civilian and economic resources for total war' (*DNB*, p. 22).
5 'vindictive regime': see letter 327. 'Vindictive' was a word RT rarely used. Anderson's reply to RT was non-committal, though he did offer to use his influence 'towards the policy of general appeasement which, if circumstances permit, my ministers would like to pursue' (Anderson to RT, 18 Aug. 1937 [RB]).

310

To Immanuel Olsvanger[1]

As already noted in letter 298, Tagore had a number of Jewish friends and was interested in the Jewish settlement of Palestine and the achievements of the Zionists. But he was not pro-Zionist in the political sense. Speaking in New York in 1930 to a Zionist interviewer, he said, 'What we poets have dreamt, the Jews can create in Palestine if they free themselves of the western concept of nationalism.'[2]

This orientation was probably the underlying reason why his hope of developing links between Shantiniketan and the Zionists never bore fruit. A few Zionists, such as Schlomith Flaum, spent time in Shantiniketan and became his friends – but there was no settlement of Jewish farmers at Shriniketan, as Tagore proposes in this letter to Immanuel Olsvanger, a Jewish emissary (and Sanskritist) who visited India in 1936 and met Indian leaders, hoping to make them more sympathetic to the Zionist cause. Apart from Sarojini Naidu, Olsvanger found little understanding of Jews and some hostility to Zionism among Indians.[3] Indian leaders such as Jawaharlal Nehru remained lifelong sympathisers of Arab, rather than Jewish, nationalism.

Santiniketan, [West Bengal, India]
8 September 1937

Dear Dr Olsvanger

I was happy to have from my friend Amiya Chakravarty the good wishes you have sent me and which I very sincerely reciprocate. What he tells me about recent developments in Jewish cultural enterprise in Palestine is very impressive; I sincerely hope that as a result of such beneficial activities an era of goodwill and cooperation will soon be inaugurated enabling the people to lay the basis of a new Palestinian civilisation. What interests me perhaps more than any other aspect of the work done by the Jewish settlers is the agricultural development of the country, the reclamation of marshy and sandy stretches, the application of modern scientific methods in dealing with problems of soil and cultivation. As you know from your own visit to India, our agricultural problems have become formidable, and they can be tackled only by an advanced technique and organisation. In the rural reconstruction department of our institution, you have seen, we are attempting to demonstrate new methods of agricultural development; our aim is to help the neighbouring villages by dealing with their problems and also to provide an example to our country by means of model farms, settlements etc. as to the possibilities of improvement which lie along advanced technique and planning.

It struck me and many of our workers while listening to Dr Chakravarty that some form of cooperation between our institution and the Zionist organisation would be very desirable. I would like this cooperation to take a practical form on the basis of help rendered to the cause of rural development in India; the inspiration that your workers can give us if some of them would join us here and start settlements of their own would be invaluable; their experience and example would, I feel sure, bring untold benefit both to our village organisers and to the villages themselves. With this object in view I have taken the liberty of outlining a scheme of agricultural settlement which would provide a few plots of land in our neighbourhood to Jewish pioneers from Palestine, and offer them every scope to develop the land and build farms following the advanced technique which they have already used with unique success.

As you will note, our scheme is a modest one, our aim being not to initiate settlements on a large scale but to show with your help, by concrete examples how India can master her own rural problems with resolute will and by the exploitation of scientific resources. I cherish the hope that the creative spirit which inspires the Zionist workers will not be restricted to the very necessary work that lies in Palestine but also be allowed to play its part in helping the eastern countries to develop their own civilisation in the modern age.

I am also considering other schemes of cooperation between our workers and your own – but I feel that if we can start a nucleus in India where Zionist enterprise would join hands with the creative movements in new India, many fruitful avenues of cultural interchange will be opened.

I am enclosing the outline scheme in separate sheets.[4] May I request you to place this letter and enclosure before Mr Shertok who, I am told, has a deep love for India, and other leaders at the Jewish Agency?[5] I would request you also to forward a copy of this letter to Dr Weizmann with my regards.[6]

With cordial remembrances and my kind regards,

Yours sincerely
Rabindranath Tagore

Source: MS copy at Rabindra Bhavan, Shantiniketan.

1 Immanuel Olsvanger (1888–1961): folklorist and Hebrew translator; he was among the first to translate Sanskrit and Japanese literary texts into Hebrew.
2 Interview with Joseph Brainin, *Jewish Standard*, Toronto, 28 Nov. 1930. RT commented:

> I understand Zionism in the same sense as my great friend Einstein. I regard Jewish nationalism as an effort to preserve and enrich Jewish culture and tradition. In today's world this programme requires a national home. It also implies appropriate physical surroundings as well as favourable political and economic conditions. I realise this. Palestine, however, can provide these only if the Jews will include the Arabs in their political and economic programme. Your spiritual and cultural programmes do not need to sacrifice anything to obtain this political cooperation. I visualise a Palestine Commonwealth in which the Arabs will live their own religious life and the Jews will revive their resplendent culture, but both will be united as one political and economic entity.

3 See Joan G. Roland, *Jews in British India: Identity in a Colonial Era* (Hanover and London, 1989), pp. 192–5.
4 The outline scheme stated:

> The Visva-Bharati offers four pieces of land, 30 acres each, in the vicinity of Santiniketan to Jewish settlers. There would be no initial payment to be made for the land by the settlers; no rent

will be charged for the first year, the rent after that period will be a very nominal one, being the usual amount paid by villagers under local law . . .

The Jewish farms will serve as demonstration farms for the Indian peasant.

5 Shertok: Moshe Sharett (1894–1965): Zionist leader; he was Israel's first foreign minister. He sent Olsvanger to India in 1936, but there is no evidence that India was of special importance to him.
6 Weizmann: Chaim Weizmann (1874–1952): head of the Jewish Agency for Palestine from 1929; he was the first president of Israel.

311

To Mahatma Gandhi

In mid-September 1937, Tagore almost died. He was in Shantiniketan, preparing to leave for Gwalior at the invitation of the maharaja, when he was struck down by an attack of erysipelas. For some sixty hours he was in a coma, without any proper medical help to begin with, since there was no telephone in Shantiniketan with which to summon it from Calcutta.[1] As word of his illness spread, messages of concern began to come in, including one from Mahatma Gandhi. It was to Gandhi whom Rabindranath wrote first on his recovery. The letter is in a shaky hand.[2]

Gandhi replied, 'You are not a mere singer of the world. Your living word is a guide and an inspiration to thousands. May you be spared for many a long year yet to come.'[3]

A week later Tagore also wrote to Leonard Elmhirst (letter 312).

Santiniketan, [West Bengal, India]
19 September 1937

Dear Mahatmaji

The first thing which welcomed me into the world of life after the period of stupor I passed through was your message of affectionate anxiety and it was fully worth the cost of sufferings which were unremitting in their long persistence.

With grateful love,

Yours sincerely
Rabindranath Tagore

Source: MS copy at Rabindra Bhavan, Shantiniketan; letter published in *Rabindra-Biksha*, Paush 1398 [Dec. 1991], p. 28.

1 The circumstances of the attack were described by P. C. Mahalanobis in an unpublished letter to E. J. Thompson:

As you know, the Poet was very seriously ill in September. Just before this he was staying with us in Calcutta. I left for Simla for a committee meeting; two days later, after a great deal of hesitation, he went back to Santiniketan, and the same night became unconscious. As the telegraph office was then closed, the railway people sent a telephonic message to our house at one o'clock at night asking that doctors should be sent to Santiniketan immediately without waiting for the morning train as otherwise it might be too late. Rani [Mrs Mahalanobis] telephoned to my uncle Sir Nil Ratan Sarkar [a famous physician]; [they] left for Santiniketan at two o'clock by car and reached there early in the morning. Poet was then completely unconscious and the local doctors thought it was a case of apoplectic stroke. He however recognised Rani, smiled and said 'So you have come'; and again became unconscous. When doctors arrived from Calcutta they found that it was a very bad attack of erysipelas complicated by kidney trouble. For sixty-two hours he was completely unconscious, and all hopes were given up. Rani was near him all this time almost continuously as nobody else could administer medicine or food. He apparently retained a subconscious touch with her and it was only she who could manage to do anything. Once he regained consciousness recovery was very rapid. As soon as he could speak he said that he wanted to write a poem or to paint a picture. As writing a poem would be more strenuous, he asked for his pigments and brushes. Within a few hours he painted quite a large picture. The whole of the foreground is a dark and ill-defined veil of primitive forest; a warm flood of golden light breaks through in the centre showing the distant view on the other side. (Mahalanobis to Thompson, 9 March 1938 [RB])

The painting is reproduced as the frontispiece of *VBQ*, 3, No. 3, Nov. 1937; the yellow light is paler and more ghostly than Mahalanobis stated.
2 A facsimile of the letter appears in Kripalani, *Rabindranath Tagore*, opp. p. 393.
3 Gandhi to RT, 23 Sept. 1937, *CWMG*, LXVI, pp. 156–7.

312

To Leonard Knight Elmhirst

Santiniketan, [West Bengal, India]
26 September 1937

Dear Leonard

Returning from this my first and latest voyage to the limitless dark I seem to realise in a brighter light a clearer vision of all the precious gifts of life that had come to my share. One of these which appeared to my mind was your friendship for which let me offer you my thanks with a renewed freshness and fervour.[1]

With my love to you and yours
Rabindranath Tagore

Source: MS original in Dartington Trust archives [Dartington]; letter published in Dutta and Robinson (eds.), *Purabi*, pp. 112–13.

1 Elmhirst's reply appears in Dutta and Robinson (eds.), *Purabi*, p.113.

313

To Rash Behari Bose[1]

In October 1937, Tagore received a cable from Rash Behari Bose, a Bengali revolutionary long settled in Japan whom he had met during his visits to Japan. It read:

> Indian merchants students residents here meeting request you prevent Congress and Nehrus anti-Japanese activities for sake Indian interests Indo-Japanese friendship.[2]

Tagore, in his reply, is torn between his old admiration for Japan and his horror at Japan's militarism in China.

Santiniketan, [West Bengal, India]
10 October 1937

Dear Rash Behari,

Your cable has caused me many restless hours, for it hurts me very much to have to ignore your appeal. I wish you had asked for my cooperation in a cause against which my spirit did not protest. I know, in making this appeal, you counted on my great regard for the Japanese, for, I, along with the rest of Asia, did once admire and look up to Japan and did once fondly hope that in Japan Asia had at last discovered its challenge to the West, that Japan's new strength would be consecrated in safeguarding the culture of the East against alien interests. But Japan has not taken long to betray that rising hope and repudiate all that seemed significant in her wonderful, and, to us symbolic awakening, and has now become itself a worse menace to the defenceless peoples of the East. Worse than its economic exploitation, worse indeed than its geographical aggression, is this daily perpetration of pitiless massacres and its unashamed championship of its inhumanity. Countries have been conquered before in history, and, seen in wider perspective, there is nothing very inhuman or shocking in a virile race overstepping the dilapidated fences built by the previous victories of an earlier race; and, until science had made man's inhumanity so effective, such fighting, like all life, seemed only half cruel. All that is changed, and today when one nation invades another, its wrong is not only that of mere imperialist ambition, but of human butchery more indiscriminate than any plague. And if the outraged conscience all over the world cries out against such a wrong, who am I to recall such righteous protest? This protest has not been engineered by any single individual, it is as spontaneous and heartfelt as the admiration that the peoples of the East felt for Japan thirty years ago. I should be powerless to check it even if I dared to attempt it.

You must therefore forgive me that I am unable to oblige you, and believe me when I say that I have great sympathy with my countrymen in Japan, as indeed I have with the Japanese themselves; but the cry that comes from China of broken hearts and broken heads and broken bones is far too piercing and awful.

With kind regards,

Yours sincerely,
Rabindranath Tagore

Source: MS copy at Rabindra Bhavan, Shantiniketan.

1 Rash Behari Bose (1885–1945): revolutionary. He organised the throwing of the bomb that wounded Lord Hardinge, the viceroy, during his state entry to Delhi on 23 Dec. 1912. In 1915, he left India for Japan, pretending to be a nephew of Rabindranath, P. N. Tagore. There, much to the indignation of the British, he was sheltered by arch-nationalists in Tokyo led by Toyama Mitsuru and married the daughter of one of them. During the late 1930s, he agitated for Indian freedom, founding an Indian Friendship Association and a branch of an overseas Indian organisation, the Indian Independence League, in 1937. See Peter Heehs, *The Bomb in Bengal: The Rise of Revolutionary Terrorism in India 1900–1910* (New Delhi, 1993), pp. 245–7, and Leonard A. Gordon, *Brothers against the Raj: A Biography of Indian Nationalists Sarat & Subhas Chandra Bose* (New York, 1990), pp. 462–3.
2 Rash Behari Bose to RT, 9 Oct. 1937 [RB].

314

To Subhash Chandra Bose[1]

During the late 1930s, the need for a nationalist song that would unite all communities in India became apparent. One obvious candidate was 'Bande Mataram' (Hail to the

Motherland), the rallying cry of nationalists during the Swadeshi Movement. But the words of this song, written in Bengali half a century earlier by Bankim Chandra Chatterji [Chattopadhyay] for his novel *Anandamath*, were clearly linked to Durga, the terrible ten-armed Hindu goddess worshipped every autumn in Bengal at Durga Puja, and the descriptions of India in the song were more true of Bengal than of India as a whole. Muslims could not be expected to sympathise with the song, nor indeed could all Hindus.

The Congress leaders were initially not aware of the problem. Nehru, not having read the words of the song in English, believed that there was no problem, though he soon changed his mind after reading an English translation.[2] Subhash Chandra Bose, as a Bengali who also knew Muslim sensitivities, was more aware of the potential conflict. Bose consulted Tagore, whose letter on the subject leaves no doubt as to his opinion.

As a result of these discussions, 'Bande Mataram' was dropped as a candidate for India's nationalist song and its potential national anthem. After Independence in 1947, Tagore's song 'Jana Gana Mana' was adopted as the national anthem.

Belgharia, [Calcutta, India]
19 October 1937

Shuhridwar

The core of 'Bande Mataram' is a hymn to the goddess Durga; this is so plain that there can be no debate about it. Of course Bankim does show Durga to be inseparably united with Bengal in the song, but no Mussulman can be expected patriotically to worship the ten-handed deity as 'Swadesh'. This year many of the special [Durga] Puja numbers of our magazines have quoted verses from 'Bande Mataram' – proof that the editors take the song to be a hymn to Durga. The novel *Anandamath* is a work of literature, and so the song is appropriate in it. But parliament is a place of union for all religious groups, and there the song cannot be appropriate. When Bengali Mussulmans show signs of stubborn fanaticism, we regard these as intolerable. If we too copy them and make unreasonable demands, it will be self-defeating.

The article on 'Bande Mataram' is by Krishna Kripalani. I had no idea he would publish it in the Visva-Bharati journal.[3] This debate has no connection with Visva-Bharati. The word was that he would write about it to Jawaharlal.

I am still under the orders of the doctors. Not yet dismissed; my health not yet properly restored for work.[4]

Tomader
Rabindranath Thakur

PS Bengali Hindus have become agitated over this matter, but it does not concern only Hindus. Since there are strong feelings on both sides, a balanced judgement is essential. In pursuit of our political aims we want peace, unity and goodwill – we do not want the endless tug of war that comes from supporting the demands of one faction over the other.

Source: Copy at Rabindra Bhavan, Shantiniketan; letter published in Nepal Majumdar, *Bharate Jatiyata o Antarjatikata ebang Rabindranath*, IV (rev. edn, 1398 [1991]), pp. 191–2.

1 Subhash Chandra Bose (1897–1945): politician; he was the leading political figure of Bengal in the 1930s, and in 1938 became president of the Congress. In the Second World War, he founded and led the Indian National Army against British rule.
2 See Nehru to Subhash Chandra Bose, 20 Oct. 1937, in Jawaharlal Nehru, *Selected Works of Jawaharlal Nehru*, VIII (second series) (New Delhi, 1984), pp. 186–7.
3 Krishna Kripalani, '"Bande Mataram" and Indian nationalism', *VBN*, Oct. 1937, p. 31. Kripalani openly disagreed with Nehru's opinion that 'Bande Mataram' was harmless, and supported the Muslim objections.
4 On RT's recent illness, see letter 311.

315

To Edward John Thompson

Tagore with age was increasingly drawn to Buddhism (see, for instance, letter 267). In 1935, at the birthday celebrations of the Buddha, he said, 'I . . . bow my head in reverence to him whom I regard in my inmost being as the greatest man ever born on this earth.'[1]

In 1937, E. J. Thompson, while writing his book about the first days of Buddhism, *The Youngest Disciple*, commented to Rabindranath:

> To me it is increasingly clear that what the world needs is to take both Buddha's and Christ's teaching – the pity and tenderness of Buddhism supplies what Christianity lacks, in a certain 'hard-boiledness' (perhaps the fault of Christian nations). The subtle and many-coloured beauty of your own wonderful life interprets Buddhism as nothing else does, and I am glad that I have known you.[2]

Tagore, in his reply, shows his sympathy for this view of religion.

Santiniketan, [West Bengal, India]
27 October 1937

Dear Thompson,

Thanks for your letter and the good wishes. I am much better now and should feel perfectly normal if the doctors by continuing the treatment did not keep on reminding me that I was still a patient. I agree with you that both Christ and Buddha embodied in their lives the only true principles that can work for men's common good; Buddha's insistence on the renunciation of greed creates the necessary condition of the mind in which the love of others ceases to conflict with one's own good. Do you know I have often felt that if we were not Hindus (in the wide sense of Hinduism which includes Buddhism as well) I should like my people to be Christians? Indeed, it is a great pity that the Europeans have come to us as imperialists rather than as Christians and so have deprived our people of their true contact with the religion of Jesus Christ. A few individuals like C. F. Andrews, whom we have known as true followers of their teacher, have created in us a respect for Christianity which the most brutal lathi charges, shootings and detentions without trial of the British Government in India have failed totally to dissipate.[3] What a mental torture it is to know that men are capable of loving each other and adding to one another's joy, and yet would not!

With kindest regards,

Yours sincerely,
Rabindranath Tagore

Source: MS original in Thompson Papers [Bodleian].

1 'Buddhadeva', *VBQ*, 22, No. 3, Winter 1956–7, p. 169.
2 Thompson to RT, 25 Sept. 1937 [RB].
3 On the religion of C. F. Andrews, see letter 257.

316

To Gertrude Emerson Sen

Although Gandhi and Tagore continued to be poles apart in temperament, they came to understand each other somewhat better during the last decade of Tagore's life. However, when approached by his friend Gertrude Emerson Sen for a piece on Gandhi that would 'sum up Gandhi the man, not merely Gandhi the saint or Gandhi the politician, or Gandhi the thorn in the side of the British Government', for publication in *Asia*, Tagore shied away, for reasons that he explains in this letter.[1]

Nevertheless, in January 1938, Tagore wrote 'Gandhi the man', his best piece of writing on the Mahatma, which was published in the *Sunday Statesman* of Calcutta, and later in *Asia*.[2]

[Shantiniketan, West Bengal, India]
[26? November 1937]

My dear Gertrude

I am quite sensible of the honour you do me in inviting me to write an article for *Asia* on Mahatma Gandhi, but, fortunately or unfortunately, I am even more sensible of my incompetence for the task. I doubt if I could at any time have done justice to the subject had I attempted it, but now, with my present health, it is out of the question. I am not even what I was at Almora, when I could still sit and write for hours.[3] Now I hold the pen very reluctantly, though I still keep on playing pranks with the brush. Moreover, though I hold Gandhiji dear and cannot but feel the force of his personality, I can hardly be said to know him intimately. We have never lived together or worked together for any length of time. What understanding and appreciation we have of each other is more or less intuitive. I hope, therefore, you will excuse me.

When are you coming to Calcutta? Give my love to Boshi.[4] With kindest regards,

Yours sincerely
Rabindranath Tagore

Source: MS copy at Rabindra Bhavan, Shantiniketan.

1 Sen to RT, 14 Nov. 1937 [RB].
2 *Sunday Statesman*, 13 Feb. 1938; *Asia*, Oct. 1938, pp. 579–80; see appendix 3.
3 See letter 308.
4 Boshi: Basiswar Sen.

317

To Leonard Knight Elmhirst

Almost as soon as he established them, Tagore's school and university started to depart from his cherished educational ideals: they acquired the examination mentality. His interest shifted progressively to Shriniketan and his hope of developing an education suitable for the mass of Indians, who mainly lived in villages, which would not aim to fulfil the aspiration of the western-influenced urban class to obtain a university degree. Like Gandhi, Tagore had no faith in the established Indian educational institutions based mostly on British models. In the words of Leonard Elmhirst, thinking back to his own experience at Shriniketan in 1924:

> Out of [Tagore's] own experience as a teacher of boys and girls from mainly middle-class families in Calcutta and from his study of our work at Sriniketan with village boys, he was convinced that some new form of schooling could be worked out for village children in India, based upon immediate contact with the world of nature and with the life, the beauty and the problems of the countryside. He urged us to establish a weekly boarding school for village boys. This he named Siksha-Satra, and invited me to collaborate with him over a statement of the principles and practice that could be applied within such a group, if for five nights and days each week they left home and were free to engage in a variety of practical enterprises – such as gardening, weaving, carpentry, painting and cooking.[1]

When Gandhi paid a visit to Siksha-Satra some years later, he was so impressed that he wanted to borrow the headmaster to help him in planning primary education for the whole of India. 'Tagore laughingly volunteered on the spot to be Gandhi's first minister of education,' Elmhirst wrote.[2] But though Gandhi's scheme of 'Basic Education', put into practice in the 1930s, was partly based on Siksha-Satra, it was too impoverished, utilitarian and inartistic for Tagore. As he makes clear in this letter to Elmhirst – thereby prefiguring similar educational debates in Britain (and other western countries) from the 1960s onwards – Tagore did not believe in one form of education for the well-off and another, inferior form of education for the poor.[3]

Santiniketan, [West Bengal, India]
19 December 1937

Dear Leonard,

You know how for a long while I have been cherishing my hope of establishing an ideal centre of education at Sriniketan – an ideal which is not curtailed [by] the strict measure of a narrow village environment, which is not specially set apart to be doled out as famine ration carefully calculated to be just good enough for emaciated life and dwarfed mentality. It is well known that the education which is prevalent in our country is extremely meagre in [its] spread and barren in [its] quality. Unfortunately this is all that is available for us and that has set up an artificial standard proudly considered as respectable. Outside the *bhadralogue* class, pathetic in their struggle [to fix] a university label on their name, there is a vast obscure multitude who cannot even dream of such a costly ambition.[4] With them we have our best opportunity if we know how to use it, and there only we can have our freedom for offering to our country the best all-round culture not mutilated by the official dictators. I have generally noticed that when charitably minded city-bred politicians talk of education for the village folk they mean the little left over in the bottom of their cups after diluting them copiously. They are callously unmindful of the fact that the kind and the amount of food that is needful for mental nourishment must not be apportioned differently according to the social status of those that receive it.

I am therefore all the more keen that Siksha-Satra should justify the ideal I have entrusted to it and should represent the most important function of Sriniketan in helping students [towards] the attainment of manhood complete in all its various aspects. Our people need more than anything else a real scientific training that could inspire in them the courage of experiment and initiative of mind which we lack as a nation. Sriniketan should be able to provide for its pupils an atmosphere of rational thinking and behaviour which alone can save them from stupid bigotry and moral cowardliness. I myself attach much more significance to the educational possibilities of Siksha-Satra than to the school and college at Santiniketan, which are every day becoming more and more like so many schools and colleges elsewhere in this country, borrowed cages that treat the students' minds as captive birds whose sole human value is judged according to the mechanical repetition of lessons prescribed by the education dispensation foreign to the soil. It would indeed give me great joy if Sriniketan could at last make use of its opportunities to realise my dream and I would welcome Dhiren with his vigorous masterfulness to rouse the Siksha-Satra to a new course of fruitful adventure.[5] In that case not only will he have my blessings but as much guidance as is possible for me to offer him with the last flicker of my life.

With love for you and Dorothy

Affectionately yours
Rabindranath Tagore

Source: MS original in Dartington Trust archives [Dartington]; letter published in Dutta and Robinson (eds.), *Purabi*, pp. 114–15.

1 'Preface' by Elmhirst to Rabindranath Tagore and Leonard K. Elmhirst, *Rabindranath Tagore: Pioneer in Education* (London, 1961), p. 13. This book includes the 'statement of principles' and 'Siksha-Satra' on pp. 66–84 (Siksha-Satra means simply '(charitable) institution for education'). See also Uma Das Gupta, 'Rabindranath Tagore on rural reconstruction: the Shriniketan programme, 1921–41', in Dutta and Robinson (eds.), *Purabi*, especially p. 135.
2 'Preface' to Tagore and Elmhirst, *Pioneer in Education*, p. 13.
3 The draft of this letter at Rabindra Bhavan, Shantiniketan, shows that RT omitted two paragraphs criticising Gandhi:

> Today Mahatma Gandhi has focussed the attention of the whole nation to the value of rural education as the most essential factor in the progress of our people and has inspired a band of enthusiastic workers to take up the cause. Mahatma Gandhi has the rare gift of making an ideal effective which I cannot claim; nevertheless I cannot help feeling sorry that though I took up the cause and worked [at] it long before others even considered it, lack of true workers should have rendered my ideal ineffectual so far.
>
> Education specially labelled as rural education is not my ideal – education should be more or less of the same quality for all humanity needful for its evolution of perfection.

4 *bhadralogue*: *bhadralok* (modern spelling), i.e. the respectable class.
5 Dhiren: Dhirendra Mohan Sen (1901–87): educationist and government official; he was principal and rector at Shantiniketan, 1930–9, and secretary for education, Government of West Bengal, 1948–65. Between 1925 and 1928, he studied in London and obtained a Ph.D in philosophy and psychology at University College. Leonard and Dorothy Elmhirst supported him financially at various times, both in Britain and at Shantiniketan/Shriniketan. Leonard, on his last visit to Shantiniketan while RT was alive, wrote home to Dorothy, 'All admit that Dhiren acted as surgeon and operated, not without cruelty, in such a way as to bring in fresh air and new health . . . His sarcasm and lack of tact are mentioned, but his achievement at Santiniketan is respected and all admit that experience has mellowed him' (6 Jan. 1939 [Dartington]). D. M. Sen's uncle was Kshiti Mohan Sen.

318

To Sven Hedin[1]

Tagore was greatly attracted to the writings of Sven Hedin, the Swedish explorer of Central Asia. The two men met at least twice, in 1921 (when Tagore visited Stockholm formally to receive his Nobel prize) and in 1926. After the first meeting, Hedin hoped to visit Tagore in India, but the Government would not give him a visa because of his pro-German sympathies during the First World War. This letter was prompted by a letter from Hedin mentioning his forthcoming book *The Silk Road*.

[Shantiniketan, West Bengal, India]
1 February 1938

My dear Sven Hedin

Your letter has brought me the pleasant news that I may look forward to a new book of yours in the near future. I love your books and your explorations even as I love you and I have read almost all your available books in English, not excluding the latest, *The Big Horse's Flight*.[2]

I often wonder if you wouldn't some day include Santiniketan in your explorations; we could not however give you the thrill that the Gobi has for you. It is a mere poet's refuge which can offer no stimulation of danger but some experience which is a novelty for you, that of rest.

With love,
Rabindranath Tagore

Source: MS copy at Rabindra Bhavan, Shantiniketan.

1 Sven Hedin (1865–1952): explorer; he began exploring the Gobi desert in 1899 and continued into the 1930s.
2 RT dedicated the Swedish edition of *Fireflies* to Hedin.

319

To Edward John Thompson

In 1937, in a public appeal for the republican side in the Spanish civil war, Tagore wrote that 'this devastating tide of International Fascism must be checked . . . come in your millions to the aid of democracy, to the succour of civilisation and culture' – and earned a public rebuke from Joseph Goebbels, speaking at the Nazi Party's Nuremberg rally.[1]

As war in Europe drew closer, fuelled by Britain and France's policy of appeasement, Tagore's letters became preoccupied with the political situation; he followed the newspaper reports closely, though he seldom referred to specific events in his letters. This letter was written a month after the *Anschluss*, Germany's annexation of Austria, 'ratified' by a plebiscite of Austrians on 10 April.

Santiniketan, [West Bengal, India]
14 April 1938

My dear Thompson,

The heat is oppressive and both body and mind feel depressed.

Aldous Huxley's latest book *Ends and Means* came as a great consolation at this trying time of iconoclastic nihilism.[2] It is a torture for me to have to witness, in the last chapter of my life, the nauseating sight of maniacs let loose making playthings of all safeguards of human culture. They seem to have an extraordinary cunning in occupying the best vantage grounds of history from where to compel their neighbours, gone out of breath by the accumulated loads of their possessions, humbly to come to terms with them after a feeble tragicomedy of futile bluffs. From the high platform of the western political stage reaches us in two different discordant pitches a prolonged duet of diplomacy between the fiercely pugnacious and the meekly accommodating.

In the meanwhile such gifts as were poured upon us in merciful profusion in our young days, are callously trodden underfoot with a savage bravado and man's faith in their values which have so long given meaning and dignity to his life [is] reduced to dust, and hooliganism wins fond embrace at every trampling step from those who are menaced.

With this worldwide cataclysm hanging over our heads, we, who are powerless, are merely waiting in a humiliating position of passive inaction. And men and messages pour in to congratulate me for measuring my seventy-seventh year!

I am sending you herewith a small poem I wrote today.[3]

Yours sincerely,
Rabindranath Tagore

Source: MS original in Thompson Papers, [Bodleian].

1 'To the conscience of humanity', *Spain*, Calcutta, 1937 (pamphlet also containing statements by Romain Rolland and Henri Barbusse). On Goebbels' reaction, see Dutta and Robinson, *Rabindranath Tagore*, p. 351.
2 RT wrote to Huxley that he was 'very greatly impressed' by *Ends and Means* (RT to Huxley, 3 March 1938 [copy at RB]).
3 The poem, which echoes the disillusioned sentiments about humanity that RT expresses in his letter, was first published in *Rabindra-Biksha*, Paush 1403 [Dec. 1996], pp. 2–3, with a note by Krishna Dutta (p. 4).

320

To Ernest Rhys

Having edited Tagore's *Collected Poems and Plays*, Ernest Rhys, as editor of Everyman's Library, asked Tagore to write a foreword to a new Everyman translation of the Hindu scriptures. Rabindranath was reluctant but felt he could not refuse Rhys.[1] The foreword appeared in 1938.[2]

Rhys, a poet himself with an interest in Indian philosophy, was not satisfied with the book. He wrote:

> Between ourselves ... Professor Macnicol [the translator and editor] is a fine scholar, but he is not, and one could not expect him to be, something of an artist as well. For such a volume it needs almost a touch of genius, and I suppose it could only be done perfectly by a pundit and a poet collaborating and preparing it under Indian skies.[3]

In his reply, Tagore heartily agrees.

[Mangpoo, Kalimpong, West Bengal, India]
12 June 1938

My dear Ernest Rhys

Your misgivings are well founded and I should not hestitate to tell you that, [like] you, I have felt disappointed with Prof. Macnicol's translation. He is no doubt a considerable scholar in his subject but unfortunately lacks the true artist's delicate sensibility, which has robbed his work of much of its merit. *Upanishads* in some of their parts are incomprehensible owing to the symbolic language used which has utterly lost its significance. These portions should have been avoided, for grammar and lexicon are no proper guide to them and there are no means whatever today for realising their spirit.[4]

I wish I had myself undertaken the task when I was younger and had greater confidence in my powers; I would have liked nothing better than to translate my favourite *Isha Upanishad* but my last serious illness has left me very helpless and I do not think I can do justice today to the work or to myself were I to really undertake the responsibility.

I am holidaying with my son and daughter-in-law.[5] It is a nice quiet place and a comfortable elevation and I am feeling much better and rested.

Yours ever,
Rabindranath Tagore

Source: MS copy at Rabindra Bhavan, Shantiniketan.

1 RT to Rhys, 31 Dec. 1936 [copy at RB].
2 Nicol Macnicol (ed.), *Hindu Scriptures* (London, 1938). RT's foreword is reprinted in Dutta and Robinson (eds.), *Anthology*, pp. 245–7.
3 Rhys to RT, 1 June 1938 [RB]. In 1937, W. B. Yeats and Purohit Swami published their translation of the *Upanishads*, which Rhys reviewed, at RT's request, for the *Visva-Bharati Quarterly* ('The ten chief Upanishads', *VBQ*, 3, No. 3, Nov. 1937, pp. 219–23). RT commented on the review – with oblique reference to the difference between himself and W. B. Yeats – in a letter to Rhys:

> Yes, I [too] believe there is a mystic tendency in the Celtic mind which makes it somewhat akin to our own – with this difference, perhaps, that the tradition of western thinking, with its implicit

faith in the intellect, prevents you from trusting it to the extent to which we in India have learnt to do. Which is wiser I do not know. (RT to Rhys, 9 Oct. 1937 [copy at RB])

4 On this point, see RT's 'Notes and Comments', *VBQ*, 2, No. 2, July 1924, pp. 175–9. Speaking to Duke Gallarati Scotti in 1925, RT said:

> My father used to teach me to repeat during my early morning meditation certain sayings he had strung together from the *Upanishads*... How often, when I was young, did I think this perpetual repetition just a bore!... And then quietly, and through the light of my own experience, I began at last to understand something of their inner meaning. I found too that my own interpretations of the texts... did not at all coincide with that of my teacher. I still believe that mine had the elements of a deep truth within it. (*VBQ*, 28, No. 2, 1962–3, p. 104)

RT much admired the translations of the *Upanishads* by Juan Mascaró, who was both a poet and a mystic. Mascaró sent some of them to him in 1938/9, and received a letter of appreciation which is part-quoted on the back cover of the edition he published in 1965: 'Your translation... has caught from those great words the inner voice that goes beyond the boundaries of words.' Mascaró dedicated his translation 'To the Spirit of Rabindranath Tagore, 1861–1941'.

5 RT was then living at the house of Maitraye Devi and her husband. For details of his stay, see Maitraye Devi, *The Great Wanderer* (Calcutta, 1961).

321

To Charles Freer Andrews

C. F. Andrews was always a poor judge of literature – a failing that Tagore allowed to create unnecessary muddle at various moments in his English literary career. But while Rabindranath was aware of it (see letter 97, for instance), he generally overlooked it, out of loyalty to his friend. Then in 1938 he was brought face to face with Andrews' literary incompetence when Andrews became enthusiastic over a forthcoming biography of Tagore by a mutual friend and wrote a foreword to it stating that 'we have at last a full and comprehensive idea of [Tagore's] works'.[1]

The book was an English translation of a book written in Czech by Vincenc Lesny, an Indologist at the Charles University in Prague, who taught himself Bengali and began to read Tagore's works in the original and translate them. In the 1920s, he lived at Shantiniketan for a substantial period, where he was able to hold many discussions with Rabindranath himself.

While there was no doubt that Lesny was a considerable scholar of oriental languages, he was no biographer or literary critic; and his approach to Tagore and his work was entirely admiring. Furthermore, the requirements of the Czech readership were very different from those of the English readership, who already had available to them E. J. Thompson's study of Tagore and much other writing on him. But even allowing for these weaknesses, Lesny's book is still a feeble and misleading book, as Tagore shows himself to be aware in both this letter and letter 323. Andrews' praise for the book tells us only what a sentimentalist Andrews could sometimes be, and how careless of facts.[2]

Santiniketan, [West Bengal, India]
31 August 1938

Dear Charlie

There are good many minor mistakes in Lesny's book, most of which may be allowed to pass. Those which are too glaring have been corrected by Amiya.[3] I am sure you have noticed that the translations are not at all good and the abstracts of the stories and plays are invariably inadequate. However, this cannot be helped. Lesny has gone too much into details which it is impossible for him to handle properly and I think it makes tedious reading. Amiya thinks it may help readers to form a fairly good idea of my personality and works.[4] I am fearfully busy with tasks that are not important and yet unavoidable, and am constantly tired – you know what that means.

With love
Rabindranath Tagore

[PS] Krishna is reading the typescript copy of Lesny's book. It will be sent back to you when it will be done.[5]

Source: MS original at Rabindra Bhavan, Shantiniketan.

1 Foreword to Vincenc Lesny, *Rabindranath Tagore, his Personality and Work* (Guy McKeever Phillips trans.; London, 1939), p. 8. Andrews seems to have arranged the publishing of the English translation of Lesny's book.
2 Andrews responded to RT's criticism of the book not by defending its literary value but by lauding Lesny's great effort in learning Bengali simply in order to understand RT's work. 'If I had not been always going off to Fiji or South Africa, I might have done something of the same kind, but that was not to be allowed me' (Andrews to RT, 2 Sept. 1938 [RB]). As always with Andrews, it was the devotion that impressed him, never mind the result.
3 Amiya: Amiya Chakravarty.
4 The book received a respectful review in the *Listener* (24 Aug. 1939) and a mixed review in the *Times Literary Supplement*, which noted that 'some . . . of [the author's] summaries, particularly of the plays, are valuable as showing the parables implicit in them. But too often they are superfluous to those who have read the originals and unenlightening to those who have not' (15 April 1939). Fortunately, most of the publisher's stock of the English translation was destroyed by a bomb in the Second World War.
5 Krishna: Krishna Kripalani. Despite RT's reservations, Kripalani praised Lesny's book in his own biography of RT (Kripalani, *Rabindranath Tagore*, p. 350).

322

To Yone Noguchi[1]

In 1915, the year before his first visit to Japan, Tagore told C. F. Andrews, 'I am almost sure that Japan has her eyes on India. She is hungry . . . Japan is the youngest disciple of Europe – she has no soul – she is all science – and she has no sentiment to spare for other people than her own.'[2] Tagore's condemnation of Japanese militarism is clear enough from letter 313, written to Rash Behari Bose in 1937. A year or so later, after the merciless Japanese bombing of Guangzhou (Canton), whatever doubts Tagore may have had had disappeared.

He was therefore stunned to receive a letter from a Japanese poet whom he knew and respected, arguing vociferously for Japan's spiritual and moral role in sending its army to China. Yone Noguchi is now almost forgotten in the West (certainly as compared to his son, the sculptor Isamu Noguchi), but in the first two or three decades of this century he was among the best-known Japanese writers (many of his books were written in English), and the associate of Yeats and Pound.[3] His poetry was, if anything, more romantic and devoid of martial spirit than Tagore's poetry: yet here Noguchi was, in mid-1938, a spokesman – and, it seems, a convinced spokesman – for carnage on a grand scale. His hope was to enlist Tagore's support in India.

Noguchi published his letter in the press in India, and so Tagore published this reply. Noguchi then wrote again, and Tagore replied once more, again in print.[4]

Santiniketan, [West Bengal, India]
1 September 1938

Dear Noguchi,

I am profoundly surprised by the letter that you have written to me: neither its temper nor its contents harmonise with the spirit of Japan which I learnt to admire in your writings and came to love through my personal contacts with you. It is sad to think that the passion of collective militarism may on occasion helplessly overwhelm even the creative artist, that genuine intellectual power should be led to offer its dignity and truth to be sacrificed at the shrine of the dark gods of war.

You seem to agree with me in your condemnation of the massacre of Ethiopia by Fascist Italy but you would reserve the murderous attack on Chinese millions for judgement under a different category. But surely judgements are based on principle, and no amount of special pleading can change the fact that in launching a ravening war on Chinese humanity, with all the deadly methods learnt from the West, Japan is infringing every moral principle on which civilisation is based. You claim that Japan's situation is unique, forgetting that military situations are always unique, and that pious warlords, convinced of peculiarly individual justification for their atrocities have never failed to arrange for special alliances with divinity for annihilation and torture on a large scale.

Humanity, in spite of its many failures, has believed in a fundamental moral structure of society. When you speak, therefore, of 'the inevitable means, terrible it is though, for establishing a new great world in the Asiatic continent' – signifying, I suppose, the bombing of Chinese women and children and the desecration of ancient temples and universities as a means of saving China for Asia – you are ascribing to humanity a way of life which is not even inevitable among the animals and would certainly not apply to the East, in spite of her occasional aberrations. You are building your conception of an Asia which would be raised on a tower of skulls. I have, as you rightly point out, believed in the message of Asia, but I never dreamt that this message could be identified with deeds which brought exaltation to the heart of Tamerlane at his terrible efficiency in manslaughter. When I protested against 'westernisation' in my lectures in Japan, I contrasted the rapacious imperialism which some of the *nations* of Europe were cultivating with the ideal of perfection preached by Buddha and Christ, with the great heritages of culture and good neighbourliness that went [in]to the making of Asiatic and other civilisations. I felt it to be my duty to warn the land of *bushido*, of great art and traditions of noble heroism, that this phase of scientific savagery which victimised western humanity and led their helpless masses to a moral cannibalism was never to be imitated by a virile people who had entered upon a glorious renascence and had every promise of a creative future before them. The doctrine of 'Asia for Asia' which you enunciate in your letter, as an instrument of political blackmail, has all the virtues of the lesser Europe which I repudiate and nothing of the larger humanity that makes us one across the barriers of political labels and divisions. I was amused to read the recent statement of a Tokyo politician that the military alliance of Japan with Italy and Germany was made for 'highly spiritual and moral reasons' and 'had no materialistic considerations behind it'. Quite so. What is not amusing is that artists and thinkers should echo such remarkable sentiments that translate military swagger into spiritual bravado. In the West, even in the critical days of war madness, there is never any dearth of great spirits who can raise their voice above the din of battle, and defy their own warmongers in the name of humanity. Such men have suffered, but never betrayed the conscience of their peoples which they represented. Asia will not be westernised if she can learn from such men: I still believe that there are such souls in Japan though we do not hear of them in those newspapers that are compelled at the cost of their extinction to reproduce their military master's voice.

'The betrayal of intellectuals' of which the great French writer spoke after the European war, is a dangerous symptom of our age. You speak of the savings of the poor people of Japan, their silent sacrifice and suffering and take pride in betraying that this pathetic sacrifice is being exploited for gun running and invasion of a neighbour's hearth and home, that human wealth of greatness is pillaged for inhuman purposes. Propaganda, I know, has been reduced to a fine art, and it is almost impossible for peoples in nondemocratic countries to resist hourly doses of poison, but one had imagined that at least the men of intellect and imagination would themselves retain their gift of independent judgement. Evidently such is not always the case: behind sophisticated arguments seems to lie a mentality of perverted nationalism which makes the 'intellectuals' of today go blustering about their 'ideologies' dragooning their own 'masses' into paths of dissolution. I have known your people and I hate to believe that they could deliberately participate in the organised drugging of Chinese men and women by opium and heroin, but they do not know; in the meanwhile, representatives of Japanese culture in China are busy practising their craft on the multitudes caught in the grip of an organisation of wholesale human pollution. Proofs of such forcible drugging in Manchukuo and China have been adduced by unimpeachable authorities. But from Japan there has come no protest, not even from her poets.

Holding such opinions as many of your intellectuals do, I am not surprised that they are left 'free' by your Government to express themselves. I hope they enjoy their freedom. Retiring from such freedom into 'a snail's shell' in order to savour the bliss of meditation 'on life's hopeful future', appears to me to be an unnecessary act, even though you advise Japanese artists to do so by way of change. I cannot accept such separation between an artist's function and his moral conscience. The luxury of enjoying special favouritism by virtue of identity with a Government which is engaged in demolition, in its neighbourhood, of all salient bases of life, and of escaping, at the same time, from any direct responsibility by a philosophy of escapism, seems to me to be another authentic symptom of the modern intellectual's betrayal of humanity. Unfortunately the rest of the world is almost cowardly in any adequate expression of its judgement owing to ugly possibilities that it may be hatching for its own future and those who are bent upon doing mischief are left alone to defile their history and blacken their reputation for all time to come. But such impunity in the long run bodes disaster, like unconsciousness of disease in its painless progress of ravage.

I speak with utter sorrow for your people; your letter has hurt me to the depths of my being. I know that one day the disillusionment of your people will be complete, and through laborious centuries they will have to clear the debris of their civilisation wrought to ruin by their own warlords run amok. They will realise that the aggressive war on China is insignificant as compared to the destruction of their inner spirit of chivalry of Japan which is proceeding with a ferocious severity. China is unconquerable, her civilisation, under the dauntless leadership of Chiang Kai-shek, is displaying marvellous resources; the desperate loyalty of her peoples, united as never before, is creating a new age for that land.[5] Caught unprepared by a gigantic machinery of war, hurled upon her peoples, China is holding her own; no temporary defeats can ever crush her fully aroused spirit. Faced by the borrowed science of Japanese militarism which is crudely western in character, China's stand reveals an inherently superior moral stature. And today I understand more than ever before the meaning of the enthusiasm with which the big-hearted Japanese thinker Okakura assured me that 'China is great'.[6]

You do not realise that you are glorifying your neighbour at your own cost. But these are considerations on another plane: the sorrow remains that Japan, in the words of Madame Chiang Kai-shek which you must have read in the *Spectator*, is creating so many ghosts.[7] Ghosts of immemorial works of Chinese art, of irreplaceable Chinese institutions, of great peace-loving communities drugged, tortured, and destroyed. 'Who will lay the ghosts?' she asks. Japanese and Chinese people, let us hope, will join hands together, in no distant future, in wiping off memories of a bitter past. True Asian humanity will be reborn. Poets will raise their song and be unashamed, one believes, to declare their faith again in a human destiny which cannot admit of a scientific mass production of fratricide.

Yours sincerely,
Rabindranath Tagore

PS I find that you have already released your letter to the press; I take it that you want me to publish my answer in the same manner.

Source: MS copy at Rabindra Bhavan, Shantiniketan; letter published in *VBQ, 4*, No. 3, Nov. 1938, pp. 202–5.

1 Yone Noguchi (1875–1947): poet and writer; he was professor of English literature, Keio University, Tokyo. From 1893 to 1904, he lived in the USA. In 1913, he lectured at Oxford on Japanese poetry and may have met RT. He visited Shantiniketan and stayed with RT in the mid-1930s. During the Second World War, he changed his mind about Japanese militarism. See Yone Noguchi, *Selected English Writings of Yone Noguchi: I, (Poetry)* (Yoshinobu Hakutani ed.; London, 1990) (introduction by Yoshinobu Hakutani).
2 RT to Andrews, 12 July 1915 [RB].
3 Noguchi produced nearly one hundred books, about a quarter of which were written in English.
4 The four letters appear in 'Poet to poet', *VBQ, 4*, No. 3, Nov. 1938, pp. 199–212.
5 In April 1938, RT sent a message of goodwill to Chiang Kai-shek, and in 1940, they exchanged letters [RB]. In 1942, after RT's death, Chiang Kai-shek and his wife visited Shantiniketan. Such was RT's bias towards Chiang that he kept silent about Chiang's drowning of hundreds of thousands of his own people in June 1938 when he ordered the dykes holding the Huang He (Yellow River) to be broken so as to stop the southward movement of the Japanese army; this incident was mentioned by Noguchi in his first letter, but ignored by RT in his reply.
6 Okakura: Okakura Kakuzo.

7 'What war is teaching China', a series of articles by Madame Chiang Kai-shek in the *Spectator*. The first, published on 1 July 1938, opened with this statement: 'The myriads of ghosts they have made will take a lot of laying – ghosts of men, women and children; of ancient cities, towns and villages; of workshops, and factories; of the little shops – the places of handicraft of the millions. You never saw such monstrous criminality.'

323

To Charles Freer Andrews

In early September 1938, Czechoslovakia began to fall apart under pressure from Nazi Germany. On 29 September, by the terms of the Munich Agreement, the Sudetenland was ceded to Germany, and Britain's prime minister, Neville Chamberlain, on returning to London the next day, made his notorious statement that the agreement with Hitler would bring 'peace for our time'. On 1 October, German troops occupied the Sudetenland and a few days later, the president of Czechoslovakia, Eduard Beneš, resigned in protest against the British and French appeasement of Hitler and Mussolini.

Tagore, watching from afar, was horrified. His reservations about the English translation of the Czech biography of him by Vincenc Lesny (see letter 321) seemed suddenly irrelevant. This letter to Andrews on that subject was written in the run-up to Munich. By the time Tagore wrote the second letter (324), to Lesny himself in Prague (in which he kept totally silent about the biography), it was obvious that the political fate of Czechoslovakia was sealed.

Santiniketan, [West Bengal, India]
8 September 1938

Dear Charlie

Lesny's book about me has not been a happy one. I wish he had not allowed it to be translated and published in England. It is full of mistakes which could not have been helped but the summary which he has given of my works is hopelessly inadequate and it cheapens the value of my writings. However I am anxious for the fate of Czechoslovakia and I earnestly hope that Chamberlain will not betray that country in the guise of a friend.

Have you read my letter to Noguchi?[1] His own letter was utterly unworthy of a poet of his reputation. I feel very anxious for China. In the present state of entanglements in Europe the only help which could have come to her from the West through the Soviet Government [will] I fear be diverted.

With love

Ever yours
Rabindranath Tagore

Source: MS original at Rabindra Bhavan, Shantiniketan.

1 See letter 322.

324

To Vincenc Lesny[1]

Santiniketan, [West Bengal, India]
15 October 1938

Dear Friend,

I feel so keenly about the suffering of your people as if I was one of them. For what has happened in your country is not a mere local misfortune which may at the best claim our sympathy, it is a tragic revelation that the destiny of all those principles of humanity for which the peoples of the West turned martyrs for three centuries rests in the hands of cowardly guardians who are selling it to save their own skins. It turns one cynical to see the democratic peoples betraying their kind when even the bullies stand by each other.

I feel so humiliated and so helpless when I contemplate all this, humiliated to see all the values, which have given whatever worth modern civilisation has, betrayed one by one, and helpless that we are powerless to prevent it. Our country is itself a victim of these wrongs. My words have no power to stay the onslaught of the maniacs, not even the power to arrest the desertion of those who erstwhile pretended to be the saviours of humanity. I can only remind those who are not yet wholly demented that when men turn beasts they sooner or later tear each other.

As for your own country, I can only hope that though abandoned and robbed, it will maintain its native integrity and, falling back upon its own inalienable resources, will recreate a richer national life than before.

I am sending you a copy of my English rendering of a recent poem of mine, yet unpublished, in which my outraged sentiment had found its expression. You may use it as you like, though it will also be published in the November issue of the *Visva-Bharati Quarterly*. If you like I can also send you the Bengali original.[2]

With best wishes and regards,

Yours sincerely,
Rabindranath Tagore

Source: MS copy at Rabindra Bhavan, Shantiniketan; letter published in *VBN*, Nov. 1938, p. 38.

1 Vincenc Lesny (1882–1953): Indologist; he was professor of Indology and Iranian studies, Charles University, Prague. A student of Moriz Winternitz, he joined Winternitz as a visiting professor at Shantiniketan in 1923, and in 1928 paid a second visit. He translated some of RT's work from Bengali into Czech, as well as writing a study of his life and works.
2 'Retribution', *VBQ*, 4, No. 3, Nov. 1938, pp. 157–8/*Nabajatak*, *RR*, XXIV, pp. 9–11. The poem was composed in the wake of the Munich Agreement.

325

To Rash Behari Bose

Rash Behari Bose, the Bengali revolutionary living in Tokyo who had tried to persuade Tagore to visit Japan in 1937 (see letter 313), tried again a year later, with an all-expenses paid invitation. But this time, with the bombing of China fresh in his mind – on 21 October, Guangzhou (Canton) fell to the Japanese and was ravaged by fire – Rabindranath was much firmer in his rejection of Bose's offer.

> Santiniketan, [West Bengal, India]
> 24 October 1938

Dear Rash Behari,

I have just received your letter dated 26.9.38 with an invitation for me to visit Japan. Though the present state of my health is hardly favourable for any strain of a long foreign journey I should seriously consider your proposal if proper opportunity is given me to carry out my own mission while there, which is to do my best to establish a civilised relationship of national amity between two great peoples of Asia who are entangled in a desolating mutual destruction. But as I am doubtful whether the military authorities of Japan, which seem bent upon devastating China in order to gain their object, will allow me the freedom to take my own course, I shall never forgive myself if I am tempted for any reason whatever to pay a friendly visit to Japan just at this unfortunate moment and thus cause a grave misunderstanding. You know I have a genuine love for the Japanese people and it is sure to hurt me too painfully to go and watch crowds of them being transported by their rulers to a neighbouring land to perpetrate acts of inhumanity which will brand their name with a lasting stain in the history of man.[1]

With kind regards,

Yours affectionately,
Rabindranath Tagore

Source: MS copy at Rabindra Bhavan, Shantiniketan.

1 On 10 May 1941, with Fascist victories in Europe at their height and Japan getting ready to join the war, Bose issued an 'Appeal to Indians!' on behalf of the India Independence League of Japan, which concluded that 'bloodshed has been and still is the only remedy, and never was the time more favourable for its use than now. May God grant us the right mind to grasp this golden opportunity.'

326

To Jawaharlal Nehru

Indian politics of the late 1930s was dominated by the struggle between Mahatma Gandhi and Subhash Chandra Bose, a believer in non-violence versus a believer in violence, with Jawaharlal Nehru cleaving more to Gandhi than to Bose. During 1938, Bose was president of the Congress and thus in a position of considerable influence, but he was unable to carry Gandhi and the Congress working committee with him – nor could he bring down the Muslim-led non-Congress ministry in Bengal, elected in 1937 as a consequence of the seat allocation decided in the 1932 Poona Pact. Like the Hindu *bhadralok* of Calcutta to which he belonged, Bose found himself powerless and increasingly frustrated.[1]

Tagore, despite strong initial reservations about Bose, had by 1937 come to view him as the only hope for principled leadership in Bengal. He was distressed to see Bose failing politically and the increasing factionalism of Bengali politics. Hoping to discuss these delicate matters with Nehru, he wrote him this letter.

Santiniketan, [West Bengal, India]
28 November 1938

My dear Jawaharlal

I asked you to come and meet me not because I had any definite plan to discuss or any request to make. I merely wanted to know your opinion about Bengal whose present condition puzzles me and makes me despair. My province is clever but morally untrained and supercilious in her attitude towards her neighbours, she breaks into violent hysteric fits when least crossed in her whims.[2] I know her weakness but I cannot maintain my detachment of mind and passively acquiesce in her doom of perdition. But I am quite willing to settle down to my special work and leave your Congress organisation to deal with her as it thinks fit. But I myself believe in some personal force for tightening screws that are loose and sawing off parts that obstruct, a head-worker, who may not be perfect as a man but expert as a mechanic. However, I want to talk to you and more than that I want to hear you talk, though all this may not lead to anything practical. Truth is I want to see you but it may wait till you have some time to spare.[3]

I am anxious about Indira's state of health.[4] I hope her spending the winter months in India will help her.

Yours affectionately
Rabindranath Tagore

Source: MS copy at Rabindra Bhavan, Shantiniketan; letter published in *VBQ*, *29*, Nos. 2–3, 1963–4, p. 108.

1 On Gandhi, Bose and Nehru, see Leonard A. Gordon, *Brothers against the Raj*, and also Chaudhuri, *Thy Hand*, pp. 459–529.
2 'It is a curious paradox but the very fact of Bengal being clever and advanced in many ways has brought about various crises' (Nehru to RT, 1 Dec. 1938, *VBQ*, *29*, Nos. 2–3, 1963–4, p. 109).
3 Nehru eventually came to Shantiniketan on 31 Jan. 1939 and opened the Hindi Bhavan (department of Hindi studies). He stayed a few days and on 2 Feb. he and Bose met for a discussion in the presence of RT.
4 Indira Nehru contracted pleurisy while travelling in Europe with her father and required a spell in hospital in Britain in Sept. 1938, before returning to India in the winter.

327

To Leonard Knight Elmhirst

In December 1938–January 1939, Leonard Elmhirst paid his last visit to Shantiniketan during Tagore's lifetime, after being away from the place and the man for a long while. Elmhirst wrote home to his wife Dorothy in Dartington:

> Most days I see the Poet for a few minutes. His humour and his mind are not dimmed and he is as good fun as ever, 'Cable Dorothy to come out and join you and stay another

month, both of you.' 'Send her my love.' So much of the strain of the old days is gone out of the political situation that the atmosphere has quite changed.[1]

While this last remark was perhaps true of the strain in the Indo-British relationship, compared to the early 1920s when Elmhirst first came to Shantiniketan, it was most certainly not true, indeed it was an almost purblind misjudgement, of the internal political situation, particularly in Bengal. Not only were Hindu–Muslim relations gradually coming to boiling point, the Congress was split down the middle between the supporters of Gandhi and those of Subhash Chandra Bose. Tagore, thinking to help Bose, came out with a rousing article in which he crowned Bose 'Deshanayak' (The Leader of the Country).[2] But Gandhi, and increasingly Nehru, were not to be persuaded. On 22 February, a month after Bose by a small majority was re-elected president of the Congress against Gandhi's wishes, the entire Congress working committee resigned, except for Bose and his brother. Just over two months later, at the end of April, Bose felt obliged to tender his resignation as president.

This letter to Elmhirst appears to have been written partly in response to the resignation news. Rabindranath mocks himself for venturing into politics, with results that are the opposite to those he intended.

Santiniketan, [West Bengal, India]
[24 February 1939]

Dear Leonard

I have an inborn talent that generally manages to entangle me in meshes which lie outside my own sphere of life while my guardian planet rarely delays in exercising its influence to counteract the mischief seemingly made [as] a joke. I do not know [in what form] the news [may] have reached you that my incorrigible optimism has betrayed me into politics. You know Bengal just now is in a most unhappy state of demoralisation and for a moment I foolishly imagined that I could help her by some political jungle clearing. In a similar mood of mind Mahatmaji once believed that by cutting down palm trees he could cure the country of the vice of intemperance. But I am sure there is hope for me, for sooner or later the bird, however silly it may be, is sure to find out that it can better attain its end not by running but by using its wings.

You know some time ago my [right of occupancy] in this land of the living was rudely challenged and I received a definite notice to quit.[3] I was afraid that enough time would not be allowed to me for meeting you once before I left for good. But in this crisis my benignant planet lent its hand to rescue me from the impasse and following my own revival the memory of the old time had the opportunity to be revived again. Your seat here had been waiting all these days, not with the vain expectation [of] being occupied but to be freshly recognised. This short visit of yours has renewed our lease of happiness. I only wish you had brought Dorothy with you whom we expected and whom we were certain to be able to please.

The sad news of Lord Brabourne's death has reached us just now and deeply grieved me.[4] He was one of the noblest representatives of your nation and his loss is sure to be mourned with a genuine feeling of sorrow by [the] whole [of] Bengal. After the vindictive regime of his predecessor his administration brought to us profound relief. We are

The Great Sentinel 505

unfortunate in [so] rarely having such a friend and then [losing] him with such a cruel stroke of destiny.

With my best love to you and Dorothy

Ever yours
Rabindranath Tagore

Source: MS original in Dartington Trust archives [Dartington]; letter published in Dutta and Robinson (eds.), *Purabi*, p. 116.

1 Leonard to Dorothy Elmhirst, 6 Jan. 1939 [Dartington].
2 See extract in Leonard A. Gordon, *Brothers against the Raj*, pp. 402–3/Tagore, *Kalantar* (rev. edn, 1367 [1961]), pp. 371–3. The essay was originally intended as an address to a meeting in Calcutta, but it was not delivered.
3 See letters 311 and 312.
4 Lord Brabourne (1895–1939): governor of Bengal, 1937–9. He died on 23 Feb. His predecessor was Sir John Anderson (see letter 309).

328

To Victoria Ocampo

By 1939, Tagore's stay in Argentina hosted by Victoria Ocampo had acquired mythical proportions in his mind. The way he speaks of it in this letter is reminiscent of one of his paintings of women: near, and intense, yet far, and remote.

Santiniketan, [West Bengal, India]
14 March 1939

Dear Vijaya

How often I feel that your nearness which once was so untrammelled and close, now that it has receded into a hopeless distance, has come poignantly closer to me, its gifts disclosing value that teases the mind by its rarity. Unfortunately the paths that accidentally had reached some preciousness can never be retraced and when the heart longs to own it back [it] realises that it is lost for ever. The picture of that building near the great river where you housed us in strange surroundings with its cactus beds that lent their grotesque gestures to the atmosphere of an exotic remoteness, often comes to my vision with an invitation from across an impossible barrier.[1] There are some experiences which are like treasure islands detached from the continent of immediate life, their charts ever remaining vaguely deciphered – and my Argentine episode is one of them. Possibly you know that the memory of those sunny days and tender care has been encircled by some of my verses – the best of their kind – the fugitives are made captive, and they will remain, I am sure, though unvisited by you, separated by an alien language.[2]

With dearest love
Rabindranath Tagore

Source: MS copy at Rabindra Bhavan, Shantiniketan; letter published in Dyson, *Flower-Garden*, pp. 455–6.

1 The building was Miralrío, the house overlooking the River Plate at San Isidro.
2 Verses: *Purabi* (see letter 205).

329

To Ramakrishna Dalmia[1]

The burden of raising money for Visva-Bharati continued until the end of Tagore's life. One of the lesser benefactors was a Jain industrialist and philanthropist, Seth Ramakrishna Dalmia. He combined respect for Tagore's unworldliness with a certain worldly shrewdness in obtaining recommendation letters from Tagore when setting up new businesses.[2] In early 1939, he requested Tagore to be present at the opening ceremony of one of these. In this letter, Rabindranath (who had often acceded to similar requests during the 1930s in Calcutta) explains why he cannot oblige him.

Santiniketan, [West Bengal, India]
24 March 1939

My dear Sethji

I have learnt with great pleasure about your paper mill which you are formally going to set into operation in April. Believing as I do in the compelling necessity of planned industrial development in the country, I read with keen interest reports about your enterprise in this direction. And I assure you I would have come to participate in the opening ceremony, if circumstances were more propitious. Unfortunately, I have to admit my physical difficulties which stand in the way; it is a torture for me even to move out of my cottage.

Moreover, there is [a] particularly heavy programme awaiting me at Santiniketan during the next month. We conclude our financial year on 31 March and we have to take our stock and know our exact position. It is strange to think that a poet and a dreamer like me should have to bother about these material affairs, but such indeed is my fate. I am so alone; my cry for help seems to fall on deaf ears.

With kind regards,

Yours sincerely
Rabindranath Tagore

Source: MS copy at Rabindra Bhavan, Shantiniketan.

1 Ramakrishna Dalmia (1893–1978): industrialist and philanthropist.
2 There are many letters from Dalmia to RT. 'I am anxious to meet you and spend some time with you. But I do not know when this will come to pass, for I am engrossed in sordid things and verities of life elude me' (Dalmia to RT, 20 April 1937 [RB]).

330

To Mahatma Gandhi

During March and April 1939, the split between Gandhi and Subhash Chandra Bose, who was still president of the Congress, deepened. At the 1939 Congress session, which began at Tripuri on 10 March, a motion of confidence in Gandhi's leadership – with its implication of no confidence in Bose – was carried. Bose retired defeated and bitter against Jawaharlal Nehru for his lack of support, and went away to try to shake off a mysterious illness, while carrying on a heavy correspondence with Nehru, Gandhi and others. Tagore, for his part, sent this letter to Gandhi, followed by a telegram three weeks later, as the crisis deepened.[1] Throughout 1939, he tried to persuade Gandhi and Nehru to back Bose.

Santiniketan, [West Bengal, India]
29 March 1939

Dear Mahatmaji

At the last Congress session some rude hands have deeply hurt Bengal with an ungracious persistence; please apply without delay balm to the wound with your own kind hands and prevent it from festering.[2]

With love,

Ever yours
Rabindranath Tagore

Source: MS copy at Rabindra Bhavan, Shantiniketan; letter published in *Rabindra-Biksha*, Paush 1398 [Dec. 1991], p. 29.

1 RT to Gandhi, 18 April 1939, *Rabindra-Biksha*, Paush 1398 [Dec. 1991], p. 32.
2 Gandhi replied, 'I have your letter full of tenderness. The problem you set before me is difficult. I have made certain suggestions to Subhas. I see no other way out of the impasse' (2 April 1939, *CWMG*, LXIX, p. 99).

331

To Sir William Rothenstein

In the summer of 1939, William Rothenstein wrote to Tagore from his country home in Gloucestershire:

> It is just 27 years since you spent the summer with us here. Do you remember how it poured with rain and how you said, where a stranger is it is always exceptional weather? That was two years before the war, then unimaginable. Now we are living in a fearful expectancy. Yet life goes on from day to day, the small and great troubles, the small and great pleasures still the basis of our thoughts and doings. Happily nothing can change the beauty of the face of the world which is to me a source of perpetual wonder.[1]

Rabindranath's reply is the last letter he wrote to his oldest English friend.

Santiniketan, [West Bengal, India]
25 June 1939

My dear Rothenstein,

I thank you for your letter which recalls back to my mind the never-to-be-forgotten memories of my stay in your village, where practically for the first time I had my real contact with the English country.[2] It is now a quarter of a century that stands athwart my mind and yet I can almost see today the undulating downs and the luscious green of the meadows. Sometimes I have so irresistibly felt like visiting the places once again before I take my farewell but Europe today is a powder magazine and I wonder if it has a place for a mere poet like myself. Anyway I would seem rather a weird figure in a gas mask and therefore I must desist. In my country my people are steadily gaining in self-respect and faith in our destiny but I cannot be happy when I know that the very ideals which were the foundations of a great civilisation are daily vanishing.

As regards your using my letters in your third volume of autobiography, you have most certainly my enthusiastic consent but do be discreet about the material you use. I have of course every faith in your judgement.[3]

I have just returned after my summer holidays on the Himalayas; the rains have set in and you have to see for yourself to realise the gorgeous beauty of the chasing raven-black clouds on the sky of Santiniketan.[4]

Yours ever
Rabindranath Tagore

Source: MS original in Rothenstein Papers [Harvard]; letter published in Lago (ed.), *Imperfect Encounter*, pp. 367–8.

1 Rothenstein to RT, 7 June 1939, in Lago (ed.), *Imperfect Encounter*, p. 367.
2 His very first contact with the English countryside was in 1879, in Torquay (see letter 1).
3 In his letter, Rothenstein mentioned his wish to quote some of RT's letters in his third volume of memoirs, *Since Fifty: Recollections, 1922–1938*, which appeared in late 1939.
4 RT stayed at Kalimpong from 17 May to 17 June.

The crisis in civilisation (1939–1941)

Introduction

The outbreak of the Second World War had comparatively little effect on Bengal. Tagore continued to maintain contact with his British friends, as far as possible, and in August 1940 an honorary degree from Oxford University was conferred on him at Shantiniketan in a special ceremony. But his mind was torn between his long-held admiration for the British character and his conviction that the war was the result of western and Japanese imperialism. He hoped that, terrible as it was, the war would have a purifying effect on Britain and her relationship with India. When no increased British sympathy for Indian nationalism was forthcoming, he became deeply disillusioned with western civilisation. His last essay, 'Crisis in Civilisation', read publicly at Shantiniketan just before his eightieth birthday, in April 1941, expressed his tortured feelings.

At the end of July, suffering in both mind and body, he was taken from Shantiniketan to Calcutta for an operation. He died in the Tagore family house at Jorasanko, on 7 August 1941.

332

To Jawaharlal Nehru

In late August 1939, just before the outbreak of war in Europe, Jawaharlal Nehru set off by plane on a goodwill mission to China, to see for himself the Chinese resistance to Japanese aggression. Before he left India, he received this letter of advice from Tagore, and also met him in Calcutta.[1]

It is a significant letter, because it clearly shows Tagore's (fallacious) belief in Indo-Chinese unity, which both coincided with and strengthened Nehru's own sympathies. Both men believed, contrary to much evidence, that Chiang Kai-shek was the inevitable leader of all China; neither man understood the power of the Chinese Communists. And in 1962, when Tagore was long dead, Nehru persisted in believing that China would not fight India over its border dispute, because of the underlying friendship between the two countries. Although Tagore does not specifically mention Buddhism in this letter, he (and Nehru) believed that the Buddhist heritage in China, which of course had its source in India, was the dominant influence in Chinese culture – again

19 The funeral of Rabindranath Tagore, Calcutta, 7 August 1941

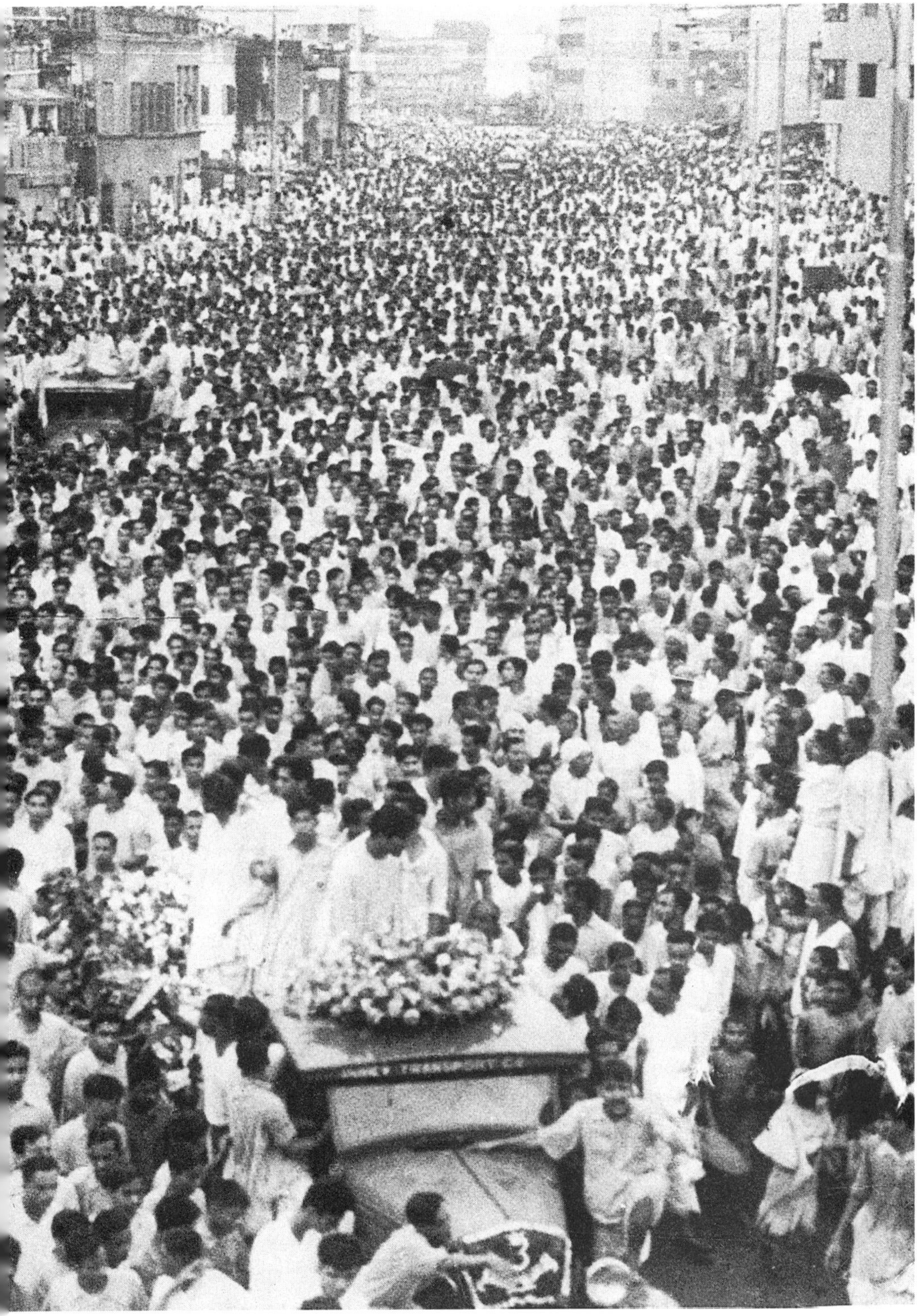

despite much evidence to the contrary. This shared heritage would, in Tagore's and Nehru's view, restrain the two countries from western-style nationalistic quarrels.

Furthermore, Tagore persisted in believing, on the basis of his visits to Japan in 1916 and after, that the same Asian unity extended to Japan, despite its recent rapacity (see letter 322). Japanese imperialism, he said to Nehru, was 'essentially a case of borrowed pugnacity' – borrowed, that is, from the western nations. He therefore urged Nehru to visit Japan too, after he had been to China, to remind the Japanese of their true selves. This was despite his own refusal to visit Japan in 1937 and 1938 when invited by Rash Behari Bose (see letters 313 and 325). Not surprisingly, Nehru took roughly the same view of this proposal as Tagore had of Bose's, feeling that such a visit to Japan would be inappropriate in a war situation.[2]

Santiniketan, [West Bengal, India]
17 August 1939

My dear Jawaharlal,

Amiya has just been telling me about his talks with you and giving me some details regarding your impending visit to China.[3] As to the present crisis in Congress I fully share your deep concern at the turn that affairs have taken; I have no doubt also that the creative forces of our nation will pass this test and come out stronger after the main issues have been clarified even if we have to pass through a temporary phase of painful adjustment.[4]

My warmest good wishes are with you in your mission of good neighbourliness to China. I feel proud that the new spirit of Asia will be represented through you and our best traditions of Indian humanity find their voice during your contacts with the people of China. My tours in the Far East have convinced me that in the main our peoples have maintained an Asiatic tradition of cultural exchange: we have not fought with each other in the name of hungry nationalism as the western countries have been doing in Europe. Japanese aggression, therefore, seems to me essentially a case of borrowed pugnacity which I feel sure has not touched the deep heart of their people. Let Japan take warning not to betray the basis of her civilisation which she shares with China and with us in India; far greater than the fearful hurt she is inflicting on China would be the inevitable wrecking of her own humanity which her militarists seem determined to achieve.

I would request you to include Japan in your itinerary: India will be with you in your appeal to the moral conscience of Asia which Japan cannot afford to kill in a mania of spiritual suicide. The pathway which led from India to her great neighbours is partly closed through centuries of neglect; we have to remove the weeds, and also the recent barriers erected by fratricidal politics so that once more the traffic of human interchange can continue, linking our country with Japan and China. India's great awakening had crossed deserts and mountains, the overflow of her glorious epoch of culture touched far continents and left permanent deposits in distant shores of Asia. In my visits to China and Japan, and to Siam, Java and Bali, I felt profoundly moved to find how the communion of our culture had persisted even up to our own days and I cannot help hoping that as a messenger from India's youth you would give strength to the historic forces of Asiatic unity, bringing new urge of neighbourly understanding to our eastern peoples.[5] India herself is passing through an eclipse when her own reality is lost to her in a haze of parochial politics, sectarianism, and domestic contention: contact with a greater world of eastern culture will, I fervently hope, help in removing her obsessions and enliven her national existence with a new humanity.

With affectionate regards,

Yours
Rabindranath Tagore

Source: MS copy at Rabindra Bhavan, Shantiniketan; letter published in *VBQ*, 29, Nos. 2–3, 1963–4, pp. 111–12.

1 Nehru describes his meeting with RT on 20 Aug. in his 'Diary of a journey', *Selected Works*, X (first series), pp. 87–8.
2 Nehru wrote: 'just after a visit in war time to the Chinese Nationalist headquarters I do not think it would be quite suitable for me to visit Japan immediately' (Nehru to RT, 19 Aug. 1939, *ibid.*, p. 84).
3 Amiya: Amiya Chakravarty.
4 The Congress crisis was the clash between Gandhi and Subhash Chandra Bose. With the outbreak of the European war in early Sept., the Congress had to face a further crisis: what attitude to adopt to the western Allies.
5 On RT's impressions of South-east Asia, see Dutta and Robinson (eds.), *Anthology*, pp. 108–19.

333

To Mahatma Gandhi

(telegram)

Tagore had made various efforts to resolve the differences between Subhash Chandra Bose and the other Congress leaders (see letters 326 and 330). But by late 1939, the split was becoming deeper, not narrower: in August, the Congress working committee disqualified Bose as president of the Congress in Bengal, and banned him from being a member of any elective Congress committee for three years. Before abandoning hope of an agreement, Tagore sent this telegram to Gandhi.

Santiniketan, [West Bengal, India]
20 December 1939

Owing gravely critical situation all over India and especially in Bengal would urge Congress working committee immediately remove ban against Subhash and invite his cordial cooperation in supreme interest national unity.[1]

Rabindranath

Source: MS copy at Rabindra Bhavan, Shantiniketan; letter published in *VBQ*, 35, Nos. 1–4 (Gandhi Number), May 1969–April 1970, p. 246.

1 Gandhi responded by telegram that the working committee could not lift the ban, adding, 'My personal opinion is you should advise Subhas Babu [to] submit [to] discipline if ban is to be removed' (Gandhi to RT, *CWMG*, LXXI, p. 56). To C. F. Andrews, Gandhi wrote on the 15 Jan. 1940:

514 Selected letters of Rabindranath Tagore

If you think it proper tell Gurudev that I have never ceased to think of his wire and anxiety about Bengal. I feel that Subhas is behaving like a spoilt child of the family. The only way to make up with him is to open his eyes. And then his politics show sharp differences. They seem to be unbridgeable. I am quite clear that the matter is too complicated for Gurudev to handle. Let him trust that no one in the committee has anything personal against Subhas. For me, he is my son. (*CWMG*, LXXI, pp. 113–14)

334

To Leonard Knight Elmhirst

The proper role of science (and its attendant statistics) in development and public policy making had always been a matter of some disagreement between Tagore and Leonard Elmhirst (see letter 259). Essentially, Elmhirst trusted scientific objectivity as a guide to the management of human affairs more than Tagore did. Thus, although Elmhirst was a founder member of the executive of PEP (Political and Economic Planning) from 1931, and was intimately involved in its activities, acting as chairman of Pep from 1939 to 1952, Pep does not figure in his correspondence with Tagore until the outbreak of war.[1] In November 1939, Elmhirst sent Tagore a copy of a Pep pamphlet, *European Order and World Order*, which was a 'vision statement' for the world to come when the Allies had won the war.[2] He commented in his covering letter: 'How we shall fare in war I don't know, but if those of us who are still free to think and plan fail now we have no excuse when the day of opportunity arrives. How important every activity at Santiniketan and Sriniketan looks from here in the light of world conditions!'[3]

Tagore, in his reply, was inspired and, as usual, optimistic about the future. He asked how Pep's activities might be spread to India, in order to find rational solutions to, for example, the communal problem. But despite some efforts in that direction by Elmhirst and others, mainly after the war, an Indian equivalent of Pep never took off.[4]

Santiniketan, [West Bengal, India]
27 December 1939

My dear Leonard,

My warmest good wishes to Dorothy and yourself for the New Year.

I have read your letter and the Pep pamphlet with profound interest – it does one good to know that all civilised thought and planning have not been submerged by war passions. Your letter gives me new hope and is a confirmation of the spiritual integrity of the European civilisation in which I have always believed – the wide-awake humanity of the West that diplomatic machinations can never crush. I can realise from your brochure on *European Order and World Order* that the best minds of Europe are being put to a severe test, that they have the sanction of the peoples of Europe in trying to formulate a federal union which will unite the peoples in spite of the ring-leaders of blind nationalism who, sitting safely in the citadels of power, send the youth of the land to destroy each other [on] the battlefield. In Europe the real battle goes on – that between organised passion and the unconquerable majesty of the human heart – and your people have the vitality to live through this struggle. I cannot believe in the victory of any belligerent power – as belligerents they are doomed – but I can hope for the triumph of the united peoples of Europe under some such system as you propose in your letter to Lord Halifax and in the programme sponsored by Pep.[5]

But what about India? It does not need a defeatist to feel deeply anxious about the future of millions who with all their innate culture and their peaceful traditions are being simultaneously subjected to hunger, disease, exploitations foreign and indigenous, and the seething discontents of communalism. Our people do not possess the vitality that you have in Europe and the crisis, even before this war started in the West, had become acute in India. Needless to say, interested groups led by ambition and outside instigation, are today using the communal motive for destructive political ends. Could the Pep give us a lead in planning for a united India in which the minority problem shorn of its manufactured complexities could be tackled at root? We do not want ready-made solutions by diplomats but a working basis for discussion such as you have planned, in which some of the best minds of your country and ours – and of the United States – could participate. Not Round Table Conferences with politicians manipulating their hidden purposes – but a genuine fact-finding and explorative group to which intellectuals with statesman-like gifts and possessing sober judgement could come and confer. An extension of Pep activities in India. We from Visva-Bharati could contribute and a few representative intellectuals from different provinces could join with us.

My path, as you know, lies in the domain of quiet, integral action and thought, my units must be few and small, and I can but face human problems in relation to some basic village or cultural area. So in the midst of worldwide anguish, and with the problems of over three hundred millions staring us in the face, I stick to my work in Santiniketan and Sriniketan hoping that our efforts will touch the heart of our village neighbours and help them in reasserting themselves in a new social order. If we can give a start to a few villages they would perhaps be an inspiration to some others – and my life work will have been done.

Yours affectionately,
Rabindranath Tagore

Source: MS original in Dartington Trust archives [Dartington]; letter published in Dutta and Robinson (eds.), *Purabi*, p. 117.

1 Pep's original objectives were to be an independent, non-party organisation, which would act 'as a bridge between research on the one hand and policy making on the other, whether in government, the social services or industry. Its aim is a practical one: to study problems of public concern, to find out the facts, to present them impartially, to suggest ways in which the knowledge can be applied.' (Quoted in John Pinder (ed.), *Fifty Years of Political and Economic Planning: Looking Forward 1931–1981* (London, 1981), p. 9). In the 1970s, Pep merged with the Centre for Studies in Social Policy to form the Policy Studies Institute.
2 The 'brochure' (or rather broadsheet, as Pep called it) was largely written by Max Nicholson, a founder member of Pep's executive. Michael Young, secretary of Pep during the war, looking back on this broadsheet in 1981, quoted its statement that 'despite its immense achievements, western civilisation now finds itself left without a dynamic and simple faith'. Young commented ironically, 'Western civilisation did not include Queen Anne's Gate' [London Headquarters of Pep], (Young, 'The Second World War', in Pinder (ed.), *Looking Forward*, p. 83).
3 Elmhirst to RT, 23 Nov. 1939, in Dutta and Robinson (eds.), *Purabi*, p. 116.
4 During his visit to India in early 1939, Elmhirst set up the Social and Economic Planning Association (Sepa), patterned on Pep, but because of the war, 'Sepa could hardly take off the ground' (Sudhir Sen,

'India loses a rare friend', *VBN*, Aug. 1974, pp. 25–6). Elmhirst's post-war efforts to establish a Pep-driven Indian Institute of Planning are mentioned in Pinder (ed.), *Looking Forward*, p. 113.
5 Halifax: Lord Halifax, then foreign secretary, formerly viceroy of India.

335

To Henry Woodd Nevinson[1]

Under pressure from Jawaharlal Nehru, in 1936 Tagore consented to become president of the Indian Civil Liberties Union, with Sarojini Naidu as the driving force.[2] Four years later he was approached on a similar subject by an Englishman he admired almost as much as Nehru, H. W. Nevinson, the veteran essayist, journalist and advocate of freedom and human rights, who had sent out a circular letter to influential people asking for their support in the worldwide struggle against tyrannous governments.[3] This letter was his response, to which Nevinson then replied personally asking Tagore to be a vice-president of the National Council for Civil Liberties in Britain.[4]

Santiniketan, [West Bengal, India]
8 January 1940

Dear Nevinson,

I have read your circular letter with great interest and entirely associate myself with the freedom of mind which you advocate. As you know, by accepting presidentship of the Indian Council of Civil Liberties, I have publicly associated myself with organised effort to further democratic ideals for our peoples. The European and the Far Eastern wars, as well as the complications in the Indian situation, have made our task more imperative.

My age and the work that I have been doing in this corner of Bengal where we have our educational and rural development centres, make it difficult for me to extend my activities in other fields. But I join you in your crusade for the liberty of the human spirit and share your hope that the western civilisation will yet triumph over the ordeal that it has set for itself. In some ways it is even harder for India to pursue the path of freedom; not only our unnatural political situation which hampers free national expression, but the legacies of medieval habits and thought will have to be overcome. It is, therefore, all the more necessary that leaders of thought in your country and ours should counteract the passions of the day and maintain close contact in our human endeavour.

Yours sincerely,
Rabindranath Tagore

Source: MS original in Nevinson Papers [Bodleian].

1 Henry Woodd Nevinson (1856–1941): essayist, journalist and philanthropist; from 1897 to 1926, he was a war correspondent for various national newspapers in Britain.
2 RT to Nehru, 28 July 1936 [copy at RB].
3 In 1921, on his return to Britain from the USA, RT wrote to C. F. Andrews:

> One of the first men I happened to meet here was Nevinson and I felt that soul was alive in this country which had produced such a man as him. A land should be judged by its best products and

I have no hesitation in saying that the best Englishmen are the best specimens of humanity. With all our grievances against the English nation I cannot help loving your country which has given me some of my dearest friends. (RT to Andrews, 10 April 1921 [RB])

4 RT consented, adding that he could do nothing but lend his name: '80 is after all a very advanced age in the tropics' (RT to Nevinson, 31 March 1940 [copy at RB]).

336

To Mahatma Gandhi

In February 1940, Mahatma Gandhi paid his last visit to Shantiniketan while Tagore lived, a quarter century after his first, when he came to collect his boys who had stayed with Tagore after leaving Gandhi's ashram in South Africa in 1914. During that period, despite his strong differences with Tagore in almost every sphere, Gandhi had visited him at Shantiniketan, had always recommended the place to others, especially foreigners, and had saved the institution from financial collapse in 1936. Now, there were long and sympathetic talks between the two men, a special ceremony in the mango grove with Rabindranath present, followed by a tour of the institution without him. Overall the visit lasted two days. In Gandhi's words, a few years after Tagore's death, 'I started with a disposition to detect a conflict between Gurudev and myself but ended with the glorious discovery that there was none.'[1]

As Gandhi came to depart for Calcutta, Tagore placed this letter in his hands.

Santiniketan, [West Bengal, India]
19 February 1940

Dear Mahatmaji

You have just had a bird's-eye view this morning of our Visva-Bharati centre of activities. I do not know what estimate you have formed of its merit. You know that though this institution is national in its immediate aspect it is international in its spirit, offering according to the best of its means India's hospitality of culture to the rest of the world.

At one of its critical moments you saved it from an utter breakdown and helped it to its legs. We are ever thankful to you for this act of friendliness.

And, now, before you take your leave from Santiniketan I make my fervent appeal to you. Accept this institution under your protection giving it an assurance of permanence if you consider it to be a national asset. Visva-Bharati is like a vessel which is carrying the cargo of my life's best treasure and I hope it may claim special care from my countrymen for its preservation.[2]

With love,
Rabindranath Tagore

Source: MS copy at Rabindra Bhavan, Shantiniketan; letter published in *VBQ*, 35, Nos. 1–4 (Gandhi Number), May 1969–April 1970, pp. 247–8.

1 Quoted in 'The Santiniketan pilgrimage', *VBN*, Feb. 1946, p. 43.
2 In his reply, written on the train to Calcultta, Gandhi affectionately accepted the responsibility. He added: 'Though I have always regarded Santiniketan as my second home, this visit has brought me nearer to it than

ever before' (19 Feb. 1940, *CWMG*, LXXI, p. 228). During the next few years, he did his best to raise money for the institution. In Dec. 1947, a month before his assassination, in a letter to Rathindranath, son of RT, he said, 'Of course, wherever I am, Santiniketan is always in my heart' (27 Dec. 1947, *CWMG*, XC, p. 303).

337

To Ajit Singh Khatau[1]

At the end of 1939, Rabindranath's granddaughter Nandini, the adopted daughter of Rathindranath and Pratima, married into a Bombay mill-owning family. This letter, written to her husband, shows Tagore's deep gratitude to Gandhi for accepting the responsibility of Visva-Bharati after his death (see letter 336).

Santiniketan, [West Bengal, India]
10 March 1940

Dear Ajit

I am extremely busy with our own affairs and with other peoples' innumerable claims. On the top of it I am eighty and the burden of age has bent my back. But I am not allowed rest, for the work I had begun has its impetus which is ceaselessly driving me on – I do not know to what end. I have had enough empty applause from my countrymen and I am afraid I shall have to thank them for it when I take my departure. The other day Mahatmaji came to our ashram and his generous sympathy and assurance of help has given a new strength to my tired endeavour. He is great and he has unerring appreciation for whatever has genuine merit and I have felt sure he would never allow me to drag my load of heavy responsibility unaided till I drop down on the road away from the final realisation. However I do not complain and I feel happy that I have my own source of strength within myself.

I find it very difficult to carry on correspondence but I constantly [get] your news from *Bouma*[2] and am glad to know that both of you are living a life of happiness which I hope with God's blessings may continue to the end.

With love and blessings to you both
Grandfather

Source: MS copy at Rabindra Bhavan, Shantiniketan.

1 Ajit Singh Khatau: Bombay mill-owner; he was the eldest son of Seth Mulraj Morarji Khatau. The latter's father was one of the pioneers of the mill industry in Bombay; he founded the Khatau Mills in 1874. The family had a reputation for philanthropy; in 1920, Mulraj Khatau and his two brothers donated Rs 250,000 for a women's hostel at the Benares Hindu University.
2 *Bouma*: Pratima Tagore.

338

To Edward John Thompson

In 1940, more than a quarter of century after it was first mooted, Oxford University conferred an honorary degree upon Tagore. E. J. Thompson, who was closely associ-

The crisis in civilisation

ated with Oxford in the 1920s and 1930s, had long been canvassing for it to be done, and at last got his way. The fact that Oxford's chancellor, Lord Halifax, the former Lord Irwin, admired Tagore no doubt smoothed the way. Although the approach to Tagore was first made in 1938, the decision was not ratified until 1940, because Rabindranath was unable to come personally to Oxford to accept the degree; eventually, however, the university agreed to make a rare exception to its rules, and award the degree in absence.[1] The ceremony thus finally took place in Shantiniketan on 7 August 1940, with the chief justice of India, Sir Maurice Gwyer, an Oxford graduate, presiding.[2]

In this letter Tagore replies to Thompson's congratulations.

Santiniketan, [West Bengal, India]
11 April 1940

My dear Thompson,

Many thanks for your letter. It is indeed kind of you to congratulate me on adding to the number of my honorary degrees but I must confess that I value the latest honour much, coming as it does from such a centre of learning and culture as Oxford. I have just learnt from Sir Maurice Gwyer that he has been asked by Oxford University to act as delegate on their behalf for the conferment of the degree.

You must have got the shocking news of the death of Charlie Andrews.[3] It has been a great personal loss to me – for, as you know, he was one of my closest of friends and associates. Sorrows like these are the penalty of a long life and I believe I cannot complain.

It is indeed good news that you will come out once again to India. We shall be glad to see you here at Santiniketan.[4]

Yours sincerely
Rabindranath Tagore

Source: MS original in Thompson Papers [Bodleian].

1 The first letter from Oxford's registrar was dated 10 Feb. 1938, the second 6 Feb. 1940 and stated: 'In the disturbed conditions at present prevailing the university wishes to exercise the power only used very rarely to confer the degree upon you in absence' [RB]. According to Thompson, the original decision to award the degree was unanimous and cordial, but there was reluctance to confer it outside Oxford, which caused the delay. 'Since then your friends at the university, who include the heads of two of our greatest colleges, have not let the matter rest, and the Rhodes Trust also took it up' (Thompson to RT, 10 March 1940 [RB]).
2 The proceedings were printed in *VBN*, Sept. 1940. On the background to the degree, see Dutta and Robinson, *Rabindranath Tagore*, pp. 20, 352.
3 C. F. Andrews died in Calcutta on 5 April 1940.
4 Thompson, in his letter, spoke of coming back to Shantiniketan in the autumn, with a view to filming its life and history. He never returned to India before his death in 1946. By a curious coincidence, E. P. Thompson was planning to return to Shantiniketan to make a film about his father and RT, a few years before his death in 1993.

339

To Robert Fleming Rattray[1]

When Tagore visited Harvard in early 1913, T. S. Eliot, who was then studying Indian philosophy there, heard him speak. Eliot's professor, James Houghton Woods, with whom he got on well, greatly admired Tagore's lectures (later published as *Sadhana*). But Eliot himself left no record, either in 1913 or subsequently, of his reaction to Tagore.[2]

In 1940, one of Eliot's fellow students at Harvard, R. F. Rattray, later a Unitarian minister in Britain, wrote an article, 'With Tagore in 1913' and sent it to Tagore, along with a letter mentioning Eliot and suggesting that 'it may be that it was impressions of you that worked into his poem *The Waste Land*: "Shanti! Shanti! Shanti!" I am not an admirer of his poetry but his fame makes the point interesting.'[3]

Rabindranath's reply to Rattray shows that he was intrigued.

Mangpoo, [Kalimpong, West Bengal, India]
3 May 1940

Dear Mr Rattray

I am deeply touched by your friendly tribute and thank you for your kind thoughts which I very sincerely reciprocate.[4] It gives me profound pleasure to share with you happy days spent in Europe still unregarded by war passions. I am interested to read what you say about Mr T. S. Eliot. Some of his poetry [has] moved me by [its] evocative power and consummate craftsmanship. I have translated – that was some time ago – one of his lyrics called 'The Journey of the Magi'.[5]

With my cordial regards and good wishes.

Yours sincerely
Rabindranath Tagore

Source: MS copy at Rabindra Bhavan, Shantiniketan.

1 Robert Fleming Rattray (1886–1967): Unitarian minister; he was minister, Memorial Church (Unitarian), Cambridge, 1931–45, and later president, Manchester College, Oxford.
2 On Eliot and RT, see Dutta and Robinson, *Rabindranath Tagore*, p. 173.
3 Rattray to RT, 22 March 1940 [RB].
4 'With Tagore in 1913', *Inquirer*, 16 March 1940.
5 'Tirthajatri', *Punashcha*, *RR*, XVI, pp. 95–7.

340

To Leonard Knight Elmhirst

In May 1940, as the whole of western Europe seemed to be about to fall to the German armed forces, Leonard Elmhirst wrote to Tagore:

> These are not easy times but I like to think of them as the birth pangs of a great age that is to be, the struggles of that chicken in the egg you used to tell me about before the shell cracks open and a new world appears. Whether we shall be permitted to get a glimpse of that promised land or not I don't know . . .
> The war does not simplify life but we are not afraid, even though we face as in 1066, 1588, and 1810 the realities of invasion. Our best love to you and Pratima and Rathi.[1]

Britain's predicament and Elmhirst's response provoked two letters from Tagore, written on 2 and 3 June, in which he expressed his hope that at last British heroism would win out over British mercantilism: a Tagorean version of Churchill's 'finest hour'.

Gouripur Lodge, Kalimpong, [West Bengal, India]
3 June 1940

Dear Leonard,

It needs a few more remarks to follow up the letter that I wrote to you yesterday. Your people belong to a tremendously vital race. The self-deluding optimism and the nervous watchfulness over the stupendous hoard of belongings of an unbroken period of prosperity which prompted your ruling power to an easy surrender of self-respect belie your heroic tradition and the pure strain of true aristocracy that possibly still has survived the cult of commercialism in your blood. And now when there is no [chance] of a diplomatic escape into a safe corner, the true fighter in you will come out in full force and will guide a war in which defeat and victory have the same value of glory. In your history you have never once lost your ground when attacked and the same history will this time repeat itself, bringing you out of the congregated disaster that is raging round you today.

It will lead you into greater wisdom and a saner estimation of your power and its generous disposal which only can ensure its perpetuity.

Charlie is dead. His loss is being mourned by the whole of India thus offering [him in] death [the] ample recompense which [he] deserves.[2] Suren is no more.[3] Those of us who loved him know that his greatness was genuine and could have won wider aceptance if it [had not been] obstructed by the meanness of his fate.

Ever yours
Rabindranath Tagore

Source: MS original in Dartington Trust archives [Dartington]; letter published in Dutta and Robinson (eds.), *Purabi*, p. 119.

1 Elmhirst to RT, 19 May 1940, in Dutta and Robinson (eds.), *Purabi*, pp. 117–18.
2 Elmhirst mentioned the death of C. F. Andrews (on 5 April) in his letter, and commented, 'I envied the secure place he had, not without toil, won for himself in India, as I admired the indomitable courage of the man, barefaced nonstop courage. But he could be exasperating.' The position of Andrews in India was ambiguous: the crowds did not turn out for his funeral in Calcutta, nor did Tagore and Gandhi find it easy to collect money in his name, but Andrews remains the only one of the English friends of Tagore/Gandhi who is known to most Indians. His Indian name is Deenabandhu Andrews ('Friend of the Poor').
3 Suren: Surendranath Tagore. He died on 3 May 1940. Elmhirst mentioned him also in his letter, with much affection: 'How tenderly he treated me, . . . and with what calm assurance he gazed out on a world that had never treated him too well.' See Rathindranath Tagore, 'Surendranath Tagore', *VBQ*, 4, No. 2, Aug.–Oct. 1940, pp. 173–8.

341

To Franklin Delano Roosevelt[1]

(telegram)

While staying at Kalimpong in June 1940, in the shadow of the Himalayas, Tagore had an amazing experience. On the night before Paris fell to the Germans on 14 June, he heard French radio broadcast from Paris his little play *The Post Office* in André Gide's translation. A French friend staying with him, the superintendent of the girls' hostel at Shantiniketan, wrote, 'We could listen clearly to its recital on the radio and marvel at this heroic display of the spiritual resistance to despondency by Parisians at the most fateful moment of their destiny.'[2]

Perhaps this event, at least in part, was what triggered Tagore to send a telegram to President Roosevelt on 15 June, urging the United States to enter the war against the Nazis. The telegram was given to the news agency Reuters and was widely publicised.

Kalimpong, [West Bengal, India]
15 June 1940

Today we stand in awe before the fearfully destructive force that has so suddenly swept the world. Every moment I deplore the smallness of our means and feebleness of our voice in India so utterly inadequate to stem in the least the tide of evil that has menaced the permanence of civilisation.[3] All our individual problems of politics today have merged into one supreme world politics which I believe is seeking the help of the United States of America as the last refuge of the spiritual man and these few lines of mine merely convey my hope even if unnecessary that she will not fail in her mission to stand against this universal disaster that appears so imminent.

[Rabindranath Tagore]

Source: MS copy at Rabindra Bhavan, Shantiniketan; letter published in the *New York Times*, 16 June 1940.

1 Franklin Delano Roosevelt (1882–1945): thirty-second president of the USA, 1933–45. RT met Roosevelt briefly in 1930, in New York. Dorothy and Leonard Elmhirst were close to Roosevelt; Dorothy's son, Michael Straight, was for a while a White House speech-writer. In late 1939, Leonard Elmhirst sent RT, in confidence, an account of a discussion with Roosevelt (Elmhirst to RT, 23 Nov. 1939, in Dutta and Robinson (eds.), *Purabi*, p. 117).
2 Letter to the editor from Christiane Bossennée, *Amrita Bazar Patrika*, 22 June 1940.
3 This sentence was omitted from RT's statement as published on 17 June 1940 in the London *Times*!

342

To Victoria Ocampo

Tagore's last letter to Victoria Ocampo continues the nostalgic theme of his earlier letters (such as letter 328), made bitter-sweet by war and extreme old age. He signed himself with rare intimacy, just Rabindranath. And he continued to think of her: a few months before he died, he wrote a poem about her.[1]

Santiniketan, [West Bengal, India]
[10 July 1940]

Dear Vijaya

How very sweet of you to think of me after such a length of time. When the world atmosphere is darkened the distracted heart naturally yearns for the nearness of those friends [with] whom [is] associated the memory of happier days the value of which enhances with time. Often [there] comes to my mind the picture of that riverside home and the regret that in my absent-minded foolishness I failed to accept fully the precious gift offered to me. However the time favoured by destiny is passed and it will never return.

You have asked me for the title of the book which I dedicated to you.[2] It is named *Puravi* (the East in its feminine gender).[3]

Love
Rabindranath

Source: MS copy at Rabindra Bhavan, Shantiniketan; letter published in Dyson, *Flower-Garden*, p. 458.

1 *Shesh Lekha* (Last Writings) (5), *RR*, XXVI, pp. 42–3.
2 Ocampo to RT, 8 June 1940, in Dyson, *Flower-Garden*, pp. 456–7.
3 Puravi/Purabi is also the name of an evocative twilight ragini in classical music; and it reminds one of Tagore's own name 'Rabi'.

343

To Leonard Knight Elmhirst

This is the last letter from Rabindranath to Leonard Elmhirst.

Santiniketan, [West Bengal, India]
9 March 1941

Dear Leonard,

Letters from across the sea have become painfully scarce. Now, when [we crave] mutual touch with distant friends with such hunger, your letter this morning gave me a complete surprise of delight.[1] As for the condition of my body it is very similar to that of world politics today. It has stood eighty years of buffeting and yet is not unseaworthy. My organs are in perfect harmony with each other, only some intolerable hooligans come to deliver sudden blows from unexpected directions. But still I have not lost my courage and am pretty nearly in the same mental condition as your Great Churchill. I have decided to win at last. But when I speak like this I must take into account the paucity of the numbers of years still left to me, however friendly their attitude may be.

Our breakfast table remains still unaffected by war unlike yours. The meagreness of its fare is not owing to any miserliness of human agency but owing to scarcity of rain [which is] holding off its ministrations [with] unseasonable persistence. But you know we are used all through our days to half-rations and are reconciled to such further curtailments of our needs. Our Visva-Bharati just now has [had] the good luck [to receive] a pecuniary grant from our central Government for a year which will help us to tide over to some extent our difficulties for the present season. I believe you have heard about the visit of the Chinese ambassador of goodwill mission to our ashram and we have been greatly impressed by the old-world graciousness beaming out of his countenance. His presence has been a real source of inspiration to our people.[2]

Please give my love to Dorothy and share it yourself with her. My pen is helplessly lame and therefore I have to borrow help from others when I write letters which have become necessarily scarce.

Ever yours
Rabindranath Tagore

Source: MS original in Dartington Trust archives [Dartington]; letter published in Dutta and Robinson (eds.), *Purabi*, p. 120.

1 Elmhirst to RT, 15 Jan. 1941, in Dutta and Robinson (eds.) *Purabi*, p. 120.
2 The Chinese goodwill mission, led by Tai Chi-Tao, reached Shantiniketan on 9 Dec. 1940. In 1942, Chiang Kai-shek and his wife visited Shantiniketan in person.

344

To Mahatma Gandhi

(telegram)

On the eve of Tagore's eightieth birthday, Mahatma Gandhi sent him a telegram, 'Four score not enough. May you finish five.'[1] Rabindranath's reply was his last direct communication with Gandhi.

> Santiniketan, [West Bengal, India]
> 13 April 1941

Thanks message. But four score is impertinence. Five score intolerable.

Rabindranath

Source: MS copy at Rabindra Bhavan, Shantiniketan; telegram published in *Rabindra-Biksha*, Paush 1398 [Dec. 1991], p. 33.

1 Gandhi to RT, 12 April 1941, *CWMG*, LXXIII, p. 438.

345

To Rt. Revd Foss Westcott[1]

Although Tagore was now clearly dying, he continued to take an interest in world affairs. On 4 June 1941, he issued a vitriolic statement from his sick-bed, after reading an open letter to Indians sent by Eleanor Rathbone, an Independent MP, pleading for more cooperation from Indians in the fight against Fascism. Echoing his earlier comments about British commercialism to Elmhirst (see letter 340), he announced:

> It is not so much because the British are foreigners that they are unwelcome to us and have found no place in our hearts, as because, while pretending to be trustees of our welfare, they have betrayed the great trust and have sacrificed the happiness of millions in India to bloat the pockets of a few capitalists at home.[2]

A few days later, he received a letter from Foss Westcott, the bishop of Calcutta (and head of the Anglican Church in India), an old friend of C. F. Andrews, who had made India his home, which attempted to explain Rathbone's open letter in more sympathetic terms.[3] Tagore replied in measured words that may stand for his ultimate verdict on the deeply contentious subject of British rule in India.

Santiniketan, [West Bengal, India]
16 June 1941

My dear Lord Bishop

I thank you for the trouble you have taken to acquaint me with your reaction to my recent reply to Miss Rathbone's open letter. I respect your sentiments and share your conviction that never was mutual understanding more necessary between your people and ours than today. I have, as you are no doubt aware, worked all my life for the promotion of racial, communal and religious harmony among the different peoples of the world. I have also, at considerable personal cost and often at the risk of being misunderstood by my own people, set my face against all claims of narrow and aggressive nationalism, believing in the common destiny and oneness of all mankind. I hold many of your people in the highest regard and count among them some of my best friends. Both my faith and my practice during the last so many decades should be ample guarantee that I was not carried away by any racial, religious or merely national prejudice in my recent statement. I have neither the right nor the desire to judge the British people as such; but I cannot help being concerned at the conduct of the British Government in India, since it directly involves the life and well-being of millions of my countrymen. I am too painfully conscious of the extreme poverty, helplessness and misery of our people not to deplore the supineness of the Government that has tolerated this condition for so long. I have nothing against Miss Rathbone personally, and I am glad to be assured by you of her estimable qualities and of her love for our people. But I had hoped that the leaders of the British nation, who had grown apathetic to our suffering and forgetful of their own sacred trust in India during their days of prosperity and success, would at last, in the time of their own great trial, awake to the justice and humanity of our cause. It has been a most grievous disappointment to me to find that fondly cherished hope receding farther and farther from realisation each day. Believe me, nothing would give me greater happiness than to see the people of the West and the East march in a common crusade against all that robs the human spirit of its significance.

With kind regards,

Yours sincerely
Rabindranath Tagore

Source: MS copy at Rabindra Bhavan, Shantiniketan.

1 Rt. Revd Foss Westcott (1863–1949): bishop of Calcutta and metropolitan of India, Burma and Ceylon, 1919–45. On Westcott's view of RT, see his obituary, 'A totalitarian in religion', *CMG*, p. 24.
2 'Tagore's reply to Miss Rathbone, MP', *ibid.*, p. 107. Rathbone's view is explained in Mary D. Stocks, *Eleanor Rathbone: A Biography* (London, 1949), which also reproduces Jawaharlal Nehru's pungent response to Rathbone's letter as an appendix.
3 Westcott to RT, 14 June 1941 [RB].

346

To Kamla Chowdhury[1]

This condolence letter addressed to a mother on the other side of India, of whom little is known, was one of the last letters written by Tagore before his own death on 7 August 1941.

Santiniketan, [West Bengal, India]
10 July 1941

Dear Child

I am deeply grieved to learn of the tragedy that has overtaken your life. I will not insult your sorrow by any cheap consolation. We are all tragically helpless before Fate, since we cannot protect the happiness of those we care for. We can only sympathise. You have to bear the weight of your sorrow till your own strength and the mercy of time help you to rise over it.

Yours sincerely
Rabindranath Tagore

Source: MS copy at Rabindra Bhavan, Shantiniketan.

[1] Mrs Chowdhury was living in Lahore. Since RT addressed her in English, she was presumably not a Bengali. We have been unable to find out any more about her.

Appendixes

Appendix 1: Tagore and Einstein

This article, by Dipankar Home and Andrew Robinson, was published as 'Einstein and Tagore: man, nature and mysticism' in the *Journal of Consciousness Studies*, 2, No. 2, Summer 1995, pp. 167–79. It appears here in a slightly shortened and modified form.

In 1983, when the astrophysicist Subrahmanyan Chandrasekhar accepted the Nobel prize in Stockholm, he spoke some much-quoted lines of poetry in English translation that he had learnt more than sixty years before, as a boy in India:

> Where the mind is without fear and the head is held high;
> Where knowledge is free;
> Where words come out from the depth of truth;
> Where tireless striving stretches its arms towards perfection;
> Where the clear stream of reason has not lost its way into the dreary desert sand of
>   dead habit . . .
> into that haven of freedom, Let me awake.[1]

The lines are from Tagore's *Gitanjali* – except, that is, for the last line. This line Chandrasekhar, being an atheist, had altered, by neatly substituting 'haven' for Tagore's original 'heaven'.[2]

Science and philosophy, leave alone science and religion, have made uncomfortable bedfellows during the twentieth century. In the emphatic words of Steven Weinberg, particle physicist and Nobel laureate, writing in 1992, 'I know of *no one* who has participated actively in the advance of physics in the postwar period whose research has been significantly helped by the work of philosophers.'[3]

Nevertheless, many of the greatest physicists, including four of the founders of quantum theory, Einstein, Bohr, Heisenberg and Schrödinger, are well known for their keen interest in philosophy. Fundamental conceptual weaknesses in quantum theory disturbed Einstein until his death in 1955. Now there is an even greater need for new ideas: laboratory experiments at the subatomic level, inspired by the theoretical work of John Bell, claim to have shown that Einstein's notion of 'local reality' – that any individual object, however small, possesses dynamical properties (at all instants) which cannot be affected by an instantaneous action at a distance – is untenable.[4] It seems that quantum reality differs profoundly from macroscopic reality. And as history reminds us, metaphysics does periodically become physics. 'The best-known example is the interior of the atom, which was considered to be a metaphysical subject before Rutherford's proposal of his nuclear model, in 1911,' wrote Eugene Wigner in 1962, in an influential article speculating on the role of mind/consciousness in quantum physics.[5] Today consciousness, which until recently was felt to be 'either purely "philosophical" or too elusive to study experimentally' (Francis Crick), has become an area of serious scientific study.[6]

As a result of this interest, Einstein's discussions with Tagore in 1930 concerning the nature of reality and the relationship of determinism to free will are now seen to merit more than a tiny footnote in the history of quantum theory. Publicised at the time – initially in the *New York Times* – they continue to provoke comment among a wide range of people because they tackle some of the fundamental questions debated within science over the past half-century. The *Encyclopaedia Britannica* quotes from one of their conversations in its entry on Einstein, for instance;[7] so did Ronald W. Clark in his major biography of Einstein (a book admired by Heisenberg for its carefulness);[8] and the physicist Abraham Pais, Einstein's scientific biographer, devoted several pages of his 1994 book *Einstein Lived Here*, to Tagore (though his account contains serious inaccuracies).[9] Among other scientists, Brian Josephson, a physics Nobel laureate at Cambridge University, has commented that, 'Tagore is, I think, saying that truth is a subtler concept than Einstein realises';[10] while Ilya Prigogine, a chemistry Nobel laureate, in 1984 went so far as to say, 'Curiously enough, the present evolution of science is running in the direction stated by the great Indian poet.'[11]

Tagore was interested in science from an early age. His first ever essay (published in serial form), written in the 1870s when he was barely a teenager, was on astronomy. In his late thirties and forties, around the turn of the century, he strongly advocated the work of the physicist and plant physiologist Jagadish Chandra Bose.[12] In Britain, in 1920, Tagore made a special point of visiting the observatory in Greenwich, where the Astronomer Royal showed him the photographic plate of the solar eclipse that had apparently confirmed Einstein's theory of general relativity in 1919.[13] And in the mid-1930s, when he was in his mid-seventies, encouraged by the astrophysicist Meghnad Saha and others, Tagore took up the study of science in earnest and wrote a short book in Bengali for young students (translated as *Our Universe*), which he dedicated to his fellow Bengali S. N. Bose (of boson fame), who had earlier won Einstein's recognition for his work on light quanta. Tagore was very disappointed to miss, through illness, meeting Arthur Eddington on his visit to India in late 1937. (In a letter to him, Eddington observed, unprompted, 'I think it is true that as scientific thought goes deeper it finds much in common with Indian philosophy.'[14])

Tagore did however meet the German physicist Arnold Sommerfeld and his former student Heisenberg, when they lectured in India in 1928 and 1929 respectively. Sommerfeld visited Tagore's university at Shantiniketan and later published a vivid description of Tagore, comparing him to 'old Goethe' in his 'infinite diligence'.[15] Heisenberg spent an afternoon talking to Tagore about Indian philosophy at his mansion in Calcutta. Though neither man wrote about the encounter, Heisenberg did speak of it much later on several occasions. One of these was in conversation with his doctoral student Helmut Rechenberg, who is now in charge of Heisenberg's papers at the Max Planck Institute for Physics in Munich; Rechenberg remembers it 'quite vividly'.[16]

Tagore and Einstein first met during his second visit to Germany in mid-1926, though Einstein was certainly aware of Tagore by 1919 (probably earlier), when together they had signed an antiwar 'declaration of the independence of the spirit'.[17] Their conversation in 1926 was not recorded as it would be later, but Einstein's (German) letter written to Tagore afterwards, survives. Its tone of respect testifies to more than mere courtesy: 'If there is anything in Germany that you would like and which could be done by me, I beg you to command me at any time.'[18] This was followed by a kind of love letter to Tagore, written in broken English by Einstein's young step-daughter Margot: 'At once, I ran to father with your letter to read to him, father loves you too, you know, he was happy with me.'[19]

The second meeting with Einstein took place in July 1930, when Tagore arrived in Germany from Britain. He had just given the Hibbert lectures in Oxford, later published as *The Religion of Man* with an appendix including his conversation with Einstein. These lectures drew freely upon science and maintained that 'We can never go beyond man in all that we know and feel.'[20] Tagore was undoubtedly charged with such thinking when he talked to Einstein.

They met at least four times in 1930. In view of the confusion that has surrounded these meetings, the dates and places are worth noting. The first occasion was on 14 July in Einstein's villa at Caputh, near Berlin; the second was on 19 August, at Berlin; the third was in late September, also at Berlin, after Tagore's return from Moscow (where he was accompanied by a party including Margot Einstein); and the fourth took place in mid-December in New York City. Here, the *New York Times* reported, Einstein and Tagore spent a morning in 'animated' conversation; a striking photograph showed them together, with the teasing caption, 'A Mathematician and a Mystic Meet in Manhattan'.[21]

The earlier two conversations were published: the first one (that on 14 July) in the *New York Times* magazine on 10 August, the second (that on 19 August) in the New York-based magazine *Asia*.[22] Both conversations concern science, but the first, on reality, is more significant. The newspaper featured it prominently beneath the headline 'Einstein and Tagore Plumb the Truth'. The byline was given as Dmitri Marianoff, a Russian journalist known to the Einsteins for several years, who married Margot Einstein in November 1930. In his preamble, Marianoff wrote: 'It was interesting to see them together – Tagore, the poet with the head of a thinker, and Einstein, the thinker with the head of a poet . . . Neither sought to press his opinion. But it seemed to an observer as though two planets were engaged in a chat.'

Three months later, in October, Einstein wrote a short piece about Tagore. He did so at the request of their mutual friend and fellow Nobel laureate, Romain Rolland, who was planning a grand global *Festschrift* for Tagore's seventieth birthday (published in 1931 as *The Golden Book of Tagore*, with Einstein as one of its sponsors). But, in answering Rolland's letter, Einstein started a small controversy. He wrote (in German): 'I shall be glad to . . . add a brief contribution. My conversation with Tagore was rather unsuccessful because of difficulties in communication and should, of course, never have been published. In my contribution, I should like to give expression to my conviction that men who enjoy the reputation of great intellectual achievement have an obligation to lend moral support to the principle of unconditional refusal of war service.'[23] Rolland agreed to this offer.

Immediately, however, Einstein totally changed his mind about the content of his contribution. Instead of writing on pacifism, he wrote on causality, determinism and free will.[24] Why? And why had he changed his mind about the publication of the July conversation in the *New York Times*? He had been fully informed of the plan to publish it, indeed he had corrected a draft of the conversation in mid-July.[25] Tagore had no role in this, though he too had his reservations: when *he* published the conversation in Calcutta a few months later (and subsequently as an appendix to *The Religion of Man*), he made significant changes, restoring certain passages cut from the draft seen by Einstein and adding some new material to clarify his own point of view.[26] Were Tagore's reservations similar to Einstein's?

The answers to these questions must be largely a matter of conjecture, since neither man commented further on his reasons, at least not directly.[27] They invite us to consider the complex and baffling issues thrown up by quantum mechanics that Einstein debated at length with Bohr, Heisenberg, Schrödinger and others from 1926 onwards, during the same period as his conversations with Tagore.

A lack of philosophical communication between Einstein and Tagore certainly is evident from the published record. While the language barrier played some part in this – Einstein spoke in German, Tagore in English – its roots go deeper. The philosopher Isaiah Berlin (who was present at Tagore's Oxford lectures) commented in 1993, 'I do not believe that, apart from professions of mutual regard and the fact that Einstein and Tagore were both sincere and highly gifted and idealistic thinkers, there was much in common between them – although their social ideals may well have been very similar.'[28] During the 1930s, Einstein was not apparently influenced by Tagore, nor Tagore by Einstein, though it is said that Tagore turned down an offer of an honorary doctorate from Berlin University in protest against Nazi treatment of Einstein.[29] In later years, Einstein is known to have referred to Tagore privately by the punning name 'Rabbi'

Tagore. Isaiah Berlin again: 'I think [this] was meant to be ironical, in the gentlest way. Einstein did not hold with rabbis much; still less with quantum physics.'[30]

Instead of their minds meeting, the two men seem mostly to have talked past each other, where they did not openly disagree. A comparable mismatch occurred, famously, between Einstein and Bohr, and lasted for thirty years right up to Einstein's death. A frustrated Bohr was never able to bring Einstein round to accepting the majority view of quantum mechanics. Although the philosophical views of Bohr and Tagore differ in crucial respects, there are important similarities too. It is fruitful to compare the Einstein–Bohr and Einstein–Tagore relationships. We shall look first at that of Einstein and Bohr.

In classical physics, the macroscopic world, that of our daily experience, is taken to exist independently of observers: the moon is there whether one looks at it or not, in the well-known example of Einstein. And the same may be conceived to be true of the subatomic world. That is what is meant by 'realism': the philosophical position of, say, Descartes – that the physical world has objectivity that transcends direct experience, and that propositions are true or false independently of our ability to discern which they are.

But in quantum physics – at least according to the 'standard' interpretation of quantum theory, the Copenhagen interpretation (named after its Danish origin and father, Bohr) – reality looks different, particularly at small scales. An electron, for instance, no longer has properties such as position, momentum, energy, in the absence of an observation/measurement. In the words of Heisenberg, whose uncertainty principle lies at the heart of the Copenhagen interpretation, 'The laws of nature which we formulate mathematically in quantum theory deal no longer with the elementary particles themselves but with our knowledge of the particles.'[31] The nature of reality in the Copenhagen interpretation is therefore essentially epistemological, that is all meaningful statements about the physical world are based on knowledge derived from observations. 'No elementary phenomenon is a phenomenon until it is a recorded phenomenon,' to quote a dictum of the quantum theorist John Wheeler.[32] This philosophical stance contains elements of positivism, the point of view strongly developed in the later nineteenth century before the advent of quantum theory by physicists such as Ernst Mach (who argued against the concept of the atom as being a mystical entity).

Einstein was at first a staunch positivist, but during the 1920s he became an equally staunch realist, and remained so thereafter. In 1950, he told the philosopher Karl Popper that he regretted no 'mistake' (Einstein's word) more than his original belief in positivism.[33] His turn to classical realism began, according to Helmut Rechenberg, with the success of his general relativity theory, i.e. after 1916; but probably his earliest unequivocal assertion of this shift in his thinking occurred in 1926 in his conversations with Heisenberg. According to the latter, Einstein declared himself sceptical of quantum theory because it concerned 'what we know about nature', no longer 'what nature really does'. In science, said Einstein, 'we ought to be concerned solely with what nature does'.[34] Both Heisenberg and Bohr disagreed: in Bohr's view, it was 'wrong to think that the task of physics is to find out how nature *is*. Physics concerns what we can say about nature.'[35] At the Solvay conferences in 1927 and 1930, Einstein pressed his point of view, and in 1935 published (with Boris Podolsky and Nathan Rosen) the famous EPR paper, in which he argued with the help of a 'thought experiment' that 'If, without in any way disturbing a system, we can predict with certainty . . . the value of a physical quantity, then there exists an element of physical reality' – in other words a 'local' reality – 'corresponding to this physical quantity'.[36]

Bohr, however, refuted this reasoning – to the apparent satisfaction of the majority of physicists.[37] How many really understood him is dubious, considering that even a leading theorist such as John Bell did not, as he freely admitted repeatedly in various writings.[38] However, in the light of all the experiments that have so far tested Bell's theorem, many physicists (though not all) accept that the locality condition used by Einstein, Podolsky and Rosen in their analysis is not valid in the quantum world. (Nevertheless, we should note that the experiments on Bell's theorem do not negate the concept of realism *per se*, but only a particular form of realism based on Einstein's locality condition. The general idea behind realism – that quantum entities have well-defined objective properties even in the absence of any measurement – remains a logically tenable proposition. This is most convincingly shown by the formulation of an alternative interpretation of quantum mechanics – à la de Broglie and David Bohm – based on a realist model, objective but nonlocal – which explains in a perfectly consistent way all known quantum phenomena.[39])

Schrödinger was the only one among the founders of quantum theory who was sympathetic to Einstein's position, but he could not entirely accept it. In their correspondence, Einstein accused the Copenhagen interpretation of being a 'tranquilising philosophy', metaphysical, nothing more than 'a soft pillow on which to lay one's head', rather than engaging reality face to face; Bohr, Einstein told Schrödinger in 1939, was a 'mystic, who forbids, as being unscientific, an inquiry about something that exists independently of whether or not it is observed'.[40]

Einstein's conversations with Tagore in 1930, shortly before he tussled with Bohr at the Solvay conference in October, express his hardening adherence to realism in a remarkably clear-cut fashion. This extract is from the conversation (as vetted by Einstein) reported in the *New York Times*:

> E: There are two different conceptions about the nature of the universe – the world as a unity dependent on humanity, and the world as reality independent of the human factor . . .
> T: This world is a human world – the scientific view of it is also that of the scientific man. Therefore, the world apart from us does not exist; it is a relative world, depending for its reality upon our consciousness.

A little later, Einstein took up the point again:

> E: Truth, then, or beauty, is not independent of man?
> T: No.
> E: If there were no human beings any more, the Apollo Belvedere no longer would be beautiful?
> T: No.
> E: I agree with regard to this conception of beauty, but not with regard to truth.
> T: Why not? Truth is realised through men.

(Here, according to a later account by the note-taker Marianoff, there was a long pause. Then Einstein spoke again very quietly and softly.[41])

> E: I cannot prove my conception is right, but that is my religion.

After some further discussion – in which Einstein asserted, 'I cannot prove, but I believe in the Pythagorean argument, that the truth is independent of human beings,' and Tagore countered with a reference to ancient Indian philosophy, to 'Brahman, the absolute truth, which cannot be conceived by the isolation of the individual mind or described in words, but can be realised only by merging the individual in its infinity' – Einstein became concrete:

> E: The mind acknowledges realities outside of it, independent of it. For instance, nobody may be in this house, yet that table remains where it is.
> T: Yes, it remains outside the individual mind, but not the universal mind. The table is that which is perceptible by some kind of consciousness we possess.
> E: If nobody were in the house the table would exist all the same, but this is already illegitimate from your point of view, because we cannot explain what it means, that the table is there, independently of us. Our natural point of view in regard to the existence of truth apart from humanity cannot be explained or proved, but it is a belief which nobody can lack – not even primitive beings. We attribute to truth a superhuman

objectivity. It is indispensable for us – this reality which is independent of our existence and our experience and our mind – though we cannot say what it means.

T: In any case, if there be any truth absolutely unrelated to humanity, then for us it is absolutely nonexisting.

E: Then I am more religious than you are!

(Here, said Marianoff, Einstein 'exclaimed in triumph'.)

The position of Einstein in this last extract is reminiscent of his well-known paradox: 'The most incomprehensible fact about nature is that it is comprehensible.'[42] Nature, for Einstein, had to be independent of man and mind. As he insisted in his question printed in *The Golden Book of Tagore*, 'Man defends himself from being regarded as an impotent object in the course of the Universe. But should the lawfulness of events, such as unveils itself more or less clearly in inorganic nature, cease to function in front of the activities in our brain?'[43]

Einstein could not accept any idea that a universal mind might control nature. Tagore, by contrast, could accept this. As he said to Einstein, 'What we call truth lies in the rational harmony between the subjective and objective aspects of reality, both of which belong to the superpersonal man.' In other words, Tagore did not adhere either to Einstein's realist, essentially objective position or to Bohr's quasi-positivistic, essentially subjective view of nature, a position that, taken to its logical extreme, denies the existence of the physical world – or at least its dynamical properties – until they are measured. Tagore did not deny the existence of the table when nobody was in the house, but he argued that its existence becomes meaningful for us only when it is perceived by some conscious mind. And he said, further, that there is a universality in the nature of consciousness (contrary to our normal sense of consciousness as being essentially private). Galileo's experiments with falling stones would be interpreted in the same way by all humans who today perform the experiment, notes Ilya Prigogine. 'In a sense, this is a result of a common structure of consciousness for all humans.'[44]

What did Tagore mean by this concept of a universal human mind? He once wrote, 'The Universe is like a cobweb and minds are the spiders; for mind is one as well as many.'[45] He tried to amplify and clarify his meaning in his own version of the conversation with Einstein published in *The Religion of Man*. (He did so partly by restoring two passages cut from the draft of the conversation before it was printed in the *New York Times*.) Pursuing the example of the table, he said:

> Science has proved that the table as a solid object is an appearance and therefore that which the human mind perceives as a table would not exist if that mind were naught. At the same time it must be admitted that the fact that the ultimate physical reality of the table is nothing but a multitude of separate revolving centres of electric force, also belongs to the human mind.
>
> In the apprehension of truth there is an eternal conflict between the universal human mind and the same mind confined in the individual. The perpetual process of reconciliation is being carried on in our science, philosophy, in our ethics.[46]

This statement resembles remarkably one made by Einstein's friend, the physicist Max Born: 'All religions, philosophies, and sciences have been evolved for the purpose of expanding the ego to the wider community that "we" represent.' Ironically, Born wrote it in 1920 in his famous introduction to Einstein's *Theory of Relativity*.[47]

If mind/consciousness, the first-person perspective, is somehow to be incorporated into physics, as certain physicists believe it should be, this would entail consequences as dramatic as those involved in the introduction of relativity by Einstein, for it would mean an acceptance that 'the lawfulness of events, such as unveils itself more or less clearly in inorganic nature' may, at least in principle, 'cease to function in front of the activities in our brain' – to answer Einstein's sceptical question addressed to Tagore in the affirmative. But Einstein could never accept this:

he was committed to the realism, determinism and strict causality of classical physics, as he made plain to Tagore in their second, more free-ranging conversation on 19 August 1930. Tagore, who was staying with a scientific friend of Einstein in Berlin, introduced the subject:

T: I was discussing with Dr Mendel today the new mathematical discoveries which tell us that in the realm of infinitesimal atoms chance has its play; the drama of existence is not absolutely predestined in character.

E: The facts that make science tend towards this view do not say goodbye to causality.

T: Maybe not; but it appears that the idea of causality is not in the elements, that some other force builds up with them an organised universe.

E: One tries to understand how the order is in the higher plane. The order is there, where the big elements combine and guide existence; but in the minute elements this order is not perceptible.

T: This duality is in the depths of existence – the contradiction of free impulse and directive will which works upon it and evolves an orderly scheme of things.

E: Modern physics would not say they are contradictory. Clouds look one from a distance, but, if you see them near, they show themselves in disorderly drops of water.

T: I find a parallel in human psychology. Our passions and desires are unruly, but our character subdues these elements into a harmonious whole.

Interestingly, Bohr made a similar point to Einstein, writing in *Albert Einstein: Philosopher-Scientist* at the time of Einstein's seventieth birthday in 1949: 'Actually, words like "thoughts" and "sentiments", . . . indispensable to illustrate the variety and scope of conscious life, are used in a similar complimentary way as space-time coordination and dynamical conservation laws in atomic physics.'[48] Einstein did not concur.

Tagore continued:

T: Are the elements rebellious, dynamic with individual impulse? And is there a principle in the physical world which dominates them and puts them into an orderly organisation?

E: Even the elements are not without statistical order; elements of radium will always maintain their specific order, now and ever onwards, just as they have done all along. There is, then, a statistical order in the elements.

T: Otherwise the drama of existence would be too desultory. It is the constant harmony of chance and determination which makes it eternally new and living.

E: I believe that whatever we do or live for has its causality; it is good, however, that we cannot look through it.

Here, in this short exchange, would appear to be the kernel of Einstein's ambivalence towards Tagore: why he changed his mind about the publication of their first conversation (on 14 July), and why he unexpectedly chose to write on determinism and free will, rather than on his promised pacifism, in Tagore's birthday *Festschrift*. Significantly, Bertrand Russell, Einstein's friend and collaborator, was ambivalent about Tagore too. Although Russell praised Tagore highly in the *Festschrift* and published in his *Autobiography* (1967) an appreciative philosophical letter on himself from Tagore, he wrote privately about the letter at the same time to a Bengali contact: 'I regret I cannot agree with Tagore. His talk about the infinite is vague nonsense. The sort of language that is admired by many Indians unfortunately does not, in fact, mean anything at all.'[49]

'I suspect Einstein . . . thought Tagore was talking nonsense,' remarks Brian Josephson (who, as we know, finds Tagore the subtler thinker about truth).[50] This is most likely correct, but it is also probable – given Einstein's undoubtedly genuine respect for Tagore – that Einstein was slightly stung by what seemed to be Tagore's (and even more Bohr's) dogmatic unwillingness to perceive what he, Einstein, effortlessly saw: a profound order in nature, 'out there', quite independent of the human mind. Einstein's seventieth birthday message to Tagore in effect reproves him for his dogmatism in the gentlest way; as does Einstein's later punning reference to Tagore as 'Rabbi'.

To summarise, then, we can discern three philosophical positions concerning the relationship between man and nature arising from the Einstein–Tagore conversations. The first, held by Einstein, is that nature exists, objectively, whether we know it or not. Hence Einstein thought it was essential to describe 'what nature does' instead of merely speaking of 'what we know about nature' (to repeat his earlier comments to Heisenberg). The second position, held by Bohr, is that the objective existence of nature has no meaning independent of the measurement process. The third position, held by Tagore, is more complex, because it requires mind/consciousness – in contrast to Bohr's (and of course Einstein's) position, but in line with certain subsequent interpretations of quantum theory that invoke the existence of 'many worlds'. Tagore says, centrally, that nature can be conceived only in terms of our mental constructions based on what we think we perceive: 'This world is a human world – the scientific view of it is also that of the scientific man' (to repeat his earlier statement). Tagore says further – and it is a separate though dependent point – that there exists a universal mind: 'What we call truth lies in the rational harmony between the subjective and objective aspects of reality, both of which belong to the superpersonal man . . . if there be any truth absolutely unrelated to humanity, then for us it is absolutely nonexisting' (to reiterate what he told Einstein).

Tagore's position has some similarity with the work of various contemporary philosophers. Hilary Putnam, in particular, has attempted to break what he calls the 'stranglehold' on our thinking of the dichotomy between objective and subjective views of truth and reason, by inserting mind into reality. In *The Many Faces of Realism*, he argued that, metaphorically speaking, 'the mind and the world jointly make up the mind and the world'.[51] And he went on to reject the existence of 'intrinsic' properties – e.g. the position and momentum of an electron ('local realism') – of the kind integral to classical physics and to Einstein in the EPR experiment, properties that, in the words of Putnam, 'something has "in itself", apart from any contribution made by language or the mind'.[52]

Another relevant philosopher is Thomas Nagel. Though his position differs more from Tagore's than does Putnam's, Nagel shares Tagore's fundamental concern: to create a world view that reconciles the objective viewpoint – what Nagel calls 'the centreless universe' – with that of the self, by integrating the two viewpoints with consciousness. He argues that, 'The subjectivity of consciousness is an irreducible feature of reality – without which we couldn't do physics or anything else – and it must occupy as fundamental a place in any credible world view as matter, energy, space, time and numbers.'[53]

Obviously these are extremely difficult problems with an ancient philosophical and scientific pedigree. In 1611, Galileo noted that 'it would seem ridiculous to me to believe that things in nature begin to exist when we begin to discover and understand them'.[54] Einstein went on worrying at 'the reality question' until the day he died; so, less conspicuously, did Tagore. Neither came to a definite conclusion. (In 1950 Einstein even informed Schrödinger that determinism was 'a thoroughly nebulous concept anyway'.[55]) All three of the above philosophical positions have adherents throughout science today, with Bohr's predominating among quantum physicists and Tagore's the least accepted of the three. None the less, towards the end of his life, Schrödinger came to a view analogous to Tagore's, that 'The world is a construct of our sensations, perceptions, memories. It is convenient to regard it as existing objectively on its own. But it certainly does not become manifest by its mere existence.'[56] – while David Bohm, in later years, believed that 'it is the brain that creates the illusion of location' of physical matter in the macroscopic world.[57]

It will be interesting to see how the balance of scientific opinion on these great questions alters as science changes. Will Ilya Prigogine's bold prediction – that science is evolving according to Tagore – come true during the next century? Or, as many scientists hope, will increasing knowledge of brain functioning and deeper insights into quantum mechanics and molecular biology make consciousness amenable to being understood in terms of the existing laws of physics, these having been suitably modified?[58] Perhaps, for the purposes of this paper, Tagore should have the last word. Here is virtually the last poem he wrote, aged eighty, shortly before he 'lost consciousness':

> The sun of the first day
> Put the question
> To the new manifestation of life –
> Who are you?
> There was no answer.
> Years passed by.
> The last sun of the last day
> Uttered the question on the shore of the western sea,
> In the hush of evening –
> Who are you!
> No answer came.[59]

Notes

1 *Gitanjali*, pp. 27–8/*Naivedya*, *RR*, VIII, pp. 56, 58.
2 The last two lines, as written by Tagore, read, 'Into that heaven of freedom, my Father, let my country awake.' We thank the late Subrahmanyan Chandrasekhar for drawing our attention to his version (Chandrasekhar to Andrew Robinson, 3 March 1993). 'Perhaps, I may venture to say that Tagore's use of "heaven" is a mild mixed metaphor: on land, one can reach a haven but not Heaven' (Chandrasekhar to Andrew Robinson, 15 March 1994).
3 Steven Weinberg, *Dreams of a Final Theory* (London, 1993), p. 134 (italics are Weinberg's).
4 An overview of studies relating to Bell's work is provided in A. F. van der Merwe, F. Selleri and G. Tarozzi (eds.), *Bell's Theorem and the Foundations of Modern Physics* (Singapore, 1992).
5 Wigner, 'Remarks on the mind-body question', in I. J. Good (ed.), *The Scientist Speculates – An Anthology of Partly-Baked Ideas* (London, 1962), p. 299.
6 Francis Crick and Christof Koch, 'The problem of consciousness', *Scientific American*, Sept. 1992, p. 153.
7 *Encyclopaedia Britannica*, 15th edn, XVIII, p. 157.
8 Ronald W. Clark, *Einstein: The Life and Times* (New York, 1971), pp. 414–15.
9 Abraham Pais, *Einstein Lived Here* (New York, 1994), pp. 99–108. Pais makes many errors about RT's life, confuses the various meetings between RT and Einstein and, most importantly, does not use the *New York Times* version of the Einstein–Tagore conversation, which Einstein vetted.
10 Brian D. Josephson to Andrew Robinson, 11 Dec. 1992.
11 Ilya Prigogine and Isabelle Stengers, *Order out of Chaos: Man's New Dialogue with Nature* (London, 1984), p. 293.
12 See letter 27.
13 Rathindranath Tagore, *Edges of Time*, p. 113.
14 Eddington to RT, 7 Feb. 1938 [RB].
15 'Arnold Sommerfeld: his life, work and an impression of his recent visit to India', *MR*, June 1929, pp. 738–9. This article contains translated extracts from an article by Sommerfeld on his Indian visit.
16 On the Tagore–Heisenberg relationship, see Dutta and Robinson, *Rabindranath Tagore*, pp. 442–3.
17 See Rolland, *Selected Letters*, pp. 10–12.
18 Einstein to RT, 25 Sept. 1926 [RB]. The letter is in German.
19 Margot Einstein to RT, 20 Sept. 1926 [RB].
20 *Religion of Man*, p. 114.
21 *New York Times*, 21 Dec. 1930. According to Subrahmanyan Chandrasekhar, the physicist A. H. Compton used to keep this photograph of Einstein and Tagore in his office.
22 The *New York Times* conversation appears in Dutta and Robinson (eds.), *Anthology*, pp. 230–33. The *Asia* conversation appears in the issue of March 1931, pp. 140–2. Gertrude Emerson (Sen), then an editor for *Asia*, was responsible for publishing it. She was present at the Dec. 1930 meeting between RT and Einstein in New York; see her account in Ramananda Chatterjee (ed.), *Golden Book*, p. 80.
23 Einstein to Rolland, 10 Oct. 1930, in Otto Nathan and Heinz Norden, *Einstein on Peace* (New York, 1960), p. 112.
24 Einstein, 'About free will', in Ramananda Chatterjee (ed.), *Golden Book*, pp. 11–12; a slightly modified translation of Einstein's contribution appears in the *Journal of Consciousness Studies*, 2, No. 2 Summer 1995, p. 172.
25 See Dutta and Robinson, *Rabindranath Tagore*, p. 446.

26 The conversation was published as 'The nature of reality', *MR*, Jan. 1931, pp. 42–3, and later in *The Religion of Man*. The original draft, sent to RT by the *New York Times* before publication, is kept at Rabindra Bhavan, Shantiniketan.
27 RT wrote an article about his meetings with Einstein, which was published in *Asia*, March 1931, pp. 139–40. It contains some interesting hints about their philosophical disagreement but nothing definite about it.
28 Berlin to Andrew Robinson, 15 March 1993.
29 See Dutta and Robinson, *Rabindranath Tagore*, p. 344.
30 Pais, *Einstein Lived Here*, p. 99; Berlin to Andrew Robinson, 24 May 1993.
31 Werner Heisenberg, *The Physicist's Conception of Nature* (London, 1955), p. 15; see also Wolfgang Pauli (ed.), *Niels Bohr and the Development of Physics*, (Oxford, 1955), pp. 12–29.
32 John Wheeler, *At Home in the Universe* (New York, 1994), p. 120.
33 Quoted in Karl Popper, *Unended Quest* (Glasgow, 1976), p. 97.
34 Quoted in Werner Heisenberg, *Physics and Beyond* (London, 1971), p. 68.
35 Quoted in Abraham Pais, *Niels Bohr's Times in Physics, Philosophy, and Polity* (Oxford, 1991), p. 427.
36 A. Einstein, B. Podolsky and N. Rosen, 'Can quantum mechanical description of physical reality be considered complete?', *Physical Review*, 47, 1935, p. 777.
37 Bohr, 'Can quantum mechanical description of reality be considered complete?', *Physical Review*, 48, 1935, pp. 696–700.
38 For instance, J. S. Bell, *Speakable and Unspeakable in Quantum Mechanics* (Cambridge, 1987). This paper was first published in 1981.
39 See, for example, P. Holland, *The Quantum Theory of Motion* (Cambridge, 1993), and David Bohm and B. J. Hiley, *The Undivided Universe* (London, 1993).
40 Quoted in K. Przibram (ed.), *Letters on Wave Mechanics* (New York, 1950), p. 44.
41 Quoted in Dmitri Marianoff, *Einstein: An Intimate Study of a Great Man* (New York, 1944), pp. 73–7, a not wholly reliable account of the Einstein–Tagore meeting in July 1930, at which Marianoff was a note-taker.
42 Quoted in, for example, Subrahmanyan Chandrasekhar, 'Science and scientific attitudes', *Nature*, 344, 1990, pp. 285.
43 Einstein, 'About free will', in Ramananda Chatterjee (ed.), *Golden Book*, p. 12.
44 Prigogine to Andrew Robinson, 26 July 1993.
45 Quoted in Schlomith Flaum, 'At the feet of my master', *Palestine News*, 23 Aug. 1941 (original source unknown).
46 Appendix to *Religion of Man*, pp. 224–5.
47 Introduction to Albert Einstein, *Einstein's Theory of Relativity* (Max Born ed., Henry L. Brose trans.; London, 1924), p. 4.
48 Bohr, 'Discussion with Einstein on epistemological problems in atomic physics', in Paul Arthur Schilpp (ed.), *Albert Einstein: Philosopher-Scientist* (Evanston, 1949), p. 224.
49 Russell to N. Chatterji, 26 April 1967 [copy at McMaster].
50 Josephson to Andrew Robinson, 17 June 1993.
51 Hilary Putnam, *The Many Faces of Realism* (La Salle, 1987), p. 1. We thank Amartya Sen for suggesting the idea of comparisons with the work of Putnam and Nagel.
52 *Ibid.*, p. 8.
53 Thomas Nagel, *The View from Nowhere* (New York, 1989), pp. 7–8, 55.
54 Galileo to Pietro Dini, quoted in A. van der Merwe et al. (eds.), *50 Years of the EPR Paper* (Dordrecht, 1985), p. 262.
55 Quoted in Przibram, *Letters*, p. 40.
56 'The physical basis of consciousness', in Erwin Schrödinger, *What is Life?* (Cambridge, 1992), p. 93.
57 Conversation with Dipankar Home, 1991.
58 See, for example, Roger Penrose, *Shadows of the Mind: A Search for the Missing Science of Consciousness* (Oxford, 1994), and discussions of his work in the *Journal of Consciousness Studies*, 1994–.
59 *Shesh Lekha*, *RR*, XXVI, pp. 49–50 (27 July 1941). The translation is by Krishna Dutta and Andrew Robinson.

Appendix 2: the Bihar earthquake

As described in letter 272, Tagore and Gandhi disagreed about the significance of the Bihar earthquake of January 1934. Gandhi, while on a tour of south India preaching against untouchability, stated that the earthquake was 'divine chastisement sent by God for our sins'. Tagore's response to this, and Gandhi's reaction to Tagore's response, were published together in Gandhi's newspaper, *Harijan*, on 16 February 1934.

Tagore

It has caused me painful surprise to find Mahatma Gandhi accusing those who blindly follow their own social custom of untouchability of having brought down God's vengeance upon certain parts of Bihar, evidently specially selected for His desolating displeasure. It is all the more unfortunate, because this kind of unscientific view of things is too readily accepted by a large section of our countrymen. I keenly feel the iniquity of it when I am compelled to utter a truism in asserting that physical catastrophes have their inevitable and exclusive origin in certain combinations of physical facts. Unless we believe in the exorability of the universal law in the working of which God himself never interferes, we find it impossible to justify His ways on occasions like the one which has sorely stricken us in an overwhelming manner and scale.

If we associate ethical principles with cosmic phenomena, we shall have to admit that human nature preaches its lessons in good behaviour in orgies of the worst behaviour possible. For, we can never imagine any civilised ruler of men making indiscriminate examples of casual victims, including children and members of the Untouchable community, in order to impress others dwelling at a safe distance who possibly deserve severer condemnation. Though we cannot point out any period of human history that is free from iniquities of the darkest kind, we still find citadels of malevolence yet remain unshaken, that the factories that cruelly thrive upon abject poverty and the ignorance of the famished cultivators, or prison-houses in all parts of the world where a penal system is pursued, which most often is a special form of licensed criminality, still stand firm. It only shows that the law of gravitation does not in the least respond to the stupendous load of callousness that accumulates till the moral foundation of our society begins to show dangerous cracks and civilisations are undermined. What is truly tragic about it is the fact that the kind of argument that Mahatmaji uses by exploiting an event of cosmic disturbance far better suits the psychology of his opponents than his own, and it would not have surprised me at all if they had taken this opportunity of holding him and his followers responsible for the visitation of Divine anger. As for us, we feel perfectly secure in the faith that our own sins and errors, however enormous, have not enough force to drag down the structure of creation to ruins. We can depend upon it, sinners and saints, bigots and breakers of convention. We, who are immensely grateful to Mahatmaji for inducing, by his wonder working inspiration, freedom from fear and feebleness in the minds of his countrymen, feel profoundly hurt when any words from his mouth may emphasise the elements of unreason in those very minds – unreason, which is a fundamental source of all the blind powers that drive us against freedom and self-respect.

Gandhi

When at Tinnevelly I first linked the event with untouchability, I spoke with the greatest deliberation and out of the fullness of my heart. I spoke as I believed. I have long believed that physical phenomena produce results both physical and spiritual. The converse I hold to be equally true.

To me, the earthquake was no caprice of God, nor a result of a meeting of mere blind forces. We do not know the laws of God nor their working. Knowledge of the tallest scientist or the spiritualist is like a particle of dust. If God is not a personal being for me like my earthly father, He is infinitely more. He rules me in the tiniest detail of my life. I believe literally that not a leaf moves but by His will. Every breath I take depends upon His sufferance.

He and His Law are one. The Law is God. Anything attributed to Him is not a mere attribute. He is Truth, Love, Law, and a million things that human ingenuity can name. I do believe with

Gurudev [Tagore] in the inexorableness of the universal law in the working of which God Himself never interferes. For, God is the Law. But I submit that we do not know the Law or all the laws fully, and what appears to us as catastrophes are so only because we do not know the universal laws sufficiently.

Visitations like droughts, floods, earthquakes and the like, though they seem to have only physical origins, are, for me, somehow connected with man's morals. Therefore, I instinctively felt that this earthquake was the visitation for the sin of untouchability. Of course, Sanatanists [i.e. the most orthodox Hindus] have a perfect right to say that it was due to my crime of preaching against untouchability. My belief is a call to repentance and self-purification. I confess my utter ignorance of the working of the laws of nature. But, even as I cannot help believing in God though I am unable to prove his existence to the sceptics, in like manner, I cannot prove the connection of the sin of untouchability with the Bihar visitation even though the connection is instinctively felt by me. If my belief turns out to be ill founded, it will still have done good for me and those who believe with me. For we shall have been spurred to more vigorous efforts towards self-purification, assuming, of course, that untouchability is a deadly sin. I know full well the danger of such speculation. But I would be untruthful and cowardly, if, for fear of ridicule, when those that are nearest and dearest to me are suffering, I did not proclaim my belief from the house-top. The physical effect of the earthquake will be soon forgotten and even partially repaired. But it would be terrible, if it is an expression of the divine wrath for the sin of untouchability and we did not learn the moral lesson from the event and repent of that sin. I have not the faith that Gurudev has that 'our sins and errors, however enormous, have not good enough force to drag down the structure of creation to ruins'. On the contrary, I have the faith that our own sins have more force to ruin that structure than any mere physical phenomenon. There is an indissoluble marriage between matter and spirit. Our ignorance of the results of the union makes it a profound mystery and inspires awe in us but it cannot undo them. But a living recognition of the union has enabled many to utilise every physical catastrophe for their own moral uplifting.

With me the connection between cosmic phenomena and human behaviour is a living faith that draws me nearer to God, humbles me and makes me readier for facing Him. Such a belief would be a degrading superstition, if out of the depth of my ignorance I used it for castigating my opponents.

Appendix 3: Gandhi the man

As described in letter 316, this article by Tagore was written in January 1938 and printed in the *Sunday Statesman*, Calcutta, on 13 February 1938.

After my return to India from some months' touring in the West, I found the whole country convulsed with the expectation of an immediate independence – Gandhiji had promised Swaraj in one year – by the help of some process that was obviously narrow in its scope and external in its observance.

Such an assurance, coming from a great personality, produced a frenzy of hope even in those who were ordinarily sober in their calculation of worldly benefits; and they angrily argued with me that in this particular case it was not a question of logic, but of a spiritual phenomenon that had a mysterious influence and miraculous power of prescience. This had the effect of producing a strong doubt in my mind about Mahatmaji's wisdom in the path he chose for attaining a great end through satisfying an inherent weakness in our character which has been responsible for the age-long futility of our political life.

We who often glorify our tendency to ignore reason, installing in its place blind faith, valuing it as spiritual, are ever paying for its costs with the obscuration of our mind and destiny. I blamed

Mahatmaji for exploiting this irrational force of credulity in our people, which might have had a quick result in a superstructure, while sapping the foundation. Thus began my estimate of Mahatmaji, as the guide of our nation, and it is fortunate for me that it did not end there.

Gandhiji, like all dynamic personalities, needed a vast medium for the proper and harmonious expression of his creative will. This medium he developed for himself, when he assumed the tremendous responsibility of leading the whole country into freedom through countless social ditches and fences and unlimited dullness of barren politics. This endeavour has enriched and mellowed his personality and revealed what was truly significant in his genius. I have since learnt to understand him, as I would understand an artist, not by the theories and fantasies of the creed he may profess, but by that expression in his practice which gives evidence to the uniqueness of his mind. In that only true perspective, as I watch him, I am amazed at the effectiveness of his humanity.

An ascetic himself, he does not frown on the joys of others, but works for the enlivening of their existence day and night. He exalts poverty in his own life, but no man in India has striven more assiduously than he for the material welfare of his people. A reformer with the zeal of a revolutionary, he imposes severe restraints on the very passions he provokes. Something of an idolator and also an iconoclast, he leaves the old gods in their dusty niches of sanctity and simply lures the old worship to better and more humane purposes. Professing his adherence to the caste system, he launches his firmest attack against it where it keeps its strongest guards, and yet he has hardly suffered from popular disapprobation as would have been the case with a lesser man who would have much less power to be effective in his efforts.

He condemns sexual life as inconsistent with the moral progress of man, and has a horror of sex as great as that of the author of *The Kreutzer Sonata*, but, unlike Tolstoy, he betrays no abhorrence of the sex that tempts his kind. In fact, his tenderness for woman is one of the noblest and most consistent traits of his character, and he counts among the women of his country some of his best and truest comrades in the great movement he is leading.

He advises his followers to hate evil without hating the evil-doer. It sounds an impossible precept, but he has made it as true as it can be made in his own life. I had once occasion to be present at an interview he gave to a certain prominent politician who had been denounced by the official Congress party as a deserter. Any other Congress leader would have assumed a repelling attitude, but Gandhiji was all graciousness and listened to him with patience and sympathy, without once giving him occasion to feel small. Here, I said to myself, is a truly great man, for he is greater than the party he belongs to, greater even than the creed he professes.

This, then, seems to me to be the significant fact about Gandhiji. Great as he is as a politician, as an organiser, as a leader of men, as a moral reformer, he is greater than all these as a man, because none of these aspects and activities limits his humanity. They are rather inspired and sustained by it. Though an incorrigible idealist and given to referring all conduct to certain pet formulae of his own, he is essentially a lover of men and not of mere ideas; which makes him so cautious and conservative in his revolutionary schemes. If he proposes an experiment for society, he must first subject himself to its ordeal. If he calls for a sacrifice, he must first pay its price himself. While many Socialists wait for all to be deprived of their privileges before they would part with theirs, this man first renounces before he ventures to make any claims on the renunciation of others.

There are patriots in India, as indeed among all peoples, who have sacrificed for their country as much as Gandhiji has done, and some who have had to suffer much worse penalties than he has ever had to endure: even as in the religious sphere, there are ascetics in this country, compared to the rigours of whose practices Gandhiji's life is one of comparative ease. But these patriots are mere patriots and nothing more; and these ascetics are mere spiritual athletes, limited as men by their very virtues; while this man seems greater than his virtues, great as they are.

Perhaps none of the reforms with which his name is associated was originally his in conception. They have almost all been proposed and preached by his predecessors or contemporaries.

Long before the Congress adopted them, I had myself preached and written about the necessity of a constructive programme of rural reconstruction in India; of handicrafts as an essential element in the education of our children; of the absolute necessity of ridding Hinduism of the nightmare of untouchability. Nevertheless, it remains true, that they have never had the same energising power in them as when he took them up; for now they are quickened by the great life-force of the complete man who is absolutely one with his ideas, whose visions perfectly blend with his whole being.

His emphasis on the truth and purity of the means, from which he has evolved his creed of nonviolence, is but another aspect of his deep and insistent humanity; for it insists that men in their fight for their claims must only so assert their rights, whether as individuals or as groups, as never to violate their fundamental obligation to humanity, which is to respect life. To say that, because existing rights and privileges of certain classes were originally won and are still maintained by violence, they can only be destroyed by violence, is to create an unending circle of viciousness; for there will always be men with some grievance, fancied or real, against the prevailing order of society, who will claim the same immunity from moral obligation and the right to wade to their goal through slaughter. Somewhere the circle has to be broken, and Gandhiji wants his country to win the glory of first breaking it.

Perhaps he will not succeed. Perhaps he will fail as the Buddha failed and as Christ failed to wean men from their iniquities, but he will always be remembered as one who made his life a lesson for all ages to come.

BIBLIOGRAPHY

In order to keep this bibliography manageable, only those manuscript sources and books cited in the text are included in it, with very occasional additions. Other useful books, consulted by us but not cited, may be found in the bibliography of our biography, *Rabindranath Tagore: The Myriad-Minded Man*, in Katherine Henn's *Rabindranath Tagore: A Bibliography* and in the bibliographies of other major studies of RT in both English and Bengali listed below.

Articles are fully referenced in the notes.

The place of publication of all cited books in Bengali is Calcutta.

Manuscript sources

We have quoted from unpublished papers in the following collections (the abbreviation used in the notes is given first):

[Adyar] Theosophical Society archives, Adyar (Madras) (Annie Besant)
[BL] British Library, London (Macmillan Company, Charlotte Shaw)
[Bodleian] Bodleian Library, Oxford (Robert Bridges, Henry Nevinson, Edward J. Thompson)
[Cambridge] Cambridge University Library
[Chicago] Joseph Regenstein Library, University of Chicago (Harriet Monroe, Harriet Moody)
[Dartington] Elmhirst archives, High Cross House (Dorothy and Leonard Elmhirst)
[Edinburgh] National Library of Scotland (Patrick Geddes)
[Harvard] Houghton Library, Harvard University (William Rothenstein)
[IOL] India Office Library and Records, London (Viceroys/secretaries of state for India, William Rothenstein)
[London] Senate House Library, University of London (Thomas Sturge Moore)
[McMaster University] Mills Memorial Library (Bertrand Russell)
[Manchester] John Rylands University Library (*Manchester Guardian*/C. P. Scott)
[New York] New York Public Library (Macmillan Company)
[RB] Rabindra Bhavan, Shantiniketan (the chief repository of RT's papers and papers relating to RT.)
[Rabindra Bharati] Rabindra Bharati University, Calcutta
[Reading] Reading University Library (Macmillan Company)
[Yale] Beinecke Rare Book and Manuscript Library, Yale University (Ezra Pound)
[Michael Yeats] Personal papers of Michael Yeats (W. B. Yeats)

Books

Books by Rabindranath Tagore (including anthologies and compilations)

Only those Bengali writings not included in the *Rabindra Rachanabali* are listed. For translated writings, where no translator is given, the translation is generally by RT.

542   Bibliography

Amal et la Lettre du Roi, André Gide trans., Paris, 1922 (drama)
Binodini, Krishna Kripalani trans., New Delhi, 1959 (novel)
Broken Ties and Other Stories, translated by various hands, London, 1925
The Centre for Indian Culture, Adyar (Madras), 1919
Chhanda, rev. edn, 1369 [1962] (essays on prosody)
Chhinnapatra, 1319 [1912] (letters)
Chhinnapatrabali, 1367 [1960] (letters)
The Child, London, 1931 (poem)
Chithipatra: I, rev. edn, 1400 [1993]; II, 1349 [1942]; III, 1349 [1942]; IV, 1350 [1943]; V, 1352 [1945]; VI, 1364 [1957]; VII, 1367 [1960]; VIII, 1370 [1963]; IX, 1371 [1964]; X, 1374 [1967]; XI, 1381 [1974]; XII, 1393 [1986]; XIII, 1399 [1992]; XIV, 1401 [1994]; XV, 1402 [1995]; XVI, 1402 [1995] (letters) [revised editions of some volumes expected]
Chitra, London, 1914 (drama)
Chitralipi, I, 2nd edn, Calcutta, 1962 (paintings)
Collected Poems and Plays, London, 1936
Creative Unity, London, 1922 (essays)
The Crescent Moon, illus. edn, London, 1913 (poems)
Crisis in Civilization, Calcutta, 1941 (essay)
The Curse at Farewell, E. J. Thompson trans., London, 1924 (drama)
The Cycle of Spring, London, 1917 (drama)
Drawings and Paintings of Rabindranath Tagore, New Delhi, 1961 (introduction by Prithwish Neogy)
The English Writings of Rabindranath Tagore, Sisir Kumar Das ed.: I, *Poems*, New Delhi, 1994; II, *Plays, Stories, Essays*, New Delhi, 1996; III, *A Miscellany*, New Delhi, 1996.
Fireflies, New York, 1928 (epigrams)
Four Chapters, Surendranath Tagore trans., Calcutta, 1950 (novel)
Fruit-Gathering, London, 1916 (poems)
The Fugitive, London, 1921 (poems)
The Gardener, London, 1913 (poems)
Gitabitan: I, 1374 [1967]; II, 1375 [1968]; III, 1373 [1966] (songs)
Gitanjali (Song Offerings), London, 1912 (introduction by W. B. Yeats) (poems)
Glimpses of Bengal, Krishna Dutta and Andrew Robinson trans., London, 1991 (letters)
Gora, [W. W. Pearson/Surendranath Tagore trans.], London, 1924 (novel)
The Home and the World, [Surendranath Tagore trans.], London, 1919; London, 1985 (introduction by Anita Desai) (novel)
The Hungry Stones and Other Stories, translated by various hands, London, 1916
I Won't Let You Go: Selected Poems, Ketaki Kushari Dyson trans., Newcastle upon Tyne, 1991
Kalantar, rev. edn, 1367 [1961] (essays)
The King of the Dark Chamber, [Kshitis Chandra Sen trans.], London, 1914 (drama)
Letters from Russia, Sasadhar Sinha trans., Calcutta, 1960
Letters to a Friend, C. F. Andrews ed., London, 1928
Lover's Gift and Crossing, London, 1918 (poems)
Mashi and Other Stories, translated by various hands, London, 1918
My Boyhood Days, Marjorie Sykes trans., Calcutta, 1940
My Reminiscences, London, 1991
Nationalism, London, 1991 (introduction by E. P. Thompson) (essays)
L'Offrande Lyrique (Gitanjali), André Gide trans., Paris, 1913 (poems)
Our Universe, Indu Dutt trans., London, 1958 (science primer)
The Parrot's Training, Calcutta, 1918 (fable)
The Post Office, Devabrata Mukerjea trans., London, 1914 (preface by W. B. Yeats); Krishna Dutta and Andrew Robinson trans., New York, 1996 (preface by Anita Desai) (drama)
Rabindra Rachanabali, I–XXVII, 1346–72 [1939–65]; XXVIII, 1402 [1995] (collected writings)
Rabindra Rachanabali: Achalita Shangraha, 1347–8 [1940–1] (addenda)

Rabindranath Tagore on Art and Aesthetics, Prithwish Neogy ed., New Delhi, 1961 (compilation)
Rabindranath Tagore: An Anthology, Krishna Dutta and Andrew Robinson eds., London, 1997
Rabindranath Tagore: Pioneer in Education, London, 1961 (essays and exchanges between RT and Leonard K. Elmhirst)
Red Oleanders, London, 1925 (drama)
The Religion of Man, London, 1931 (essays)
Sacrifice and Other Plays, London, 1917
Sadhana: The Realisation of Life, London, 1913 (essays)
Selected Poems, William Radice trans., rev. edn, London, 1987
Selected Short Stories, Krishna Dutta and Mary Lago trans., London, 1991
Selected Short Stories, William Radice trans., rev. edn, London, 1994
Shiksha, rev. edn, 1397 [1990] (essays on education)
Stray Birds, New York, 1916 (epigrams)
A Tagore Reader, Amiya Chakravarty ed., New York, 1961 (anthology)
Three Plays, Ananda Lal trans., Calcutta, 1987 (drama)
Towards Universal Man, translated by various hands, Bombay, 1961 (essays)
Tripura's Ties with Tagore, Chiranjiv Kaviraj trans., Agartala (India), 1969 (speeches, letters and songs)
The Wreck, [J. G. Drummond trans.], London, 1921
Yurop Jatrir Diary, 1368 [1961] (travel diary in Europe, 1890)
Yurop Prabashir Patra, 1368 [1961] (letters)

Books about Rabindranath Tagore

Aronson, Alex and Krishna Kripalani, eds., *Rolland and Tagore*, Calcutta 1945
Calcutta Municipal Gazette (Tagore Memorial Special Supplement), 13 Sept. 1941
Chander, Jag Parvesh, ed., *Tagore and Gandhi Argue*, Lahore, 1945 (selected writings)
Chatterjee [Chatterji], Ramananda, ed., *The Golden Book of Tagore*, Calcutta, 1931
Das Gupta, R. K., ed., *Rabindranath Tagore and W. B. Yeats: The Story of a Literary Friendship*, New Delhi, 1965 (booklet)
Das Gupta, Uma, *Santiniketan and Sriniketan*, Calcutta, 1983 (booklet)
Dutta, Krishna and Andrew Robinson, *Rabindranath Tagore: The Myriad-Minded Man*, London, 1995
Dutta, Krishna and Andrew Robinson, eds., *Purabi: A Miscellany in Memory of Rabindranath Tagore, 1941–1991*, London, 1991 (foreword by Javier Pérez de Cuéllar)
    Rabindranath Tagore: An Anthology, London, 1997
Dyson, Ketaki Kushari, *In Your Blossoming Flower-Garden: Rabindranath Tagore and Victoria Ocampo*, New Delhi, 1988
Elmhirst, Leonard K., *Poet and Plowman*, Calcutta, 1975
Gnatyuk-Danil'chuk, A. P., *Tagore, India and the Soviet Union: A Dream Fulfilled*, Calcutta, 1986
Hay, Stephen N., *Asian Ideas of East and West: Tagore and his Critics in Japan, China and India*, Cambridge, Mass., 1970
Henn, Katherine, *Rabindranath Tagore: A Bibliography*, Metuchen, N. J., and London, 1985
Kämpchen, Martin, *Rabindranath Tagore and Germany: A Documentation*, Calcutta, 1991
Kripalani, Krishna, *Rabindranath Tagore: A Biography*, 2nd edn, Calcutta, 1980
Kundu, Kalyan, et al., eds., *Rabindranath Tagore and the British Press (1912–1941)*, London, 1990
Lago, Mary M., ed., *Imperfect Encounter: Letters of William Rothenstein and Rabindranath Tagore, 1911–1941*, Cambridge, Mass., 1972
Lesny, Vincenc, *Rabindranath Tagore, his Personality and Work*, Guy McKeever Phillips trans., London, 1939

544 Bibliography

Majumdar, Nepal, *Bharate Jatiyata o Antarjatikata ebang Rabindranath*, IV, rev. edn, 1398 [1991]
Mukherjee, Sujit, *Passage to America: The Reception of Rabindranath Tagore in the United States, 1912–1941*, Calcutta, 1964
Paul, Prashanta Kumar, *Rabijibani*, I (1861–1878), rev. edn, 1400 [1993]; II (1878/9–1884/5), 1391 [1984]; III (1885/6–1893/4), 1393 [1986]; IV (1894/5–1900/1), 1395 [1988]; V (1901/2–1907/8), 1397 [1990]; VI (1908/9–1913/14), 1399 [1993]; VII (1914/15–1918/19), 1403 [1996] [further volumes and revised volumes expected]
Pearson, W. W., *Shantiniketan: The Bolpur School of Rabindranath Tagore*, London, 1917
Radhakrishnan, Sarvepalli, *The Philosophy of Rabindranath Tagore*, London, 1918
Rhys, Ernest, *Rabindranath Tagore: A Biographical Study*, London, 1915
Robinson, Andrew, *The Art of Rabindranath Tagore*, London, 1989 (introduction by Satyajit Ray)
Roy, Basanta Koomar, *Rabindranath Tagore: The Man and his Poetry*, New York, 1915
Roy, Dilip Kumar, *Among the Great*, 4th edn, Pondicherry, 1984
    Tirthankar, rev. edn, 1382 [1975]
Sahitya Akademi, *Rabindranath Tagore: A Centenary Volume, 1861–1961*, New Delhi, 1961 (introduction by Jawaharlal Nehru)
Tagore, Rathindranath, *On the Edges of Time*, 2nd edn, Calcutta, 1981
    Pitrismriti, 1373 [1966]
Thompson, Edward J., *Rabindranath Tagore: His Life and Work*, Calcutta, 1921
    Rabindranath Tagore: Poet and Dramatist, New Delhi, 1991 (introduction by Harish Trivedi)
Thompson, Edward P., *Alien Homage: Edward Thompson and Rabindranath Tagore*, New Delhi, 1993

Other books

Some of these books have sections or even chapters on RT, and most (except those on science) make some reference to him or his works.

Appasamy, Jaya, *Abanindranath Tagore and the Art of his Times*, New Delhi, 1968
Archer, W. G., *India and Modern Art*, London, 1959
Banerjee, Sumanta, *The Parlour and the Streets: Elite and Popular Culture in Nineteenth Century Calcutta*, Calcutta, 1989
Basham, A. L., *The Wonder That Was India*, London, 1954
Bell, J. S., *Speakable and Unspeakable in Quantum Mechanics*, Cambridge, 1987
Berlin, Isaiah, *The Sense of Reality: Studies in Ideas and their History*, Henry Hardy ed., London, 1996
Boardman, Philip, *The Worlds of Patrick Geddes: Biologist, Town planner, Re-educator, Peace-Warrior*, London, 1978
Bohm, David and B. J. Hiley, *The Undivided Universe*, London, 1993
Born, Irene, trans., *The Born–Einstein Letters*, London, 1971 (foreword by Bertrand Russell)
Bose, Buddhadeva, *An Acre of Green Grass: A Review of Modern Bengali Literature*, Calcutta, 1948
Bose, Jagadish Chandra, *Patrabali*, 1958 [1365]
Bose, Manjula, ed., *Leonard Elmhirst*, Calcutta, 1994
Bridges, Robert, ed., *The Spirit of Man*, London, 1916
Brittain, Vera, *Search after Sunrise*, London, 1951
Broomfield, J. H., *Elite Conflict in a Plural Society: Twentieth-Century Bengal*, Berkeley, 1968
Brown, Judith M., *Gandhi's Rise to Power: Indian Politics 1915–1922*, Cambridge, 1972
Case, Frank, *Tales of a Wayward Inn*, New York, 1938
Chakravarty, Punya Lata, *Chhelebelar Dinguli*, 1365 [1958]

Chatterji, Joya, *Bengal Divided: Hindu Communalism and Partition, 1932–1947*, Cambridge, 1994
Chatterji [Chattopadhyay], Aghorenath and Jnanendranath Chatterji [Chattopadhyay], *Shantiniketan Ashram*, 1357 [1950]
Chaudhuri, Nirad C., *Thy Hand, Great Anarch!: India 1921–1952*, London, 1987
Chirol, Valentine, *Indian Unrest*, London, 1910
Clark, Ronald W., *Einstein: The Life and Times*, New York, 1971
Coomaraswamy, Ananda K., *Art and Swadeshi*, Madras, 1912
Cottis, Nicholas and John Lane, *A Dartington Anthology 1925–75*, Dartington, 1975
Cousins, J. H. and M. E., *We Two Together*, Madras, 1950
Das, Frieda Hauswirth, *A Marriage to India*, London, 1931
  Purdah: The Status of Indian Women, London, 1932
Das, Suranjan, *Communal Riots in Bengal 1905–1947*, New Delhi, 1991
Datta, Sudhindranath, *The World of Twilight: Essays and Poems*, Calcutta, 1970
Dickinson, Goldsworthy Lowes, *Appearances: Being Notes of Travel*, London, 1914
  An Essay on the Civilisations of India, China and Japan, London, 1914
Dignan, Don, *The Indian Revolutionary Problem in British Diplomacy 1914–1919*, New Delhi, 1983
Draper, Alfred, *Amritsar: The Massacre that Ended the Raj*, London, 1981
Dunbar, Olivia Howard, *A House in Chicago*, Chicago, 1947
Dutta, Krishna and Andrew Robinson, eds., *Noon in Calcutta: Short Stories from Bengal*, London, 1992 (preface by Anita Desai)
Einstein, Albert, *Einstein's Theory of Relativity*, Max Born ed., Henry L. Brose trans., London, 1924
Field, Michael, *Works and Days: From the Journal of Michael Field*, T. and D. C. Sturge Moore eds., London, 1933
Finneran, Richard J., George Mills Harper, William H. Murphy, eds., *Letters to W. B. Yeats*, II, London, 1977
Fisher, David James, *Romain Rolland and the Politics of Intellectual Engagement*, Berkeley, 1988
Forster, E. M., *Selected Letters of E. M. Forster*, Mary Lago and P. N. Furbank eds., II (1921–1970), London, 1985
Fox Strangways, Arthur H., *The Music of Hindostan*, Oxford, 1914
Foxe, Barbara, *Long Journey Home: A Biography of Margaret Noble*, London, 1975
Furrell, James W., *The Tagore Family: A Memoir*, Calcutta, 1882
Gandhi, Mohandas Karamchand, *The Collected Works of Mahatma Gandhi*, I–XC, Ahmedabad, 1958–84 (especially XV–LXXIV, 1918–41)
  The Story of my Experiments with Truth, II, Mahadev Desai trans., New Delhi, 1930
Gandhi, Sonia, ed., *Freedom's Daughter: Letters between Indira Gandhi and Jawaharlal Nehru, 1922–1939*, London, 1989
Gangulee, Nagendranath, *India: What Now?*, London, 1933
  The Indian Peasant and his Environment (The Linlithgow Commission and After), Oxford, 1935
Gangulee, Nagendranath, ed., *The Russian Horizon*, London, 1943 (foreword by H. G. Wells)
  Thoughts for Meditation, London, 1951 (foreword by T. S. Eliot)
Geddes, Patrick, *The Life and Work of Sir Jagadis C. Bose*, London, 1920
Ghosh, J. C., *Bengali Literature*, London, 1976
Good, I. J., ed., *The Scientist Speculates – An Anthology of Partly-Baked Ideas*, London, 1962
Gordon, A. D. D., *Businessmen and Politics: Rising Nationalism and a Modernising Economy in Bombay, 1918–1933*, New Delhi, 1978
Gordon, Leonard A., *Brothers against the Raj: A Biography of Indian Nationalists Sarat & Subhas Chandra Bose*, New York, 1990
Gouda, Frances, *Dutch Culture Overseas: Colonial Practice in the Netherlands Indies, 1900–1942*, Amsterdam, 1995

Green, Gretchen, *The Whole World and Company*, New York, 1936
Gurney, Ivor, *Ivor Gurney: War Letters*, R. K. R. Thornton ed., Manchester, 1983
Gwynn, Frederick L., *Sturge Moore and the Life of Art*, London, 1952
Haeberlin, John, *Kavyasangraha: A Sanscrit Anthology*, Calcutta, 1847 (includes *slokas* of Chanakya)
Hajnóczy, Rózsa, *Fire of Bengal*, Eva Wimmer and David Grant trans., William Radice ed., Dhaka, 1993
Hamilton, Daniel, *New India and How to Get There*, London, 1930
Hatcher, John, *Laurence Binyon: Poet, Scholar of East and West*, Oxford, 1995
Havighurst, Alfred F., *Radical Journalist: H. W. Massingham*, Cambridge, 1974
Heehs, Peter, *The Bomb in Bengal: The Rise of Revolutionary Terrorism in India 1900-1910*, New Delhi, 1993
Heisenberg, Werner, *The Physicist's Conception of Nature*, London, 1955
  Physics and Beyond, London, 1971
Holland, P., *The Quantum Theory of Motion*, Cambridge, 1993
Holmes, Edmund, *The Creed of Buddha*, London, 1908
Inge, W. R., *Diary of a Dean*, London, 1949
Ingrams, Richard, *Muggeridge: The Biography*, London, 1995
Jones, Ernest, *The Life and Work of Sigmund Freud*, Lionel Trilling and Steven Marcus eds., London, 1961
Kalidasa, *The Dynasty of Raghu*, Robert Antoine trans., Calcutta, 1972
Kawabata, Yasunari, *The Existence and Discovery of Beauty*, V. H. Viglielmo trans., Tokyo, 1969
Keyserling, Hermann, *The Travel Diary of a Philosopher*, J. Holroyd Reece trans., London, 1927
Kopf, David, *The Brahmo Samaj and the Shaping of the Modern Indian Mind*, Princeton, 1979
Kübler-Ross, Elisabeth, *On Death and Dying*, New York, 1969
Lal, Prem Chand, *Reconstruction and Education in Rural India*, London, 1932 (introduction by Rabindranath Tagore)
Legge, Sylvia, *Affectionate Cousins: T. Sturge Moore and Marie Appia*, Oxford, 1980
Lévi, Desirée, *Dans l'Inde (de Ceylan au Nepal)*, Paris 1925
London, Christopher W., ed., *Architecture in Victorian and Edwardian India*, Bombay, 1994
Lopez, Donald S., Jr, ed., *Curators of the Buddha: The Study of Buddhism under Colonialism*, Chicago, 1995
MacBride White, Anna and A. Norman Jeffares, eds., *The Gonne-Yeats Letters*, London, 1992
MacDonald, Ramsay, *The Awakening of India*, London, 1910
Macnicol, Nicol, ed., *Hindu Scriptures*, London, 1938 (foreword by Rabindranath Tagore)
Maitraye [Devi], *The Great Wanderer*, Calcutta, 1961
Marianoff, Dmitri, with Palma Wayne, *Einstein: An Intimate Study of a Great Man*, New York, 1944
Mascaró, Juan, trans., *The Upanishads*, London, 1965
Mayo, Katherine, *Mother India*, New York, 1927
Milward, Marguerite, *An Artist in Unknown India*, London, 1948
Mitter, Partha, *Art and Nationalism in Colonial India: Occidental Orientations*, Cambridge, 1994
Monk, Ray, *Ludwig Wittgenstein: The Duty of Genius*, London, 1990
Moore, Thomas Sturge, *The Sea is Kind*, London, 1914
Mukherji [Mukhopadhyay], Manashi, *Atul Prashad*, 1378 [1971]
Nagel, Thomas, *The View from Nowhere*, pbk edn, New York, 1989
Nanda, B. R., *Gokhale*, New Delhi, 1977
Nandy, Ashis, *Alternative Sciences: Creativity and Authenticity in Two Indian Scientists*, 2nd edn, New Delhi, 1995
Nathan, Otto and Heinz Norden, *Einstein on Peace*, New York, 1960
Nehru, Jawaharlal, *An Autobiography*, 2nd edn, London, 1989
  The Discovery of India, New Delhi, 1946; centenary edn, 1989

Bibliography

Selected Works of Jawaharlal Nehru, I–XV (first series), New Delhi, 1972–82; I– (second series), New Delhi, 1984–
Nethercot, Arthur, *The First Five Lives of Annie Besant*, London, 1961
Noguchi, Yone, *Selected English Writings of Yone Noguchi: I, (Poetry)* Yoshinobu Hakutani ed., London, 1990
Nowell-Smith, Simon, ed., *Letters to Macmillan*, London, 1967
Nussbaum, Martha C. et al., *For Love of Country*, Boston, 1996
Pais, Abraham, *Einstein Lived Here*, New York, 1994
   Niels Bohr's Times in Physics, Philosophy, and Polity, Oxford, 1991
Patel, Jehangir P. and Marjorie Sykes, *Gandhi: His Gift of the Fight*, Rasulia (India), 1987
Pauli, Wolfgang, ed., *Niels Bohr and the Development of Physics*, Oxford, 1955
Penrose, Roger, *Shadows of the Mind: A Search for the Missing Science of Consciousness*, Oxford, 1994
Pickett, Clarence, *For More Than Bread*, Boston, 1953
Pinder, John, ed., *Fifty Years of Political and Economic Planning: Looking Forward 1931–1981*, London, 1981
Pollard, Patrick, ed., *André Gide et l'Angleterre*, London, 1986
Popper, Karl, *Unended Quest*, Glasgow, 1976
Popplewell, Richard J., *Intelligence and Imperial Defence: British Intelligence and the Defence of the Indian Empire 1904–1924*, London, 1995
Pound, Ezra, *The Letters of Ezra Pound 1907–1941*, D. D. Paige ed., London, 1951
Pound, Omar and A. Walton Litz, eds., *Ezra Pound and Dorothy Shakespear: Their Letters: 1909–1914*, London, 1985
Prigogine, Ilya and Isabelle Stengers, *Order out of Chaos: Man's New Dialogue with Nature*, London, 1984
Przibram, K., ed., *Letters on Wave Mechanics*, New York, 1950
Putnam, Hilary, *The Many Faces of Realism*, LaSalle, Ill., 1987
Ray, Satyajit, *Jakhan Chhoto Chhilam*, 1982 [1389]
   Our Films Their Films, New Delhi, 1976
Report of the Calcutta University Commission, Calcutta, 1919
Rhys, Ernest, *Everyman Remembers*, London, 1931
   Letters from Limbo, London, 1936
Robinson, Andrew, *Satyajit Ray: The Inner Eye*, London, 1989
Roland, Joan G., *Jews In British India: Identity in a Colonial Era*, Hanover (New England) and London, 1989
Rolland, Romain, *Inde: Journal (1915–1943), Tagore Gandhi Nehru et les Problèmes Indiens*, Paris, 1951
   Selected Letters of Romain Rolland, Francis Doré and Marie-Laure Prévost eds., New Delhi, 1990
Ronaldshay, Lord, *The Heart of Aryavarta: A Study of the Psychology of Indian Unrest*, London, 1925
Rothenstein, William, *Men and Memories: Recollections, 1900–1922*, London, 1932
   Since Fifty: Recollections, 1922–1938, London, 1939
Roy, Biren, *Marshes to Metropolis: Calcutta (1481–1981)*, Calcutta, 1982
Russell, Bertrand, *The Autobiography of Bertrand Russell, 1872–1914*, London, 1967
   The Selected Letters of Bertrand Russell: I, The Private Years (1884–1914), Nicholas Griffin ed., London, 1992
Sadleir, Michael, *Michael Ernest Sadler: A Memoir by his Son*, London, 1949
Salvadori, Massimo (Max), *The Labour and the Wounds*, London, 1958
Salvemini, Gaetano, *The Fascist Dictatorship in Italy*: I, *Origins and Practices*, London, 1928
Sarkar, Sumit, *The Swadeshi Movement in Bengal, 1903–1908*, Calcutta, 1973
Schilpp, Paul Arthur, ed., *Albert Einstein: Philosopher-Scientist*, Evanston, Ill., 1949

Schrödinger, Erwin, *What is Life?* (with *Mind and Matter* and *Autobiographical Sketches*), Cambridge, 1992 (foreword by Roger Penrose)
Sehanobis, Chinmohan, *Rabindranath o Biplabi Samaj*, 1392 [1985]
Sen, Dibakar, *Patrabali*, 1401 [1994]
Sen, K. M. [Kshiti Mohan], *Hinduism*, London, 1961
   Medieval Mysticism of India, Manomohan Ghosh trans., London, 1930
Sengupta, Padmini, *Sarojini Naidu: A Biography*, London, 1966
Shaw, George Bernard, *Collected Letters*, IV (1925–1950), Dan H. Laurence ed., London, 1988
Sinclair, Upton, *My Lifetime in Letters*, Missouri, 1960
Sircar, N. N., *Sir N. N. Sircar's Speeches and Pamphlets*, B. N. Dutta Roy ed., Calcutta, 1934
Som, Shobhan, ed., *Rabindraparikar Surendranath Kar*, 1400 [1993] (preface by K. G. Subramanyan)
Speaight, Robert, *William Rothenstein: The Portrait of an Artist in his Time*, London, 1962
Stock, Noel, *The Life of Ezra Pound*, London, 1970
Stocks, Mary D., *Eleanor Rathbone: A Biography*, London, 1949
Suu Kyi, Aung San, *Freedom from Fear and Other Writings*, London, 1991
Tagore, Debendranath, *The Autobiography of Maharshi Devendranath Tagore*, Satyendranath Tagore and Indira Devi trans., Calcutta, 1909 (with appendices); London, 1914 (without appendices)
Tagore, Jyotirindranath, *Twenty-Five Collotypes from the Original Drawings by Jyotirindra Nath Tagore*, Hammersmith (London), 1914 (preface by William Rothenstein)
Tendulkar, D. G., *Mahatma: Life of Mohandas Karamchand Gandhi*, I–VIII, Bombay, 1951-4
Tharu, Susie and K. Lalita, eds., *Women Writing in India: 600 BC to the Present:* I, *600 BC to the Early 20th Century*, New York, 1991
Thompson, Edward J., *The Other Side of the Medal*, London, 1925
Tinker, Hugh, *The Ordeal of Love: C. F. Andrews and India*, New Delhi, 1979
van der Merwe, A., et al., eds., *Microphysical Reality and Quantum Formalism*, I, Dordrecht, 1985
van der Merwe, A., F. Selleri and G. Tarozzi, eds. *Bell's Theorem and the Foundations of Modern Physics*, Singapore, 1992
Vidyasagar, Iswar Chandra, *Kathamala*, in *Rachanashambhar*, Pramathanath Bisi ed., 1364 [1957]
Visva-Bharati, *Mrinalini Devi*, 1381 [1974]
Wallis, Jill, *Mother of World Peace: The Life of Muriel Lester*, London, 1993
Watt, George, *Dictionary of the Economic Products of India*: V, *Linium to Oyster*, Calcutta and London, 1891
Webb, Beatrice, *Diaries 1912–1924*, Margaret I. Cole ed., London, 1952
Weinberg, Steven, *Dreams of a Final Theory*, London, 1993
Wheeler, John, *At Home in the Universe*, New York, 1994
Wolff, Kurt, *Kurt Wolff: A Portrait in Essays and Letters*, Michael Ermarth ed., Chicago, 1991
Yeats, W. B., *The Letters of W. B. Yeats*, Allan Wade ed., New York, 1955
Young, Michael, *The Elmhirsts of Dartington: The Creation of an Utopian Community*, Dartington/London, 1982

INDEX

Page numbers in *italic* type indicate main entries. Text references to Calcutta and Shantiniketan have not been indexed, because they are too frequent.

Aden (Yemen), 19, 411
Adhikari, Ranu, 297n2, 448
Adyar (Tamil Nadu), 212, 327n1
Aesop, *35*, 36n6
Afghanistan, 400, 401n5
'Africa' (RT), *474*, 477
Africa Answers Back (Nyabongo), 477
Aga Khan (III), 232n3, *379–80*
Ahmed, Rafiuddin, *467*
Ahmedabad (Gujarat), 305, 475–76
Ajanta paintings, 140, 176
Akbar (emperor) 76, 77n4, *251*
Albert Einstein: Philosopher-Scientist (Schilpp), *533*
Algonquin, Hotel (New York City), *241*, *242–43n3*, 245, 246, 248, 250, 252, 255
Ali, Aruna Asaf, 68n4
Ali, Hashim Amir, 412, 414n3
Alien Homage (Thompson), 130n1, *348*
Allahabad (Uttar Pradesh), 433, 442, 465
Almora (Uttar Pradesh), 59, 442n4, 447, 478, 479, 480n5, 489
Ambedkar, B. R., *415*
Amiel, Henri Frederic, *38–39*
Amrita Bazar Patrika (newspaper), 183n1
Amritsar (Punjab), 473, 474n6
Amritsar massacre (1919), xix, *215–16*, *218–24*, 226n1, 233, 238n4, 249, 250, 320n1, 440
Anandamath (Chatterji), 487
Andaman Islands, 435n3, *480–82*
Anderson, James Drummond, 160, 161n2, *196–97*, 230
Anderson, Sir John, 397, 434, *435*, *480–82*
Andrews, Charles Freer, xviii, xxiv, xxv, 2, 85, *105*, *127–28*, 129, 133, 134, 143, *150*, 152n3, *155–57*, 158n2, 162, *163–64*, 166, 170, 177n3, 178, 179, 186, 187n7, 195, 200n3, 201, 202n5, *212–14*, *219–24*, 225, *231*, 232n5, 234, *235*, *236–37*, *239–40*, 243, *245–47*, 249–51, *252–53*, *255–61*, 265, *266–67*, *273–75*, 293n5, *297–300*, 304, 317, *330*, 332, 336, 337, 338, 339n5, 356n6, 361, 380, 381n6, 384, 385n5, 391, 392, 397, *409–10*, 415, *457*, *461–62*, 474, 488, *495–96*, *500*, 513n1, 516n3, *519*, *521*, 525
Anna Karenina (Tolstoy), *43*, 44n1
Antwerp (Holland), 239
Arabian Nights, The, 41

Arai, Kampo, *175–76*
Archer, W. G., *177n4*
Argentina, 313–17, 322, 367, 439, *505*
Art and Swadeshi (Coomaraswamy), *79–80*
Artist in Unknown India, An (Milward), 375n1
Arup Ratan (RT), *460*
Aryanayakam, E. W., *379n2*, 384, 385n4, *391*, 392
Asia (journal), 319n1, 455n8, 479, 380n6, 489, 529, 535n22
Asoka (emperor), 76, 77n4
Athenaeum, The (journal), *101*
Athens (Greece), 377n3
Atlantic Monthly (journal), 388, 390n1
Aurangzeb (emperor), 251
Austria, 233, 329, 330, 332, 337, 339, 493
Autobiography, An (Nehru), *465–66*
Autobiography, An (Russell), *533*
Autobiography of Devendranath Tagore, The, 94, 284n4, 286n1
Awakening of India, The (MacDonald), *416*
Aziz, Doctor (Forster's character), *250*

Bach, Johann Sebastian, 328n2
Balak (journal), 84n1
Balaka (RT), *290*, *350n5*, 402n1
Balatonfüred (Hungary), *340*, *341n2*
Baldwin, Stanley, 416n4
Bali (Indonesia), 351, 353n2, *366*, 367n6, 512
Ball, Sir Robert Stawell, *82n1*
Ballygunj (Calcutta), 82n3, 84
Banamali (servant of RT), 153n5, 367n8
Banbhatta, *38–39*
'Bande Mataram' (Chatterji), *486–88*
Banerji, Surendranath, 183
Bangadarshan (journal), 61, 62, 64, 65n6 and n13, 71, 229
Bangalore (Karnataka), 214
Bankura (West Bengal), 130, 137n1, 144n1
Baranagar (West Bengal), 467, 479, 480n8
Barbusse, Henri, 493n1
Barcelona (Spain), 317
Barddhaman (West Bengal), 64, 65n17
Barisal (Bangladesh), 62, 67
Baudelaire, Charles, 314, *315n4*
Bela – *see* Madhurilata Chakravarty
Belgharia (Calcutta), 487

549

Belgium, 153, 233
Beliaghata (Calcutta), 71n7
Bell, John, 527, 530, 535n4
Bena, G. A., 313n2
Benares Hindu University, 243n7, 518n1
Benavides, Gustavo, *342n1*
Beneš, Eduard, 500
Bengal, Partition of (1905), xix, *61*, 64, 65n9
Bengal Legislative Council, 49, 50n3, 65n17
Bengal School (of artists), *139*, *176–78*, 345, 375n7, 398
Bengalee, The (newspaper), 183n1 and n2, 187n3
Berahimpur (Bangladesh), 42–43, 165, 166n1
Berhampur (West Bengal), 190, 191
Berlin (Germany), 270, 275n6, 374, 375, 383, 384, 398, 467n1, 529, 533
Berlin University, 273, 529
Berlin, Sir Isaiah, xx–xxi, *529–30*
Besant, Annie, 174n1, 181, *182–85*, *211–14*
Bhagavad Gita, 269, 286n1
Bharati (journal), 7, 142n5
Bhattacharya, Hem Chandra, 56n19
Bhattacharya, Vidhu Shekhar, 69
Bible, *146*
Bichitrita (RT), 457n1
Biday-Abhisap (RT), 444n5
Big Horse's Flight, The (Hedin), 492
Birla, G. D., 464n5
Birmingham (UK), 397
Birth Control Review (journal), 320, 321
Bismarck, Prince Otto von, 264n2
Blavatsky, Madame, 184n1
Bodhgaya (Bihar), 56n14
Boer War, 55n10
Bohm, David, 531, *534*
Bohr, Niels, 527, 529, *530–1*, 532, *533*, 534
Bolpur (West Bengal), 29, 56, 62, 64, 65, 67, 70, 71, 78, 84, 87, 117, 118, 119, 133, 135, 143, 156, 158n2, 179, 203, 210, 360, 480n3
Bomanji, Shavaksha Ratanji, 231, 270, *379–80*
Bombay (Maharashtra), 127, 158, 231, 275, *298*, 300, 305, 380n1, 411, 424, 430, 436, 518n1
Bombay University, 290
Borges, Jorge Luis, 315n1
Born, Max, *532*
Bose, Lady Abala, xix, 56n18, *71–72*, 73n5
Bose, Abinash Chandra, 264n8, 455n1
Bose, Aurobindo Mohan, *71*, *73n1*
Bose, Buddhadeva, *1*, *346*
Bose, Chandranath, 51, 52n6
Bose, Sir Jagadish Chandra, xix, 2, *52–55*, 70, 71, 73n3, 80, 290–91, 376, 401, 480n5, 528
Bose, Kumudini, 298
Bose, Nanda Lal, *313*, 420, 457n1, 473
Bose, Raj Narain, 62, 65n8, 81
Bose, Rash Behari, xx, *485–86*, 496, *501–2*, 512
Bose, S. N., 528
Bose, Subhash Chandra, 2, 182, *400*, 471, *486–88*, *502–3*, 504, 506–7, *513–14*
Bose Institute (Calcutta), 55n1
Bossennée, Christiane, 522n2
Boston (USA), 106, 107, 109, 110, 243, 244n2, 247, 248, 249n1, 390, *391*, 392
Boulogne-sur-Seine (France), 263
Bourdelle, Emile, 374n1

Bourdette, Miss, 78, *79n3*
Brabourne, Lord, *504–5*
Bradley, Andrew Cecil, 419, 420n8
Brahmoism/Brahmo Samaj, 13, *14*, 49, 52n5, 57n3, 61, *62*, 64, 66, *67*, 78, *80–81*, 114, 132, 153n6, 286n5, *356n2*
Brahms, Johannes, 14n2
Brass Check, The (Sinclair), *304*, 305n1
Brett, George Platt, 169n4, *198*, *199n2*, *200n1*, 203n4, *224–25*, 283n1
Bridges, Edward, 172n3
Bridges, Robert, 2, *147–48*, 149, *161–62*, *166–69*, *171–72*, 418
Brighton (UK), 7
British Indian Association, 49, 50n2
Brittain, Vera, 68n1
Broglie, Louis de, 531
Broken Wing, The (Naidu), *182*
Brooke, Stopford, 419, 420n8
Brooks, Morgan, 99n4
Brussels (Belgium), 240
Budapest (Hungary), *340*, 438, 439n1
Buddhism, *72*, 171, 217, *245*, 246n1, *259–60*, 274, 286n1, *293*, *294n5 and n6*, 295, 307, *342n1*, 353, 354n1, *426*, 427, 472, 479, 480n3, *488*, 497, 509, 540
Buenos Aires (Argentina), 307, 313, 318
Bulgaria, 339
Bunting, Basil, 454n3
Burman, D. K. Dev, 419, 420n11
Burman, Somendra Chandra Dev, 91 (photo), *179n5*
Burns, Robert, *94–95*
Burroughs, John, 246
Byron, Lord, 146

Calcutta Corporation, 2, 49, *400*
Calcutta Municipal Gazette, 362, 364n1
Calcutta University, 71, 134, 143, 155, 178, 214n3, 256n6, 263, 282, *302–3*, *383*, *436*
Calcutta University Commission (1919), 206n3, 207n5, 209, *210–11*, *256n6*, 262
Calicut (Kerala), 421
Cambridge (UK), 95, 96n2, 102n2, 116n6, 150, 159, 196, 210, 230
Cambridge (USA), 106, 107, 109
Cambridge University, 71, 116n2, 196, 358n1, 528
Canada, 362n1, 375, 395
Cap Martin (France), 374, 375, 376, 377
Caputh (Germany), 438n5, 529
Carmichael, Lord, *160–61*, 209n4, 262, 263
Carnegie Hall (New York City), 373, 394
Case, Frank, *242–43*
Cathleen Ni Houlihan (Yeats), 105
Centre of Indian Culture, The (RT), 211n3
Ceylon – *see* Sri Lanka
Chaitanya, 76, 77n4, 473, 474n3
Chakravarty, Ajit Kumar, *80n7*, 178, 276, *277n2*, 278, *279n4*
Chakravarty, Amiya, 199n3, *354–56*, 383, 384n5, 393n1, 408, 409n5, 429, *436*, *443–44*, *446*, *447n3*, 450–51, *452–55*, *461*, *474*, 481, 482, 483, 495–96, 512
Chakravarty, Bihari Lal, 57, 59n1
Chakravarty, Byomkesh, 224n2

Chakravarty, Haimanti, *354–56*
Chakravarty, Madhurilata, 7, *19*, *27–28*, 47 (photo), 51, *57–58*, 59n6, 71n7, *108–9*, *110n1*, 111, *197*, 198, *206*, 207, 213n1
Chakravarty, Naresh Chandra, 25n1
Chakravarty, Sharat Chandra, 57, 59n1, 108, 109
Chamba (Himachal Pradesh), 68
Chamberlain, Neville, 500
Chanakya, 85, *86n8*, 109, 214
Chanda, Anil, 384n2, 468n1
Chandannagar (West Bengal), 449n5, *450*
Chandrasekhar, Subrahmanyan, *527*, *535n2* and n21
Chapman, John Jay, 97, *107*, *108n3*
Char Adhyay – see *Four Chapters*
Chatterji, Aghoranath, 30
Chatterji, Bankim Chandra, 7, 62, 65n6, 99n1, 278, 279n5, *487*
Chatterji, Harindranath, 311n6
Chatterji, Kedarnath, 115, *116n2*
Chatterji, Ramananda, 2, 85, 86n6, 91, *115–16*, *187n3*, 249, *297*, 401, *428–29*
Chatterji, Sarat Chandra, 2, 196, 254, 255n3, *346–47*
Chatterji, Shanta, 116n10
Chatterji, Sita, 116n10
Chatterji, Suniti Kumar, 2, *358–60*, *367–70*, 375
Chattopadhyay – *see* Chatterji
Chaudhurani, Indira Devi – *see* Indira Tagore
Chaudhuri, Anath Bandhu, *193*
Chaudhuri, Arya, 141
Chaudhuri, Sir Ashutosh, *50n2*, 64, *65n17*, 142n6
Chaudhuri, Jogesh, 64, *65n16*
Chaudhuri, Nirad C., 39n5, 80n1, *209n5*, *369–70n1*
Chaudhuri, Pramathanath, 2, 18n1, 33, 48, 51, 52n6, 65n16 and n17, *118–19*, *152–53*, 160, 355
Chaudhuri, Pratibha, 65n17
Chauri Chaura (Uttar Pradesh), 285
Chelmsford, Lord, 202, *203*, *219*, *220*, *222–24*, 226n1, 238n4
Chhinnapatra – see *Glimpses of Bengal*
'Chhuti' (RT), 80
Chiang Kai-shek, 471, *499*, 509, 524n2
Chiang Kai-shek, Madam, 499, *500n7*
Chicago (USA), 89, 103, 107, 108n2, 109, 110, 111, 112, 115, 116n7, 124, 135, 137n1, 233, 248, 249, 253n1, 256, 259
Chicago University, 109
Child, The (RT), 444n2
China, xxiv, 160n2, 307, 308, 310–11, 312, *352*, 353, 368n3, 387n2, 405, 406n6, 437, 438n1, 463, 464n6, 471, 485, *486*, *497–500*, *502*, *509*, *512–13*, 523
Chirol, Sir Valentine, 77n5, 138, 139n5, 140
Chitra (RT), *139–40*, 156n1, 461, 462n6, 464
Chitrangada (RT), 402n1, 444n5
Chittagong (Bangladesh), *404–5*
Chowdhury, Kamla, *526*
Christ, Jesus, 295, 334, *409*, 427, *488*, 497, 540
Churchill, Sir Winston, 521, 523
'City and village' (RT), 312
Clark, Ronald W., 528
Collected Poems and Plays (RT), 149, *443–44*, *446–47*, *450–51*, *453–54*, 459, *461–62*, *468*, 494

Colombo (Sri Lanka), 436
Comilla (Bangladesh), 327
Compton, A. H., 535n21
'The Conclusion' (RT), *23–24*, 25n1
Constantinople (Turkey), 340
Coomaraswamy, Ananda Kentish, *79–80*, *390–91*
Cooper, Edith, 139, *140n9*
Cornell University, 264n7, 287
Cousins, James H., *173–74*, 208, 209n3, 211–12, 213, *214*
Creative Unity (RT), *290*
Creed of Buddha (Holmes), 72, *73n8*
Crescent Moon, The (RT), 121, 122n8, 139, 140n8, *272*
Crick, Francis, *527*
'Crisis in Civilisation' (RT), 509
'The cult of the *charka*' (RT), *364*
cummings, e. e., 1
Curzon, Lord, 49
Cuttack (Orissa), 33, 34
Cycle of Spring, The (RT), 186, 187n4
Czechoslovakia, 233, *500*

D'Abernon, Viscount, *274–75*
Dak Ghar – see *The Post Office*, 89
Dakshineswar (Calcutta), 480
Dalmia, Ramakrishna, *506*
Dandi (Gujarat), 370
Dans l'Inde (Lévi), 286n3, *354n8*
Dante Alighieri, 102, *289*, 290n1
Darjeeling (West Bengal), *54*, *56n13*, 58, 59n6, 403, 425, 427, 428
Darmstadt (Germany), 270, 273, *274*
Dartington (UK), 11, 318, 322, 343n5, 371n4, 381, *412*, 503
Dartington Trust, *289n1*, 318n1, 370
Darwin, Charles, 290
Das, Ashamukul, 180 (photo), 187n6
Das, Chitta Ranjan, 183, 187n3, *223*, *319–20*, 364n1, 369
Das, Frieda Hauswirth, *422–24*
Das, Sarangadhar, 422
Das Gupta, Aparna, 25
Das Gupta, Kedarnath, 243–44
Datta – see Dutta
Dattatreya, Kakasaheb Karlekar, *163*, *165n7*
Delhi, 127, 216, 219, 222, 301, 371n3, 464, 465n4, 475, 486n1
Denmark, 233, 384n5
Desai, Mahadev, 279, 280n1, *471–73*
Descartes, René, 530
'Deshahit' (RT), 71
'Deshanayak' (RT), 504
Devi (film by Ray), 175n2
Devon (UK), *11–12*
Dewey, John, 414
Dey, Mukul, 177, *178n5*, 311
Dhaka (Bangladesh), 46, 64, 65n12, 375n7, *406n4*
Dhaka University, 328n3
Dickens, Charles, 44n1, 347n1
Dickinson, Goldsworthy Lowes, 95, 96n2, *159–60*, *249–52*, *275n5*
Draper, Alfred, 224n3
Drummond, John Graham, 229, 273n2
Drummond, William Hamilton, 377, 378n4

Duhamel, Georges, 329
'Duranta Asha' (RT), 31
Dürer, Albrecht, 98
Durga (goddess), 315n3, *487*
Dutta, Charu Chandra, 11n5
Dutta, Kamala, 460n4
Dutta, Kshetra Mohan, 120n15
Dutta, Michael Madhushudan, *13n2*, 278, 279n5
Dutta, Rajeshwari, 376n1
Dutta, Sudhindranath, *375–76*

Eddington, Sir Arthur, *528*
Edison, Thomas, 246
Eeden, Frederik van, *122–23*
Egypt, 222, 339, 340
Einstein, Albert, *xxiii*, 1, 27n1, 39, 227, 307, 373, 376, 399, 401, 437, 438n5, 466, 483n2, *527–36*
Einstein, Margot, *528*, 529
Einstein Lived Here (Pais), 528
Elephant Boy (film by Flaherty), 445n3
Eliot, George, 44n1
Eliot, T. S., 68n1, 108n1, 462n3, *519–20*
Ellis, Havelock, 321n3
Elmhirst, Dorothy Whitney, 191n4, 194n2, *253n1*, 285, *288*, 289n6 and n7, *296–97*, *317–19*, 322, 324n4 and n7, 370, 371n2, *377–78*, *387–88*, 410n4, 412, 463, 479, 491, 492n5, *503–4*, 522n1, 524
Elmhirst, Leonard Knight, xxi, 2, *11*, 191n4, 194n2, *264n7*, 285, 287 (photo), *287–89*, *296–97*, *305–6*, 307, *311–15*, *317–19*, *321n3*, *322–24*, *330–31*, 336, 340–41, 364, 370, *371*, 377, *378*, 387, 397, *411–14*, 439, 440n2, 463, 479, 480n2, *485*, *490–92*, *503–5*, *514–15*, *520–21*, 522n1, *523–24*
Encyclopaedia Britannica, 528
Ends and Means (Huxley), 493
Engel, Mrs George, 438, 439n1
Engel, P., 439n1
Essay on the Civilisations of India, China and Japan (Dickinson), *159–60*, *249–52*
'The essence of religion' (Russell), *95–96*
Ethiopia, 474, 497
European Order and World Order (Pep), 514, *515n2*
Eyesore (RT), 142n3
Ezra, Nissim Ezra Benjamin, *437*, *438n1*

Faizpur (Maharashtra), 473, 474n7
Farr, Florence, 90
Faust (Goethe), 271n2
Feisal, King (of Iraq), 420n4
Fiji, 187n7, 258n1, 496n2
Fire of Bengal (Hajnóczy), 356n1, 362n1
Fireflies (RT), 444n2, 480n6, 492n2
Firestone, Harvey, 246
Flaherty, Robert, 445n3
Flaubert, Gustave, 138
Flaum, Schlomith, 460n3, *466–67*, 482, 536n45
Flexner, Simon, 98n6
Flower Garland, The (Ghoshal), 119
'For India' (Pearson), *202*, 203n5, 296n1
Ford, Henry, 246
Formichi, Carlo, 328, *336–37*, 338, 393, 394
Forster, E. M., 160n2, *249*, 251n2
Fortnightly Review, The (journal), 115

Four Chapters (RT), 452–53, 454n4, 455n8
Fox Strangways, Arthur H., *36n4*, 103, *104n2*, 105
France, 75, 233, 234, *263–65*, 310, 373, *374–78*, 380n1, 448, 493
Freud, Sigmund, *407*, *408n3*
Frost, Robert, 388
Fruit-Gathering (RT), 83n2, 169, 173n5
Fugitive, The (RT), 83n2, 173n5, 219n5
Fuller, Sir Bampfylde, 62, *65n9*
Fultala (Bangladesh), 58

Gahdr party, *428–29*
Galerie Pigalle (Paris), 56n12
Galileo Galilei, 532, *534*
Gandhi, Indira – *see* Indira Nehru
Gandhi, Mohandas Karamchand, xix, *xxii–xxiii*, 1, 2, 27n1, 55n10, 61, 62, 81n1, 133, 149, *155*, *158–59*, 182, *187n6*, 212, *213*, *215–16*, *218–19*, 229n1, 231, 233, *236–38*, *247*, *258*, 261n9, 275, 279, 281, 282, 285, 289n6, 299, 306n3, 320, *321–22*, 326n4, 345, *358n1*, 360n3, 362n1, 364, 369, 370, 371n1, 373, 376, 380n1, 381, 397, 401, *409*, *414–17*, 418, *421–22*, *424–30*, *433–34*, *457–58*, 464n5, 465, 470 (photo), *471–72*, 473, 474n7, *475–76*, 481, *484*, *489*, *490*, *491n3*, *502*, 503n1, *504*, *506–7*, *513*, *517–18*, 521n2, *524*, *536–40*
Ganesh (god), 32
Gangulee, Mira, 47 (photo), 57, 65, *66n1*, 67, 78, *82*, *84*, 92–93, 113, *114*, *121*, 179, 213, *226–27*, 231, 232n5, *233–35*, *238*, *383–84*, 409, *410–11*, 460n1, 462
Gangulee, Nagendranath, xxi, 65, *66–68*, *70*, 79, *82*, *84*, *86–87*, 93n2, 108, *113–14*, 115, 156, *165–66*, 209n5, 212, *213*, *214n3*, *226–27*, 232n5, *238–39*, 371n3, 409, 410n1, 460n1
Gangulee, Nitindranath, *93n2*, 114n5, 121, 213, 234, *383–84*, 402–3, 409, *410–11*, 415
Gangulee, Upendranath, 68n4
Ganguli, Mani Lal, 160, 161n3
Ganguly, Promode Lal, 467
Gardener, The (RT), *45*, 103n5, 104n1, 106n4, 122n7, 132, 140n8, 154, 155n2, 169n4
Geddes, Arthur, *327–28*
Geddes, Sir Patrick, 2, *52*, *290–93*, 327
Geneva (Switzerland), 266, 268, 311n4, 384
Genoa (Italy), 317
Germany, 99, 233, 234, 235, 239, *270–75*, 307, 310, 331, 340, 373, *383–84*, 387, 390, *402–3*, 415, 447, 464, 498, 500, 528
Ghare Baire – see *The Home and the World*
Ghosh, Aurobindo, 445n4
Ghosh, Barindra, 445
Ghosh, Gour Gopal, *296–97*
Ghosh, Jyotish Chandra, *190–92*, 194
Ghosh, Kali Mohan, 69, *115*, *116n3*, *123*, 124, 297
Ghosh, Mira, 286n3
Ghosh, Moti Lal, *182–83*, 187n3
Ghoshal, Jyotsnanath, 120n14
Ghoshal, Swarna Kumari, *119*, *141–42*
Gide, André, 155n3, 266n1, *272*, *379*, 522
Gitali (RT), 277
Gitanjali (Song Offerings) (RT), xviii, 43, 83n2, 89, *90n3*, *91*, 93, 95, 96, *99–101*, 102, 105, 107,

108, 115, *117–19*, 122, 127, 128, *132*, 136n4, *138*, *140–41*, 149, 155, *161–62*, *167–69*, 184, 196, 197n3, 208, 253n1, 254, 299, 374, *418–19*, 453, 527
Glimpses of Bengal (RT), 3, *209n5* and n7, 231n2
Goebbels, Joseph, 493
Goethe, Johann Wolfgang von, 264n2, 271n2, 290n1, 528
Gokhale, Gopal Krishna, *133–34*, 158n2
Golden Book of Tagore, The (Chatterjee), 376, *401–2*, 406, 529, *532*
Gonne, Iseult, *154–55*, 170n5
Gonne, Maud, 154–55
Gora (RT), 44n1, 294, *310–11*
Gosaba (West Bengal), *381*
Gosse, Edmund, 181, 182n2
Gourlay, William Robert, *190–91*, 192, 193, 194n2, 195n1, 286
Govinda, Guru, *473*, 474n5
'The great sentinel' (Gandhi), *281*
Greece, 339, 340
Green, Gretchen, 289n7, 297, *305*, 306n4, 392, *463–64*
Greenwich (London), 528
Greenwich Village (New York City), 252
Gregory, Lady, *105n4*, 169
Guangzhou (China), 496, 502
Gupta, Bihari Lal, *34–35*, *36n5*, 286n8
Gurney, Ivor, 172n1
Gwalior (Madhya Pradesh), 484
Gwyer, Sir Maurice, 519

Hafiz, 232n3, 283, 379
Hailey, Sir Malcolm, *442*
Hajnóczy, Rózsa, 356n1
Haldar, Asit Kumar, 323, 324n4
Halifax, Lord – *see* Lord Irwin
Hamburg (Germany), 270
Hamilton, Sir Daniel, *381–82*
Hardinge, Lord, *85*, 127, 133, 134, 160, 224n5, 486n1
Hardy, Thomas, 127, 130, 138
Harijan (journal), 422
Harvard University, 89, 108n1, 109, 116n8, 118, 249n3, 390n5, 519
Havell, Ernest Binfield, 139n6, 177n1 and n4
Hedin, Sven, *492*
Hegel, Georg Wilhelm Friedrich, xviii
Heisenberg, Werner, 527, 528, 529, 530, 534
Herder, Johann Gottfried von, xviii
Hesse, archduke of, 274
Hibbert Journal, The, 82n6, 95, 115, 118
Hibbert lectures, 373, 375n4, 528
Higginbottom, Sam, 287
Hijli (Bangladesh), 396
Hindi Bhavan (Shantiniketan), 503n3
Hindu Mahasabha, *417*, 445n1
Hindu Mela, 62
Hinduism (Sen), 69
Hitabadi (magazine), 32, 33n1
Hitler, Adolf, *437*, 471, 500
Holbein, Hans, 98
Holland, 233, 237, 238, *239–40*, 242n2
Home, Amal, *364n1*, 370n1
Home, Dipankar, 527

Home and the World, The (RT), xx, 225, *264*, 310, 346, 379, 404, 406, 453
Home Rule League, 183, *212*, 380n1
Hornell, W. W, *303n5*
Houston (USA), 256
Howrah (West Bengal), 266
Hsu Chih-mo, 313n5
Hungary, 339, 340
Hungry Stones and Other Stories, The (RT), 143n3, 145n1
Hunter report (1920), 233, 236, *238n4*
Huxley, Aldous, 493
Huxley, T. H., 290
Hyderabad (Andhra Pradesh), 182n1, 212, 213, 381n5, 435

Ibsen, Henrik, 321
Illinois, University of (Urbana), 61, *66–67*, 78, 87, *98–99*, 113, 138n2
Imperfect Encounter (Lago), 5n4
Imperial Legislative Council, 215
Inde (Rolland), 329n1
India and Modern Art (Archer), *177n4*
India Society (London), 89, 90n3, 93, 105, 139n7, 142n1
Indian Civil Liberties Union, 516
'The Indian ideal of marriage' (RT), *356n7*
Indian National Congress, 62, 64, *182–83*, *185–86*, 187, 211, 212n1, 238n4, 258, 362, 469n4, 471, 487–88, 503, *504*, *506–7*, 512, *513*, 539, 540
ingabangas, *8–10*
Inge, Dean W. R., *410n4*
Ireland, 222
Irwin, Lord, *370–71*, 515, 516n5, *519*
Israel's Messenger (journal), 437, *438n1*
Italy, 307, 314, 317n2, 324n8, 328–337, 394, 498
Izura (Japan), 176n4
Izvestia (newspaper), xxiv, xxv

Jackson, Sir Stanley, 370, *371n2* and n4
Jacobson, N., 414
Jallianwala Bagh (Amritsar), 215
'Jana Gana Mana' (RT), 487
Japan, *xx*, xxiv, 2, 149, 151, 159, 160n2, 161, *175–77*, 179n1, 181, 204, 251, 307, 310, 311, 335, 353, 368n3, 400, 471, *485–86*, *497–500*, *502*, 512
Java (Indonesia), *351–52*, 353, 367, 512
'Jay-parajay' – *see* 'Victorious in Defeat'
Jerusalem (Israel), 466
'Jete Nahi Dibo' (RT), 27
Jewish Agency (Palestine), 483, 484n6
Jinnosuke, Sano, 400
Jorasanko (Tagore houses in), 7, 13, 19, *45–46*, 47, 49, 57, 78, 108, 129, 135, 144, 153n6, 176n2, 177n1, 178n6, 180, 183, 187n4, 209, 270, 286, 370n6, *392–93*, 424n3, 509
Josephson, Brian, *528*, *533*
'The Journey of the Magi' (Eliot), 520

Kabir, 76, *77n4*, 116n3, 408
'Kabulioala' – *see* 'The Kabuliwallah'
'The Kabuliwallah' (RT), 27, 52, 80, 85
Kadambari (Banbhatta), *38–39*

Kadoorie, Sir Elly, 312, *313n3*
Kahn, Albert, 252n6, *375n9*
Kala Bhavan (Shantiniketan), 313n6
Kalamazoo (USA), 463
Kali (goddess), 32, 175n2, 473, 474n6
Kalidasa, 32, *33*
Kaligram (Bangladesh), 20, 46, 88n4
Kalimpong (West Bengal), 494, 508n4, 521, 522
Kalka (Himachal Pradesh), 82
Kamta (Bangladesh), 87
Kant, Immanuel, 264n2
Kar, Surendranath, 448, *449n4*, 457, 458n2
Karachi (Pakistan), 81, 467n4
Karakhan, L. M., 385, 387n2
Karpelès, Andrée, 393n3, *448–49*, 466
Karpelès, Suzanne, 197n6, 449n1
'Kartar Bhoot' (RT), xxi
Kashmir, 54, 159, 170
Kasmunda (Uttar Pradesh), 463n1
Kathiawar (Gujarat), 305, 306n3
Kautilya – *see* Chanakya
Kawabata, Yasunari, *176n1*
Keats, John, 289
Kellogg, Edith, 124, 125n3
Kelvin, Lord, 52
Keyserling, Count Hermann, *270–71*, 274
Khatau, Ajit Singh, *518*
Khatau, Seth Mulraj Morarji, 518n1
Khilafat Movement, 236, 237n1
Khulna (Bangladesh), 62
Kim-Taro Kasahara, *324*
King of the Dark Chamber, The (RT), 102n3, 124, *150*, 152n5, *155–56*, 444n2, *460*
Kipling, Rudyard, 136, *351*, 445n3
Kleist, Heinrich von, 264n2
Kobe (Japan), 312
Konarak temple (Orissa), 140
Konow, Sten, *293–94*, 337n1
Kopai, River (West Bengal), 30, 236
Korda, Alexander, 444, *445*
Kreutzer Sonata, The (Tolstoy), xxii, 539
Kripalani, Krishna, 142n3, 202n2, 447n1, 460n1, 467n4, 487, *488n3*, 496n5
Kripalani, Nandita, 179n9, 234, *460*, 466, 467n4
Krishna (god), 30, 76
Krishnamurti, Jiddu, 212n2
Kshanika (RT), 278, 279n4
Ku Klux Klan, 334
Kübler-Ross, Elisabeth, *83*
Kurseong (West Bengal), 178
Kushtia (Bangladesh), 166n5
Kusumoto, S., *66n4*

Lago, Mary M., *169n3*
Lahore (Pakistan), 465n4, 526n1
Lakshmi (goddess), 366
Lal, Madho, 301
Lal, Prem Chand, *324*, 387, 388n1
Lamont, Thomas, 253n1
Lansbury, George, 184
Laurie, T. Werner, 142n5
Lawrence, T. E., 136
Lawrence, Will, 136
Leap-Home and Gentlebrawn (Das), 424n6
Leipzig (Germany), 383

Lesny, Vincenc, *495–96*, *500*, *501*
Lester, Muriel, *434–35*, *440–41*, 452
Letters from John Chinaman (Dickinson), 159
Letters from Russia (RT), *xxiv*, 385, 387
Letters to a Friend (RT), 2
Lévi, Desirée, *354n8*
Lévi, Sylvain, 2, *160–61*, 197n6, 266n1, 285, *286*, 293, 337n1, *353–54*, 441n3, 449n1, 466
Lewis, Edwin H., *269n3*
Lewis, Isle of (UK), 328n2
Lima (Peru), 313
Lincoln (USA), 195
Listener, The (journal), 496n4
Liszt, Franz, 14n2
Liverpool (UK), 123
Lives of a Bengal Lancer (film), *445*
Livingstone, David, 363
London (UK), *8–10*, 11, 53, 89–90, 91, *92n3*, 93, 95, 97, 112, 113, 115, 117, 121, 122, 124, 127, 207, 233, 238, 239, 242n2, 262, 267, 378, 380, 434, 440
Los Angeles (USA), 178, 429
Lover's Gift (RT), 169, 173n5
Loyola, Ignatius, 258
Lucknow (Uttar Pradesh), 300
Lytton, Lord, 303n4

Macbeth, Lady (Shakespeare's character), 153
MacDonald, Ramsay, 135n1, 136, *415–16*
Mach, Ernest, 530
Macmillan and Co. (London), 89, 103, 104, 108, *111*, 115, 118, 122n7, 123n2, 124, 128n4, 139n7, 142n1, *150*, 154, *157*, *166–68*, 171, *172*, 202n5, *254*, 310, *311*, 433, 443, 453, 461, *468*, 479
Macmillan and Co. (New York), *199–200*, 203, *224–25*, 283n1
Macnicol, Nicol, *494*
Madanapalle (Karnataka), 174n1, 214
Madras (Tamil Nadu), 212, 214, 227, 327n1
Maffey, Sir John, 203n4, *220n4*
Mahalanobis, Nirmal Kumari (Rani), 309 (photo), 356n2, *364*, 367n1, 385, 480, *484–85n1*
Mahalanobis, Prashanta Chandra, 115, 116n2, *277–79*, 280, *285–86*, 309 (photo), 319, 320n4, *339n3*, 343n4 and n6, *348*, *354–56*, 364, 480, *484–85*
Mahendra (servant), 152–53
Mahmudabad (Uttar Pradesh), 300
Maitra, D. N., 91, 163, 178
Maitra, Heramba Chandra, 356n2
Maitra, Nirmal Kumari – *see* Nirmal Kumari Mahalanobis
Maitra, S. N., 197n6
Maitraye Devi, 495n5
Majumdar, Kshitindranath, 479n2
Majumdar, Santosh Chandra, 68n3, 137, 138n2, 297
Majumdar, Shailendra, 36–37, *42–43*
Majumdar, Sharbesh Chandra, 242, 243n7
Majumdar, Shrish Chandra, 37, 68n3, 268n2
Malaviya, Madan Mohan, 417n4, 445
Malaya, 367
Malini (RT), 102n3

Manchester Guardian, The (newspaper), 152n3, *156n1*, 226n1, 241, 336n1, 337n2 and n4, *338*, 339n5, 394
Manu, 153, 423, 472
Marconi, Guglielmo, 52
Marianoff, Dmitri, *529*, 531
Marriage to India, A (Das), 423
Mascaró, Juan, *426n5*, *495n4*
Massingham, H. W., 136n4
'The Master's will be done' (RT), *185*
Mayar Khela (RT), 56n18
Mayo, Katherine, 423
Mead, George Robert Stour, *183–85*
'The meeting of the East and the West' (RT), *241*
'Megh o Roudra' (RT), 230, 254
Meghduta (Kalidasa), 119, 286n1
Meghnad (*Ramayana*), 86
Men and Memories (Rothenstein), *418*, 420n7
Mendel, Bruno, 399, 533
Mendel, Hertha, *398–99*
'Meyeli chhara' (RT), 42n2
Meyer-Benfey, Heinrich, *262–63*, 449–50
Meyer-Franck, Helene, *262–63*, *264n2*, 449–50
Milan (Italy), 332, 340, 408n2
Milward, Marguerite, *373–74*, 375n1
Miraben, 425
Mitra, Krishna Kumar, 286
Mitra, Naba Gopal, 62, 64n5
Mitsuru, Toyama, 486n1
Modern Review (journal), 79–80, *115*, 116, 140, 172, 187n3, 190, 191n5, *249*, 290, 297, 388, 401, 420n9, 428
Monk, Ray, 156n1
Monroe, Harriet, 2, 89, 102, 103n5, 104n1, 105, 135, 136n1
Montagu, Edwin, 190, 194, *195n1*, 207n5, 233, *262–63*, 275n6
Montessori, Maria, *326–27*
Moody, Harriet, *107*, 109–10, 112n3, 123n3, *124–25*, 136, *137*, 142n2, *203–4*, 206n1, 256
Moody, William Vaughan, 107
Mookerjee, Sir Ashutosh, *302–3*, *319*, 417n4
Mookerjee, Lady Ranu – *see* Ranu Adhikari
Mookerjee, Shyama Prasad, 417n4
Moore, Marie Sturge, 140n10, 272–73
Moore, Thomas Sturge, 95n6, 121n5, 122n8, 127, *138–40*, 140, 142n1, *145*, 173, 230n3, 231n2, *272–73*, 275n5, *281–82*, *310–11*, 398, 418, 420n1, 443, 447n3, *450–52*, 453, 468n1, 478
Morgan Co., 253n1, 455n10
Morgenthau, Henry, 394
Morrell, Lady Ottoline, 96n3
Morris, William, 245
Morriswala, Hirjibhai Pestonji, 361n1
Moscow (Russia), *385–86*, 398, 529
Mother India (Mayo), 423
Muggeridge, Malcolm, 160n3
Mukerjea, Devabrata, 102n3, 154–55, *208–9*, 444n2
Mukherjee, Sujit, 110n5
Munger (Bihar), 462
Munich (Germany), 270, 383, 402, 528
Music of Hindostan, The (Fox Strangways), 36n4
Mussolini, Benito, 2, 307, 328, 330, 331n3, 332, 333, *335–36*, 337n4, 339, *393–94*, 407, 471, 474, 500

Muzaffarpur (Bihar), 57
My Reminiscences (RT), *170n6*, *172–73*, *208*, 310, 406
Mysore University, 282

Nabyabharat (journal), 70
Nag, Kalidas, 116n10, 341n1
Nagel, Thomas, *534*
Naidu, Sarojini, *181–82*, 242n3, 311, *430*, 482
Naivedya (RT), 402n1
Nanak, 76, 77n4
Naples (Italy), 330
Nara (Japan), 293, 294n6
Nashtanirh (RT), 379
Nation, The (UK journal), 124, 136n4, *262*
Nationalism (RT), *188–89*, 199n4
Natir Puja (RT), 424n3, 460
Natore (Bangladesh), 404
Naukadubi – *see* The Wreck
Nazi party, 383, 402, 437
Nehru, Indira, 442, *447*, 458, 459n3, *465*, *468–69*, 503n4
Nehru, Jawaharlal, xix, xxvn4, 2, 307, 432 (photo), 433, *442*, *447*, 457, *458*, *464–66*, *468–69*, 471, 480, 481, 482, 487, 488n2 and n3, *502–3*, *507*, *509*, *512–13*, 525n2
Nehru, Kamala, *442*, *447*, *464–65*
Nepal, 353, 361, 400
Nevinson, Henry Woodd, *516*
New Haven (USA), 391
New India (newspaper), 183
New Republic (journal), 319n1
New Statesman, The (journal), *138*, 326n4
New York City (USA), 73, *97*, 107, 110, 112, 124, 225n2, 233, 240–41, *243*, *246*, 248, 250, 252, 254, 255, 264n7, 267, 270n3, 285, 287, 296, 334, 372, 373, *388–89*, *390–91*, 392, 393n3, *394–95*, 482, 529, 535n22
New York Times, The (newspaper), *388–89*, *390*, 394, 528, *529*, *531–32*, 535n9 and n22, 536n26
Newcastle-under-Lyme (UK), 92
Newson, Ranald, 5n2
Nicholson, Max, 515n2
Nilmani – *see* Banamali
Nivedita, Sister, 50n6, 56n14, 79, 85
Noailles, Countess Anna de, 344 (photo)
Nobel prize, xvii, 89, 91, 105, 113, 114n2, 116, *127–40*, 144n6, 148, 149, 165, 206n1, 214n4, 227, 233, 234, 302, 394, 416, 436n4, 492, 527
Noble, Margaret – *see* Sister Nivedita
Noguchi, Isamu, 496
Noguchi, Yone, *496–99*, 500
Noncooperation Movement, xix, 61, 62, 233, 246, *247*, *258–61*, 275, 279, *285–86*, 288, 321, 326n4, 471
Norway, 234, 293, 331, 340, 392
Nuremberg (Germany), 493
Nussbaum, Martha, *xxv*
Nyabongo, Prince Akiki, *477*

Ocampo, Victoria, 307, *313–17*, 323, *325*, 344 (photo), 375n3, *378*, *439*, 440n2, 448, *505*, *522–23*
O'Dwyer, Sir Michael, 220n1
Offrande Lyrique (Gitanjali), L' (RT), 379n1

Okakura Kakasu/Kakuzo, 66n3, 151, 175, *176*, 375n5, 499
Okuma Shigenobu, Marquess, 198, 199, *200–1*, 202, 203
Olsvanger, Immanuel, *482–84*
Omaha (USA), 195
Omar Khayyam, *54*, 56n17
On Death and Dying (Kübler-Ross), *83*
Ortega y Gasset, José, 314, 315n6
Other Side of the Medal, The (Thompson), 325
Our Universe (RT), 480n7, 528
Oxford (UK), xvii, 116n6, 147–48, 202n2, 210, 374, 376, 436n7, 474, 477, 499n1, 528, 529
Oxford Book of Modern Verse, The (Yeats), 161
Oxford University, 325, 373, *518–19*
Owen, Wilfred, 172n1

Padma (houseboat of the Tagores), 15, 449–50
Padma, River, *24–25*, *26–27*, *36–37*, *42–44*, 54, 135, 137, 242
Pais, Abraham, 528, 535n9
Palamás, Kostís, *376–77*, 401
Palestine, *466*, *482–83*
Palit, Lokendranath, *19*, 38, 53, *54*, 66n5, 120n15, 130
Palit, Mabel, 120n15
Palit, Sir Taraknath, *66n5*, 166n5, *178*
Parasara, 472
Parichay (journal), 376n1
Paris (France), 53, 56n12, 139, 233, 236, 237, 238, 239, 240, 250, 262, 264, 344, 354n8, 373, 374, 377, 379, 407, 439, 448, 449n1, 522
Parrot's Training, The (RT), 52n4, 206, *207n5*
Pasadena (USA), 305n5
Pashchatya Bhraman (RT), 8
'Pashu priti' (Balendranath Tagore), *37–38*
Passage to India, A (Forster), *249–50*, 252n5
Pather Dabi (Chatterji), *346–47*
Pather Shanchay (RT), 93n1
Patisar (Bangladesh), 37, 87, 113
Patna (Bihar), 433
Paul, Prashanta Kumar, 11n1
Pearson, William Winstanley, 38n2, *163–64*, *170–71*, 176n4, *185–87*, 194, 196n2, *202–3*, 239, 240, 242n2, *243–44*, *247–49*, 257, 258n1, 286, *294–96*, *307–11*, 317, 361, 429
Peking (China), 202, 307, 310
Penrose, Sir Roger, 536n58
Perera, Nina, 398n4
Persia, 381n5, 397, *419*, 420n4
Personae (Pound), 105, *106*
Peru, 307, *313*
Petavel, J. W., 211n5
Petrov, Fedor Nikolaevich, *387n3*
Phalguni – see The Cycle of Spring
Phatik (RT's cook), 38–39
Phelps, Myron H., *73–74*, 116
Philadelphia (USA), 390, 392
Philosophy of Rabindranath Tagore, The (Radhakrishnan), *201*, *202n2*
Phoenix Settlement (South Africa), *155–56*, 157n6, *158*
Phoutrides, Aristides E., 377n2
Picasso, Pablo, 399
Pickett, Clarence, *390n4*

Pigalle, Galerie (Paris), 344 (photo), 375n3, 393n3
Pithapuram (Andhra Pradesh), 211, 212–13
Plato, 288
Podolsky, Boris, 530
Poems of T. Sturge Moore, The, 452n4
Poetry (journal), 89, *102*, 103, 104n1, 105
Poland, 331
Political and Economic Planning (Pep), *514–15*
Pond, James B., 198, 200n1, 203, 239, *240*, 248n2, 255
Poona Pact (1932), 397, 404, 417n2, *429–30*, 471, 502
Popper, Sir Karl, 530
Portsmouth (UK), 38
Post Office, The (RT), 89, 102n3, *118*, 121n5, 154, 180, *186*, *187n6*, 209n4, 351n4, 379n1, 444n2, *522*
'The Postmaster' (RT), *32*, 41
Pound, Ezra, xviii, 1, 2, 89, 91, *102–3*, 104, *105–6*, 107, 115, 116n3, 173n1, 407, *452*, 464n7, 496
Prabasi (journal), 70, 80n1, 82, 115, 348
Prague (Czech Republic), 338, 339n3, 495, 500
Prague University, 293
Presidency College (Calcutta), 210
Prigogine, Ilya, *528*, *532*, 534
Priyam Bada Devi, 33
Probsthain, Arthur, 383
Pune (Maharashtra), 158n2, 409, 415, 429
Purabi (RT), *314*, *325*, 326, 506n2, 523n3
Purdah (Das), *423*, 424n6
Puri (Orissa), *34–35*, *54*, 56n20
Purohit Swami, 494n3
Putnam, Hilary, xxiii, *534*
Pythagoras, 531

Quakers, 388
Quest, The (journal), 115, 185n1

Rabindranath Tagore (Dutta and Robinson), *4*
Rabindranath Tagore (film by Ray), *15*, 224n4
Rabindranath Tagore (Rhys), 149
Rabindranath Tagore (Thompson, 1921), *276–78*, 280–81, *283*
Rabindranath Tagore (Thompson, 1926), 276, 289, 290n1, 345, *348–50*
'Race conflict' (RT), 115
Radha (consort of Krishna), *30*
Radhakrishnan, Sir Sarvepalli, *201–2*, 463n1
Radice, William, 11n6
Raghuvamsa (Kalidasa), *33*
Raj Lakshmi Devi, 79n10
'The Raj Seal' (RT), 36n2
Raja – see The King of the Dark Chamber
Rajshahi (Bangladesh), 64
'Rajtika' – *see* 'The Raj Seal'
Rakta Karabi – see Red Oleanders
Ramachandra (*Ramayana*), 76
Ramakrishna Paramahansa, 229n1
Raman, Sir C. V., *55n3*
Ramanuja, 76, 77n4
Ramanujan, Srinivasa, 52
Ramayana, 56, 86n10, 102n6
Ramgarh (Uttar Pradesh), 156, 163
Ranchi (Bihar), 82, 140, 286
Ranjitsinhji Vibhaji, 232n3
Rapallo (Italy), 407n4

Raphael, 54
Ratcliffe, S. K., 331n4
Rathbone, Eleanor, *524–25*
Rattray, Robert Fleming, 116n8, *519–20*
Ratwal (Bangladesh), 87
Ravana (*Ramayana*), 86n10
Ray, Annada Shankar, 21n1, *393n1*
Ray, Hemanta Bala, 2, 370n2, 404, *406n1*
Ray, Jagadananda, 164, 165n9, 303n5
Ray, Nepal Chandra, 164, 165n9, 255, 256n3, 267
Ray, P. K., 56n18
Ray, Sarala, *54, 56n18*
Ray, Satyajit, xxiv, xxv, *3*, *15*, 25, *30*, 175n2, *177n2*, 224n4, *252n5*, *390n2*, 401n5, *445*, *452*
Ray Chaudhuri, Debi Prashanna, 71n3
Ray Chaudhuri, Nagendranath, 82n5
Ray Chaudhuri, Sudhakanta, 227n1
Rayleigh, Lord, 52
Rechenberg, Helmut, 528, 530
Reconstruction and Education in Rural India (Lal), 324n7
Red Oleanders (RT), 297n2, 305n4, 444n2
Religion of Man, The (RT), 375n4, *528*, 529, 532, 536n26
Reményi, Eduard, *14*
Reza Shah Pehlavi, 420n4
Rhys, Ernest, 116n6, 123, *149–50*, *152*, 254, 433, 443, *453–54*, 455n9, *461–62*, 468, 478, *494*
Richard, Paul, 179n1
Roberts, Lord, 53
Rochester (USA), 104, 109
Rockefeller, John D., 246
Roerich, Nicholas, 452
Rolland, Madeleine, 309 (photo), *330n4*
Rolland, Romain, 2, 179n1, *227–29*, 233, 266n1, 307, 308, 309 (photo), 321–22, *328–30*, 339, *377n3*, 401, 493n1, 529
Romania, 339
Ronaldshay, Lord, 181, 185n4, 190, *192–94*
Roosevelt, Franklin Delano, 394, *522*
Rosen, Nathan, 530
Ross, Sir Ronald, *345–46*
Rothenstein, Lady Alice, 97, 98n4, 100, 131, 141
Rothenstein, Sir John, 91 (photo)
Rothenstein, Rachel, *207–8*
Rothenstein, Sir William, 2, 79, 80n7, 89–90, 91 (photo), *91–92*, 93, 94, *95–104*, *107–8*, 111, *112*, 116n3, 118, 121n5, *123–24*, 127, *128–29*, *130–31*, *134–35*, 136n4, *140–42*, 147, 150, 152, 159, *161–62*, 166, 167, *188–89*, *205–6*, 207, 209, 213n2, *225–26*, 249, *252n4*, 256, *262–66*, *268–69*, 291, 342, *348–50*, 351n3, *373–74*, *375n8*, 376, *397–98*, 406, *418–20*, *478*
Rowlatt report (1918), *215*
Roy, Basanta Koomar, 152n2
Roy, Bidhan Chandra, 400, *401n1*
Roy, Dilip Kumar, 2, 48n2, 356–57, *358n1*
Roy, Dwijendra Lal, 358n1
Roy, Janakinath, 87, 88n2
Roy, Rammohun, 36, 37, 62, 67
Roy, Sharat Kumar, 163
Roy, Shatish Chandra, *59–60*, 68, 187n5
Rudra, Sudhir, 156
Rudra, Susil, *128n5*, 156, 219
Ruskin, John, 291

Russell, Bertrand, 2, *95–96*, *101*, 159, 280n3, *533*
Russia (USSR), *xxiv*, 304, 373, *385–88*, 391n4, *392–93*, 500
Russiar Chithi – see *Letters from Russia*
Rutherford, Ernest, 527

Sabarmati (Gujarat), 222, 421
Sadhana (journal), 64, 65n10
Sadhana (RT), 89, 116n6, 122n7, 149, 159n4, 185n1, *410n4*, 461, *462n7*, 520
Sadler, Sir Michael, 2, *206*, *209–11*, 262, 283n1
Saha, Meghnad, 528
Sahitya (journal), 370n1
St Xavier's College (Calcutta), *22–23*
Salvadori, Guglielmo, 329, *330n2*, *336n2*, 338, 394n1
Salvadori, Madam, 329, 337
Salvadori, Max, 330n2
Salvemini, Gaetano, 330n2
Samajpati, Suresh, *370n1*
San Francisco (USA), 181, 198, 199, 200, 202, 204, 428–29
San Isidro (Buenos Aires), 313, 316, 323, 325, 506n1
Sanger, Margaret, *320–21*
Sangharakshita, Urgyen (D. P. E. Lingwood), *294n6*
Sanskrit Siksha (RT), 56n19
Santals, *295*, 296n3
Sapru, Sir Tej Bahadur, 458, *459n2*
Saraswati (goddess), 10
Sarkar, Kunja, 23
Sarkar, Nil Ratan, 70, *71n7*, 408n1
Sarkar, Sir Nripendranath, *429–30*
Sarkar, Sharashi Lal, *407–8*
Sarkar, Sumit, *113*
Sastri, V. S. Srinivasa, 419, 420n6
Sastri, Vidhu Sekhar, 417n1
Schelling, Friedrich von, xviii
Schiller, Friedrich von, 264n2
Schlegel, August Wilhelm von, xviii
Schopenhauer, Arthur, xviii
Schrödinger, Erwin, 527, 529, 531, *534*
Scott, Charles Prestwich, 2, *338–39*
Scott, Leroy, 71n4
Scott, Paul, 194n2
Scotti, Duke Gallarati, 408n2, 459n4
Sea is Kind, The (Moore), *145*, 146
Seal, Sir Brajendranath, 2, 95, 96n6, 206, *282–84*, 301
Seattle (USA), 178
Sedgwick, Ellery, *388–90*
Sen, Atul Prashad, *300–1*
Sen, Basiswar, *479–80*, 489
Sen, Dhirendra Mohan, 491, 492n5
Sen, Dinesh Chandra, 61, *64n1*, 303
Sen, Gertrude Emerson, 454n5, 455n8, 479n3, *479–80*, *489*, 535n22
Sen, Keshub Chandra, 62, 64n4, 81n1
Sen, Kshiti Mohan, 2, 61, *68–69*, 81, 90, 93, 101, 153n4, 312, 341, 492n5
Sen, Kshitish Chandra, 150, 152n6, 255n3
Sen, Mohit Chandra, 56n16
Sen, Nabin Chandra, 278, 279n5
Sen, Priyanath, *13–14*, *50–51*, 57

Sen, Ramprasad, *174*, *175n2*
Sen, Snehalata, 286n8
Sen Gupta, Sudhanshu, 452n2
Serbia, 340
Seymour, Arthur, 99n4, 205n1
Seymour, Mayce, 99n4, *110n4*, 121n2, 203, *204–5*, 253n1, 264n7
Shabuj Patra (journal), 153n1, 197
Shadhu Charan (servant of RT), 153n5, 238
Shaha, Gopal, 25n1
Shahibag (Ahmedabad), 305, *306n1*
Shahjahan (emperor), 306n1
Shahzadpur (Bangladesh), 15, 16, 21, 22, *23*, 24, 25, 29, 32–33, 34, *41–42*
Shakespear, Dorothy, 102
Shakespeare, William, 290n1, 349, *350*
'Shamapti' – *see* 'The Conclusion'
Shanghai (China), 311–13, 437, 438n1
Shanibarer Chithi (journal), *368*
Shankara, 76, 77n4
Shapmochan (RT), 460n2
Sharadotsav (RT), 256n2
Shaw, Charlotte, 351
Shaw, George Bernard, *350–51*
Shelidah (Bangladesh), 15, 21, 25, *26–27*, 31, *36–37*, *39–40*, 42, *43–44*, 46, 49, 51, 52, *53–55*, 56, 69, 73, 77, 79n3, 81, 82, 84, 87, 113, *117*, 133, *134–35*, 137, 138, 140, 143, 144, 166n5, 245, 258, 288, 360
Shelley, Percy Bysshe, 146, 289
Shertok (Sharrett), Moshe, 483, 484n5
Shesh Shaptak (RT), 455n1
Shillong (Assam), 305n4, 460
Shimla (Himachal Pradesh), 54, 219
Shishu – *see* The Crescent Moon
Shishu Bholanath (RT), 282n3
Shiva (god), 32
Shriniketan, 116n3, 154, 285, *296–97*, 305, 312–13, *324*, 327, *370–71*, 381, 388n1, *393*, *411–14*, 463, 466, 481, 482, *490–92*, *514–15*
Shudarshana (RT's character), 155, *156n1*, 460
Shurangama (RT's character), *460*
Shyamali (Shantiniketan), 448–49
Siam – *see* Thailand
Siggard, Hiordis – *see* Haimanti Chakravarty
Sikhism, *472–74*
Siksha-Satra, *490–91*
Silk Road, The (Hedin), 492
Since Fifty (Rothenstein), 508n3
Sinclair, Upton Beall, *304–5*
Singapore, 195
Sinha, S. P., 139n5
Sinha family (of Raipur), 287
Sircar – *see* Sarkar
Slade, Madeleine – *see* Miraben
Smaran (RT), 48n3
Solo (Indonesia), 352
Sommerfeld, Arnold, *528*
'Sonnet Panchashat' (Chaudhuri), *118–19*
Sorbonne University (Paris), 239
South Africa, *133*, 134, 149, 158, 213, 496n2, 517
Southampton (UK), 8
Speaight, Robert, *96*
Spectator, The (journal), 326n4, 406n4, 420n9, 477, 499, *500n7*

Spender, J. A., 330
Spinoza, Benedict de, 96n3
Spirit of Man, The (Bridges), 148n3, 149, 161, 162n1, *172n1*, 418
Sri Lanka, 397, *435–36*, 439
Srikanta (Chatterji), 255n3, 347n1
Statesman, The (newspaper), 219, 220n1, 331n4, 404, 428, 489
Stein, Gertrude, 242n3
Stockholm (Sweden), 272, 492, 527
Stopes, Marie, 321n3
Story of my Experiments with Truth, The (Gandhi), 219n1
Straight, Dorothy Whitney – *see* Dorothy Elmhirst
Straight, Michael, 522n1
Straight, Willard, 318n1, 479
Strait is the Gate (Gide), *379*
Stray Birds (RT), 83n2, 480n6
Strickland, C. F., *414n2*
Stroud (UK), 92
Subramanyan, K. G., 375n5
Suhrawardy, Hasan Shahid, *147–48*, 167n4
Sunderbans (West Bengal), 381
'The Sunset of the Century' (RT), 55
Sur (journal), 313, 315n1
Surabaya (Indonesia), 353n2
Surul (West Bengal), 153, *153–54*, 258, 277, 285, *287–89*, *296–97*, 305, 306n4, 324n6
Swadeshi Movement, 49, *61–64*, *69*, *71–72*, 73, 120, 182, 215, *260*, 263, 366, 487
Sweden, 233, 234, 331
Swinburne, Algernon, *94n4*, 169
Switzerland, 233, 234, 266, *267*, 308, 309, 326, 328, 331, 336, 459n3, 468
Symons, Arthur, 181

Tagore, Abanindranath, 2, 79n1, 139, 161n3, 175, *176–78*, 180 (photo), 186, 187n6, 207n5, 324n4, 345, 398, 457n1
Tagore, Ajindranath, 395, 460n5
Tagore, Amita, 395, 460
Tagore, Balendranath, *37–38*, 64, 165, 166n5
Tagore, Binayini, 79n1
Tagore, Birendranath, 38n3
Tagore, Maharshi Debendranath, 10n1, 13, 14n3, 42, 46, 49, 57n3, *62*, 64n4, 65, 94, *153n6*, 165, *262n10*, *283*, 379, *392–93*, 421
Tagore, Dwarkanath, 297
Tagore, Dwijendranath, 7, 8, 11n4, 62, 64n5, 79n8, 165, 166n2, *261*
Tagore, Dwipendranath, 78, 79n8
Tagore, Gaganendranath, 2, *49–50*, 66n5, 78, 79n1, 173n4, *175–76*, 178n6, 180 (photo), 186, 187n6 and n8, 457n1
Tagore, Gunendranath, 62, 64n5
Tagore, Hemendranath, 142n6
Tagore, Indira, 3, 11n4, 15–17, *18n1*, 20–44, 52n6, *84*, 116–20, 152–53, 208, 209n5, 286n1, 356n4
Tagore, Jnanadanandini, 59n6, 82, *84*, 286n7
Tagore, Jotendra Mohan, 49, *50n3*
Tagore, Jyotirindranath, 7, *10n1*, 50n4, *62*, 65n9, 71n7, 82, 84n5, *98–99*
Tagore, Kadambari, 7, 10n1, 11, 59n1, 83, 84n5
Tagore, Madhurilata – *see* Madhurilata Chakravarty

Tagore, Manjushri, 286
Tagore, Mira – *see* Mira Gangulee
Tagore, Mrinalini, 7, *18–19*, 27–28, *45–48*, 51, 54, 56–59, 66n3, 78, 79n10, 82n5, 84n5, 328
Tagore, Nandini, *384–85*, 395, 518
Tagore, P. N., 486n1
Tagore, Pratima, 47 (photo), *77–79*, 82, *83*, 92, *98–99*, 110, 118, 121, 122, 140, 156, 178n6, 203, 204, 309 (photo), 384, *394–95*, 448, 454, 479, 494, 518, 520
Tagore, 'Rabbi', 529–30, 534
TAGORE, RABINDRANATH: major references only (For RT's relationships with individuals, institutions and places, see entry under relevant heading, e.g. 'Yeats, W. B.', 'Gandhi, Mohandas Karamchand', 'Calcutta University', 'Shriniketan', 'Japan', 'Bombay'.)
   and **academe**, 4, 107–9, 273, 282–84, 293, *302–3*, *353–54*, *518–19*
   as **actor**, 186, 187n6, *369*
   appearance, physical, *1*, *147*, 508
   as **art critic**, *98*, 139, *175–77*, 293, 323, *399*, *420*
   as **autobiographer**, 7–8, *169–70*, *172–73*, 208–9
   and **Bengali literature**, 13n2, *30*, *278*
   relationship with **Bengalis**, *8–11*, 34, *41–42*, *49–51*, *67*, 72, *127*, *134–35*, *163–64*, *185–86*, 319, *368–69*, *402*, *452–54*, 503
   relationship with the **British** (in UK), *8–11*, *89–90*, *92–93*, *100–1*, *115*, *128–29*, *138–39*, *147–48*, 455, 469, 478, 521
   relationship with the **British** (in India), *15–18*, *25–26*, *34–35*, 54, *138–40*, *159*, 160, *203*, *210*, *249–51*, 397, 504
   on **British rule** in India, *xix*, *49–50*, *75–77*, *85–86*, 181, *184*, *190–95*, 215, *219–24*, *249–51*, *347*, *434–35*, *524–25*
   on **cinema**, *444–45*, 459
   on **Communism**, *385–87*, 392, *403*
   as **dance composer**, *459–60*
   on **death**, *25*, *83*, 197, *410–11*, 416, *438*, *462*, *464–65*, *484–85*, *526*
   on **East–West** encounter, *xviii*, 3, *37*, *53*, 67, *74–77*, *90*, *115*, 122, *136*, *228*, *241*, 338, *351–52*, *389–90*, *497–99*
   as **editor**, *38*, *70*
   as **educationist**, *xxiii–iv*, 23, *60*, 61, *65–69*, *75–77*, 78, *82*, 156, 158, *179*, 206, *210–11*, 256, *263–69*, *281–83*, *291–92*, *293–94*, *308–10*, *312–13*, 327, *341–43*, *370–71*, *440–41*, *517*
   on **English language**, *65–66*, 78, 90, 106, *115*, *118*, 122, *141*, 167, *168*, *171*
   and **European literature**, 1, *38*, *43–44*, 50, *51*, *93–95*, 101, *106*, *146*, 147, *173–74*, *289*, 304, 314, *376–77*, *379*, *519–20*
   relationship with **family**, 4, *7*, 13, *18–19*, *27–28*, *45–52*, 54, *56–60*, *65–68*, *77–78*, *82–84*, *86–87*, *92–93*, *98–99*, *109–11*, *113–14*, *117–19*, *120–21*, *141*, 152, *165–66*, 197, 206, 213, *227*, *234*, *238*, *302*, *383–85*, *395*, *410–11*, *459–60*, *518*
   on **Fascism**, 330, *332–37*, *403*, *437*
   as **fundraiser**, 3, *143*, *166n5*, *178*, *224–25*, 231, *239–43*, *246*, *248–49*, *252–53*, *255*, *297–98*, *300–1*, *380*, 391, *395*, 433, *435–36*, *457–58*, *475–76*, *506*, *517*, *523*

   on **ghosts**, *32–33*
   health/illnesses, *120–21*, *323*, 325, 326, 331, 460
   on **history of Bengal/India**, *61–65*, *74–77*, 81, *423*
   personal **income**, 106, *113–14*, *165–66*
   knighthood, xix, *223–24*
   as **lecturer**/essayist, xviii, *109*, 110n4, 178, *242*, 274, 329, 509
   as **letter writer**/diarist, *xvii*, *xviii–xix*, *1–4*, *7–8*, *209*
   as **literary critic**, 1, *44*, *182*, 290, 345, *346–50*, *465–66*, 492, *494–96*
   on **marriage**, *13*, *46–48*, *56–58*, 227, *355–58*
   as **music critic**, *13–14*, *35*
   as **nationalist leader**, *xix–xxii*, *61*, *71–72*, *85–86*, 133, 216, 218, *223–24*, 345, 397, *414–17*, *424–30*, *442*, 471, *480–81*, *486–87*, *525*
   as **novelist**, xviii, *xx*, 229, 310, 346, *452–53*
   as **painter**, xviii, 54, 323, *367*, *373–75*, *390–91*, 392, *397–98*, *408*, *478*
   as **philosophical/religious thinker**, *xxiii*, *38*, *39–40*, *42–44*, *95–96*, 108n7, *132*, 148, *170–71*, *201*, *225–26*, *238*, 240, *245*, *257–58*, *260–61*, *276–77*, *279–80*, *283*, *294–96*, *299–300*, *407–8*, *409–10*, *425–27*, *433–34*, *488–89*, *527–38*
   as **playwright**, 101, 150, *155–56*, *186*, *460*, *522*
   as **poet**, xvii, 15, *45*, *79–80*, *90–92*, *93–94*, *99–108*, *117–18*, *132*, *139*, *147–48*, 168, 282, 325, *443–44*, *461*, *474*, *477*
   as **political thinker**, *xviii*, *xxii*, *xxiv*, *61–64*, *69–70*, *71–72*, *74–77*, *182–95*, 211, *216*, 218, *236–37*, *247*, *258–60*, *274–75*, *322*, 339, *340–41*, *358–60*, *361–62*, *364–66*, *381–82*, *392–93*, *403–6*, *418–19*, 466, *493*, *496–99*, *501*, *503–4*, *507*, *509*, *512–16*, *521*, *522*, *525*, *538–40*
   as **religious reformer**, 72, *80–81*, *420–22*, *471–73*
   and Indian **revolutionaries**, *xx*, 70, 181, *198–201*, *202–5*, *242*, *255–56*, *428–29*, *485–86*, *501–2*
   as **rural developer**, *15*, 70, *86–87*, *113–14*, 285, *287–88*, *296–97*, 324, *411–14*, *482–83*, *490–91*, *515*
   on **Sanskrit literature**, *32–33*, *38–39*, 54, 56, 119
   and **science**/technology, *xxii–iii*, 42, *52–55*, *82*, 394, *407–8*, 413, *527–36*
   relationship with **servants**, *152–53*
   as **short story writer**, xviii, 15, 21, 23, *25n1*, *27–28*, 32, 40, 52, *79–80*, 85, *142–43*, *145*, 157, 230, 254
   as **singer/song composer**, xviii, 301, *327–28*, *486–87*
   as **social reformer**, *xviii*, *xx*i, xxii, *xxiv*, *62–64*, *74–77*, *320–21*, *355–60*, *361–64*, *364–66*, *400–1*, *420–23*, *471–73*
   on **translation** (by RT and others), 3, *79–80*, *91–92*, *102–6*, *117–19*, *131–32*, *136*, *138–39*, *142–45*, 149, *150*, 154, 157, *161–62*, *166–69*, *171–72*, 174, *196–97*, 229, 230, 254, *272–73*, *275–76*, *289*, *310–11*, *418–19*, 433, *444*, 446, *450–52*, *452–54*, 468, 474
   travels (main tours only), *7–12*, *19*, *89–125*, *175–79*, *233–75*, *310–19*, *328–43*, *373–95*
   on **women**, *xxii*, *23–24*, *314–17*, *430–31*, *448*, *522–23*
   as **zamindar**, *15–18*, *20–21*, 26, *32–33*, *36–37*, *41–44*, 46, *165*, *261*, *392*

Tagore, Rathindranath, 7, *19*, 27, *28*, *29*, 47 (photo), *56*, *59–60*, 61, 62, *67*, *77–79*, 82, 84, *86–87*, 91 (photo), 93n3, 101, 102n4, 108, 110n3, 113, 118, 122, *123n2*, 138n2, *142n2*, 156, 160–61, 165, 176, 178n6, *178–79*, 187n6, *197*, 203, 204, 207, *209n5*, *226–27*, *235n2*, 243, 244n3, *253n1*, *259*, *264n7*, 268, 270, 297, 314, 319, 327n1, 343n6, 384, *390–93*, 394, 436, 448, 454, 467, 476n1, 494, 518, 520
Tagore, Renuka, 28, 45, *57–59*
Tagore, Satyendranath, 7, 14n4, 18n1, 64, 82, 84n1, *285–86*, 306n1
Tagore, Saudamini, 83
Tagore, Shamindranath, 45, 49n6, *411*, *462–63*
Tagore, Shanjna, 93
Tagore, Shubir, 286
Tagore, Surendranath, 48, *49n6*, 51, 53, 93n4, 98, *118*, 140, 153, 173, 178n6, 209, 231, 286n7, 310, *311n4*, 453, 454n5, 455n8, *521*
Tagore, Swarna Kumari – *see* Swarna Kumari Ghoshal
Tagore and Co., *166n5*
Tai Chi-Tao, 524n2
Taikan, Yokoyama, *175–76*
Takagaki, Shinzo, *400–1*
Talks in China (RT), 311n5
Tamerlane, 497
Tapati (RT), 370n6
Tarkachudamani, Shashadhar, 62, 65n7
Tata, Sir Ratan, 301n2
Tattvabodhini Patrika (journal), 62, *81*
Techniques of Judo (Takagaki), 400, 401n3
Tennyson, Alfred, 1
Terauchi Masatake, Count, 199, 200–1
Thacker Spink and Co. (Calcutta), 51, *52n4*, 78, 207n5
Thadani, N. V., 195
Thailand, 367, 512
Thakur – *see* Tagore
Theory of Relativity (Einstein), 532
Theosophy, 211–12
Thompson, Edward John, 2, 3, *129–30*, *131–33*, *137*, *142–45*, *147*, 150, 152n3, 154, 157n3, 162n5, 166, *174–75*, 197n2, *202n2*, 212n2, *230*, *253–55*, *275–77*, *280–81*, *283*, 284n3, 285, *289–90*, *325–26*, 345, *348–50*, *360–61*, 397, *401–2*, 424n1, *443–47*, 450, 453, 455n10, *459*, 468n1, *488*, *492–93*, 495, *518–19*
Thompson, E. P., xviii, xx, xxiii, 130n1, *142*, 189n2, *254*, *348*, *350n7*, *381*
Thompson, Theodosia, 255n3
Thoreau, Henry, 122
Timbres, Harry, *391–92*
Times, The (newspaper), 53, 115, 220n1, 522n3
Times Literary Supplement, The, *100*, 189n2, 468n2, *496n4*
Tinker, Hugh, *409*
Tokyo (Japan), 176, 354n8, 400, 401n3, 486n1, 498, 501
Tolstoy, Leo, xxii, 1, *43*, 539
'Toomai of the Elephants' (Kipling), 445n3
Torquay (UK), 7, 11, 92, 508n2
Travancore (Kerala), 54, 298
Travel Diary of a Philosopher, The (Keyserling), *270*

Tripura, 53, 419
Tripuri (Madhya Pradesh), 507
Trivedi, Harish, 130n1, *348*
Tucci, Giuseppe, 328, 337n1, *341–43*, 349, 353, 441n3
Tucker, Boyd W., *361–62*, *421–22*
Tunbridge Wells (UK), 11
Twain, Mark, 51
Twenty-Five Collotypes from the Original Drawings by Jyotirindra Nath Tagore, *98–99*

Uma Charan (servant of RT), 152–53
Unfinished Song, An (Ghoshal), 142n5
United States of America, 37, *66–67*, 70, 73–75, *86–87*, *97–112*, 149, 153n4, 175n3, *178–79*, *198–200*, *202–5*, 233, *239–50*, *252–56*, 257, 259, 263, 266, *268–69*, 270, 273, 287, 305, 312, 318, 320n1, 326, *334*, 362n1, 373, 375, 380n1, 383, *387–91*, 392–93, *394–95*, *428–29*, 463, 466, 479, 515, *522*
Upanishads, 62, *95*, 164, 165n10, 245, 266, *279–80*, *283*, *425*, *494–95*
Uttarayan (Shantiniketan), 331n7

Vadodara (Gujarat), 227, 436
Vaishnavism, *30*, 173, 245
Varanasi (Uttar Pradesh), 69n1, 300–1, 305, 327n3
Vaswani, Thanwardas Lilaram, 81n1
Vedas, 62
'Vera Sazanova' (Gangulee), *70*, *71n4*
Vichitra club (Calcutta), 176n2, 177, *178n6*, 187n6
Victoria, Queen, 14n2
'Victorious in Defeat' (RT), 85
Vidyarnava, Pandit Shivadhan, 51, *52n5*, 54
Vidyasagar, Pandit Iswar Chandra, 36n6, 64, 65n15
Vidyavati Devi, Maharajkumari, *462–63*
Vienna (Austria), 329, 330, 331, 332, 337, 407
Vijayanagar (Karnataka), 212
Villeneuve (Switzerland), 308, 309
Visarjan (RT), 42n1
Visva-Bharati University, 56n20, 60n1, 73n1, 177n1, 178, *179*, 211, 215, 231, 233, 239, 241, 256, *262–69*, 279n1, *281–82*, *285*, *290–94*, *297–98*, *300–1*, 304, 307, 311, *312–13*, 328, 330, 331, 336–37, 343n4, *353–54*, 355, 361n1, *370–71*, 373, *379–80*, 391, 395, 433, *435–36*, 457, *458*, 462, 463n1, 464n5, 471, *475–76*, 482–84, 487, 506, 515, *517*, 518, *523*
Visva-Bharati News (journal), 440, 487, 488n3
Visva-Bharati Quarterly (journal), 229n2, *298–99*, 321n4, 420n9, 446–47, 501
Visva-Parichay – *see Our Universe*
Vivekananda, Swami, 229n1
Vizianagaram (Andhra Pradesh), 463n1
Voiceless India (Emerson), 480n1

Walker, Emery, 99n2
Wardha (Madhya Pradesh), 458n2
Waste Land, The (Eliot), 520
'Wayside' (RT), 231n2
Webb, Beatrice, 234n1
Weil, Miss, 479, 480n6
Weinberg, Steven, *527*
Weizmann, Chaim, 483, 484n6
Wells, H. G., 68n1

Index

Westcott, Right Reverend Foss, 2, *524–25*
What I Owe to Christ (Andrews), *409–10*
Wheeler, John, *530*
Whole World and Company, The (Green), *463*
Wigner, Eugene, *527*
Wilberforce, William, 477n6
Wilde, Oscar, 97n3, 153n1
William, Prince (of Sweden), *143–44*
Williams, Ariam – *see* E. W. Aryanayakam
Williamstown (USA), 389
Willingdon, Lord, 434
Wilson, Woodrow, 2, 198, *199*, 200, 202, 203
Winternitz, Moriz, 293, *294n8*, 501n1
Wittgenstein, Ludwig, *96n5*, 156n1
Wolff, Kurt, 235 (photo), *271*, *273–74*, 300n1
Woodroffe, Sir John, 52n5
Woods, James Houghton, *108*, 519
Woolworth's, 480n6
Wordsworth, William, 11, *94n4*, 136n4, 289
Works and Days (Cooper), 140n9
Wreck, The (RT), 197n3, *229–30*, 272

Yama (god), 40n1
Yama Farms (USA), *246*, 248
Yeats, William Butler, xviii, 2, 3, 45, 89, *90*, *93–95*, 96, 102n3, *103n6*, *105*, 107, 108, 116n3, 117, 118, 123, 127, 128n4, *132*, 138, 139n1 and n5, 140, *145*, 147, 149, *154–55*, *161–62*, 166, *168–70*, 171, *172–73*, 181, 185n1, *208–9*, 264n8, 272, 311n6, *406–7*, *418–19*, 420n2, 439, 443, *455–57*, 468n1, 494n3, 496
Yeats-Brown, Francis, 445n1
Yogayog (RT), 406n1
Yokohama (Japan), 176
Young, Michael, *515n2*
Young India (newspaper), 320
Youngest Disciple, The (Thompson), 488
Yugoslavia, 339
Yurop Prabashir Patra (RT), *7–12*

Zionism, 482, *483*
Zurich (Switzerland), 329, 337
Zwager, N., *351–52*

University of Cambridge
Oriental publications published for the
Faculty of Oriental Studies

1. *Averroes' commentary on Plato's Republic*, edited and translated by E. I. J. Rosenthal
2. *FitzGerald's 'Salaman and Absal'*, edited by A. J. Arberry
3. *Ihara Saikaku: the Japanese family storehouse*, translated and edited by G. W. Sargent
4. *The Avestan Hymn to Mithra*, edited and translated by Ilya Gershevitch
5. *The Fuṣūl al-Madanī of al-Fārābī*, edited by D. M. Dunlop (out of print)
6. *Dun Karm, poet of Malta*, texts chosen and translated by A. J. Arberry; introduction, notes and glossary by P. Grech
7. *The political writings of Ogyū Sorai*, by J. R. McEwan
8. *Financial administration under the T'ang dynasty*, by D. C. Twitchett
9. *Neolithic cattle-keepers of south India: a study of the Deccan Ashmounds*, by F. R. Allchin
10. *The Japanese enlightenment: a study of the writings of Fukuzawa Yukichi*, by Carmen Blacker
11. *Records of Han administration.* Vol. I *Historical assessment*, by M. Loewe
12. *Records of Han administration.* Vol. II *Documents*, by M. Loewe
13. *The language of Indrajit of Orchā: a study of early Braj Bhāṣā prose*, by R. S. McGregor
14. *Japan's first general election, 1890*, by R. H. P. Mason
15. *A collection of tales from Uji: a study and translation of 'Uji Shūi Monogatari'*, by D. E. Mills
16. *Studia semitica.* Vol. I *Jewish themes*, by E. I. J. Rosenthal
17. *Studia semitica.* Vol. II *Islamic themes*, by E. I. J. Rosenthal
18. *A Nestorian collection of Christological texts.* Vol. I *Syriac text*, by Luise Abramowski and Alan E. Goodman
19. *A Nestorian collection of Christological texts.* Vol II *Introduction, translation, indexes*, by Luise Abramowski and Alan E. Goodman
20. *The Syriac version of the Pseudo-Nonnos mythological scholia*, by Sebastian Brock
21. *Water rights and irrigation practices in Lajh*, by A. M. A. Maktari
22. *The commentary of Rabbi David Kimḥi on Psalms cxx–cl*, edited and translated by Joshua Baker and Ernest W. Nicholson
23. *Jalāl al-dīn al-Suyūṭī.* Vol. I *Biography and background*, by E. M. Sartain
24. *Jalāl al-dīn al-Suyūṭī.* Vol. II *'Al-Tahadduth bini'mat allāh'*, Arabic text, by E. M. Sartain
25. *Origen and the Jews: studies in Jewish-Christian relations in third-century Palestine*, by N. R. M. de Lange
26. *The 'Vīsaḷadevarāsa': a restoration of the text*, by John D. Smith
27. *Shabbethai Sofer and his prayer-book*, by Stefan C. Reif
28. *Mori Ōgai and the modernization of Japanese culture*, by Richard John Bowring
29. *The rebel lands: an investigation into the origins of early Mesopotamian mythology*, by J. V. Kinnier Wilson
30. *Saladin: the politics of the holy war*, by Malcolm C. Lyons and David Jackson
31. *Khotanese Buddhist texts* (revised edition), edited by H. W. Bailey

32 *Interpreting the Hebrew Bible: essays in honour of E. I. J. Rosenthal*, edited by J. A. Emerton and Stefan C. Reif

33 *The traditional interpretation of the Apocalypse of St John in the Ethiopian orthodox church*, by Roger W. Cowley

34 *South Asian archaeology 1981: proceedings of the sixth international conference of South Asian archaeologists in western Europe*, edited by Bridget Allchin (with assistance from Raymond Allchin and Miriam Sidell)

35 *God's conflict with the dragon and the sea. Echoes of a Canaanite myth in the Old Testament*, by John Day

36 *Land and sovereignty in India. Agrarian society and politics under the eighteenth-century Maratha Svarājya*, by André Wink

37 *God's caliph: religious authority in the first centuries of Islam*, by Patricia Crone and Martin Hinds

38 *Ethiopian Biblical interpretation: a study in exegetical tradition and hermeneutics*, by Roger W. Cowley

39 *Monk and mason on the Tigris frontier: the early history of Ṭur 'Abdin*, by Andrew Palmer

40 *Early Japanese books in Cambridge University Library: a catalogue of the Aston, Satow and Von Siebold collections*, by Nozomu Hayashi and Peter Kornicki

41 *Molech: a god of human sacrifice in the Old Testament*, by John Day

42 *Arabian studies*, edited by R. B. Serjeant and R. L. Bidwell

43 *Naukar, Rajput and Sepoy: the ethnohistory of the military labour market in Hindustan, 1450–1850*, by Dirk H. A. Kolff

44 *The epic of Pābūjī: a study, transcription and translation*, by John D. Smith

45 *Anti-Christian polemic in early Islam: Abū 'Īsa al-Warrāq's 'Against the Trinity'*, by David Thomas

46 *Devotional literature in South Asia: current research, 1985–8. Papers of the fourth conference on devotional literature in new Indo-Aryan languages*, edited by R. S. McGregor

47 *Genizah research after ninety years: the case of Judaeo-Arabic. Papers read at the third congress of the Society for Judaeo-Arabic Studies*, edited by Joshua Blau and Stefan C. Reif

48 *Divination, mythology and monarchy in Han China*, by Michael Loewe

49 *The Arabian epic: heroic and oral storytelling*, volumes I–III, by M. C. Lyons

50 *Religion in Japan: arrows to heaven and earth*, edited by P. F. Kornicki and I. J. McMullen

51 *Kingship and political practice in colonial India*, by Pamela Price

52 *Hebrew manuscripts at Cambridge University Library: a description and introduction*, by Stefan C. Reif